D0151389

LABOR IMMIGRATION
UNDER CAPITALISM

LABOR IMMIGRATION UNDER CAPITALISM

ASIAN WORKERS IN THE UNITED STATES BEFORE WORLD WAR II

Edited by
LUCIE CHENG
and
EDNA BONACICH

UNIVERSITY OF CALIFORNIA PRESS
Berkeley   Los Angeles   London

UNIVERSITY OF CALIFORNIA PRESS
Berkeley and Los Angeles, California

UNIVERSITY OF CALIFORNIA PRESS, LTD.
London, England

COPYRIGHT © 1984 BY THE REGENTS OF THE UNIVERSITY OF CALIFORNIA

Library of Congress Cataloging in Publication Data

Main entry under title:
Labor immigration under capitalism.

   1. Alien labor, Asian—United States—History—
Addresses, essays, lectures. 2. Asian Americans—
Employment—History—Addresses, essays, lectures.
3. United States—Emigration and immigration—History—
Addresses, essays, lectures. I. Cheng, Lucie
II. Bonacich, Edna.
HD8081.A8L3   1983   331.6'2'5073   82-21765
ISBN 0-520-04829-6

PRINTED IN THE UNITED STATES OF AMERICA

1 2 3 4 5 6 7 8 9

Contents

Preface

Immigrants from Asian countries came to the United States and Hawaii beginning in the 1850s. They came mainly as laborers, working in the most back-breaking, lowest paying jobs. They were subjected to severe discriminatory efforts, which sometimes peaked in violence and death. And, in successive stages, each group was denied the right to send any more immigrants.

This volume represents an effort to describe and, more importantly, to understand this history in the pre-World War II era. Before the war, exclusion of all Asian immigrants had been achieved. The war marked a low point in the treatment of the "Asian question," particularly with respect to one group, the Japanese. As is well known, they were interned in concentration camps, the ultimate form of exclusion, which included even native-born American citizens.

Since the war, the position of Asian immigrants and their progeny has changed dramatically. Instead of being seen as part of a dreaded "yellow peril," the later generations are seen as "model minorities" that have assimilated effectively into United States society. While the model minority image is fraught with problems, they are very different from the prewar hostility that Asian American communities had to endure. Further, since the war and particularly since the mid-1960s, American immigration policy has undergone a major shift, resulting in a new wave of immigration from Asian countries. These new immigrants represent a somewhat different set of forces and circumstances than did the prewar immigrants. For these reasons, we have chosen to limit our topic to the pre-World War II era.

This volume is the product of a five-year research project conducted at the Asian American Studies Center at the University of California, Los Angeles. The inspiration for the project lay in our criticisms of almost all the existing literature on Asian Americans. While often useful for providing an accurate description of parts of the Asian experience, this literature generally lacks a strong theoretical focus. In particular, it fails for the most part to place Asian immigration in the larger political and economic context in which it arose, namely, the development of capitalism in Europe and the United States and the emergence of imperialism, especially in relation to Asia.

Our purpose, then, is to provide a theoretical framework within which Asian immigration can be understood. The volume is not intended to show all that such an orientation can achieve. Rather, it is meant as a first step toward framing a theory and generating empirical findings and interpretations. We hope it will inspire others to pursue some of the myriad themes it raises and to expand upon our work.

This book is the product of the contributions of several researchers, most of them students in Asian American studies who shared our general theoretical orientation. Each researcher was responsible for completing a paper on a particular topic. We met regularly as a group to define and redefine the goals, to discuss theoretical issues, and to hear reports from the participants. Since the two of us who are the editors developed our theoretical position over the years of the project, the guidance we were able to give, especially in the beginning, was often not as clear as it might have been. Consequently, some of the papers proved to be unusable in the final volume. The people who wrote them did contribute enormously to the collective development of ideas, and we acknowledge them at the end of this preface in the list of participants.

A few of the papers presented in this volume were written by nonparticipants in the project, though almost all were or are affiliates of the Asian American Studies Center. Because some of the original papers did not work out, we were left with some important lacunae. Fortunately some of the research being done by others seemed to fill these holes rather well, and we asked to use their papers. We are grateful that they agreed.

A minority of the papers are reprints of previously published essays or slightly different versions of such papers. In all cases, the original was either written under the auspices of this project or was influenced by our suggestions for developing it for the project. Authors could not always wait for the time it would take for the entire volume to be ready for publication and, with our concurrence, submitted their work to journals. That they were favorably reviewed as independent pieces encouraged our belief in the usefulness of our framework.

One of the biggest problems we encountered in conducting this project was its dual goals. We wanted both to make a theoretical statement and to conduct original research, and these two aims were not always compatible. We often struggled over which should have the higher priority. Original research is difficult to do in this field. Language differences limit accessibility to original sources, a difficulty we tried to overcome by recruiting people with some proficiency in the various Asian languages. Moreover, there is a scarcity of sources, and most of our research assistants were not trained as historians, so they had difficulties learning how to find what sources there are. As sociologists, the two of us were better equipped to give theoretical than empirical guidance, yet the researchers were responsible for finding the facts.

The participants in this project tended to be either sociologists or historians by training. The two disciplines have different approaches to footnoting their sources, let alone minor stylistic differences within disciplines. After a futile effort at trying to make everyone conform to a sociological style, we decided to let each author use the style they were most comfortable with. As a result, this book is not uniform in its notation style.

Despite these and other difficulties in the process of creating this volume, we hope the product will prove itself worthwhile to the reader. To reiterate, our goal is less to write a definitive work than to chart a direction. We hope to stimulate further work along these lines in the study not only of Asian immigrants in the United States but also of other ethnic and racial minorities here and in other countries.

The structure of the volume is as follows: We begin in chapter 1 with a theoretical introduction that provides our basic orientation to labor migration under capitalism. The theory is stated in general terms, with no effort to apply it specifically to the Asian American case. We hope the theory is of use to all students of labor migration under capitalism, regardless of the particular countries of origin and destination they are studying. The remainder of the volume uses the ideas developed in chapter 1 to analyze the particular situation of Asian immigration to the United States. Needless to say, the fit between theory and empirical reality is imperfect, and at times we need to modify the theory in accordance with this particular historical case. Still, the theory serves as an important guide for helping us select from the welter of historical detail those events and processes that are significant in Asian American history. It is an indispensable tool for directing our research, and we hope its usefulness is demonstrated by the new questions it has caused the researchers to explore.

The empirical part of the volume is divided into three sections. Part I examines capitalist development in the United States in an effort to understand the context into which Asian immigrants were moving. The first essay, chapter 2, establishes some of the basic facts of Asian immigration, where Asians fit in the political economy of the United States, and the treatment they received. Chapter 3 attempts to place the phenomenon of Asian immigration within the broad sweep of capitalist development in the United States and, particularly, to show how that development affected the treatment of racial minorities. In chapter 4 we turn to California and Hawaii, the loci of major Asian immigrant settlement, in an effort to examine how these territories were integrated into the larger American political economy. While they shared some similarities, there were also important differences between them, and the final chapter of the section focuses on Hawaii to explore the particular role of Asian labor in that territory.

Part II considers the Asian countries of origin and the effects of both internal development and Western imperialism that might have led to a rise in emigration to the United States. Each of the five essays addresses one of the five countries of origin, namely, China, Japan, Korea, India, and the Philippines. The essays vary in their comprehensiveness. For those dealing with Korea (chap. 8) and India (chap. 9), where the emigration to the United States was small and research on the causes of the emigration virtually nonexistent, the authors attempt a broad overview of the question. For China, Japan, and the Philippines, where the numbers of emigrants were substantial and considerably more research has been done, the studies are more specific. The essays on Japan (chap. 7) and the Philippines (chap. 10) focus on the migration to Hawaii, while the essay on China (chap. 6) concentrates on the particular region of emigration without attempting to place it within the total context of Chinese development. Clearly, more work needs to be done on the important and understudied question of the roots of emigration from these countries.

In part III we turn to the immigrant workers themselves, examining some of the occupations they filled and how classes developed in their communities. Again we cover all five Asian groups, though this time we did not limit ourselves to one essay per group. An exception was made because of a desire to cover the special situation of immigrant women workers; hence, two essays, chapters 12 and 14, deal with Chinese and Japanese women. As in the case of the previous section, the least research has been conducted on Koreans and Indians, leading our authors, in chapters 15 and 16, to develop broad essays covering what little is known and to uncover some new sources. The three larger groups, Chinese, Japanese, and Filipinos, have received more research attention, which permitted the authors to conduct more focused research on a section of these communities. Thus, the essay on Filipinos, chapter 17, concentrates on Hawaii, while that on the Chinese, chapter 11, focuses on Chinatown in San Francisco. The essay on the Japanese (apart from the paper on women) deals with a specific occupation in which the immigrants concentrated, namely, gardening (chap. 13). These essays do not pretend to cover all that can be said about Asian immigrant workers. They are, instead, a sampling of the kinds of studies that need to be done.

Not all aspects of the theory are covered by the empirical sections. For example, it would have been useful to have a chapter that provided a broad analysis of United States imperialist activity in Asia. Further, we do not provide studies on the impact of Asian immigrant labor on local workers or the rise of the anti-Asian movement, a topic that is perhaps better covered by the existing literature than most. Another gap in our coverage concerns the development and content of political movements among the immigrants. We hope that these and similar holes will be filled in later by other researchers.

In sum, the empirical section of the book presents studies on three facets of the theory. Part I examines the development of the receiving country and how it led to a demand for immigrant labor. Part II explores developments within the sending countries, attempting to explain why emigration arose at a particular time and place. And part III presents selected studies of the immigrant workers themselves and the development of their communities and internal class structures. The purpose of these studies is not to prove the theory but to demonstrate its utility for developing research questions and topics to study. Eventually the theory will have to be modified in light of research findings, and the modified theory will generate new questions to be researched. This volume represents the first stage in that process.

This research would not have been possible without a grant from the Institute of American Cultures at the University of California, Los Angeles. Typing and duplicating funds were provided by an intramural grant at the University of California, Riverside. We are grateful to Clara Dean for a fine typing job on the final draft, to Kiyoshi Ikeda of the University of Hawaii for providing typing support and a forum for developing some of the ideas presented here, and to the staff of the Asian American Studies Center at the University of California, Los Angeles, for various support services over the years of the project. The following friends have read parts of the manuscript and provided helpful criticism: Johanna Brenner, Ronald Chilcote, Norma Chinchilla, James Geschwender, Richard Gordon, Nora Hamilton, Barbara Laslett, Ivan Light, James Matson, Alejandro Portes, Alexander Saxton, Alvin So, and Julia Wrigley. In addition, as a reviewer for the University of California Press, Mark Selden provided an amazingly careful critique and detailed suggestions for revision, while an anonymous reviewer provided some very helpful criticisms. Finally, we express our gratitude to copy editors Betsy Alexander and Carol Leyba for working with a difficult manuscript.

LIST OF PARTICIPANTS

Linda Bell
Helen Chen
Remy Galedo
Evelyn Nakano Glenn
Ardis Kuniyoshi
Henry Lah
John Liu
Sucheta Mazumdar
June Mei
Walter Morita
Alan Moriyama
Wing Cheung Ng
Linda Pomerantz
Miriam Sharma
Nobuya Tsuchida
C.Y. Wong
Sun Bin Yim

1

Introduction: A Theoretical Orientation to International Labor Migration

Edna Bonacich
Lucie Cheng

The study of immigration is undergoing rapid change. Until recently it was dominated by demographers who concentrated on specifying discrete "push" and "pull" factors in the sending and receiving countries, respectively. Sociological concern has tended to focus upon the adjustment and assimilation of newcomers, including problems of prejudice and discrimination directed toward them by members of the receiving society. To the extent that authors have considered the systemic aspects of immigration, they have tended to take a functionalist or developmentalist perspective, assuming that migration will equilibrate resources and labor needs, to the benefit of both sending and receiving countries. (For more detailed descriptions and criticisms of these positions, see Bach 1978b, Portes 1978a:5-11.)

A new approach to immigration is now emerging (e.g., Bach 1978a; Breman 1978, 1979; Burawoy 1976; Castells 1975; Castles and Kosack 1973; Freeman 1979; Gonzales and Fernandez 1979; Gorz 1970; History Task Force 1979:33-63; Maldonado-Denis 1980; Nikolinakos 1975; Omvedt 1980; Petras 1980; Portes 1978a; Ward 1975a, 1975b; Zolberg 1978). These authors and others like them place the processes of emigration and immigration in a broader context, showing how they are part of an interconnected world capitalist system. Rooted in Marxist theory, contributions to this approach see many forms of international migration as a product of the logic of capitalist development. The present volume attempts to contribute to this new approach by studying in some detail one example of such migration: the movement of Asian workers to the United States Pacific Coast states and Hawaii during the later nineteenth and early twentieth centuries. In the process we hope both to advance the perspective theoretically and to elucidate an important aspect of Asian American history.

The central idea is schematically presented in figure 1.1. Capitalist development leads to imperialism (1A), which in turn distorts the development of colonized territories. As a result, many people are displaced from their traditional economic pursuits, becoming available for emigration (2A). Meanwhile, as the original capitalist society develops, its requirements for labor, especially cheap labor, increase (1B). These two conditions, the displacement of colonized peoples and the requirement of more labor in the capitalist economy, arise out of the logic of capitalist development. And both result in pressure for people to migrate as workers to the more advanced capitalist countries (2A, 2B).[1] In other words, migration is a product not of discrete and unconnected factors in the sending and receiving societies but of historical connections between the countries. It is not fortuitous; it is systemic.

Immigrant workers contribute to the development of the country to which they have moved (3A), while their country of origin loses some of its most ablebodied and productive members (3B). Thus labor migration reinforces discrepancies in development between sending and receiving societies. Based in part on immigrant labor, the developed society becomes increasingly developed, while the poorer societies are likely to remain underdeveloped.

Within the receiving country, immigrant workers face a mixed reception. Employers want to keep them as an especially exploitable sector of the working class, a position rationalized by such ideological concomitants of imperialism as racism. Local workers, however, are fearful of being undercut by the presence of an especially exploitable group of workers. These competing interests give rise to anti-immigrant movements, which exaggerate ethnic and racial differences among workers and result in a special status for the immigrants. They are cut off from the mainstream of the working class movement and are forced into enclaves that are like "internal colonies." Thus, the treatment of immigrant workers, including the prejudice and discrimination they face, must also be seen as part of the world capitalist system.

This essay is intended as a theoretical introduction. It discusses the dynamics of capitalism, showing how they produce the various processes we have been describing. It does not go into historical specifics, which always condition and modify the ways that various forces and processes work themselves out. In the remainder of the book we do

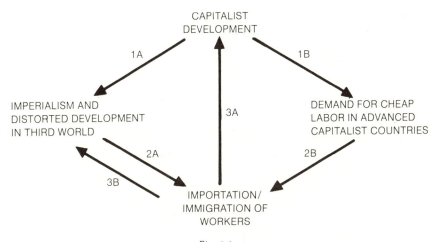

Fig. 1.1
Development of labor migration.

describe the historical developments for one particular case: the immigration of Asians to the United States. This theoretical essay covers three topics: the origins of imperialism, the consequences of imperialism for the dominated countries that lay the foundations for labor emigration, and the changing labor needs of advanced capitalist countries that lead to immigration.[2]

The topics of this essay are interconnected so that what is cause in one instance may be effect in another. Unfortunately, since writing is a linear process, one must make clear one point before moving on to the next. This violates the interconnectedness of reality but is unavoidable. Therefore, at certain points in the text, the reader should be tolerant of simplifications that hold other things constant. We hope we have succeeded in restoring some of the complexity as we move along. As we proceed, we shall occasionally insert diagrams (like fig. 1.1) that attempt to show some of the interconnections in one picture, even if we cannot discuss them all at once.

IMPERIALISM

Most authors writing on immigration from the developing Marxist or world systems perspective recognize that imperialism is a vital force in loosening potential emigrants from their homelands. Yet while the effects of imperialist penetration are discussed (e.g., Burawoy 1976: 1058; Portes 1978*a*:11-23), its causes are not developed. We believe that the roots of imperialist expansion are closely linked to the roots of labor immigration/importation. Thus a thorough understanding of the latter is predicated on a good understanding of the former.

As with other sections of this essay, there are major debates within the Marxist tradition on the roots of imperialism. For one thing, there is no general agreement on what the term refers to (Owen and Sutcliffe 1972:3; Sutcliffe 1972:313-315; Arrighi 1978:9-19). Does it encompass the entire period of European expansionism, including the seventeenth-century trading companies and early colonial settlements in the New World? Or should it be restricted, as in Lenin (1939), to finance capitalism of the late nineteenth and twentieth centuries? While not wishing to enter this debate, we do want to treat the tendency for capitalism as a system to expand overseas as a unitary phenomenon, albeit one that goes through very different stages as capitalism evolves.

For most authors, the roots of imperialism lie in the tendency of the capitalist system to move toward crisis, both long-term and cyclical. Imperialism can be seen as one very important way in which capital, often backed by the state, alleviates this tendency. There are several important and competing theories of capitalist crisis, though almost all theorists agree that it arises from a decline in the rate of profit, leading capitalists to reduce their investments, which in turn leads to rising unemployment, and so on, in a downward spiral.

Weisskopf (1978)[3] distinguishes three major Marxist perspectives on the question of capitalist crises: the tendency for the organic composition of capital to rise;[4] the inability of a population to consume all that advanced capitalism produces, or underconsumptionism;[5] and the tendency for the reserve army of labor to become depleted.[6] While it is unnecessary to choose between the competing theories, we feel that some shed more light on our topic than do others. Specifically, the theory of the exhaustion of the reserve army of labor and its linkages to a rising organic composition of capital seems most relevant to that aspect of imperialism that concerns us here, namely, the search for cheap labor abroad.

The Rising Cost of Labor Power

As capitalism develops, the cost of labor power to the capitalist (variable capital) tends to rise for at least five reasons.[7] These reasons tend to correspond to different stages of capitalist development, with some more likely to arise at earlier and some at later stages. There is considerable overlap as well, however.

First, as capitalism develops, increasing numbers of people are drawn from precapitalist modes of production into the proletariat until the potential national labor force is completely absorbed. We can see this process in the decline of independent farming, the rise of large cities, and the movement from self-employment to wage and salary work. Gradually the potential national labor force is completely incorporated, but since the drive toward capital accumulation continues, the demand for labor comes to exceed the supply.[8] Wages are driven up as capitalists compete for a limited number of workers (Sweezy 1970:83-87).

A second factor is that as capitalism develops, national natural resources become depleted. Thus the amount of necessary labor time required to extract or develop them increases. For example, the labor required for coal mining in a coal-rich country is much less than the labor required in a country where coal near the surface has already been mined. (The search for raw materials abroad may, of course, also derive from their simple unavailability in the home country.)

Third, as workers become increasingly proletarianized, they are decreasingly able to provide any of the means of subsistence for themselves and their families. These must be purchased with wage earnings that have to be gradually increased simply for the workers to reproduce themselves. In other words, during transitional phases of incomplete labor absorption, part of the cost of subsistence and reproduction of the work force is sustained by the worker and his/her family, reducing the cost of the worker's labor power to the employer. Even in apparently highly advanced capitalist countries, this transition may not be complete, especially if women are still working in the home. An indication of the rise in real wages is the concomitant rise of the service sector, reflecting a shift from unpaid services supplied by the family to paid-for services supplied by capitalists. The wage bill needs to cover an increasingly large number of such services.

Fourth, as capitalism develops, the social conditions of production are conducive to the political organization of workers, who can then demand a greater share of the surplus. In particular, the concentration of capital in large factories enables workers to compare their grievances and form organizations. And their growing separation from the creation of their own means of subsistence gives them the motivation to demand more, for they now have nothing to lose. In addition, since advancing capitalism is associated with a tremendous rise in productivity, there is a larger "pie" from which workers can demand a share. The notion of what constitutes a decent, or even minimal, standard of living tends to rise.

Fifth, the increasing demands of workers may receive limited state support. Such programs as unemployment and old-age insurance, health and accident protection, minimum wages, overtime compensation, child labor laws, compulsory education, and the recognition of independent labor unions and their right to engage in collective bargaining all bolster the price of labor power. The emergence of welfare provisions for the destitute also acts as a protection for workers against competition. In other words, the state helps to set national standards of working and living.

As should be evident, a rise in the cost of labor power to capital does not necessarily mean that workers are better off in an absolute sense. As we have indicated, part of the reason for the higher cost of labor power is a rising cost of living that also accompanies capitalist development. The cost of subsistence goes up as it becomes increasingly dependent upon commodities. The quality of life of workers may actually decline, even as wages climb. But from the point of view of capital, the rising wage bill, when not compensated for by increasing labor productivity, puts pressure on the rate of surplus value. One of Marx's great insights was that wages reflect the cost of workers' subsistence, not what the worker earns from his productivity. Productivity and wages are independent. Proletarianization increases subsistence costs while not necessarily affecting productivity. Hence profits become squeezed.

As mentioned earlier, the various features of a rising cost of labor are associated with different developmental stages of capitalism. For instance, the impact of complete proletarianization (with the exception of certain pockets), may be a relatively early phenomenon, while the protections of the welfare state are associated with late capitalism.[9] Labor organizations gain strength as the system moves from competitive to monopoly capitalism, since the conditions for organization are enhanced in large, centralized plants. Similarly, as crafts are eroded and labor is "degraded" (Braverman 1974), worker organizations shift from craft to industrial unionism, accompanied by increasing inclusiveness and militancy.

The rise in the cost of labor associated with capitalist development helps to account for national differences in wages and levels of living. Generally speaking, the more developed a country is in terms of its productive forces, the higher will be the price of labor power. Conversely, the less developed a national economy, the cheaper will be its labor power.

An interesting elaboration of this tendency is found among colonial emigrants from advanced capitalist countries. Because they frequently moved to territories that were sparsely settled, they were often able to reestablish a precapitalist way of life, particularly as small, independent farmers. They became deproletarianized. Yet the price of their labor power tended to remain high, in part because of earlier experiences of a certain standard of living and of labor organizing and also because of some level of mother-country state protection. Thus the British government did not permit the outright enslavement of her emigrants to the British West Indies although the planters there might have wanted to bind them for life. Once these settlers could establish their independence from enforced labor, the relative accessibility of land pushed the price of their labor power up, since they could resist working for low wages. Colonial conditions thus modify the tendencies we are speaking of but have a similar effect to capitalist development of putting pressure on profits because of high wage levels among the colonizers.

While the secular tendency is for the cost of labor power to rise with the development of capitalism, there are several countertendencies or ways that capital can try to halt the decline in the rate of profit. One is to increase the rate of exploitation by lengthening the workday, thereby increasing the proportion of value produced that can be appropriated by capital. This strategy is termed increasing *absolute surplus value*. A second approach is to increase the productivity of labor by increasing its intensity, for instance, by speedups. And third, capitalists can reduce the cost of variable capital, or real wages, by paying workers below their level of subsistence. These latter two approaches involve increasing *relative surplus value* (Sweezy 1970:64-65).

Another approach to increasing relative surplus value is to increase the organic composition of capital (i.e., the proportion of capital invested in machinery and raw materials as opposed to labor) through technical innovations and the like. Raising the organic composition of capital has several effects on the rate of surplus value. It increases productivity, thereby reducing the labor time necessary to produce a given number of commodities. As a consequence the price of the commodities tends to fall. This occurs because the value of a commodity is determined by the amount of living labor time put into it. As necessary labor time falls, the value of the commodity falls. Prices will generally follow but may be kept artificially high if the producer does not face competition. Hence it may be rational to introduce technical innovations, in the short run, to gain temporary advantage over one's competitors even if, in the long run, prices will decline to the level of their true value. During the interim, the rate of surplus value goes up as the capitalist continues to pay his workers the cost of their subsistence.

More important, increased productivity cheapens commodities and thus reduces the costs to workers of the necessities of life. If these necessities remain essentially stable, a general rise in the organic composition of capital throughout the economy will lower the cost of living, reducing variable capital (wages) and increasing the rate of surplus value. Of course it is possible for necessities to expand as fast as productivity, in which case the benefits of the new technology to capitalists would be negated.

A third consequence of increasing the organic composition of capital is that workers are displaced by machinery. Machines are "laborsaving." This may be the most important force that pushes capitalists continually to improve the implements of production, more important even than the short-run competitive advantage over other capitalists. Introducing machinery is a very effective way of getting rid of troublesome and demanding workers who organize, go on strike, halt production, and hurt the accumulation process. At the same time, machinery increases the productivity of the workers who remain. Thus it seems like an ideal solution to the problem of the rising cost of labor power.

In addition, the labor displacement feature of the rising organic composition of capital leads to a replenishment of the reserve army of labor, as increasing numbers of workers are thrown out of jobs. This, in turn, puts pressure on the wages of those who remain employed, since labor scarcity is reduced (Sweezy 1970:87-92). There are now masses of people eager to take the jobs of those who have them. We should note, however, that the working class has been able, in recent times, to protect itself somewhat from this effect by erecting barriers against easy replacement by the reserve army (Bonacich 1976).

In the long run, the rising organic composition of capital contributes to the declining rate of profit, as many theorists have noted. The basic reason is that profits are essentially derived from labor through the extraction of surplus value. Thus reducing one's reliance on labor ultimately reduces profits.[10] Moreover, the introduction of machinery is often associated with greater education and training needs on the part of the work force, contributing to the costs of reproducing the work force and again putting pressure on the cost of variable capital. The labor power of educated workers is more costly than that of the untrained because of the increase in labor time necessary to reproduce the former. Thus the "cure" for rising labor costs and a falling rate of profit ultimately contributes to the disease.

Still another effect of the rising organic composition of capital is that it contributes to the concentration of capital. Technological innovations mean larger initial investments that squeeze out smaller capitals or lead to their consolidation. The result is a decrease in competition or the emergence of what is sometimes termed *monopoly capitalism*. The development of massive firms able to collaborate and avoid deadly competition is another factor that acts as a countertendency to the declining rate of profit. The monopolies can pass on wage increases to the consumer in the form of price increases, thereby bolstering sagging profits. This in turn, however, pushes up subsistence costs and the price of labor power. It also makes national monopolies vulnerable to international competition. But in the short run, monopolies can sustain their profit rate by this means, especially if other sectors of the economy are not monopolized and cannot engage in collusive price fixing.

To summarize all these complex forces and counterforces, there are essentially two strategies for dealing with the rise in the cost of labor power. One is to increase absolute surplus value by lengthening the workday, a strategy that is likely to meet resistance by workers, exacerbating the class struggle. The other is to increase relative surplus value by raising the intensity of labor or the organic composition of capital. In the first case, again, workers are likely to resist. The latter solution produces more contradictory results but in the end, when we balance them off against one another, is unable to prevent the profit rate from falling.

One can see in these tendencies and countertendencies a basis for the cyclical development of capitalism. For example, when the rising cost of labor leads to increased mechanization, it is followed by the laying off of workers, or a rise in unemployment. At this point, the "underconsumptionist" thesis comes into play in that rising unemployment reduces the purchasing power of workers, shrinking the available market. As a result, warehouses remain full, more workers have to be laid off, and the downward spiral continues. The roots of recovery can also be seen in these processes. As the reserve army grows, real wages drop, increasing the rate of surplus value. It becomes profitable once more to hire new workers and step up production. The recovery occurs at a higher level of mechanization, however, so profit rates show a secular trend downward even if, in the short run, things have picked up again. At each stage of the development process, the particular strategies of capital and labor may change, as the former tries to protect against the erosion of the profit rate, while labor tries to protect and improve its level of subsistence.

Because of the inability of capitalism to cope with this tendency on an internal level, pressure arises to seek the solution outside. Imperalist expansionism is another reaction to the cyclical and long-term fall in the rate of profit. It can be seen, in large measure, as an effort to harness the cheap labor of less developed societies.

Cheap Labor

The cost of labor power is considerably lower in less developed societies than it is in the advanced capitalist countries. The reason lies partly in the obverse of the conditions that lead to a rise in the cost of labor power as capitalism advances and partly in the effects of imperialism. Here we shall only treat the former of these on the assumption that the initial discrepancy in development helps to explain imperialism, which then contributes to the discrepancy in development and cost of labor power. The effects of imperialism will be dealt with in part II.

The main reason for the lower cost of labor power in less developed societies lies in the nature of precapitalist modes of production. In precapitalist systems, people work mainly for their own subsistence. When confronted with capitalist employers, they are likely, at first, to work for capital only on a supplementary basis. Most of their subsistence is provided by precapitalist forms. As a result, the capitalist employer need not pay the worker his/her complete subsistence, but only that portion of it that is necessary to sustain the worker at that moment. In other words, the subsistence of his/her family, including health care, education, and housing, can be left out of labor costs. This enables employers in transitional economies to appropriate extraordinary rates of surplus value and at the same time to undersell competitors who use fully proletarianized work forces.

Other features of attachment to precapitalist modes of production also contribute to the cheapness of labor power. New proletarians are likely to be unfamiliar with trade unions. And because they are less dependent on the wage-earning job, they have less incentive to form or join organizations to further their long-term collective interests as workers. Stable labor organizing goes hand in hand with permanent proletarianization. In general, the more completely dependent a group of workers is upon wage labor, the more developed will be its labor organizations.

Another factor that lowers variable capital in less developed countries is a lower standard of living. This may partly reflect differences in necessities; for example, an urban worker must have a means of transportation to get to work, must have a radio to find out certain kinds of information, must have a can opener because some food comes in cans, must have a refrigerator to preserve store-bought foods, and so on. But it also reflects different experiences and expectations, or what Marx termed a historical and moral element (Emmanuel 1972:109-123). For example, housing standards may vary from one society, where straw huts or shacks are perfectly acceptable, to another, where they are not permitted.

Generally, the more advanced capitalist countries have higher minimally acceptable standards of living. Such items as housing, bedding, diet, and gadgetry of all kinds tend to be more substantial. Undoubtedly this reflects a higher level of productivity. Advanced capitalism spews forth tons of commodities, many of which come to be defined as necessities, in part through capitalist efforts. In poor, undeveloped countries these "necessities" are luxuries that people have lived without from time immemorial. Imperialists can capitalize on these lower expectations by lowering wages accordingly.

Roots of Imperialism

It is in the tendency for the rate of profit to decline, leading to crises, that the roots of expansionism of capitalist societies lie. All the forms of imperialism can be seen as a means of coping with the declining rate of profit.

We can divide imperialist expansion into four major themes, corresponding roughly to historical sequence (Barratt-Brown 1972:25). The first is foreign trade, with an emphasis on bringing in cheap commodities. Second is the search for foreign markets in order to sell manufactured goods. Third is the search for cheap raw materials. And fourth is the search for investment opportunities.[11]

All four of these themes share a common element. Because of the lesser development of other societies, the lower cost of labor power there enables capitalists in more advanced economies to take advantage of the discrepancy and reap larger profits than they would at home. Going overseas is therefore a way of coping with the declining rate of profit. Let us consider each type of imperialism in turn.

Marx (1959:232-233) treats foreign trade as one of the important "counter-acting influences" to the tendency for the rate of profit to fall: "Since foreign trade partly cheapens the elements of constant capital, and partly the necessities of life for which the variable capital is exchanged, it tends to raise the profit rate by increasing the rate of surplus-value and lowering the value of constant capital." In other words, foreign trade reduces the cost both of raw materials and of some consumer items, which can be translated into a reduction in wages. As a result, profits are enhanced. These benefits are predicated on the notion that the commodities purchased in foreign trade are cheaper than those produced and sold at home.

The second theme concerns the search for overseas markets. While underconsumptionists stress that the impetus for this comes from overproduction, one can look at it another way: foreign markets provide an opportunity for making especially advantageous exchanges. As Marx (1959:232) states,

> Capitals invested in foreign trade can yield a higher rate of profit, because, in the first place, there is competition with commodities produced in other countries with inferior production facilities, so that the

more advanced country sells its goods above their value even though
cheaper than the competing countries

The idea here is that because of greater mechanization in the more
advanced country, the productivity of labor is increased. Each commodity requires less labor time and is thus cheaper to produce. In "backward" economies, however, more labor power is needed to produce the
same goods. Thus when traders from more advanced capitalist countries bring their industrial products to the less developed countries, they
can undersell local producers, even though they may be able to charge
higher prices than they could in their home market.

In this second case, advanced capitalist countries produce goods more
cheaply than backward countries and take advantage of the discrepancy.
In the case of simple importing, however, the opposite is true; namely,
the goods produced overseas are cheaper. How can we account for this
contradiction? The answer lies in the kinds of commodities that are
being exchanged and, particularly, the importance of variable capital in
them. If the proportion of constant capital invested in the production of
a particular commodity is about the same in both countries, the lower
labor costs in the poorer country will enable that country to produce the
commodity more cheaply. But when the organic composition of capital
is higher in a particular industry in one country than in another, the
advantage of cheapness goes to the former. It thus follows that more
advanced countries will advantageously export capital-intensive goods,
while poorer countries will export labor-intensive goods.

This adds up to the probability that foreign trade between advanced
and backward nations will, at least initially, take the form of manufactured goods produced in the former being sold cheaply in the latter
(thereby undermining indigenous industries), while raw materials that
depend heavily on the application of labor are likely to be exported from
poorer countries where they can be produced more cheaply. This is a
function not only of labor costs but also of the depletion of raw materials (including available land) in the advanced capitalist countries, making their profitable use require increasing quantities of capital and labor
time.

The relative cheapness of labor in backward countries is an advantage
even when technology is applied to the labor. In other words, holding
constant the organic composition of capital, the cheaper labor of
undeveloped areas enables them to undersell more advanced economies.
This explains the current exodus of some high technology industries,
such as electronics, to cheap labor countries.

Ultimately this kind of exchange is to the disadvantage of the backward country. "The favoured country recovers more labour in exchange for less labour, although this difference, this excess is pocketed, as in any exchange between labour and capital, by a certain class" (Marx 1959:233). Thus simple free trade between more developed and less developed countries redounds to the benefit of the former. It is therefore not surprising that, once certain countries achieved a resounding lead in industrialization (after having used coercive mercantilist policies to achieve that lead), the principle of free trade came to receive support from the capitalist class in the most advanced countries. This discrepancy in trade is an important reason for uneven development, or the tendency for the rich to get even richer and the poor to get poorer (Emmanuel 1972). Of course, the existence of a free trade advantage does not preclude the persistence of coercive policies as well, including those associated with a monopoly position.

The third theme of imperialist expansion is the search for raw materials. We have touched on this already. Another way to deal with the declining rate of profit is to search for ways to cheapen means of production, or constant capital. Raw materials produced in less developed countries or regions are likely to be cheaper to the extent that they are less depleted and to the extent that the labor required to extract or grow them is cheaper. Both of these conditions are more likely to hold in less developed areas.

Finally, the fourth theme is the search for investment opportunities. While this can be interpreted from an underconsumptionist perspective, it can also be viewed as a direct effort to improve the profit rate, or simple accumulation. Marx (1959:233) comments on this point: "As concerns capitals invested in colonies, etc., . . . they may yield higher rates of profit for the simple reason that the rate of profit is higher there due to backward development, and likewise the exploitation of labour, because of the use of slaves, coolies, etc." In other words, lack of development means that the organic composition of capital is lower, which means that profits are higher (holding constant the rate of exploitation). In addition, the rate of exploitation, or surplus value, is also likely to be higher, especially in the colonies, so that profits are even more enlarged. The role of colonial domination in this is clearly critical, and we consider it in some detail in the next section. But even apart from the effects of colonialism, the rate of surplus value is still likely to be higher in undeveloped economies to the extent that labor costs are low. Thus, setting aside such complexities as shipping costs or the development of infrastructure, the combined effect of a high ratio of labor to constant capital and of a high ratio of surplus to necessary labor makes investment in undeveloped societies highly profitable. Therefore, they become attractive objects of imperialist expansion.

Figure 1.2 summarizes the impetus to imperialist expansion. The most direct push comes from the rising cost of labor power, leading to a decline in the rate of profit (1), which leads to a search for alternative, cheaper sources of labor power in less developed areas (4). Contributing to this process is a secondary response to the rising cost of labor power, that is, an increase in the organic composition of capital (2), which ultimately adds to the falling rate of profit (3) and the search for cheap labor (4). Simultaneously, the rising organic composition of capital leads to an increase in labor productivity (5), hence a cheapening of commodities and a trade advantage with less developed nations (6). We thus see that the two apparently contradictory features of imperialism, cheap labor and cheap products, both derive from the same origins.

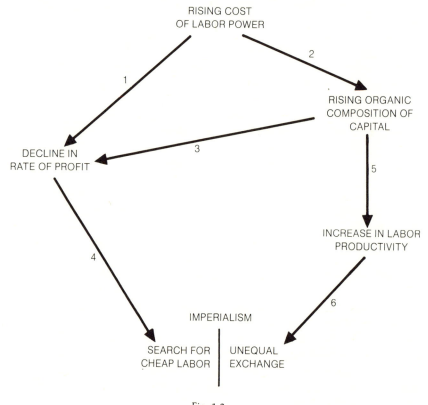

Fig. 1.2
Forces leading to imperialism.

Imperialist expansion is not simply an economic phenomenon. It is associated with another product of capitalist development, the emergence of states, which act at least in part to promote the interests of the dominant capitalist class. Thus imperialism is backed by state action, in such forms as political annexation and military takeover. Competition among several imperialist powers tends to increase state involvement as each expands more quickly than it otherwise might in order to cut off competitors and preserve future opportunities for expansionism.

Imperialism has also had a strong ideological component. The expansion is justified by a "civilizing" and "developing" mission. The noncapitalist world came to be defined as backward and uncivilized, justifying its conquest and exploitation. Because capitalism first emerged in western Europe, the distinction between civilized and uncivilized came to have a racial connotation. Thus various beliefs about racial inferiority became inextricably linked to imperialism as a justification for the takeover of a great part of the world.

A fifth theme in imperialist expansion can also be mentioned, namely, the search for colonies the surplus population of Europe could settle. British mercantilists supported the export of population as a means of countering the declining rate of profit (Portes 1978a:3). While this seems at odds with a theory of imperialism that focuses on the rising cost of labor power as the prime impetus to expansionism, the discrepancy is more apparent than real. The mercantilist promotion of labor exportation had the dual character of alleviating excessively high unemployment rates at home while being able to utilize that labor more cheaply in the colonies. In the first instance, while the presence of a reserve army serves to lower wages, at some point too large a reserve army becomes an excessive burden on the state and threatens political upheaval. Thus labor exportation can coincide with a desire to lower wages. On the second point, provided that labor from the homeland could be restricted to the production of raw materials and could be bound (by indentures, for instance), it could be kept cheaper than it could be in the mother country. Colonial settlement thus would contribute to unequal exchange and accumulation in the metropolitan nation.

These mercantilist policies gave way to free trade and to efforts to restrict emigration. Presumably, free trade proved more beneficial and easier to enforce once western European industrialization was in full swing. It was no longer necessary to use coercion to gain a trade advantage. Meanwhile, with industrial growth, labor surpluses quickly shrank and threatened to become shortages. Better to save domestic workers for the domestic labor market, where their numbers could be used to keep wage levels in check.

The emigration of Europeans to the colonies was not merely a product of capitalist policy; it also reflected the goals and ambitions of Europe's poor. In part they fled to the colonies to escape what was happening in Europe, without particularly receiving the support of their home governments. This type of colonization can hardly be seen as imperialism. While it was an outgrowth of the dynamics of capitalism, it was not part of the drive to accumulate capital.

In sum, the dynamics of capitalist development lead to a declining rate of profit and a tendency toward cyclical crisis. One way of dealing with this is outward expansion or imperialism. In expanding outward, capital is able to take advantage of less developed economies where variable capital is cheaper, thereby compensating for declining profits. We should note here that the roots of immigration are closely related to the roots of imperialism. In both cases, capital makes use of, or absorbs, workers from less developed societies. The major difference lies in the locus of the absorption.

UNDERDEVELOPMENT

Imperialism distorts the development of societies that are subjected to it. Their national development, which would presumably proceed if they were left to their own devices, is subverted and altered, with the not uncommon consequence of their becoming "underdeveloped" (Dietz 1979; Frank 1967, 1969; Palma 1978).

Imperialist penetration can take many forms, from direct colonial domination and the imposition of foreign political rule to less direct forms of foreign penetration, such as foreign investments or unequal trade agreements. These less overt forms can still create such dependency that the dominated country cannot determine its own course of development. Throughout this paper we shall use the term *colonized* to connote the receiving end of imperialist domination, even if that domination does not take the form of direct governmental takeover.

The particular effects of imperialism depend on many factors, including the level of development of the dominant society, its colonial policy, the degree of competitiveness among world capitalist powers, the level of development of the colonized society, population density and climate, and so on. A few generalizations can be made, however.

First of all, imperialism has often led, especially in the early phases of contact, to the exaction of tribute or simple stripping of some of the wealth of the invaded area. This can take the form of looting, payment of war indemnities, or taxation. Whatever the form, the effect is an initial transfer of some wealth from the colonized people to the colonial power.

A second effect is unequal exchange, discussed in the previous section. Even if no special barriers to free trade (such as protective tariffs) are set up, exchange between more and less advanced economies will redound benefit of the former. As a result, indigenous craftsmen and incipient entrepreneurs are undermined. Because the imperialist power can produce the goods more cheaply, they can undersell local producers. If left alone, these local potential capitalists would undoubtedly attempt to protect themselves by limiting the access of foreign-made commodities to the local market. But since imperialism is typically associated with some degree of political domination, local capitalists are unable to protect themselves. Even the establishment of unequal treaties, such as the forced opening of a port for free trade, can be devastating to local industry.

Furthermore, imperialist powers can use their political advantage actively to subvert industrial development in the colonized societies. They can, through selected tariff and other policies, force dominated countries to concentrate in raw material production and prevent them from producing manufactures that could compete with the advanced capitalist country.

One of the chief attractions of imperialist expansionism, as suggested earlier, is the access that it gives capitalists to cheaper labor, enabling them to extract a higher rate of surplus value in order to counter the falling rate of profit in the metropolitan society. Gaining access to that labor is by no means a simple matter, however. In some cases, especially when the political economy of the indigenous people was at a relatively simple level of development (hunting and gathering, or nonsettled agriculture), the colonizers had difficulties getting the "natives" to work for them at all and ended up decimating or annihilating them (e.g., Frazier 1957; Harris 1964:1-24; Marchant 1966). Such is the story of the Brazilian Indians, Tasmanians, Bushmen of Southern Africa, Indians of the West Indies, and so on. If the indigenous people were of no use to the conquerors, they were pushed off the land like wild animals.

But even when those colonized were engaged in settled agriculture, getting them to work freely for capitalists was not easily achieved. The indigenous peoples, not unreasonably, were attached to their own cultures and political economies and were reluctant to forsake them (Portes 1978a:11-23).[12] Capitalists devised various methods for dealing with this problem, from allowing precapitalist modes to continue while extracting surplus from them through taxation or trade, to coercing people through enslavement to work for capitalists. Most colonial labor policies lay somewhere in between. It was common practice, for example, to try to break up precapitalist forms by altering the land tenure system (creating private property) and by instituting a cash tax that forced people to enter the cash economy for at least a brief period of time (Furnivall 1956; Wilson 1972; Amin 1976:204).

Partially as a result of the decimation of indigenous people and partially because of other difficulties with internal labor supplies, colonial situations were often associated with the importation of labor from other territories that had experienced imperialist domination. Major examples include the African slave trade, Indian indenture system, and Chinese "coolie" trade. Using workers from other territories enabled colonial capitalists to break their ties with precapitalist modes, at least temporarily. In some cases, as with migrant labor, the retention of ties to precapitalist forms was encouraged as a mechanism for shifting the cost of reproduction of the labor force to that sector (e.g., Burawoy 1976; Meillassoux 1972; Wolpe 1972). In these cases, the price of labor power could be even lower than that of simple enslavement.

The use of imported labor was also associated with various forms of coercion to bind the worker to the capitalist. While fully developed capitalism depends on free wage labor, colonial conditions made this unrealizable. Even if workers could be effectively broken away from precapitalist modes of production, colonial situations often were associated with "open resources," vast expanses of land to which the newly created proletariat could escape. In order to obtain any workers, capitalists had to bind them (Domar 1970; Evans 1970; Petras 1976:22).

These distortions in colonial labor systems limit capitalist development.[13] Whether the employer uses coerced or migrant labor or a semifeudal type of arrangement, the engine that drives capitalism toward becoming an ever more productive system is lacking. For example, in the case of plantation slavery, the investment in ownership of the labor force restricts the flexibility of the plantation owner to increase relative surplus value. Mechanization would decrease his dependence upon slaves, thereby undermining the value of his investment in them. Labor productivity is likely to be increased only through intensification of labor or by migration to more fertile land (Post 1982). Other colonial labor systems have similar rigidities built into them.

Because of the coercive aspects of colonial labor systems, another force for economic development is thwarted, namely the class struggle. Workers under colonial domination are severely limited in their ability to demand any improvements. As a result, employers have little incentive to introduce laborsaving devices. The means of production are unlikely to be continually revolutionized, since there is no declining rate of profit to react against. The result is a stagnant economy.

Contributing to stagnation is the dependent position of colonial capital. Since it often depends on foreign investment and loans, profits and interest tend to be drained from the colonized society. In addition, investment decisions are made in relation to the requirements of imperialist capital and are not necessarily oriented toward internal development (e.g., Dos Santos 1970:231).

Perhaps more important is the fact that colonial societies are forced into specializing in exports. According to Amin (1976: 200):

> The distortion toward export activities (extraversion), which is the decisive one, does not result from "inadequacy of the home market" but from the superior productivity of the center in all fields, which compels the periphery to confine itself to the role of complementary supplier of products for the production of which it possesses a natural advantage: exotic agricultural produce and minerals.

The emphasis on exports forces colonial capital to enter the highly competitive world market, which leaves little room for controlling the price of its commodities.[14]

In contrast, industrial capital of the metropolitan territories becomes monopolized, in part because of control over technologies and in part because the costs of massive industrialization require mergers into increasingly large capitals. As a result, metropolitan capital can charge monopoly prices, while colonial capital is engaged in deadly price wars, often between different colonial territories engaged in the production of the same raw materials and other exports.

The competitive nature of colonial production contributes to the peculiarities of its labor systems. The use of coercion to keep labor suppressed seems essential, given capital's lack of ability to control the market. Slave owners may prefer the flexibility of a free wage labor system but have no choice in the matter because of the commodities they are producing. Thus coercive colonial labor systems can persist even within a world capitalist economy.

In sum, colonial conditions, including open resources, the attachment of indigenous peoples to precapitalist modes of production, and the competitive nature of colonial markets, distort capitalist development even though they are creations of the world capitalist system. Because a true capitalist mode of production tends not to be created, colonial areas become stagnant. Unequal development becomes increasingly so as accumulation continues in the metropolitan countries and the colonies become underdeveloped. Whatever potential the colonized societies had for evolving capitalism themselves is undermined. Thus, while unequal exchange is a direct result of different levels of development, imperialist domination exacerbates the problem.

Figure 1.3 summarizes the main processes. The fact that colonial and semicolonial societies are precapitalist leads to an initial trade disadvantage (1), which is greatly exacerbated by imperialist domination and the imposition of free trade (2). Open resources (3) and attachment to precapitalist modes of production (4) contribute to the use of coercion in mobilizing labor, which is backed by imperialist political force (5). Thus a special colonial labor system, or colonial mode of production, is created that is neither feudal nor capitalist in the European sense of these terms. Unequal exchange exacerbates the unevenness of development by undermining local industries (6), a process that is supported by the presence of foreign capital (7). The use of coerced labor hinders the development of productive forces, helping to maintain unequal exchange

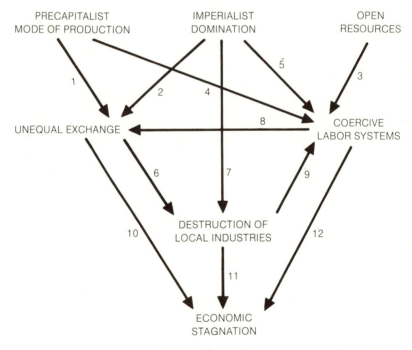

Fig. 1.3
The development of underdevelopment.

(8), while the destruction of local industries forces the economy increasingly into export-oriented production that relies on cheap, coerced labor (9). We see here a kind of self-perpetuating cycle (6, 8, 9) of cheap labor, lack of development, and unequal exchange. All three help keep the colonized society in a state of economic stagnation (10, 11, 12). Thus arises underdevelopment.

Class Relations

Imperialism affects class relations both within colonized and metropolitan societies and across national lines. Figure 1.4 illustrates the major class relations that arise from imperialism. Some authors (e.g., Fanon 1968; Baran and Sweezy 1966) stress the importance of the line of national division, emphasizing the oppression of one nation by another.[15] Some would even go so far as to suggest that national

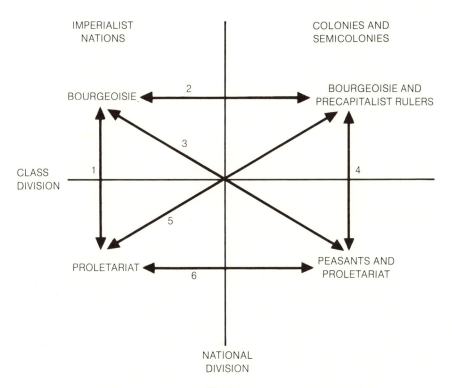

Fig. 1.4
National and class relations resulting from imperialism.

oppression is the major form of exploitation under imperialism. Third World nations are the new proletariat, while metropolitan societies as a whole play the part of capitalists and their "lackeys." An alternative emphasis is to stress the importance of class relations, emphasizing the commonality of exploitation of all workers across national boundaries and the joint interests of the international bourgeoisie.

We believe that any complete understanding of the world capitalist system must take full account of both national and class domination and the relations between them. Various authors have, of course, attempted to do this (e.g., Nicolaus 1970; Wolpe 1975), and our effort here is aimed at contributing to this understanding.

The fundamental colonial exploitation lies in the relationship between the imperialist bourgeoisie and the workers (including peasants and other precapitalist, subordinate classes) of the colonies (fig. 1.4, 3). The use of coercion, backed by the imperialist state and justified by ideologies of racism and national chauvinism, enables imperialist capital to keep colonized labor power especially cheap. Because of the retention of precapitalist forms, the nature of this exploitation may be obscured. Surplus is extracted from colonized workers but not always in the form of surplus value deriving from the strict wage relationship. Even so, the level of worker exploitation (used loosely here to mean the proportion of the value of their labor that is expropriated) is likely to be especially high, leading some to use the term *superexploitation* in relation to colonized workers.

It is possible to argue (e.g., Bettelheim 1970; Evansohn 1977:57) that colonized workers are less exploited than the workers in metropolitan countries because labor is more productive in the latter, owing to heavier capital investment in machinery. The higher productivity of labor in the capitalist centers enables capitalists to expropriate a higher proportion of the surplus generated by labor. But measuring the rate of exploitation is difficult in colonial situations where precapitalist relations persist. Surplus is expropriated through many indirect channels, as well as through the wage relationship. For example, a small artisan shop may have a low profit rate, hence the workers would appear to be less exploited. Yet the goods produced in this shop may work their way through many hands to the point of final sale where the discrepancy between the earnings of the direct producer and the earnings of nonproducers is multiplied many times. Despite the "unproductiveness" of colonized labor power, huge profits can result from its employment. It is at this level that a discrepancy in level of exploitation can be found.[16]

Imperialism has a dual impact on the relations between the imperialist ruling class and the colonized ruling class (fig. 1.4, 2). On the one hand, as we have seen, the potential industrial bourgeoisie is undermined by the introduction of cheap products into the colonial market. On the other hand, the colonial powers have created intermediary leaders, such as a comprador class, or used traditional ruling classes to help them exploit the masses (4). These classes act in alliance with imperialist capital, fostering class as opposed to national oppression. But the incipient national bourgeoisie of the colonized people shares with the workers an interest in overthrowing imperialist domination.[17]

The use of an intermediary class helps make the cheap labor of colonial territories even cheaper by aiding in the suppression and coercion of workers. This suppression can take place at a variety of levels, from the individual entrepreneur or landholder to the state, where oppressive national regimes can keep labor subdued for the benefit of foreign capital. These intermediary classes often play a critical part in keeping the relations of production partially precapitalist. But the profits that flow to metropolitan capital as a result become part of modern capital, to be invested in industrial capitalist enterprises. The compradors place the colonized peasants and workers under a double level of oppression, making it more difficult for them to gain liberation (e.g., Wallerstein 1975).

Although the national bourgeoisie in colonized countries is typically weak and often has economic ties with imperialism and colonial political rulers, segments of the class frequently play an important role in anti-imperialist movements. They have an interest in ridding the territory of foreign capital that undermines their own development and exploits their national resources, including labor. They form alliances with workers and peasants who want to get rid of foreign domination. In other words, they join together in movements of national liberation. But this coalition should not belie the fact that essentially class forces are at work: the exploitation of colonized labor and the undermining competition between metropolitan and colonial bourgeoisies.

Considerable debate has centered on the kinds of alliances that are desirable in colonial, semicolonial, and neocolonial societies and on who the "true enemy" really is, each approach being linked to a particular analysis of the effects of imperialism (e.g., Fernandez and Ocampo 1974; Mandel 1970; Mao 1967:305-334; Petras 1976; Romagnolo 1975). One issue is whether colonized societies need two-stage revolutions: first, a bourgeois-democratic revolution to overthrow colonialism and enable the national bourgeoisie to develop the productive forces along capitalist lines, which must be a precursor to socialist revolution (Omvedt 1973:7). This was the position of the Communist party for a long time and has been severely criticized, especially by dependency theorists.

Part of their contention that the colonies were really capitalist was to argue that peasants and workers are ready for socialist revolution now and need not wait through a bourgeois-democratic revolution. Besides, the very nature of dependent capitalism makes it highly unlikely that such a revolution would occur.

Critics of dependency theory, such as Fernandez and Ocampo (1974), who see colonial backwardness as rooted in the incomplete transition to capitalism, argue that a bourgeois-democratic phase must still be passed through. Feudal class relations must be destroyed, for instance, by breaking up land monopolies through land reforms that give land to the immediate producer, a democratic rather than strictly socialist policy. Only when feudal class relations are destroyed will it be possible to move to a socialist revolution. But because the Latin American (and presumably other colonial) bourgeoisie failed in its historic task of accomplishing this transition, it is up to the proletariat.[18]

We do not wish to enter this debate, which seems highly polemical and often takes the form of each group denouncing others as betraying true Marxism-Leninism. We suspect that such sectarianism arises out of the difficulties of finding workable alliances and strategies in highly oppressed societies. Our main point is simply that class relations within colonized and semicolonized nations are distorted by imperialism. Class antagonisms are somewhat diluted in the face of a common oppressor, at least for a time. The main axis of revolutionary struggles thus often appears to be along national rather than class lines.

Imperialism also affects class relations within the metropolitan societies (fig. 1.4, 1). As suggested earlier, a major impetus for imperialist expansion lies in the rising price of labor power and the development of class struggle in the advanced capitalist countries. Imperialism lowers labor costs and thus must have an important impact on the working class of imperialist nations.

As usual, there is debate about the nature of this effect. Some argue that metropolitan workers benefit from imperialism. Part of the super-profits extracted from colonized workers is used to buy off metropolitan workers, who are, therefore, implicated in the oppression of Third World nations. The lines of oppression coincide with nationality, more than with class, even though there are class divisions within national groups. The main axis of exploitation is national, with oppressor nations and oppressed (or proletarian) nations (e.g., Emmanuel 1970; Nicolaus 1970).

This point of view is associated with an extension of the concept *aristocracy of labor*. Originally used to describe segments within the working class of advanced capitalist countries, notably craft unionists, who protected themselves against competition from other workers and thereby inflated the price of their labor power above its true value, the concept has been extended to all workers in imperialist countries who are seen to reap the benefits of the predations of their national bourgeoisie.

We disagree with this analysis (as do Barratt-Brown 1972:79-138; Bettelheim 1970; Dobb 1940:223-269; Evansohn 1977; and Mandel 1970, among others). The effects of imperialism on metropolitan workers and their class struggle are far more complex than this model suggests. For one thing, the greater earnings of metropolitan workers cannot simply be attributed to transfer payments from those colonized, the "spoils of imperialism." As we said at the start of this essay, they result in large measure from the greater evolution of productive forces, or uneven development (Evansohn 1977:57; Bettelheim 1970). In other words, the higher wages in metropolitan societies are a product of the evolving capitalist mode of production, including the cheapening of commodities, a greater dependence upon commodities, and, perhaps most important, the development of proletarian class consciousness and class struggle.

The main beneficiaries of imperialism are the capitalists of imperialist countries, not the working class. Imperialism helps save the capitalist class from its worst crises, which are partly induced by class struggle. In this sense it is against the long-term interests of the metropolitan working class.

Imperialism also encourages capital accumulation, which in turn encourages investment in constant capital in the metropolitan societies. While this process improves the productive forces, enabling metropolitan labor power to be more productive, it also leads to technological unemployment and the recreation of a reserve army of labor in the metropolitan societies.

Finally, the exodus of capital overseas to the colonies drains job opportunities in the metropolitan societies. To the extent that capitalists can invest more profitably in the colonies, they will not invest in the metropolitan nation, which leads to the displacement of the workers of the imperialist nation (Barratt-Brown 1972:104-107). In other words, the two groups of workers are forced to compete with each other (fig. 1.4, 6). The cheapness of colonial labor gives it an edge that threatens the employment opportunities and hard-won labor standards of metropolitan workers.

Because of imperialism, the class struggle cannot be fought within national borders. Capital is far more mobile than labor, and, instead of staying in the territory to fight it out, capital can escape, leaving labor with declining job opportunities and no way to protect itself. It is caught in a situation of decaying class struggle and is forced into compromises with the capitalist class. Compromises with capital often take the form of business unionism and other moderate forms of labor unionism. These compromises, again, fall along national lines, so capital and labor appear to share an interest in the metropolitan societies as well. As in the colonies, the axis of nationality seems to predominate.

Meanwhile, not only are the relations of metropolitan workers with colonized workers competitive and potentially hostile but their relations with the compradors and colonized national bourgeoisie (fig. 1.4, 5) are also hostile. This latter class helps keep colonized labor cheap and, as such, helps prevent the kind of class struggle that would equalize the workers and decrease their competition with one another. And it helps perpetuate imperialist rule, which is so harmful to metropolitan workers.

In sum, we deny that imperialism has resulted in a basic shift from class exploitation to national oppression in a simple sense. True, the worst exploitation occurs in the oppression of colonized workers by imperialist capital. But the two remaining classes, the metropolitan proletariat and the colonial bourgeoisie, are by no means united in their interests with the other major classes in their nation. Imperialism distorts class conflicts in both types of society, leading to occasional alliances along national lines. But this does not mean that class struggle is not a serious and continuing issue within each type of nation or that international class alliances are impossible or undesirable.

The weakness of international working class solidarity results mainly from the activities of the national bourgeoisies, not from a natural chauvinistic sentiment or even from one group of workers gaining at the expense of the other. Rather, they are pitted against each other, which keeps both from successfully overthrowing the capitalist system.

Since metropolitan workers are often caught between attempting to improve their position vis-à-vis capital and fearing displacement from beneath by colonized labor, they seem immobilized for true revolutionary action. This has led some authors to believe that the most revolutionary class of all is colonized labor, reversing the standard Marxist prediction that capitalism must reach its most advanced stages before the proletariat can engage in a successful socialist revolution.

Revolutions by colonized peoples have the benefit of attacking international capital at its weakest link. To the extent that colonized workers can overthrow imperialist capital, they weaken the ability of that class to escape from crisis. Therefore, they ultimately benefit workers in the metropolitan society, who can confront capital head-on. Thus, as Marx and Engels (1972) said years ago in relation to the Irish question, the working class in imperialist countries should support movements for national liberation in the colonies.

Labor Emigration

The underdevelopment associated with imperialism lays the groundwork for labor emigration. As we saw earlier, considerable displacement occurs as a result of imperialist intrusion (Dietz 1979:18-19; Portes 1978a:11-23). Local crafts workers are driven out of their trades by competition from cheap manufactured imports. Peasants either are forced off their land or retain an increasingly tenuous hold on it. Peasant families must often supplement their meager livelihood by sending members to work at least part-time in capitalist-run enterprises. Thus, as a result of imperialism, a population is created that desperately needs employment in order to survive.

Another characteristic of underdeveloped societies is that capitalist development does not keep pace with rural decline. There are not enough jobs available in the cities or in capitalistic agriculture. Of course this was true in metropolitan societies as well, but the fact that their nation was a colonial power gave workers an outlet: they could flee to the colonies as settlers and reestablish a peasant, or independent producer, way of life. The colonized people had no such outlet and were therefore available for recruitment to any work that was available.

In a sense colonial labor emigration can be seen as the spilling overseas of the migrant labor system. The typical emigrant would be a young adult male who retained a base in subsistence agriculture where his family lived in a peasant village. He was a family representative, sent to work in the capitalist economy for a limited period of time in order to supplement the family's declining subsistence base. At the same time it was hoped that his savings would enable the family to reestablish itself, perhaps by paying off debts or repurchasing lost land, at which time he would return. Thus the emigrant was not a permanent settler in the capitalist sector. He was a sojourner, much like the person who worked for part of the year on a plantation within the colonized society and went home at harvesttime.[19]

The temporary nature of colonial labor emigration was completely rational from the point of view of the emigrant and his family. First of all, while comparative riches could be earned in the capitalist sector, they could easily be eaten up by the high cost of living. It was much wiser for a single worker to go, leaving behind his family, who could more or less support themselves by subsistence agriculture. His supplementary remittances meant a great deal to the well-being of his family in the subsistence sector, while they could only support the most degraded style of life within the capitalist economy.

Second, retaining a foothold in the peasant village acted as a form of social security (Wilson 1972:148). Early capitalism provided few guarantees that a sick, disabled, elderly, or unemployed worker would be cared for. The village community, however, could care for such people. It was a place to return to when things were bad. But in order to maintain this social security, the emigrant worker would have to "pay his dues" by maintaining ties with the village. This could be done by sending remittances and, if possible, by occasional visits. Leaving a wife behind also secured one's ties. Thus, colonial labor emigrants often planned to return and made sure that their right to return was guaranteed.[20]

We should note briefly here a point that will be raised in more detail later, namely, that both the needs of capitalist labor importers and the needs of emigrant workers rather neatly complement and reinforce each other. For example, the fact that workers keep a tie to the subsistence sector enables employers to pay wages that do not take account of family subsistence or social security, while low wages keep the worker's tie to the village a necessity.

Because imperialism is associated with various degrees of political domination, colonized ruling classes often had difficulty controlling the terms on which their emigrant laborers went abroad. Imperialist power could be used to introduce coercion into the terms of labor emigration. For instance, recruits could be bound to contracts for several years, preventing them from exercising the right to search for the best paying job once they reached the country of immigration. Sometimes the government of semicolonized territories tried to intercede on behalf of their nationals, but their weakened condition, resulting from imperialist domination, often limited their ability to control the situation.

Labor emigration from colonized territories frequently took the form of a transfer of elements of the colonial mode of production to the capitalist sector. Often when workers arrived, they were neither true proletarians who had been completely removed from the means of subsistence nor free wage laborers in the sense that they were truly free to sell their labor power for the most advantageous terms. They came from a situation in which capitalist relations of production were incompletely developed, and they were introduced into capitalist labor markets with some of the bonds of precapitalist relations still upon them. We shall return a little later to examine some of the strictures that were placed on immigrant workers at the point of entrance, but for now we want to emphasize that many of these strictures were already present at the point of departure.

The bourgeoisie of the imperialist societies played a variable role in labor recruitment in the colonies. Sometimes it sent agents who were actively involved in the process. At other times labor emigration was left largely in the hands of the comprador class or colonized rulers, who, acting as middlemen, also played an important role in maintaining the precapitalist social relations with emigrant workers. For instance, they could provide loans to prospective emigrants and bind them to contracts that required that they pay off the loan by working for a specific employer. In such a case, a semicoercive element, not unlike debt peonage, enters in, preventing the emigrant worker from being free wage labor.

In sum, imperialism helps create in the colonies a reserve army of labor that is available for emigration to and wage labor in the metropolitan territories or capitalist sector of other colonies. But the conditions of labor emigration often retain features of a colonial mode of production; that is, they are not fully capitalistic and often have a coercive element. Thus colonized workers move into capitalist labor markets at a definite disadvantage relative to other workers.

LABOR NEEDS OF ADVANCED CAPITALIST COUNTRIES

At the beginning of this essay we noted that as capitalism develops, the price of labor power tends to rise, a fact that contributes to the emergence of both cyclical and long-term crises. We argued that imperialist expansionism is one way that capital can deal with crises, by seeking out cheaper factors of production, notably labor. Instead of moving capital to cheaper labor, another way of dealing with the same situation is to move cheaper labor into the metropolitan capitalist economy. Immigration and importation of cheap labor power from colonized territories can be seen as a phenomenon parallel to colonization. In both cases, to deal with the tendency for the rate of profit to fall, metropolitan capital increases the rate of exploitation by making use of an especially exploited group of workers. The main difference is the locus of this exploitation.

The recent rise of "guest workers" in Western Europe has led many people to believe that labor immigration to metropolitan societies is only a recent phenomenon. In fact, at least in the case of Great Britain, it has been a long-standing practice, with Irish immigrant workers a familiar part of the British scene in the days of Marx and Engels (1972; see also Jackson 1963). The importation and immigration of labor, however, was far more common in colonial societies, such as the United States, Brazil, South Africa, and Malaysia, than in Western Europe, leading to some confusion.

Essentially we can distinguish three types of labor immigration: migration from metropolitan societies to their own colonies (e.g., British workers moving to the United States or Australia), migration of colonized workers to other colonial territories (e.g., Indian workers moving to Natal or the Fiji Islands), and migration of colonized workers to metropolitan societies (e.g., West Indians or Nigerians moving to Great Britain). While in all these cases the relative cheapness of immigrant labor is an attraction to capital, the level of development of both receiving and sending societies makes a difference in the role immigrant labor plays.

When immigrant labor moves from one colonized society to another, for instance, the chances are high that conditions will be relatively coercive. This is partially the case because the immigrants are entering a colonial mode of production, based on dependent capitalism, in which capital must use coerced workers to stay afloat. Various forms of indenture and contract are typical of intercolonial labor movements.

Movements by workers from metropolitan to colonial societies are more ambiguous. These movements created "white settler" societies, which often burgeoned into developing and developed capitalist economies. While in the early phases, such movements may have had a coercive character, as the receiving societies developed, they came to take the form of free labor immigration. Workers could be absorbed in large numbers because these societies were colonial territories and had not yet been fully developed. Often there was plenty of available land (after it had been wrested from the indigenous population) and natural resources that were ripe for exploitation by new capital, which in turn required a labor supply.

Most of the new literature on labor immigration concentrates on the third type of movement, of colonized workers to advanced capitalist economies. When we began this project, we assumed that Asian immigration to the United States before World War II fit into this pattern. Yet on closer examination, it proved to be a more ambiguous case, falling somewhere between intercolonial emigration and movements to advanced capitalist countries. The problem is that the United States shifted, in the course of its history, from a colonial to an advanced capitalist status. Even when formal independence from Great Britain had been achieved, sectors of the economy remained dependent on Great Britain at least until the Civil War. Thus, while European workers moving into the northeast in the late nineteenth century were entering a capitalist system, a full-blown colonial labor system based on the semicoercion of black sharecroppers existed in the south. In the case of Asian immigration to California and Hawaii, the precise status of these territories is problematic.

The particulars of the case of the United States and its changing patterns of development will be examined in part I of this volume. Here we concentrate on the "pure" case of colonial workers entering an advanced capitalist economy. Our goal in this section is to consider why capitalists in such economies would encourage labor immigration from colonized societies. Despite our concentration on this pure type, we should keep in mind the applicability of these principles to transitional or intermediate cases of the American type.

Looking broadly, we can conceive of labor immigration to advanced capitalist countries as the absorption of new sources of labor power. This process infuses the reserve army of labor with new blood, replenishing it rather than recycling workers already in the system. The immigration of peasants (and other precapitalist workers) from Third World countries can be seen as an extension of the process of capitalist societies absorbing their own peasantries. Gradually all indigenous peasants are displaced from the land, and the search for new workers to absorb spills overseas. The peasantry of less developed societies is encouraged, induced, or coerced to enter the orbit of the capitalist mode of production.[21] As peasants enter they become a new source of cheap labor power.

The Cheapness of Immigrant Labor Power

As we have already seen, emigrants from colonized countries have certain fetters upon them arising both from the low level of development of their homeland and from the impact of imperialism upon it. They are frequently desperately poor and therefore ready to accept terms that workers in advanced capitalist countries would consider unacceptable. They often have ties to precapitalist systems and tend to be single young men in the peak of health and work capacity. Their ties to precapitalist modes of production mean that they are accustomed to a relatively low standard of living and have had little or no exposure to proletarian organization such as labor unions. Furthermore, their plans to return to the peasant economy limit their interest in joining the local proletarian movement in the country of immigration. The immigrants are eager to earn money as quickly as possible and are therefore likely to protest low wages. But the protest is more apt to take a spontaneous, short-term form than to be a protracted struggle since, unlike local workers, the immigrants have no interest in improving conditions for future generations (Castells 1975:53). All of these characteristics of immigrant workers help make them cheap labor on arrival.[22]

Conditions in the country of immigration exacerbate the disadvantages with which immigrants arrive and perpetuate their distinctive situation. The process of immigration itself contributes to the cheapness of immigrant labor. Newcomers suffer all kinds of adjustment problems, including language disabilities and unfamiliarity with how to find housing or how to get around in the society. Under such conditions of stress, immigrants may be forced to take undesirable jobs at low pay, at least until they can settle down. If they do not know the local language, this settling-in period can be quite extended, with immigrant workers experiencing great difficulties obtaining jobs commensurate with their talents.

Far more important than adjustment problems, or indeed any of the disabilities immigrants bring with them from the homeland, is the fact that immigration permits the receiving state to place these workers in a special legal category. They can be treated differently from nationals (Castells 1975:53; Petras 1980:440-445). This profoundly influences not only the initial cheapness of immigrant labor but also the ability of the receiving society to keep immigrant labor cheap for a longer period of time. No matter how low a person's initial standard of living, one would expect that entry into a country where the standard of living is higher would rather quickly lead to a readjustment in expectations. The legal category of immigrant allows capitalists in the receiving society to interfere with this process and perpetuate a cheap labor status for immigrants.

The receiving national bourgeoisie exercises its influence to keep immigrant workers suppressed in three major ways, all of which involve the intervention of the state, at least to some extent. First, it can be selective about who can enter. For instance, immigration law can select for ablebodied young men while excluding all dependent populations, such as women, children, the elderly, the sick, and paupers. The cost of reproduction of the work force can be left to the sending society (Burawoy 1976; Castells 1975:47; Gorz 1970:29). Meanwhile, maintenance of the immigrant workers can be minimal. Thus, because immigrant workers are healthier than the average worker, health care costs can be minimized (Castells 1975:46). When they are not permitted to bring families, they can be housed in bunkhouses, compounds, or other substandard housing, while educational facilities need not be supplied, and so on. In sum, the normal social costs associated with a complete population, such as housing, education, and health care, can be minimized for immigrants.

Second, capital and the capitalist state can keep immigrant workers in a special legal category. As noncitizens, they are vulnerable to being shipped home at the slightest provocation. On these grounds they can also be denied welfare and other forms of social insurance, and when they cease to be productive workers (because of either personal disability or economic downturn), they can be subject to deportation. Further, if they appear to be the least bit politically dangerous, they can also be removed, an obvious disincentive to their engaging in open protest (e.g., Castells 1975:53; Portes 1978a:31-33).

The existence of a special legal status for immigrants creates the possibility of an extralegal status: the illegal immigrant. The disabilities of all immigrant workers are multiplied for illegal immigrants, who risk disclosure and deportation if they attempt to protest or improve their situation in any way (e.g., Portes 1978b; Samora 1971).

Third, and most direct, capitalists in immigrant-importing societies can actively engage in the recruitment process. In so doing, they may be able to bind workers to contracts while they are still in their home country. The workers may be unaware that the provisions of the contracts they sign are highly unfavorable when compared with conditions of other workers in the country of immigration. Yet on arrival they are subject to threats of legal action if they break their contracts.

Castells (1975:52) sums up the special control capital can exercise over immigrant labor:

> The utility of immigrant labour to capital derives primarily from the fact that it can act towards it as though the labour movement did not exist, thereby moving the class struggle back several decades. A twenty-first century capital and a nineteenth-century proletariat —such is the dream of monopoly capital in order to overcome its crisis.

One might add that the condition of immigration enables capital to introduce nonmarket factors into the wage determination. Immigrant workers are not fully free wage labor, though their degrees of freedom vary over time and place. In other words, precapitalist or noncapitalist features accompany the immigrant worker status and limit the workers' choices and their ability to develop fully as a proletariat. A colonial mode of production is, to some extent, replicated in the metropolitan society.

Because of their disabilities, immigrant workers can be subjected to especially onerous work conditions compared to other workers, including longer hours, lower wages, worse living conditions, greater intensity of labor, more dangerous work situations, and so on. They do the "dirty work" of the society (Oppenheimer 1974). Given a certain level of capital investment, the rate of exploitation of immigrant labor is higher than that of local workers. The average rate of profit is thereby increased, enabling capital to mitigate the worst economic crises.

The members of the immigrant petite bourgeoisie can play a pivotal role in the situation of immigrant workers. Like the colonial ruling class, they have a dual relationship with metropolitan capital. On the one hand, it can be conflictive and competitive, as their own ability to develop as capitalists is hindered by unequal exchange and legal/political disabilities. On the other hand, they can play an invaluable role for local capital in keeping immigrant workers suppressed, while at the same time gaining benefits themselves.

An illustration of the middleman role played by this group is the position of the labor contractor, which is often filled by members of the immigrant community. The labor contractor can have two faces. He can represent the workers in his negotiations with capital, trying to get the best possible bargain for them, and at the same time enhance his own commission or earnings. Or he can play an invaluable role for the employer by bearing the costs of labor recruitment, providing housing and food for the workers, and finding alternative jobs for them during the off-season. On top of these cost-saving features he may have pre-capitalist ties with his workers, such as familial, village, or regional bases of affiliation. These elements reflect bonds of mutual obligation that make it difficult for workers to develop an antagonistic relationship to the contractor. They enable him to gain unusual control over his work force, to the benefit of the chief employers. These ties can also restrict the ability of different groups of workers, especially those of different national backgrounds, to join together since their contractors, as petty capitalists, are in competition with one another.

The role of the immigrant middleman extends to other forms of small business (Bonacich 1978, 1979a). For example, even an independent service or retail store owner can perform a labor-control function. His use of unpaid family labor is a prime example of the extension of precapitalist relations into a capitalist setting. But even when he hires wage workers, precapitalist elements are likely to enter in the form of paternalistic ties based on family, region and so on. While not, perhaps, directly useful to big capital, the cheap immigrant small shop enables the local bourgeoisie to engage in cost-reducing exchanges with the immigrant community. In sum, both metropolitan capitalists and the immigrant petite bourgeoisie participate in keeping immigrant workers in a superexploited position.

Sectoral Concentrations

Immigrant workers are not uniformly distributed throughout the economies to which they move. They tend to be regionally concentrated and to be overrepresented in certain industries, firms, and jobs. Apart from obvious characteristics of immigrants that might lead to such concentrations, such as proximity leading to regional concentrations or the correspondence between the skills of immigrant workers and the skill requirements of jobs, can anything more be said about the requirements of advanced capitalism and its influence on the distribution of immigrant workers?

On the one hand, we can see immigrants as concentrating in the competitive sector of a dual or segmented labor market (e.g., Portes 1978a:37-39). On the other hand, they are likely to be excluded from monopoly-sector industries.[23] The reasons for this division lie in the labor needs of the different sectors. Because of their heavier investment in technology and mechanization, monopoly-sector firms require higher levels of training. This is most evident among the technocrats who plan the production process. But even assembly line work requires some training. Monopoly-sector firms develop large bureaucracies of clerical workers who must be at least literate. Thus the general education as well as specific training requirements of workers in the monopoly sector tend to rise (e.g., Gordon 1972; Aronowitz 1978).[24] Such issues as worker stability become increasingly important since the costs of retraining, when one is running a very complex and interconnected production process, become prohibitive. The acceptance of a fully developed, permanent proletariat divorced from any precapitalist ties is more likely under such conditions.

The type of labor force required by the monopoly sector and the conditions under which it works are conducive to the formation of workers' organizations. Unionization is likely to develop, leading to increased wages and improved work conditions. In other words, monopoly-sector firms tend to face a continual rise in the cost of labor power. They deal with it, in part, by introducing more labor-saving devices, increasing the productivity of their remaining workers still further, and gaining a competitive advantage over firms in similar product lines because they can produce the goods more cheaply. More important, perhaps, because of their oligopolistic position, they can engage in price-fixing agreements and pass on increasing labor costs to the consumer, thereby not endangering their profits. Thus monopoly-sector firms are able to cope with the rising cost of labor power without being greatly threatened by it.

Firms in the competitive sector, in contrast, have little capital and a high labor-to-capital ratio (labor intensity). They have insufficient capital to introduce substantial technological innovation. Hence labor productivity is low. These tend to be small-scale firms. Since little capital is required to enter them, their industries of concentration tend to be overcrowded. Indeed, when the reserve army of labor is augmented by the laying off of workers in the monopoly sector (because of technological innovation), the number of small, competitive-sector firms is likely to rise; some of the unemployed are able to scrape together the capital to open one of these low-capital enterprises. Thus competitive capitalism is continually reproduced at the margins of society.

These features help to determine the nature of the labor supply competitive-sector firms require. Instability of production leads to the need for seasonal and part-time workers. Since these firms have less invested in machinery, keeping the machines running at all times is neither necessary nor possible. Thus the investment in the training of any particular worker is minimal. Worker turnover is relatively less important and may even be desirable as a means of continually lowering labor costs. (One can pay a new worker beginning wages. An established worker may expect continual wage increases.) The productivity of each worker is much lower in competitive than in monopoly firms, not so much because of training differences as because of the amount of capital applied to each worker. The workers in different sectors may, in fact, be substitutable in terms of their personal characteristics. But the jobs themselves create vastly different productivities.

The diverse labor requirements of different sectors within advanced capitalism have important consequences for the concentration of immigrant workers. While all capitalists want to reduce their costs of production, competitive-sector firms have a more pressing need for cheap labor power (e.g., Castells 1975:58). Thus many authors predict that immigrants will concentrate in competitive-sector firms and industries and in regions where such firms predominate.

A segmented labor market approach may be useful for understanding current concentrations of immigrant workers, but we question its generality. Labor market segmentation tends to be a post-World War II phenomenon, having partially arisen in response to the emergence of protective labor legislation (Bonacich 1980). If we consider earlier labor migrations, such as that of millions of southern and eastern Europeans to the United States in the late nineteenth and early twentieth centuries, we see that workers concentrated not in peripheral small businesses but in the largest, most advanced industries of the time. Indeed, their labor helped transform these businesses into giant monopolies. Since the Asian immigration with which this volume deals is a pre-World War II phenomenon, we need to develop a broader understanding of the concentrations of immigrant labor.

We start with the principles that all industries and firms would like to cheapen production as much as possible and that the cheapening of labor power is a fundamental component of cheapening production. Production costs can be reduced by the direct employment of lower-wage labor. They can also be reduced indirectly by the purchase of raw materials or capital goods from enterprises that employ cheap labor.

And they can be reduced by the availability of cheap consumer goods or services from cheap labor-based firms that can be translated by the employers or the consumers into lower wages.

Put another way, the presence of cheap labor is beneficial to capitalists even if they do not directly employ that labor. The relationship between monopoly-sector firms and those that rely on cheap labor is parallel to the relationship between imperialist and colonized enterprises. Surpluses can be drained from the latter to the former by mechanisms discussed before: unequal exchange (based on different levels of productivity of labor), reduction in the cost of inputs, the simple appropriation of surpluses (as in rent and interest payments), and dependency (as in cases of subcontracting and other instances where monopoly capital can dominate the production process). Thus, the presence of cheap immigrant labor power, even if concentrated in certain industrial sectors and regions, is likely to have ramifications throughout the economy.

While all firms and industries could benefit from the use of cheaper immigrant labor power, at least two factors affect their need and ability to do so. First, firms and industries differ in the degree to which their workers are organized to prevent them from using immigrant labor. Local workers, backed by the state in some instances, may be able to prevent capitalists from using immigrant labor to undercut them. (This topic will be discussed in more detail under Class Relations below.)

The types of industries that are cut off from access to immigrant labor power vary by historical period and economic stage of development. For example, in earlier phases of capitalist development, crafts workers, often employed in small shops, were among the best organized workers. Consequently, the crafts were least likely to employ cheap immigrant labor, which was more prone to be concentrated in unskilled jobs, often in large plants that were able to engage in deskilling (or breaking complex skills down into elementary component activities requiring little training). After World War II, in contrast, industrial unions in large plants were better able to prevent access by employers to cheap immigrant labor power. The dual labor market of today reflects this latter phase. It is backed by state regulations that provide better protection for labor standards in larger-scale enterprises (Bonacich 1980). Hence, immigrants are now more likely to be concentrated in small-scale firms, which are able to avoid unionization and evade state inspections.

Employer access to cheap labor power may be an issue of continued struggle and change. Periods of temporary accommodation to a highly priced labor supply may be followed by renewed efforts to lower the cost of variable capital. These, we would predict, are associated with threats to the profit rate generated by cyclical swings or threats to monopoly position (such as a rise in international competition). Therefore, businesses that at one point in time did not employ immigrant labor may at another seek to bring in immigrant workers. The industrial distribution of immigrants is thus a somewhat changeable phenomenon, depending upon both the determination of labor to keep immigrants out and the determination (or immediate need) of capital to bring them in.

This brings us to the second factor that affects the likelihood of immigrant concentration, namely, the immediate need of different industries to employ cheap labor power directly. Many factors contribute to the degrees of freedom under which firms operate: their control over sources of capital, their ability to control markets, and so on. Generally, monopoly-sector firms are better able to exercise control over their environments and are less pressed to hire cheap labor power. Even when they do employ immigrant workers, they are in a better position to grant them concessions (Castells 1975:58).

We would like to characterize industries that are unable to control capital and markets as dependent rather than competitive. The competitive sector, as described in dual labor market literature, implies small-scale, marginal enterprises typically catering to local markets. Dependent firms need be neither small-scale nor local (though they can be). They need not even participate in highly competitive markets. For example, the slave plantations of the southern United States were often large in scale and produced for national and international markets. Yet they were forced to operate within the constraints of outside investments and a market whose price structure they could not control, even though it was not necessarily competition that accounted for the lack of control. In general, then, we predict that cheap immigrant labor is likely to be more concentrated in industries and firms that are in a relatively dependent position.

The concentration of immigrant labor in certain industries, particularly when that labor is kept under special political constraints, has an impact on the development of those industries. To the extent that precapitalist (coercive, semicoercive, or paternalistic) relations prevail in these industries, they have little incentive to mechanize. A cyclical process sets in: need for cheap labor power — failure to mechanize — need for cheap labor power. The industry becomes stagnant, and the workers caught in that sector have limited opportunities for advancement. In other words, the concentration of precapitalist or colonial-type labor systems within advanced capitalist countries contributes to uneven development (Bluestone 1972; Vietorisz and Harrison 1973) as some sectors fall increasingly behind.

Uneven development, in turn, permits the more advanced sector to take advantage of the backward sector. There is an articulation of modes of production, with monopoly capital able to make use of the presence of precapitalist modes within the same national territory. The introduction of cheap immigrant labor thus reproduces internally the relations between metropolitan capital and colonized labor.[25] And in the same way, the use of colonized, cheap labor power is a mechanism by which capital avoids crisis and a declining rate of profit.

In sum, it can be stated as a law that all capitalists, regardless of degree of monopolization, will seek the cheapest labor supply possible. But the pressure is likely to be greater and more continuous on dependent than on monopoly-sector firms. The former are less likely to be restricted by their own workers and the state from seeking out new sources of labor power. Indeed the state, backed by monopoly capital, may actively aid dependent firms in this endeavor. We would expect, therefore, that immigrant labor would be more concentrated in dependent firms. Meanwhile, to the extent that monopoly-sector firms are free to use cheap immigrant labor power, they will do so, either directly or indirectly.

Class Relations

Figure 1.5 shows the major class relations that surround immigrant workers. As is evident, this figure parallels figure 1.4 and does so intentionally. It is our contention that labor immigration from colonized countries essentially reproduces imperialist class relations, though now on metropolitan soil. Of course we must be careful not to overstate this parallel, since there are some important differences between the situations, too.

We have already covered arrows 1 through 4 in the previous discussion. The rising price of labor power, partially caused by class struggle (1), drives the bourgeoisie of metropolitan societies to seek out cheaper immigrant labor power (3), particularly under conditions of special control that sometimes extend to outright coercion. The immigrant petite bourgeoisie can play an important role in helping to keep immigrant labor controlled (4) to the benefit of local capitalists (2).

The local working class is potentially threatened by the introduction of immigrant workers (6). As we have seen, immigrant labor power is used by local capital to reduce labor costs and to lower labor standards. This is its major purpose (e.g., Gorz 1970:28-29). Since the capitalist class can act toward immigrant workers as if no labor movement existed, members of the labor movement are threatened.

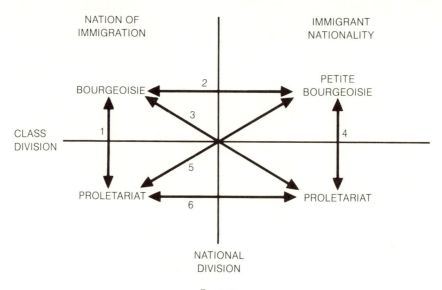

Fig. 1.5
National and class relations resulting from labor immigration.

The threat can be both direct and indirect.[26] The direct threat takes the form of capitalists using immigrants to break strikes or to displace local workers. Employers can use immigrants as a club to get local workers to temper their demands or be fired (Castells 1975:59). The issue of direct displacement is one around which local workers often rally and attempt to protect themselves. It is not unusual for local workers to develop mechanisms for preventing their employers from hiring immigrants in this or any capacity, as a means of protecting themselves against being undercut. Since workers in the monopoly sector are the most organized, they are best able to protect themselves from immigrant competition. Their protectionism thus helps to ensure that immigrants will be forced to look for work in dependent-type firms. Meanwhile, because immigrant opportunities are restricted, their position is weakened still further, and the cheapness of their labor power is exacerbated.

Indirect threat arises when immigrants are used in sectors where there is no established labor movement and they are therefore not in direct competition with local workers. Some authors (e.g., those writing from an internal colonialism perspective) argue that the use of immigrant labor in segregated industries redounds to the benefit of local workers, since some of the surplus extracted from the immigrants can be passed on to monopoly-sector workers. As is evident, this argument runs parallel to the idea that there is an international labor aristocracy and that metropolitan workers gain from imperialism. Let us briefly reiterate our response as it applies to the local level. The high wages and better work conditions of monopoly-sector workers are a result, in part, of the generally higher level of productivity in that sector owing to the development of the productive forces and in part, to the class struggle waged by those workers, rather than simply to expropriation from the dependent sector (Gorz 1970). While it is true that immigrants and dependent-sector workers earn much less and work under much more onerous conditions, it is unclear that the benefits go to anyone but monopoly capitalists and, to a lesser extent, to dependent capitalists.

The presence of a cheap labor sector, even if segregated in dependent industries, however, acts as a threat to the entire labor movement. It acts as a damper on wages for all and permits capital to force local labor to compromise on issues under threat of displacement. Put another way, the access of capital to cheap labor power, even indirectly, hinders the development of the class struggle and the overthrow of capital. The presence of immigrant labor power has thus hindered the development of socialist movements.

Industries based on cheap labor act as an attraction to capitalists, who can earn a higher rate of profit from such labor power. They are tempted to move capital from highly unionized plants and regions to areas where they can get cheaper labor power. Although workers in the established plants are not directly displaced, they are indirectly displaced by the movement of capital. The internal runaway shop (or flight of plants to cheap labor regions) is the result.

Finally, as mentioned previously, the presence of cheap immigrant labor acts as a disincentive for capital in dependent firms to improve the means of production. Given semicoercive, precapitalist relations in these firms, the rate of surplus value is not immediately threatened. There is little incentive to introduce laborsaving devices that would simultaneously upgrade work conditions and improve productivity. Thus these industries remain stagnant. Because the jobs in them are so unattractive when judged by recognized labor standards, the jobs themselves are "displaced."

Castells (1975:54) makes this point cogently. He notes that it is often argued that immigrant workers are necessary because the local population is unwilling to do certain kinds of work. He continues:

> In fact this is only a half-truth. While it is certain that immigrants do carry out the most arduous, the worst-paid and the least-skilled jobs, it does not follow from this that these jobs though necessary, have been

given up by other workers. Such jobs are not given up because they are "dirty" and "soul-destroying" (since the jobs taken instead can hardly be said to be "fulfilling") but because they are less well-paid. Whenever arduous work is relatively well-paid (e.g., miners) nationals, in particular, are found doing it. It remains true, however, that these jobs are badly paid and are most arduous, but *in relation to what standard?* To the historical standard of the balance of power established by the labour movement in each country, to what would be unacceptable to a working class which had the necessary strength to impose better working conditions and higher wage levels. In brief, then, *immigrant workers do not exist because there are "arduous and badly paid" jobs to be done, but, rather, arduous and badly paid jobs exist because immigrant workers are present and can be sent for to do them.* (Castells's italics.)

Of course if these jobs were, in fact, improved, the average rate of profit would decline, and capital would be unable to bail itself out of impending crises (Gorz 1970:31).

One segment of the local working class is especially vulnerable to the competitive use of immigrant labor power by capital, and that is the local reserve army of labor. Both groups have great difficulty gaining access to monopoly-sector jobs and thus compete, to some extent, for the limited alternatives: welfare, petty entrepreneurship, and dependent-sector employment. Since these opportunities are already in short supply, they are squeezed still further as more individuals compete for them. In addition, since immigrants have more difficulty gaining access to welfare and other social subsidies (and sometimes show less motivation to do this), they are contrasted with those in the national reserve army, who are pictured as unwilling to work and as social drains.

Protectionist reactions by local workers toward immigrants are not inevitable. They could, and sometimes do, integrate immigrants fully into the labor movement, thereby combating the use by capital of immigrant workers to divide the working class. Clearly it is in the long-term interests of local workers to follow this approach. That they often do not is less a product of their being bribed labor aristocrats than of the fact that bringing immigrants into the labor movement can prove to be extraordinarily difficult. Three layers of oppression intervene between immigrants and local labor. First, the precapitalist ties of immigrants themselves, especially to homeland communities, act as a disincentive to their joining with local workers. Second, the immigrant petite bourgeoisie can keep immigrant workers controlled and thereby divided from locals, which is a basis for antagonism along this axis (fig. 1.5, 5). Third, and most important, capital and the state can keep immigrant workers in an especially vulnerable category so that they must risk much more than local workers when they participate in labor militancy. Thus the objective conditions of immigrant workers are different from those of local workers, making coordination difficult.

Protectionist reactions by local workers exacerbate the division, driving immigrant workers to seek aid from their home governments, their local national petite bourgeoisie, or even the local capitalist class. In the latter two cases, paternalistic protections can sometimes be found, since both groups of employers would be happy to take full advantage of the immigrants while keeping them docile. Whatever the particular recourse, immigrant workers are further divided from the local labor movement, and the line of national division within the working class becomes more deeply etched than ever. (See Bonacich 1976 for an illustration of this process in connection with black workers in the United States.)

Discrimination by local workers plays into the hands of the immigrant petite bourgeoisie to some extent. Since immigrant workers cannot find jobs in the monopoly sector, they are often forced to offer their services to employers in their own community. Because they lack options, these workers must accept whatever terms are offered. Thus levels of pay, work conditions, and so on are likely to be especially onerous in immigrant enterprise, supporting its competitive status in relation to other businesses.

Figure 1.6 summarizes the interplay between national and international uneven development and the role played by immigrant labor in advanced capitalism. We start with international uneven development and its creation of a source of cheap labor power (1). Because of national uneven development within the receiving country, the locus of demand for immigrant labor is in the dependent sector (2), where immigrant labor tends to locate (3). The need for cheap labor by this sector is supported by economic and political restrictions on the ability of monopoly-sector firms to gain access to cheap immigrant labor directly (4); but there is a concomitant need on the part of these firms to have cheap labor enter the system somewhere to alleviate the falling rate of profit. The concentration of immigrant workers in dependent industries (and the imposition of special political disabilities to keep them there) contributes importantly to their maintenance as cheap labor (5).

Meanwhile, in the monopoly sector, for a variety of reasons discussed earlier, the working class has been able to forge protections for itself against direct displacement (6). Since immigrant workers are an especially cheap labor pool, monopoly-sector workers are likely to erect protective barriers against their employment (7). Protectionism drives immigrant workers into the dependent sector, thereby helping to maintain their cheap labor status (8).

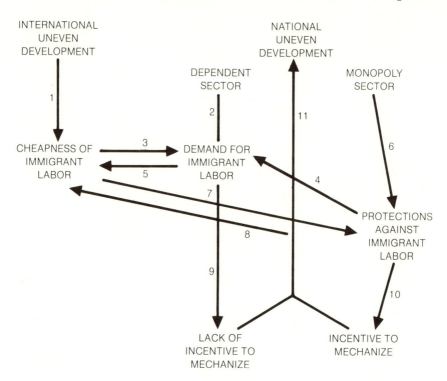

Fig. 1.6
Immigrant labor and uneven development.

The ability of dependent firms to make use of cheap labor and thereby maintain a high rate of exploitation acts as a lack of incentive to mechanize (9), while precisely the opposite is true in the monopoly sector (10). The latter continues to invest more capital in improving the means of production and increasing the productivity of its labor force. Thus uneven development is perpetuated and recreated (11).

Immigrant Political Movements

Immigrant workers are the most oppressed segment of the working class, a condition that leads them to form political movements of protest. Their situation is parallel to that of colonial workers: they are at the bottom of a chain of exploitation and hence have most to gain and least to lose from the overthrow of the entire system.

At the same time, the very oppression of immigrant workers handicaps them in their struggle. They suffer the following disabilities: first, as a form of migrant labor, their composition continually changes, making organizing a never ending process. Unlike the labor organizations of monopoly-sector workers who have a stable work force with a small minority of new entrants who can easily be absorbed into the labor movement, immigrant worker organizations face formidable rates of turnover. The ties to precapitalist villages in the homeland make the problem worse, since workers can express their dissatisfactions by withdrawal from the labor market altogether.

Second, the location of immigrant workers in highly competitive, dependent industries means that they participate in the most competitive labor market. Unlike workers in monopoly industries, workers here are continually competing with one another merely to keep a job and maintain an income that is far less than adequate. In general, unionization is much more difficult to achieve in this sector, whether workers are immigrants or not. Since immigrants are forced to congregate here, the problem is exaggerated by the heterogeneity of the work force. Language and cultural barriers pose additional obstacles to the formation of unified workers' organizations.

The exercise of precapitalist or nonmarket controls over immigrant workers acts as a third barrier to immigrant political movements. These precapitalist controls can be imposed by both the immigrant petite bourgeoisie and the local ruling class. In either case, they inhibit the ability of immigrants to act as free agents to form political movements.

Fourth, the lack of coordination between immigrants and the local working class acts as a further disability to the organization of immigrants. For not only must they organize against capital but they must also overcome the discriminatory (racist, chauvinist) reactions of local workers. A vicious circle of mutual mistrust between local trade unions and immigrant workers can develop with devastating consequences for the working class (Castells 1975:60).

These special disabilities shape the nature of immigrant political movements. They tend to encourage intense but sporadic outbreaks of protest (Castells 1975:59, Petras 1980:445). The intensity is explained by the high level of deprivation experienced by these workers, while their sporadic nature is accounted for, in large measure, by the ability of capital to coercively destroy long-term organizations (e.g., by the threat of deportation). Of course, sometimes immigrants are able to overcome this tendency and to form or join stable political movements. We merely point out that they face greater obstacles in doing so.

Another way that immigrant movements are shaped is that immigrants are often pushed into the hands of the immigrant petite bourgeoisie and ruling class. This tendency is, of course, parallel to the colonial situation where workers are pushed to form temporary coalitions with their national bourgeoisies in movements of national liberation. Since immigrant workers and the petite bourgeoisie both suffer from national oppression, they share an interest in working together, at least temporarily, even though the immigrant petite bourgeoisie plays a role in helping to exploit the immigrant working class. Of course, the emergence of nationalist movements among immigrants inhibits still further the possibility of a unified working class movement, which, one might add, ultimately redounds to the benefit of the capitalist class.

Despite the special disabilities of immigrant workers, they can represent the most progressive and class-conscious segment of the working class. Just as peasant-based revolutions in the Third World have led the way in attacking the world capitalist system while the metropolitan proletariat has been caught in a series of compromises, so immigrant workers may also come to lead movements for radical social change.

CONCLUSION

This paper has attempted to sketch some of the underlying processes that lead to international labor immigration. We have argued that labor immigration grows out of the logic of capitalist development, which creates a tendency for the profit rate to fall and a cyclical tendency toward crises. This leads to an effort to solve these problems by seeking to increase the rate of exploitation by absorbing new and cheaper sources of labor power. In the course of such absorption, either on an international level (imperialism) or in the national arena (immigration), the initial uneven development that attracted capital becomes reinforced not only because of the efforts of capital to keep colonial workers in a superexploited position but also because of the intervening activities of colonial middlemen and metropolitan/monopoly-sector workers. For both of these classes, national development and class struggle are distorted by the ability of metropolitan capital to make use of colonial labor. These distortions mean that nationalist movements, in both colonial and advanced capitalist societies, often appear to take precedence over class-based movements. The most oppressed people in the entire system, both within the colonies and as immigrants, are the superexploited colonial workers. This volume studies one example of such immigrant workers: the Asians in the United States.

NOTES

1. International labor migration can, in a sense, be conceived of as a spilling overseas of processes that have been occurring within the capitalist nation-state, that is, rural underdevelopment and the absorption of rural populations by urban industry. Capitalist countries first "use up" their own peasants and then move abroad in search of more peasants to absorb.

2. Regrettably, we are unable to deal with the impact of international labor migration on the development or underdevelopment of the sending societies (arrow 3B of figure 1.1). This topic is being studied with respect to emigration from China in another University of California, Los Angeles, Asian American Studies Center project.

3. See also Wright (1975), who develops a similar breakdown but includes a fourth theory on the role of state expenditures.

4. The concept *organic composition of capital* comes from Marx's basic value formula: $c + v + s = P$; where c = constant capital, or machinery and raw materials; v = variable capital, or the amount invested in labor, or real wages; s = surplus value, or additional labor from which profits are derived; and P = total value produced. The organic composition of capital is defined as:

$$q = \frac{c}{c + v} ,$$

that is, the proportion of investment in constant capital. The theory states that as capitalism develops, the organic composition of capital (i.e., the proportion of capital invested in machinery and raw materials rather than labor) tends to increase. The profit rate is expected to fall, assuming that the rate of exploitation of the workers remains the same, because profits are derived from the surplus labor time of living workers. If the proportion of all value comes decreasingly from living labor, the proportion of surplus value must also decrease. The profit rate is defined as: $p = s/(c + v)$, namely, the ratio of surplus to total investment. It can be mathematically derived that $p = s(1 - q)/v$. The component s/v refers to the rate of exploitation, or the proportion of the total labor time that goes to the production of surplus value rather than to wages for the worker. Holding this constant, we can see that the profit rate varies inversely with the organic composition of capital (Sweezy 1970:67-69).

5. This problem is endemic to capitalism because exploiting workers necessarily means that their earnings cannot match the increasing productivity of the economy. Consequently, capitalism is given to overproduction, which in turn leads to falling prices, falling profits, and crisis.

6. The depletion can be both quantitative and qualitative (e.g., Boddy and Crotty 1975; Glyn and Sutcliffe 1971). Quantitatively, as capitalist accumulation expands, more and more workers are absorbed. Reproduction of the population cannot keep up with the increasing demand for labor. As labor becomes scarcer, real wages are driven up, putting pressure on the proportion of living labor that goes to surplus. On the qualitative side, labor becomes increasingly organized, the class struggle is intensified, and again, the rate of surplus value or exploitation declines, putting pressure on the profit rate, which leads capitalists to limit their investments, thereby precipitating crisis.

7. Such a rise may or may not affect the rate of surplus value, defined as $s' = s/v$ (also known as the rate of exploitation), depending on the productivity of labor. If labor is increasingly productive, then surplus value and real wages can rise together. They need not rise together, however, and when real wages rise without a concomitant rise in labor productivity, surplus value (and profits) will be squeezed.

8. Pockets of precapitalist relations can coexist with a capitalist mode of production and resist full proletarianization. At a later date these people may be released into the labor force, even though they may have been inaccessible to capital before. This is now happening with women in many advanced capitalist countries. Thus the potential national reserve can apparently be used up at one point in time, only to be expanded at another.

9. Even here, state involvement in the protection of labor standards may have arisen at a fairly early date, with such actions as setting limits on the length of the workday. Extensive state involvement only flowered in late capitalism, however.

10. While this idea is based on the presumption that the rate of exploitation (or surplus value) remains constant, which, as we have seen, is not a viable assumption, nevertheless there are real limits on the degree to which the rate of profit can be increased (Wright 1975:16). If all surplus is derived from living labor and if the proportion of living labor to the dead labor embodied in machinery goes down, then there is a logical limit to the possible extension of the surplus. Consider the following example. If $c = 5$, $v = 5$, and $s = 5$, then $P = 15$. If we increase c to 10, then even if v goes down because of the greater productivity of labor, there is a limit on how large s can be. Under these circumstances, $v + s$ must total 5, in which case s must be less than 5, or reduced.

11. Lenin emphasized this fourth to the exclusion of the other three. Yet, as will be shown, they all reduce to a common denominator and are not easily separable.

12. A similar reluctance was shown among Europeans, many of whom fled to the colonies to become independent producers rather than succumb to "free" wage labor.

13. Considerable debate has developed around the issue of whether these colonial labor systems are capitalist (Harding 1976). Frank (1967), Wallerstein (1974), and other dependency theorists argue that they are capitalist, and have been since the onset of European expansion, because they have been integrated into the world capitalist market. Their critics (e.g., Brenner 1977; Fernandez and Ocampo 1974; Laclau 1971) contend that the essence of capitalism lies in the fact that it is a mode of production, based on specific relations of production, rather than a marketing system. The key characteristic of the capitalist mode of production is seen to be the existence of free wage labor separated from its own means of subsistence. Since colonial labor systems either perpetuate some attachment by the worker to his/her means of subsistence or entail some degree of coercion (or both), they are by definition not capitalistic. Our own position is that while colonial labor systems are indisputably a product of world capitalist expansion and their purpose is one of capital accumulation, they include precapitalist or noncapitalist elements and so do not develop along the same lines as the pure capitalist mode of production.

14. A well-known counter to this tendency arose in the late 1950s with an import substitution strategy of development adopted by several Third World countries once they were free from formal colonial domination. The strategy proved generally unsuccessful, and exports again predominated in the 1970s and early 1980s.

15. This is essentially the point of view of the internal colonialism school of thought (see Wolpe 1975). It is also the predominant position of non-Marxist scholars of race relations, for instance, writers in the plural society tradition (e.g., Kuper and Smith 1969; van den Berghe 1967).

16. Another approach to this issue is to treat the price of labor power as somewhat independent from the amount of capital applied to each source of labor. There is no question that colonial workers earn less than metropolitan workers for the same amount of effort. But workers in metropolitan societies labor under conditions of greater investment in constant capital, hence greater productivity. If capital transfers from metropolitan to colonial labor and if wages and standard of living of the latter remain, at least temporarily, as they are, the rate of exploitation of colonial labor is higher. It is this difference that leads to displacement

(Bonacich 1972, 1975, 1976). Without additional capital, however, colonial labor is indeed unproductive, often producing low levels of surplus.

17. Needless to say, class formation in colonized areas is far more complex than this brief sketch describes. For a more detailed portrait of the various classes that emerge in colonial society, see Omvedt 1973.

18. This debate has its counterpart in discussions of the black question in the United States (Geschwender 1978:70-105).

19. Note that the emigrants could move to capitalist enterprises either in the metropolitan societies or in other colonial territories. In the early period of colonial labor emigration the latter predominated.

20. For the period of Asian immigration that this volume covers, the pattern of single male migrants predominated. More recent labor migrations, especially since the mid-1960s, are more likely to encompass whole families or even to be preponderantly women. Since these shifts are not pertinent to our major topic we shall not attempt to deal with them here. But even in the most advanced capitalist countries, including the United States, the pattern of single male migrants persists (as in Mexican migration to the American Southwest and some North African migration to Western Europe). The phenomenon we are describing here has not disappeared.

21. In the case of the United States West and Hawaii, the destruction of precapitalist forms was not complete at the beginning of Asian immigration. Indeed, part of the impetus for the immigration lay in the inability of capitalists to loosen local workers from precapitalist forms. The underlying commonality between this situation and the one described in the text is that, in both cases, local labor was costly to employ, threatening profitability. Under these circumstances, immigrants could be more profitably employed.

22. Immigrants, in fact, vary in the degree to which they have these features on arrival. Generally, the more colonized the society of origin, the more these features are likely to be present. Thus they are more characteristic of Third World than European immigrants and more characteristic of Eastern than Western Europeans.

23. Dual or segmented labor market theory (e.g., Gordon 1972; Edwards, Reich, and Gordon 1975; O'Connor 1973:13-39; Vietorisz and Harrison 1973) maintains that industries are bifurcated or subdivided, depending on such characteristics as capital intensity, size, degree of concentration, perishability of products, and scope of market. These features of industries, it is argued, help determine their labor requirements and the strategies they have used to control labor. For instance, monopoly-sector firms have been able to institute internal job ladders as a mechanism of labor control.

24. This is a point of much debate, in fact. Some argue that the much-touted educational needs of advanced capitalism are a fraud. We believe there is some confusion on the point because of a focus on different stages of development. It is true that mechanization has eroded the individual skills of craftsmen (Braverman 1974), a feature of early capitalist development. But once this phase is passed and industrial plants have been installed, their increasing complexity demands a different kind of education, though admittedly the educational requirements are unevenly distributed over the firm.

25. One might say that immigrant labor forms an "internal colony" (e.g., Blauner 1972). While the internal colonialism model has much to recommend it, we are not particularly wedded to it, in part because it tends to emphasize national oppression to the detriment of examining the class forces that underlie national oppression.

26. Bonacich has dealt with this issue at length in studies of the split labor market (Bonacich 1972, 1975, 1976, 1979*b*), and we shall not dwell on it here.

References

Amin, Samir
    1976   Unequal Development. New York: Monthly Review Press.
Aronowitz, Stanley
    1978   "Marx, Braverman, and the logic of capital." Insurgent Sociologist 8 (Fall): 126-146.
Arrighi, Giovanni
    1978   The Geometry of Imperialism. London: New Left Books.
Bach, Robert L.
    1978a   "Mexican immigration and U.S. immigration reforms in the 1960s." Kapitalistate 7:63-80.
    1978b   "Mexican workers in the United States: A study of migration and social change." Ph.D. diss., Duke University.
Baran, Paul A., and Paul M. Sweezy
    1966   Monopoly Capital. New York: Modern Reader.
Barratt-Brown, Michael
    1972   Essays on Imperialism. Nottingham, England: Spokesman.
Bettelheim, Charles
    1970   "Economic inequalities between nations and international solidarity." Monthly Review 22 (June):19-24.
Blauner, Robert
    1972   Racial Oppression in America. New York: Harper and Row.
Bluestone, Barry
    1972   "Economic crises and the law of uneven development." Politics and Society 2 (Fall):65-82.
Boddy, Raford, and James Crotty
    1975   "Class conflict and macro-policy: The political business cycle." Review of Radical Political Economics 7 (Spring):1-19.
Bonacich, Edna
    1972   "A theory of ethnic antagonism: The split labor market." American Sociological Review 37 (October):547-559.
    1975   "Abolition, the extension of slavery, and the position of free blacks: A study of split labor markets in the United States, 1830-1863." American Journal of Sociology 81 (November):601-628.
    1976   "Advanced capitalism and black/white race relations in the United States: A split labor market interpretation." American Socialogical Review 41 (February):34-51.
    1978   "U.S. capitalism and Korean immigrant small business." Paper delivered at annual meeting of International Sociological Association, Uppsala.
    1979a   "Immigrant small business as a form of cheap labor." Paper delivered at annual meeting of American Association for Advancement of Science, Houston.
    1979b   "The past, present, and future of split labor market theory." Pp. 17-64 in Cora B. Marrett, ed., Research in Race and Ethnic Relations. Greenwich, Conn.: JAI Press.
    1980   "The creation of dual labor markets." Paper presented at conference on the Structure of Labor Markets, Athens, Georgia.

Braverman, Harry
    1974   Labor and Monopoly Capital. New York: Monthly Review Press.
Breman, Jan
    1978   "Seasonal migration and co-operative capitalism: The crushing of cane and
    &   labour by the sugar factories of Bardoli, South Gujarat." Parts 1 and 2. Journal
    1979   of Peasant Studies 6 (October):41-70; 6 (January):168-209.
Brenner, Robert
    1977   "The origins of capitalist development: A critique of neo-Smithian Marxism."
           New Left Review 104 (July-August):25-92.
Burawoy, Michael
    1976   "The functions and reproduction of migrant labor." American Journal of Soci-
           ology 81 (March):1050-1087.
Castells, Manuel
    1975   "Immigrant workers and class struggles in advanced capitalism: The western
           European experience." Politics and Society 5(1):33-66.
Castles, Stephen, and Godula Kosack
    1973   Immigrant Workers and Class Structure in Western Europe. London: Oxford
           University Press.
Dietz, James L.
    1979   "Imperialism and underdevelopment: A theoretical perspective and a case study
           of Puerto Rico." Review of Radical Political Economy 11 (Winter):16-32.
Dobb, Maurice
    1940   Political Economy and Capitalism. New York: International Publishers.
Domar, Evsey D.
    1970   "The causes of slavery or serfdom: A hypothesis." Journal of Economic History
           30 (March):18-32.
Dos Santos, Theotonio
    1970   "The structure of dependence." American Economic Review 60 (May):231-236.
Edwards, Richard C., Michael Reich, and David M. Gordon, eds.
    1975   Labor Market Segmentation. Lexington, Mass.: D.C. Heath.
Emmanuel, Arghiri
    1970   "Economic inequalities between nations and international solidarity." Monthly
           Review 22 (June):13-19.
    1972   Unequal Exchange: A Study of the Imperialism of Trade. New York: Monthly
           Review Press.
Evans, Robert Jr.
    1970   "Some notes on coerced labor." Journal of Economic History 30 (December):861-
           866.
Evansohn, John
    1977   "Workers and imperialism: Where is the aristocracy of labor?" Insurgent Soci-
           ologist 7 (Spring):54-63.
Fanon, Frantz
    1968   The Wretched of the Earth. New York: Grove Press.
Fernandez, Raul, and Jose Ocampo
    1974   "The Latin American revolution: A theory of imperialism, not dependence."
           Latin American Perspectives 1 (Spring):30-61.
Frank, Andre Gunder
    1967   Capitalism and Underdevelopment in Latin America. New York: Monthly
           Review Press.
    1969   Latin America: Underdevelopment or Revolution. New York: Monthly Review
           Press.

Frazier, E. Franklin
    1957   Race and Culture Contracts in the Modern World. Boston: Beacon Press.
Freeman, Gary P.
    1979   Immigrant Labor and Racial Conflict in Industrial Societies. The French and
            British Experience, 1945-1975. Princeton, N.J.: Princeton University Press.
Furnivall, J. S.
    1956   Colonial Policy and Practice. New York: New York University Press.
Geschwender, James A.
    1978   Racial Stratification in America. Dubuque, Iowa: Wm. C. Brown.
Glyn, Andrew, and Bob Sutcliffe.
    1971   "The critical condition of British capital." New Left Review 66 (March-
            April):3-33.
Gonzales, Rosalinda M., and Raul A. Fernandez
    1979   "U.S. imperialism and migration. The effects on Mexican women and families."
            Review of Radical Political Economy 11 (Winter):112-123.
Gordon, David M.
    1972   Theories of Poverty and Underemployment. Lexington, Mass.: D. C. Heath.
Gorz, Andre
    1970   "Immigrant labour." New Left Review 61 (May-June):28-31.
Harding, Timothy F.
    1976   "Dependency, nationalism and the state in Latin America." Latin American
            Perspectives 11 (Fall):3-11.
Harris, Marvin
    1964   Patterns of Race in the Americas. New York: Walker.
History Task Force, Centro de Estudios Puertorriqueñas
    1979   Labor Migration Under Capitalism. The Puerto Rican Experience. New York:
            Monthly Review Press.
Jackson, John Archer
    1963   The Irish in Britain. London: Routledge and Kegan Paul.
Kuper, Leo, and M. G. Smith, eds.
    1969   Pluralism in Africa. Berkeley and Los Angeles: University of California Press.
Laclau, Ernesto
    1971   "Feudalism and capitalism in Latin America." New Left Review 67 (May-
            June):19-38.
Lenin, V. I.
    1939   Imperialism: The Highest Stage of Capitalism. New York: International
            Publishers.
Maldonado-Denis, Manuel
    1980   The Emigration Dialectic: Puerto Rico and the USA. New York: International
            Publishers.
Mandel, Ernest
    1970   "The laws of uneven development." New Left Review 59 (January-February):
            19-40.
Mao, Tse-Tung
    1967   Selected Works of Mao Tse-Tung. Vol. 2. Peking: Foreign Language Press.
Marchant, Alexander
    1966   From Barter to Slavery. Gloucester, Mass.: Peter Smith.
Marx, Karl
    1959   Capital. Vol. III. Moscow: Foreign Languages Publishing House.
Marx, Karl, and Frederick Engels
    1972   Ireland and the Irish Question. New York: International Publishers.

Meillassoux, Claude
    1972   "From reproduction to production." Economy and Society 1 (February):93-105.
Nicolaus, Martin
    1970   "The theory of the labor aristocracy." Monthly Review 21 (April):47-56.
Nikolinakos, Marios
    1975   "Notes towards a general theory of migration in late capitalism." Race and
           Class 17 (Summer):5-17.
O'Connor, James
    1973   The Fiscal Crisis of the State. New York: St. Martin's Press.
Omvedt, Gail
    1973   "Towards a theory of colonialism." Insurgent Sociologist 3 (Spring):1-24.
    1980   "Migration in colonial India: The articulation of feudalism and capitalism by the
           colonial state." Journal of Peasant Studies 7 (January):185-212.
Oppenheimer, Martin
    1974   "The sub-proletariat: Dark skins and dirty work." Insurgent Sociologist 4
           (Winter):7-20.
Owen, Roger, and Bob Sutcliffe, eds.
    1972   Studies in the Theory of Imperialism. London: Longman.
Palma, Gabriel
    1978   "Dependency: A formal theory of underdevelopment of a methodology for the
           analysis of concrete situations of underdevelopment?" World Development 6
           (July/August):881-924.
Petras, Elizabeth McLean
    1980   "Towards a theory of international migration: The new division of labor." Pp.
           439-449 in Roy Bryce-Laporte, ed., Sourcebook on the New Immigration. New
           Brunswick, N.J.: Transaction Books.
Petras, James F.
    1976   "Class and politics in the periphery and the transition to socialism." Review of
           Radical Political Economics 8 (Summer):20-35.
Portes, Alejandro
    1978a "Migration and underdevelopment." Politics and Society 8(1):1-48.
    1978b "Toward a structural analysis of illegal (undocumented) immigration." Interna-
           tional Migration Review 12 (Winter):469-484.
Post, Charles
    1982   "The American road to capitalism." New Left Review 133 (May-June):30-51.
Romagnolo, David J.
    1975   "The so-called 'law' of uneven and combined development." Latin American
           Perspectives 2 (Spring):7-32.
Samora, Julian
    1971   Los Mojados: The Wetback Story. Notre Dame: University of Notre Dame
           Press.
Sutcliffe, Bob
    1972   "Conclusion." Pp. 312-330 in Roger Owen and Bob Sutcliffe, eds., Studies in
           the Theory of Imperialism. London: Longman.
Sweezy, Paul M.
    1970   The Theory of Capitalist Development. New York: Modern Reader.
van den Berghe, Pierre L.
    1967   Race and Racism. New York: John Wiley.
Vietorisz, Thomas, and Bennett Harrison
    1973   "Labor market segmentation: Positive feedback and divergent development."
           American Economic Review 63 (May):366-376.

Wallerstein, Immanuel
  1974   The Modern World-System. New York: Academic Press.
  1975   "Class-formation in the capitalist world-economy." Politics and Society
          5(3):367-375.
Ward, Antony
  1975a   "European capitalism's reserve army." Monthly Review 27 (November):17-32.
  1975b   "European migratory labor: A myth of development." Monthly Review 27
          (December):24-38.
Weisskopf, Thomas E.
  1978   "Marxist perspectives on cyclical crises." Pp. 241-260 in Crisis Reader Editorial
          Collective, U.S. Capitalism in Crisis. New York: Union for Radical Political
          Economics.
Wilson, Francis
  1972   Migrant Labour in South Africa. Johannesburg: South African Council of
          Churches and SPRO-CAS.
Wolpe, Harold
  1972   "Capitalism and cheap labour-power in South Africa: From segregation to apar-
          theid." Economy and Society 1 (November):425-456.
  1975   "The theory of internal colonialism: The South African case." Pp. 229-252 in
          Ivar Oxaal, Tony Barnett, and David Booth, eds., Beyond the Sociology of
          Development. London: Routledge and Kegan Paul.
Wright, Erik Olin
  1975   "Alternative perspectives in Marxist theory of accumulation and crisis." Insur-
          gent Sociologist 6 (Fall):5-39.
Zolberg, Aristide R.
  1978   "International migration policies in a changing world system." Pp. 241-286 in
          William H. McNeill and Ruth S. Adams, eds., Patterns and Policies. Blooming-
          ton: Indiana University Press.

PART I
The Development of United States Capitalism and Its Influence on Asian Immigration

In chapter 1 we presented a theoretical orientation to international labor migration in the world capitalist system. That effort was, by its very nature, general and ahistorical. We were searching for principles regarding the logic of capitalist development and its consequences for labor migration. Now, and for the remainder of the volume, we turn from the general to the particular, from theory to history. Theory is a guide to understanding history, providing us with reasons for considering certain facts and not others important and worthy of our attention. But theory does not determine what we shall find. Each historical case has its own unique features that modify the way the theory works in practice. This is very evident in the following section of the volume, which turns to the United States as a capitalist power importing immigrant labor from Asia, for the United States is not a "pure" case of the theory. Thus, in recounting how this country came to import workers from Asia before World War II, we shall, on occasion, take short excursions away from the main road, only to return to our theory as the principal path for cutting through the wealth of historical detail.

Our purpose in this section is to establish the context into which Asian immigrants were moving. We want to understand what was going on in the United States that would lead to a demand for Asian labor. That demand, we should note, was not general; it was localized in time, place, and sector of the economy. Furthermore, the demand for Asian labor was not indefinite. Indeed, after each nationality group was brought to the United States, it was subjected to exclusionary pressures until, eventually, the immigration was cut off. This pattern of inducement, localization, and curtailment of immigrant labor from Asia needs to be accounted for. We believe the explanation lies in the development of United States capitalism.

Before attempting to explain the facts, we need to make sure we know what they are. Chapter 2 presents, in broad outline, some of the major facts of Asian immigration. It shows the pattern of arrival of each nationality group in a series of waves. It examines the regional distribution of the immigrants, showing their heavy concentration in Hawaii and the Pacific Coast states, particularly California. It presents some of the very limited available data on industrial distribution of Asian immigrants as compared to the surrounding population. And it briefly traces the pattern of exclusion of each group over time. These, then, are some of the major facts that need to be explained.

In chapter 3 we present a broad interpretive overview of United States capitalist development. The purpose of the essay is to establish the national context in which Asian immigration arose and fell. The United States does not fit our theory perfectly because, unlike the capitalist countries of western Europe, it began as a European colony. The colonial origins of the United States had an important impact on the character of its development, bringing it much closer to other "white settler" colonies, such as South Africa, Australia, and Canada, than to the metropolitan countries of Europe.

The interpretation of United States capitalist development presented here concentrates on understanding the meaning of *race* in this country. Essentially we argue that the early colonial status of the country established a pattern of using racial minorities as coerced or semicoerced labor. This colonial labor system was at odds with other aspects of United States development, notably, wide-scale settlement by the surplus population of western Europe. Racial minorities, particularly the blacks, became a focus of conflict between competing ideals of development. This was most evident prior to and during the Civil War but continued to be played out in the postwar settlement of the West.

After the Civil War, development in the United States took on more of a standard capitalist form. Our theory applies better to this period, and we utilize it to help account for United States imperialist expansion across the Pacific and into Asia. Still, remnants of pre-Civil War themes retained a certain vitality (and seem alive, to some extent, even today). Thus, Asian immigration occurred not only in a context of simple capitalist development but in a society where *nonwhite* carried reverberations of long-standing struggles over the initial purpose and direction of national development.

The next two chapters turn to those areas of greatest Asian concentration, namely, California and Hawaii. Chapter 4 focuses mainly on the former state, bringing in Hawaii at the end for comparative purposes, while chapter 5 turns to a more detailed analysis of Hawaii. The main purpose of chapter 4 is to demonstrate that the themes developed in the analysis of United States development as a whole (in chap. 3) were, to a large extent, recapitulated in California. California became an arena of struggle between large-scale capital, which wanted to employ cheap, racially oppressed labor, and white small producers who wanted to counter the power of the monopolies. In the East the battle was mainly fought over black labor; on the West Coast, Asians took the place of blacks as the chief object of exploitation and struggle.

Hawaii presents an important contrast to California since it lacked a substantial small producer, white settler class. In a sense Hawaii can be seen as a United States colony, plain and simple. The use of semicoerced immigrant labor was completely compatible with this status, and the absence of white small producers and workers meant that the system went unchallenged by any significant class except the Asian workers themselves. Chapter 5 shows how the productive system in Hawaii evolved under these circumstances until the time of annexation, when Hawaii became more closely integrated with the United States and hence more directly subject to the political fallout of mainland struggles. Although we have not included an analysis of post-1900 Hawaiian developments here, we are able to demonstrate how the development of the plantation economy was closely linked to the use of Asian labor.

This section of our volume raises many questions that require further research. We have presented our analysis in broad strokes, and many details need to be painted in, some of which may alter the composition in significant ways. We hope that others will follow some of the ideas presented here with more detailed research, even if they prove us wrong on some points. We hope, however, to have provided a new, and more comprehensive way of understanding the Asian American experience.

2

Some Basic Facts: Patterns of Asian Immigration and Exclusion[1]

Edna Bonacich

During a period spanning the 1860s to the 1920s thousands of Asian immigrants came to the United States from a variety of countries. These immigrants settled mainly in the Pacific Coast states, especially California, and in Hawaii in large numbers. They tended to enter the country as laborers, although many managed to work their way into independent small business and farming. And they were subjected to a vitriolic exclusion effort that sent many back to Asia and prevented untold numbers from ever arriving.

Several aspects of Asian immigration need to be explained. These include patterns of immigration (numbers, time of arrival, country of origin), regional concentrations within the United States over time, occupational and industrial concentration, and the history of anti-Asian agitation and legislation (including their exclusion). The purpose of this chapter is to establish some of the basic facts; subsequent chapters will focus on explaining them.

IMMIGRATION PATTERN

There are two chief ways of examining the rise and fall of Asian population in the United States. One is to study the annual immigration statistics, and the other is to look at the decennial census enumerations. Both have their pitfalls. On the one hand, the immigration authorities gave a more detailed annual accounting but did not enumerate Koreans separately until 1948 and only began counting Filipinos in 1936. (See U.S. Bureau of Census 1975, Part I:108 for the data available on immigration from China, India, and Japan.) The census, on the other hand, probably grossly undercounted Asians at times. Since it did enumerate each Asian group separately, however, it presents a better picture of Asian immigration for our purposes.

We present the census data on the five Asian groups that comprise the heart of this study: Chinese, Japanese, Filipinos, Indians (from India, not to be confused with Native Americans), and Koreans. This means that a few Asian groups, such as Malays and Samoans, are omitted from the count. Prior to 1940, however, they had come to the United States in such tiny numbers as to make almost no difference to the totals.

Table 2.1 shows the population of each Asian group in the United States over time. Overall the picture is one of gradual growth in the total number of Asians in this country until 1940, when there is a drop of about 10,000. But within each group there tends to be a rise and fall. The number of Chinese rose to a peak of almost 110,000 in 1890, then dropped precipitously until, in 1930, it began to show a slight climb, probably reflecting the emergence of a second generation. The Japanese population peaked at close to 140,000 in 1930, the same year in which Indian and Korean populations hit their maximum numbers. Filipinos, who began arriving in substantial numbers later than the others, were still on an upward trend by 1940.

If we were to generalize, the overall pattern seems to be one of over-lapping groups, each of which shows a growth and decline. Speaking only of the three major groups (in terms of numbers), first came the Chinese; as they began to decline, the Japanese began coming; as their numbers began to go down, the Filipinos started arriving.

Generally, Asians have always been a minuscule proportion of the United States population. Table 2.2 shows their numbers in comparison to totals for the whole country. During the entire period they never reached even one-quarter of 1 percent. Nevertheless they came to play an important part in the development of United States capitalism, as well as becoming the object of considerable political agitation.

Regional Distribution

Asian immigrants concentrated in the western region of the mainland and in Hawaii. During the period under consideration Hawaii was, of course, not yet a state so we treat it separately. Table 2.3 shows the proportion of each group on the mainland living in California and the

TABLE 2.1

ASIAN POPULATION IN THE UNITED STATES, 1860 TO 1940

(EXCLUDING HAWAII AND ALASKA)

	Chinese	Japanese	Filipino	Indian	Korean	Total
1860	34,933					34,933
1870	63,199	55				63,254
1880	105,465	148				105,613
1890	107,488	2,039				109,527
1900	89,863	24,326				114,189
1910	71,531	72,157	160	2,545	462	146,855
1920	61,639	111,010	5,603	2,505	1,227	181,984
1930	74,954	138,834	45,208	3,130	1,860	263,986
1940	77,504	126,947	45,563	2,405	1,711	254,130

SOURCE: U.S. Census of Population 1890, pt. I: 401; U.S. Census of Population 1900, vol. I, pt. I: 487; U.S. Census of Population 1930, vol. III: table 2 for each state; U.S. Census of Population 1940, vol. II, pt. I: 52.

TABLE 2.2

ASIAN POPULATION AS PERCENT OF TOTAL UNITED STATES POPULATION

(EXCLUDING HAWAII AND ALASKA), 1860 TO 1940

	Total Asian	Total U.S.	Percent Asian
1860	34,933	31,443,321	0.11
1870	63,254	38,558,371	0.16
1880	105,465	50,155,783	0.21
1890	109,527	62,947,714	0.17
1900	114,189	75,994,575	0.15
1910	146,855	91,972,266	0.16
1920	181,984	105,710,620	0.17
1930	263,986	122,775,046	0.22
1940	254,130	131,669,275	0.19

SOURCE: For total Asian, see table 2.1. For total U.S., see U.S. Bureau of Census, Historical Statistics, 1975, vol. I:14.

TABLE 2.3

PERCENTAGE OF ASIAN GROUPS RESIDING IN CALIFORNIA AND THE WEST, 1860 TO 1940

	1860	1870	1880	1890	1900	1910	1920	1930	1940
California									
Chinese	100.0	78.0	71.2	67.4	50.9	50.7	46.7	49.8	51.0
Japanese		60.0	58.1	56.3	41.7	57.3	64.8	70.2	73.8
Filipino						3.1	47.7	67.4	68.9
Indian						76.5	68.8	59.8	61.4
Korean						65.8	62.9	59.0	53.6
West									
Chinese	100.0	99.4	96.8	90.1	75.4	72.6	62.6	59.9	60.4
Japanese		60.0	63.5	76.5	96.1	94.4	93.9	94.8	95.3
Filipino						21.9	70.1	80.5	77.0
Indian						97.4	78.3	67.4	68.1
Korean						93.1	85.2	79.1	77.2

SOURCE: Same as table 2.1.

West as enumerated by the census. As can be seen, almost three-quarters or more of every Asian group lived in the West, and typically at least half lived in California.

There is some variation by ethnic group. For instance, Japanese have increasingly concentrated in California and the West, while Chinese have tended to disperse over time, moving especially to New York. Still the overwhelming fact is one of western, especially California, concentration. As a consequence, Asians formed a more substantial proportion of the population in the West than elsewhere. Table 2.4 shows that in 1860, Asians comprised almost 10 percent of the California population, a figure that has steadily declined over the decades. Still, even in 1940 they were a more significant segment of California than of the nation as a whole. Thus the story of the role of Asian labor in United States capitalism must be understood in a framework of the relationship of California and the West to the whole.

Large numbers of Asians also settled in Hawaii (see table 2.5). In the case of the Japanese, Filipinos, and Koreans, larger numbers settled in Hawaii than in the entire continental United States (refer back to table 2.1).[2] As with California, then, the relationship of Hawaii to the mainland is critical to understanding the significance of Asian labor.

Industrial Concentrations

Hard data on Asian industrial concentration prior to World War II are difficult to obtain since the census typically included Asians in a general category of "nonwhites." But we have been able to find such information for two census years: 1870 and 1910.

Table 2.6 shows the occupational distribution of Chinese and Japanese in California in 1870. More precisely, the count is of those whose place of nativity was China or Japan, but since few second-generation people could have been born, let alone could have entered the labor force at this early date, the data probably do cover the Asian population. In 1870 only thirty-three Japanese were enumerated in California, so the table mainly reflects Chinese industrial concentrations.

Perhaps the first thing to note is that a much higher proportion of Asians than of the population of the state as a whole was gainfully employed. Asians had a much smaller dependent population, suggesting that the reproduction of the labor force had been relegated to their homeland. This means that fewer social costs, in the form of education, housing, health care, and so on, would be incurred by the state and employers for this particular group of immigrant workers.

TABLE 2.4
ASIAN POPULATION OF CALIFORNIA AS PERCENTAGE OF TOTAL
CALIFORNIA POPULATION, 1860 TO 1940

	Total Asian	Total California	Percent Asian
1860	34,933	380,000	9.2
1870	49,310	560,000	8.8
1880	75,218	865,000	8.7
1890	73,619	1,213,000	6.1
1900	55,904	1,485,000	3.8
1910	79,861	2,378,000	3.4
1920	105,933	3,427,000	3.1
1930	168,257	5,677,000	3.0
1940	167,245	6,907,000	2.4

SOURCES: Total Asian, same as table 2.1; Total California, Historical Statistics, pt. 1, 1975:25.

TABLE 2.5
ASIAN POPULATION OF HAWAII, 1853 TO 1940

	Chinese	Japanese	Filipino	Korean	Total
1853	364				364
1860	816				816
1866	1,306				1,306
1872	2,038				2,038
1878	6,045				6,045
1884	18,254	116			18,370
1890	16,752	12,610			29,362
1896	21,616	24,407			46,023
1900	25,767	61,111			86,878
1910	21,674	79,675	2,361	4,533	108,243
1920	23,507	109,274	21,031	4,950	158,762
1930	27,179	139,631	63,052	6,461	236,323
1940	28,774	157,905	52,569	6,851	246,099

SOURCE: Nordyke 1977:135.

TABLE 2.6
INDUSTRIAL DISTRIBUTION OF CHINESE AND JAPANESE,
TEN YEARS AND OLDER, CALIFORNIA, 1870

	Chinese & Japanese	Percent	California Total	Percent Chinese & Japanese
*Agriculture**	3,481	10.3	51,331	6.8
Agricultural laborers†	1,637	4.8	16,231	10.1
Gardeners, nurserymen, and vine growers	663	2.0	2,648	25.0
Professional and personal services	15,867	47.0	76,112	20.8
Domestic servants	4,343	12.9	15,472	28.1
Laborers (in services)	7,800	23.1	37,586	20.8
Launderers	2,899	8.6	4,043	71.7
Trade and transportation	1,861	5.5	33,165	5.6
Traders and dealers	817	2.4	10,734	7.6
Mining‡	9,087	26.9	36,473	24.9
Manufacturing	3,472	10.3	41,567	8.4
Cigar makers and tobacco workers	1,705	5.0	1,902	89.6
All occupations	33,768	100.0	238,648	14.1
Population 10 yrs. +	46,070		430,444	10.7
Percent gainfully employed	73.3		55.4	

SOURCE: Ninth Census 1870, vol. I, Population.
* Includes fishermen, oystermen, lumbermen, raftsmen, and woodchoppers, although these are listed under manufacturing in the original.
† Nonitalicized titles are subcategories of broader industrial titles. Only those with 500 or more Asians are presented.
‡ Mining is subsumed under Manufacturing and Mining in the original. Quarrymen are counted as miners.

Asian workers were most heavily concentrated in the service industries, with almost half their numbers in this category. In contrast, less than one-third of the state total were engaged in services. Asians were especially overrepresented in laundries, with over 70 percent of laundry workers coming from Asian countries. They were substantially overrepresented as domestic servants, making up 21 percent of the workers in this line of work although they made up only 14 percent of the labor force.

The next largest field of concentration was mining. Over one-quarter of Asian workers were miners, and they accounted for almost a quarter of all workers in this line of endeavor. Approximately equal numbers were engaged in agriculture and manufacturing, with about one-tenth in each. At this point, Asians were underrepresented in both of these categories though overrepresented in particular lines of work within them. Finally 5 percent were engaged in trade and transportation, where they were underrepresented.

Within manufacturing, Asians were unevenly distributed (see table 2.7). Virtually half of all Asians in manufacturing were cigar makers and tobacco workers, and they accounted for close to 90 percent of all workers in this industry. For California as a whole, in contrast, manufacturing workers were distributed over a wide range of occupations, with carpenters being the most numerous.

Asians were overrepresented in only three other manufacturing lines: as boot and shoemakers, brick and tile makers, and cotton and woolen mill operatives. They were notably absent from construction work, in which only 5 percent of Asian manufacturing workers were engaged. In contrast, almost 30 percent of all workers in manufacturing were employed in construction.

TABLE 2.7
CHINESE AND JAPANESE IN MANUFACTURING IN CALIFORNIA, 1870

	Chinese & Japanese	Percent	California	Percent
Bakers	26	.075*	870	2.09*
Blacksmiths	30	0.86	3,310	7.96
Bookbinders and finishers	0	0.00	72	0.17
Boot and shoemakers	392	11.29	2,502	6.02
Brewers and maltsters	5	0.14	568	1.37
Brick and stonemasons, marble and stonecutters	21	0.60	1,159	2.79
Brick and tile makers	62	1.79	415	1.00
Butchers	79	2.28	1,686	4.06
Cabinetmakers and upholsterers	10	0.29	704	1.69
Car, carriage, and wagon makers	3	0.09	526	1.26
Carpenters and joiners	151	4.35	7,413	17.83
Cigar makers and tobacco workers	1,705	49.11	1,902	4.58
Clerks and bookkeepers (in mfg. establishments)	1	0.03	119	0.29
Confectioners	1	0.03	128	0.31
Coopers	11	0.32	451	1.08
Cotton and woolen mill operatives	254	7.32	484	1.16
Curriers, tanners, and leather finishers	0	0.00	229	0.55
Distillers and rectifiers of liquors	0	0.00	79	0.19

TABLE 2.7 (Continued)
CHINESE AND JAPANESE IN MANUFACTURING IN CALIFORNIA, 1870

	Chinese & Japanese	Percent	California	Percent
Harness and saddle makers	1	0.03	719	1.73
Hat and cap makers	0	0.00	34	0.08
Iron and steel workers	1	0.03	565	1.36
Machinists	6	0.17	290	0.70
Millers	11	0.32	457	1.10
Milliners, dress and mantua makers	20	0.58	1,507	3.63
Painters and varnishers	5	0.14	1,850	4.45
Paper mill operatives	0	0.00	21	0.05
Plasterers	0	0.00	499	1.20
Plumbers and gas fitters	0	0.00	361	0.87
Printers	4	0.12	1,045	2.51
Sawmill operatives	39	1.12	1,156	2.78
Ship riggers, caulkers, carpenters, and smiths	0	0.00	693	1.67
Tailors and seamstresses	138	3.97	1,798	4.32
Tinners	10	0.29	998	2.40
Wheelwrights	2	0.06	398	0.96
Total	3,472		41,567	

SOURCE: Same as table 2.5.
*Percentages do not total 100.0 because some occupations are not listed in the original.

In sum, in 1870 Asian workers were not evenly distributed in the California economy. They were confined mainly to service work, mining, and a narrow range of manufacturing. They were largely excluded from the bulk of manufacturing activities — that sphere of the economy that was most developed or developing and in which wages were likely to be highest.

For 1910 complete occupational data are available for Chinese and Japanese in the United States as a whole. Less complete data are available by state. The national information is presented in table 2.8. Within broad occupational categories Asians were substantially overrepresented only in domestic and personal service. They were at parity in trade and transportation and were underrepresented in all other fields. At a more detailed level, Asian workers congregated in farm labor and gardening (totaling about 22 percent of Asian jobs), laundry work (15 percent), and household service (16 percent). This is quite a skewed distribution within the national labor force.

TABLE 2.8

INDUSTRIAL DISTRIBUTION OF CHINESE AND JAPANESE,
TEN YEARS AND OLDER, UNITED STATES, 1910

	Chinese & Japanese	Percent	United States	Percent
Agriculture, forestry, animal husbandry	*32,168*	*26.0*	*12,659,203*	*33.2*
Farmers*	1,750	1.4	5,865,003	15.4
Farm laborers	15,235	12.3	5,975,057	15.6
Fishermen and oystermen	1,041	0.8	68,275	0.2
Gardeners, florists, fruit growers, nurserymen	2,898	2.3	139,255	0.4
Garden, greenhouse, fruit orchard, nursery laborers	9,800	7.9	133,927	0.4
Extraction of minerals	*1,944*	*1.6*	*964,824*	*2.5*
Manufacturers	*16,461*	*13.3*	*10,658,881*	*27.9*
Laborers, building and hand trades	5,099	4.1	934,909	2.4
Laborers, saw and planing mills	1,729	1.4	260,142	0.7
Laborers, fish curing and packing	3,171	2.6	4,870	0.0
Transportation	*8,944*	*7.2*	*2,637,671*	*6.9*
Laborers, steam railroad	7,916	6.4	543,168	1.4
Trade	*12,028*	*9.7*	*3,614,670*	*9.5*
Retail dealers	6,677	5.4	1,195,029	3.1
Salesmen and women	2,649	2.1	921,130	2.4
Public service	*194*	*0.2*	*459,291*	*1.2*
Professional service	*1,249*	*1.0*	*1,663,569*	*4.4*
Domestic and personal service	*49,852*	*40.3*	*3,772,174*	*9.9*
Laundry operatives	12,453	10.0	111,879	0.3
Laundry owners, officials, managers	6,400	5.2	18,043	0.0
Porters (except in stores)	1,390	1.1	84,128	0.2
Restaurant, cafe, and lunchroom keepers	1,977	1.6	60,832	0.2
Servants	19,731	15.9	1,572,225	4.1
Waiters and waitresses	2,696	2.2	188,293	0.5
Clerical Occupations	*971*	*0.8*	*1,737,053*	*4.6*
Total	*123,811*	*100.0*	*38,167,336*	*100.0*

SOURCE: Thirteenth Census of U.S. Population 1910, vol. IV, Occupation
Statistics:91-94; Bureau of the Census, Bulletin 127, Chinese and Japanese in the United
States 1910:21-22.

* Detailed occupations presented when Chinese and Japanese totaled 1,000 or more.

Within manufacturing, Asians were not only grossly underrepresented overall; they were also more concentrated in unskilled laborer jobs. Of 16,461 Asians in manufacturing, 11,754 (71.4 percent) were laborers. For the United States as a whole, 2,489,706 out of 10,658,881 manufacturing workers (23.4 percent) were laborers. Asians were largely absent from skilled and semiskilled manufacturing jobs.

As noted, the available data on California are not as good. The census presents only selected occupations for Chinese and Japanese and does not provide the totals for the broad occupational categories. We present what is available in table 2.9. In 1910 these two Asian groups made up 5.8 percent of the gainfully employed of the state, so whenever this figure is exceeded in the last column, they are overrepresented. Undoubtedly the occupations selected by the census reflect those in which Asians were found in fairly large numbers. Thus the table gives us a better picture of Asian over- than underrepresentation.

TABLE 2.9

SELECTED OCCUPATIONS OF GAINFULLY EMPLOYED CHINESE AND JAPANESE, TEN YEARS AND OLDER, CALIFORNIA, 1910

	Chinese & Japanese	Percent	Total California	Percent Chinese & Japanese
Agriculture, forestry, animal husbandry				
Farm and dairy farm laborers	12,994	20.2	91,029	14.3
Farmers and dairy farmers	943	1.5	64,240	1.5
Fishermen and oystermen	889	1.4	3,802	23.4
Garden, greenhouse, orchard, and nursery laborers	8,592	13.3	22,199	38.7
Gardeners, florists, fruit growers, nurserymen	2,173	3.4	18,625	11.7
Lumbermen, raftsmen, and woodchoppers	205	0.3	8,852	2.3
Mining				
Gold and silver mine operatives	439	0.7	15,827	2.8
Manufacturing				
Laborers in building and hand trades	1,540	2.4	38,896	4.0

TABLE 2.9 (Continued)
SELECTED OCCUPATIONS OF GAINFULLY EMPLOYED CHINESE AND JAPANESE,
TEN YEARS AND OLDER, CALIFORNIA, 1910

	Chinese & Japanese	Percent	Total California	Percent Chinese & Japanese
Laborers in fish curing and packing	1,100	1.7	1,243	88.5
Laborers in fruit and vegetable canning	416	0.6	931	44.7
Dressmakers and seamstresses	169	0.3	14,151	1.2
Transportation				
Laborers in steam railroads	853	1.3	18,470	4.6
Trade				
Clerks in stores	380	0.6	14,805	2.6
Laborers, porters, helpers in stores	448	0.7	3,137	14.3
Retail dealers	4,124	6.4	47,097	8.8
Salesmen (in stores)	1,734	2.7	38,793	4.5
Domestic and personal service				
Barbers, hairdressers, manicurists	380	0.6	8,614	4.4
Boarding and lodging house keepers	455	0.7	8,612	5.3
Cleaners	518	0.8	1,272	40.7
Laborers in domestic and private service	333	0.5	2,102	15.8
Launderers (not in laundries)	239	0.4	4,282	5.6
Laundry operatives	3,481	5.4	10,359	33.6
Laundry owners and managers	709	1.1	1,482	47.8
Porters (except in stores)	577	0.9	2,949	19.6
Restaurant, cafe, lunchroom keepers	519	0.8	3,289	15.8
Servants	11,539	17.9	50,100	23.0
Waiters and waitresses	1,061	1.6	11,705	9.1
Clerical				
Clerks and bookkeepers	489	0.8	45,722	1.1
Total	64,374		1,107,668	5.8

SOURCE: Thirteenth Census of U.S. Population 1910, vol. IV, Occupation Statistics: 96-109; Bureau of the Census, Bulletin 127, Chinese and Japanese in the United States 1910:30.

Looking at the first two columns we find that the major Asian occupations, in terms of sheer numbers, were farm laborers (representing a
change from 1870) and household servants (representing a continuity).
The third largest occupational category was gardening. In a comparison
with the state as a whole, Asian concentrations stand out in gardening,
fishing, fish packing, fruit and vegetable cannery work, laundry work,
cleaning, and household service. Clearly this is a very distorted occupational distribution in a state where 26.5 percent of the gainfully employed
worked in manufacturing and only 12.6 percent were in the entire field
of domestic and personal service. (Just for the selected occupations
presented, 41.2 percent of gainfully employed Asians were in domestic
and personal service.)

The state data in the census bulletin also reveal some other interesting concentrations in other states, including coal-mining operatives in
Wyoming (476), Colorado (366), and Utah (128);[3] farm laborers in several western states (especially Oregon, Washington, and Colorado); fish
packing in Oregon (1,359) and Washington (707); lumber mill laborers
in Washington (1,503); and railroad workers in many of the western
states (Colorado, Idaho, Montana, Nevada, Oregon, Utah, Washington,
and Wyoming). Service workers (including those in laundries) and
workers in trade (such as retail dealers) were generally found all over.

Hawaii reveals a different picture, with a much higher proportion of
Asian workers in agricultural labor, especially on sugar plantations (see
table 2.10). In large measure this reflects the nature of the Hawaiian
economy as a whole; but even within it, Asian workers were overrepresented in agriculture and, as usual, in domestic and personal service,
while they were underrepresented in the limited manufacturing of the
islands and virtually absent from professional and public service.

When we combine the occupational structure of the Chinese and
Japanese in California and Hawaii, we find the Asian workers occupying
a few economic niches: agricultural labor, domestic and personal service, some retailing, and heavy labor in a few manufacturing lines. They
were more or less absent from the more advanced sectors of the economy, including most of manufacturing, the professions, and public service. To some extent their skewed occupational distribution can be
accounted for by the economic character of the territories in which they
resided, which was probably not fortuitous. But allowing for this, we
find that even within California and Hawaii they were more likely than
other workers to concentrate in the same few occupations. The significance of these occupations in the development of United States capitalism is, therefore, a subject that we must address.

TABLE 2.10
INDUSTRIAL DISTRIBUTION OF GAINFULLY EMPLOYED CHINESE AND JAPANESE,
TEN YEARS AND OLDER, HAWAII, 1910

	Chinese & Japanese	Percent	Total Hawaii	Percent Chinese & Japanese
Agriculture, forestry, animal husbandry	40,490	61.7	56,329	71.6
Farm laborers*	33,357	50.9	45,027	74.1
General farms	4,469	6.8	6,479	69.0
Rice	1,825	2.8	1,962	93.0
Sugar	26,358	40.2	35,947	73.3
Farmers and planters	2,329	3.6	3,026	77.0
Extraction of minerals	133	0.2	282	47.2
Manufacturing	8,393	12.8	15,345	54.7
Carpenters	1,267	1.9	2,078	61.0
Laborers, building and hand trades	1,516	2.3	3,828	39.6
Laborers, sugar factories	1,708	2.6	1,974	86.5
Transportation	2,389	3.6	6,723	35.5
Laborers, steam and street railroad	1,024	1.6	1,345	76.1
Trade	3,950	6.0	5,831	67.7
Retail dealers	2,073	3.2	2,491	83.2
Salesmen	1,297	2.0	1,838	70.6
Public service	126	0.2	2,842	4.4
Professional service	357	0.5	2,601	13.7
Domestic and personal service	7,270	11.1	9,434	77.1
Servants	4,572	7.0	5,317	86.0
Clerical occupations	470	0.7	1,807	26.0
Total	65,572†	100.0	101,194	64.8

SOURCE: 1910 Census, vol. IV:293-294; Census Bulletin 127:23.
* Detailed occupations for cases where Chinese and Japanese total 1,000 or more.
† The subcategories do not add up to the total, as presented in the original.

EXCLUSION

Agitation against Asian immigrants on the mainland began almost at the moment of their arrival. Starting in the 1850s California passed a series of acts against the Chinese. These acts typically involved the imposition of special taxes or regulations, some of which specified the Chinese while others were aimed at them without singling them out by name (Garis 1927:287). The laws were generally found to be unconstitutional by the federal courts, and it was only in 1875 that a preliminary exclusion law was enacted. This law prohibited "the transporting into the United States of residents of China, Japan or any Oriental country, for the purpose of holding them to a term of service" (Garis 1927:292). It also prohibited the importation of women for purposes of prostitution.

In 1882 Congress passed the Chinese Exclusion Act, prohibiting the immigration of all Chinese laborers for the next ten years (Bennett 1963:17). This was the first federal law restricting the immigration of a national group. Several other laws and treaties followed (Bennett 1963:19-20); for instance, in 1892 Chinese exclusion was extended for another ten years. Finally, in 1904 it was extended without a time limitation. Chinese exclusion was repealed in 1943, in part because of the wartime strategy of alliance with China (Riggs 1950).

Efforts to restrict immigration from Japan followed a similar pattern. Agitation arose at the local level, with Californians organizing legal and extralegal campaigns to exclude the Japanese (Daniels 1966). The federal government took action by negotiating a "Gentlemen's Agreement" with Japan in 1907-1908, in which Japan was to undertake control over the emigration of laborers to the United States. At the same time, the president issued an executive order restricting the movement of Hawaiian Japanese to the mainland. The Gentlemen's Agreement permitted the wives of local Japanese residents to enter the United States, and many brought in picture brides. Based on an old Japanese custom of arranged marriages, the picture bride system extended such agreements abroad by allowing emigrant men to select brides in Japan through the exchange of photographs. Thus the Japanese population continued to grow. And along with it came continued agitation until, in 1924, Japanese exclusion was enacted as part of the Immigration Act of 1924.

Koreans were subjects of Japanese imperialism, and the exclusion of Korean immigrants was affected by more complex forces. The Japanese prohibited Koreans from emigrating to the United States in 1905 (Houchins and Houchins 1976:135), while on the United States side they were treated more or less as Japanese. For instance, the Asiatic Exclusion League was first named the Japanese and Korean Exclusion League

(Daniels 1966:126). And the presidential executive order restricting the flow of Japanese from Hawaii to the mainland also cut off Koreans (Houchins and Houchins 1976:136-137). Thus Koreans did not come under a distinct and separate exclusion effort.

Indians, like Koreans, were treated less directly than the Chinese and Japanese, although they, too, faced agitation (Hess 1976:160-163). In terms of legal action, Congress passed an Immigration Act in 1917 that set up a literacy test and numerous other restrictions on immigration. This act established a "barred zone," a geographical area defined by latitude and longitude from which immigration (with minor exceptions for professionals, merchants, and diplomats) was prohibited. The barred zone was aimed at Asia and encompassed most of China, all of India, and several other Asian countries. Japan was not included because it was felt to be adequately covered by the Gentlemen's Agreement (Bennett 1963:27). According to Garis (1927:307), the most important effect of this regulation was the exclusion of Indians.

Filipinos were in a situation somewhat different from that of other Asians. Since the United States owned the Philippines, the immigrants were nationals who traveled under United States passports and who could therefore not be excluded. This problem was bypassed in 1935 with the passage of the Tydings-McDuffie Act, granting future independence to the Philippines. The act may have been passed primarily to effect Filipino exclusion, since it received strong support from exclusionists (Daniels and Kitano 1970:66).

To summarize, Asian immigration to the mainland before World War II tended to follow a pattern. Asians from a particular country would begin arriving in small numbers. Very soon, agitation and harassment would develop against them at a local level. At first these efforts would not receive federal sanction, but finally the federal government would step in and arrange treaties or enact legislation to prohibit further immigration from that country.

It is possible to correlate the arrival of a new group with the establishment of restrictions on a previous nationality. Referring back to table 2.1, we see that the commencement of Japanese immigration corresponds to the period of Chinese exclusion. Chinese exclusion was first enacted in 1882, and small numbers of Japanese began arriving in the 1880s. They came in substantial numbers in the 1890s, a period of Chinese decline. Similarly, the decade of the Gentlemen's Agreement with Japan (1900 to 1910), which also cut off Korean immigration, marked the start of immigration from India and the Philippines. Filipino immigration really got going, however, in the 1920s after the 1917 exclusion of Indians and especially after the 1924 exclusion of the Japanese. We shall attempt to explain this pattern of ebb and flow, of exclusion and replacement, in the course of this volume.

Hawaii presents a very different pattern. That territory engaged in virtually uninterrupted open recruitment of immigrant laborers from wherever they could be obtained. While the United States mainland banned the importation of contract labor in 1885 (Garis 1927:91-92), Hawaii continued recruiting workers under contract until the territory was annexed by the United States in 1900. At that point Hawaiian immigration policies were affected by mainland laws (Lind 1968:226-227). The one exception to an open immigration policy was an effort to restrict Chinese. This movement never reached anywhere near the pitch of the anti-Chinese movement in California, and the actual enforcement of Chinese exclusion for a brief period in the late 1880s may have been more a consequence of conditions laid down by Japan in her negotiations for sending laborers to Hawaii than of the strength of the indigenous anti-Chinese movement. The marked differences between Hawaiian and Californian reactions to Asian immigration are another issue we shall attempt to explain.

Asian immigrants received unique treatment in the United States in many ways. While eastern and southern European immigrants received a less than hospitable welcome to the East Coast, the depth of antagonism never reached the degree faced by Asians in the West. These Europeans were, in a sense, excluded in 1924 but only after millions had come. Such numbers of Asians were never permitted to enter. In addition, the Europeans never faced the kind of racial and national ban enforced against the Asians. No barred zone was set up across Europe or, for that matter, anywhere else. Perhaps most important was the definition of Asians as "aliens ineligible for citizenship," a status that marked them off from all other immigrants, and even from blacks after the Civil War. In sum, Asians were treated as a class apart by the United States immigration system. Both the causes and consequences of their unique status are critical to an understanding of their role in United States capitalist development.

NOTES

1. I would like to thank Ivan Light, John Liu, Linda Pomerantz, Miriam Sharma, and the members of Red Wednesday, Johanna Brenner, Norma Chinchilla, Nora Hamilton, Barbara Laslett, and Julia Wrigley, for their very helpful comments on this and the next two chapters.

2. An exception to the pattern is 1920, when Japanese were more numerous on the mainland than in Hawaii.

3. These were probably mainly Japanese as opposed to Chinese, since by the late 1880s, the Chinese had largely left the coal fields (Ichioka 1979). There may be other such ethnic concentrations masked by the combining of data by the census.

References

Bennett, Marion T.
 1963   American Immigration Policies. Washington, D. C.: Public Affairs Press.
Daniels, Roger
 1966   The Politics of Prejudice: The Anti-Japanese Movement in California and the
           Struggle for Japanese Exclusion. Gloucester, Mass.: Peter Smith.
Daniels, Roger, and Harry H. L. Kitano
 1970   American Racism. Englewood Cliffs, N.J.: Prentice-Hall.
Garis, Roy L.
 1927   Immigration Restriction. New York: Macmillan.
Hess, Gary R.
 1976   "The forgotten Asian Americans: The East Indian community in the United
           States." Pp. 157-177 in Norris Hundley, Jr., ed., The Asian American: The
           Historical Experience. Santa Barbara: ABC-Clio.
Houchins, Lee, and Chang-su Houchins
 1976   "The Korean experience in America, 1903-1924." Pp. 129-156 in Norris Hund-
           ley, Jr. ed., The Asian American. Santa Barbara: ABC-Clio.
Ichioka, Yuji
 1979   "Asian immigrant coal miners and the United Mine Workers in America: Race
           and class at Rock Springs, Wyoming, 1907." Amerasia Journal 6 (Fall):1-23.
Lind, Andrew W.
 1968   An Island Community: Ecological Succession in Hawaii. New York: Greenwood
           Press. First published in 1938.
Nordyke, Eleanor C.
 1977   The Peopling of Hawaii. Honolulu: East-West Center.
Riggs, Fred W.
 1950   Pressures on Congress: A Study of the Repeal of Chinese Exclusion. New York:
           King's Crown Press.
U. S. Bureau of the Census
 1975   Historical Statistics of the United States, Colonial Times to 1970. Washington,
           D. C.: U. S. Government Printing Office.

3

United States Capitalist Development: A Background to Asian Immigration

Edna Bonacich

Asian immigration to the United States arose within a particular context: the development of capitalism in this country. While the development of California and Hawaii, the areas of greatest Asian immigrant concentration, has the most direct bearing on the immigrant experience, both the development of these regions and the treatment of Asian laborers occurred within the wider context of United States development. This chapter, therefore, presents a brief history of United States capitalist development.

It is, of course, beyond the scope of this book to present a complete history of United States economic development. My goal is restricted to presenting a highly selective interpretation of United States development that seems best to explain Asian immigration in the pre-World War II period.

PRE-CIVIL WAR

The United States began its history as a British colony. The colonization of the United States (and many other territories around the globe) was a product of the development of capitalism in Great Britain and its concomitant, imperialism. European imperialism led to the creation of two major kinds of colonies: those that produced raw materials for the growing industries of Europe and those that became areas of settlement for the displaced, surplus population generated by capitalist development.[1] European colonies sometimes specialized in one or the other of these two functions. Thus, the British West Indies produced mainly raw materials, while Australia was principally an area of "white" settlement. The United States served both purposes, and therein lies a contradiction that is of major consequence for the "race" question, including the treatment of Asians, in this country.

The producers of raw materials for Great Britain came to the United States with hopes of developing the new territory, both to provide fodder for British industries using the cheapest means possible and to make fortunes for themselves in the process. They were capitalist in orientation, wanting to invest capital in the production of commodities to be sold in British and other markets for a profit. Under normal circumstances they would have hired "free labor," as was evolving in Western Europe, and participated in the simple capitalist mode of production.

But the colonies were not normal circumstances. While there was considerable variation from one British colony to the next, they all shared the problem of securing a labor supply. In some instances, efforts were made to pry the indigenous people from their own economy in order to have them work for the Europeans. In others, including the United States and the West Indies, the indigenous people were too sparsely settled or ravaged by European diseases and the conquest itself to provide an adequate labor supply.

One option was simply to recruit free wage labor from Europe. In territories where the indigenous population was sparse, however, the availability of vast expanses of land, or "open resources" (Domar 1970), meant that wage labor could not readily be hired on a voluntary basis. Any free person would rather strike out on his own and had little reason not to. In order to induce people to work for them, employers had to offer wages that were 30 to 100 percent higher than in Great Britain. And even then, as soon as they had accumulated enough to purchase their own farms or tools, most colonial workers would quit wage labor (Morris 1946:45, 48).

The high price of free labor in the colonies was incompatible with the production of raw materials for the European market. In addition to the high cost of labor power, heavy transportation costs had to be borne. Using free labor, the colonies could only produce very costly raw materials and not the required cheap goods. Commodity prices were set in the European market, and colonial producers were constrained to match them.

Given both the constraints of producing for a foreign, uncontrollable, distant market and the fact that free labor could rarely be secured no matter how high its price in a situation of open resources, colonial "capitalists" were forced to turn to some form of coercion in order to secure reasonably priced labor power. Efforts were made to enslave the Native Americans, while the indenture system and the use of convict labor bound many European immigrants to their employers for several years (Williams 1966:3-19; Morris 1946). The solution ultimately arrived at was the enslavement of Africans, a system that proved to be the cheapest and most reliable of all (Evans 1970:865).

Although colonial producers of raw materials came to depend upon coerced labor, their orientation was essentially capitalist. They were involved in the investment of capital in an enterprise whose purpose was the production of commodities for a market, while profits were created by the extraction of surplus from labor by having the slaves work longer hours than was necessary for their own subsistence. Profits were reinvested for the accumulation of greater quantities of capital. Still, the fact that they depended upon coerced labor ultimately acted as a brake on full-blown capitalist development, a point to which we shall return shortly.

The second strain of settlement in the American colonies consisted of people who were escaping from Great Britain. In the course of British capitalist development, millions of small farmers were displaced from the land. Many of them entered the new urban proletariat. Craftsmen, too, were displaced by mechanization, and urban unemployment became a chronic problem. Thus a large surplus population was created, many of whom fled to the colonies. These people were mainly trying to escape from the ravages of capitalist development. They hoped to recreate a precapitalist way of life in which people could maintain their independence and produce their own subsistence. Shepperson (1957:5) describes these British emigrants as follows:

> Agriculturalists romantically pictured the past and the "good old days" before the advent of the new industry, and by way of contrast saw America with her vast stretches of rich soil as a haven of hope where sturdy farmers could find opportunities no longer available in once "merry England."

Skilled artisans, too, came in response to the opportunity of setting up their own independent enterprises or acquiring homesteads (Morris 1946:26).

These settlers were, in a sense, anticapitalist. They glorified self-sufficiency, establishing what Merrill (1976) calls the "household mode of production." They had experienced the negative aspects of capitalist development and feared it. They clung tenaciously to a rough egalitarianism, knowing that the wealth of the few would lead to impoverishment and loss of autonomy for the many. Emmanuel (1972) describes this element among the white population in Africa, pointing out their antagonism to the metropolitan capitalist class and, indeed, to imperialism. The Boer War is a classic example of such anti-imperialist, white settler sentiment. Yet despite their anticapitalism, the settlers were essentially a backward-looking class, hoping to escape proletarianization rather than pass through capitalist development and on to socialism.

The United States thus had a duality, a fundamental division of purpose, from its inception. This division was a continuous source of struggle, reaching a pinnacle of intensity at the time of the Civil War but flaring up again and again thereafter. The struggle was between two different modes of production,[2] neither of which was a pure replica of European modes. Of the two, slavery represented the more advanced form, since it entailed capital accumulation. Indeed, during colonial times slave plantations were the largest form of enterprise and employed the most labor (Morris 1946:38). In contrast, the household mode of production tried to maintain precapitalist social relations, with a minimal use of hired labor of any kind.

The two modes of production were on a collision course. The slave-based enterprise was a threat to the independent household producers, which it tended to drive out. The process was similar to the ouster of yeoman farmers by the introduction of capitalist agriculture in Great Britain. Put simply, the employment of wage labor in capitalist production meant that employers could eke more value out of their workers than subsistence producers would squeeze out of themselves. When on top of this is added a coerced, slave labor force, the competition becomes deadly. In order to hold onto his land, a subsistence farmer would have to be willing to live and work like a slave. In addition, economies of scale made the slave plantation even more efficient, so working like a slave would not ensure the subsistence farmer's survival. Thus the two modes of production could not easily coexist, and as a result, one major impetus for United States westward expansion was the desire of small farmers to flee the negative impact of slavery.

One can think of the two competing modes of production as two competing ideals for the development of the United States territory. On the one hand was the ideal of a few wealthy men and a mass of slaves making raw materials for Europe, amassing riches for the former. Such was the development pattern of the West Indies and of Brazil in its early years. On the other hand was the Jeffersonian ideal of a more or less egalitarian society with many small, independent farmers and artisans, all of whom were generally self-sufficient. The latter ideal permitted extensive white settlement, while the former did not.

The evils of the first ideal, from the point of view of the second, were symbolized by slavery. Slavery allowed a few families to become excessively wealthy and to drive out the ordinary people. The slaves themselves were not to blame for this fact, of course, but their presence was the basis of the wealth and power of the plantation owners. Part of the antagonism toward the slave system was thus directed against the slaves. Their very helplessness made them objects of easy exploitation and the generators of large fortunes for the plantation owners.

The fact that the slaves were racially distinctive added another layer of ideology to this conflict. Because blacks had been enslaved, so some whites reasoned, they must be servile. No self-respecting white man would permit himself to be enslaved. It must be that blacks were naturally more exploitable. They were really only fit for slavery. And so on. These were the kinds of racist ideas that arose in a situation where slave status and race coincided.

The struggle between the two modes of production thus became partially phrased in racial terms. The question was whether the United States would become a "white man's country." This did not simply refer to the racial composition of the population but to a whole way of life. A white man's country really meant the Jeffersonian ideal of independent household producers. It meant the opportunity for extensive settlement. Most important, it meant a society in which labor had dignity and where people were free.

That blacks came to be seen as racially inferior made other nonwhite racial groups suspect. Only white men, and particularly white men from northwestern Europe, were believed indomitable. This suspicion was probably not based solely on assumptions about racial inheritance. It could also be a cultural theory and still have the same consequences. Africans, for instance, could be seen as having been enslaved because of their sociocultural condition (e.g., the political and economic weakness of west African societies relative to those in western Europe). The roots of their exploitability were of less relevance than the fact itself. It was the fact that was felt to be dangerous. One's theory of origins only had relevance to long-term policy in that, if one held a nongenetic theory, presumably blacks could be ultimately educated to become like free white men. Similarly other nonwhite groups, as well as Europeans of nonwestern origin, had to prove that they were not servile, either for racial or cultural reasons.

In sum, the question of race became interwoven in the conflict between two modes of production in the colonial United States. Black people were associated with the more capitalistic slave system, which was seen as antipathetic to the mass settlement of nonpropertied whites. As we shall see in the next chapter, this conflict between modes of production moved westward across the continent and was replayed in California.

Regional Differences

The northern and southern regions of the United States accommodated to this struggle in different ways, with important consequences for their development. The South, needless to say, became a stronghold of the coerced labor mode of production in the form of plantation agriculture based on African slave labor, which produced raw materials mainly for the British market. Table 3.1 shows the value of cotton exports relative to total exports from the United States prior to the Civil War. Almost half of these exports were destined for Great Britain (North 1966a:77). The dominance of cotton suggests the greater development of the South and also reveals its dependence on uncontrollable markets, hence its need to rely on coerced labor.

Yet even in this region where the slave mode of production predominated, the settler mode had its representatives in the form of nonslave-owning white farmers and artisans, who made up almost three-quarters

TABLE 3.1
VALUE OF TOTAL EXPORTS AND COTTON EXPORTS, 1816 TO 1860
(in thousands of dollars)

	Total	Cotton	Percent cotton
1816-1820	402,708	121,459	30.2
1821-1825	343,982	123,432	35.9
1826-1830	350,328	133,122	38.0
1831-1835	458,822	207,614	45.2
1836-1840	576,682	321,191	55.7
1841-1845	506,307	256,847	50.7
1846-1850	689,253	296,562	43.0
1851-1855	1,015,342	491,477	48.4
1856-1860	1,473,532	744,587	50.5

SOURCE: Adapted from North 1966a:233.

of the free population of the region (e.g., Shugg 1972:22-24). "A large percentage of the [southern white] population made very little cash income and cannot be thought of as a regular part of a market economy" (North 1966a:130). One author (Rothstein 1967) goes so far as to suggest that the South was a "dual economy," with a modern, commercial sector in the plantations and a "traditional," subsistence sector among the nonslave-owning poorer whites.

As has happened time and again, the people who did not have the capital to command the labor of others were forced off the best lands. Many fled to the hills, becoming the "hillbillies," "crackers," and poor whites of the South. They despised the plantation system, as shown by their high rate of desertion from the Confederacy during the Civil War, since it threatened their noncommercialized way of life (Genovese 1975:335).

Artisans, too, had difficulty surviving in the South. According to Mandel (1955:29),

> A mechanic in the South could not make a go of it because the local market was continually evaporating through the process of engrossing the land, driving out the small farmers, and replacing them with slaves, who were not good customers. . . . There was nothing left for him and his children but to move away or die.

One might add that artisans had to compete with much cheaper slave labor, too. Plantation owners preferred to train their slaves in the crafts instead of using less reliable free white labor (Spero and Harris 1966:5). And when not needed on the plantations, skilled slaves would be hired out or sent to the cities.

The dominance of slavery in the region meant that it was an unattractive area of settlement for free immigrants. Table 3.2 shows the distribution of foreign-born whites by region prior to the Civil War. Although these data are available only from 1850, they are based on the census and reflect cumulative settlement by immigrants over the previous decades. As can be seen, the South was much less attractive to immigrants than other sectors of the country, both in absolute numbers and relative to the population already settled there.

Similarly, because of slavery, the South was less able to keep the white population it did have. Table 3.3 shows the proportion of the native-born white population living in their regions of birth before the Civil War. The northern region clearly had a substantially lower loss rate than the South, especially the South Atlantic and East South Central states. (The West South Central area was one of the sections of the

TABLE 3.2
FOREIGN-BORN WHITE POPULATION BY REGION, 1850 AND 1860
(in thousands)

| | 1850 | | | 1860 | | |
	Total population	Foreign-born whites	Percent foreign-born	Total population	Foreign-born whites	Percent foreign-born
Northeast	8,627	1,324	15.3	10,594	2,016	19.0
North Central	5,404	650	12.0	9,097	1,543	17.0
South	8,983	240	2.7	11,133	392	3.5
West	179	27	15.1	619	179	28.9
Total	23,193	2,241	9.7	31,443	4,130	13.1

SOURCE: Derived from Historical Statistics of the United States 1975:22-23.

TABLE 3.3

LOSS OF NATIVE-BORN WHITE POPULATION, BY REGION, 1850 AND 1860

	1850		1860	
	No. of whites born in region	% living out of region of birth	No. of whites born in region	% living out of region of birth
New England	2,822	16.1	3,145	17.8
Middle Atlantic	5,484	16.7	6,944	19.6
East North Central	2,757	6.3	4,563	11.4
West North Central	374	10.4	849	10.9
South Atlantic	3,765	25.3	4,265	24.1
East South Central	2,180	21.8	2,781	26.3
West South Central	286	2.1	550	5.7
Mountain	60	0.0	101	0.0
Pacific	10	1.0	102	3.4
Total	17,737	17.1	23,299	18.6

SOURCE: Derived from Historical Statistics of the United States 1975:91.

new frontier to which white southerners were fleeing, hence its low loss rate.) Thus, the slave mode of production in the South tended to drive out free (white) laborers and the independent mode of production to which many of them aspired.

Of course, the slaves themselves were the people who suffered most from the system of coerced labor. In a sense they can be seen as the first major proletariat of the United States. Apart from the fact that they were not free to bargain over wages and work conditions, they were a proletariat in every other sense of the word: they had been completely separated from any vestige of ownership of the means of production, they had no control over the labor process, and their labor was completely alienated in the sense that they did not benefit from its fruits. The slaves were far more truly proletarianized than many of the white artisans, teamsters, and small farmers who still owned some of the tools of their trades.

It was upon the backs of the slaves that the whole edifice of southern production was erected. Slave labor produced the basic commodities that supported all else, including banks, merchants, and professionals as well as plantation owners. Slaves also staffed the service sector, providing cheap services that would otherwise have drained accumulated profits and permitting southern capitalists to live luxuriously. Their position in the economy was quite similar to that of Asians on the West Coast, as described in the previous chapter.

As we have said, during the colonial era the slave system was the most advanced mode of production. In the first two hundred years of European settlement in North America, the South was its wealthiest region (Perloff et. al. 1960:110). For example, in 1774, the net per capita wealth of free people was £32.7 in New England, £51.3 in the middle colonies, and £131.9 in the South (U.S. Bureau of the Census 1975:1175). The coerced labor mode of production had within it the seeds of its own destruction, however. Because of its heavy reliance on coerced labor, the South ultimately became a relatively stagnant region in terms of economic development. In this sense it was similar to other dependent territories in the colonial world that produced staples and raw materials for the world market and that at first were developed, only to become backward and underdeveloped in the long run (Dowd 1956).

The development of the South was largely stultified by the nature of its labor system. The principal reason, according to Anderson and Gallman (1977), lay in the fact that slave labor was a form of fixed capital. Slave owners had a heavy investment in their labor force and consequently had an interest in keeping their workers steadily employed. This led plantation owners to diversify their production so slave labor could be put to work during the slack season. Plantations often produced their own food, and slaves did various forms of skilled work. As a result, the region failed to develop highly specialized firms that could each maximize efficiency and trade with one another. Internal commerce was restricted, which in turn limited economic development. The key to this lay in the need of slave owners to keep their workers occupied. In a free labor system, in contrast, workers can be laid off when they are unneeded. The employer does not bear the burden of unemployment, making it easier to specialize.

One way to deal with the inflexibility of slave labor and the need to keep slaves occupied was to rent them out. Indeed a slave rental market did develop in the South, enabling slave labor to be used in industrial production (Starobin 1970; Wade 1964). But the rental market was limited and much less flexible than a system that simply permitted unneeded workers to fend for themselves.

Since slave labor was a fixed cost for the slave owner, when slaves were used in economic activities other than the production of the basic cash crop of the plantation, there was little incentive to invest in machinery to increase the productivity of labor. In the off-season there was a surplus of slave labor that could not be laid off. Labor was cheap during these periods, leading to the economically rational choice of labor-intensive methods of production. As a result, the productivity of slave labor remained low; there was no incentive to raise it (Anderson and Gallman 1977:37-38).

Post (1982) presents a somewhat different account of the failure of the slave system to become fully capitalistic. According to him, the essence of capitalism lies in "the continual technical reorganization of the labor process in order to continually reduce the share of necessary labor in relation to the share of surplus labor in the total social product. More precisely, the capitalist labor process is characterized by the increasing production of relative surplus labor, in the form of relative surplus-value."[3] In contrast, the slave plantation is characterized by the appropriation of absolute surplus value, that is, an effort to increase the intensity of exploitation but not to transform its character. Increasing relative surplus value would entail the displacement of labor, which is anathema to the slave owner with his heavy investment in the workers themselves. In order to increase labor productivity, then, the slave owner was limited to such efforts as increasing the pace of work, increasing the acreage worked by each slave, or moving to fresher, less exhausted soil. Herein lies the root of the tendency of the slave system to expand territorially.

One might add that the use of coercion in the slave system severely restricted the ability of the workers (slaves) to organize and demand improved working and living conditions. Their domination was a disincentive for slave owners to invest in laborsaving devices since labor was so cheap. Thus capitalist development was retarded so long as the owners of capital could earn big profits off the unchanging use of coerced labor.

The North followed a development path very different from that of the South. There the independent producers gained the upper hand and were able to contain and eventually abolish slavery before it could become the dominant mode of production (Mandel 1955:62-63). While it is common to argue that slavery did not take hold in the North mainly for geographical and climatic reasons that made plantations producing raw materials impractical, I suspect that social and political considerations were more significant. In particular, the fact that the northern colonies were, from the outset, areas where a high proportion of the immigrants were without substantial capital meant that a strong antislavery sentiment was implanted early. Once established, antislavery tended to snowball. If a region can keep slavery at a minimum, it becomes a more attractive area for poorer immigrants, who add to the ranks of those who oppose slavery, and so on.

Put another way, there is an unstable equilibrium between the two competing modes of production. If coerced labor establishes a foothold, it tends to drive out the small producers, who are no longer attracted to the region. Conversely, once small producers become established in a territory, it becomes a magnet for more of their kind, swelling the ranks of those who would keep out coerced labor. There is a difference between the two situations, however. Coerced labor tends to drive out the small producers for mainly economic reasons. The small settlers, in contrast, could only drive out slavery by political means because slavery was, in fact, the more efficient (cheaper) system. The ace the independent producers held was demographic: by attracting many more people, they could gain the numbers to push for a political victory and exclude slavery from their region.

Ironically, despite the fact that most of the settlers in the North were seeking to escape European capitalism, it was in this region that full-blown, industrial capitalism emerged. The independent household mode of production had within it the seeds of competitive capitalism[4] and, ultimately, of monopoly capitalism, a mode of production that threatened the independent producer at least as much as did slavery.

There is some debate whether industrial capitalism emerged before or after the Civil War (Hacker 1970), but along with North (1966a) and Bruchey (1975) I would argue that at least some growth in manufacturing was evident before the Civil War, especially after 1840. Thus between 1840 and 1860, the number of workers in factory production grew from 500,000 to 1,530,000, and their proportion rose from 13.9 to 18.5 percent of all workers (Bruchey 1975:44). These figures are for the country as a whole, but most of the growth in manufacturing occurred in the Northeast where, in 1850, 75 percent of the nation's manufacturing workers were employed (Bruchey 1975:46). Relative urbanization statistics, shown in table 3.4, are an indicator of the regional differentiation.[5]

The reasons for the emergence of capitalism in the North are obviously complex. One important reason would appear to be that the North did not rely on coerced labor. As we have seen, because of the availability of

TABLE 3.4
URBAN POPULATION AS A PERCENTAGE OF TOTAL POPULATION, BY REGION,
1820 TO 1860

	1820	1830	1840	1850	1860
New England	10.5	14.0	19.4	28.8	36.6
Middle Atlantic	11.3	14.2	18.1	25.5	35.4
East North Central	1.2	2.5	3.9	9.0	14.1
West North Central	0.0	3.5	3.9	10.3	13.4
South Atlantic	5.5	6.2	7.7	9.8	11.5
East South Central	0.8	1.5	2.1	4.2	5.9

SOURCE: North 1966a:258.

land, free labor was costly. Northerners could not easily acquire such labor and were forced to develop laborsaving devices in order to bypass it. English investigators in the United States in the 1850s were impressed by northern industrial innovations. The firms were not necessarily large, but they used a lot of machinery. "The constant concern with labor-saving machinery was considered . . . to be a fundamental explanation of the indigenous development of such innovations, and the relatively high price of labor was considered the driving force" (North 1966a:173). Since industry could not utilize cheap slave labor, there was an incentive for industrial development.

Furthermore, because labor was free in the North, this was an attractive area to European immigrants. Immigrants were available as a labor supply at least until they could amass sufficient capital to become independent. "In a society where the problem of relative labor scarcity was augmented by aspirations of the native born for independent employment, the supply of European labor provided a workforce ready and willing to enter industrial employment" (North 1966a:206-207). The coincidence of immigration and the rise of industrialization is shown in the following figures: between 1820 and 1840, 700,000 immigrants entered the United States; between 1840 and 1860 the figure was 4,200,000 (Bruchey 1975:39). Immigrants thus provided the new manufacturers with the needed labor force to begin to accumulate capital.

While immigrants were mainly attracted to the North because of opportunities for homesteading, their swelling numbers made this possibility increasingly remote. The more densely settled the region, the more the conditions of Western Europe were recreated, with people forced to sell their labor for a wage because they had no independent means of subsistence. Immigration helped create an industrial proletariat of truly "free" labor (i.e., labor that was "free" from ownership of the means of production), a necessary condition for the development of full-blown industrial capitalism.

Another factor in the industrialization of the North was its relationship to the South. Not only did British industrialism depend on cheap raw materials based on slave labor from the southern United States (Williams 1966); the northern United States, too, was able to accumulate capital through the slave trade (Dowd 1977:62) by shipping cotton to Great Britain and by financing and providing insurance to southern plantations (Foner 1941; North 1966a:113-113).[6] The first major northern industry was the production of cotton textiles in Massachusetts, using cheap southern cotton (North 1966a:160-161). Thus the development of the North depended, to some extent, on the underdeveloped labor system of the South. Northern as well as southern capitalists rested upon the backs of slaves.

Although the roots of industrial capitalism lay mainly in the independent household mode of production, it was a system that threatened to
destroy that way of life as surely as slavery. For, like slavery, capitalism
was a more advanced system of production that faced the independent
producer with deadly competition and ultimately forced him out of his
independence and into the labor market. Just as the slave plantation,
with its army of workers from whom surplus could be wrenched, drove
the small farmer off the land, so the factory, with its army of industrial
workers, threatened to drive out the independent artisan. As with slavery, the independent producer would have to work himself as hard as a
proletarian from whom surplus value was being extracted in order to
compete, and even then he would ultimately be driven out. The factory
had the advantage of a complex division of labor that made much more
efficient use of labor time. Moreover, it came to have capital invested in
machinery that drastically reduced the labor time necessary to produce
a particular commodity. A small producer, without capital to invest in
machinery or to hire labor, could not survive.

There was one important difference between displacement in the
North and South, however. Under slavery, there was no place for white
small farmers and artisans to go but out of the plantation area. Their
displacement did not push them into the slave "proletariat." Since they
never became slaves, they could not identify with them and join forces.
The whole slave system, including the slaves, were seen as the enemy.
In contrast, in the North, displacement had two possible consequences.
It pushed some independent producers into fleeing westward to escape
capitalist development. But it also drove some people into the new
industrial proletariat.

In the North, then, unlike in the South, the distinction between independent producer and proletariat was often blurred. There was considerable exchange in personnel between the two classes, in both directions. Independent artisans would find themselves driven into selling
their labor power for a wage, only to try to amass the capital to "buy"
their freedom. Even immigrants brought in as wage labor sought to
become petty producers (an option that was much less available to
slaves). Single families would often combine both petty producers and
proletariat, as in the practice of New England farmers sending their
daughters to work in the textile mills (Wertheimer 1977). And it was
sometimes difficult to determine whether an individual belonged to one
or the other class, especially during the early phases of capitalist development when artisans could keep their skills and some of their tools
while being hired by the owners and controllers of capital.

For example, in trying to determine the size of the industrial proletariat before the Civil War, Mandel (1955:13-15) runs into some difficulty

distinguishing this group from independent producers. In 1850, for instance, there were 1,288,000 mechanics, artisans, and skilled laborers in the United States. He has to examine the nature of their crafts in order to estimate whether they were self-employed. Thus, most of the 100,000 blacksmiths worked in two-person establishments, and he assumes they were mainly petty producers, while among the 185,000 carpenters he concludes that three-quarters were wage earners. In this year there were only 11,000 factory hands, though the 910,000 unskilled workers could be assumed to be wage earners. He concludes that not counting their families, about 12 percent of the free population were in the proletariat proper. But their stability in that class is questionable.

In the long run, the class differences between independent producers and proletariat are very important. The former group was essentially a reactionary class, seeking to reestablish a precapitalist golden age, while the latter was ultimately progressive, seeking to confront and challenge the reality of capitalist power. But for a time there was a basis for a coalition between them, even apart from the ambiguity of their boundaries. This lay in the fact that both classes were anticapitalist and especially opposed to big capital or the monopolies. Whether forward or backward looking, they shared a common enemy. This coalition of independent producers and industrial proletariat has been of major importance in United States history. It formed the basis of Jacksonian Democracy in the pre-Civil War period when the Democratic party rested upon it. And it provided the foundation of the populist movement later in the century.

Because big capital was often able to exploit racial minorities and, to a lesser extent, immigrants, the coalition often expressed its anticapitalism in racist terms or anti-immigrant movements. The superexploited were seen as the tools of big capital. As such they were dangerous, even though they suffered most from the system. In the pre-Civil War North, white workers expressed antipathy not only to slavery as a system but also to freed blacks, whom they saw as still vulnerable to domination by capital. Indeed, free blacks were more threatening to northern workers because they were available for exploitation by northern industrialists (Mandel 1955:65-66). Draft riots in New York during the Civil War reflected fears by northern workers that emancipation of the slaves would lead to a major, detrimental influx of blacks into the North (Lofton 1949; Man 1951).

Of the two anticapitalist classes, the petty producers were more likely to be racist. To them the whole system of capitalists accumulating wealth through the employment of cheap labor was threatening. They wanted to escape from it all and prevent cheap labor from following them. In contrast, segments of the industrial proletariat were capable of seeing past divisions in the working class to the possibility, indeed necessity, of a united working class movement. Since racial minorities, especially blacks, tended to be the most proletarianized segment of the population, the closer white workers came to complete proletarianization, the more they could find common cause. For a long time, however, the "working class" in the United States contained many people in transition between independent producers and true proletariat, such as craft workers in construction, who still owned some of their tools and controlled aspects of the labor process. Incomplete proletarianization meant that people would still want to fight the reactionary battle against displacement and therefore support racist movements.

Territorial Expansionism

As capitalism developed in the North, cyclical crises began to emerge. North (1966a:70) describes three major cycles from 1815 to the Civil War, each starting with a boom and ending in a depression: 1815 to 1823, 1823 to 1843, and 1843 to 1857. "Each surge of expansion during this period consisted of extensive movement into new territory, with all the concomitant internal migration and investment in transportation and construction which accompanied the opening up, settlement, and integration of the area into the economy" (North 1966a:13). In other words, imperialist expansion westward was a way of dealing with depressions; and capitalist development, with its inherent cyclical tendency, is one important factor in the westward movement.[7]

Table 3.5 shows the acquisition of land during the first half of the nineteenth century. Imperialist expansionism did not stop at the Pacific border, as we shall see, but continued across the ocean to Hawaii, the

TABLE 3.5
CUMULATIVE UNITED STATES TERRITORIAL ACQUISITIONS BEFORE THE CIVIL WAR.

		Total sq. miles (approximate)
1790		850,000
1803	Louisiana Purchase	1,700,000
1819	Florida	1,800,000
1845	Texas	2,100,000
1846	Oregon	2,480,000
1848	Mexican Cession	2,990,000
1853	Gadsden Purchase	3,010,000

SOURCE: North 1966a:99-100.

Philippines, and ultimately the Asian mainland, though not always in the form of territorial acquisition. What is important, however, is that the expansion of the small producer class more or less ceased in California. For a variety of reasons, the Pacific Islands and, especially, Asia proved unsuitable for large-scale white settlement. Capital, in contrast, moved more freely to wherever profits could be found.

Southern capitalists had an expansionist tendency as well, though for different reasons. As we have seen, the slave system depended upon the extraction of absolute surplus value (Post 1982). This led plantation owners to use their lands to their fullest capacity, which often resulted in soil exhaustion. In order to increase labor productivity, hence profits, the slave system moved toward increasing the amount of land under cultivation, as well as toward incorporating more fertile land. Although the roots of expansionism in the South were thus not identical to those in the North, the effect was similar, namely, territorial acquisition.

There were thus essentially two strains involved in westward movement in the United States, paralleling the two strains that left Great Britain to settle on the eastern seaboard (Kiernan 1978:4-5). There was, first, the capitalist expansion of both the North and South. These two areas had competing modes of production based on different labor systems. But they also shared a great deal in common, namely, the tendency to expand in the face of declining profitability. In a way, the competition between them for the Western territories is similar to that between two European nations competing for colonies in Africa. Both were driven by a similar expansionist dynamic and came into conflict over dividing the spoils.

The second strain of westward movement was of people seeking to escape the negative effects of capitalism of both varieties. As with the British poorer classes, these people moved to the frontier in an effort to reestablish an independent household mode of production. Their interests were very different from those of the capitalist expansionists. For example, Shannon (1957:44) describes agitation from the late 1820s to the 1850s by the eastern labor parties, which sought to preserve easy access to the land for potential homesteaders. One proposal, which gained widespread support, was as follows:

> End all selling of public land and . . . dispose of it in maximum lots of 160 acres to persons who would farm it. Such tracts should remain free of any threat of monopoly control even by seizure for debts. In order that eastern laborers could get their share, the government was to pay for necessary equipment and for transportation to the land (Shannon 1957:44).

This reveals a certain socialist strain in the homesteading class.[8] Despite their backward-looking orientation, they were fiercely anti-big capital and wanted a rough equality, at least for white men.

Federal land policy reflected the conflicting interests represented by these two very different sources of western expansionism. While many historians see the state as having essentially given in to capitalist interests (e.g., North 1966b:125), particularly revealed in the "donation of a tenth of the area of the United States to railroad corporations" (Shannon 1957:45), there are also signs of important concessions to settler interests. For instance, the Preemption Act of 1841 gave some protection to "squatters," people who settled on new land before it had been surveyed for public auction, granting them first rights of purchase (North 1966b:124) before the "speculators and monopolists" could buy it all up.

The most important piece of legislation was the Homestead Act of 1862, under which "a bonafide settler could receive title to 160 acres free and clear (or 320 acres if he were married) provided that he lived on the land and improved it for a certain period and in certain terms" (North 1966b:125). This act reflected a compromise and did not prevent the monopolization of much of United States territory. But the fact that it was passed reveals that the independent producer class was not without political clout.

Both northern and southern capitalists were at odds with the independent producers over land policy in the West. The former wanted to be able to purchase large tracts for commercial purposes. They wanted land to be costly enough to be beyond the reach of those who possessed no capital in order to create a surplus of free labor (O'Connor 1975:50). "Opposition [to free land] came from the entrenched Atlantic seaboard interests, . . . both north and south, who wanted to maintain land prices, [and] prevent mobility of labor" (Shannon 1957:44). But in the mid-1850s, the Republican party was able to forge a coalition between homesteaders and northern capitalists in opposition to the expansion of slavery, thereby isolating the southern capitalists. Both could agree on the dangers of the expansion of slavery, though for different reasons (Hacker 1970:186; Foner 1970).

One can see in these conflicting interests some of the roots of the Civil War. By that time, there were essentially three modes of production in the United States: southern dependent capitalism, tied to British and northern United States markets and sources of capital and relying upon coerced labor; northern incipient industrial capitalism, seeking to establish independence in relation to Great Britain and using free labor; and the independent household mode of production, found most clearly in the West but with strong segments in the North and, to a lesser extent, the South.

The war mainly represented a conflict between the two regional capitalisms. Not only were they both expansionist and therefore competing over the carving up of the western territories, like any two imperialist nations, but the differences between their productive systems also put them in conflict. For one thing, northern capitalists wanted protection for their young industries by the institution of tariffs against cheap British manufactured imports, while the South, because of its high levels of trade with Great Britain and reliance on cheap British goods, not to mention goodwill, was opposed to protectionism (e.g., Aglietta 1978:21). Another source of friction was the different labor systems, with the South having a competitive edge in some industries because of its cheaper labor supply (Mandel 1955:63; Bonacich 1975). Furthermore, because the North relied on free labor, which in turn depended on extensive settlement and the filling up of open resources so that some independent producers would be forced to "freely" sell their labor power for a wage, the expansion of slavery was detested, since slavery precluded wide-scale settlement. Similarly, the expansion of slavery limited the development of an internal market, which northern industries depended upon in their early days when they could not yet compete in the world market. For all these reasons, and there are probably others, northern and southern capitalists were on a collision course.

The independent producers, as we have seen, were in conflict with both of these modes of production. But their conflict with the slave system was more severe than it was with northern capitalism. If a western territory became a slave area, it would be unavailable for homesteading. Northern capitalism was still in its infancy at this stage and posed less of a threat in the western territories (with the important exceptions of the railroads and the land speculators). Besides, northern capitalists had an interest in a densely settled interior, as we just mentioned. Thus there was a basis for a temporary coalition between these two modes of production. As Aglietta (1978:21) states,

> The reasons for the political alliance between the [northern] capitalists and the agricultural small producers are clear enough. The latter feared above all else the extension of the slave system to the free lands of the West, and the blocking of the sales of public land by a Congress dominated by the slaveowners' representatives. . . . Yet they were soon to find out to their cost that this was an alliance with the devil himself.

Meanwhile, it proved to be a winning coalition, and the slave system was demolished.

POST-CIVIL WAR

The period after the Civil War marks the rise of monopoly capitalism in the United States. During this period the United States emerged as the world's leading industrial power. Giant corporations became an important part of the United States economic scene. With them came a rise in capital investment, an increase in the organic composition of capital, increased class struggle, major cyclical crises, and a growth in imperialist expansion. While these developments were mainly centered in the northeastern sector of the country, they had implications for the West and Hawaii, the areas of major Asian settlement. In brief, crisis in the industrial centers spurred investment in the West and encouraged the importation of cheap labor power that could be used to deal with the declining rate of profit.

Rise of Monopoly Capitalism

Although industrialization had begun in the United States before the Civil War, it was only after the war, particularly in the last two decades of the century, that United States capitalism was transformed into what is termed by some *monopoly capitalism*. The Civil War itself marked an important shift in relations with Great Britain. Despite formal independence in 1776, the United States, especially the South, remained heavily dependent on British capital, manufactured imports, and markets. The defeat of the South enabled the federal government to institute high tariffs against manufactured imports, giving an important boost to local industrialization (Scheiber et al. 1976:284-287).

The hallmark of monopoly capitalism is the concentration of capital in fewer and larger business enterprises to the point where they can exercise considerable control over access to inputs, including raw materials and financing, and over markets and prices. In 1865, the typical United States business was a family owned and operated firm producing for a local market (Scheiber et al. 1976:221). The concentration of capital is indicated by a dramatic reduction in self-employment and the transformation of independent operators into wage and salary workers. Table 3.6 shows the decline in self-employment from 1900 to 1940. By 1900, over half of the economically active population were already nonowners. The process of proletarianization continued until World War II, when close to three-quarters of the labor force were wage and salary workers. Most of this shift is accounted for by the destruction of family farming.

Consolidation of the railroads began in the 1850s and continued until, by 1904, 90 percent of the rail mileage of the country was under the control of six financial groups. Financial institutions, such as insurance

TABLE 3.6
PERCENT DISTRIBUTION OF CLASS OF WORKER, FOR EMPLOYED PERSONS
FOURTEEN YEARS AND OLDER, 1900 TO 1940.

	1900	1910	1920	1930	1940
Self-employed	35.9	31.4	27.8	25.5	22.9
Unpaid family workers	11.2	7.2	4.5	4.0	4.0
Wage and salary workers*	52.9	61.4	67.7	70.6	73.2
Total numbers (in thousands)	26,956	34,559	39,208	44,183	47,520

SOURCE: Lebergott 1964:513.
*Includes domestic service employees.

companies and investment banks, also showed early signs of consolidation and were among the largest of business establishments during the 1860s (Scheiber et al. 1976:231).

Industrial concentration, however, was a phenomenon that largely began in the 1870s and reached a peak in the 1890s. The process continued in an erratic way, well into the twentieth century, with major merger movements arising in the late 1920s and mid-1950s (Nelson 1959:3-7). Indeed, another seemed to be in progress in the early 1980s.

Capitalist concentration took several forms. First there were simple mergers in which one firm bought out others. Mergers occurred either by vertical or horizontal integration. In the latter, competitors would be incorporated, while in the former, control was extended over industrial inputs (Scheiber et al. 1976:231-232). The merger movement reached its peak after the depression of 1893 to 1897 and was especially evident in the years 1898 to 1902. Table 3.7 shows the annual mergers from 1895 to 1920. According to Nelson (1959:100-102), most of the mergers from 1895 to 1904 led to the acquiring by a firm of a dominant share of the market in its industry.

A second means of consolidation was the creation of pools and cartels. These were organizations of businesses in a specific industry that attempted to impose agreements on component firms to limit competition, fix prices, and sometimes set up territorial agreements. While the railroads formed pools in the 1850s, manufacturing pools reached their zenith in the 1870s. Pools and international cartels are found well into the twentieth century, however (Scheiber et al.1976:233).

Trusts, a third form of consolidation, emerged in the mid-1880s and remained in wide use until 1897. Trusts were more efficient than pools and depended less on unenforceable agreements and more on the actual

TABLE 3.7
FIRM DISAPPEARANCES BY MERGER, 1895 TO 1920.

Year	No. of firm disappearances
1895	43
1896	26
1897	69
1898	303
1899	1,208
1900	340
1901	423
1902	379
1903	142
1904	79
1905	226
1906	128
1907	87
1908	50
1909	49
1910	142
1911	103
1912	82
1913	85
1914	39
1915	71
1916	117
1917	195
1918	71
1919	171
1920	206

SOURCE: Nelson 1959:37.

transfer of stock so that ownership was consolidated. John D. Rocke-
feller's Standard Oil, formed in 1879 and reorganized in 1882, is an
early example of a successful trust (Scheiber et al. 1976:233).

In 1890 the Sherman Antitrust Act was passed, leading capital consolidation to take a new form: the holding company. In this instance, an
outside organization was formed that held stock in several corporations
and was thus able to coordinate their activities even while not formally
owning them. An 1895 Supreme Court decision supported the legality
of this form, stimulating the further concentration of capital (Scheiber
et al. 1976:233).

Using concentration ratios that measure the percentage of total sales
in an industry controlled by the four largest firms in the industry,

Scheiber et al. (1976:235) estimated that by 1901 nearly one-third of the value added in manufacturing was accounted for by industries with concentration ratios of 50 or higher. Among the most concentrated industries at the time were steel (78.8), paper and allied products (71.0), and transportation equipment (57.3). Thus, even before the major merger movement was over, the United States was a highly concentrated economy.

Endemic to capitalist development is a tendency toward cyclical crises. These are clearly evident in the late nineteenth century, with two major depressions, 1873 to 1878 and 1893 to 1897, and a recession from 1882 to 1885 (Scheiber et al. 1976:193-194; Kirkland 1961:4-8). Marxist theory would also predict a decline in the rate of profit accompanying a rise in the organic composition of capital. Clearly the latter phenomenon was proceeding at a rapid pace in the last decades of the nineteenth century, as indicated by a rise in manufacturing.

Table 3.8 presents one measure of the rise in manufacturing, namely, the distribution of the labor force. As can be seen, at the time of the Civil War, well over half of the labor force was engaged in agriculture, while only 15 percent worked in manufacturing. Even as late as 1900, despite considerable growth in manufacturing employment and a decline in the proportion working in agriculture, the latter still outnumbered the former two to one. It was only in 1920 that the absolute numbers working in agriculture began to decline; in the same year, the number employed in manufacturing finally exceeded agricultural workers.

Proportion employed in manufacturing is not an unalloyed indicator of the rising organic composition of capital. For one thing, other industries, including agriculture, may also develop an increased relative investment in machinery and raw materials. Manufacturing almost certainly was associated with such increases, however, and thus its tremendous growth in this period suggests increased capital investment in the means of production. The percentages in table 3.8 mask the extent of this growth, since they only present relative distributions. In fact, between 1860 and 1900, employment in manufacture grew 285 percent (compared to 99 percent in agriculture) and grew 631 percent from 1860 to 1920.

Seltzer (1979:105) reports on a study that attempted to measure the organic composition of capital and purported to find that it rose substantially between 1880 and 1920. There are questions, however, about the validity of the approach. Seltzer (1979:105) also investigates whether the profit rate was falling. Using data from banking, the only industry for which such information is available, he finds that net profits fell from an average of 7.7 percent in the 1870s to 5.8 percent in the 1890s.

TABLE 3.8

INDUSTRIAL DISTRIBUTION OF UNITED STATES LABOR FORCE, 1860 TO 1940
(percentage).

	1860	1870	1880	1890	1900	1910	1920	1930	1940
Agriculture	59.0	52.1	51.7	45.0	42.8	35.5	30.7	28.7	25.4
Fishing	0.3	0.2	0.2	0.3	0.2	0.2	0.1	0.2	0.2
Mining	1.8	1.4	1.6	2.0	2.3	3.2	3.4	2.7	2.4
Construction	5.2	6.0	5.2	6.8	6.1	5.9	3.5	5.4	5.0
Manufacture	15.4	19.0	19.1	19.8	21.6	25.1	31.8	26.9	29.9
Trade	8.9	10.1	11.2	13.4	14.5	16.0	16.6	22.1	24.7
Transport*	2.3	2.3	3.1	3.9	4.2	6.0	6.9	4.9	3.5
Service†	7.2	9.0	7.9	8.7	8.2	8.1	6.9	9.0	9.0
Total (in thousands)	9,967	13,023	17,262	22,120	27,297	33,197	35,144	36,769	37,769

SOURCE: Lebergott 1964:510.

*Combines ocean and railroad transportation. May omit other forms.

†Combines teachers and domestic service workers. May omit other forms.

Over the same period, the average yield on stock investments fell from 6.1 percent in the 1870s to 4.1 percent in the 1890s. Perhaps more important is evidence from such leading economists of the time as one of Grover Cleveland's chief financial advisors, David Wells, who in the 1880s spoke of a falling "rate of profit on even the most promising kinds of capital" (cited in McCormick 1967:27).

As discussed in the introductory chapter of this volume, the rising organic composition of capital and the falling rate of profit can be linked to a rise in cost of labor power (or variable capital). In a later section of this essay we shall examine the nature of the United States labor force and the working class movement. For now we turn to an examination of the effects of these developments, namely the rise of United States imperialism.

Imperialism

The rise in monopoly capitalism is temporally linked to the rise of United States imperialism. Imperialism needs to be distinguished from simple territorial expansion, which, as we have seen, can have many roots, including efforts to escape capitalist development. By imperialism I mean that form of expansionism that is rooted in the contradictions of advanced capitalism, including cyclical crises and the tendency for the rate of profit to fall.

There is some question of the precise timing of the emergence of the United States as an imperialist nation. According to Seltzer (1979:102), the United States became a full-blown imperialist power at the turn of the century (1898 to 1901). But early signs of imperialist activity began in the 1870s, after the Civil War and once the hegemony of capitalism had been unquestionably established.

Imperialist expansion can be seen in a rise in United States international trade and particularly in a shift in the content of that trade from the export of raw materials and import of manufactured goods to the reverse. It can be seen in a rise in American investments abroad. And it can be seen in various overt political and military moves in relation to other countries. Let us look at each of these in turn.

Changing Trade Relations

The post-Civil War period marks a major expansion of United States overseas trade. "By 1920 exports had increased 24-fold over the level of 1860 and imports had increased 16-fold" (Scheiber et al. 1976:280). Table 3.9 presents the raw figures on trade, and the first two columns

TABLE 3.9

UNITED STATES INTERNATIONAL TRADE, 1866 TO 1940

(in millions of dollars).

Years	Exports	Imports	Exports / Imports
1866-1870	1,539	2,042	.75
1871-1875	2,429	2,889	.84
1876-1880	3,319	2,463	1.35
1881-1885	3,873	3,337	1.16
1886-1890	3,628	3,585	1.01
1891-1895	4,381	3,925	1.12
1896-1900	5,680	3,708	1.53
1901-1905	7,134	4,861	1.47
1906-1910	8,755	6,724	1.30
1911-1915	11,659	8,561	1.36
1916-1920	33,471	17,557	1.91
1921-1925	21,552	17,251	1.25
1926-1930	23,439	20,167	1.16
1931-1935	9,944	8,539	1.16
1936-1940	15,832	12,201	1.30

SOURCE: Historical Statistics of the United States, Colonial Times to 1970, Washington, D.C.: U.S. Government Printing Office, 1975: 889-890.

TABLE 3.10

COMPOSITION OF UNITED STATES INTERNATIONAL TRADE, 1866 TO 1940

Years	Ratio exports/imports		Percent manufactures	
	Raw materials	Manufactures	Imports	Exports
1866-1870	2.01	.33	75.1	33.3
1871-1875	1.68	.48	69.7	39.6
1876-1880	2.07	.93	63.4	43.8
1881-1885	1.83	.80	65.1	45.2
1886-1890	1.40	.77	61.6	46.9
1891-1895	1.34	.95	57.8	49.1
1896-1900	1.55	1.52	55.4	55.0
1901-1905	1.35	1.57	53.7	57.5
1906-1910	1.16	1.42	54.5	59.4
1911-1915	1.13	1.57	52.3	60.4
1916-1920	1.01	2.89	47.9	72.5
1921-1925	.96	1.52	51.5	62.7
1926-1930	.72	1.59	50.6	69.2
1931-1935	.89	1.38	55.6	65.9
1936-1940	.64	1.86	53.8	77.2

SOURCE: Same as table 3.9.

reveal tremendous growth in both imports and exports up to 1920. The ratio of exports to imports shows that exports overtook imports in the mid-1870s and that the United States balance of trade remained favorable until World War II.

More important as an index of imperialism is a shift in the composition of trade. The unequal exchange of imperialism is predicated on the export of capital-intensive goods and the import of labor-intensive goods and raw materials. Until 1890, the leading United States exports were agricultural products, such as wheat, corn, and meat, and processed foods, such as flour, vegetable oils, and dairy products. Meanwhile, imports were dominated by manufactured goods, such as iron and steel products and textiles, mainly from Great Britain and other European countries. Manufactured exports began to rise after the Civil War, however, while imports revealed a shift toward foods and raw materials and away from manufactures (Scheiber et al. 1976:281-282).

Table 3.10 suggests these shifts. The data presented in Historical Statistics are divided into five types of imports and exports: crude materials, crude food, manufactured food, semimanufactures, and finished manufactures. In table 3.10 the cutting point lies between the first two categories (raw materials) and the latter three. Undoubtedly the results would look different if we defined raw materials and manufactures differently.

The table shows that, on the one hand, raw materials tended to be an important export for the United States up to 1920, and, indeed, raw materials exports predominated over imports until this time. On the other hand, manufactured exports grew rapidly relative to imports, and by the turn of the century the United States exported more manufactures than it brought in (columns 1 and 2). If we look at the percentage of all imports and exports that are manufactured (columns 3 and 4), we find a steady decline in the former and a steady rise in the latter, with the crossover occurring around the turn of the century. All of this suggests a shift in the United States position in the world economy from raw materials supplier to industrial power. The long-lasting export of raw materials and foodstuffs suggests, however, that the shift was not total and that sectors of the vast United States hinterland continued to remain unindustrialized.

The rise in manufactured exports can be seen as an indicator of imperialism in that it was a reaction to internal problems and contradictions. According to McCormick (1967:21-52), overproduction was the key to the recurrent crises and declining rate of profit of the late nineteenth century, at least in the eyes of business leaders and politicians. In addition, the social dislocations associated with early competitive capitalism were generating major protest movements by farmers and workers.

These developments led business and political leaders to push for expansion of overseas markets, both as a direct method of dealing with overproduction and as an effort to "export" the social problems.

The Pacific basin became one increasingly important arena of United States commerce. New England whalers, merchants, and missionaries established a foothold in Hawaii in the 1820s. By the Civil War, the Monroe Doctrine, demanding the noninterference of European powers in Western Hemisphere affairs, had been implicitly extended to Hawaii. The takeovers of Hawaii and even of California can be seen as efforts to establish stepping-stones to the vast China market (LaFeber 1963:5, 7). Some of the major developments in transportation of the time, including the construction of a transcontinental railway system and the digging of the Panama Canal, were also at least partially aimed at the reaching of the Far Eastern market by northeastern industries (McCormick 1967:18-19).

Trade with Asia began as early as 1783 when the first United States trading vessel stopped at Canton. Thereafter, United States traders continued to carry both American and European exports to Canton and Calcutta. In 1821, United States exports to China were valued at $4.3 million, and that country was the fourth largest recipient of American goods. An 1836 census of Canton, the only Chinese city open to foreign trade at the time, found that nine of the fifty-five foreign firms there were from the United States (Lewis 1938:175-176).

The United States led the way in opening Japan to Western commerce with the arrival of Commodore Matthew Perry in 1853. A treaty was signed in 1854 opening Japanese ports to United States merchants, but trade with Japan grew slowly until the end of the century (Lewis 1938:176-177). Efforts were made to open Korea to United States influence in a similar way in 1871, but they failed, only to succeed in 1882 following the successful establishment of a treaty with Korea by Japan (Williams 1956:330).

While the majority of United States manufactured exports went to Europe, the European proportion of the export market (which included raw materials) decreased from 81 percent in 1870 to 65 percent in 1910. Meanwhile, United States manufactures were gradually penetrating Third World markets, especially in Latin America and Asia (Scheiber 1976:282). In the 1870s, Asia accounted for less than 2 percent of the United States export trade. By the turn of the century, it had doubled to 4 percent. After World War I, exports to Asia rose to about 9 percent of total exports, climbing to over 16 percent by 1940. The Asian trade was even more important as a means of supplying raw materials. By the 1870s over 10 percent of United States imports derived from Asian countries, rising to 15 percent at the turn of the century, 27 percent during World War I, and over 30 percent by 1940 (Gideonse 1951:547-548).

These overall trends mask important shifts in the Asia trade, particularly a marked rise in the 1890s. According to McCormick (1967:300), growing commercial interests in the Far East during this decade were very important in explaining the Spanish-American War and its aftermath. For instance, in the early 1890s, United States exports to China were valued at $4 million per annum. In 1896 they jumped to $6.9 million and in 1897 to $11.9 million. Similarly, exports to Japan climbed from $3.9 million in 1894 to $7.6 million in 1896 and $13 million in 1897 (McCormick 1967:301). Certain industries were especially dependent upon Asian markets, notably, cotton goods, kerosene, wheat flour, iron, and steel (McCormick 1967:354). Thus trade, as an index of imperialism, was burgeoning with Asia by the late nineteenth century.

Overseas Investments

Standardizing for changing currency values, Seltzer (1979:103-104) reports that United States overseas investments grew from $250 million (1967 dollars) in 1869 to $2.8 billion in 1897, for an annual growth rate of 9 percent. By 1908, the value of foreign investments had grown to $9.26 billion. In 1869, foreign investments were 1.4 percent of the gross national product; in 1897 they were 4.8 percent; and in 1908, 9.0 percent. Clearly, in the late nineteenth and early twentieth centuries there was a major shift in the nature of United States involvement abroad.

According to Wilkins (1970:71-72), the largest wave of capital exports prior to World War I occurred after the panic of 1893 and the depression of 1893 to 1897. Indeed, the heaviest period of foreign investments, 1898 to 1901, coincides with the first major merger movement, which created massive banking houses and giant corporations that were in a position to move overseas.

Table 3.11 shows the geographic distribution of American overseas investments. Before World War II Asia was not a major source of United States investment compared to other areas. Yet even proportionally, investments in that continent jumped from 3.4 percent of total United States investments in 1897 to 9.3 percent in 1908. Thereafter the Asian proportion stabilized at around 7 percent. In dollar value, however, overall investments were growing dramatically, the amount invested in Asia growing more than ten times from 1897 to 1914 and quadrupling between 1914 and 1929.

TABLE 3.11

DIRECT AND PORTFOLIO INVESTMENTS BY REGION, 1897 TO 1935

(in millions of dollars).

	1897	1908	1914	1919	1924	1929	1935
Europe	151.0	489.2	691.8	1,986.8	2,652.8	4,600.5	3,026.0
Canada	189.7	697.2	867.2	1,542.8	2,631.7	3,660.2	3,657.6
Latin America*	308.3	1,068.2	1,648.7	2,406.1	3,672.9	5,429.2	4,551.0
Africa	1.0	5.0	13.2	31.2	58.7	119.2	125.8
Asia	23.0	235.2	245.9	309.5	671.8	1,040.4	915.3
Oceania	1.5	10.0	17.0	54.2	140.7	403.0	413.1
International	10.0	20.0	30.0	125.0	125.0	140.1	151.9
Total†	684.5	2,524.8	3,513.8	6,455.6	9,953.6	15,392.6	12,840.7

SOURCE: Lewis 1938:606.

*Includes Cuba and other islands of the West Indies, Mexico, Central America, and South America.

†Excludes short-term credits.

It is interesting to note that even as the United States moved to export capital, it continued to be a recipient of investments from Europe, especially Great Britain. As late as 1910, over $6 billion in European capital was invested here (Faulkner 1943:565). Indeed, the United States remained a debtor nation, owing more on external loans than it earned from its own overseas investment activities, until World War I. It was only at the time of the war that the United States became a creditor nation, and New York replaced London as the financial center of world capitalism (Dowd 1977:227; Faulkner 1951:86-87). Again this reveals the dual character of the United States, combining both colonial and advanced capitalist features until quite late.

Imperial Wars and Takeovers

The expansion of foreign trade and investments coincided with active state intervention in the affairs of other countries. This most visible aspect of imperialism emerged with full force at the turn of the century, particularly with the Spanish-American War of 1898. Certainly the United States government had not been completely passive in foreign affairs prior to the war, but the late nineteenth century was marked by the rise of full-blown western European imperialism and the carving up of the world into European colonies. Within this context, the United States was a relatively minor imperialist power, jostling to maintain a position among the stronger powers (Iriye 1977:53). It was only with the Spanish-American War that the United States became a significant colonizer. And even then it was not until World War I that the United States joined the Europeans as a leading imperialist power.

United States capitalism had two principal targets of expansionism: Latin America, particularly the Caribbean area, and the Pacific, including both the Pacific islands and the countries of Asia ringing the Pacific basin. In the latter, even before the Spanish-American War, expansionary moves were occurring. For instance, in 1867 the United States claimed Midway. A United States harbor was secured in Samoa in 1878, in part by supporting the islands against the domination of European powers; finally, in 1899, Germany, Great Britain, and the United States established a joint protectorate in Samoa. Meanwhile, United States penetration of Hawaii continued, leading to a revolution in 1893 and ultimately to annexation in 1898 (Williams 1956:329-330).

The Spanish-American War enabled the United States to wrest Cuba, Puerto Rico, Guam, and the Philippines from the dying Spanish empire. The form of takeover differed from one territory to the next: Puerto Rico and the Philippines were openly annexed, while Cuba was more subtly reduced to a virtual protectorate by forcing a constitutional amendment upon her in 1901 (Scheiber et al. 1976:289). United States troops landed in Cuba in 1906, 1912, and 1917 to preserve control (Faulkner 1951:71).

Acquisition of the Philippines gave the United States yet another stepping-stone to Asia, particularly China. There the United States had to compete with the more advanced European imperialist powers as well as a rising Japan. In this case, expansionism took the form of the United States asserting its equal access to Far Eastern markets and investment opportunities. The "open door notes" of 1899 announced the determination of the United States to gain access to China. While the notes formally expressed concern for China's political integrity, they were strongly supported by business and financial interests that foresaw not only commercial but also investment potential in China (Scheiber et al. 1976:288-289).

In Central America, the United States instigated a revolution in a sector of Colombia that became Panama. A puppet regime permitted the United States to build a canal through the isthmus, which aided the opening of access to the Pacific. In 1904 Theodore Roosevelt enunciated the "Roosevelt corollary" of the Monroe Doctrine that asserted that the United States would act as an international police force to maintain certain kinds of regimes in Latin America. This was quickly acted upon in the Dominican Republic in 1905, when the United States became heavily involved in that country's financial affairs. Finally, in 1916, the marines were sent to take direct control (Scheiber et al. 1976:290).

Other areas of direct United States intervention included Haiti (1915) and Nicaragua (1912). Giant American corporations, especially the United Fruit Company, dominated Guatemala, Honduras, and Costa Rica (Scheiber et al. 1976:290-291). And in 1917 the United States purchased the Virgin Islands (Faulkner 1951:70). In sum, at the end of the nineteenth century and during the first two decades of the twentieth, the United States emerged as a leading imperialist power in competition with western European countries and Japan.

Labor

As suggested in the introductory theoretical essay, an important source both of capitalist crises and of imperialist expansion is a change in the nature of the labor force. In particular, as capitalism advances, labor power becomes more costly, in part because workers come to organize themselves politically. This section examines developments in the United States labor movement in the post-Civil War period. I then consider one of the major ways that capital dealt with this problem, namely, the encouragement of large-scale immigration from southern and eastern Europe. The reasons for this course and its consequence of perpetuating a white/nonwhite race line are evaluated. Finally, I examine the persistence of a small producer class well beyond the Civil War and its continued antimonopoly coalition with labor. This coalition, I believe, was crucial for the perpetuation of racism as a major organizing principle of the United States political economy until well into the twentieth century.

Indigenous Labor Movement

The working class in the United States had formed organizations from the beginning of the nineteenth century, but until the Civil War they tended to be small-scale and local in scope (Faulkner 1943:460). The postbellum period marks a sharp rise in labor organizing. From the Civil War until 1873 the number of national unions rose dramatically. Unions appeared among construction workers, skilled railroad workers, cigar makers, telegraphers, iron and steelworkers, and shoemakers (Kirkland 1961:357).

Increasing unionization corresponded to shifts in the structure of United States capitalism. The rise of large corporations in urban centers provided the conditions for labor organizations to emerge. First of all, workers were increasingly removed from ownership of the tools of their trade. The sheer size of the proletariat grew dramatically, from

957,000 in 1849 to 4,252,000 in 1889 and 7,036,000 in 1914. Second, as capital became concentrated, investment in machinery proceeded, threatening crafts workers with deskilling (or the reduction of their crafts to more simplified processes that could be quickly learned) and displacement. It is no accident that the earliest workers to organize were the skilled, since their way of life was most threatened by the rise of giant monopolies (Faulkner 1943:459).

The rise of monopoly capitalism provided other impetuses to labor organizing. The congregation of workers in large plants and the concentration of these plants in the growing cities of the Northeast permitted workers to communicate their grievances and combine their efforts. Furthermore, by establishing a national market supported by an extensive communications network that included newspapers as well as transportation linkages, capital unwittingly created the means by which workers, too, could communicate across vast stretches of territory. An aggressive labor press, for example, formed early (Faulkner 1943:459-460).

Movements toward the formation of a national labor federation also appeared right after the war in response to the emergence of a national economy. The first, the National Labor Union, was formed in 1866. Among other things, it pushed for limiting the workday to eight hours and achieved some legislative success. The organization disappeared in 1872 after having formed a political party that stressed currency reform at the expense of trade unionism (Foner 1947:370-432).

A more long-lasting and important federation, the Knights of Labor, was formed in 1869 and reached its peak in the 1880s (Foner 1975:47-92). The Knights incorporated unskilled as well as skilled workers and, unlike much of the rest of the labor movement, organized immigrants, women, and blacks. Its inclusiveness did not, however, extend to the Chinese (Foner 1975:58-60).

Meanwhile in the 1880s a new federation of nationally based unions emerged, the American Federation of Labor. Unlike the Knights of Labor, which tried to organize the entire working class into a single union and whose structure tended to emphasize regional organization, the AFL was a loose federation of nationally based unions usually organized around the principle of a common trade. While the Knights sought fundamental change of the wage labor system, the AFL was willing to work within the structure of capitalism but pushed for economic gains for its members (Grob 1971).

The AFL, of course, came to dominate the United States labor movement at least until the 1930s, while the Knights of Labor disappeared. There are at least two reasons for the shift, which can be seen as a triumph of craft unionism. First, given the level of development of the United States proletariat at the time and the fact that the major transformations that were occurring tended to threaten skilled workers, perhaps organization along craft lines was inevitable. One of the important contributing factors to the demise of the Knights was its conflict with the trade unions and inability to deal with the particular problems of workers in specific trades and industries (Foner 1975:157–161).

Second, in the late 1880s there was a major counteroffensive by the capitalist class against the labor movement. Starting with the Haymarket affair in 1886, employers engaged in a reign of terror to crush the movement. They formed associations, hired Pinkerton detectives, and engaged in lockouts, blacklisting, and red scares. The police and courts backed capital in these efforts (Foner 1975:116-117). An organization like the Knights, which promoted labor solidarity across many of the divisions in the working class, was a special anathema to capital and thus an important target of their counteroffensive (Foner 1975:157). An organization like the AFL, although also antagonistic to capital, was less threatening and could be more tolerated. Thus, given the inevitability of class struggle, United States capital, backed by the state, could exercise some selectivity over the kind of labor movement that would survive.

The AFL and nonmember unions grew rapidly as the nineteenth century drew to a close. In 1897, after a major depression, total trade union membership was 447,000. In 1900 it had risen to close to 900,000. And by 1901, it had reached over 1 million (Kirkland 1961:360). In other words, the period of major United States imperialist expansion abroad coincides with the growth of a powerful trade union movement. As we have suggested, this is no accident. Imperialist expansion was one way that United States capital could deal with increasing labor militancy at home.

Immigration

Another way of dealing with the high cost of domestic labor, including its militancy, was to seek out alternative sources of labor power. In the post-Civil War period one obvious source for northeastern capitalists would have been the recently emancipated slaves of the South. Indeed, there were those who believed that one of the major motives behind northern support for abolition was to gain access to the large labor reserve of the South (Lofton 1949).

Had this effort succeeded, the course of United States racism would have been very different indeed. Blacks would have become an important segment of the new industrial proletariat, and even though racial friction would have undoubtedly accompanied their movement north, in all likelihood they would have been eventually absorbed into the working-class movement. The equation between color and coerced (or colonized) labor would have been broken.

That black labor was not brought north at this time but much later, after World War I, has less to do with the desires and plans of northern capitalists than with those of the southern oligarchy. After the brief period of Reconstruction, the dominant class of landowners in the South reasserted their control over the black work force. By various devices, including forms of debt peonage, they were able to bind the majority of ex-slaves to the land. Although nominally free, black workers were again subjected to a coercive labor system, backed by the state governments, which denied them political rights (Woodward 1974).

It is conceivable that some northern capitalists also had an interest in this arrangement. Just as cotton manufacturers in the North depended upon cheap southern cotton before the Civil War, so the same interests would continue to have an interest in the maintenance of a cheap-labor system after the war. But many northern capitalists probably had no vested interest in maintaining the southern system of labor control and would have happily used black labor if it had become available. They also had no particular interest in using black labor, per se, however; and if other sources of labor were more readily available and if their use did not entail a struggle to get them released, those sources would serve the purpose just as well.

The source that was tapped was, of course, southern and eastern Europe. Why this area of the world should have become a generator of surplus population during the late nineteenth and early twentieth centuries is beyond the scope of this study. I can only surmise that the region was affected by forces similar to those of imperialism. In other words, the region was being penetrated by western European capitalism, which led to distortions in its internal development and the consequent displacement of the peasantry. Poland, for instance, came at least partially under German domination and became a wheat producer in support of German industrialization. Eastern and southern Europe were never as fully colonized as the Third World, however, a fact that had a major impact on the development of racism in the United States.

Most of the typical features of labor migration apply to the movement of southern and eastern Europeans to the United States. They were brought here or encouraged to come voluntarily because of the high price of indigenous labor power. Given the explosive growth of United States industry in the late nineteenth century, the short supply of free labor (i.e., labor that was unattached to farms or independent crafts) inevitably drove up labor costs. But, in addition, as we have seen, local workers were organizing themselves increasingly in unions and political parties. They were demanding a shorter workday, higher wages, and better working conditions. Added to this, and probably linked to it, was the emergence of recurrent cyclical crises. The late nineteenth century, as we saw earlier, had two major depressions and a recession.

Cheap immigrant labor was a solution to these problems. And the Europeans came with many of the features that typically make immigrants cheap labor: they were poor and desperate; they came from peasant societies and had had little experience as a proletariat; their societies of origin had lower standards of living than the United States; they sometimes came under the control of labor contractors or padrones; their composition emphasized the young and ablebodied, while dependent populations could be kept out by law; the polyglot character of the work force inhibited communication and working-class organization; they often planned to return to their homelands, leading them to work especially hard in order to accumulate savings rapidly and to eschew long-term labor militancy; and they were noncitizens on arrival and hence subject to deportation if they caused trouble. All of these features made immigrant labor especially desirable to United States capital as it expanded in the late nineteenth and early twentieth centuries.

The pattern of immigration is depicted in table 3.12. Total European immigration began to climb in the decade of the 1840s, but it was mostly from western Europe. Eastern European immigration, which was much more likely to provide cheap labor, is a post-Civil War phenomenon and only predominated from the 1890s up to World War I. Significantly, this migration corresponds to the period of the ripening of monopoly capitalism and emergence of United States imperialism.

European immigrant labor was used, in part, to undermine the local labor movement and to lower labor standards. The immigrants were used directly as strikebreakers. In some instances local workers were simply displaced by the Europeans, who would work for longer hours at lower wages. The immigrants were also useful to capital in the process of deskilling; unskilled immigrants could take the place of high-priced local crafts workers by performing simplified parts of the production process at a fraction of their wages.

Because of these types of threat, large-scale European immigration provoked nativist reactions. Segments of the local labor force became adamantly anti-immigrant and pushed for legislation to limit the flow. An early instance of this was the Contract Labor Law, or Foran Act of 1875, which made illegal the importation of immigrant labor under

TABLE 3.12
IMMIGRATION FROM EUROPE TO THE UNITED STATES, 1821 TO 1940

Years	Total Europe	Eastern Europe*	Percent Eastern Europe
1821-1830	98,797	520	0.52
1831-1840	495,681	2,948	0.59
1841-1850	1,597,442	2,542	0.16
1851-1860	2,452,577	10,883	0.44
1861-1870	2,065,141	24,136	1.17
1871-1880	2,271,925	181,203	6.22
1881-1890	4,735,484	934,772	19.74
1891-1900	3,555,352	1,875,499	52.75
1901-1910	8,056,040	6,048,256	75.08
1911-1920	4,321,887	3,176,689	73.50
1921-1930	2,463,194	1,081,272	43.90
1931-1940	347,552	136,454	39.26

SOURCE: Adapted from Dinnerstein and Reimers 1975:162-164.
Based on Annual Report of U.S. Immigration and Naturalization Source.
*Rough estimate, based on adding Austria-Hungary, Bulgaria, Czechoslovakia, Estonia, Greece, Italy, Latvia, Lithuania, Poland, Romania, Soviet Union, and Yugoslavia.

contract, a situation that put the immigrants more easily under the thumb of capital and thus made them especially threatening to local labor.

But in the long run, European immigrants were absorbed by the local labor movement and proved to be among its staunchest supporters. They no longer could serve capital as a source of cheap labor, which helps explain why anti-immigration legislation was successfully passed in the 1920s.

Several factors account for their absorption. First, as suggested earlier, their countries of origin were less colonized than those of Africa, Asia, and Latin America. As a result (and perhaps also as a cause) of this, their homelands were more economically developed than much of the Third World. Workers from eastern and southern European countries came to the United States with lower standards of living than Americans or western Europeans but higher minimal standards than Third World immigrants.

Proximity to western Europe added another dimension. Eastern Europe was exposed to the radical movements of the mid-nineteenth century. A tradition of radical thought and politics was available to the immigrants (Miller 1974). Indeed, United States capitalists became increasingly alarmed at the radicalism of the immigrants, and the "Americanization movement" can, in part, be seen as an effort to expunge such so-called foreign notions as socialism and anarchism from their new workers. At least some sectors of the immigrant community were even more radical than local workers. Immigration law increasingly made efforts to screen out these "troublemakers."

The Russian revolution was seen as the ultimate corrupter of this source of labor by United States capital. The latest flood of immigrants came filled with revolutionary ideology. It is no coincidence that the doors from eastern Europe were firmly slammed shut by a selectively restrictive immigration policy shortly after this momentous event.

A third factor contributing to the absorption of Europeans into the local labor movement was the fact that they came with the possibility of attaining citizenship. This was partially a historical accident. After the United States had gained independence from Great Britain, it passed a naturalization act in 1790 that granted the right of all "free white" aliens to acquire citizenship under specified conditions (Konvitz 1946:79-80). That citizenship was limited to "free whites" would appear to reflect the political and social realities of the times. Almost all blacks in the United States were slaves, and granting the vote to slaves was tantamount to giving them freedom. The same would apply to nonfree white indentured servants. *Free white* was less a racial than a social category, corresponding closely to *free labor*. That it was cast in racial terms reflects the correlation between race and social conditions at the time.

The fact that the framers of the law used the term *white* instead of *northern and western European* gave a special advantage to southern and eastern Europeans. It seems unlikely that the framers of the law wanted to include such immigrants. They were not an element of the United States population in 1790 and so were probably not considered. The "free white" limitation was mainly aimed at excluding blacks (and Native Americans) rather than at including other categories of whites. But the choice of the word *white* in the original law gave the latter legal protection. Thus, even though eastern European immigrants were, for a period, considered "racially" inferior, the presumption of the law was on their side.

A fourth factor in their absorption is the concentration of these immigrants in the most advanced industrial sector of the national political economy. Indeed, their labor power was an important contributor to the evolution of monopoly capitalism in the northeastern United States. The fact that their cheap labor helped fuel industrialization, deskilling, and the concentration of firms into giant corporations helps account for some of the nativist sentiment that arose against them. In a sense they played a similar role to that of the blacks: they were seen as the tools of big capital, in opposition to the interests of small producers and local workers. Unlike the blacks, however, they were tools of the most advanced capitalists, and this provided them with opportunities that the blacks lacked.

The advantage of being located in the most advanced industrial sector lies in the conditions of labor in that sector. From the point of view of capital, workers in that sector had to be free to provide the necessary flexibility for an ever-changing economy. The factory system permitted immigrants to experience alienation from their work, observe the gulf between owners and workers, and compare grievances. Thus the immigrants found themselves in a context conducive to labor organizing. Finally, the market advantage of many of the industries and firms they worked for permitted capital the flexibility to concede some of their workers' demands, since increased costs could be passed on to consumers. Although monopoly capitalists fiercely resisted the organization of their workers until World War II, they nevertheless were not in such a dependent position in the world economy that their firms would fold if they made concessions. European immigrants thus benefited from their industrial location, which proved conducive to the formation of their own labor organizations and to their joining with the local labor movement.

In sum, several factors contributed to the absorption of eastern Europeans into the United States labor movement. Some of these were fortuitous, having to do with accidents of timing and location. But regardless of its causes, the experience of these immigrants fostered the perpetuation of an equation between *white* and *free labor*. The term *white* was extended to cover peoples who were marginally white in skin color and questionably similar in "racial" origins to the founding fathers, but its extension helped place the race line of the United States rather firmly between peoples of European origin and non-Europeans. The presumption that nonwhites were potentially servile while whites were not thus remained unchallenged.

Antimonopoly Movements

Despite industrial development in the Northeast in the post-Civil War era, much of the country remained heavily rural in the South and West. The ideal of the independent small producer remained vital even as the industrial proletariat grew. True, most small farmers were unable to engage in self-sufficient agriculture and mainly grew crops for the market. But many were still not full-blown capitalists, for they did not simply invest capital in their farms as a means of maximizing profits. They were committed to a way of life and resisted ouster from the land even if their capital could be more profitably invested elsewhere. These petty producers thus continued to resist capitalist encroachment and often fought bitterly against it.

According to Mayhew (1972), for instance, the roots of farmer protest in the United States between 1870 and 1900 lie not so much in the actual financial condition of farmers as in their negative reaction to the process of commercialization itself. They denounced the railroads, bankers, farm equipment producers, and other middlemen less because of the particular rates they charged and more because the farmers were becoming increasingly dependent on these corporate institutions. Pre-Civil War farmers had sold their surpluses when opportunities presented themselves, but they were not dependent upon commercial inputs. After 1870, farmers increasingly had to become businessmen, and they resisted the change (see also Kelly 1979:46).

As was the case prior to the Civil War, small producers and workers continued to form antimonopoly political alliances, since both were engaged in class struggle against big business. A prime illustration of such a coalition is the Populist movement that flourished in the 1890s (e.g., Pollack 1962).[9]

The roots of populism can be traced back at least to the Civil War, when farmers began to form such organizations as the Grange (founded in 1867), political parties such as the Independent, Reform, Anti-Monopoly, and Farmers parties (active in 1874), and various alliances (in the late 1870s and 1880s) (Shannon 1945:309-314). The backbone of these movements was white, southern small farmers, who were indebted to merchant capital and threatened with sliding into tenancy or share-cropping, and western farmers faced with debt and foreclosure of their mortgages (Shannon 1945:314).

The People's or Populist party was formed in 1892 and brought together various farmer alliances and worker organizations, including the declining Knights of Labor (Foner 1975:300-303). Among other things, it called for the breaking up of railroad domination of the government; the confiscation of excessive railroad landholdings; the confiscation of huge lands held by monopolists, which made a mockery of the Homestead Act; stronger laws against unrestricted immigration and contract labor; a shorter workday; and the eradication of Pinkerton labor spies (Foner 1975:303; Shannon 1945:321, 327).

Some leaders in both the Socialist Labor party and the AFL were skeptical of a farmer-worker coalition, on the grounds that the farmers were really small businessmen who sometimes employed and exploited wage labor. The farmers were seen as essentially reactionary (Foner

1975:303-309). Still, despite these criticisms, sufficient commonality existed between farmers and labor for many workers and working-class organizations to support the populist movement.

In their first national election the Populists garnered over one million votes, 9 percent of those cast. Analysis of voting returns reveals that the party received its greatest support in western rural communities but also got a considerable number of votes from working-class city dwellers in the West (Foner 1975:309). The panic of 1893 and subsequent depression contributed to Populist support, especially among laborers. Eastern industrial states that had previously failed to provide electoral support for the party began to do so. In the 1894 election, the People's party picked up approximately 500,000 more votes despite successful efforts by the Democrats to lure away labor votes by adopting some prolabor positions (Shannon 1945:323; Foner 1975:311-326). The populist movement eventually died as an organized political party in 1896 in the face of partial fusion with the Democrats and intimidation of unorganized workers by capital (Foner 1975:327-344). But a farmer-worker coalition in one form or another survived long past the turn of the century (Youngdale 1975).

Farmers and workers, separately and in concert, strove to curb the power of the monopolies. One approach was antitrust legislation. The Sherman Anti-Trust Act was passed in 1890, probably with more support from the small business and farming sector than from organized labor (Kirkland 1961:132-134; Foner 1975:370). The law was a compromise, however, calling for government regulation rather than government expropriation, as called for by many populists and labor organizations. It preserved the myth of competitive capitalism more than it effectively curtailed monopolization (Kirkland 1961:314-319).

Another way of attacking big capital was to attack imperialism.[10] United States labor expressed strong opposition to the annexation of Hawaii, partially on the grounds that it would permit big capital to extend the contract labor system to the United States (Foner 1975:407; Appel 1956). Indeed, the majority at the 1897 AFL convention believed that annexation would be tantamount to admitting a slave state to the union (Whittaker 1976:35). Labor leaders generally opposed war on the presumption that the working class would have to do the fighting and bear the taxes for the benefit of capital. Besides, "the working people know no country," according to Samuel Gompers, and only share one common enemy: capital (Foner 1975:405-407).

The Cuban question raised some problems for the AFL since some members wanted to support the Cuban movement for liberation from Spain. The majority, however, felt that active support by the labor movement would be playing into the hands of United States imperialists and militarists (Foner 1975: 408–409). Imperialism, it was believed, "means slavery . . . [and] the exploitation of cheap labor as a club to strike down American labor" (Whittaker 1976:34).

Similarly, the takeover of the Philippines had a dual character and could be interpreted as aiding an oppressed people in their revolutionary struggle against Spanish tyranny. Although many labor leaders fully realized the imperialist character of the Spanish-American War, they supported it anyway, both to avoid accusations that labor was unpatriotic and, after years of depression, to gain the immediate economic benefits resulting from a military build-up (Foner 1975: 413–416). Once the war was over and the suppression of Philippine independence undertaken, anti-imperialism again predominated and became the majority position of the labor movement. For instance, the capitalist argument that imperialism was necessary to expand overseas markets was countered by the argument that internal markets should be improved by raising wages (Foner 1975:418-424). In other words, labor perceived a link between capitalist domination at home and imperialist domination abroad. Attacking the latter was a means of attacking the former.

As with Hawaii, however, some of the concern over the domination of the Philippines was protectionist in character. American workers were fearful that the Philippines would provide capital with cheap labor to use both in the islands and in the United States (Whittaker 1976). Thus the anti-imperialism of the labor movement, much like the anti-slavery views before it, had more than a tinge of racism in it. Filipinos were viewed by Gompers as "millions of semi-barbaric laborers" who threatened United States labor with "close and open competition" (cited in Whittaker 1976:38). The cutting off of capitalist access to cheap Asian labor was thus an important motive in the anti-imperialist drive.

Farmers' organizations, too, showed support for an anti-imperialist position (Foner 1975:418). While some populists supported expansionism for immediate economic gain, as in the case of midwestern grain farmers seeking better access to the British market, many populist leaders opposed imperialism (Youngdale 1975:12). Anti-imperialism was thus another basis for an antimonopolist coalition.

The coalition of small producers and workers, according to O'Connor (1975), was able to retard capitalist development in the United States. By continually taking action to weaken the monopolies small producers and aspiring small producers were able to extend the process of complete proletarianization, which continued at least until World War II. Even after the war, the ideology of the small producer still pervaded sections of the country, especially the South and West, affecting the character of the labor movement.

Racism

Small producers and proletarians, both separately and in coalition, developed ambivalent positions toward racial minorities. As we saw earlier, before the Civil War, black slaves and even free blacks were seen as tools of the monopolies. This equation persisted after the war, in large measure because southern capitalists were able rather quickly to reestablish their hegemony over black workers and sharecroppers. Although formally free, blacks remained a rightless group, stripped of the franchise, often bound by debt to landed capital, and subjected to pervasive and degrading segregation.

The especially disadvantaged position of black workers posed a dilemma for both small producers and white workers. On the one hand, since blacks could be used by the monopolies to displace or undercut both of these classes, they needed to be brought into antimonopoly movements. They were natural allies since, of all segments of the population, they were the most crushed by the monopolies. And, indeed, both the labor and populist movements in the post-Civil War period went through periods of joining with blacks in antimonopoly struggles. Within the labor movement, the Knights of Labor is noteworthy for its efforts to join with black workers, while even the AFL, during its early history, took a strong antiracist stand (Foner 1976:47-69). Similarly, the populist movement of the 1890s incorporated black farmer organizations, at least in its early phases (Woodward 1974). In both cases, joining with blacks was not merely an ideological position but a practical response to material interests. If blacks could be used against them by the monopolies, then blacks needed to be brought into the working class-populist fold (e.g., Allen 1975:52-54).

On the other hand, that blacks could be used by the monopolies against white workers and small producers fed the racism of these two classes. Blacks were seen as too dominated and subservient, too much under the thumb of capital, and therefore unreliable as allies. They were thought to be unorganizable. Better to draw a narrow circle of protection around white workers and farmers, reasoned leaders who followed this logic, than attempt to organize blacks. One way to protect white labor was to form craft unions and limit black access to apprenticeships. Employers would then find it much more difficult to replace white workers with blacks. Similarly, many white populists in the South supported the disfranchisement of black sharecroppers when the latter were coerced into voting for the Democratic party by their landlords (Allen 1975:61-62). Other provisions limiting black rights and privileges had a similar meaning (Bonacich 1972, 1975). Both the labor and farmer movements thus contained a strong protectionist strain.

The coalition of small producers and workers contained both strains simultaneously. There were always some segments that pushed for incorporating blacks and promoting full racial equality and other segments that pushed for the opposite. It is my suspicion that the small producer class, including, importantly, the nonfarming sectors of it that were active in the labor movement (such as teamsters and crafts unionists who still owned some of their tools and had greater control over the labor process), predominated in the tendency toward racial exclusiveness, while fully proletarianized white workers, with no hope of reestablishing themselves as independent producers, would have been most likely to support racially inclusionist strategies. In the latter instance, nothing was to be gained by keeping blacks out. Rather, it was the truly proletarianized sector that was most directly threatened with displacement and thus had most to gain by forming a united position with the black proletariat. Small producers, in contrast, still hoped to stem the full-blown development of capitalism, and the best way to do this seemed to be to limit the access of capital to an exploitable proletariat.

The perpetuation of a protectionist strain in worker-small producer movements in the United States was ultimately of benefit to the capitalist class. It was able to utilize racial divisions to weaken and, in the end, destroy various progressive movements by pitting one racial group against another. For example, the Populist movement was effectively destroyed by the ability of capital to attack black farmers more fiercely than they did the whites, knowing that the latter's weak support for the blacks could be easily broken. Simultaneously, blacks would easily feel betrayed by the white farmers, given the legacy of racism and their possible cooptation by capital in support of racism.

In sum, the problems of racial division in the working class, which were manifested in the very origins of this country, persisted well after the Civil War. True, the emergence of monopoly capitalism transformed certain aspects of this division. For one thing, an increasing segment of the white working class became irreducibly proletarianized, while its numbers were greatly extended with European immigration. The increasing proletarianization of white workers, once they ceased resisting the process, was bound to lead to more interracial solidarity, a phenomenon that began to emerge with increasing force around the time of World War II. Another impact of the development of monopoly capitalism was the gradual decline of colonial labor systems in the South and the increasing absorption of black workers into the industrial proletariat, especially in the Northeast. This process, too, contributed to increasing interracial labor solidarity, as black and white workers found themselves in a more similar situation. This is not to suggest that racial divisions have been eradicated in the United States since World War II. Far from it. But the climate has shifted somewhat, and organized labor has become more aware of the need for interracial cooperation.

CONCLUSION

The purpose of this essay has been to describe the context into which Asian immigrants were moving. During the period of Asian immigration (roughly 1860 to 1935) the United States was undergoing a major transformation from early capitalism, with remaining colonial and pre-capitalist sectors, to monopoly capitalism, during which the country became one of the leading industrial and imperialist powers of the world. Indeed, by the end of the period in question, the United States had emerged as the most dominant capitalist nation in the world. This transformation helps to explain both United States expansionism in Asia and the need for cheap labor immigration from territories such as Asia.

The development of capitalism in the United States was not, however, a simple linear progression. Because of its early colonial status and dependent ties to Great Britain and because the United States had served as a "white settler" colony for Great Britain's surplus population, there was considerable conflict regarding the ultimate goals of this country. A strong antimonopoly strain existed, growing out of the small-producer class of settlers and joined by the rising industrial proletariat. These classes fought hard against the dominance of the giant corporations and financial institutions.

Unfortunately, racial minorities became an important factor in this struggle. Because the monopolies were able to exploit their labor with special effectiveness, racial minorities were seen as tools they used to undermine the white small producers and proletariat. Many of the progressive, antimonopoly efforts in United States history thus took on a racist tinge (Allen 1975), paradoxically combining racism with their anticapitalism.

The major target of racism was the large black minority, but the ideology that was generated in this case could easily be extended to other racially distinctive peoples — and was. Every racial minority (and even some nonracial ones) was suspected to be a possible tool that monopoly capital could use to displace whites. It was into this context of complex class struggles and racial hostility that Asian immigrants moved.

NOTES

1. A third type of colonization can also be distinguished, namely, trading centers. Since this is less pertinent to United States history I have omitted it here.

2. There is considerable debate on whether the term *mode of production* is appropriately used in this context. Some authors (e.g., Sherry 1976; Dowd 1977; Post 1982) contend that the United States was capitalist from its inception and that the independent producers were really early petit bourgeois capitalists. As is evident, I agree with O'Connor (1975, 1976) and Kelly (1979) on this question. The essence of a mode of production, in my view, lies in the way labor is organized and surplus extracted. The fact that independent producers occasionally produced commodities for a market does not belie the fact that they were essentially engaged in production for subsistence rather than accumulation and that they did not make significant use of wage labor to accumulate surplus value. While the slave system did resemble capitalism in many ways, its labor system and hence its method of accumulation were sufficiently distinctive to generate different "laws of motion" (Brenner 1977), which warrant distinguishing it as a different mode of production.

3. This quote is taken from the prepublication manuscript and does not appear in this precise form in the published version.

4. That capitalism could evolve out of the independent mode of production has led authors like Post (1982) and Sherry (1976) to argue that it is therefore not a mode of production at all. Their argument rests on the idea that a separate mode of production must have antagonistic principles of surplus extraction so that the presence of one mode retards the development of the other. It seems to me that there is plenty of evidence of the antagonism of small farmers, artisans, and so on to the emergence of capitalism but that, nevertheless, capitalist social relations could develop from within and be imposed upon the petty producers. The theoretical issues are complex and beyond the concerns of this study, which focuses more on the relationship of these social forms to racism than on their precise character and correct label.

5. There is some question of the timing of the dominance of industrial capitalism over the independent mode of production, as opposed to the timing of the emergence of industrial capitalism. In O'Connor's (1975) view, the hegemony of capitalism was established in the late nineteenth century, and even then, the struggle between the two modes of production remained vital, as demonstrated by the Populist movement. The vitality of the independent mode of production, according to O'Connor (1975:50-51), acted as a curb on the emergence of capitalism in the United States.

6. I have tended to downplay the importance of mercantile capital in the emergence of industrial capitalism in the North. Some authors argue that the presence of merchant capital is evidence of the dominance of capitalism in the United States from its inception. Others contend that mercantile capital can and has existed within various precapitalist modes of production and does not itself constitute either a distinctive mode of production or capitalism. I agree with the latter position. Merchant capital can be used to help finance industrial capitalism and undoubtedly was so used in the North. This type of capital, however, can finance other types of production as well, including slavery, and thus in itself cannot account for the emergence of capitalism in the North.

7. There is some question whether United States territorial expansion can be seen as imperialist in the pre-Civil War period. Since monopoly capitalism only emerged in the late nineteenth century, "true" imperialism as represented by the activities of finance capital can be seen as a later phenomenon. While the dynamics of land grabbing are somewhat different from those of imperialist investment, there is also considerable overlap. I have chosen not to make a sharp distinction between them in this essay, but it should be noted that the importance of small producers in the pre-Civil War territorial expansion of the United States makes it a mixed case. Similarly, the expansionist tendency of slavery is also not identical in its dynamics to the imperialism of developed capitalism (Post 1982).

8. A similar equalitarian, almost socialist, strain is found among Afrikaner "homesteaders" in South Africa (Bonacich 1981).

9. Both Pollack (1962) and Youngdale (1975) point to socialist elements in the populist movement, paralleling the point we made for the pre-Civil War period.

10. The anti-imperialist movement was not restricted to the worker-farmer coalition but also received support from some wealthy, prominent citizens (Harrington 1956).

References

Aglietta, Michel
  1978 "Phases of United States capitalist expansionism." New Left Review 110 (July-August):17-28.
Allen, Robert L.
  1975 Reluctant Reformers: Racism and Social Reform Movements in the United States. Garden City, N. Y.: Doubleday Anchor.
Anderson, Ralph V., and Robert E. Gallman
  1977 "Slaves as fixed capital: Slave labor and southern economic development." Journal of American History 64 (June):24-46.
Appel, John C.
  1956 "American labor and the annexation of Hawaii: A study in logic and economic interest." Pp. 407-413 in William Appleman Williams, ed., The Shaping of American Diplomacy. Chicago: Rand McNally.
Bonacich, Edna
  1972 "A theory of ethnic antagonism: The split labor market." American Sociological Review 37 (October):547-559.
  1975 "Abolition, the extension of slavery, and the position of free blacks: A study of split labor markets in the United States, 1830-1863." American Journal of Sociology 81 (November):601-628.
  1981 "Capitalism and race relations in South Africa: A split labor market analysis." Pp. 239-277 in Maurice Zeitlin, ed., Political Power and Social Theory. Vol. 2. Greenwich, Conn.: JAI Press.
Brenner, Robert
  1977 "The origins of capitalist development: A critique of neo-Smithian Marxism." New Left Review 104 (July-August):25-92.
Bruchey, Stuart W.
  1975 Growth in the Modern American Economy. New York: Dodd, Mead, and Co.
Dinnerstein, Leonard, and David M. Reimers
  1975 Ethnic Americans: A History of Immigration and Assimilation. New York: Harper and Row.
Domar, Evsey D.
  1970 "The causes of slavery or serfdom: A hypothesis." Journal of Economic History 30 (March):18-32.
Dowd, Douglas F.
  1956 "A comparative analysis of economic development in the American West and South." Journal of Economic History 16 (December):558-574.
  1977 The Twisted Dream: Capitalist Development in the United States Since 1776. 2d ed. Cambridge, Mass.: Winthrop.
Emmanuel, Arghiri
  1972 "White-settler colonialism and the myth of investment imperialism." New Left Review 73 (May-June):35-57.
Evans, Robert Jr.
  1970 "Some notes on coerced labor." Journal of Economic History 30 (December):861-866.

Faulkner, Harold U.
  1943 American Economic History. 5th ed. New York: Harper.
  1951 The Decline of Laissez Faire, 1897-1917. New York: Rinehart & Co.
Foner, Eric
  1970 Free Soil, Free Labor, Free Men: The Ideology of the Republican Party Before the Civil War. London: Oxford University Press.
Foner, Philip S.
  1941 Business and Slavery: The New York Merchants and the Irrepressible Conflict. Chapel Hill: University of North Carolina Press.
  1947 History of the Labor Movement in the United States. Vol. I. New York: International.
  1975 History of the Labor Movement in the United States. Vol. II. 2d ed. New York: International.
  1976 Organized Labor and the Black Worker, 1619-1973. New York: International.
Genovese, Eugene D.
  1975 "Yeoman farmers in a slaveholders' democracy." Agricultural History 49 (April):331-342.
Gideonse, Max
  1951 "Foreign trade and commercial policy." Pp. 534-550 in Harold F. Williamson, ed., The Growth of the American Economy. 2d ed. Englewood Cliffs, N. J.: Prentice-Hall.
Grob, Gerald N.
  1971 "Knights of Labor versus American Federation of Labor." Pp. 30-43 in David Brody, ed., The American Labor Movement. New York: Harper & Row.
Hacker, Louis M.
  1970 The Course of American Economic Growth and Development. New York: John Wiley.
Harrington, Fred Harvey
  1956 "The anti-imperialist movement in the United States, 1898-1900." Pp. 401-407 in William Appleman Williams, ed., The Shaping of American Diplomacy. Chicago: Rand McNally.
Iriye, Akira
  1977 From Nationalism to Internationalism: U. S. Foreign Policy to 1914. London: Routledge & Kegan Paul.
Kelly, Kevin D.
  1979 "The independent mode of production." Review of Radical Political Economics 11 (Spring):38-48.
Kiernan, V. G.
  1978 America: The New Imperialism: From White Settlement to World Hegemony. London: Zed Press.
Kirkland, Edward C.
  1961 Industry Comes of Age: Business, Labor, and Public Policy, 1860-1897. New York: Holt, Rinehart & Winston.
Konvitz, Milton R.
  1946 The Alien and the Asiatic in American Law. Ithaca: Cornell University Press.
LaFeber, Walter
  1963 The New Empire: An Interpretation of American Expansion, 1860-1898. Ithaca: Cornell University Press.
Lebergott, Stanley
  1964 Manpower in Economic Growth: The American Record Since 1800. New York: McGraw-Hill.

Lewis, Cleona
    1938 America's Stake in International Investments. Washington, D. C.: Brookings
         Institution.
Lofton, Williston H.
    1949 "Northern labor and the Negro during the Civil War." Journal of Negro History
         34 (July):251-273.
Man, Albon P. Jr.
    1951 "Labor competition and the New York draft riots of 1863." Journal of Negro
         History 36 (October):375-405.
Mandel, Bernard
    1955 Labor: Free and Slave. New York: Associated Authors.
Mayhew, Anne
    1972 "A reappraisal of the causes of farm protest in the United States, 1870-1900."
         Journal of Economic History 32 (June):464-475.
McCormick, Thomas J.
    1967 China Market: America's Quest for Informal Empire, 1893-1901. Chicago:
         Quadrangle Books.
Merrill, Michael
    1976 "Cash is good to eat: Self-sufficiency and exchange in the rural economy of the
         United States." Radical History Review 3 (Fall):42-71.
Miller, Sally M.
    1974 The Radical Immigrant. New York: Twayne.
Morris, Richard B.
    1946 Government and Labor in Early America. New York: Columbia University
         Press.
Nelson, Ralph L.
    1959 Merger Movements in American Industry, 1895-1956. Princeton: Princeton
         University Press.
North, Douglass C.
    1966a The Economic Growth of the United States, 1790-1860. New York: W. W.
         Norton.
    1966b Growth and Welfare in the American Past. Englewood Cliffs, N. J.: Prentice-
         Hall.
O'Connor, James
    1975 "The Twisted Dream." Book review. Monthly Review 26 (March):41-54.
    1976 "A note on independent commodity production and petty capitalism." Monthly
         Review 28 (May):60-63.
Perloff, Harvey S., Edgar S. Dunn, Jr., Eric E. Lampard, and Richard F. Muth
    1960 Regions, Resources, and Economic Growth. Baltimore: Johns Hopkins Press.
Pollack, Norman
    1962 The Populist Response to Industrial America. Cambridge, Mass.: Harvard Uni-
         versity Press.
Post, Charles
    1982 "The American road to capitalism." New Left Review 133 (May-June):30-51.
Rothstein, Morton
    1967 "The antebellum South as a dual economy: A tentative hypothesis." Agricultu-
         ral History 41 (October):373-382.
Scheiber, Harry N., Harold G. Vatter, and Harold Underwood Faulkner
    1976 American Economic History. New York: Harper & Row.

Seltzer, Rick
    1979   "An analysis of the empirical evidence on the origins of American imperialism: 1871-1900." Review of Radical Political Economics 11 (Winter):102-111.
Shannon, Fred A.
    1945   The Farmer's Last Frontier: Agriculture, 1860-1897. New York: Rinehart.
    1957   American Farmers' Movements. Princeton: Van Nostrand.
Shepperson, W. S.
    1957   British Emigration to North America. Minneapolis: University of Minnesota Press.
Sherry, Robert
    1976   "Comments on O'Connor's review of The Twisted Dream. Independent commodity production versus petty bourgeois production." Monthly Review 28 (May):52-60.
Shugg, Roger W.
    1972   Origins of the Class Struggle in Louisiana. Baton Rouge: Louisiana State University Press. First published in 1939.
Spero, Sterling D., and Abram L. Harris
    1966   The Black Worker: The Negro and the Labor Movement. Port Washington, N.Y.: Kennikat. First published in 1931.
Starobin, Robert S.
    1970   Industrial Slavery in the Old South. New York: Oxford University Press.
U. S. Bureau of the Census
    1975   Historical Statistics of the United States, Colonial Times to 1970. Washington, D. C.: U.S. Government Printing Office.
Wade, Richard C.
    1964   Slavery in the Cities: The South, 1820-1860. New York: Oxford University Press.
Wertheimer, Barbara Mayer
    1977   We Were There: The Story of Working Women in America. New York: Pantheon.
Whittaker, William George
    1976   "American labor and the Philippines: A perspective." Bulletin of the American Historical Collection 4 (July):33-51.
Wilkins, Mira
    1970   The Emergence of Multinational Enterprise: American Business Abroad from the Colonial Era to 1914. Cambridge, Mass.: Harvard University Press.
Williams, Eric
    1966   Capitalism and Slavery. New York: Capricorn Books. First published in 1944.
Williams, William Appleman, ed.
    1956   The Shaping of American Diplomacy. Chicago: Rand McNally.
Woodward, C. Vann
    1974   The Strange Career of Jim Crow. New York: Oxford University Press.
Youngdale, James M.
    1975   Populism: A Psychohistorical Perspective. Port Washington, N. Y.: Kennikat.

4

Asian Labor in the Development of California and Hawaii

Edna Bonacich

The previous chapter examined the overall development of United States capitalism in an effort to establish the broad context in which Asian immigration emerged and was terminated. This chapter turns to California and Hawaii, areas of special concentration of Asian labor prior to World War II, in order to understand their relationship to the rest of the country. My purposes are to explain why Asian immigrants concentrated in these areas, to account for their industrial concentrations within these territories, and to explore the roots of reaction to the immigrants.

CALIFORNIA

As in the East, the two major United States modes of production, independent settlers and capitalism, had their representatives in California. Like the East, capitalism in California developed a dual form of dependent capitalism tied to external markets and using cheap, semi-coerced labor, on the one hand, and indigenous industrial capitalism, on the other. Also like the East, in California these modes of production were in conflict with each other, and the question of racial minorities, in this case mainly from Asia, became one of the major terms of the conflict. Let us examine in turn each mode of production as it developed in California.

Independent Producers

The independent producer class first came to California with the gold rush. Gold was discovered in January 1848. By April there were 4,000 men mining gold. By the following year the number had jumped to 100,000 (Heizer and Almquist 1971:92). Most were people without means (McWilliams [1976:26] called it the last "poor man's gold rush"), who were seeking to escape the constraints of eastern economic development. They were joined by, or became themselves, small farmers and artisans, thus creating from the outset a substantial anticapitalist class in California.

Miners. The anticapitalism of the miners is revealed in their early regulations:

> In 1848, the California miners adopted their own rules and regulations in which they were careful to safeguard the equality of opportunity which had prevailed at the outset. . . . The rules adopted in the California camps carefully emphasized the policy of "one miner, one claim." . . . These same rules also narrowly limited the size of mining claims. Later, the California miners successfully resisted, for some years, a series of measures by which the federal government sought to convey fee titles to mining claims. These measures, the miners contended, would make for monopoly. Hence in California . . . the free miner remained, at least until 1873 or later, the foundation of the whole system (McWilliams 1976:28).

McWilliams draws a parallel between these miners and homesteaders. The miners were a class that knew that if a few men were to get very wealthy, the independence of the majority would be lost. Because of the gold rush, California had a large population in this class from the state's inception.

As we have seen, the small independent producers were strongly opposed to slavery. Indeed, many had fled west to escape its ravages. The issue of permitting slavery in the state was discussed at the California constitutional convention of 1849. According to McWilliams (1976:47) this was a miners' convention (though many gave their occupations as what they had done before coming to California). Their ideology encompassed the notion of the "dignity of labor," in part because they viewed themselves as "workmen" (McWilliams 1976:46). Such a view was incompatible with slavery. Thus they decided unanimously against it, putting the following provision into the constitution:

"Neither slavery, nor involuntary servitude, unless for the punishment of crimes, shall ever be tolerated in this State" (Bean 1973:130; Heizer and Almquist 1971:94).

The convention also debated whether to permit free blacks into California. They feared that slave owners would bring in slaves who had nominally been freed but were still under the domination of their former owners, thereby driving out free labor that included the independent producer. In the words of one delegate,

> I desire to protect the people of California against all monopolies — to encourage labor and protect the laboring class. Can this be done by admitting the negro race? Surely not; for if they are permitted to come, they will do so — nay they will be brought here. Yes, Mr. President, the capitalists will fill the land with these living laboring machines, with all their attendant evils. Their labor will go to enrich the few, and impoverish the many; it will drive the poor and honest laborer from the field, by degrading him to the level of the negro (cited in Heizer and Almquist 1971:107).

This theme was continually reiterated by other delegates (see also Lapp 1977:126-129; McWilliams 1946:47).

The convention initially adopted an exclusion provision but took it out for pragmatic reasons, fearing the constitution would be rejected by the federal government. Suffrage was only granted to "free white males," however, with the possibility of its extension to Native Americans later (Bean 1973:130), since it was also feared "that large landowners who employed a great many Indians might on election day lead scores of 'docile' Indians to the polls" (Heizer and Almquist 1971:96).

From the start, then, race was an issue in California, and it was linked to the competition between two modes of production: the independent producer mode, which sustained the dignity of free labor, and capitalism, which permitted the development of monopolies based on subjugated labor and driving out the independent farmers, miners, and artisans. *Free labor* was equated with *white labor*, while racial minorities, starting with both Native Americans and blacks, were seen as the tools of the monopolists. It was into this environment that the Chinese began to immigrate.

The Compromise of 1850 extended the line dividing the United States into slave and nonslave states to the Pacific Ocean. Under it California would have been divided. An agreement was reached to admit California to the union as a free state, while New Mexico and Utah would be left to decide whether they would accept slavery (Heizer and Almquist 1971:94; Bean 1973:134). For the time being, the small producers had won the day.

Farmers. While the small producers successfully prohibited slavery from California, they were less successful on another key ingredient of their way of life: access to free or cheap land. Unlike what happened in many other areas of the Midwest and West, where settlers were given free homesteads when the territory was transferred to United States control, California residents were not granted free land. Surveying of government lands was slow, which delayed the ability of settlers to gain access to them. Finally, in 1853, settlement was authorized on unsurveyed public land; but since most of the valuable land in California had been privately claimed and was being slowly adjudicated by the Board of Land Commissioners, only limited acreage was available for settlement. Not until 1856 did the board finish its task and make clear which land was available to the public. Thereafter, challenges to claims and efforts to evict squatters continued to fill the California courts into the 1870s (Gates 1960:387-390).

Much California land was privately claimed because of the granting of huge ranchos, of 4,500 to 49,000 acres each, to cattle ranchers by the Mexican governors. In addition, several missions had been given grants of up to 133,000 acres. Hardly any of the claimants had perfect titles, and typically the land had not been surveyed and the boundaries were vague. Before the United States took over the territory, a good deal of the land had been turned over to Anglo-Americans. Altogether 813 land claims came before the Board of Land Commissioners (Gates 1960:388-389). They totalled between 13 and 14 million acres, 13 to 14 percent of the state (Gates 1978:7).

Adding to the problem of land monopolization was the granting to the state of California by the federal government, under the Swamp Act of 1850, of over 2 million acres of rich swamplands to be reclaimed. Instead of treating this as a public task, the state sold the land cheaply before it had been surveyed, setting up conflicts between squatters and buyers (Gates 1960:395). Furthermore, the federal government granted huge areas to the railroads, amounting to 16 percent of federally owned lands in the state. By 1880 the railroads owned over 11 million acres, some of which were in desert areas while others were in valuable agricultural regions (McWilliams 1976:95). By these and other means, 35 million acres, or over one-third of California and most of its best land, was excluded from the restrictions of the Pre-emption and Homestead Acts (McWilliams 1976:97; see also McWilliams 1971:11-39 for a general description of land monopolization in California).

The unavailability of free land was more crucial in California than elsewhere because of the early rapid growth of population there. Not only were large numbers of disappointed gold miners seeking farming opportunities but their numbers were swelled by 250,000 immigrants in the 1850s, "drawn to the state by tales of rich soil, high wages, and unexampled economic opportunities" (Gates 1978:8). In the face of land monopolization, many took to unauthorized settlement:

> Squatters, disappointed because they found no land open to pre-emption and contemplating the great areas of uncultivated land within the private claims, settled upon them, made their improvements, and started farming operations. In a short time they had spread over most of the northern claims and were reported to be killing the cattle, cutting down the trees, and threatening the life of claimants if they were disturbed. Ejectment proceedings were attempted but not always with success, for settlers had learned long since that, if united, they could resist the law effectively, at least for a time (Gates 1960:389-390).

Here we see the formation of one of the major class struggles in California, that between small farmers and large landholders. It was essentially a struggle between two competing modes of production: capitalism (including both capitalist agricultural production and simple land speculation) and independent household production. Indeed, for a while it might be described as class warfare, for violence flared up between squatters and claimants well into the 1870s (Gates 1962, 1978:8-10). The independent producers even formed their own political party, the Settlers' or Squatters' party, which was influential in state politics (McWilliams 1976:89).

In 1860, 35 percent of California farms were smaller than 100 acres (Gates 1960:396), demonstrating that a small-farmer class was still in existence. The introduction of fruit and vegetable farming, especially in the 1870s and 1880s, increased the viability of smaller farms. Thus despite extensive land monopolization and the creation of huge land empires in California, there persisted an important class of small farmers. The distribution of farm acreage in 1910, for example, is shown in table 4.1. As can be seen, over 50,000 farms were smaller than 100 acres, while the median farm size was about 50 acres. There were still agricultural small producers in California.

Artisans. So far we have seen the presence of a small producer class in California in the form of miners and small farmers. A third segment consisted of independent artisans and tradesmen. As in other parts of the country, the distinction between artisans who were independent producers and those who were members of the proletariat is fuzzy. Both were free labor, and their level of living was probably not dissimilar, in part because employers of free wage labor would have to pay wages comparable to the earnings of independent producers to induce anyone to become an employee. Occupational titles like *carpenter* prob-

TABLE 4.1
NUMBER OF FARMS BY SIZE, CALIFORNIA, 1910

Acres	Number	Percent
Under 3	1,269	1.4
3-9	9,324	10.6
10-19	11,932	13.5
20-49	20,614	23.4
50-99	10,680	12.1
100-174	12,015	13.6
175-259	4,689	5.3
260-499	7,862	8.9
500-999	5,119	5.8
1000+	4,693	5.3
Total	88,197	100.0

SOURCE: U.S. Census of 1910, vol. VI, Agriculture:148.

ably combine both categories. While some may have been strictly employees, others probably owned their own tools and hired themselves out by the job. In the latter case, wages would consist of the fees they charged for their services. Craft unions thus may have been more like guilds of small producers than true "labor" unions.

Table 4.2 presents the occupations of all males in California as listed by the 1850 census. Information on females was not collected. The occupations were listed alphabetically, so a rough attempt was made to categorize them, with some probable error. The biggest group by far was the miners, accounting for almost three-quarters of all workers in the state. Here is where the bulk of the small producers were first located.

All rural occupations are combined under *Farmers, etc.* It is impossible to assess how many of them were small producers and how many were huge landholders, but it seems safe to assume that the rancheros fall into the latter category. Other occupations perhaps belong here, including some blacksmiths, overseers, and laborers, who may have been employed by the land barons. The size of the farmer category suggests that many of them were settlers and squatters.

The remainder of the occupations would appear to be urban. Their great diversity and the small number of people in many of them suggest the dominance of small producers at this early date. This is especially true for the craftsmen, with fifty-six distinctive occupations. Of course, in some cases they could be employees. For instance, all fifty-five printers could have worked for one large printing establishment. Yet in many cases the very nature of the occupation makes it unlikely that it

TABLE 4.2

OCCUPATIONS OF THE MALE POPULATION OF CALIFORNIA, 1850

Total	77,631	100.00%
Miners	57,797	74.45
Farmers, etc.	2,157	2.78
Dairymen	18	
Farmers	1,486	
Fishermen	61	
Gardeners and florists	111	
Hunters	55	
Herdsmen and graziers	197	
Lumbermen	19	
Rancheros	210	
Professionals	1,109	1.43
Actors	14	
Apothecaries and druggists	29	
Architects	3	
Artists	7	
Civil engineers	6	
Clergymen	36	
Dentists	20	
Editors	7	
Engineers	53	
Interpreters	4	
Lawyers	191	
Musicians	46	
Newsmen	7	
Physicians	626	
Professors	21	
Publishers	1	
Surgeons	3	
Surveyors	18	
Teachers	17	
Traders, dealers, etc.	7,189	9.26
Agents	28	
Auctioneers	62	
Barkeepers	147	
Bankers	3	
Bath tenders	2	
Boardinghouse keepers	126	
Booksellers	3	
Billiard saloon keepers	16	
Cattle dealers	6	
Clothiers	37	
Contractors	6	
Grocers	109	
Hay dealers	60	

TABLE 4.2 (Continued)
OCCUPATIONS OF THE MALE POPULATION OF CALIFORNIA, 1850

Innkeepers	598	
Merchants	3,284	
Milkmen	6	
Peddlers	7	
Produce dealers	12	
Refectory keepers	202	
Storekeepers	43	
Traders	2,410	
Wood dealers	2	
Craftsmen	3,778	4.87
Agricultural implement makers	2	
Bakers	264	
Barbers	27	
Black and white smiths	457	
Bookbinders	1	
Brewers	22	
Brickmakers	6	
Builders	9	
Butchers	298	
Cabinet and chair makers	42	
Carpenters	1,172	
Caulkers	2	
Chandlers	7	
Chemists	1	
Coach makers	9	
Confectioners	11	
Coopers	44	
Cooks	413	
Coppersmiths	2	
Cordwainers	117	
Dyers	2	
Engravers	4	
Gilders	2	
Gold and silversmiths	20	
Gold washer manufacturers	17	
Gunsmiths	17	
Hat and cap manufacturers	14	
Jewelers	46	
Joiners	19	
Locksmiths	2	
Machinists	21	
Manufacturers, not specified	6	
Masons and plasterers	72	
Mathematical instrument makers	1	
Mechanics, not specified	26	
Millers	46	

TABLE 4.2 (Continued)

OCCUPATIONS OF THE MALE POPULATION OF CALIFORNIA, 1850

Millwrights	15	
Moulders	2	
Painters and glaziers	80	
Pianoforte makers	1	
Printers	55	
Rope makers	3	
Saddle and harness makers	31	
Sail makers	5	
Sash makers	1	
Sawyers	31	
Ship carpenters	5	
Stone and marble cutters	2	
Tailors	112	
Tanners and curriers	15	
Tinsmiths	99	
Tobacconists and cigar makers	4	
Undertakers	2	
Upholsterers	11	
Vinegar makers	3	
Watchmakers	30	
Wheelwrights	49	
Woolen manufacturers	1	
Transport workers	1,891	2.44
Boatmen	64	
Carters	60	
Drivers	15	
Drovers	19	
Expressmen	19	
Livery stable keepers	22	
Mariners	482	
Muleteers	431	
Ostlers	15	
Pilots	10	
Porters	29	
Teamsters	725	
Unskilled labor	2,767	3.56
Laborers	2,159	
Packers	199	
Servants	295	
Washers	64	
Woodcutters	50	
Government workers	270	0.35
City, county, town officers	84	
Soldiers	140	
U.S. officers	46	

TABLE 4.2 (Continued)
OCCUPATIONS OF THE MALE POPULATION OF CALIFORNIA, 1850

Other	673	0.87
Clerks	526	
Overseers	22	
Students	2	
Unspecified	123	

SOURCE: Adapted from U.S. Census 1850:976.

was centralized under the control of capitalists. A case in point would be tailors. There may be some misclassifications here too; for instance, cooks could be private household servants, restaurant entrepreneurs, or, like carpenters, people who sold a skill for a while to a variety of buyers.

The transport workers seem quite similar in character to the craftsmen. One can imagine many of them owning their own conveyances, or the tools of their trade, and therefore able to retain some control over their labor. An exception is the mariners, who probably worked as proletarians for large shipping companies.

The category of dealers and traders refers mainly to people who sold rather than produced commodities. Judging from their occupational titles, one could say that most seem independent. Some would probably fall in the small producer class (e.g., boardinghouse keepers and refectory keepers) with a blurred distinction between simply selling and selling a service that required labor. Undoubtedly some people in this category were capitalists (e.g., the bankers and some of the merchants and traders), though they were more mercantile than industrial. Given the numerical preponderance of merchants and traders, one might conclude that most in this category were not small producers.

Like some of the dealers and traders, the professionals were more likely to sell a service than a commodity. Some, such as the publisher, may have been employers; and others, such as the newsmen, employees; but they were probably mainly independents, falling into the small producer mode of production.

The three remaining categories, government workers, unskilled laborers, and other, would seem unambiguously not to be small producers. Unskilled labor is the most problematic category since other occupations may belong here, while some of those I have included may not.

Still, the three categories combined account for less than 5 percent of the California labor force, suggesting how undeveloped the state was at this early date.

By 1860 the occupational structure of the state had become considerably more complex. In that year, 306 separate occupations were listed for 219,192 California workers. The largest category remained miners, with 82,573 (38 percent). They were followed by laborers with 25,394 (12 percent), farmers with 20,836 (10 percent), and farm laborers with 10,421 (5 percent). The remaining 302 occupations are widely dispersed, and many of them appear to include independent craftsmen. For example, the list includes 34 bookbinders, 75 daguerreotypists, 125 harness makers, 91 plumbers, 619 wheelwrights, and so on. Of course, those in many of the occupations, including laborers and farm laborers, undoubtedly worked for others, but the continuation of small producer craftsmen (let alone miners and farmers) seems evident in this census too (U. S. Census of Population, 1860:34-35).

In sum, there was a substantial class of small producers in California from the time of the gold rush. Members of this class had experienced displacement in the East, whether they were European immigrants who had ultimately been displaced in their homelands and were ousted by native workmen in eastern cities, old stock from rural backgrounds "in flight from constant encroachment of a more complex and commercialized community," or urban craftsmen who had been "displaced by industrialization" (Saxton 1971:13). They brought with them a strong anticapitalist, antimonopolist position that was to play a crucial role in the reception and treatment of Asian immigrant workers.

Capitalism

Again as in the eastern United States, capitalism in California developed along two distinctive lines. On the one hand there was a kind of colonial or dependent capitalism, relying on eastern and European investments and mainly producing raw materials for those markets. On the other hand was an indigenous, multifaceted, manufacturing capitalism that grew out of the small-producer class, much as in the northern states. This distinction had important consequences for the kind of labor that could be and was used, with Asian labor generally concentrating in the dependent sector. Let us first consider this sector, turning afterwards to indigenous manufacturing.

Dependent Capitalism

Dependent capitalism in California was mainly represented by three industries: mining, railroads, and agriculture. While each of these operated under somewhat different conditions, they shared a strong link to the East or Europe as a source of capital, markets, or both. This linkage to distant areas meant that these sectors had to be competitive by national or international standards. To attract outside capital they had to be profitable relative to eastern and European investment opportunities. To be able to sell in these distant markets they had to produce cheaply enough to compensate for added transportation costs and still have their products competitively priced.

It is no accident that the dependent sector of the California economy tended to produce raw materials rather than manufactured goods. Eastern and European capital was already invested in manufacturing and was seeking not to create competitors but to cheapen their own production by lowering the cost of raw materials (including food for their workers). In addition, California manufacturing was in its infancy, lacking developed technology or economies of scale. It was highly uncompetitive, as is typical of the early stages of manufacturing. The natural tendency was for advanced capitalist areas to exchange cheaper manufactured goods with the cheaper raw materials of the less developed areas. And this is what happened in California.

The dependent character of mining, railroads, and agriculture conditioned the kind of labor they could use. Since they had to compete in international and national markets for both capital and sales, they operated under severe constraints. On the one hand, prices had to be kept low so the products would sell. On the other hand, profits had to be high in order to attract investment. The major area of flexibility lay in labor costs, and the constraints under which they operated drove them to seek the cheapest possible labor. As we shall see later, the available white labor supply in California was too costly, for several reasons, to be profitably employed in these industries.

As in the East, dependent capitalism started as the most advanced sector. Like the slave plantations of the South, dependent capitalist industries were the largest and most concentrated industries of California. Here is where most capital was invested, where commercialization had progressed furthest, and where a propertyless proletariat first emerged. Here also is where capital consolidated most rapidly to form monopolies. We should note, however, that they were limited monopolies. While they might have tremendous power and concentration of wealth within the state, they could not control their financing or markets. Indeed, as we have indicated, they operated in a highly competitive out-of-state environment. Thus they did not have the power of the true monopoly to pass on higher costs to the consumer and ensure high profits that way. Rather, they were forced to curb expenses.

We now turn to a closer examination of each of the three dependent industries to see the particular conditions under which they operated.

Mining. Although gold mining began as an activity of independent small producers, it evolved into a highly capitalized industry, requiring equipment, advanced technology, and employed labor. The age of the individual miner corresponds with abundant surface deposits, when gold was easily accessible with simple tools and no advantage could be gained in combination (McWilliams 1976:29). This was known as placer mining, which was the only form of mining from 1848 to 1851. Although other types of mining emerged during the 1850s, most individuals were still engaged in placer mining, though declining surface deposits made it less rewarding (Paul 1967:144-145; McWilliams 1976:28)

The new types of mining that emerged to reach deeper gold resources included river mining, where rivers were diverted to reveal gold-bearing riverbeds; quartz mining, where the gold had to be stamped out of rock; deep mining, involving tunneling into hillsides; and hydraulic mining, in which jets of water wore down gold-bearing hillsides (Paul 1967). Each of these emerged in the mid- or late 1850s and required heavy capital investment as well as the employment of hired labor. In addition, hydraulic mining required the development of a subsidiary industry, water companies, which brought large quantities of water to the mining areas and themselves required considerable capital and labor.

Table 4.3 shows the value of gold production in California over more than two decades. There was a tremendous rise through 1852, during the heyday of the placers. The amount of gold produced gradually declined through the 1850s and early 1860s, until 1865 when it reached a stable plateau. The decline reflected diminishing gold resources and was accompanied by an increase in efforts made by company mining to reach the less accessible sources profitably. From 1865 on, mining was mainly a big company business, producing steadily. This level of production lasted at least until 1884 (Paul 1967:254).

The 1860 census reflected the trend away from independent mining and toward concentration in capitalist mining companies. In that year there were 7,042 gold mining establishments employing 42,616 miners. Since the average number of employees per firm is small (six), only a small proportion of these firms could have been very large. The census listing of occupations gives 82,573 persons as miners. While some may have worked in mines other than gold, a substantial proportion must have been independent gold miners. Meanwhile, the companies that employed wage labor had a total capital investment of $11,005,876 and paid $15,860,809 for raw materials. In the former case, the figure totaled half of all capital invested in manufacturing in the state, while

TABLE 4.3

GOLD PRODUCTION IN CALIFORNIA, 1848 TO 1874

Year	Value ($)
1848	245,301
1849	10,151,360
1850	41,273,106
1851	75,938,232
1852	81,294,700
1853	67,613,487
1854	69,433,931
1855	55,485,395
1856	57,509,411
1857	43,628,172
1858	46,591,140
1859	45,846,599
1860	44,095,163
1861	41,884,995
1862	38,854,668
1863	23,501,736
1864	24,071,423
1865	17,930,858
1866	17,123,867
1867	18,265,452
1868	17,555,867
1869	18,229,044
1870	17,458,133
1871	17,477,885
1872	15,482,194
1873	15,019,210
1874	17,264,836

SOURCE: Paul 1967:345-346.

raw materials expenditures were 58.6 percent of the state total (U. S. Census of Population, 1860:34-35; U. S. Census of Manufactures, 1860: 35-36). The mining industry was clearly on its way to becoming big business.

Large mining companies often grew out of the combinations of smaller miners. But typically they did not have enough capital to undertake the risks entailed in opening new resources and constructing costly equipment. It was often difficult to raise capital in San Francisco; thus they turned to the eastern United States and Great Britain. In the 1850s, British investment in quartz mining was substantial. "In the beginning of 1853, there were at least twenty Anglo-Californian gold-quartz mining companies in the London market, representing nearly 2,000,000 shares, and the investment of about $10,000,000" (Paul 1967:145-146). Many of these early quartz mines failed, scaring foreign capital away for a period.

It was not until the mid-1860s that California mining was established on a firm capitalist footing. Unlike the Comstock Lode in Nevada, which immediately attracted large-scale investment accompanied by such trappings of finance capitalism as incorporation, the selling of shares, and the emergence of banking, California mining developed slowly (Paul 1967:182-184). Thus in 1863, there were 203 incorporated mining companies in the Far West, only 30 of which were in California, and most of these were in newly opening mining areas of the state (Paul 1967:298). Perhaps this slowness reflects the resistance of the small producer class. For instance, mine workers fought against the introduction of gunpowder, which they feared would displace them (Paul 1967:326-327). This kind of dispute can be interpreted as a resistance to the advance of capitalism since it retarded technical innovations that lowered the cost of production. The spirit of resistance probably arose out of the miners' recent history of independence. Newer mining areas, however, lacked this tradition and so could introduce capitalist innovations without resistance.

In any case, by the mid-1860s, whatever resistance there was had been overcome. In 1867 California mining stock began to be placed on the San Francisco stock exchange (Paul 1967:300). British capital began to return to the California mines, though in unknown quantities. Eastern interests were mentioned less often, but at least one important instance was the purchase of a major mining water company by New York interests in 1865. It was incorporated for $2,250,000 (Paul 1967:301-302).

Reliance on external or even city capital undoubtedly acted as a constraint on mining companies. They had to be responsive to their shareholders and therefore had an added incentive for cutting costs. Indeed, the rate of bankruptcy was very high, suggesting that many failed to be profitable enough to repay loans. Perhaps more important than their capital sources in this regard is the fact that gold was a commodity largely produced for "export" to the East. In fact it was the chief export of California for the first few decades of the existence of the state. Table 4.4 shows the amounts of gold appearing in San Francisco for export each year and the percentage of annual production (based on the figures in table 4.3) that was for export. When the figure exceeds 100 percent it reflects accumulation from previous years. As can be seen a very high proportion of California gold was exported.

I have been unable to find any information on how gold prices were determined. But it seems safe to conclude that they could not be con-

TABLE 4.4
CALIFORNIA GOLD EXPORTS, 1848 TO 1860.

Year	Manifested in San Francisco for export (in thousands of dollars)	Percent exported
1848	—	—
1849	4,921	48.5
1850	27,676	67.1
1851	42,583	56.1
1852	46,588	57.3
1853	57,330	84.8
1854	51,329	73.9
1855	45,183	81.4
1856	48,881	85.0
1857	48,977	112.3
1858	47,548	102.1
1859	47,649	103.9
1860	42,203	95.7

SOURCE: North 1966:255.

trolled by either individual miners or the mining companies even as the industry was becoming concentrated. Rather, the price was probably determined in either the eastern or the world market. In this sense, gold mining was a dependent industry, unable to control its profit rate and forced to turn to cheap sources of labor if possible.

Railroads.   Unlike mining, which underwent a gradual transition from small independent production to big business, the railroads were big business from the start. Indeed, they were the first big business of California and the largest employer of wage labor through 1880 (Chiu 1967:40). The capital requirements of railroad construction are obviously huge, which helps account for its tendency quickly to become a concentrated industry.

In further contrast to the situation in mining (or in agriculture, as we shall see in a moment), railroad builders were less directly constrained by prices determined in distant markets. Their chief profits derived not from the direct sale of commodities but from the freight rates they could charge. Thus they were indirectly bound by market conditions. Local railroad companies in California, for instance, could charge higher freight rates than the transcontinental railroad, since the goods they were hauling did not have to compete in the international market.

The major commodities the transcontinental railroad was expected to haul were gold, a low-bulk product that would bring limited freight rates (Chiu 1967:40-41), and wheat, a high-bulk commodity with its price fixed in the world market. Ping Chiu (1967:42-43) describes the consequences of this latter fact for railroad construction:

> As world market determined the price of wheat, it indirectly set the upper limit of potential local transportation costs. Above these the farmer would be compelled to withhold the commodity from the market. This potential maximum freight rate, or the expected income of the railroad, decided its optimum capitalization, or fixed costs. These in turn formed the basis for the calculation of maximum wage rates above which capital would not be invested and the road not be built.

Even a railroad monopoly had to operate within constraints.

The system of capitalization also set limits on the construction costs of the transcontinental railroad. Because it was a very risky business, initial efforts to raise the necessary capital simply to form a corporation under California law, let alone to raise the capital for actual construction, foundered (McCague 1964:18-19). San Francisco capitalists refused to invest on the grounds that they had much safer enterprises, such as mining, trade, and real estate, with higher and more immediate returns in which to invest (Bean 1968:209). The Sacramento merchants who formed the "Big Four" of the Central Pacific were only persuaded to capitalize incorporation because they saw an opportunity for quick profits in a line to the Comstock Lode (silver mines) of Nevada (Bean 1968:210).

The financing of actual construction came mainly from federal loans based on the issuance of thirty-year bonds. The railroads were given $16,000 per mile of track to cover flat land, $48,000 per mile in the Sierra Nevada and the Rocky Mountains, and $32,000 per mile between these two ranges. These were loans, not grants, and the railroads not only had to keep costs within these figures but also to pay them back. In addition, the federal subsidy was only forthcoming after the completion of a forty-mile unit of construction. This put the two major companies, the Union Pacific, building west from Omaha, Nebraska, and the Central Pacific, building east from Sacramento, in a kind of competition, each seeking to build as quickly as possible in order to get maximum government loans, as well as the land grants that accompanied them (Bean 1968:213-214; Saxton 1971:61). Time pressure was thus greater for the first transcontinental railroad than for local lines in California and created a more immediate need to deal with labor shortages (Chiu 1967:42).

The Central Pacific operated under additional cost constraints. Iron rails and locomotives had to be purchased in the United States, according to the terms under which government subsidies were granted. This meant that they had to be purchased in the East at inflated wartime prices, since construction began in the middle of the Civil War. Furthermore, they had to be transported long distances by sea at wartime freight and insurance rates. This put the Central Pacific at a disadvantage relative to the Union Pacific (Bean 1968:214; Lewis 1959:86-88).

The Central Pacific also tried to raise capital from private sources but ran into difficulty:

> Interests hostile to the railroad did everything they could to discourage private investors from lending it money. The Pacific Mail Steamship Company, the California Steam Navigation Company, Wells Fargo and Company, and the Sacramento Valley Railroad, as well as all the bankers who had money invested in one or more of these enterprises, naturally anticipated that the building of the Central Pacific would injure them, and they joined in denouncing it (Bean 1968:214).

Thus, it faced competition not only from other railroad companies but also from alternative means of transportation.

To suggest that the railroads operated under constraints is not to say that they did not earn huge profits. They did, using numerous devious means including redefining where the foothills of the Sierra Nevada began in order to garner a bigger government subsidy (McCague 1964:76-77; Rolle 1969:339-340). They were able to exert tremendous influence over the California state government. Leland Stanford, for example, became governor in 1862 and used his position to get the state to provide further subsidies to the Central Pacific (Bean 1968:213-214). Indeed the "Octopus" dominated state politics for decades after the Civil War.

With the expansion of the Central Pacific, the railroads in California became more of a monopoly than any segment of capital. It was quickly able to absorb most competitors in the state, including water as well as rail competition. In the latter case Central Pacific took over the Southern Pacific and eventually built another transcontinental line in 1883. The Big Four consolidated their monopoly interests into the Southern Pacific Company in 1884 (Orsi 1975:197). But at least in the early days of constructing the first transcontinental railroad, which correspond to the period when the railroads most relied upon Chinese labor, they were a monopoly within limits. Within the state they might reign supreme, but the transcontinental construction occurred within a competitive framework, where they were constrained by the size of government subsidies and by the market prices for the products they would haul (Chiu 1967:50). These constraints had an effect on the labor they could employ in construction.

Agriculture.   Early California agriculture, too, was a dependent form of capitalism not unlike the slave plantations of the old South. Large landholders invested capital first in the production of wheat and later in irrigated crops, such as fruit, to be sold in the national or world market. These capitalists were thus constrained by outside competition, outside market prices (Chiu 1967:69), and the disadvantage California suffered in terms of its great distance from major markets (Rothstein 1975).

Wheat production dominated California agriculture from the 1860s to the turn of the century. Indeed, by 1889 California was the second largest wheat producer in the nation (Paul 1958:397). Since the Midwest and the East were also wheat producers and were closer to populated areas, California could not compete with them for eastern markets. Even after the transcontinental railroad was completed in 1869, it was not profitable, given the bulkiness and low value of grain relative to rail freight rates, to ship grain eastward across the country (Paul 1958:391-392, 395).

The major outlet for California wheat and wheat products came to be Great Britain. Although that country was even more distant than the eastern states, demand for grain was growing more rapidly there as the country industrialized and farming declined. In addition, Great Britain was accessible by sea, and though the voyage from California around Cape Horn was exceedingly long, it could be navigated by sailing ships, which was cheaper than other means of transportation (Paul 1958:391-392). Between 1871 and 1895, over two-thirds of the value of domestic exports from Pacific Coast ports was accounted for by wheat and wheat products (Rothstein 1975:275).

Competing in the British market put major constraints on California growers. Wheat prices were set at the Liverpool Corn Exchange and were unresponsive to California costs of production and transportation. California wheat had to compete with exports from the eastern United States, Canada, India, Russia, and Germany (Paul 1958:391-393). As Chiu (1967:69) points out, "farm prices in California were determined not by local supply and demand but by world market conditions. As a consequence, commodity price set the upper limit of both profit and wages." Thus, keeping the cost of production low was a paramount consideration.

Because of the distance of their market and their inability to control it, grain producers tended to come under the domination of an oligarchy of British and San Franciscan merchant-shippers, the so-called Grain Kings (Rothstein 1975:278). Most of the shipping was in British hands, while British insurance companies set up offices in San Francisco and dominated the insuring of the wheat trade. Finally, much of the capital advanced as loans on wheat shipments came from Great Britain and other European sources (Paul 1958:403-404). These features point to the dependent character of California wheat production, which was probably similar to cotton production in the pre-Civil War South. Indeed, Paul (1958:405) describes the situation as one of British "economic imperialism," and rural California and San Francisco merchants as "almost a colonial appendage" of Great Britain (Paul 1958:412).

Wheat production was brought to an end in California by a combination of declining prices beginning in the mid-1880s and declining productivity of the land because of continued cropping without fertilization (Paul 1958:410-411). Furthermore, more profitable uses for the land were emerging in the form of irrigated crops, which mainly included fruits with the addition of sugar beets, hops, cotton, and vegetables. Table 4.5 demonstrates the shift, with *extensive* crops referring to wheat and other grain products dependent on dry farming and *intensive* crops referring to those produced under irrigation. As can be seen, by the turn of the century, irrigated crops were increasingly dominating California agriculture; and although grain production experienced another surge around 1920, fruit production had by that time clearly outstripped it.

The introduction of irrigation is another chapter in California capitalist development and the class conflict surrounding it. According to Chan (1978:7), irrigation was seen by progressive forces as a means of breaking up land monopolies and establishing small farms according to the Jeffersonian, small producer ideal. Needless to say, the idea backfired, and irrigation brought tremendous accumulation and concentration of wealth in its wake. The struggle over whether water rights

TABLE 4.5
EXTENSIVE AND INTENSIVE AGRICULTURE IN CALIFORNIA, 1869 TO 1929

Year	Value of crop ($) Extensive	Intensive	Percent Intensive
1869	35,006,614	2,444,259	6.6
1879	69,304,191	2,813,997	3.9
1889	62,603,721	—	—
1899	53,111,131	40,441,677	43.3
1909	70,246,078	68,886,694	49.5
1919	204,692,315	346,249,327	63.4
1929	109,902,741	397,030,268	78.4

SOURCE: Taylor and Vasey 1936:286.

should be allocated on a "democratic" basis, limiting the amount per farm, continues in California to this day, showing the vitality of the conflict between these two modes of production.

Fruit was grown more for the national than international market but was still an export crop for California. As Shannon (1959:262) points out, "While the easterner grew fruits mainly for local consumption, the Pacific states were in the business of supplying the nation." Since much of the produce was shipped by rail to compete in eastern markets, again the dual constraints of competition and high transportation costs set a ceiling on profitable production costs. These problems are described for the California citrus industry for the period 1869 to 1900 by Bean (1968:274):

> [The farmer] seldom had enough information about the market to know what a fair price would be, and speculators took every possible advantage of his ignorance. The markets for citrus fruits and other California specialty crops were from 2,000 to 3,000 miles away, and they were developing only gradually. With many growers and packers sending haphazard shipments, prices were so erratic that the commission merchants demanded the use of the consignment system, under which the growers bore all the risk.

Thus farming capitalists had strong incentives to cut costs, the major variable in which was the cost of labor.

Like mining and the railroads, agriculture was big business in California. According to Nash (1972:319), agriculture dominated the economic growth of the state in the last three decades of the nineteenth century. As big business, agriculture became a major employer of wage labor. In other words, a proletariat emerged in this industry. Table 4.6 presents an estimate of the size and proportion of this proletariat, based on the number of farm laborers relative to the number of gainfully employed persons in agriculture. As can be seen, the numbers rise steadily, while the proportion fluctuates but shows a secular trend upward. Taylor and Vasey (1936:286-289) compared these trends with the numbers of farm laborers in Iowa and Mississippi during the same period. They found that California patterns were closer to those of Mississippi, with both states having a higher proportion of farm laborers than Iowa, again suggesting similarities with the dependent South.

In summary, all three of the major capitalist industries of California shared certain features. They involved large investments of capital for the purposes of earning a profit. Like all capitalist enterprise, they tended to become concentrated in fewer and fewer hands, as competitors knocked one another out of the running and as technology

TABLE 4.6
FARM LABORERS COMPARED TO ALL PERSONS GAINFULLY EMPLOYED IN
AGRICULTURE, CALIFORNIA, 1860 TO 1930

Year	Farm laborers	Total gainfully employed in agriculture	Percent farm laborers
1860	15,014	37,785	39.7
1870	19,239	47,863	40.2
1880	28,546	79,346	36.0
1890	59,145	129,715	45.6
1900	71,867	145,801	49.3
1910	119,611	211,898	56.4
1920	125,248	260,612	48.1
1930	196,812	332,024	59.3

SOURCE: Taylor and Vasey 1936:288.

advanced, requiring increasingly large investments of capital. In other words, all three industries tended to become monopolized. But unlike true monopolies, which are able to set prices, California big businesses were limited by their participation in highly competitive national and international markets while suffering the disadvantage of great distance from those markets especially while transportation was poorly developed. Thus California industries had a dependent cast, making them resemble colonial enterprises in certain respects.

Local Labor

The dependent character of California big business set a limit on the kind of labor it could employ. Labor costs had to be below a certain level in order for it to be profitable to continue the enterprise at all. But the price of available "free white" labor in California was high. This was true because of the persistence of opportunities for the small producer class, the most notable of which was mining. As we have seen, placer gold mining continued late into the nineteenth century even after the most lucrative finds had been exhausted. The discovery of the Comstock Lode provided another major opportunity for independent producers. In addition, squatters and other small farmers, and artisans in the towns, could still maintain their independence, as we saw earlier.

In other words, in its early history, California was a land of open resources. These resources may have been partially monopolized but not so completely as to force all or even most settlers to sell their labor power for a wage. And as long as people had the option to work for themselves and maintain their independence, most would choose to do so. Again we can see the applicability of a colonial analogy to early California development, since the southern plantations faced a similar problem.

The availability of open resources pushed up the price of California labor. In order to induce people to sell their labor power, capitalists had to offer wages equal to if not higher than workers could expect to earn on their own (Cross 1935:10-14). Thus the earnings of independent miners tended to set the level of wages in California, and these were generally high. Table 4.7 compares average wage levels of the states in 1869 and 1879. In the former year, the California average was $519, well over the national average of $378 per annum and ranking seventh only behind other western states with open resources. By 1879, the California wage level had begun to decline, but so had the national average. Now down to $468, compared with $343 for the nation as a whole, California had risen to fifth place.

The high price of local labor was also influenced by the early development of a labor movement in California (Cross 1935). From the start, workers in California refused to be intimidated by capital and organized to protect their interests. According to McWilliams (1976:128), "The most striking characteristic of the labor movement in California is its deep-rooted and indigenous character. Unions are as old as the state itself . . . . No one organized San Francisco; it organized itself."

Undoubtedly the early emergence of a labor movement is linked to open resources and the presence of a sizable small producer class. Those in the latter group were unwilling to submit to "wage slavery" and were determined to protect themselves against complete subordination. "Long after the gold rush had vanished, the tradition of high wages, of the honor and dignity of labor, continued to create a congenial social milieu for trade union activity" (McWilliams 1976:132). The fact that open resources were still available provided some material basis for resistance. The early labor movement probably contained a substantial independent producer segment. For instance, early crafts unions, such as that of carpenters, would be combinations of people who owned their own tools and did not spend their work life in a single factory. In a sense their unions would be closer to guilds of small producers than simple labor unions. For example, even after 1900, labor unions included "butchers, barbers, bakers, picture frame makers, cloak makers, tailors, milk wagon drivers, art glass blowers, blacksmiths, and many similar occupations which usually fall into the 'little business' category" (McWilliams 1976:141). Their desire to resist complete proletarianization probably contributed to their militancy.

TABLE 4.7
AVERAGE WAGES IN MANUFACTURING ESTABLISHMENTS, BY STATE, 1869 AND 1879

	1869			1879		
	Number of wage earners (in hundreds)	Total wages paid (in thousands of dollars)	Average wage (in dollars)	Number of wage earners (in hundreds)	Total wages paid (in thousands of dollars)	Average wage (in dollars)
United States	18,612	704,298	378.4	25,400	870,712	342.8
Alabama	71	1,936	272.7	92	2,282	248.0
Arizona	1	32	320.0	1	55	550.0
Arkansas	26	583	224.2	40	761	190.2
CALIFORNIA	228	11,835	519.1	385	18,007	467.7
Colorado	6	388	646.7	45	1,882	418.2
Connecticut	849	36,826	433.8	1,085	41,617	383.6
Delaware	83	3,064	369.2	120	4,055	337.9
District of Columbia	33	1,358	411.5	61	3,455	566.4
Florida	23	834	362.6	54	1,218	225.6
Georgia	155	4,201	271.0	228	4,699	206.1
Idaho	2	94	470.0	3	80	266.7
Illinois	738	27,944	378.6	1,306	51,525	394.5
Indiana	503	15,983	316.1	636	20,003	314.5
Iowa	200	5,898	294.9	242	8,199	338.8
Kansas	53	1,878	354.3	99	3,175	320.7
Kentucky	267	8,493	318.1	337	10,419	309.2
Louisiana	287	3,984	138.8	105	3,494	332.8
Maine	464	13,603	293.2	510	13,093	256.7
Maryland	409	11,619	284.1	693	16,692	240.9

TABLE 4.7 (Continued)
AVERAGE WAGES IN MANUFACTURING ESTABLISHMENTS, BY STATE, 1869 AND 1879

	1869			1879		
	Number of wage earners (in hundreds)	Total wages paid (in thousands of dollars)	Average wage (in dollars)	Number of wage earners (in hundreds)	Total wages paid (in thousands of dollars)	Average wage (in dollars)
Massachusetts	2,644	110,113	416.5	3,343	120,428	360.2
Michigan	559	18,666	333.9	719	23,328	324.5
Minnesota	95	3,490	367.4	178	7,261	407.9
Mississippi	48	1,295	269.8	52	1,038	199.6
Missouri	522	25,383	486.3	572	21,270	371.9
Montana	6	344	573.3	5	227	454.0
Nebraska	21	1,227	584.3	35	1,252	357.7
Nevada	27	2,408	891.9	5	359	718.0
New Hampshire	391	13,274	339.5	471	14,187	301.2
New Jersey	674	28,885	428.0	1,186	43,044	362.9
New Mexico	3	147	490.0	4	104	260.0
New York	3,265	131,797	403.7	4,950	181,414	366.5
North Carolina	124	1,933	155.9	172	2,544	147.9
N. and S. Dakota	1	19	190.0	7	255	364.3
Ohio	1,216	44,506	366.0	1,692	57,263	338.4
Oregon	22	942	428.2	31	1,461	471.3
Pennsylvania	2,892	115,478	399.3	3,667	126,581	345.2
Rhode Island	464	17,802	383.7	601	20,041	333.5
South Carolina	71	1,365	192.3	144	2,499	173.5
Tennessee	164	4,713	287.4	200	4,569	228.5
Texas	65	1,502	231.1	106	2,816	265.7

Utah	13	354	272.3	22	718	326.4
Vermont	169	5,822	344.5	164	4,829	294.5
Virginia	235	4,621	196.6	363	6,660	183.5
Washington	9	525	583.3	10	465	465.0
West Virginia	107	4,105	383.6	136	4,118	302.8
Wisconsin	401	12,713	317.0	522	17,132	328.2
Wyoming	5	316	632.0	3	138	460.0

SOURCE: Derived from Lee et al. 1957:684, 688.

Labor in California was not only organized early; it was politically oriented from the outset. For example, as early as 1853, organized labor managed to get a ten-hour-day law passed (McWilliams 1976:128). In 1877 the Workingmen's party was able to elect many state and local officials and to exert substantial influence on the state constitutional convention of 1879 (Kauer 1944). The Union Labor party dominated San Francisco politics for several years at the turn of the century (McWilliams 1976:129; Bean 1968:289).

In addition, labor politics in California tended to be radical. Some of the most important San Francisco labor leaders were socialists (Bean 1968:286-287). In the 1880s a socialist organization, the International Workingmen's Association, played an important role in the labor movement. The International Workers of the World (IWW) was prominent from 1905 to 1920. And from 1920 to 1940 the Communist party exerted an important influence. Meanwhile in Los Angeles the Socialist party was influential in the development of the local labor movement (McWilliams 1976:129).

McWilliams (1976:134) attributes California labor militancy in part to the kind of workers who were immigrating into the state:

> A large part of the skilled labor force of San Francisco was made up of foreign-born workers who brought a knowledge of trade union organization to California. For example, there were unions of German-speaking cigar-makers, brewers, bakers, and cabinet-makers. The Sailors' Union, which served as a training school for trade unionists in San Francisco, was largely made up of men who were natives of Sweden, Norway, and Finland.

Developments in their countries of origin contributed to their ability to organize. The acquisition of California by the United States in 1848 of course corresponds to major developments for European labor (McWilliams 1976:136).

Thus big capital faced a labor force highly priced not only because of market conditions but also because it would not tolerate highly exploitative work conditions. Clearly California export capitalists could not pay the prevailing or negotiated wages and still hope to compete in the national and international market.

There were essentially two ways to deal with this dilemma. One was to introduce labor-saving devices into production and, indeed, California was noted for its great technological innovations along these lines. In mining, new and ingenious methods for extracting increasingly inaccessible gold were continually being invented (Paul 1967). California wheat farmers were acclaimed for their high level of mechanization

(Paul 1958:397, Rothstein 1975:276, Nash 1972:318). Mechanization is very costly, however, and involves high levels of capital investment. Given limits on market prices, the profitablity of such investment might be questionable. Indeed a declining rate of profit, partially induced by mechanization, may have contributed to the demise of large-scale wheat production in California.

The second alternative to high labor costs was to search for cheaper, more controllable labor. This had been the solution devised by southern planters in the face of similar circumstances. Had slavery been an option for California big capital, it is unlikely it would have refrained from using it. But, as we have seen, California quickly became a nonslave state, and the Civil War and abolition of slavery brought an end to any such possibility. It was under these circumstances that Asian labor, starting with the Chinese and moving on to the Japanese, Koreans, Indians, and finally Filipinos, entered the labor force of California.

Asian Labor

While the high price of local labor dictated that California capitalists would seek sources of cheap labor power elsewhere, it by no means followed that they would necessarily turn to Asia. Why did they not use other sources, such as American blacks, European immigrants, or Mexicans? I do not have a complete answer to this question but can suggest some possibilities. First of all, California capitalists did try to tap these sources and to some extent were successful in doing so. (For example, a Mexican labor force eventually became dominant in the California fields.) But there were reasons why each group was not an ideal answer to the problem.

Blacks were unsuitable because after the Civil War they had essentially the same rights as whites. They could not be bound to a particularly rightless status that would force them to work for low wages in the dependent sector. For example, Bean (1968:294) reports that in the 1890s, efforts were made by agricultural capital to bring in black workers from the southern states. "But agricultural wages were so low that they soon found better pay in unskilled labor or domestic service in the cities."

Another possible labor source was Mexico, a territory even more subject to the effects of United States imperialism than most Asian countries. When the United States took over the southwestern states from Mexico, a fairly substantial indigenous population was present that might have been used as cheap labor. Under the Treaty of Guadalupe Hidalgo, however, Mexican residents of United States territories were granted citizenship (Almaguer 1971:11) and many retained landholdings for a period, so they were less exploitable than immigrants. Immigrant workers could be imported from Mexico, and undoubtedly some did come before the turn of the century; but substantial numbers began coming only after 1900, increasing especially after the revolution in 1910 and the labor shortages associated with World War I (Samora 1971:17-18; McWilliams 1968:162-163).

Several reasons can be suggested for the relatively low usage of Mexican immigrant labor during the late nineteenth century. First, the northern region of Mexico was sparsely settled, and transportation to the more populous southern region was not developed. Second, because Mexicans were Catholics, they were culturally closer to United States whites than were Asians. The ideological similarities may have made it more difficult to subject the Mexicans to a coerced or semicoerced status. Third, the level of development in Mexico in the second half of the nineteenth century may have played a part. As long as Mexico remained primarily a peasant society, few people would be available for emigration. Major emigration movements depend upon economic dislocations leading to large numbers of people who need to seek a livelihood elsewhere. I suspect this transformation occurred later in Mexico. Finally, as McWilliams (1968:163) states, the very fact that Asian labor was used extensively in California delayed the use of Mexican labor there, as opposed to Texas, until about 1917. The fact that Asian labor was available earlier thus tended to set a pattern in California.

In contrast to the situation in Mexico, displacement of the peasantry was occurring on a massive scale in Europe, contemporaneously with Asia if not earlier. European labor was being used extensively in the East. Why then was it not used in the same way in the West? Again, I can only guess at the answer. Apart from the obvious factor of proximity, we should recall that in the East, European labor was mainly used in the northern indigenous capitalist sector, not in the dependent capitalism of the South. The coercion applied to black labor could not be used against the immigrant whites. They came mainly as free labor in the late nineteenth century, a status that was highly useful to emerging industrial capitalism but not to the southern plantations. Because of their status as free labor, Europeans, let alone native whites, could not be bound to work in the dependent industries. Employers often expressed a preference for white labor but felt it could not be acquired at a profitable rate. Thus in 1906 the California Fruit Growers Association stated, "Sincerely as our growers would prefer loyal and efficient services by those of Caucasian blood, it is incontestable that such labor is not to be had at a price which the present margin of profit in fruit operation can allow" (cited in Jones 1970:30). They passed a resolution calling for a modification of the Chinese Exclusion Act that would permit the immigration of workers irrespective of nationality.

There are, however, some similarities between European and Asian immigrants. The Irish, for instance, worked in railroad construction. Italians were brought in under the padrone system, which bound them to contracts for a period. Many of the eastern and southern Europeans were sojourners who came to the United States with the intention of earning money quickly and returning to their homelands. All these are features that characterized the Asians, as we shall see, and made them desirable to California capitalists.

Still, in general, Asian immigrants experienced these disabilities in more extreme form and were therefore especially desirable as workers. For instance, Black (1963:60) reports several instances of pro-Chinese Californians making invidious comparisons to the "violent, lawless" Irish. As she explains, "The Irish, having served their apprenticeship as outsiders and strikebreakers . . . were becoming enough at home to form an integral part of the trade union movement; and since they were, apart from the Negroes, the last hired and first fired, the most militant part." Asians were seen by potential employers as more controllable than European immigrants. And given the additional burden of distance from markets and their low level of development relative to the East, California capitalists would have a special incentive to seek the cheapest, most tractable labor possible.

This question can be turned around the other way; namely, why did eastern capitalists not make use of Asian labor? The answer, again, is that to some extent they did. For instance, Chinese were imported into Mississippi during Reconstruction as a means of undercutting ex-slaves (Loewen 1971). And there were other southern efforts to deal with abolition in this manner. In the North in 1870, Chinese were brought into a shoe factory in North Adams, Massachusetts in an effort to break a strike by the largest trade union of the time, the Secret Order of Saint Crispin. This shoemakers union was resisting mechanization. When the factory owner tried to bring in local and European immigrant scabs, they were quickly organized. Finally he imported Chinese from San Francisco, under three-year contracts at low wages, housing them within the factory grounds. They were an especially coerced labor force, inaccessible to the Crispins because of extraordinary employer control. By using Chinese labor, the owner saved the factory $40,000 in the first year and helped break the union. This incident received widespread attention in the Northeast, contributing to labor's antagonism to Chinese immigration while helping make Chinese exclusion a national rather than regional issue (Rudolph 1947, Hill 1973:45).

In summary, Asian labor was probaby concentrated in the West for much the same reasons that blacks were concentrated in the South. As an especially disadvantaged group, they could be used to fill the peculiar needs of California dependent capitalism. California did, in fact, attract European immigrant labor as well, but this was mainly in the indigenous capitalism sector. In other words, a racial division of labor emerged in California that was similar to that of the East, where "colored" labor worked in the dependent sector and white free labor worked in the emerging industrial sector.

Now let us turn to the peculiar status of Asian labor that made it both available and cheap for California big businesses. Essentially this boils down to the fact that Asian countries were the object of United States, especially West Coast (Cox 1969), imperialism (as well as that of other European countries). As such, their political economies were severely dislocated, which put pressure on the peasantry and other classes and created a substantial population whose means of livelihood were so disrupted as to make them candidates for emigration. This process will be dealt with extensively, on a country-by-country basis, in part II.

As an imperial power in Asia, the United States could not only impose unequal treaties in terms of trade and tariffs. It could also impose unequal conditions on the flow of personnel, or labor power. United States and Hawaiian capital could send representatives to Asian countries to actively recruit labor and could play an important, sometimes determinative role in setting the conditions under which the workers emigrated. Of course, there was variation by country. In China, where the government lacked control of the situation, Chinese citizens could be bound to contracts that they could not comprehend and would never agree to freely. In some cases they could even be kidnapped off the streets. The notorious "coolie trade" throughout the colonial world suggests the level of inability of the Chinese government to control this "emigration."

A very different case is Japan, with a much stronger government better able to control emigration. But Japan, too, was forced by the Western countries not only to open its doors to trade but also to permit labor emigration, a thing it had refused to do for centuries. When Japan agreed to a labor convention with Hawaii in 1868, it was hardly a contract between two free and equal parties. The Japanese government could exercise more restraints on the conditions imposed from without than could China, but it was not in complete command of the situation.

In general, imperialist activity in Asia helps explain why this area became a major source of cheap labor in the western United States. This was not an isolated phenomenon. In the second half of the nineteenth century Asian labor was moving, or being moved, to many parts of the colonial world. Perhaps the most dramatic instance was the Indian indenture system, in which Indians were sent as laborers to such diverse territories in the British Empire as South Africa, Fiji, Trinidad, and Malaya. Chinese emigration may have been less well orchestrated by a dominant colonial power, but the net effect was much the same. Asian immigration to the United States and Hawaii was part of a more widespread trend.

The opening up of Asia as a source of labor corresponds to the ending of African slavery. The Indian indenture system arose on the heels of abolition in the British Empire in 1834. Similarly, the beginning of Asian immigration to the United States roughly corresponds to the termination of slavery in the early 1860s. This is not to say that Asian labor in California and Hawaii was somehow a substitute for black labor in the South but that capitalists in California and Hawaii did not have access to the type of labor supply that the South could command. They had to seek out what was available at the time. The opening up of Asia by Western imperial powers at this time made it a logical source.

It should be noted that there is a correspondence between sources of emigration and degree of colonial influence. The major Asian sources of immigration to the United States, China, Japan, and the Philippines, were all areas of major United States influence. Countries like Malaya, India, or Indonesia, however, did not become important suppliers of labor power to the United States. Their domination by Great Britain or the Netherlands and the competition among the various colonial powers probably determined this. That Indians did not go to Hawaii in any significant numbers partly reflects British unwillingness to have them used to develop a rival colony, as well as United States reluctance to enhance British influence in the islands. The few Indians who came to the mainland were, in large part, a spillover from a British colony, Canada. Similarly, as a Japanese territory, Korea could not be fully tapped for labor by the United States; Japan wanted to keep control over its own colonial work force.

Ultimately the selection of Asia rather than eastern and southern Europe as a source of labor for the West comes down to the fact that capital in California and Hawaii, varyingly backed by different levels of government, could impose harsher conditions on Asian immigrants than it could on the Europeans. This was partly a product of the ideological trappings of imperialism, which enabled Westerners to see "people of color" as inferiors who deserved no better. Added to this was a difference in the political power of the home countries, which varied in their ability to demand certain standards in the treatment of their emigrants. For instance, although Portugal was a poor and backward country in Europe, it could still command considerably more favorable conditions for its emigrant laborers to Hawaii than could Japan, let alone China or the Philippines. This difference made Asian labor attractive, especially to the highly competitive monopolies of the western United States, which suffered the additional disability of distant markets.

The major advantage to big capital of using immigrant Asian laborers was that capitalists could exercise some control over their legal and political status on entry. Immigrant labor is typically far more controllable than native labor for this reason, though, of course, special pockets of disadvantaged workers can be created within nation-states as well (e.g., women). The special disability imposed upon Asian immigrants was their ineligibility for citizenship; they were a completely disfranchised group. The implications of this peculiar status are so staggering, in terms of the ability of capital to control them, that it alone can explain why Asians were cheap labor. There were other factors contributing to their "cheapness," however, which we shall consider after briefly describing the evolution of their being denied the possibility of citizenship.

As we saw in the previous chapter, the first United States naturalization law of 1790 limited citizenship to free whites, with the chief aim of denying it to blacks and nonfree whites. Since there were no persons of Asian ancestry present in the country at the time, the status of Asian immigrants was undefined. China and the United States signed treaties in 1844 and 1858 that opened up and regulated trade relations but left the issue of immigrant status unspecified. Presumably Chinese immigrants were like all others, and some did become naturalized citizens.

The Burlingame Treaty of 1868 clarified the issue. For the first time, the right to free migration (as opposed to free trade, which had been established earlier) was promulgated. China was, in essence, forced to open her doors not only to Western goods and merchants but also to the free flow of her populace. Presumably this freedom extended to labor recruiters as well. The treaty acted as a stimulus to Chinese immigration to the United States, as shown in table 4.8.

Certain events in California coincided with the passage of this treaty:

> In 1868 various labor organizations had been strong enough to secure the passage of a state law providing for an 8-hour day in public works contracts, and unions had been able to persuade many private employers to agree to the same policy. But in order to roll back this advance on the part of labor, certain employers in San Francisco established a "California Labor and Employment Exchange" and an "Immigrant Aid

TABLE 4.8
NUMBER OF CHINESE ARRIVING IN THE UNITED STATES, 1857 TO 1882

1857	4,524	1870	15,740
1858	7,183	1871	7,135
1859	3,215	1872	7,788
1860	6,117	1873	20,291
1861	6,094	1874	13,776
1862	4,174	1875	16,437
1863	5,280	1876	22,781
1864	5,340	1877	10,591
1865	3,702	1878	8,992
1866	1,872	1879	9,604
1867	3,519	1880	5,802
1868	6,707	1881	11,890
1869	12,874	1882	39,579

SOURCE: Coolidge 1968:498.

Association," through which they carried on a nation-wide propaganda campaign designed to bring in as many new workers as possible to California and thus to weaken labor's bargaining power (Bean 1968:220).

We might add that the Burlingame Treaty also roughly coincided with the termination of black slavery. Discussions of substituting Chinese for blacks were being held in the South at the time, only to die down several years later when it became clear that black labor could still be controlled by southern capital (Konvitz 1946:11-12). Perhaps it is coincidental that Chinese immigration was encouraged by the federal government at this particular time, but there may also be a connection.

The Burlingame Treaty granted "most favored nation" status to China. During its ratification, however, the Senate imposed only one amendment (Bean 1968:233):

Nothing herein contained shall be held to confer naturalization upon citizens of the United States in China, nor upon the subjects of China in the United States.

According to Coolidge (1968:148-149), this amendment reflected debates in Congress over black suffrage and the parallel between blacks and Chinese. At the time, the clause was understood not as forbidding naturalization to the Chinese but as not conferring it automatically by the treaty.

In 1870 naturalization privileges were extended to blacks. But the term *free white persons* was left standing as the basis for citizenship and only *"persons of African descent"* was added to the list of eligibles. This, according to Konvitz (1946:83), was in response to agitation by Pacific Coast senators who wanted to prevent Chinese immigrants from becoming citizens.

California passed numerous anti-Chinese bills, many of which were declared unconstitutional by the courts. But "denial of the privileges of citizenship by exclusion from naturalization, suffrage, giving testimony for or against white persons in courts, and exclusion from public schools" remained legal because of the phrase in the Burlingame Treaty denying automatic conferral of citizenship (Coolidge 1968:80). Formal federal denial of the right to become naturalized was finally declared as part of the Chinese Exclusion Act of 1882 (Konvitz 1946:80).

The question of eligibility of Asians for citizenship was continually raised in court cases and legislation, with contradictory and confusing results (see, for instance, Melendy 1977:47-48). An act would fail to mention free white persons in one of its sections, and the issue would be taken to court, only to have various courts make different determinations.

Overall, each Asian immigrant group faced the issue of denial of naturalization rights, fought it in the courts, and lost. The circumstances surrounding each group were slightly different. Filipinos had the peculiar status of being United States nationals after 1898 when the United States acquired the Philippines. But they were found to be ineligible for citizenship in a series of court fights lasting until 1918 because they were not "free white persons." An exception was made for persons who served in the armed forces. As nationals, Filipinos were permitted to immigrate freely until 1934 when they were excluded under the Tydings-McDuffie Independence Act (Melendy 1977:47-48). Thus they had the unique status of being a rightless group that could still immigrate without restriction.

Indians also fought for citizenship in the courts, with mixed results in individual cases. The final determining case, *United States* v. *Thind,* was heard by the Supreme Court in 1922. Because Indians were considered to be racially Caucasian, they could argue that they fell into the category "free white," which had been interpreted in some courts to mean Caucasian. The Supreme Court ruled against Thind, invalidating the claim of Indians on the basis of their color (Konvitz 1946:88-97; Melendy 1977:216-221; Hess 1976:169-171).

Although the Supreme Court did not deal with the issue of citizenship for Japanese until the Ozawa case in 1922, when it ruled unfavorably (Konvitz 1946:80-88), lower courts generally assumed that Japanese fell under the ban against non-"free whites." When California passed its Alien Land Laws, barring from purchasing land those who were "aliens ineligible to citizenship," the Japanese were clearly the chief target (Daniels 1966:50-51). Koreans were usually treated like Japanese. Though individual Koreans fought for citizenship rights in the courts, they were denied on the grounds of being "Mongolian" (Melendy 1977:136).

In summary, Asian immigrant workers were placed in a unique category of people who could not become citizens and who could therefore never enjoy the rights of citizens. Needless to say, this was of tremendous advantage to their employers, who could act without restraint in their efforts to control the immigrant workers. It is difficult to discover whether California capitalists actively contrived to create or uphold this status for Asians, but since it was so markedly in their interests, it seems highly likely that they would have. For instance, one wonders whether, when the 1870 naturalization law was extended to blacks, the Pacific Coast senators who lobbied against striking the phrase "free white persons" were not responsive to these interests.

The interests of big capital in Asian immigration need to be distinguished from the interests of labor. While labor would generally push for exclusion, big capital would want Asians to continue coming but in an especially rightless status. In this sense, the peculiar status of Filipinos would be highly suitable to capital. As nationals they could not easily be excluded, yet they could still be denied citizenship rights. Capital was, perhaps, getting wiser about how to play the labor immigration game.

Apart from the workers' lack of rights, certain other features of Asian immigrant labor contributed to its cheapness for capital. First, a certain selectivity could be exercised in terms of who was permitted to enter. For instance, people who were sick or likely to become a public charge could be denied entry. Furthermore, the most ablebodied predominated, namely, young, single males. While the latter was partially a function of self-selection, since it corresponded so well to the requirements of the capitalists, they probably had some influence on the process. For instance, recruitment agents in Asia no doubt actively sought out such immigrants.

The advantage to big capital of single, healthy, young adult males need scarcely be stated. Such workers could be easily moved about in response to the changing needs of capital. For instance, they would be especially suitable for railroad construction or migrant farm work. They could be housed cheaply, while their burden of dependency (in the form of families they helped support at home) could be ignored in the wage calculation, let alone the provision of social services. In other words, the reproduction of the labor force was left in Asia, freeing local capital of this expense.

A second feature of Asian labor that contributed to its cheapness was the fact that these workers could be expelled if they proved undesirable to capital. This is a feature of all immigrant labor but is exaggerated when immigrants lack political and legal rights to challenge such actions. Thus Asians could be deported or denied admission during times of depression. Perhaps more importantly, they could be excluded if and when they became "unsuitable" as laborers either by beginning to organize or by moving out of the laboring class in search of other opportunities that might compete with local capital. In any case, the very threat of deportation must have acted as a curb on the ability of Asian workers to organize.

The needs of Asian laborers corresponded somewhat to those of capital, making some of the features of their employment that favored capital easier to enforce. Thus most Asian immigrants came to the United States with the intention of saving some money and aiding their families back home. They planned to return after their tour of overseas duty. Under the circumstances it was sensible to leave the family behind, since the cost of living in California corresponded to the higher wages there. Besides, life in California was very insecure; there were no assurances that one would be taken care of in old age or sickness. Keeping ties with the village in Asia, retaining family connections there, acted as a form of social insurance.

The actions of capital and Asian labor on this issue of providing for the reproduction of the work force were mutually reinforcing. As long as Asians provided for it themselves, capital did not have to. But as long as capital did not provide for it, communities in Asia had to sustain it. The result was a kind of vicious circle, perpetuating a form of migrant labor or sojourning. Essentially capitalist development in California, at least of the dependent variety, made use of the persistence of a precapitalist sector in Asian countries. Needless to say, this pattern is found elsewhere in the world as well.

A final benefit to California capitalists lay in the role played by middlemen. They were often of the same ethnicity as the immigrant workers, though they need not have been. Thus Chinese merchants or Japanese immigration companies played an active role in bringing Asian workers to California, but so also did "white" steamship companies. The middlemen helped bind immigrant workers to contracts, often by various forms of indebtedness. They also helped discipline the workers for capital. For example, the role of labor contractor, another important middleman function, was pivotal in providing land owners and the railroads with a steady and disciplined labor supply. They contributed to making Asians a semicoerced work force, exactly what the dependent capitalists of California needed and wanted.

An illustration of the desires of capitalists was the Tingley Tariff Bill of 1852, introduced into the California legislature in an effort "to legalize and make possible the enforcement of contracts by which Chinese laborers could sell their services to employers for periods of ten years or less at fixed wages" (Paul 1938:185). Although the bill failed to pass, it clearly represented what capital was after: in the face of high local labor costs and open resources, capitalists wanted workers they could bind. While this could not be achieved legally in California, it could nevertheless be achieved in modified form by the introduction of a rightless group of workers.

It is possible to trace the way in which each of the major dependent capitalist industries in California faced the problems of securing a labor supply locally and came to use Asian labor. The pattern was similar in each case. An industry would hire white labor, only to find that it would disappear in the face of better opportunities or would prove too costly. For instance, the Central Pacific found that its railroad builders would leave for the Comstock Lode as soon as they could. The level of wages needed to make them stay would be prohibitive. Employers would then experiment with Asian labor, find it to be far preferable to white labor, and actively pursue an Asian labor force. Thus did Asians come to concentrate in these industries.

Indigenous Capitalism

As had happened in the northern United States, out of the independent producers gradually evolved industrial capitalism. California only began to industrialize in a major way after the turn of the century. Before that time most of its industries were subsidiaries of the dependent sector engaged in the processing of raw materials, namely, sugar refineries, flour mills, sawmills, and canneries (Nash 1972:321). These, too, were areas of concentration for Asian labor (e.g., Ichihashi 1932:150-156).

After 1900, and especially by World War I, industrial diversification was under way with the development of the oil industry (providing much-needed power for local plants), tourism, the movie industry, and large-scale manufacturing, including automobile assembly and aircraft construction. By 1940, manufacturing provided about $1 billion, one-third of the total state income (Nash 1972:321-322).

An indicator of the internal development of California was the emergence of large-scale banking. "Until the First World War California was dependent to a large extent on eastern as well as foreign capital. Indeed, the state's position was not wholly unlike that of an underdeveloped nation, a colony subject to control by outside financiers such as Wall St." (Nash 1972:323). But after the war, and especially with the emergence of the Bank of America as a major financial institution in 1919, California was able to become free from a heavy reliance on outside capital (Nash 1972:323-324).

Long before this, however, in the latter part of the nineteenth century, the state had a variety of developing small manufacturing industries, especially in San Francisco. Thus in 1865 San Francisco ranked ninth among United States cities in terms of the amount of capital invested in manufacturing and value of manufactured products (McWilliams 1976:229). Typical manufactures between 1850 and 1870 were boots, shoes, clothing, chemicals and drugs, furniture, iron and steel, distilled liquors, soap, candles, tobacco, leather goods, gas, planed wood, bricks, tile, and pottery (Cleland and Hardy 1929:134). But as a contemporary pointed out, "The factories of California are few and small, relatively high wages make it impossible to compete successfully with the cheap labor of the Eastern States" (cited in Cleland and Hardy 1929:134-135). For example, according to the 1860 Census of Manufactures (Secretary of Interior 1865:35-36), there were in the state 1,426 manufacturing establishments, excluding mining, having an average of 4.6 workers per firm and paying an average wage of $830 per annum.

As these figures suggest, the transition between the small producer and competitive capitalist modes of production was gradual, and the boundary between them far from clear. Thus for a long time, many of the small manufacturing firms in San Francisco were somewhere between the two modes, and the workers in them were neither completely proletarianized nor completely free from having to sell their labor power for a wage. Still, a small capitalist class was gradually emerging that could invest in production for a profit and could afford to hire the labor power of others.

In contrast to the monopoly industries, indigenous capitalism in California grew from the accumulation of capital within the state. It did not depend on outside investment. Nor was it geared to distant markets. Instead, production was mainly for the local market. As a result, these businesses did not have to concern themselves with the costs of long-distance transportation. Nor did they have to face price competition in eastern and international markets. Even though wages were high on the West Coast, they could pass on this cost to their customers. The entire West Coast economy was inflated by the combination of gold production and high wages. But the region was protected from competition by distance (McWilliams 1976:216).

The completion of the first transcontinental railroad in 1869 brought an end to this protection. Some local capitalists foresaw this result with dread, which helps account for some of the difficulties the railroad faced in trying to raise capital in San Francisco. Even though eastern manufacturers had to pay transportation costs to export their products to the West, they had developed more advanced techniques and could produce the same commodities more cheaply. (This was less true for the production of raw materials, which helps explain why these became California's exports.) Eastern imports thus posed a threat to the industrial development of California and probably contributed to the depression of the 1870s.

The impact of eastern imports was variable, however. Some industries, such as shipping or construction, were by their very nature local. Such industries remained unaffected by the completion of the railroad and could still afford to sustain high-wage labor. Other industries, notably cigar, garment, and shoe manufacturing, directly faced eastern competition and were threatened by it.

All emerging capitalists in California would have an interest in using Asian labor if they could. It would give them at least a temporary advantage over their competitors, enabling them to earn high profits. The pressure would be most intense in industries threatened by competition from cheaper imports, however. Here sheer survival dictated that they cheapen production somehow, and Asian labor seemed the best available possibility (Saxton 1971:75–76). Thus in 1870, within manufacturing, Asian labor was primarily concentrated and overrepresented in three industries: boot and shoemaking, cigar making, and textile mills and sewing.

Turning to Asian labor spurred the transition from small producers to competitive capitalism, since Asian laborers were, at least in the beginning, mainly a propertyless group. In this sense they were more completely proletarianized than most white workers. When a budding capitalist hired Asian laborers, he could appropriate all the surplus value they generated. When, however, he hired white laborers, they sometimes owned their own tools and controlled aspects of the work process, so his ability to generate and appropriate surplus value was restricted. Since these workers were organized to resist their complete reduction into the proletariat, employing them entailed not only paying a high price for labor but also having to temper changes in the production process that would increase efficiency.

Perhaps even more important, many of the small manufacturing firms were probably owned and operated by the same people; that is, they were still at the small-producer level of development. These firms would find themselves in competition with businesses organized along more efficient capitalist lines. A capitalist firm could eke much more labor out of each worker by the division of labor into monotonous but quickly repeatable tasks, by making him work long hours, and by closely monitoring his activities. In addition, the firm could get this greater amount of labor by paying less than the independent producer "paid" to himself, a discrepancy that was exaggerated if the work force was Asian. In order to survive, the small producer would have to reduce his level of living and increase his work output to the level of a proletarian.

The urban areas of California were thus somewhat confusing centers of two kinds of class struggle. On the one hand was the simple struggle between capital and labor. On the other was the struggle by independent producers against the development of capitalism as a mode of production. Both proletarians and independent producers were anticapitalist, though for somewhat different reasons. They formed a potent political coalition that was able to set limits on the newly developing capitalist class. And perhaps the most important limit they could set was on the access of that class to Asian labor. In other words, probably the most important reason for the restricted use of Asian labor in most manufacturing industries was the opposition to it by white labor and small producers. Since white labor was already concentrated in these fields, it was here that political opposition could be most easily mobilized.

The two kinds of California capitalism were similar to those in the northern and southern areas on the East Coast. Indigenous capitalism was like that of the North, emerging out of the small-producer class and resistant to institutions like slavery. The dependent sector was like the South, relying for its very existence on some degree of coercion and binding of its labor force. That Asians concentrated in the latter was in part a product of their exclusion from the former.

The ouster, or denial of entry of Asians from most segments of local manufacturing had tremendous ramifications for them. If they were cheap labor on arrival, it was not a status that had to last. Indeed, one would expect it to have disappeared rather quickly as the immigrants learned of the local level of wages and standard of living. But their exclusion from the sector of the economy that was most rapidly developing (in terms of technical innovation and hence productivity of labor) set severe limits on their ability to improve their condition. Like blacks in the South they were essentially confined to the low wage sector and therefore had to accept low wages. They were victims of a vicious circle: because they were cheap labor they were kept out of high wage jobs, and because they were kept out of high wage jobs they remained cheap labor. The fact that they had a severely restricted set of job choices only added to this difficulty. Needless to say, the vicious circle served the interests of capital in the monopoly sector, helping secure a continued supply of the kind of labor it needed.

Service and Self-Employment

As we saw in an earlier chapter, Asians tended to concentrate heavily and were overrepresented in household and personal service occupations. In the former category they tended to work as housecleaners, cooks, and gardeners. These kinds of jobs are typical of colonial settings and were common among blacks in the South, too. While these occupations did not contribute to the accumulation of wealth in the state, they reflect the process of accumulation by representing one of the ways in which profits were spent. In all likelihood, this servant class worked mainly for capitalists who used some of the wealth they were accumulating in productive activities to support a fairly luxurious life-style.

Unlike some colonial labor forces, Asians also entered personal service occupations in which they ran their own small businesses. Examples include laundries, restaurants, and boardinghouses. They also moved into other forms of self-employment, such as retailing, market-gardening, fishing, and farming. The reasons for this move are complex (e.g., Light 1972; Bonacich and Modell 1980) and need not concern us here. The main point is that self-employment or the running of a small business proved to be an outlet for many Asian immigrants, who were thereby able to escape the role of laborer.

Asian small businesses tended to serve the population at large, particularly the working class. Asians provided essential services cheaply. In this, they also played an important part in the development of California capitalism. On the one hand, by providing workers with cheap foodstuffs (from market-gardens and farms) and key services, they enabled capital to lower the wage bill of their employees. Thus, even though big capital did not directly control Asian small businesses, it could benefit from their presence. On the other hand, the development of a small business class also put Asians in competition with some sectors of capital, as well as with segments of labor, a phenomenon that could fill another volume.

Linkages Between Sectors

Asian immigrants were clearly a superexploited segment of the California work force. They tended to be concentrated in the worst kinds of jobs, those that were most dangerous, entailed the worst living and working conditions, and had the longest hours and lowest pay. This is true whether they worked in the dependent sector, in the few manufacturing lines to which they were confined, or in their own independent small businesses. Asians did the work no one else was willing to do at a rate that made these ventures viable. For instance, had only local white labor been available for constructing the transcontinental railroad, it is questionable whether it could ever have been completed. The high wages that would have been required to keep those workers on the job might have made the whole venture unfeasible.

An important question that can be raised regarding those in this Asian immigrant underclass is, Who benefited from their exploitation? It is clear that their immediate employers (namely, mining, railroad, and agricultural capitalists) and Asian middlemen were the direct beneficiaries, but we suspect that the benefits extended to other segments as well. Without being able to trace them here, we can at least suggest some possibilities.

First of all, eastern and British capitalists who invested in California monopolies probably benefited from the use of Asian labor, since the profits they earned were higher than they would have been with more expensive labor and were higher than the profits they could earn at home. Second, and less directly, the eastern and British trading partners of the California monopolies benefited from being able to purchase the goods in question cheaply. They could engage in *unequal exchange*. For example, eastern and British industrial capitalists could purchase cheap California grains and produce, enabling them to lower their wage bill.

Perhaps most interesting are the benefits that accrued to the indigenous capitalists in California. They, too, engaged in trade with the dependent sector. As manufacturers utilizing highly priced but efficient labor (because technology was applied to it), they had a trade advantage in relation to the dependent sector, exchanging less labor time for more. In other words, some of the surplus extracted from Asian labor probably worked its way up to manufacturing capitalists. At the very least, certain goods and services were made available at cheap rates, which, as in the East, could be translated into lower wages. Thus, because of the presence of Asian laundries, for instance, employers could cut wages commensurate with the lower cost of cleaning clothes. Asian restaurants served a similar function, while Asian agricultural labor had a major impact on the food bill. The ultimate effect was to lower the costs of California manufacturing, enabling it to compete more effectively in the national market.

An important question is whether white labor benefited from the presence of an Asian underclass. Aside from possible political benefits, such as providing local workers with an issue around which to rally (e.g., Saxton, 1971), it can be argued that they, too, had an economic stake in this oppression: as consumers they would be able to purchase cheaper goods and services, and as workers they would be protected from having to do the most arduous and unpleasant jobs. I contend that this is unlikely. In the first place, the benefits to consumers would, in all likelihood, be translated by their employers into lower wage rates. Wages were calibrated to the cost of living rather than the productivity of labor, and if that cost declined, employers would not simply let the benefits go to their employees.

On the second point, it can be argued that the jobs Asians occupied were unpleasant mainly because employers had no incentive to upgrade them. Agricultural production did not have to be organized on the principle of migrant, bunkhouse labor. The fact that capitalists were able to impose this organization made these jobs undesirable. But local labor ideally would have liked to dispense with that whole system of production, transforming agriculture into an activity in which anyone could engage.

The fact that white labor continually agitated for Asian exclusion seems to be fairly clear evidence that it, at least, did not perceive itself benefiting from the exploitation of Asian immigrants. It was a capitalist argument that white laborers were "pushed up" a labor hierarchy, but it was an argument that they did not accept. If local workers had benefited from the presence of an underclass, would they have pushed for its exclusion? This seems highly unlikely.

The question of linkages between sectors clearly deserves much more examination, at both a theoretical and an empirical level. It is beyond the scope of this volume, but should provide an important line of inquiry for future research.

Exclusion

Each Asian group came to face hostile reactions of multiple kinds from the surrounding population, including riots, anti-Asian legislation, and ultimately, exclusion laws or efforts to prohibit further immigration. These came in sequence, with each group arriving and then facing mounting hostility and, finally, exclusion. How are we to account for this pattern and, particularly, for the fact that Asian immigration was so severely restricted?

I shall argue that exclusion was mainly the product of class struggle in California and was fostered by the anticapitalist coalition of small producers and white labor. A case can be made that the capitalist class also played a part in the exclusion movements, however, so let us start by considering its interests.

First, it can be argued that as capitalism developed, the kind of labor power represented by Asian immigrants was no longer required. Asian immigrant labor was especially useful for the colonial phase of California's development. Once the state became industrialized, this kind of cheap, migrant labor was no longer useful. Instead, stability on the job became a desirable trait. Further, once the indigenous industries developed some economic power and increased their productivity, they could afford to pay higher wages. Meanwhile, as California developed, its open resources dried up. Once small producers resigned themselves to a life of wage labor, wages and labor militancy would decline. In other words, local labor would now be perfectly suitable to the capitalists of the state. There was no longer a need for an immigrant underclass.

While this may be true as a general trend, with a declining proportion of the labor force concentrated in the dependent sector, and while it may be true for particular occupations, as when railroad construction was completed, it is inadequate as a complete explanation of Asian exclusion. For one thing, despite the exclusion of each particular immigrant group, the next came in to fill essentially the same slot. More important, even after Asian immigration was completely terminated, Mexican immigrants continued to be brought in to work in the same occupations. This suggests that the demand for a cheap labor sector did not dry up in California. Indeed it persists to this day.

Another possible interest of capitalists in exclusion would be its use as a method of dealing with the business cycle. In general one would expect them to favor Asian immigration in times of boom; but when depression led to high unemployment, they ought to have supported exclusion. Not only would this be a mechanism for shifting the burdens of unemployment back to Asia but it would also be a means of diverting the attention of white labor from the systemic problems of capitalism. By focusing on Asian immigrants as a possible source of unemployment (because they were presumably "taking white jobs"), local labor would not threaten to overthrow the system itself.

There is no simple correspondence between depressions and Asian exclusion. Using Dowd's (1977:92) table of business cycles in the United

States we find that 1882, the year of Chinese exclusion, was a year of prosperity; that 1907-1908, when the Gentlemen's Agreement with Japan was made, were years of panic and depression; that 1917, when the barred zone in Asia excluded Indians, was a year of wartime prosperity; that 1924, when the Japanese were finally excluded, was a recession year; that Filipino exclusion in 1934 was effected during the depths of the Great Depression. Clearly downward swings predominate in this list, but they do not correspond to all cases, nor did all depressions over the entire period produce exclusion legislation. This does not invalidate the hypothesis, however. The year of enactment of an exclusion decree is but one point in the development of exclusion as a movement. The precise timing of enactment may be accidental to a certain degree. For instance, the passage of the Chinese Exclusion Act of 1882 followed a serious depression in the 1870s and may be more a product of the movement generated during that time than of events concurrent with passage.

This interpretation of exclusion seems to make considerable sense even if its empirical validation may require more research. Although the prime thrust for exclusion may have come from white workers and small producers, at least minimal capitalist willingness to permit the enactment of such legislation would seem to be a prerequisite to its successful passage. Depressions would provide an occasion not only of stepped up local worker opposition to competition from immigrants but also for capitalist willingness to permit limitations on the supply of immigrant laborers, who now would probably be unemployed and hence a tax burden.

A third interest capitalists might have in Asian exclusion would be to use it as a means of countering "detrimental" developments in the Asian communities. These would include the emergence of labor militancy, the exodus of Asian labor into the small business sector, the maturation of the labor force so that workers would be physically less able, and the emergence of a second generation that could not be denied the rights of citizenship. All of these features would make each immigrant group less desirable to capital over time. It would thus have an interest in dismissing members of a maturing community and replacing them with "raw recruits" from another country. Waves of entry and exclusion would have the additional benefit of enabling capital to play off one group against another and to use linguistic and cultural differences to fragment the work force.

This last possibility also makes sense. In general, I would argue, the capitalist class in California wanted cheap labor and was opposed to exclusion. They were not especially committed to any particular source of cheap labor, however. As long as the exclusion of one nationality did not cut off other options, capitalists could concur with exclusion, especially if the nationality in question was no longer as tractable and cheap as it once was.

While capitalists would occasionally have reasons to support exclusion movements, they were not the principal force behind them. Instead, I believe, the main impetus for Asian exclusion came from the populist coalition of small producers (including small farmers) and white proletarians (e.g., McWilliams 1976:139-142; Chiu 1967:86-87). As stated earlier, both classes were fiercely anticapitalist, if for different reasons, and saw the growth of monopolies as a dangerous trend that would undermine them. They formed various organizations and political parties to combat big capital, including the People's Independent party (1873), the Workingmen's party of California (1877-1880), the International Workingmen's Association of California and the Far West (in the 1880s), the Nationalist movement (around 1890), and the People's Party of California, or Populists (in the 1890s) (Griffiths 1970).

White small producers and workers saw Asian immigrants as a coerced labor force, not unlike slaves, and, as such, a tool big capital could use to their detriment. For example, the San Jose branch of the Workingmen's party saw its goal as perservering "in this struggle and agitation until we have eliminated from our midst the Asiatic serfs transported to these shores by an imperial dynasty at the behest and in the interests of soulless monopolies, by which free labor is being enslaved" (cited in Griffiths 1970:93). To the small producers, the availability of Asian labor to capitalists spelled the end of their independence. They would be forced out of business or farming and into the proletariat. To the proletariat, the use of Asian labor threatened their jobs, standard of living, and perhaps most important, their unions, which fought to sustain and increase both of these. The anti-Asian movement was less a movement against Asian workers themselves as it was against big capital. It was an expression of the class struggle.

For example, Jones (1970:24-25) reports on efforts by California farming interests to lobby on behalf of continuing Chinese immigration in 1881. The State Horticultural Society, representing commercial fruit growers, adopted a public resolution in favor of "Chinese Cheap Labor," which they said was essential to the continuation of their business, and sent a delegation to urge a new California congressman to vote for the defeat of Chinese exclusion. In contrast, the position of the Grangers and family farmers in the state was expressed in a letter to the *Pacific Rural Press*:

> Part of the matter with the vine and orchard men is "big heads." They like the Chinaman because he is their slave, and they can sit in the

shade and drive him as the old Southern overseer did the negro in the cotton field. The vineman of California . . . wants to be a lord, an autocrat, over unquestioning serfs (cited in Jones 1970:25).

The newspaper editorials propounded the alternative ideal of small, settled farm families and independent mechanics, an economy based on "free labor" rather than "developed" by servitude (Jones 1970:27).

Clearly, white labor might have taken another stand; namely, to bring Asian immigrants into their movement, fight for their rights, and present a united front to capital (e.g., Hill 1973). Indeed, some efforts were made in this direction, notably by the IWW in the 1910s. On the whole, however, white labor in California tended to support the racist-exclusionist position. While there are many reasons for this, an important one was the level of development of the white working class. That the small-producer segment was very prominent and that crafts unions were often more petit bourgeois than proletarian in orientation probably contributed importantly to this resolution (McWilliams 1976:141). Joining with Asian workers signified resignation to the triumph of capitalism as the dominant mode of production and acceptance of the inevitability of proletarianization. Once accepted, the major struggle becomes one of getting all workers to join together in a struggle to overthrow capitalism as a system. But many a California craft unionist was engaged in a different kind of battle: to prevent a full-blown capitalism from developing at all. A coalition with Asian labor would not foster that end. The only way the small producers could prevent capitalism from expanding was to cut off its labor supply.

Another critical factor in exclusion was the peculiar ability of capital to control Asian laborers, especially by denying them citizenship rights. The unusual legal status of Asian immigrants divided the working class more surely than any other factor, whether ideological or material. Having access to a rightless work force gave California capitalists a tremendous advantage in the class struggle with local labor and small producers. That the latter two classes tried to break this advantage is shown in such efforts as the defeat of the Tingley Bill, which would have enabled capitalists to bind Chinese workers to contracts with the support of the state (Paul 1938). White labor and small producers wanted to prohibit the creation of an underclass. Unfortunately, in trying to achieve this goal, they never seriously considered joining with the immigrant workers themselves in an effort to secure their rights.

Asian immigrants were subject to two quite different forms of racism, and it is important to keep them separate. On the one hand was the racial oppression of employers. This class wanted to bring in large numbers of Asian workers and to keep them in a legally disadvantaged position. They wanted to maintain Asians (and other similar groups) as a specially exploitable work force. On the other hand was the racism of white workers and small producers. This coalition was primarily exclusionist in orientation, seeking to prevent the access of capital to such a work force.

Asian immigrant workers were caught between these two forces. They suffered a double layer of oppression, having to overcome not only the superexploitation of their employers but also the hostility and exclusionism of the rest of the working class. (One might add a third layer of oppression, that of Asian middlemen.) These two forces help explain why Asian workers came to be confined to ˆertain sectors of the economy. They also help account for the cyclical pattern of Asian immigration: capital would bring in a certain group, labor and small producers would push for its exclusion, and capital would turn to a new group. The setting up of a barred zone in Asia in 1917 was a broad victory for the exclusionists, but capital was able to counter by bringing in American nationals, the Filipinos. And so it went. The current phase takes the form of undocumented immigrants crossing the southern border.

In conclusion, Asian immigrant labor played a vital part in the development of capitalism in California. Like blacks in the South these workers were, in a sense, the first true proletariat of the region. It was upon their hard work that the capitalist edifice was first erected. They provided an important basis for the early accumulation of capital in the state. And to the extent that California played a part in the development of the nation, especially by providing gold and cheap foodstuffs, they played an important role in the development of the country as a whole.

HAWAII

Hawaii provides an important contrast to California. It was much simpler. Unlike California, which attracted both independent producers and dependent capitalist industries, Hawaii was almost exclusively settled by people engaged in the latter system of production. Put another way, Hawaii was a colony of the United States and was generally unimpeded in developing a colonial mode of production. This took the form of plantation agriculture producing staples, especially sugar, for the mainland market.

The colonial nature of the Hawaiian economy, with its dependence upon distant and uncontrollable markets and its open resources (especially for the indigenous population, who could choose to farm on their own rather than sell their labor power to a plantation) led, as usual, to the need for cheap, coerced labor. Had slavery not been abolished by the time Hawaii began significant sugar production, the planters might well have adopted it. As it was, slavery was impossible, so they turned to the next best thing: labor imported under contract. That their labor force came mainly from Asia was fortuitous and, as in California, mainly reflected availability. The Hawaiian planters scoured the world looking for the cheapest labor and most advantageous contracts they could find (Lind 1968:188-209; Fuchs 1961:24-25). They ended up primarily with Chinese, then Japanese, and finally Filipinos because conditions in these countries created such a labor force.

Of course, the fact that these areas were under significant United States influence aided in the transferal of labor. That Indians, for example, were only brought to Hawaii in tiny numbers when they were, at the time, being shipped to several sugar-growing colonies around the world reflects their control by Great Britain and the unwillingness of the United States to allow a rival power to get a foothold in Hawaii by following its laborers with diplomatic and legal personnel (Rowland 1933:255-257).

Hawaii had never developed a significant white settler class before the war (Fuchs 1961:37). The reasons for this are complex and probably a product of historical accident. The westward movement of this class in the United States essentially halted at the Pacific Ocean, brought that far initially by the California gold rush. That white settlers did not move to Hawaii, the Philippines, or, for that matter, China and Japan may reflect conditions in those areas, including climate, density of settlement of the indigenous population, and so on. Once Hawaii became clearly colonial in its dominant mode of production, it lost all potential as an attractor of independent producers. The "Jacksonian ideal" had no chance as soon as the planter oligarchy became established.

Because of the lack of independent producers, no such white settler class in Hawaii could arise to develop a strong antimonopoly movement and curb the power of the plantation owners. Furthermore, without independent producers there was no gradual evolution of indigenous manufacturing capitalism and hence no development of a free proletariat to counter capital. Much like the South, Hawaii became a backward area, engaged in monocultural agriculture for another area on which it was dependent.

The absence of a white settler class made class and race relations much simpler. Once the native Hawaiians had been decimated and largely stripped of their land, the class structure essentially consisted of white capital (plantation owners and related people) and Asian labor. Class and race coincided. There was no great fissure in the working class between white free and nonwhite coerced labor as in California.

Although there were ethnic divisions among the plantation workers, these were not of the order to produce the kind of tearing struggle that emerged in California.

In a sense, Hawaii demonstrates what would probably have happened in California had there been no white small producers and workers. Capital could act in an unrestrained manner toward its immigrant workers. It openly co-opted the state, which acted as a labor recruitment agency. It obtained legal endorsement for the importation of contract labor and ensured the enforcement of contracts through the police powers of the state. Annexation in 1898 and the passage of the Organic Act making Hawaii a United States territory in 1900 brought an end to open labor contracting and were therefore opposed by the plantation oligarchy. But even after the annexation, the members of this group, like southern cotton growers, were able to regain control over their labor force by a variety of means (Fuchs 1961:206-225). In other words, the principle of coerced or semicoerced labor was not significantly contested from within Hawaii.

Similarly, Hawaii had no significant exclusion movement, with the exception of a relatively minor interlude of Chinese exclusion, until annexation, when mainland laws barring Chinese immigration were applied to the islands over the objections of plantation owners. The relative absence of an exclusion movement in Hawaii provides us with important clues to the true roots of exclusion on the mainland. First of all, the limited anti-Chinese movement in Hawaii seems to have grown out of resistance by local merchants to the competition from Chinese who had left the plantations and entered the petite bourgeoisie. The movement to exclude was not favored by plantation owners, and until annexation they continued to recruit Chinese when needed.

The plantation owners did not push for exclusion to deal with the business cycle, casting some doubt on the hypothesis that it was the major source of exclusion efforts. But since the Hawaiian economy was relatively stagnant in terms of the development of manufacturing capitalism, we cannot test the idea that exclusion would have resulted from development. What the Hawaiian case seems to demonstrate is that the major impetus for exclusion in California came not from the colonial capitalists who employed Asian labor but mainly from white labor, the small producers, and perhaps segments of the emerging capitalist class. The absence of these classes in Hawaii goes a long way toward explaining the absence of strong exclusionist sentiment there.

The simplicity of class relations in Hawaii was an advantage to Asian workers, in a sense. The enemy was clear. There were no double layers of oppression. They were not caught in the middle of someone else's struggle. This difference helps explain the higher level of development of the labor movement among Asians in Hawaii than among those on the mainland. In Hawaii the labor movement was not tainted by racism to nearly the same extent. Unambiguously, the main enemy was capital.

As a colony of the United States, Hawaii presumably had linkages to the mainland economy similar to those of the dependent capitalist sector in California. Cheap, coerced labor on the Hawaiian plantations not only benefited the plantation owners but reverberated up the system, helping mainland capitalists deal with their declining rate of profit and rising labor costs. Apart from investment opportunities in the islands, mainland capital could import cheap sugar, enabling it to lower its wage bill proportionately. In other words, Asian labor played a role in relation to mainland capitalist development similar to that which southern blacks played to northern and British capitalist development. They helped provide a cheap raw material. The development of the mainland was, to some extent, predicated on the backwardness of Hawaii and the repression of labor there.

The presence of a colonial labor system in Hawaii had ramifications for California. Apart from the stimulus it gave to California's development, as suggested above, it also provided competition for the state's sugar beet industry. As a consequence, capitalists in sugar beets could argue for the necessity of immigrant labor in that field, and they did so to justify bringing in Japanese laborers. The competition between two colonial systems of production drove both of them to the cheapest level of labor. This competition may help account for United States efforts to limit contract labor in Hawaii before annexation (Rowland 1933) and to keep Hawaiian planters from abrogating Chinese exclusion in 1920 (Fuchs 1961:232).

Another impact of Hawaii on California resulted from the discrepancy between wage levels and work conditions in the two territories. The presence of a class of white workers and small producers in California, which fought against coerced labor, tended to drive the standard of labor up, even for immigrants. Thus California was a more desirable place to work and acted as an attraction to plantation laborers in Hawaii. In a sense, California was like an area of open resources to Hawaiian residents, a place to which they could escape. This may have contributed to the efforts of Hawaiian planters to bind workers firmly to contracts. Opportunities in California may have had a negative impact on conditions for Asian immigrant workers in Hawaii. But they also drew Asians from Hawaii, adding importantly to the Asian population in California. Hawaii became a major stepping-stone for Asian immigrants who wished to come to California and thus itself became a target of exclusion.

A third effect of coerced labor in Hawaii was that it probably contributed to white workers' fears about Asian labor. If the immigrants could be bound in Hawaii, surely they could be bound by California capitalists too. The "coolie labor" image was fed by the Hawaiian example. It thus probably contributed to exclusionist sentiment on the mainland.

Conclusion

Asian labor was mainly used in the dependent sector of California and Hawaii. It was like colonial labor around the world, limited by the sector to which it was confined. Asian immigrant labor had many similarities to Afro-American slavery. Like blacks, these workers were subject to special coercion by capitalists so their labor was cheaper than that of other workers. As a result, they enabled capitalists to engage in rapid accumulation and to develop large-scale enterprises. While blacks were, in a sense, the first completely proletarianized workers on the East Coast, Asians were the first on the West Coast. Thus they played a significant role in the development of capitalism in the region.

Because of the duality of United States origins and class development, however, both blacks and Asians became the object of a complex class struggle. While capitalists in the United States and Hawaii unambiguously wanted to exploit these workers, they were at odds with the majority of people on the mainland, especially the earlier European immigrants who wanted to escape from capitalism and preserve an independent household mode of production. Constantly threatened with proletarianization or complete economic displacement, these "white settlers" saw in the use of coerced or semicoerced labor a tool that would enhance capitalist development to their detriment. Asian immigrants, as had blacks before them, thus became an object of class struggle between segments of the white community. This struggle was muted in Hawaii because the colonial mode of production was generally segregated there. But in California the struggle was fiercely fought. And no matter what the outcome, Asians (like blacks) were the losers. They were either superexploited by capital or excluded and forced into the worst jobs by white labor. This double layer of oppression helps account for many aspects of the Asian experience in the United States before World War II.

References

Almaguer, Tomás
    1971 "Toward the study of Chicano colonialism." Aztlan 2 (Spring):7-21.
Bean, Walton
    1968 California. New York: McGraw-Hill.
    1973 California. New York: McGraw-Hill.
Black, Isabella
    1963 "American labour and Chinese immigration." Past and Present 25 (July):59-76.
Bonacich, Edna, and John Modell
    1980 The Economic Basis of Ethnic Solidarity: A Study of Japanese Americans. Berkeley, Los Angeles, London: University of California Press.
Chan, Sucheng
    1978 "Japanese immigrants and the transformation of California agriculture, 1890-1920." Paper presented at Asian American Labor History Conference, University of California, Los Angeles.
Chiu, Ping
    1967 Chinese Labor in California, 1850-1880: An Economic Study. Madison: University of Wisconsin.
Cleland, Robert Glass, and Osgood Hardy
    1929 March of Industry. San Francisco: Powell.
Coolidge, Mary R.
    1968 Chinese Immigration. Taipei: Ch'eng-Wen. First published in 1909.
Cox, Thomas R.
    1969 "The passage to India revisited: Asian trade and the development of the Far West, 1850-1900." Pp. 85-103 in John Alexander Carroll, ed., Reflections of Western Historians. Tucson: University of Arizona Press.
Cross, Ira B.
    1935 A History of the Labor Movement in California. Berkeley: University of California Press.
Daniels, Roger
    1966 The Politics of Prejudice: The Anti-Japanese Movement in California and the Struggle for Japanese Exclusion. Gloucester, Mass.: Peter Smith.
Dowd, Douglas F.
    1977 The Twisted Dream: Capitalist Development in the United States Since 1776. 2d ed. Cambridge, Mass.: Winthrop.
Fuchs, Lawrence H.
    1961 Hawaii Pono: A Social History. New York: Harcourt, Brace, and World.
Gates, Paul W.
    1960 The Farmer's Age: Agriculture, 1815-1860. Economic History of the United States, vol. III. New York: Holt, Rinehart, and Winston.

1962   "California's embattled settlers." California Historical Society Quarterly 41 (June):99-130.

1978   "California land policy and its historical context: The Henry George era." Pp. 1-30 in R. E. Robie, J. T. Knox, and N. Y. Mineta, eds. Four Persistent Issues: Essays on California's Land Ownership Concentration, Water Deficits, Sub-State Regionalism, and Congressional Leadership. Berkeley: Institute of Governmental Studies, University of California.

Griffiths, David B.

1970   "Anti-monopoly movements in California, 1873-1898." Southern California Quarterly 52 (June):93-121.

Heizer, Robert F., and Alan J. Almquist

1971   The Other Californians: Prejudice and Discrimination Under Spain, Mexico, and the United States to 1920. Berkeley, Los Angeles, London: University of California Press.

Hess, Gary R.

1976   "The forgotten Asian Americans: The East Indian community in the United States." Pp. 157-177 in Norris Hundley, Jr., ed., The Asian American: The Historical Experience. Santa Barbara: ABC-Clio.

Hill, Herbert

1973   "Anti-Oriental agitation and the rise of working-class racism." Society 10 (January-February):43-54.

Ichihashi, Yamato

1932   Japanese in the United States. Stanford: Stanford University Press.

Jones, Lamar B.

1970   "Labor and management in California agriculture." Labor History 11 (Winter): 23-40.

Kauer, Ralph

1944   "The Workingmen's Party of California." Pacific Historical Review 13 (September):278-291.

Konvitz, Milton R.

1977   The Alien and the Asiatic in American Law. Ithaca: Cornell University Press.

Lapp, Rudolph M.

1977   Blacks in Gold Rush California. New Haven: Yale University Press.

Lee, Everett S., Ann Ratner Miller, Carol P. Brainerd, and Richard A. Easterlin

1957   Population Redistribution and Economic Growth, United States, 1870-1950. Philadelphia: American Philosophical Society.

Lewis, Oscar

1959   The Big Four. New York: Knopf.

Light, Ivan H.

1972   Ethnic Enterprise in America: Buisness and Welfare Among Chinese, Japanese and Blacks. Berkeley, Los Angeles, London: University of California Press.

Lind, Andrew W.

1968   An Island Community: Ecological Succession in Hawaii. New York: Greenwood Press. First published in 1938.

Loewen, James

1971   The Mississippi Chinese: Between Black and White. Cambridge: Harvard University Press.

McCague, James

1964   Moguls and Iron Men: The Story of the First Transcontinental Railroad. New York: Harper and Row.

McWilliams, Carey
1968 North From Mexico. New York: Greenwood. First published in 1949.
1971 Factories in the Field. Santa Barbara: Peregrine. First published in 1935.
1976 California: The Great Exception. Santa Barbara: Peregrine Smith. First published in 1949.
Melendy, H. Brett
1977 Asians in America: Filipinos, Koreans, and East Indians. Boston: Twayne.
Nash, Gerald D.
1972 "Stages of California's economic growth, 1870-1970: An interpretation." California Historical Quarterly 51 (Winter):315-330.
North, Douglass C.
1966 The Economic Growth of the United States, 1790-1860. New York: W. W. Norton.
Orsi, Richard J.
1975 "The Octopus reconsidered: The Southern Pacific and agricultural modernization in California, 1865-1915." California Historical Quarterly 54 (Fall):197-221.
Paul, Rodman W.
1938 "The origin of the Chinese issue in California." Mississippi Valley Historical Review 25 (September):181-196.
1958 "The wheat trade between California and the United Kingdom." Mississippi Valley Historical Review 45 (December):391-412.
1967 California Gold: The Beginning of Mining in the Far West. Lincoln: University of Nebraska Press. First published in 1947.
Rolle, Andrew F.
1969 California: A History. 2d ed. New York: Crowell.
Rothstein, Morton
1975 "West Coast farmers and the tyranny of distance: Agriculture on the fringes of the world market." Agricultural History 49 (January):272-280.
Rowland, Donald
1933 "The United States and the contract labor question in Hawaii, 1862-1900." Pacific Historical Review 2 (Number 3):249-269.
Rudolph, Frederick
1947 "Chinamen in Yankeedom: Anti-unionism in Massachusetts in 1870." American Historical Review 53 (October):1-29.
Samora, Julian
1971 Los Mojados: The Wetback Story. Notre Dame: University of Notre Dame Press.
Saxton, Alexander
1971 The Indispensable Enemy: Labor and the Anti-Chinese Movement in California. Berkeley, Los Angeles, London: University of California Press.
Secretary of the Interior
1865 Manufactures of the United States in 1860. Eighth Census. Washington, D. C.: Government Printing Office.
Shannon, Fred A.
1959 The Farmer's Last Frontier: Agriculture, 1860-1897. New York: Rinehart.
Taylor, Paul S., and Tom Vasey
1936 "Historical background of California farm labor." Rural Sociology 1 (September):281-295.

5

Race, Ethnicity, and the Sugar Plantation System: Asian Labor in Hawaii, 1850 to 1900

John M. Liu

From the middle of the eighteenth until the beginning of the twentieth century, Hawaii underwent an economic metamorphosis. In this relatively short period of time, a market economy devoted to the production and exportation of a single agricultural commodity, sugar, supplanted the native Hawaiian subsistence economy. Accompanying this transformation was the near extinction of the native populace and the importation of over 400,000 people from various parts of the globe beginning in the 1850s. More than 75 percent of these migrants came from China, Japan, and the Philippines. Prior to 1900, however, all recruited Asian laborers were either Chinese or Japanese.

The dependency of the Hawaiian sugar industry (i.e., the plantation system) upon Asian laborers is evident in their predominance in the plantation work force. In 1882, the Chinese made up 49 percent of the plantation laborers but only 20 percent of the total population (Glick 1938:32). By 1900, Chinese and Japanese accounted for 81 percent of the workers on the plantations but only 56 percent of the population (U.S. Bureau of Labor Statistics, hereafter referred to as USBLS, 1902:19, 29).

Asians dominated the work force because they were the cheapest available labor. Moreover, the agricultural economy of the islands offered few inducements to attract either skilled or unskilled white labor (USBLS 1903:716-723). Between 1886 and 1900, Portuguese, Puerto Ricans and other Caucasians never accounted for more than 15 percent of all sugar plantation employees.

186

The importation of Asians and other ethnic groups not only fulfilled the manpower needs of the plantations; it also had a fundamental impact on the *structure* of production. With the introduction of these various ethnic groups, race and ethnicity became principal factors in the organization of labor. They served as a basis for segmenting the work force. Lind (1954:3) notes,

> It was, in brief, through the plantations that the first clearly defined pattern of stratification by race was initiated in Hawaii. . . . a fairly distinct barrier of social distances separated the proprietary white from the large mass of non-white laborers on the plantations, and a further social gradation of other racial groups at the lower levels of the plantation occupational pyramid also emerged.

Race and ethnicity were also basic criteria in organizing the sugar-making process. How planters dealt with the various ethnic groups affected both the plantation's daily operations and its long-term development. Specific forms of production evolved to take into account the multiethnic composition of the plantation work force. Each of these forms also provided the planters with means to maintain the amenability of their laborers. This paper will examine the consequences the importation of Asian labor had on the division of labor, the forms of production used in making sugar, and the types of labor control that emerged during the formative years of the plantation system between 1850 and 1900.

EMERGENCE OF THE PLANTATION ECONOMY

The introduction of a plantation economy into the islands was a direct outgrowth of European and American expansion. Almost immediately following the Western discovery of Hawaii by James Cook in 1778, outside political and economic forces, especially those of the United States, influenced Hawaii's economic and social development (Morgan 1948:iv, 205). The involvement of the United States with the islands arose after the American Revolution. Independence necessitated a reorientation of overseas commerce because Great Britain had erected barriers against American shipping in British-controlled ports. American maritime commerce sought new markets to replace those that had been lost or that were no longer profitable. A number of merchants turned to Hawaii and the Far East (Bradley 1942:13).

This reorientation led to the development of the sandalwood and fur trade industries involving the Pacific Northwest, Hawaii, and China during the 1820s. Toward the end of the 1830s, the whaling industry, which was largely dominated by American citizens, replaced the earlier two industries. Together, these three enterprises profoundly affected the economic development of Hawaii. One consequence was the diversion of large quantities of labor and land from domestic agriculture. Many Hawaiian natives stopped cultivating their traditional foods to gather sandalwood or cultivate cash crops for the larders of foreign ships. The natives also left the islands in large numbers as they signed on as crew members for passing vessels. The diversion of labor caused shortages of basic Hawaiian foods and precipitated the destruction of a subsistence society based on reciprocal economic and social relationships.

Trade also meant the formation of Western settlements. Merchants organized businesses in the main ports of call, missionaries came to Christianize the native inhabitants, and governments established consulates. These representatives of Western civilization channeled social and economic change in a direction that drew Hawaii into the world capitalist market economy. This was especially true of the American missionaries who began arriving in the 1820s. Although only 52 of the 184 persons coming to Hawaii under the auspices of the American Board of Commissioners for Foreign Missions were ordained ministers, no single group was more influential in binding the fate of the islands to the concerns of the United States. Acting as personal advisors to the Hawaiian royalty and as teachers to both nobility and commoners, these missionaries were crucial in promulgating Western ideas of law and property. Under their influence, Hawaii became a constitutional monarchy, a political transition that Americans and Europeans felt was necessary to further the development of the Hawaiian economy along capitalist lines (Adler 1966:16-17).

By the 1840s, the islands were clearly emerging as part of the commercial frontier of the United States although European and American interests continued to vie with one another (Bradley 1943). This relationship also received political expression. In 1840, Daniel Webster, then secretary of state, sent a letter to Kamehameha III, asserting, "The United States . . . are more interested in the fate of the islands and of their Government, than any other nation can be" (Stevens 1945:3). He further wrote that the United States expected other nations to respect Hawaii's independence, implying that any violation of this would provoke an American reaction. In the same year, President Tyler reaffirmed this message in a speech before Congress (Stevens 1945:3).

Absorption into the American economy placed Hawaii in an economically subordinate position. From the 1840s on, fluctuating economic conditions on the mainland dictated changes in the Hawaiian economy. Hence, the island economy shifted from maritime commerce to agricultural production when settlement of the Pacific Coast created a demand for various foodstuffs. Diversified agriculture flourished for a short period between 1848 and 1851 with sugar cultivation as one of the primary beneficiaries of this shift. Although successful sugar plantations had been in existence as early as 1835, the traditional Hawaiian system of land tenure, the unwillingness of foreigners to make long-term investments, and the lack of markets hindered the growth of plantations (Morgan 1948:98).

The Great *Mahele* (land division) of 1848 resolved the land issue. The Mahele and subsequent legislation ended the Hawaiian feudal tenure system by treating land as an alienable commodity (Kelly 1981). The availability of land as private property attracted foreign capital, especially as the Pacific Coast market opened up.

Toward the end of 1851, an economic depression occurred on the mainland and spread to the islands. The economic downswing was particularly severe in Hawaii, for the growth of agriculture in California and other West Coast regions totally undermined diversified farming in the islands. Since cane could not be cultivated on the mainland, sugar was one of the few agricultural enterprises to survive the depression and the development of agriculture on the Pacific Coast. These events clearly indicated to the planters that their economic well-being was tied to the fortunes of the American market. To improve their position, the planters attempted to have a reciprocity treaty with the United States negotiated in 1855 but were unsuccessful (Taylor 1935:7; Bradley 1943:279).

The establishment of the sugar industry in the islands created a need for an adequate supply of cheap, tractable labor. Although native Hawaiians made up the bulk of the plantation work force between 1850 and 1876, planters had problems with this source of labor.[1] A sugar crop in Hawaii required eighteen to twenty-four months of constant supervision before being harvested. Hawaiian workers, however, often did not commit their labor for the entire period. In the traditional Hawaiian economy, people labored only until they fulfilled their needs and their obligations to the chiefs. The Hawaiians transferred this pattern of economic behavior to the wage system. They frequently quit the plantations and returned to their former modes of living after raising enough money to meet their immediate needs (Lind 1938; Alexander 1937).

During the early stages of the sugar industry, Hawaiian workers were also highly mobile because of the competition for their labor from other agriculturalists and the whaling industry. Under these circumstances of open resources, planters were limited in their ability to control the work force. Growers took several steps to retain their labor force.

Under pressure from island sugar interests, the Hawaiian government enacted the Master and Servant Act in 1850. Modeled after the United States Seaman Shipping Act, the Master Act committed a worker to a plantation for a fixed number of years, just as sailors were bound for specific tours of duty. For this reason, a term of service on the plantation was known as "shipping." Penalties for desertion or for failure to fulfill the terms of a contract were specified within the act (Coman 1903:8-9).

Growers also modified the method of paying wages. Learning from the experience of earlier plantations, such as Koloa, planters paid laborers in kind or in scrip. Laborers received part of their wages in cash and part in housing, fuel, and sometimes foodstuffs provided by the plantation. Scrip, which was only redeemable at the plantation store, was also issued instead of cash (Alexander 1937). Although they were intended primarily to control the native work force, both the new wage system and the Master Act were later applied to imported labor.

One difficulty with native labor could not be easily resolved: the rapid decimation of the indigenous population following the introduction of Western diseases, alcoholism, internecine warfare, and demoralization (Hormann 1954:34). At the time of Cook's discovery, the native population was estimated at 300,000. This figure declined to 107,954 in 1836 and to 70,036 in 1853. By 1878, there were barely 44,000 native Hawaiians (Lind 1967:16; Nordyke 1977:table 3). These drastic decreases placed a severe physical restraint on the further development of the sugar industry. Aware of the need for expanded sources of labor, some planters recruited contract labor.

Plantation economies evolving prior to the nineteenth century had resorted to slavery as a means of creating a controllable work force. This was not an option available to the Hawaiian sugar growers in the 1850s. Not only was slavery subject to world moral disapprobation but access to areas previously supplying slaves was also closed by this time. Hawaii turned to Asia, where Western imperialism was opening new sources of labor. Labor from Asia was cheaper because of the region's proximity to the islands, but access to Asian labor was important for another reason.

As noted earlier, native Hawaiians were often unwilling to commit their labor for nearly two years. But even when they did remain on the plantation, the sugar yields resulting from their labor were low. This reflected the inexperience of both labor and management in cultivating a commercial crop. While many Hawaiians cultivated small patches of fruits and vegetables to barter with passing vessels after the opening of trade with the West, this activity did not prepare the natives for the regimentation necessary to produce a cash crop on a large scale. Similarly, during the early stages of the industry, many of the planters had no knowledge of raising sugar on a commercial basis. In fact, many of the growers, especially the speculators, had little familiarity with agriculture (Lind 1938:62). It was therefore desirable for the growers to assemble a work force experienced in extensive cultivation of cash crops. Asians migrating to the islands fulfilled this need. In the case of the first Asian immigrants, the Chinese, many were specifically skilled in cultivating and manufacturing commercial sugar (Mei 1979:468; U.S. House Committee on Immigration and Naturalization 1921:338; Vandercook 1939:24). As early as 1852 some large planters experimented with Chinese contract labor. But as long as the West Coast market for Hawaiian sugar did not expand, Hawaiians continued to be the principal source of plantation labor, and Chinese immigration remained limited.

Production and demand for sugar stayed fairly stable following the 1851-1852 economic depression. Sugar production did not increase until 1858 when 602 tons were exported. This was 70 percent more than the previous year's export of 350 tons. Sugar exports continued to rise until the outbreak of the American Civil War, which caused the world price of sugar to drop temporarily (Taylor 1935:167). The war was a blessing to Hawaii, for the loss of Louisiana's sugar crop and the disruption of shipping between the Union and the West Indies stimulated island production.[2]

The average price of sugar rose to 10.55¢/lb., after averaging 6.95¢/lb. between 1850 and 1859, with a peak price of 17.19¢/lb. in 1864 (Taylor 1935:167-169). Sugar exports grew from 1,281 tons in 1861 to 8,865 tons in 1866 (Morgan 1948:227). In the same year, another economic depression spread from the mainland to the islands, but sugar production remained at wartime levels. Inflation resulting from the war kept the price of sugar at 10¢/lb. until 1873. More important for the planters, the market did not collapse as it had in the previous depression of 1851-1852 (Kuykendall 1953:146-149).

The stability of both price and demand established sugar as the principal crop of the islands. In 1869, the growth in sugar production enabled the total value of exports to exceed the value of imports for the first time. From 1871 on, Hawaii was to have a favorable balance of trade (Daws 1968:177).

Several technological advances accompanied and stimulated the growth of production during these years. These advances came about because, unlike almost every other type of farming, sugar plantations often had to engage in manufacturing as well as cultivation. The bulk and weight of the cane, in addition to its rapid deterioration after being cut, made the transportation of the harvest to the mill difficult.[3] In Hawaii and the South, this problem was handled by constructing and operating mills under the direction of a single plantation (Schmitz 1977:960; Adler 1966:50-58). As a result of combining these two functions, the sugar industry in both regions was more integrated in its operations than it was in other sugar-producing areas of the world where cultivation and milling were under separate management (USBLS 1940:23-24).

In contrast to the South, however, sugar plantations in Hawaii implemented new technologies, especially in mill operations, at a very early date. This partially solved some of Hawaii's labor problems. Prior to 1850, animals or water generated the power to run the mills. These mills were capable of handling the low demand for sugar prior to the 1860s.[4] In the late 1850s, a technological advance in generating power occurred as steam replaced animals and water. Steam also made possible the use of new machinery: the centrifugal device for drying sugar and the vacuum pan for more efficient extraction of sugar.

Utilizing steam mills and new machinery created an internal stimulus to expand. Mills were designed to process far in excess of what existing acreage provided. The unused capacity of the mills, therefore, prompted planters to increase the acreage under cultivation. This entailed very little additional expenditure because, after the machinery was installed, the cost of operating and maintaining mill equipment remained relatively fixed (Schmitz 1977:975-980). The access to new land resulting from the Mahele made this expansion physically possible.

These technological advances fostered the specialization of functions within the plantation system. Prior to the Civil War, independent farmers or plantation companies negotiated directly with mainland firms for the purchase of equipment and the sale of the sugar crop. Following the war, a number of plantations began relying on wholesale and retail merchandising establishments or *factors* located in Honolulu for the financing and marketing of their crops. The factors were in a position to carry out these functions because of their commercial experience, superior access to American and European capital, and familiarity with the operations of local plantations. Their assumption of these functions allowed the planters to concentrate solely on the production of sugar. This was necessary because of the increased value of fixed capital (Morgan 1948:186).

Technological and organizational advances in the plantation system and a stable market contributed to increasing production. Exports grew from 8,500 to 12,500 tons between 1865 and 1875. This expansion was modest but was sufficient to mobilize growers to prepare for a large-scale importation of labor. A basis for this mobilization had been established earlier in 1864 with the creation of the Hawaii Bureau of Immigration. The formation of this board was intended in part to assure foreign governments that Hawaii was not engaging in the slave or coolie trade (Hawaiian Islands, Bureau of Immigration, hereafter referred to as HIBI, 1886:15-16).

The events of the period between 1850 and 1875 established the basis for the rapid expansion of the sugar industry and the onset of large-scale importation of labor following the passage of the Reciprocity Treaty of 1876.

THE GROWTH OF THE PLANTATION ECONOMY: 1876 to 1900

After several earlier failures, American sugar growers in Hawaii and expansionists on the mainland combined to successfully push through a United States-Hawaii reciprocity trade treaty. The agreement allowed semirefined and lower grades of Hawaiian sugar to enter the United States duty-free. Although island sugar growers were elated with the pact, the signed treaty had one significant difference from what the planters had originally proposed.

The Hawaiian government had initially requested that all grades of island sugar be exempt from the tariff. California refiners strenuously contested this provision. They argued that allowing the entry of fully refined sugar from Hawaii would encourage the industrial development of the islands. Refineries and other industries would be established in the islands in order to be closer to the source of raw materials. Such an occurrence would be detrimental to the development of American industry on the Pacific Coast (Eichner 1969:88).

California refiners succeeded in preventing the entry of fully refined sugar and in limiting the development of diversified industry in the islands. All island economic activity was confined to the cultivation, milling, and transportation of sugar. With this singular economic focus, the plantation economy prospered as annual production increased from 12,990 tons in 1875 to 36,600 tons in 1880. Ten years later, annual production quadrupled to 133,310 tons and constituted 87 percent of the value of all Hawaiian farm products (USBLS 1902:67). In 1900, 297,000 tons were produced. Land planted in sugar increased tenfold from 12,000 acres in 1875 to 128,000 acres in 1900 (Mollett 1962:12).

Continued capital improvements, more efficient organization of the sugar industry, and the massive importation of foreign labor underlaid the rapid growth of the plantation system. Capital improvements to mill facilities prior to 1876 were sufficient to handle the increased production of this period. Therefore, new capital expenditures were made in other areas, especially in developing new sources of water and in increasing the use of fertilizers (Thrum's Annual 1882:42; Kuykendall 1967:62-71). Irrigation costs, accounting for 7 percent of all capital outlays in 1870, rose to 26 percent by 1900 (Mollett 1962:23). The use of fertilizers also expanded. In 1885, more than two million pounds of fertilizer and related material were imported at a cost of $30,569. The value of these imports grew to $154,635 in 1890 and to $579,380 in 1897 (Kuykendall 1967:70).

Nearly all plantations, with the exception of those on the largest island, Hawaii, were dependent upon extensive irrigation.[5] This meant either digging wells to tap undergound reservoirs or constructing irrigation ditches to transport water from mountain sources. The costs were enormous in both cases. Irrigation projects required huge capital outlays for physical materials and called for additional workers and managers with sufficient training and skills. Since no Hawaiian governmental aid was sought or given, these costs had to be underwritten by private enterprise (Thrum's Annual 1905:155). This was also true of expenses incurred in clearing new fields, integrating field and mill operations (e.g., constructing new roads and railroad tracks to the mills), and recruiting new labor.

Most of these expenditures were beyond the financial means of individual planters. Consequently, grower dependence upon the Honolulu factors for capital deepened. Toward the end of the 1880s, changes in plantation ownership accompanied the continuing specialization of functions between factors and planters. Following the lead of major companies on the mainland, many of the larger factors incorporated. Their assets were acquired as the factors gained control of individual plantations that failed to amortize their debts (USBLS 1940:27). By the turn of the century, the individual plantations were under the control of one of the "Big Five" factors: Alexander and Baldwin Co., Brewer and Co., Castle and Cooke, Theo Davies and Co., and Hackfeld and Co.[6] Corporate control facilitated the mobilization of capital, production on a large scale, and coordination of activities among the individual plantations. As a result of these mergers, the physical capital per plantation, averaging $70,800 in 1880, expanded to $200,700 in 1890 and $773,500 in 1900. The number of plantations stabilized at fifty-two in 1900, after having grown from twenty to seventy-three between 1870 and 1890. The average size of plantations increased from 425 to 2,462 acres (Mollett 1962:27).

The expansion in acreage and physical capital resulted in a larger number of complete plantations, that is, units controlling both cane fields and mills. In the period following reciprocity, three types of units were producing sugar: complete plantations, independent planters without milling facilities, and mill operators without their own fields. The total number of these production units reached a maximum of ninety in 1883 with complete plantations making up 57 percent of the total. This percentage rose to 91 percent by 1899 (Kuykendall 1967:51).

Another aspect of this consolidation of ownership and control was the organization of planters into a single association. In 1882, the Planter's Labor and Supply Company was formed to facilitate the exchange of technical information and to obtain additional manpower required by the expanding sugar industry.

The search for additional labor led to the recruitment of approximately 45,000 Chinese and 86,400 Japanese between 1876 and 1900. The large majority of these Asians were men who came as contract laborers, under either the auspices of the Hawaiian government or the sponsorship of private concerns. About 93 percent of the Chinese coming to Hawaii were males.[7] Glick (1980:23) estimates that between two-thirds and three-fourths of all Chinese entering the islands before 1900 began as laborers on sugar or rice plantations.

Conroy (1949:157) estimates that about 80 percent of the Japanese migrants were males. The sex ratio was less skewed than in the case of the Chinese because the convention covering Japanese immigration initially called for 30 percent of the immigrants to be women. The proportion of women was later reduced to 25 percent (Conroy 1949:137; United Japanese Society of Hawaii, hereafter referred to as UJSH, 1971:107). Although the Hawaiian government and the planters never imported women at the agreed-upon ratio, the convention nonetheless resulted in more women being brought in than the planters desired.[8] The overwhelming majority of Japanese immigrants came under government or private immigration company contracts (UJSH 1971:110-111).

A comparison of immigration figures with the growth of the Hawaiian population indicates the significance of this migration for Hawaii's development (see table 5.1). Between 1879 and 1884, the island population grew by approximately 22,000 persons. In this same interval, about 18,400 Chinese arrived. By the time of the 1884 census, the Chinese accounted for nearly half of the male population between the ages of fifteen and fifty (Glick 1980:15). In 1900, the Hawaiian populace was estimated at 154,000, an increase of 74,000 persons from 1884. This population growth included more than 49,000 Chinese and Japanese migrants. (The number of Chinese and Japanese immigrants is greater

TABLE 5.1

POPULATION, PLANTATION EMPLOYMENT, AND ASIAN IMMIGRANTS, 1876 TO 1900

Year	Total[1] population	Total men[2] employed on sugar plantations	Chinese[3] arrivals	Japanese[4] arrivals
1876			1,283	
1877			557	
1878	57,985		2,464	
1879			3,812	
1880			2,505	
1881			3,924	
1882		10,243	1,362	
1883			4,243	
1884	80,578		2,708	
1885			3,108	5,040
1886		14,539	1,766	2,693
1887			1,546	2,993
1888		15,578	1,526	4,813
1889			439	3,443
1890	89,990	17,895	654	4,453
1891			1,386	7,240
1892		20,536	1,802	5,013
1893			981	5,098
1894		21,294	1,459	7,451
1895			2,734	5,501
1896	109,020	23,280	5,280	12,438
1897		24,653	4,481	7,987
1898		28,597	3,100	14,025
1899		35,987	975	26,474
1900	154,001			2,984
			51,095	117,646

SOURCES: 1. Andrew W. Lind, *Hawaii's People*, 3d ed. (Honolulu: University of Hawaii Press, 1967), p. 28.
2. Clarence E. Glick "The Chinese Migrant in Hawaii: A Study in Accommodation" (Ph.D. diss., University of Chicago, 1938), p. 32.
3. Clarence E. Glick, *Sojourners and Settlers: Chinese Migrants in Hawaii* (Honolulu: University Press of Hawaii, 1980), p. 12.
4. United Japanese Society of Hawaii, *A History of Japanese in Hawaii* (Honolulu: United Japanese Society of Hawaii, 1971), pp. 110-111.

than the actual population increase because the figures presented in table 5.1 do not indicate the number of people who left the islands. Nor do the figures take into account the number of people who were counted more than once because of reentry into the islands.) Without this tremendous influx of people, the sugar plantations would have lacked the necessary labor for expansion. The success of the Hawaiian government and the growers in obtaining Asian labor, however, had unforeseen consequences for the organization of production.

In order to meet the growing demand for sugar created by the Reciprocity Treaty, growers expanded old fields, opened new fields, and founded plantations.[9] The clearing of this virgin land was an arduous task requiring the removal of tree stumps and large boulders, principally by human labor, and frequently consuming an entire planting season. Reluctant to use their more experienced hands in this backbreaking and time-consuming task, plantations instead assigned this work to the most recently arrived laborers, who were settled in camps constructed adjacent to the areas to be cleared and cultivated.[10]

These camps were responsible for a limited number of fields rather than for all arable plantation lands. As a result, each camp came to represent individual production units. The peopling of these camps led to the formation of production units that were ethnically homogeneous.

Between 1876 and 1900, Asian labor recruited for the islands came from a few provinces in China and Japan. Most of the Chinese coming to Hawaii originated from Zhongshan county in Guangdong province, while most Japanese migrants came from five prefectures in Japan (Hiroshima, Yamaguchi, Kumamoto, Fukuoka, and Okinawa) (Mei 1979:466; U. S. House Committee on Immigration and Naturalization 1921:338; UJSH 1971:117).[11] Upon arrival, people from the same ship were assigned to plantations in large groups. Since contracts were signed in numerical sequence, allocating laborers in this way meant that workers not only were of the same ethnicity but frequently were from the same village or district and, in many instances, were related to one another.

Private companies and the Hawaiian government assisted in creating and maintaining ethnically homogeneous camps. In addition to recruiting from only a few areas in Asia, they intentionally assigned workers to plantations and camps where people shared common geographical origins or cultural backgrounds. Immigration authorities, for instance, sent Chinese Christians to plantations where their brethren had previously settled (Glick 1980:31). Robert Irwin, the Hawaiian consul to Japan, instituted a similar practice by preventing the separation of family and friends from the same prefecture (Conroy 1949:124).

The emergence of camps containing single ethnic groups had unforeseen influences on the division of labor, the production process, and the
types of labor control utilized by the growers in their efforts to maintain the tractability of the work force. The camps accommodated the
emergence of an ethnically segmented labor force that was also divided
by different skill levels. White workers generally held skilled and super-
visory positions and were housed separately from the Hawaiians and
Portuguese, who were predominantly semiskilled workers and field
foremen.[12] These two ethnic groups lived apart from the Asian camps,
which were made up of unskilled laborers.

A measure of this occupational segregation was the confinement of
Asian labor to field and other unskilled or semiskilled positions until the
early years of the 1900s. The 1902 report of the labor commissioner to
Hawaii indicates that, although Asians made up 83 percent of the work
force, they held only 18 percent of the superintendencies and 35 percent
of the administrative jobs. The latter figure is somewhat misleading
since most of the clerical positions, usually manned by Asians, were
included in this category.[13] In comparison, Caucasians and Portuguese
held 44 and 24 percent of the superintendencies and 45 and 12 percent
of the administrative positions, respectively, although they were only
2.4 and 6.3 percent of the plantation work force (USBLS 1903:762).

Asians were preferred by planters for unskilled positions because
they could be acquired at a cheaper cost than that of white workers, as is
clearly seen in table 5.2. The costs for importing and providing board
and quarters for Chinese and Japanese were significantly lower than
they were for white unskilled laborers in each category. Proximity of
the islands to Asia is one reason Chinese and Japanese labor was less
costly. The composition of the European migration is another. Whereas

TABLE 5.2
LABOR COSTS OF HAWAIIAN PLANTATIONS BY ETHNIC GROUP, 1886 AND 1890

| | Cost to planter of Importing Board per Quarters month | | | Wages per month of men without food | | Wages per month of women and minors without food | |
	1886	1886	1886	1886	1890	1886	1890
Chinese	$ 76.83	$6.43	$31.49	$13.56	$17.54		
Germans	100.00	8.00	79.57	12.75	26.02	$ 9.95	
Japanese	65.85	6.32	41.94	9.88	17.21	8.54	$10.45
Portuguese	112.00	9.16	76.38	10.41	20.89	10.32	11.95

SOURCE: U.S. Department of Labor, *Report of the Commissioner of Labor on Hawaii, 1902*, Dept.
of Labor Bulletin no. 47 (Washington, D.C.: U.S. Government Printing Office, 1903),
p.758.

most Asian migrants were males, the majority of Europeans came as families (Lind 1967:29; W. Alexander 1896:121). This accounts for the larger amounts expended on board and quarters for white field hands. From the planters' perspective, these additional support costs were economically infeasible since neither children nor mothers significantly contributed to the productivity of the plantation.

The need of white laborers to support their wives and children also explains why they received a higher wage. This was not yet evident in 1886 when the Chinese were the best-paid workers. Their higher wages were based on the fact that they had been on the plantations for nearly a decade before other groups arrived and were therefore more experienced. By 1890, however, a clear salary difference existed between white and Asian labor, regardless of experience. The wages of German and Portuguese field hands more than doubled in four years and they earned 33 and 16 percent more, respectively, than the Chinese. Although Japanese wages increased by 74 percent, they continued to earn less than the Chinese, whose wages only rose 30 percent. The racial/ethnic wage difference resulted from growing planter awareness of the advantages deriving from manipulation of their multiethnic labor force, as will be discussed later.

Racial/ethnic differences not only provided the basis for a segmented labor force; they were also incorporated into the production process. In the years preceding reciprocity, and in the periods covered by penal contracts, sugar was produced under the *luna* or overseer system. Lunas, often ethnically different from the workers they supervised, were responsible for the pace, quality, and quantity of work performed. This responsibility frequently led to abusive labor practices by the overseers, prompting charges that plantations were reinstituting the practice of slavery (Lind 1938:215).

To counter the images evoked by the luna system, the production process was modified for workers not under penal contracts. In addition to improving the public image of life on the plantations, planters hoped that these modifications would increase the number of workers remaining on the plantation after their original contracts expired. Planter experience prior to reciprocity indicated that only a comparatively small proportion of workers "reshipped" under the luna system (Lind 1938:226). In order to get workers to continue working on the plantations, the growers provided additional inducements through the development of production methods that gave the laborers varying degrees of control over the production process and minimized the role of the lunas. Each of these changes also preserved among the workers the cohesiveness and stability that emanated from common ethnicity, geographical loyalties, and kinship ties.

The new forms of production were modifications of the Hawaiian *ukupau* (also spelled *ukepau*) system, which allocated a daily work quota or stint to individuals or groups for an agreed-upon sum of money. Two features of this system appealed to workers. First, laborers determined the pace of work in completing a stipulated task, although they were still under the supervision of lunas. Second, laborers remained in groups they were accustomed to working with even when individuals were assigned specific tasks (Glick 1938:42; USBLS 1903:734-735; Lind 1938:229-230).

During the 1880s, growers meshed specific plantation tasks with the piecework system. Furrowing, planting, and weeding, for instance, were paid per row or per acre, while other tasks, such as cutting and loading cane, were paid by the ton. Pay rates for field tasks varied depending upon the type of soil, cane, and terrain worked on. In the mills, piecework rate applied to activities such as filling, sewing, and marking sugar bags.

As with the ukupau system, workers controlled the pace of work while keeping their groups intact. But under the piecework system, workers had an opportunity to earn higher wages since there was no limit to the amount of work that could be performed in a day. "You were getting piece work, in other words, tonnage . . . da more cars you load, da more money you make. So if you was bit slow on da job, ah, dat — less you would make" (Ethnic Studies Program 1977, 8:84). In time, piecework and pay scales became the dominant form of production and payment.

The piecework system also served as a foundation for voluntary agreements known as short-term (sometimes referred to as acre) contracts. Utilizing worker desires to remain together in groups, planters contracted with a group or *hui* to perform any or all of the tasks necessary to bring a field of cane to maturity and deliver it to the mill. The contract stipulated the price for each completed operation. Unlike workers doing straight piecework, short-term contractors were not paid on the basis of work completed during each pay period. Rather, they were paid after the completion of a stipulated task or after delivery of the cane to the mill. This was to ensure that huis did not leave the plantation in the middle of a job. In contracts calling for settlement only after the cane was delivered to the mill, workers received monthly advances, credit at plantation stores, and the use of plantation housing. The advances and credit, which were both assessed interest charges, were deducted from the final settlement. The hui members determined among themselves how the remaining proceeds were distributed (USBLS 1903:737-741).

Voluntary contractual agreements were also used in a third form of production. Known as long-term or ton contracts, these agreements were similar to the short-term contracts requiring workers to tend a field of sugar until maturity. Plantations provided monthly advances, credit, and housing until all the contracted work was completed and final payment rendered. There were, however, several significant differences.

Long-term contracts were reserved for groups of workers who had gained the utmost confidence of plantation managers. This confidence was based both on length of service and on the knowledge some huis acquired from tending particular fields over a period of years. Long-established huis were often able to develop an intimate knowledge of the limited areas they cultivated. Plantation managers gave these groups almost entire control of the areas they farmed under contract. Huis were even extended the privilege of selecting one of their own members to act as an overseer or headman.

The extension of this control to the hui was based on more than confidence. Long-term cultivators had a self-interest in increasing a field's output. They were not paid piecework rates for each of the tasks performed in bringing a field to harvest but instead received a share of the proceeds from the sale of the sugar crop. This share was originally determined by "a sliding scale rated according to the net proceeds from the sugar or from last sales previous to the delivery of the cane made in the primary market, which was usually San Francisco" (USBLS 1903:746). In the years following annexation, a sliding scale was retained, but long-term contractors were guaranteed a minimum price per ton. This reduced the possibility of a long-term worker earning less than a piecework or short-term contract employee during a bad harvest. Long-term contractors were also referred to as "profit sharers" because they shared risks and gains with the planters (USBLS 1903:741-748).[14]

Each of these new forms of production preserved and assured the continued existence of racially segregated production units by keeping work groups and camps intact. The piecework system did not directly promote group labor. But equally important, it did not disrupt existing work relations. Short-term and long-term contracts, however, explicitly exploited the group nature of production.

During the 1890s, especially after the overthrow of the Hawaiian monarchy in 1893, the new forms of production came into greater use. Penal contracts signed in the 1880s were expiring and releasing a large proportion of the plantation work force from the provisions of the Master and Servant Act. Workers who chose to remain on the plantations did so under the piecework system or under voluntary contracts.

The growing number of free or day laborers and the expanding number of imported workers in the islands hastened the demise of the penal contract system. Planters found it increasingly difficult to track down individuals who broke their contracts.

The growing number of deserters from penal contracts indicate the deterioration of the penal contract system. From 1880 on, desertions were the largest single category of police work. In 1882, there were 3,454 arrests for desertion. This rose to 5,706 in 1890 (Aller 1958:128). After this year, deserters were rarely arrested or taken to court, and the Master and Servant Act rapidly became a dead letter (Goodale 1914:198). By 1897, more than 45 percent of the 23,000 field hands were employed as piece rate or voluntary contract workers (USBLS 1903:696; Maxwell 1899:151).

In 1898, the United States annexed the islands. This signaled the legal demise of the penal contract system since American laws prohibiting contract labor were eventually enforced in Hawaii. A prominent planter pondered the uneventfulness of this:

> The sudden extinction of the penal contract, while exercising great influence upon the situation, will not prove of so revolutionary a character now as it would have done ten years ago, for there has been a manifest tendency against it steadily increasing during that period and a frank depreciation by the planters of its supposed necessity, irrespective of annexation. This is proved by the fact of a material decrease since the early days of the sugar industry in the proportion of contract laborers to the total number of laborers employed (Castle 1898:88-89).

The ending of the penal contract system did not mean planters were unable to effectively prevent their workers from organizing and engaging in multiethnic collective action. The very fact that planters provided workers with food (only in the years prior to 1876 and for employees under penal contracts signed after reciprocity), housing, fuel, and medical services placed workers in a dependent position. Tate (1940:55) observes, "The well being and prosperity of a plantation economy depends upon the exchange of goods which the planter develops rather than upon a self-sufficing village culture in which products are grown for consumption. Thus workers became dependent upon the planter for products which they formerly produced themselves." Lind (1938:216) adds, "Merely to accept employment in a land several thousand miles from home and kin and among people of alien language left the recruited laborers in almost complete dependence upon the plantation system."

In addition to this obvious control, planters gradually became aware that ethnically homogeneous camps and differentiated wages and forms of production encouraged the development of group identification along regional and ethnic lines rather than upon common work experiences. "The practice of the planters to treat alike all persons recruited from the same foreign region . . . has served to create a sense of racial identity and solidarity where little or none existed before" (Lind 1969:44-45).

Planters did not immediately recognize the possibility of a "divide-and-rule" policy based on ethnicity. The first concrete evidence that planters considered such a policy appears to have been in 1883 when the *Planter's Monthly* stated, "By employing different nationalities, there is less danger of collusion" (Weingarten 1946:11). The *Planter's Monthly* hardly spoke for a unified group because three years later, the publisher of the journal, the newly formed Planter's Labor and Supply Company, was still striving to overcome strong internal pressures favoring the organization's dissolution (Hawaiian Planter's Monthly 1886:101-102).

A deliberate divide-and-rule policy did not fully crystallize until the end of the 1880s and early 1890s. By 1895, responses to questions submitted by a labor commission, formed to investigate the problem of strikes and arbitration, clearly expressed this policy. Planters were united in their desire to split the labor force along racial lines. With the exception of one manager, the responses agreed with George Fairchild's remark, "Keep a variety of laborers, that is different nationalities, and thus prevent any concerted action in the case of strikes, for there are few, if any cases of Japanese, Chinese, and Portuguese entering into a strike as a unit" (Hawaii Labor Commission 1895:36).

Importing different racial groups also enabled planters to control their labor by manipulating the racial composition of the work force. This was to prevent any single group from monopolizing the labor market. As with divide and rule, the potential advantage of a multiracial labor force was not immediately evident to the planters.

According to the Hawaiian Sugar Planters' Association (the successor to the Planter's Labor and Supply Company), growers adopted a policy of manipulating the racial composition of the work force as early as the 1860s. This is questionable. As late as 1882, many planters were unwilling to experiment with Japanese contract workers as a replacement for Chinese labor when the Hawaiian foreign minister, Walter Gibson, asked them to do so (Lydon 1961:141-142). But the responses to the Hawaii Labor Commission (1895:23-24) indicate that by the mid-1890s planters were cognizant of the benefits deriving from the manipulation of the racial composition of the labor force. Many of the planters' replies echoed George Renton's statement, "If immigrants of various nationalities would come in until there are sufficient of them in the country to offset any one nationality, we would be better off" (Hawaii Labor Commission 1895:23-24).

To implement these two policies, growers imported more laborers than were actually needed at any one time. The overabundance of labor had the additional effect of lowering wages. "The value of a labor surplus as a means of depressing wages and as a means of labor control is so well recognized that the planters have never willingly allowed the doors to immigration to be completely closed" (Lind 1938:219-220). For this reason, planters recruited more than 38,000 Japanese and 4,000 Chinese between 1898 and 1900 while Congress debated Hawaii's status in the Union, fully knowing that penal contracts would soon legally end. They recruited these laborers in the hopes that Congress would permit existing penal contracts to expire before imposing a ban. The Organic Act of 1900, which established Hawaii as a territory, however, abrogated all existing penal contracts.

CONCLUSION

By 1900, the essential features of the sugar plantation system in Hawaii were firmly established. Three distinct trends emerged in the development of this system. The first trend was that sugar plantations in the islands were more capital intensive than those in any other sugar-producing area of the world. Hawaii led other sugar producers in the application of technology and machinery to the cultivation and milling of sugar. These capital improvements, beginning with the mills, created an internal stimulus for the continued expansion of production.

The mills had to run at full capacity in order for the planters to realize a profit from these capital investments. This was only possible if the sugar acreage and the yield from the sugar crop increased. The Mahele provided the land necessary for this physical expansion. The importation of Asians supplied the needed manpower. Yields increased with the construction of irrigation systems, the application of fertilizers, and the development of new hybrids of cane.

All these improvements required tremendous amounts of money and demanded the growers' constant vigilance over the entire production process. These requirements led to a separation in the producing, financing, and marketing of the sugar crop. Growers concerned themselves solely with the production of sugar while the factors handled all business matters.

This functional division increased the Big Five's control of the industry, the second major trend of this period. The consolidation of individual plantations under the control of one or another of the major factors allowed for the development of economies of scale, which, in turn, provided additional internal stimulus for expansion. This is seen in the rising number of complete plantations, which again advanced the productive capacities of the industry. The Big Five continued introducing improvements, including the establishment of a uniform labor policy. The latter was crucial because the industry remained labor-intensive until the late 1930s.

The dependency of the sugar plantation on imported labor is the third trend. Asians and other ethnic groups entered the islands in large numbers to meet the labor needs arising from the expansion of production after the Reciprocity Treaty of 1876. Race and ethnicity became *socially significant* as a result of this migration and were used as criteria to establish social distance among the various groups. In the case of the plantation system, these criteria were a central factor in the structuring of the production process. A racially/ethnically segmented labor force emerged as workers were housed in functionally segregated camps.

New forms of production were developed by the planters to accommodate these divisions within the work force. The piecework system and short-term and long-term contracts each preserved and promoted the worker's identification with his own ethnic group rather than with laborers sharing the same occupational positions. Consequently, Chinese and Japanese workers did not easily establish common ground with one another.

The planters enhanced their control of the labor force by exploiting these ethnic and racial divisions. The various ethnic groups were paid different salaries even when performing the same work. Although the major difference was between white and nonwhite labor, growers also maintained wage differentials among Asian workers. In general, Chinese laborers received slightly higher wages than their Japanese counterparts throughout this entire period. The racial composition of the labor force was manipulated by planters to ensure that no one group gained control of the labor market. They also created labor surpluses to dampen worker demands for higher wages.

In the period following annexation, each of these trends continued. Sugar production gradually became capital-intensive. The Big Five reached the height of their power as they effectively integrated all phases of the industry, and the recruitment of labor continued.

There was a basic tension between these three trends that did not emerge until after the turn of the century, however. Both the continued capital improvements and the centralization of the industry prompted constant expansion. This eventually undermined production based on race and ethnicity. At one level, the increasing reliance on mechanization demanded a free interchangeability of labor. But production based on race hindered the movement of labor because of the occupational separation of the various ethnic groups. At another level, continued development of the industry destroyed conditions that made racial production possible. For instance, the conversion of all available lands to cane fields brought about a consolidation of the separate camps. While plantations made attempts to maintain distinct ethnic sections within these larger camps, they found it increasingly difficult to sustain segregated housing.

The tension between these two competing ways of organizing production was to be overtly expressed in the strikes conducted by Asian laborers throughout the first third of the twentieth century. That, however, is the subject of another study.

NOTES

1. As late as 1895, one plantation in Laie, Oahu, continued to use only native Hawaiian laborers (Hawaii Labor Commission 1895).

2. Prior to the Civil War, an eighteen-parish region of southeastern Louisiana accounted for 95 percent of United States sugar production (Schmitz 1979:959).

3. Cane will rapidly deteriorate if it is not processed within two or three days after cutting (Aller 1958:55-56).

4. Even with low demand and crude processing equipment William Hooper, the first manager of Koloa Plantation, frequently complained about the underutilization of the mill machinery (Alexander 1937).

5. Growing sugarcane requires massive amounts of water. The Hawaiian Sugar Planters' Association estimates that 2,000 pounds of water are needed to produce one pound of sugar (Adler 1966:33).

6. The first three factors were American owned. Theo Davies was a British-owned firm, and Hackfeld and Co. was German owned. During World War I, the United States government confiscated the assets of Hackfeld and Co. American Factors Co. (Amfac), an American-owned business, acquired the confiscated properties and promptly became one of the Big Five.

7. In one period, from 1879 to 1883, over 98 percent of the 15,846 Chinese arrivals were male (Glick 1938:175).

8. See the Hawaiian Islands Bureau of Immigration reports for 1886 and 1888. They are replete with planter objections to the importation of women. See also USBLS 1903:698.

9. According to Thurston (HIBI 1890:85) the increase in the labor force between 1880 and 1888 principally came about not by the "opening of any new plantations, but the simple expansion of existing ones.

There is no reason to believe that there will be any less expansion during the coming than last period."

10. Poor transportation was a primary reason for constructing camps next to the areas to be cleared and cultivated. According to an 1882 newspaper account,

> What are called roads are simply the most wretched trails, not only unsightly but a positive detriment to the country. They do not encourage the development of the fine lands distant from the various towns or ports . . . existing [roads] are utterly worthless and new ones are not likely to be constructed.

> The planters with their works scattered all over the land, with their great trains of laborers and the thousands who cluster about the plantations, have made the prosperity and they have waited patiently for some signs of improvement but in vain. (Hind 1951;71)

11. Many of the Chinese in Hawaii also came by way of San Francisco. Between 1852 and 1866, of the 1306 Chinese entering the islands, 900 came from Hong Kong and Macao and 406 from San Francisco (Wright 1894). In 1881, there was a temporary ban on emigrants leaving Hong Kong. Consequently, most of the Chinese coming to Hawaii were from San Francisco (Glick 1938:18).

12. At this time, Portuguese were not classified with whites on the plantations. Rather they were treated as a distinct category between Asians and other Caucasians. According to the labor commissioner (USBLS 1903:700), "this is probably because the 'white man' has always been a sort of aristocrat in the islands, and a large body of immigrants who lived in ordinary plantation quarters and worked with hoes could hardly aspire to that rank in popular estimation."

13. Approximately 69 percent of the administrative positions consisted of store clerks. Again racial pay differences appear. All clerks worked about sixty hours per week. One hundred one Japanese clerks earned an average of $1.05 per day. The average daily pay for seven Americans was $2.60; two Canadians, $2.77½; three Scots, $2.63½, and one German, $3.83 (USBLS 1903:874-895).

14. Plantations also utilized planter contracts. There were agreements between the plantation and an individual, who either owned his own or leased plantation land. This form of production is not discussed since it was not available to the large majority of plantation employees. Moreover, planter cultivation was mainly confined to the island of Hawaii, where the jagged terrain created isolated arable fields unsuitable for plantation cultivation techniques.

References

Adler, Jacob
    1966   Claus Spreckels: The Sugar King in Hawaii. Honolulu: University of Hawaii Press.

Alexander, Arthur Chambers
    1937   Koloa Plantation, 1835-1935; A History of the Oldest Hawaiian Plantation. Honolulu: Star Bulletin.

Alexander, William D.
    1896   "History of immigration to Hawaii." Thrum's Annual, pp. 114-125.

Aller, Curtis Cosmos Jr.
    1958   "The evolution of Hawaiian labor relations: From benevolent paternalism to mature collective bargaining." Ph.D. diss., Harvard University.

Bradley, Harold Whitman
    1942   The American Frontier in Hawaii: The Pioneers, 1789-1843. Palo Alto: Stanford University Press.
    1943   "Hawaii and the American penetration of the northeastern Pacific." Pacific Historical Review 12:277-286.

Castle, James B.
    1898   "The labor outlook." Thrum's Annual, pp. 88-91.

Coman, Katherine
    1903   "The history of contract labor in the Hawaiian Islands." Publications of the American Economic Association (3d series) 4:1-61.

Conroy, Francis Hilary
    1949   "The Japanese expansion into Hawaii, 1868-1898." Ph.D. diss., University of California, Berkeley.

Daws, Gavan
    1968   Shoal of Time: A History of the Hawaiian Islands. New York: Macmillan Co.

Eichner, Alfred S.
    1969   The Emergence of Oligopoly: Sugar Refining as a Case Study. Baltimore: Johns Hopkins Press.

Ethnic Studies Program. Oral History Project.
    1977   Waialua and Haleiwa, The People Tell their Stories. Honolulu: University of Hawaii, Ethnic Studies Oral History Project. 9 vols.

Glick, Clarence E.
    1938   "The Chinese migrant in Hawaii: A study in accommodation." Ph.D. diss., University of Chicago.
    1980   Sojourners and Settlers: Chinese Migrants in Hawaii. Honolulu: University Press of Hawaii.

Goodale, W. W.
    1914   "Brief history of Hawaiian unskilled labor." Thrum's Annual, pp. 170-191.

Hawaii (Republic) Labor Commission
    1895   Report of the Labor Commissioner on Strikes and Arbitration. Honolulu: R. Grieve.

Hawaiian Islands. Bureau of Immigration
    1886-   Report of the President of the Bureau of Immigration.
    1892
Hawaiian Planters Labor and Supply Company
    1886   Hawaiian Planter's Monthly 5 (May):101-102.
Hawaiian Sugar Planter's Association
    1921   Proceedings of the Annual Meetings. Honolulu-Hawaiian Sugar Planter's
            Association.
Hind, Robert Renton, ed.
    1951   John Hind of Hawi (1858-1933): His Memoirs. Manila: Carmelo and Bauermann.
Hormann, Bernard
    1954   "Rigidity and fluidity." Pp. 25-48 in Andrew W. Lind, ed., Race Relations in
            World Perspective. Honolulu: University of Hawaii Press.
Kelly, Marion
    1981   "Land tenure in Hawaii." Amerasia Journal 7(Fall):57-74.
Kuykendall, Ralph S.
    1953   The Hawaiian Kingdom. 1854-1874, Twenty Critical Years, vol. II. Honolulu:
            University Press of Hawaii.
    1967   The Hawaiian Kingdom. 1874-1893, The Kalakaua Dynasty, vol. III. Honolulu:
            University of Hawaii Press.
Lind, Andrew W.
    1938   An Island Community: Ecological Succession in Hawaii. Chicago: University of
            Chicago Press.
    1954   "Changing race relations in Hawaii." Social Process in Hawaii 18:1-9.
    1967   Hawaii's People. 3d ed. Honolulu: University of Hawaii Press.
    1969   Hawaii: The Last of the Magic Isles. London: Oxford University Press.
Lydon, Edward C.
    1961   "The movement to restrict Chinese immigration in the Hawaiian Kingdom."
            Master's thesis, Sacramento State College.
Maxwell, Walter
    1899   "Labor conditions in Hawaii." Paradise of the Pacific 12(October):151.
Mei, June
    1979   "Socioeconomic origins of emigration: Guangdong to California, 1850-1882."
            Modern China 5:463-501.
Mollett, John Anthony
    1962   "Capital and labor in the Hawaiian sugar industry since 1870: A study of eco-
            nomic development." Journal of Farm Economics 44:381-388.
Morgan, Theodore
    1948   Hawaii: A Century of Economic Change, 1778-1886. Cambridge: Harvard Uni-
            versity Press.
Nordyke, Eleanor
    1977   The Peopling of Hawaii. Honolulu: University Press of Hawaii.
Schmitz, Mark
    1977   "Economics of scale and farm size in the antebellum sugar sector." Journal of
            Economic History 37:959-980.
    1979   "The transformation of the southern cane sugar sector, 1860-1930." Agricul-
            turral History 52:270-285.
Stevens, Sylvester K.
    1945   American Expansion in Hawaii, 1842-1898. Harrisburg: Archives Company of
            Pennsylvania.

Tate, Russell S.
    1940   "Plantation production in the Pacific area." Master's thesis, Duke University.
Taylor, William Henry
    1935   "The Hawaiian sugar industry." Ph.D. diss., University of California, Berkeley.
Thrum's Annual
    1882   Thrum's Annual. Honolulu: Honolulu Star Bulletin.
    1905   Thrum's Annual. Honolulu: Honolulu Star Bulletin.
United Japanese Society of Hawaii.
    1971   A History of Japanese in Hawaii. Honolulu: United Japanese Society of Hawaii.
U. S. Bureau of Labor Statistics
    1902   Report of the Commissioner of Labor on Hawaii, 1901. Senate document no.
            169. Washington, D. C.: U. S. Government Printing Office.
    1903   Report of the Commissioner of Labor on Hawaii, 1902. Dept. of Labor Bulletin
            no. 47. Washington, D. C.: U. S. Government Printing Office.
    1931   Labor Conditions in the Territory of Hawaii, 1929-1930. Bureau of Labor Sta-
            tistics Bulletin no. 534. Washington, D. C.: U. S. Government Printing Office.
    1940   Labor in the Territory of Hawaii, 1939. Bureau of Labor Statistics Bulletin no.
            687. Washington, D. C.: U. S. Government Printing Office.
U. S. House Committee on Immigration and Naturalization.
    1921   Labor Problems in Hawaii. Hearings before the Committee on Immigration
            and Naturalization. Washington, D. C.: U. S. Government Printing Office.
Vandercook, John W.
    1939   King Cane: The Story of Sugar in Hawaii. New York: Harper and Bros.
Weingarten, Victor
    1946   Raising Cane: A Brief History of Labor in Hawaii. Honolulu: International
            Longshoremen and Warehousemen Union.
Wright, W. H.
    1894   "Chinese immigration to the Hawaiian Islands." Thrum's Annual, pp. 70-78.

PART II

Imperialism, Distorted Development, and Asian Emigration to the United States

In the late nineteenth century, as a consequence of capitalist development, western Europe and the United States found themselves unable to use the productive capacity they had built. They sought foreign markets, often backed by military force, and excluded foreign products from their own markets through protective tariffs (Dillard 1979). To win a competitive edge against each other, and driven by the profit motive, they looked for ways to gain the cheapest supply of raw materials and labor. In part I we dealt with the role of the United States in that process. We now turn to the consequence of that process for the Asian countries that supplied the largest number of workers to the United States. We argue that labor emigration from these countries was, in part, a consequence of Western capitalist expansion.

> The effect of imperialism on Third World countries has a dual character: On the one hand, the center [or imperialist power] is in a position to dominate the periphery [or "colonized" territory] by virtue of its superior power. The result can be that the center exploits the resources of the periphery to the advantage of the former and to the disadvantage of the latter. On the other hand, the center, in the process of penetrating the periphery, can break down its traditional modes of production and promote the growth of a modern capitalist social and economic order (Weisskopf 1978:500).

Whether the regressive or the progressive aspect of imperialism is predominant "depends on the particular historical context and the geographical area under analysis" (Weisskopf 1978:500).

We follow a line of scholars who have concluded that for most of Asia, Latin America, and Africa, the regressive aspect of the imperialist relationship predominated (Weisskopf 1978; Griffin 1969; Frank 1969; Baran, 1957). Yet there are tremendous differences among the Asian countries examined in this book, and these variations are a major topic of concern among area specialists. While controversies remain in each case, some general conclusions are possible. For India, Korea, and the Philippines, foreign penetration and imperialism played a pivotal role in their underdevelopment. For China, most scholars agree that although it did not succumb to foreign imperialism as did the countries mentioned above, its development was, to a great extent, affected by it.

The case of Japan is complicated by the fact that Japan itself became an imperialist power during the period that we are studying. But we should not confuse Japan's subsequent development into an imperialist power with the initial impact of foreign penetration. The fact that Japan was able to achieve greater economic development in spite of this penetration requires separate discussion beyond the scope of this study. What we want to focus on is that Japan, like other Asian countries, was the object of Western imperialist penetration. The Western powers imposed on all the Asian countries unequal treaties concerning trade, tariffs, and the flow of labor power, which governed the coming of Asian immigrants to the United States. They sent representatives to recruit for labor and set the conditions under which the workers emigrated. Even though Japan had a stronger government and was therefore better able to control the flow, it was forced by the United States to lift its 200-year-old prohibition on labor emigration.

We want to emphasize that although there were variations among the Asian countries in terms of their interaction with the West, they were all subjected to imperialist penetration and were targets of intense competition among the Western powers. Foreign penetration and imperialism shook loose a massive population from its traditional economic base, rendering it available for labor recruitment. Furthermore, the inability of industries within the Asian countries to absorb this labor, again partly resulting from foreign imperialism, made it accessible to other capitalists in need of cheap labor.

In chapter 1, we outlined some of the important ways that imperialism is linked to underdevelopment or distorted development; for example, how imperialism, through direct looting and taxation, transferred wealth from the colonized to the colonial power and how, through unequal exchange and the use of political power, the colonizers stifled the development of competitive industries and the growth of local incipient capitalism. In addition to the economic and political impact, the effect of imperialism on the peripheral countries had a cultural-psychological aspect also. It created in the minds of the indigenous peoples an image of Western superiority. The obvious economic and political power of the West impressed them. American missionaries and teachers taught them not only the English language but also an idealized image of the United States. It was no accident that when labor recruiters from the United States came with promises of a good life and equal opportunity, many fell easy prey to the propaganda. The cultural-psychological aspect was also manifested in the treatment that Asian laborers received in the United States. Since Asian countries were either colonized by or fell into the sphere of influence of Western powers, their peoples were seen as inferior by United States society and were marked off for separate treatment.

Conditions in the rural areas of many Asian countries, partly induced by imperialism, were such that thousands could not survive locally. Given the low level of industrial development relative to population increase, the urban centers could not absorb all the surplus labor from the countryside. When word got out that the United States was in need of labor, private entrepreneurs, using such existing organizational structures as clan or regional ties, began to channel this surplus labor abroad, sometimes with active government involvement. After this process was set in motion, the comparative economic advantage of working in the United States, created by the unequal relationship between the advanced capitalist country and the underdeveloped areas, induced a pattern of chain migration until the Asian exclusion movement was begun.

It is not our purpose to provide a thorough discussion of the complex relationship between imperialism and the socioeconomic development of each of the Asian countries that fulfilled the labor demand of the western United States and Hawaii. That task needs to be done, and in some cases has been done, by a number of scholars. For several Asian countries, such as India, there is some degree of consensus on the predominance of the regressive aspect of imperialism. For others, such as China, that conclusion is still controversial. In this section, we only intend to present an interpretation of the historical processes that led Asian labor to the United States. We see the demand for cheap labor in the United States and the supply of cheap labor from the Asian countries as part of the same process of capitalist development. The theory we have advanced clearly needs modification in some cases. We believe a strength of the present volume is that we treat theory as a guideline, not a dogma, pointing to things we should look for rather than determining a priori what we will find.

DIFFERENCES AMONG COUNTRIES

China

Although emigration from China occurred prior to the Opium War, one characteristic that distinguished nineteenth-century Chinese emigration from other waves of emigration in Chinese history was the direct and indirect role of Western imperialism in the promotion of the unprecedented mass emigration from Guangdong, a coastal province where domestic troubles and foreign influence converged. Western economic and military pressure on China created an unequal economic and political relationship. The burden of the peasantry, already substantial, was increased by the large indemnities which the Qing government was forced to pay to foreign states, and foreign competition in the domestic market destroyed many indigenous industries. The low level of domestic industrial development could not absorb the displaced peasantry and small craftsmen, causing thousands of them to search for employment elsewhere. The unequal political relationship made it possible for Western powers to control the flow of Chinese labor, either expediting it, or impeding it according to their own labor needs. Between 1848, when gold was discovered in California, and 1882, when the Chinese Exclusion Law was enacted, more than 200,000 came to the American West Coast to fulfill its labor needs. Chapter 6 discusses the socioeconomic origins of this wave of Chinese emigration.

Japan

In 1866, as a consequence of Western intervention, the Japanese government lifted its restrictions on emigration, thus ending the isolationist policy that had lasted for more than two hundred years. In response to the critical need for labor in Hawaii, where the sugar plantations were being developed, Japan began to send workers there, first as contract laborers and then, when that was forbidden, as free laborers. Before this immigration flow came to an end in 1924, when Congress passed the exclusion act, more than 400,000 Japanese traveled to Hawaii and the continental United States, among whom the vast majority were laborers.

This labor emigration was an outcome of the class conflict between the peasantry and the Japanese bourgeoisie intensified by Western imperialism. During the Meiji era, those in the Japanese ruling class moved to the position that to ensure survival, they must accumulate sufficient capital for industrial and military development and thereby achieve political, economic, and social parity with the Western powers. They chiefly used three means for capital accumulation: the Meiji Land Tax, rent, and the exploitation of wage labor, with the burden mainly shouldered by the agricultural sector. Thousands of peasant families were forced to send sons and daughters to search for jobs to supplement their meager incomes derived from farming increasingly smaller plots. Therefore, a large section of the Japanese labor market consisted of workers in a continuous migratory search for jobs. Emigration to the United States can be viewed as an extension of this search (Morita 1976).

For the United States, Japan was clearly a source of "colonial cheap labor," especially for Hawaii, which sent labor recruiters and worked out a convention with Japan for this purpose. Japanese emigrant contract workers were quite comparable to Indian indentured workers. Both worked on plantations in colonial territories, and both even worked on the same colonial crop, namely, sugar. As with other Asian immigrants, the status of Japanese who went to the mainland is more ambiguous. Since the mainland had abolished the immigration of contract laborers, the open importation of immigrants from Japan under such contracts could not occur. Nonetheless, some workers from Japan and other Asian countries did come to the West Coast under various under-the-table agreements. Thus, despite the fact that Japan seems like an exception to the general Asian pattern, there were, in fact, many points of similarity. The differences are in degree, not in kind. Chapter 7, which discusses one period of Japanese immigration to Hawaii, presents an analysis of the relationship between United States penetration and Japan's release of some of its labor power to the United States. We hope this introductory analysis will encourage a thorough study of this topic.

Korea

Korean emigrants to Hawaii and the United States before World War II totaled at most about 8,000. Although the number was small, the coming of Koreans reflected the rivalry among major imperialist powers that dominated eastern Asia in the late nineteenth and early twentieth century. After being forced to sign the Kanghwa Treaty with Japan in 1876, Korea was coerced by other imperialist powers to enter into unequal treaties and became "a shrimp among whales." The forced opening of trade and the subsequent penetration of foreign capitalism hastened the decline of Korean agriculture and the feudal economy, which resulted in the emergence of a large number of displaced farmers who had to seek work elsewhere. Hawaii and the United States were among the destinations to which Koreans migrated. In chapter 8 we discuss the various forms of imperialist expansion in Korea and their consequences for the local economy. In part, emigration was the outcome of imperialist rivalry for the domination of Korea.

India

During the late nineteenth and early twentieth centuries, with the expansion of colonial industries and the abolition of slavery, India became a major supplier of labor to those areas, especially within the British Empire, where there was a need for labor. Nearly 700,000 Indians were taken to the West Indies, British Guiana, and Mauritius. A small number, estimated at about 6,400 went to the United States between 1907 and 1920. While those in the first category of Indian emigrants were mainly indentured laborers, those who came to North America were mostly agricultural workers who owned some land in the Punjab. The "Hindus" as they were often erroneously called, settled predominantly in California; and though they never approached the size of the Japanese, Chinese, and Filipino groups, they were nevertheless significant as an Asian immigrant labor force on the West Coast (Hess 1974).

The process by which a pool of labor in India became available for international migration was, to a large extent, related to British colonization. Under British rule, India provided products and raw materials for British consumption or trade and markets for British manufactures (Bagchi 1973:45-56). As a consequence of the British policy, India failed to industrialize enough to absorb the large number of people in rural areas who found themselves unemployed for a substantial portion of the year. These individuals, including both laborers and those who owned small plots of land, were characteristic of those Indians who went to the United States in the early twentieth century. Chapter 9 describes the effect of British colonization on the Punjab, the area where most Indian immigrants to the United States originated.

Philippines

Filipino immigration to the United States in the early twentieth century was a result of the colonial relationship between the two countries. From 1906 to 1946 over 125,000 Filipinos, predominantly single males, came to labor on the sugar plantations of Hawaii. Of those who came, a disproportionately large number were from the Ilocos region, where the export-oriented national economy instituted by the Spanish and United States colonial governments left the area the least developed in the country. The focus on sugar and other export industries forced small farmers to sink more deeply into debt. Many lost their land and became tenant farmers who found it necessary to work on plantations during the off-season to supplement their incomes. By 1910, when Hawaii began recruiting labor from the Philippines, a ready and experienced work force was available. Chapter 10 discusses how the interests of Hawaii's planters, foreign and indigenous capital, the Philippine national elite, and the peasants of the Ilocos converged to result in emigration.

United States domination of the Philippines was not limited to the economic and political spheres. Through the public education system the United States sought to acculturate the Filipino people to American values and tastes. The favorable image of the United States as the land of milk and honey with equal opportunity for all was certainly an important factor in Filipino immigration (Galedo 1978).

In conclusion, since the social and economic conditions of each Asian country were different at the time of foreign penetration, the resulting interaction between internal and external forces differed and therefore the process and outcome of foreign penetration could not be the same. Not only did such consequences vary from country to country but they also varied from region to region within the same country. Each of the papers in this section is to some degree limited by the fact that while the discussion of the impact of imperialism often applies to the nation as a whole, the discussion of emigration is limited to those locales that produced the largest number of emigrants to the United States. Unfortunately, not much information is available on the effects of imperialism on these particular locations within each country, nor do we provide a comparative analysis of all the destinations of emigrants from these countries. Nevertheless, we believe that each paper has made a tentative assessment and given some clues on what questions need to be answered. They are presented in the hope that our framework of analysis can stimulate further inquiry into the relationship between capitalist development and international migration.

PART II

References

Bagchi, Amiya Kumar
  1973 "Foreign capital and economic development in India: A schematic view." Pp. 43-76 in Kathleen Gough and Hari P. Sharma, eds., Imperialism and Revolution in South Asia. New York & London: Monthly Review.
Baran, Paul
  1957 The Political Economy of Growth. N.Y.: Monthly Review.
Dillard, Dudley
  1979 "Capitalism." Pp. 69-76 in Charles K. Wilber, ed., The Political Economy of Development and Underdevelopment. 2d ed. N.Y.: Random House.
Frank, Andre Gunder
  1969 Capitalism and Underdevelopment in Latin America. Rev. & enlarged ed. N.Y. and London: Monthly Review.
Galedo, Remy
  1978 "U.S. colonialism and Filipino emigration." Unpub. paper.
Griffin, Keith
  1969 Underdevelopment in Spanish America. London: George Allen and Unwin.
Hess, Gary R.
  1974 "The forgotten Asian Americans: The East Indian community in the United States." Pacific Historical Review 43 (November):576-596.
Morita, Walter
  1976 "The political economy of Japanese emigration to the United States 1866 to 1924." Master's thesis, California State University, Los Angeles.
Weisskopf, Thomas E.
  1978 "Imperialism and the economic development of the Third World." Pp. 500-514 in Richard C. Edwards, Michael Reich, and Thomas E. Weisskopf, eds. The Capitalist System. Rev. ed. Englewood Cliffs, N.J.: Prentice Hall.

6
Socioeconomic Origins of Emigration: Guangdong to California, 1850 to 1882*

June Mei

A GENERAL PERSPECTIVE

By the late nineteenth century, domestic turmoil and economic decline in China resulted in the inability of the countryside to provide an adequate means of livelihood for a growing population. Agriculture was gradually shifting to the production of cash crops for commercial sale, and some indigenous industries were beginning to take shape in large towns. These developments were limited to a few parts of south China, however, and rapid progress was discouraged by state policies and conservative ideas. One result of these changes was the increasing separation of peasants from the land as growing numbers of small landowners were forced to sell all or part of their holdings and become tenant farmers, hired hands, or urban workers. This process resembled that which occurred in Europe, where an urban proletariat grew out of a dispossessed peasantry. In China, however, capitalism and technology did not develop quickly enough to absorb this potential labor force. Human dislocation and government weakness were worsened by a series of large-scale peasant revolts. With the arrival of Western imperialism in 1840, industrial growth was hampered even more by the effects of foreign wars and economic competition. Guangdong was a major center of contact with the West and also the site of a bloody antidynastic uprising; hence the effects of all these factors were especially noticeable there.

The preceding conditions might be described as *internal* factors for emigration, insofar as they explain what socioeconomic forces produced the emigrants; they do not indicate why people went where they did. For this, we must look to the rapid expansion of Western imperialism and colonialism to all continents in the nineteenth century. This created a need for a labor supply, preferable cheap, to develop the economies of newly annexed or colonized lands. The gradual abolition of slavery around the world intensified the labor shortage. Because China was politically dominated by the West and because Chinese laborers had some desirable skills (such as familiarity with excavation work in hilly terrain), they were considered a good source of labor. Protected by privileges granted in unequal treaties and aided by Chinese agents and compradors, some Western firms developed a sizable coolie trade. Areas like California and Australia were attractive enough that relatively little coercion was needed to bring men there — in such cases, voluntary emigrants generally borrowed from lenders who were known to them or who were from the same home districts, and the credit-ticket system flourished.[1] Other places where pay and working conditions were far worse, such as Cuba and Peru, had to be supplied with men who had been forcibly abducted or who were tricked. In both situations, only a minority of those who left China ever returned. Voluntary and involuntary emigration were alike, insofar as the Chinese were wanted overseas only for their labor power and not for their persons; in other words, they were needed primarily to develop rather than to settle other lands. This was recognized even in 1868 by a British consul in China, who observed that "the principal object of this emigration is not so much colonization as the supply of labour" (Campbell 1923:154).

Furthermore, emigration itself became a business, where the labor power of the emigrants was the commodity. It was not a slave trade (although the coolie trade came close to being that), for contracts were for services rather than for persons. One major exception to this pattern was the trade in Chinese women for prostitution overseas. While some contracted themselves for definite time spans (McLeod 1947:facing p. 176), it seems that a majority were bought and sold as chattels and were not free to leave after repaying a certain sum or working a fixed length of time. Trade in women, however, was a relatively small though significant fraction of total Chinese emigration in the nineteenth century.

Small-scale emigration evidently occurred even prior to the Opium War, and it might be argued that the underlying cause was the economic deterioration in south China and the resultant social upheavals. There can be no doubt, however, that Western powers hastened this decline and used their influence in China, directly and indirectly, to promote emigration in unprecedented proportions. Thus, the domestic situation (or internal factors) made emigration a viable alternative, but imperialism in China and the labor shortage in new colonies and territories (or *external* factors) were responsible for its rapid growth. In central China, farmlands were depopulated by the bloodshed accompanying the Taiping and Nien uprisings; because a return to the land was possible (at least for a while), there was relatively little need to emigrate in order to find work. Thus, although Shanghai (a major treaty port) was located in that area, the internal forces were much weaker there. In inland regions of south China and throughout most of north China, there were relatively few points of direct contact with foreigners, so external forces were even less significant in those regions. Emigration was greatest from the two provinces of Guangdong and Fujian, where both internal and external factors were strongest.

Although it is convenient to distinguish between internal and external forces in this context, it would be erroneous to treat them as separate and unrelated. Western economic and military pressure on China promoted the image of Western superiority (an external factor), but it also hastened the socioeconomic breakdown of Chinese society, which was an internal factor. Similarly, foreign firms often hired Chinese agents to act on their behalf, and such middlemen cannot be neatly classified as either internal or external factors. The political weakness of China, however, made that country more attractive to foreign labor recruiters, so internal forces could also strengthen external forces. The key feature of Chinese emigration in this period is that it was a product of events occurring both in China and abroad, and these events were often intertwined. But use of the terms *internal* and *external* is not intended to suggest that China was the principal center of the emigration process, for this in fact was taking place worldwide.

It is highly significant that foreign powers and their Chinese agents took an active role in promoting emigration. This characteristic is unique to nineteenth century Chinese emigration and sets it apart from the other waves of emigration in Chinese history. Previous Chinese expeditions to Korea, Vietnam, and central Asia were a result of deliberate military expansion. Although they resulted in the appearance of sizable Chinese populations in other countries, their purpose was conquest and settlement, undertaken at the initiative of the Chinese government. That is, they were created entirely by internal factors.[2]

The best-known instances of Chinese emigration before the nineteenth century were the exoduses to southeast Asia, the Philippines, and Indonesia, which took place during the collapse of the Ming dynasty Although these moves were largely prompted by political unrest and economic chaos at home (all internal factors), they still represented an emigration of settlers and colonizers. These people were not being employed by anyone, nor were they entering a structured economy. There was no distinction between their persons and their labor power. While the exact details are unclear, it seems quite unlikely that this wave of emigration became a business, if only because the turmoil and strife in China was too extensive to allow this to happen. Certainly the emigrants were not induced by any foreigners to leave China in this period. Once abroad, they generally controlled their own economies, whereas in the nineteenth century, Chinese laborers usually worked in enterprises or on land owned or planned by others. Finally, because the earlier emigrants were moving to relatively underdeveloped countries, they were able to become dominant economic forces in their communities.

In contrast to this, the nineteenth-century emigrant laborers were sent to areas where political and economic control was already firmly established and where they had hardly any chance of entering the channels of power. To put it another way, earlier Chinese emigrants settled in preindustrial societies, and they were often able to either establish or join the ruling classes there, with varying degrees of success. Nineteenth-century emigrants went to capitalist countries or their colonies and were compelled by many factors to remain wage laborers. In many cases, they were second-class citizens or aliens ineligible for citizenship. Their chances of entering the ranks of the ruling classes in these latter destinations were virtually nil.

The key factor that distinguished nineteenth-century emigration from earlier types was the development of capitalism, both in China and in the West. Without the creation of a *free* (i.e., not land-bound) labor force in China, there would have been little or no voluntary seeking of employment abroad. But displaced peasants do not necessarily go abroad if they can find work in their own country. In China, however, industrial development was slow and inadequate for a variety of reasons, and the domestic economy could not absorb this free labor force. At the same time, the development of Western capitalism laid the foundation for the West's military superiority over China, which created an unequal political relationship. This inequality was very significant for emigration, expediting the process through the use of treaty ports, extraterritoriality, and other diplomatic privileges or impeding it by the passage of exclusion laws. Thus colonial powers could promote or retard the flow of Chinese labor as their own conditions required. Western capitalism also accelerated the development and exploitation of new colonies and territories — without this, there would not have been as much demand for Chinese laborers abroad. The impact of capitalism is reflected in the status of nineteenth-century emigrants as wage laborers, whereas Chinese who left the country in earlier periods were generally soldiers, merchants, or peasants. The actual business transactions involved in nineteenth-century emigration were also capitalistic, with contracts, interest payments, commissions, and so forth.

It is clear, then, that there is no simple answer to the question, What caused nineteenth-century emigration from Guangdong to California? Fundamental economic changes caused peasants to be slowly separated from the land; war, foreign competition, and domestic strife made it difficult for many to find alternative work in China; and myths of quick riches and active recruitment caused some to turn to California for a livelihood. Unfortunately, these complexities have often been ignored in many studies of Chinese emigration to the United States. Stanford Lyman, for example, depicts it as a continuation of the traditional Chinese "disapora" to foreign lands (Lyman 1974:chap. 1). This view fails to take into account the very different conditions surrounding the various waves of emigration. It also tends to explain emigration solely as an aspect of Chinese history, whereas, in the nineteenth century, developments in the West were of great importance in promoting emigration.

Betty Lee Sung, in contrast, stresses the "pioneering" spirit of the men from Xinning, who comprised the majority of the emigrants to the continental United States. Again, this explanation dwells only on the Chinese and their history (Sung 1967:11). While it is possible that some men traveled to California out of a sense of adventure, it is more likely that the great majority emigrated because of pressing economic need. Furthermore, this psychological explanation disregards the active role played by foreign firms and their Chinese agents. Sung's great emphasis on Xinning makes this district sound more unusual than it actually was, for while many people from this area did indeed go to California, large numbers of Chinese were also emigrating from other districts in Guangdong as well as from Fujian to other parts of the world.

Gunther Barth recognizes that the nineteenth-century Chinese were wanted for their labor power, and he compares emigration to California with that to Malaya in the early part of the century (Barth 1971:50-55). This comparison is valid insofar as both were part of the economic development of new territories. But by focusing almost exclusively on the details of and the Chinese involvement in the various modes of emigration (indentured vs. credit-ticket vs. abducted), Barth overlooks the backing that many Chinese middlemen received from foreigners, either in China or abroad. He also ignores the role played by the West in the disruption of China, which gave rise to emigration, and instead concentrates almost exclusively on domestic problems. In other words, like Lyman and Sung, Barth fails to adequately discuss the external factors and their promotion of internal factors. The effect of such a presentation is, again, a picture of emigration in which everything takes place in an all-Chinese setting and only with Chinese participants. It does not explain why, if the Chinese were seeking fortunes abroad, they did not go to highly developed Western cities to work or do business or why merchants who were less economically hard pressed at home also went overseas with their poorer countrymen, albeit to engage in commerce rather than manual labor.

This essay is an attempt to examine the socioeconomic factors behind Chinese emigration to California. It does not, for example, dwell on the role of family and regional ties in determining the pattern of emigration from different areas, nor does this omission imply that such ties did not exist or were unimportant. It seems, however, that such ties were not themselves causes of emigration; rather, once the process started, they affected the manner in which it occurred. The growth of capitalism is a key element in understanding the dynamics of emigration, and yet it is often overlooked.

THE PATTERN OF CHINESE EMIGRATION TO CALIFORNIA, 1849 TO 1882

In the latter half of the nineteenth century, large numbers of Chinese emigrated to the Americas, southeast Asia, Australia, New Zealand, and the Caribbean islands. The majority of those bound for North America went to California and Hawaii, and most of them in turn came from a few counties near the Pearl River delta in Guangdong province. Large-scale Chinese emigration to the United States began shortly after the California gold rush started in 1849, and it continued at an uneven rate until 1882, when it was drastically reduced by passage of the Chinese Exclusion Act (see fig. 6.1). One source mentions Chinese contract laborers recruited from Guangdong and Fujian emigrating to Hawaii as early as the 1820s (Tanshan huaqiao 1929: "Huaqiaoshi" section, 1). This case (if it indeed took place) was an isolated instance, however, and the Hawaiian islands were not a United States territory at the time. In California, gold mining and construction of the transcontinental railroad were the two principal sources of employment for Chinese until 1870, and in their heydays, each accounted for a temporary sharp rise in immigration (gold mining: 1852 to 1855; railroad construction: 1868 to 1870).

ARRIVALS
(THOUSANDS)

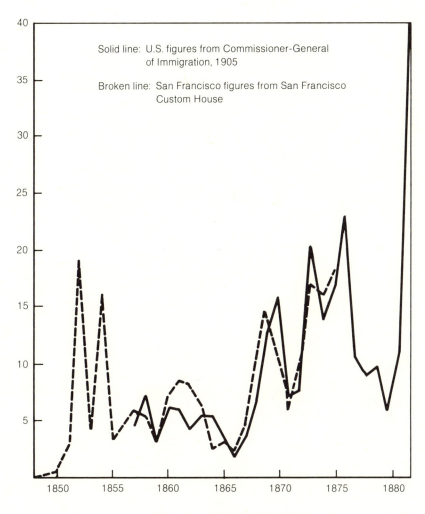

Fig. 6.1
Chinese Immigration to the United States, 1848 to 1882
(Source: Coolidge 1909:498)

The overwhelming majority of the California Chinese came from the Pearl River delta region, particularly from the following counties (see fig. 6.2):

Cantonese	*Putonghua*	
Sunning	Xinning	(Later renamed Toisan/Taishan)
Sunwui	Xinhui	
Hoiping	Kaiping	
Yungping	Enping	
Heungshan	Xiangshan	(Later renamed Chungshan/Zhongshan)
Chikkai	Chixi	
Bo-on	Baoan	(Later renamed Sun-n/Xin'an)
Punyu	Panyu	
Namhoi	Nanhai	
Shuntak	Shunde	

1. Yangjiang	7. Heshan	13. Dongguan	19. Qingyuan
2. Enping	8. Xiangshan	14. Baoan	20. Fagang
3. Kaiping	9. Shunde	15. Kaoyao	21. Conghua
4. Xinning	10. Nanhai	16. Sihui	
5. Chixi	11. Panyu	17. Sanshui	
6. Xinhui	12. Zengcheng	18. Huayuan	

Fig. 6.2
The Pearl River Delta Region.

The first four districts were known collectively as Siyi (Szeyup), and the last three as Sanyi (Samyup). Many emigrants went from Xiangshan to Hawaii as well as to California, while most Kejia emigrants originated from the two counties of Chixi and Baoan.

Of these areas, Siyi produced the largest number of emigrants to the United States (see fig. 6.3), but this numerical advantage was not overwhelming until 1868 and after. This date is closely associated with Chinese participation in the building of the transcontinental railroad, suggesting that the great majority of the Chinese railroad workers came from Siyi. The question of why other districts were not as heavily involved will be discussed later. Nonetheless, we find that those parts of China that were home to most of the United States-bound emigrants all shared several features: they were undergoing rapid and drastic socioeconomic change, they were areas with a large impoverished population, and they were near seaports where foreign trade was well established — Guangzhou, Hong Kong, and Macao. To better understand the historical forces behind the migration, it is thus necessary to examine domestic developments in the Pearl River delta and Western impact there.

THE GUANGDONG SETTING: DOMESTIC AND INTERNATIONAL FACTORS

By the nineteenth century, cash crops were extensively grown in Guangdong, wage laborers were used in some industries, and a fairly advanced monetary system based on silver was generally used (Mei 1979: 468-469). The economy, then, was moving in the direction of "protocapitalism"; but government policies favored the Chinese landowning class and slowed the development of commerce and technology, so it became increasingly difficult for production to keep pace with population growth. After the sixteenth century, economic development throughout the country was slow, and even relatively advanced areas like the Pearl River delta remained pockets in a backward whole.

The Qing government's reluctance to accept extensive contact with the West resulted in the creation of the so-called Canton system, which restricted the volume of trade and channeled it through a rigid operation designed to limit and supervise it. There emerged from this arrangement a group of Chinese merchants who had experience in dealing with Europeans (Fairbank 1959:46-53). They were the precursors of a social class that was later to play a significant role in the emigration of Chinese laborers — the compradors.

(THOUSANDS)

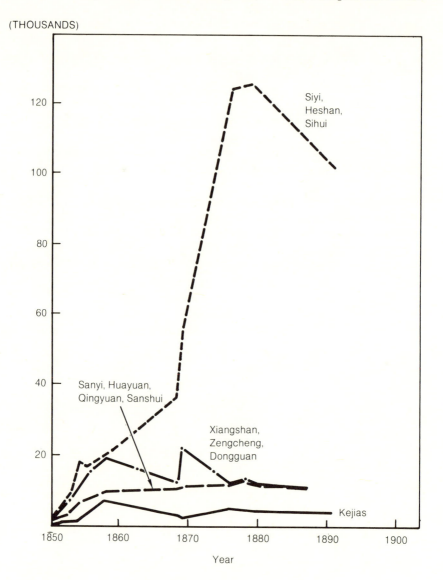

Fig. 6.3
Chinese in the U.S. by Districts of Origin
(Source: Lumei Sanyi zonghuiguan jianshi 1975)

The Opium War of 1840 to 1842 marked the coming of Western imperialism to China. The Treaty of Nanjing, which concluded the war in 1842, provided for the establishment of five treaty ports, one of which was Guangzhou. It also ceded Hong Kong to Great Britain, and that city's new status as British territory (instead of Chinese territory open to foreigners) allowed it to become a major center of Chinese emigration within a decade. Another major provision of the treaty was the granting of extraterritorial privileges to foreigners residing in China. In theory, only foreign nationals and their property were entitled to extraterritorial protection; in practice, their Chinese agents, associates, and servants were often protected as well. Hence compradors involved in the emigration business and particularly in the coolie trade, which was banned by Chinese law, often escaped punishment because they were shielded by their employers.

The Treaty of Nanjing and subsequent unequal treaties had a broad economic impact on China and further eroded Chinese sovereignty. The enormous indemnities that the Qing government was forced to pay were raised by increasing the already heavy burden of taxation. Reparations for the Opium War alone required a sum roughly equal to one-third of the annual income of the national treasury. Business in the treaty ports was conducted along the principles of free trade as practiced in the West, since trade had been one of the major goals of the foreign powers in China.

The Chinese economy could not absorb all this without changing, and the ultimate effect was the accelerated disintegration of the traditional agrarian economy. This vast and complex subject cannot be covered in any detail here, but some of the major developments are relevant to an understanding of Chinese emigration. After the Opium War, cotton goods became one of the biggest foreign export items to China, and the importation of such products naturally caused great disruption in those areas where commercial cloth manufacture had been the principal means of livelihood. Competition abroad also adversely affected local industries by decreasing China's textile exports to other countries. Since Canton had been a regional center of commercial textile production and export ever since the Ming dynasty, the negative effects of foreign imports were probably felt there as well as in the Jiangnan area, the center of the Chinese textile industry.

Ironically, China's economy in this period was still largely self-sufficient, and Western dreams of a vast Chinese market for foreign goods never materialized. Indigenous industries were concentrated in a few areas, treaty ports were established near many of them, and so imports of manufactured goods hit especially hard at these local enterprises. The volume of textiles imported into China was insignificant compared to the total volume of cloth consumed in the country; it was, however, a considerable portion of the domestic cloth trade. In the early 1850s, for example, it is doubtful if all foreign imports of cotton cloth taken together could have accounted for more than 5 percent of Chinese consumption. Yet, in absolute figures, this was a sizable volume and would have represented a considerable part of the domestic cloth business.

Other occupations in Guangdong were also affected by Western imperialism. With the opening up of Shanghai and Ningbo to foreign trade, exported teas from Zhejiang and Anhui were diverted away from Guangzhou, causing over one hundred thousand porters and boatmen in northern Guangdong to lose their jobs. Some Cantonese porters, warehousemen, shroffs, and compradors were confronted with an economic crisis (Wakeman 1966:98-100). This disruption was probably one cause of the emigration of merchants from Guangzhou to California, which will be more fully discussed below.

On the political and diplomatic level, Western imperialism also indirectly laid the groundwork for Chinese emigration. Under traditional Chinese law, emigration was forbidden. Yet in 1859, the provincial government of Guangdong was forced to officially sanction foreign recruitment of Chinese laborers. This was one consequence of the Allied occupation of Guangzhou, and it was actually acquiescence in an illegal business that had, in fact, existed for over a decade with the knowledge of the local authorities, who were powerless to stop it. The Treaty of Beijing, signed the next year, also indicated the central government's acceptance of large-scale emigration. Even when it had a strong case, the weakness of the Qing government prevented it from taking firm and effective action. For example, when the first Chinese Exclusion Act was passed by the United States Congress in 1882, it was in clear violation of both the spirit and the letter of a bilateral treaty between the United States and China (the Burlingame Treaty of 1868), which affirmed the right of Chinese and American citizens to emigrate freely to each other's country. Action by the Chinese government did not go beyond a few ineffective protests that were disregarded by the United States. In contrast, any Chinese action that was perceived by the Western powers (rightly or wrongly) to be a treaty violation was generally used as an excuse to demand more privileges, and these demands could be readily backed up with superior military force.

Although imperialism had such negative effects on Guangdong, it was not the sole cause of socioeconomic disruption. In fact, the greatest manifestations of social unrest in nineteenth-century China — peasant rebellions — were directed as much against the inept and oppressive

Qing government as against foreign intruders. The antidynastic Triad societies, whose members were identified by their red turbans, had been active in delta counties like Xiangshan, Xinhui, and Xinning as early as 1843; after a period of relative dormancy, they organized an armed revolt in the spring of 1854. After the insurrection was subdued, the local authorities attempted to purge Guangdong of the surviving rebels. Over seventy thousand executions took place in Guangzhou alone, and perhaps as many as one million people were killed throughout the province (Wakeman 1966: 136-150).

Political upheavals were not the only causes of violence in Guangdong. In 1856, merely one year after the Red Turban revolt ended, fighting broke out in the Siyi area between "locals" and Kejias. The latter were concentrated in the small county of Chixi, immediately adjacent to Xinning. The fundamental conflict was over arable land, which was relatively scarce in these two hilly districts; linguistic and social differences between the Kejias and locals worsened matters, and fighting spilled over into the neighboring counties of Yangjiang (Yeungkong) and Xiangshan. According to local accounts, these land disputes were protracted and bloody: a single battle could claim one or two thousand lives, and in a single month of almost incessant fighting in 1856, well over three thousand people were killed in the district of Xinning alone (Taishan xianzhi 1893:14:22a-26b). These feuds continued, off and on, for twelve years.

Because of the constant warfare in Guangdong, the consequences of the usual natural disasters — floods and droughts — were magnified. Even in times of comparative peace and stability, the government did little to alleviate the hardships of the peasantry; with its attention turned to domestic rebellion and foreign incursions, even token relief measures were ignored. Incessant fighting also made it difficult for peasants to maintain their farmlands. In addition, the government made few efforts to suppress banditry and piracy, both of which were extensive in the delta area. For those living in areas where cash crops were primarily grown, the interruption of normal commerce and transportation brought the threat of starvation. Xinning, for instance, produced only enough grain annually to feed its population for half a year, and the difference had been made up by importing rice (Taishan xianzhi 1893:8:6b). During the late 1840s and the 1850s, and particularly during the Kejia-local feuds, famines were not unusual. Because of the prolonged warfare in Guangdong, an increasing number of ablebodied men were faced with military conscription. After the suppression of the Triads, tax collection was turned over to the gentry, who could use the ensuing confusion between rent and taxes to squeeze more from the peasants (Wakeman 1966:155).

There were, then, several factors in Guangdong that tended to displace peasants from the land: commercialization of agriculture and development of local manufacture, competition from foreign imports, land disputes, imperialist invasions, and domestic uprisings. The Qing government was unable either to improve conditions or to prevent foreigners from taking advantage of them. For potential emigrants, working abroad offered the possibility of economic benefits; at times, it may have seemed like the only viable alternative. An official record contained the following description of the situation in Xinning: "Ever since the disturbances caused by the Red [Turban] bandits and the Kejia bandits, dealings with foreigners have increased greatly. The able-bodied go abroad. The fields are clogged with weeds. . . . Daughters are often drowned rather than raised" (Taishan xianzhi 1893:8:6b). Thus, at a time when the development and exploitation of new colonies and territories around the world required a fresh supply of labor, Guangdong's human resources were generously tapped by Great Britain, Holland, the United States, and other Western powers. This was the background of Chinese emigration to California in the mid-nineteenth century.

THE EMIGRANT MERCHANTS

Merchants were among the first Chinese to emigrate to California. As early as 1849, they were engaged in trade in San Francisco. One early observer noted that "in the fall of 1849 the Chinese in San Francisco numbered several hundred. . . . Most of the Chinese who came here were men of means enough to pay their own way and here they mainly embarked in mercantiles and trading pursuits" (Chinn 1973:9). This was corroborated by some American businessmen who had extensive dealings with Chinese merchants: one asserted that many came bringing their capital with them, while another estimated that merchants constituted roughly 2 percent of the Chinese emigrant population (U. S. Congress 1877:816, 530). Some opened restaurants that catered to miners and people of all nationalities (Taylor 1949:89). Others established stores that sold Chinese groceries and daily necessities to their fellow countrymen. Chy Lung, one of the oldest and most successful examples of the latter, was a store founded in 1850 by a partnership of several Sanyi men (Sam Yup Association 1975:179). It prospered and expanded its business to include luxury goods such as silks and lacquerwares, and it sold these to Chinese and whites alike.

In some ways, Chy Lung was typical of many of the early businesses set up in San Francisco's Chinatown: it dealt primarily in imported goods, it was jointly financed, and it was established by immigrants from Sanyi. Prior to the 1870s, most of the leading merchants in Chinatown came from Sanyi, particularly from Nanhai county (Sam Yup Association 1975:213-217, 237). Part of the city of Guangzhou lies within this county, and it was one of the most advanced commercial areas in China. There are several reasons to believe that at least some of the early emigrant Sanyi merchants had also been merchants in their home districts. First, they had (at least collectively) enough money to pay their own passage and start new businesses. Second, they had the inclination to engage in trade at a time when mining for gold was the chief attraction for most people. Third, the import-export nature of their business required some familiarity with the commodities traded; this was especially true of the merchants who handled luxury goods from Suzhou and Hangzhou. These included such things as clothing, fans, and expensive silks and brocades that were sold in China by merchants who specialized in such goods. Fourth, some of the larger stores in San Francisco had affiliated stores (*lianhao*) in Hong Kong and, more infrequently, Guangzhou (Sam Yup Association 1975:179, 184). This suggests a network of business connections that may have existed prior to the departure of the merchants from China. The more successful merchants also established their own affiliates in Hong Kong, Canada, and even Yokohama. Again, this indicates that they had associates who were knowledgeable in Chinese business practices.

This supposition gains credibility if we examine the social classes of the Sanyi area. The poorest potential emigrants — peasants and wage workers — were unlikely to have enough money to pay their way across the Pacific and still have the capital needed to start businesses in the United States. Landlords, in turn, had their assets tied up in land. Furthermore, the economic recessions of 1847 and 1853 in Guangzhou hit hardest at urban merchants, not rural landlords. Given the uncertainties of doing business in Guangzhou and its environs, at least some merchants could have decided to try their luck in California.

THE EMIGRANT LABORERS

In contrast to the early Chinese merchants, the majority of the emigrants from Guangdong were men from outlying districts rather than from the vicinity of Guangzhou. This does not necessarily mean that they were all peasants. Few contemporary sources refer to their backgrounds, but from some fragmentary evidence we can find clues that enable us to reconstruct the social origins of some of these emigrant workers.

The earliest reference to Chinese accepting employment overseas occurs in an 1839 memorial by Lin Zexu, the imperial commissioner stationed in Guangzhou (Chouban yiwu shimo buyi 1839: 8th month, 17th day). He observed that "every year at winter time, when the foreign ships return to their homelands, there are some unemployed paupers who, privately recruiting among themselves, accept employment abroad. . . . Upon arrival in those countries, they are ordered to excavate mountains and plant trees or do other kinds of heavy work." This was written a year before the outbreak of the Opium War, suggesting that even then conditions in the Guangdong countryside were bad enough to motivate the jobless to emigrate.

Various factors, however, kept the level of emigration down during this period. Since the Ming dynasty, the government had made it a criminal offense to leave China without official permission; furthermore, it was not easy to make the necessary contact with foreign ships. The port referred to in Lin's memorial was Macao, a center of Portuguese activity. Nearby Guangzhou probably handled much more foreign shipping, but supervision was also likely to have been stricter there. It is worth noting that this early emigration was apparently voluntary; or, at least, if the foreigners made any efforts to recruit Chinese workers, Lin Zexu was unaware of it. Finally, the tone of the document indicates that the number of people involved in this process was relatively small and that it occurred only seasonally. Winter being not only sailing time for foreign ships but also the slack season on farms, it appears that the "unemployed paupers" were either totally jobless or seasonally hired during the busy months. In either case, they would have had no source of income in the winter.

In contrast to the limited, semiclandestine emigration described by Lin, we find the open and notorious coolie trade that mushroomed after the opening of the treaty ports.[3] The coolie trade was centered in cities like Guangzhou and Xiamen, where foreign firms and their compradors could operate with minimal interference from Chinese authorities. Some diplomats boldly used their special status and privileges to promote the coolie trade for their own benefit (Campbell 1923:96).

By 1859, the forcible abduction of laborers had become so blatant and commonplace that even R. Alcock, British consul in Guangzhou, commented on the gravity of the situation in one of his dispatches (R. Alcock to J. Bowring, April 12, 1859, in Poole and Dickens 1894:318). The demand for labor had by this time greatly exceeded the supply of voluntary emigrants, and kidnapping became an important way of procuring men to work abroad. At the same time, the existence of such a situation indicates that would-be emigrants had developed some understanding of the different countries where they might go: abduction was necessary for the more undesirable destinations, but not for places like California and Hawaii.

Chinese documents from the same year (1859) shed more light on the social origins of a group of men who went to Guangzhou in search of work, either in China or abroad (Zhu 1959:44-67). The forty-odd men came from over twenty districts in Guangdong, but only two were from the immediate area of Guangzhou. Most were engaged in peddling or in nonagricultural manual labor such as rice carrying. Although they had jobs, they were having difficulty making ends meet, and most had gone from their rural home districts to Guangzhou hoping to find better work.

In light of this, we may surmise that they left their homes "voluntarily," in the sense that they were not taken by force from the countryside. Yet their uprooting was "involuntary" insofar as it was not a matter of choice but of necessity that they find new or better jobs elsewhere. It is worth noting that these men were not workers in indigenous industries who had lost their jobs because of foreign competition; instead, they seemed to come from a stratum of underemployed or unemployed workers from the countryside who had not been able to find a place in urban industries. In this sense, they might be termed *semiproletarian*, for it appears that they would have accepted work for wages had it been available.

The fact that no peasants are listed in the case cited above does not mean that the countryside was unaffected. Given the pressures of limited land and social disorders, it is quite possible that some of the workers mentioned above were members of peasant families who had turned to nonagricultural jobs because there was too little land to sustain them. For example, a household with landholdings just adequate to sustain itself, but with more than one son, would not be able to give the younger sons any land to support families. Of course, hired hands would have no land to begin with.

There is reason to believe that some of the emigrants who went to California came from the stratum of the peasantry that owned a marginal amount of land. In 1876 the president of the Hop-wo (Hehe) Company, whose constituency was composed primarily of emigrants from the Kaiping and Enping districts, along with members of the Yee (Yu) clan of Xinning district, testified that most Chinese in the United States had been farmers at home who did not have complete ownership of the land they tilled (U. S. Congress 1877:94). An American observer of Chinese emigration noted that in 1869, one-third of those leaving Hong Kong "belonged to that class of coolies[4] who own no property and who can scarcely live from day to day in China on their wages. The others belonged to the next higher class, who may be the owners of cabins, pieces of land, or other property sufficient to secure a passage, and yet be far from the danger of want or even of starvation in case of any accident" (Conwell 1871:180). Since this was written during the height of emigration for railroad construction, the nearly destitute workers of this period could have their passage paid by the railroad companies, when otherwise they would not be able to afford the ticket. Still, the thrust of the available evidence suggests that Chinese emigrants to California and elsewhere were generally poor men of rural background. This is further corroborated by Thomas King, an American merchant who had lived in China and become involved in the emigration business (U. S. Congress 1877:101-102): He testified that most Chinese emigrants left their country in the winter months, when they were heavily debt ridden and agricultural work was scarce. (Additional testimony that the Chinese in the United States had rural origins can be found in U. S. Congress 1877:445, 756, 887, 939, 1245.)

We find, then, that the majority of the emigrant laborers were hired hands, sharecroppers, or small landowners. Economic pressures and war had caused them to leave the land, so they had to look for new ways to make a living. The immediate reasons given by the laborers for their decision to emigrate included false arrests by the police, fear of being drafted into the army by the government, reduction of wages by landlords, and deprivation of daily necessities by tax collectors (Conwell 1871:120). The second and perhaps the first of these factors were related to the peasant rebellions and antidynastic activities in Guangdong. The increase in taxes was partially necessitated by wars with Western powers and the need to suppress domestic uprisings; the reference to landlords and wage reductions again indicates that some emigrants were hired hands or poor peasants who also worked part-time for landlords.

The previously noted testimony of Thomas King also corroborates the hypothesis that the emigrants mentioned in Lin Zexu's 1839 memorial were also hired hands or poor peasants, since their emigration was seasonal and concentrated in the winter months. Hence it appears that both before and after the Opium War, emigrant laborers came from the same social classes. Their numbers, however, went up sharply after 1840 for several reasons: China was under strong political pressure from the West to legalize emigration and not interfere with the coolie trade and the economic crisis in Guangdong had intensified because of constant warfare. Many peasants who owned some land preferred to sell their holdings and seek work abroad. A Chinese witness testified in 1876 before Congress as follows (U. S. Congress 1877:71):

"If they have means they pay their own passages; if not, they borrow from others. They sell their farms and property to get here. If they have no property and can't borrow they don't come." Families with land that was not worth the cost of passage could also pool resources with relatives to send one member of the clan abroad; in this manner, men whose immediate families were actually too poor to afford a ticket still managed to travel to California.

Over half the Chinese who had emigrated to the continental United States by 1882 came from Siyi, and of this group a majority came from the district of Xinning. Conversely, few men from Siyi emigrated to areas outside North America and Australia. A likely reason for this pattern can be found in the motivation of laborers going to the United States and Australia, compared to those bound for other parts of the world: in the former case, there was the attraction of sudden and enormous wealth in gold mining, but this was lacking in the latter. The first great wave of Chinese emigration to the United States was catalyzed by the California gold rush. One Qing poet noted that distance did not deter the miners from making the long journey and hinted that they went voluntarily (Zhang, n.d., in Qian, 1966:1). Even after the heyday of the gold rush, Chinese sought on their own to go to the United States. In fact, one of the men recruited in the 1859 case mentioned earlier had gone there of his own accord to seek passage to California (Zhu 1959:47). It therefore appears that some Siyi emigrants paid for their own voyages by borrowing from friends where possible or by selling any land they may have possessed. If these channels were exhausted, they probably turned to the credit-ticket system. In any case, they seldom resorted to unfamiliar barracoons or coolie brokers, since these offered no assurance that they would get to California or Australia.

It was quite well known in Guangdong that a few Chinese emigrants did indeed "strike it rich" during their stay abroad. Some used their money to extend loans to others who needed funds to cross the Pacific. The most likely recipients of such loans would be people known either directly or indirectly to the creditor — in other words, people from his own home district. Conversely, with a number of their kinsmen already in the United States and returning as lenders to China, job seekers from Siyi had a better chance of obtaining loans through the credit-ticket system than did men from other parts of Guangdong. The importance of clan and regional ties in expediting emigration from certain areas should not be underestimated. It is reflected in the role played by the Six Companies, which were district associations, in recruiting Chinese laborers to California. Similarly, a majority of Chinese emigrants to southeast Asia came from Fujian and from the Swatow (Shantou) district of Guangdong, where a variation of the southern Fujian dialect was spoken. It appears here that most of the creditors and their clients came from the same areas (Campbell 1923). Since many of the early Chinese laborers in the United States were from Siyi, it can be expected that their prospective clients (i.e., those hoping to borrow money from them) would also be from that region. If Siyi men had access to this channel of emigration, then it was unnecessary for them to approach unknown coolie recruiters in the cities.

Recruitment of unwilling workers by deceit or abduction was intended to supply labor to such places as Peru and Cuba, where the climate was severe, the working conditions harsh, and the pay minimal. Volunteers would hardly be attracted to such jobs or environs. Australia and California, however, held out the lure of gold (real or imagined), and most of the Chinese bound for these two sites seemed to have gone voluntarily. In the case of California, the desire to find a better job overseas was often further strengthened by the advertising of shipping firms, which stood to make large profits from the trans-Pacific traffic. These companies, through their agents and compradors in China, often overexaggerated the chances of getting rich quickly in California in order to induce potential emigrants to buy tickets. The image of the United States in China was frequently misleading. One popular myth was that after several years of hard work, the Chinese laborer could expect to return home relatively well off (Conwell 1871:chap. 12). This was reinforced by the sight of those returnees who indeed had accumulated a respectable sum to take home. Even one younger son of a landlord, upon seeing a poor neighbor come back from the United States rich and prosperous, decided to try his luck as an emigrant (Stein and Taft 1971:54-57). The effect on poorer villagers must have been even greater.

Often, however, less fortunate emigrants never managed to return to China at all, and even some of those who succeeded in paying their way home were left with little to show for their years abroad. Hosea B. Morse recalled one returned emigrant whose savings were almost completely depleted by corrupt officials and family obligations (Morse 1918:166). Those who had accumulated enough money to return and retire often lost their savings gambling in San Francisco Chinatown prior to their departure; others at times were afraid to go home lest they be robbed en route by the pirates along the Guangdong coast (Franck 1925:315). In 1876, when over 200,000 Chinese had emigrated to the United States (most of them to California), an open letter from the Six Companies admitted that most emigrants were unable to return to China because they had overestimated their own prospects in the United States (U. S. Congress 1877:38-39). The Chinese population of California in that year was estimated to be approximately 148,000 (U. S. Congress 1877:33, also Campbell 1923:33), so it appears that, at best, only about one-fourth of the emigrants who came were able to return to China. If we allow for some who died in the United States and for others who moved to different places, this figure would be even lower. While the one-fourth estimate may seem low, it is consistent with figures that can be derived from annual immigration statistics. Of course the percentage of women who returned to China was probably even lower still, since many were prostitutes who were denied even the opportunity to leave their profession, let alone the country. While it cannot be assumed that all those who were financially successful returned to China, family and regional ties probably led the vast majority of them to do so, if only for short visits. Thus, those who did return to their homeland were likely to be the success stories and not representative cases. Yet, because they were the ones perceived in China to be "typical" returnees, their presence would have the effect of promoting the "quick riches" reputation of California and further fostering emigration. In addition, those who were economically unsuccessful abroad might be prevented by a sense of guilt or shame from admitting their failure to their families and friends; hence, the bleaker side of emigrants' lives was less likely to be publicized than the stories of the wealthier few.

THE ECONOMICS OF EMIGRATION

Given the lack of great monetary rewards for the majority of the Chinese working in California, what economic incentives motivated so many men to seek work there? Deceptive advertisements alone would not have been persuasive enough. One fundamental reason was the sad state of the Chinese economy, where social change, domestic rebellion, and foreign aggression interfered with both commerce and agriculture.[5] Often the alternative to emigration was starvation. In addition, the buying power of United States wages was huge in light of the low cost of living and even lower standard of living in China. Most emigrant workers sought primarily to support themselves and their families; an optimistic but common goal would be retirement with a comfortable sum to live on. Probably very few genuinely expected to find fabulous riches abroad and return home extremely wealthy, although this could always be hoped for.

With some scrimping and saving, the average Chinese railroad worker in the United States might accumulate from $5 to $15 per month, or $60 to $180 annually (Mei 1979:487-488). Out of these savings, he had to repay a substantial debt. The most obvious one was the price of his passage to the United States and whatever interest he owed on this loan. This generally ranged from $60 to well over $100, and most records indicate that repayment of this debt alone usually took from three to five years. Of course, if the emigrant aspired to return home someday, he would have to save enough to pay his way back, although this generally cost less than the trip to California because little or no interest was incurred. Another probable debt is often overlooked — it was necessary for the would-be emigrant to acquire the legal papers needed to enter the United States before borrowing his passage from friends or through the credit-ticket system. These papers could cost more than the fare itself. Two men testified in the 1859 Guangzhou case that they had each paid $165 to procure entry papers. This sum probably included the various fees collected, legally and illegally, by United States consuls in treaty ports (U. S. Congress 1877:890-891, 93), as well as fees for one or more Chinese middlemen. One hundred sixty-five dollars was three to four times the cost of crossing the Pacific, and men who had to borrow the cost of their passage were unlikely to pay such a large sum unless it was also with borrowed money. Since the usual income of rural workers in this period was approximately $8 to $10 a year (Conwell 1871:62), their total debt upon arrival in California (emigration papers, fare, and interest on loans) may well have exceeded ten years of wages at home. The fact that they were willing to assume such a financial burden to get a job abroad is a measure both of their economic desperation and of their high expectations.

According to one contemporary observer, thirty dollars per year was the approximate remittance sent back to China by many emigrants (California State Senate 1878:101), a considerable sum in China at that time. Thirty to forty dollars would be enough to buy grain and other necessities for one year for a family of one adult and two or three children. It was therefore a significant, though not enormous, sum to the recipients. The annual wage for servants and barracoon staff was between twelve and twenty-four dollars and probably included room and board, but this was still slightly lower than the average remittance. Hence we find that remittances were roughly equal to the annual income of an urban menial worker, but even then they represented a substantial though not luxurious addition to the budget of any poor family. Further, when war or natural disasters interrupted the flow of money from abroad in the twentieth century, many who depended on such sums became refugees or were compelled to sell their belongings, homes, children, or even themselves to stay alive. For some families, remittances were the margin of survival, and while they may have been better off than those with no fiscal support from abroad, it would probably be incorrect to portray the majority of these families as "wealthy."

Emigrant workers were undoubtedly aware of the standard of living afforded by their remittances, and the fact that they did not send more suggests that they did not earn enough to do so.

Although working abroad did not greatly enrich many laborers, the crimps[6] and other middlemen involved in the emigration business often made large sums of money. A comprador coolie-broker, like the barracoon proprietor in the 1859 case, might net as much as $1000 each year (Mei 1979:490-491). Compared with the incomes of the rural peasants, hired hands, urban laborers, or even emigrant workers, this income would seem staggering. The lucrative nature of a crimp's occupation resulted as much from his status as a comprador as from any uniqueness of the coolie trade. It demonstrates how much more profitable it was to work for a foreign firm than to eke out a living like most Chinese citizens.

Although compradors handled relatively little of the emigration to California, their incomes were comparable to those of men who recruited on behalf of American shipping firms and employers, as well as credit-ticket lenders. A defaulted credit-ticket could bring the lender as much as $300 on a $40 loan. Brokers recruiting laborers for the United States were paid $10 to $27 per recruit, depending on the strength of the men they found (Conwell 1871:89). In 1862, a circular distributed by a comprador for an Oregon firm offered steamship tickets for $54, or almost double the actual cost (Conwell 1871:154-155). Given the magnitude of emigration to the United States prior to 1882, profits on loans for passage alone would have amounted to hundreds of thousands of dollars in peak years. In addition, there were interest charges on various other loans, and agents of American companies (particularly of the railroad and shipping firms) probably also received salaries as well as commissions. Hence the real wealth in the emigration business accrued not to the laborers (although such was the popular image) but to the shipping firms, brokers, and labor recruiters, some of whom acted directly or indirectly on behalf of labor-hungry United States companies. Chinese compradors, crimps, and middlemen also benefited, and they might earn from three to five times what the average railroad worker was paid in California; ironically, it was often the emigrants rather than their handlers or creditors who hoped for great wealth through emigration.

CONCLUSION

Although this study has focused on the emigration of Chinese from Guangdong to California, it must be remembered that large-scale emigration was also occurring in the same period from many parts of south

China to southeast Asia, Latin America, and elsewhere. This movement of people must be seen as a global shifting of laborers from more backward areas to newly developing colonies and territories. The relatively advanced capitalist countries were expanding (economically and geographically) at a rate faster than were their own populations, while poverty and local upheavals tended to uproot people in poorer countries. In this sense, Chinese emigration to the United States was unlike any previous Chinese emigration — it had more in common with, for example, the settling of German and Irish immigrants in the United States than it did with the earlier movement of Chinese from the mainland to Taiwan. It is therefore important to study this emigration as part of an international process than just as a Chinese phenomenon.

The United States, for its part, played two roles in the movement of Chinese laborers. It furnished both the organized capital that could recruit workers on a large scale and the labor-short territories that were ripe for development. This was unusual, for most imperialist powers that were active in China in the latter half of the nineteenth century channeled emigration to their colonies rather than to their homelands. Great Britain, for example, heavily recruited Chinese laborers for its southeast Asian possessions but discouraged workers from going to Great Britain itself. The American pattern is probably a result of uneven development within the United States: while much of the eastern part of the country had by then a rapidly developing capitalist economy, the western territories were still being acquired in stages and were economically more like the colonies of advanced capitalist nations (such as Great Britain) than like the homelands themselves.

We may note that the first major wave of Chinese emigration to California, which was a result of the gold rush, was not significantly organized in any way and that it took place just at the time California acquired statehood. At this early stage, the economic and political power of the large eastern capitalist companies had not yet been extended to the Pacific Coast. In contrast, the second large wave of Chinese immigration was directly linked to the construction of the transcontinental railroad. American companies played an active part in publicizing the need for laborers, recruiting them, and even financing their journeys. Thus, although Chinese railroad workers may have gone to the United States with the same hopes as the miners, the much more organized nature of their emigration was definitely made possible by the involvement of American capitalism.

At the diplomatic level, the United States was not as aggressive as the European powers in wresting privileges from China by war or threats of war. One possible reason for this difference is the gap in development between the United States and western Europe. When the Opium War started in 1840, Great Britain was already a well-established capitalist country with several overseas colonies, while the United States was still absorbed with the development of its own growing territory. Nevertheless, Americans in China were shielded by extraterritorial privileges, and the United States received all the favors given to European countries because of the "most-favored nation clause." Thus, while it may not have very actively sought to enjoy an unequal political relationship with China, the United States did not turn down the opportunity when it arose. Moreover, it took full advantage of China's weakness by passing the Exclusion Act of 1882, in violation of the Burlingame Treaty.

Chinese emigration to the United States was therefore a highly complex phenomenon, involving global factors as well as bilateral ones. The most significant force was the development of capitalism. In the West, this resulted in the emergence of several advanced imperialist states that were seeking overseas colonies. Their foreign policy contributed to the destabilization of the Qing dynasty, while their colonies became "labor magnets" for would-be emigrants. Because several Western powers were competing for political domination over China, that country was never totally colonized by any one state; but at the same time it was subjected to pressures from many states. This is reflected in the pattern of emigration, which brought Chinese workers to lands controlled by Great Britain, France, Holland, Spain, and Portugal, as well as to the United States.

Emigration, however, was not caused solely by imperialism. The development of capitalism within China itself also hastened the decline of the Qing dynasty in a paradoxical manner. By taking place at all, it undermined the traditional agrarian economy; by taking place so slowly (in part bacause of competition from advanced capitalist countries), it helped separate peasants from the land without absorbing them into a domestic working class. From this pool of dislocated peasants came the majority of Chinese emigrants in the nineteenth century.

Because of its sheer size, China has rarely been affected throughout the entire country by any single phenomenon; yet, because its vast expanse is ruled by one government, events in one area may indirectly affect others. For instance, many of the Chinese cloth firms forced out of business by foreign competition were located in central China, far from any major centers of emigration. But their bankruptcy diminished government tax revenues at a time when expenditures for indemnities and other costs were rising sharply. This contributed to heavier taxation, which was felt all over China. Similarly, peasant rebellions in central and north China would not dispossess Guangdong peasants, but by weakening the government, they indirectly weakened its ability to control emigration from Guangdong and to protect it citizens abroad.

It would be too simplistic to attribute emigration to any single cause. Many factors played a role: government incompetence, natural disasters, domestic uprisings, foreign encroachment, and so on. Yet the strand of imperialism runs like a thread through virtually everything that affected emigration. Although there are widely divergent assessments of the impact of imperialism on modern Chinese development, there is almost unanimous agreement that it helped destabilize traditional Chinese society. It put economic pressure on the government by demanding trading privileges and war indemnities, and it lent military support to the suppression of peasant rebellions when foreign interests were threatened. It directly and indirectly impeded the growth of industries in China that might have absorbed the uprooted peasantry, as European industries had done. It specifically promoted emigration through active labor recruitment in China, even before emigration was legalized by the Qing government.

We could say that the slow rate of capitalist development in China helps explain the existence of large numbers of unemployed people, while the aggressive imperialism of more developed capitalist countries caused these people to emigrate as indentured or wage workers rather than as agricultural settlers. The labor shortage caused by rapid development in the United States and many European colonies explains why Chinese laborers went to certain places and not others. The very process of emigration itself became closely linked to large companies such as railroad and steamship firms. The inequality of power between China and more advanced Western nations generally resulted in Chinese receiving unequal treatment abroad. The United States, for instance, barred Chinese from citizenship and subsequently excluded most of them by law. The global development of capitalism therefore explains certain features of nineteenth-century emigration, and it should be considered a necessary (though not, by itself, a sufficient) cause of emigration in this period.

NOTES

*This is an adaptation of a paper published in Modern China 5 (October 1979).

1. Under this system, the cost of passage was advanced to an emigrant, who then had to repay his debt from his earnings after finding employment.

2. The well-known expeditions of Zheng He to southeast Asia, India, Persia, Arabia, and Africa in the fifteenth century were politically motivated and did not lead to any significant emigration.

3. The term *coolie* here refers to those laborers who were taken abroad by force, deception, or both. Although very few of the Chinese emigrants who went to California were coolies, some of them had similar backgrounds.

4. Conwell uses the word *coolie* to mean a man who earns his living by doing heavy manual labor. It is unrelated to the emigration in his usage.

5. Some men who participated in the Taiping Revolution might also have left the country in fear of official reprisals; this would also be true of Triad members.

6. A crimp was a middleman who procured coolies through any means available and then transferred them to another agent who shipped them abroad. The transaction could be an outright sale or a commissioned job.

References

Barth, Gunther
1971 Bitter Strength. Cambridge, Mass.: Harvard University Press.
California State Senate
1978 Chinese Immigration: Its Social, Moral and Political Effect. Sacramento.
Campbell, Persia C.
1923 Chinese Coolie Emigration. London: P. S. King.
Chinn, Thomas W., ed.
1973 A History of the Chinese in California. San Francisco: Chinese Historical Society of America.
Chouban yiwu shimo buyi
1839 [Addenda to the Complete Account of our Management of Foreign Affairs].
Conwell, Russell
1871 How and Why. Boston: Lee & Shepard.
Coolidge, Mary R.
1909 Chinese Immigration. New York: Holt.
Fairbank, John K.
1959 Trade and Diplomacy on the China Coast. Cambridge, Mass.: Harvard University Press.
Franck, Harry A.
1925 Roving Through Southern China. New York and London: Century.
Lyman, Stanford
1974 Chinese Americans. New York: Random House.
McLeod, Alexander
1947 Pigtails and Gold Dust. Caldwell, Id: Caxton.
Mei, June Y.
1979 "Socioeconomic origins of emigration: Guangdong to California, 1850-1882," Modern China 5 (October):463-501.
Morse, Hosea B.
1918 The International Relations of the Chinese Empire. Vol. 2. London: Longmans.
Poole, S., and F. Dickens
1894 The Life of Sir Harry Parkes. London: Macmillan.
Qian Xingcun, [A Ying], ed.
1966 Fan Mei huagong jinyue wenxueji [Collected writings of opposition to the U. S. Chinese Exclusion Act]; contains Zhang Weiping (n.d.) "Jinshan pian" ["The Golden Mountains"]. Beijing: People's Publishing House.
Sam Yup Association (Lumei Sanyi zonghuiguan)
1975 Lumei Sanyi zonghuiguan jianshi [A concise history of the main branch of the Sam Yup Association in the United States]. San Francisco.
Stein, Leon, and P. Taft, eds.
1971 Workers Speak. New York: Arno.

Sung, Betty L.
   1967   The Story of the Chinese in America. New York: Collier.
Taishan xianzhi
   1893   [Local gazetteer of Taishan county].
Tanshan huaqiao
   1929   [The Chinese in Hawaii]. Honolulu: Tanshan huaqiao bianyinshe.
Taylor, Bayard
   1949   Eldorado. New York: Alfred A. Knopf.
U. S. Congress
   1877   Report no. 689 (Report of the Joint Special Committee to Investigate Chinese Immigration). Washington, D. C.
Wakeman, Frederic
   1966   Strangers at the Gate. Berkeley, Los Angeles: University of California Press.
Zhu Shijia, ed.
   1959   Meiguo pohai huagong shiliao [Historical source materials on the persecution of Chinese workers by the United States]. Beijing: People's Publishing House.

7

The Causes of Emigration: The Background of Japanese Emigration to Hawaii, 1885 to 1894

Alan Moriyama

Between 1885 and 1894, the period of government-sponsored emigration, twenty-six ships carrying Japanese emigrants landed in Honolulu. Based on the records of the Japanese consulate in Honolulu, the names of the ships, their arrival dates, and the number of emigrants in each are listed in table 7.1.

Although the purpose of this study is not to examine this group of 29,000 emigrants in detail, several characteristics of the particular situation are important in our understanding of its causes. Emigrants went to Hawaii under rules outlined in the labor convention that was signed in Tokyo on January 28, 1886.[1] Thus, responsibility for the welfare of the emigrants before they left Japan lay with the Japanese government, and their lives after reaching Hawaii were in the hands of the Hawaiian government. Labor contracts were signed by the emigrants before leaving Japan.[2] These contracts outlined the conditions of work awaiting the emigrants, their wages, and details about food and medical care. They also guaranteed free passage to Hawaii for the emigrants as well as adequate numbers of inspectors, interpreters, and doctors to help them. All of this was overseen by government-appointed officials until 1894, when the period of emigration company activity began.

Why, after more than two hundred years of isolation and the prohibition of emigration, did the Japanese government begin to allow and even sponsor emigration of laborers to Hawaii?

TABLE 7.1
JAPANESE EMIGRANTS TO HAWAII, 1885 TO 1894

Name of ship	Arrival date	Number of emigrants
City of Tokyo	Feb. 8, 1885	944
Yamashiro Maru	June 17, 1885	988
Peking Maru	Feb. 14, 1886	927
Wakaura Maru	Dec. 11, 1887	1,447
Takasago Maru	June 1, 1888	1,063
Takasago Maru	Nov. 14, 1888	1,081
Takasago Maru	Dec. 26, 1888	1,143
Omi Maru	Mar. 2, 1889	957
Yamashiro Maru	Oct. 1, 1889	997
Yamashiro Maru	Nov. 21, 1889	1,050
Yamashiro Maru	Jan. 9, 1890	1,064
Yamashiro Maru	Apr. 2, 1890	1,071
Yamashiro Maru	May 22, 1890	1,068
Sagami Maru	June 17, 1890	596
Yamashiro Maru	Mar. 11, 1891	1,093
Omi Maru	Mar. 30, 1891	1,081
Yamashiro Maru	Apr. 28, 1891	1,091
Yamashiro Maru	May 29, 1891	1,488
Miike Maru	June 18, 1891	1,101
Yamashiro Maru	Jan. 9, 1892	1,098
Yamashiro Maru	June 25, 1892	1,124
Yamashiro Maru	Nov. 28, 1892	989
Miike Maru	Mar. 6, 1893	729
Miike Maru	June 6, 1893	1,757
Miike Maru	Oct. 9, 1893	1,631
Miike Maru	June 15, 1894	1,491

Total 29,069

SOURCE: Hawai Nihonjin Iminshi Kanko Iinkai, *Hawai Nihonjin iminshi* (Honolulu: Hawaii Nikkeijin Rengō Kyōkai, 1964). pp. 99-100.

ECONOMIC BACKGROUND IN JAPAN

The Japan from which the emigrants to Hawaii left during the period from 1885 to 1894 was a country in which modernization and Westernization were occurring in all spheres of society. Under the threat of American guns, the Japanese shogunate signed a treaty in 1854 to open the country's ports to foreign trade. Subsequently, a series of treaties were concluded between Japan and the encroaching Western powers, opening more ports to trade and towns to foreign residents, fixing import and export duties, and granting extraterritorial rights. Fearful that their country might suffer a fate similar to China's, the new Meiji leaders made a conscious decision to "enrich the country" through the import of Western ideas and technology. A decision had also been made to industrialize the country at the expense of the larger agricultural sector. These decisions as well as events during this period created economic conditions within Japan that would not only affect the reasons a number of Japanese would decide to emigrate overseas but also influence the form that emigration took.

Probably the most important and far-reaching economic factors that affected the farming areas of Japan during this period were the land tax reforms initiated by the new Meiji government in 1873 and the subsequent effects during the deflationary period of the 1880s. The tax reforms affected farmers in a number of significant ways. For example, from 1878 to 1882 this land tax made up 88 percent of all of the direct taxes levied on the agricultural sector.[3] This yearly tax on agricultural land after 1873 became a fixed sum determined by the "legal value" of the land.[4] No longer did the value change from year to year as the value of the crops changed. This tax was also to be paid in money rather than in crops. This change in policy enabled the government to have some idea of the amount of money that would be coming into its coffers yearly. Plans could be made for future expenditures. The result for the average farmer in the following years was mixed. The reforms put the fortunes of the farmers at the mercy of market conditions and the prices their crops could bring. Thus, if the price of rice was high in the marketplace, the farmer would receive more money for his crops, and his fixed taxes would make up a smaller part of his income. But if the price of rice dropped, the farmer would not only get less money for his crops but would also be paying a larger portion of his income for taxes.

This land tax became essential for the industrialization process in Japan during a critical period in which government revenues were necessary for economic development. The money from this land tax accounted for more than half of government revenues until 1900 and over one-third of the revenues during the next fifteen years.[5] It is estimated that throughout this period, the tax burden on agriculture was at least twice that of other sectors.[6]

The early period following the land tax reforms was an inflationary one.[7] There were a number of reasons for this phenomenon, not the least of which was the increased amount of money spent by the central government in suppressing the Satsuma Rebellion in 1877. Over 41 million yen was spent putting down this antigovernment uprising by discontented samurai.[8] The government tried to raise funds by a note issue of 27 million yen.[9]

The Meiji government also spent a great deal of money from 1870 to 1874 paying off the stipends of former samurai. During this five-year period, while administrative expenses were 85.9 million yen and military expenses 39 million yen, the stipends for samurai totaled 88.1 million yen.[10] In all, the amount for bonds issued to pay for these stipends came to over 172.9 million yen.[11]

In addition, a foreign currency exchange had not yet been established, and Japan had problems with the exchange of silver and gold. Another problem was the imbalance of trade Japan suffered as the amount of foreign imports increased every year. Finally, the government spent a great deal of money trying to expand the industrial sector both to solve the problem of unemployed samurai and to lessen the impact of foreign imports. All of these factors resulted in an increased amount of money in circulation and thus contributed to the inflationary trend. An indication of this can be seen in the price index for rice in this period, shown in table 7.2.

Farmers growing rice during this early period did fairly well for themselves. Although the price of commodities rose, the market price of rice either kept pace with or at times rose faster than other prices. This period ended with the deflationary policies instituted by Finance Minister Matsukata beginning in 1881. By cutting down on government expenditures, curtailing the amount of paper money issued, and establishing a foreign silver exchange, the government managed to cool down the economy.[12] In the long run this was an important step in stabilizing the Japanese economy. Yet, it also resulted in severe deflation during the next several years. For example, the commodity price index and the rice price index dropped, as is shown in table 7.3.

There were several results from this deflation. First of all, a large number of farmers found that the low price of rice in conjunction with the fixed land tax made it impossible to survive. Between 1883 and 1890 over 367,000 landholding farmers were dispossessed because of their inability to pay land taxes.[13] This was a period in which a large amount

TABLE 7.2
PRICE INDEX FOR RICE, 1877 TO 1881

1877	100
1878	117
1879	156
1880	203
1881	203

SOURCE: Shindo, "The Inflation," p. 46.

TABLE 7.3
COMMODITY PRICE INDEX AND RICE PRICE INDEX, 1876 TO 1884

	Commodities	Rice
1876	100.0	100.0
1882	140.5	178.8
1883	114.1	129.5
1884	101.9	104.2

SOURCE: Ike, "Taxation," p. 174.

of land became concentrated in the hands of larger landholders who could afford taxes and survive the shift in rice prices.[14] Small landholders became tenant farmers. By 1892, tenant land had risen from 31.10 to 39.99 percent of total cultivated land.[15] Even those who ended up as tenant farmers had made previous attempts to hold on to whatever land they had. Figures show that over 260,000 persons received loans between 1881 and 1886 to pay land taxes.[16]

Because this deflationary period followed an inflationary one, it can be argued that the real income of the farmers and their purchasing power merely reverted back to earlier levels. An index for the real income of tenants shows a range from 100 in 1873 up to 191.3 in 1881 and then back down to 120.8 by 1885.[17] The important point is that the trend beginning in 1881 was downward, and from the point of view of the average farmer it did not seem as though the situation would get any better.

The price of rice kept dropping, and each time this happened, the farmers' situation worsened, with little indication that it would improve in the immediate future. There was probably another effect of the inflationary period, namely, rising expectations for these farmers. They had gone through a period in which they were relatively well-off compared to the price of goods. Suddenly, the situation changed, and farmers seemed worse off than before. For those who had tasted a better life, the thought of reverting back to their former situation must have seemed intolerable. These would be the people who would try different avenues in attempts to regain their prosperity.

The early years of the Meiji period saw the influence of foreign countries on the Japanese economy both in terms of the markets that were available and new imported goods. Several native industries suffered because the Japanese products could not compete with foreign goods in price and quality. This was particularly true of the cotton industry, sugarcane, wax tree and rapeseed oil, and homemade paper products.[18] In several cases foreign products replaced native Japanese products in the home market. Japanese cotton yarn and cotton products were unable to compete with the low price of cotton from foreign countries. One hundred pounds of cotton yarn spun by Japanese cost 42.70 yen in 1874 compared with 29.66 yen for a similar amount of foreign cotton yarn sold in Japan.[19] In the next four years, not only did the Japanese cotton industry fail to close the gap in prices but the difference increased to 45 yen for Japanese cotton compared with 25.46 yen for foreign cotton.[20] Japan's inability to compete with cotton goods from the West indicated a need for modernization in the industry and the construction of new mills. But the modernized cotton industry began to operate on a large scale only after 1885.[21]

One of the few industries to prosper because new markets were being opened in the West was the silk industry. It seems clear that its development was not enough to offset the problems in agriculture. For a number of reasons it was difficult for the silk industry to quickly develop and provide jobs that would absorb large numbers of workers. This industry tended to be quite small-scale. In 1893 only 3 out of 2,602 machine-processing enterprises employed more than 500 workers, and only 121 employed more than 100 workers.[22] As we will see later, most of those hired in the silk mills were female workers, not dislocated farmers.

Another problem for the agricultural sector of the economy was the emphasis on the military and thus the amount of money the central government spent in this area. The influence of these expenses was particularly felt in the inflationary period before 1881. The nation's farmers ended up supporting military exercises not only with their young men who were conscripted into the armed services but also monetarily through payment of their taxes. Even when the army and navy were not involved in a conflict, a large amount of money was needed for the modernization of the army and the expansion of the navy. In the period from 1877 to 1893 the former cost over 197 million yen and the latter over 112 million yen.[23] The Sino-Japanese War in 1894-1895 cost the government more than 233 million yen as well as thousands of Japanese lives.[24] All of this had to be absorbed by the Japanese taxpayers, and it contributed to the growing inflation of the time.

These economic changes played an important role both in influencing the Japanese government to change its policies on overseas emigration and in helping persuade many young Japanese to emigrate abroad. As mentioned earlier, this period saw a sharp rise in the number of foreclosures of land and the number of former landholders who began working as tenant farmers. One estimate concluded that between 1884 and 1886 lands worth over 203 million yen were foreclosed.[25] Farmers who had planted rice expecting the price to continue to rise found themselves victims of the Matsukata deflationary policies. Others, particularly those in textiles, found that competition with Western goods was a disaster. Forced to give up their land, many chose the alternative of working for a landlord. Even this did not solve the economic problems of the farmers. According to one estimate, in the period between 1878 and 1887 the average farmer getting an average price for rice was forced to divide his proceeds as follows: 11.5 percent for the state in the form of taxes, 56.5 percent for the landlord, and 32 percent for himself.[26]

The scale of tenancy at this time is an indication of the severity of the economic situation. It cannot be argued that there is a direct correlation between a growing tenancy rate and the beginning of emigration. Undoubtedly, a number of tenant farmers decided to emigrate, but the figures in table 7.4 seem to show that the prefectures that had the highest percentage of tenant farmers in 1873 and 1892 were not, as will be seen later, the "emigrant prefectures" from which an overwhelmingly large number of emigrants came. Table 7.4 ranks prefectures by the percentage figures of 1892. All of the figures for 1873 are estimates, and several of the prefectures had no reported figures.

Besides the rise in tenancy, the poor economic conditions of the time resulted in a rise in wage labor, especially in the urban centers. Mikio Sumiya in *Social Impact of Industrialization in Japan* points out that the economic conditions of this period resulted in a large number of tenant farmers leaving agriculture in one of three different ways.[27] One way was to work in the countryside, especially in silk manufacturing, silk weaving, and silk spinning. This may have absorbed some surplus labor not only from agriculture but also from the cotton industry, which had been suffering from foreign competition. This particular path probably had little relationship to later emigration because these textile industries tended to hire large numbers of young women. Of the 37,452 workers in 1,068 silk reel mills in 1882, only 2,755 were adult male workers.[28] The remainder were women and children.

Another type of farmer, when faced with impossible conditions in the countryside, merely deserted his family and left his village. Stories in Tokyo newspapers in 1885 reported that thousands of people were on the verge of starvation in the rural areas.[29] An article on Fukuoka prefecture gave an example of one town of eighty households; two-thirds of these families had disposed of their belongings by public auction and were waiting for death.[30] It seems doubtful that those who would later take the chance of traveling to work in a foreign country would be the type to resign themselves to destitution or death.

TABLE 7.4
PERCENTAGE OF TENANCY AMONG FARMERS, 1873 AND 1892

Prefecture	1873	1892
Kagawa	49	63
Toyama	40	60
Osaka	38	57
Tottori	41	54
Shizuoka	33	54
Niigata	41	52
Shimane	43	51
Chiba	18	48
Fukuoka*	43	48
Wakayama	18	47
Akita	15	47
Gifu	27	47
Yamanashi	47	47
Hyogo	42	46
Okayama	27	46
Ehime	49	46
Aiichi	38	45
Tokyo	38	45
Kumamoto*	38	43
Nagasaki	27	42
Fukui	31	42
Tokushima	31	41
Kyoto	35	40
Nara	35-38	39
Kanagawa	49	39
Mie	27	39
Oita	12	39
Hiroshima*	19	38
Yamaguchi*	24	38
Saitama	24	38
Gumma	18	38
Yamagata	34	38
Ishikawa	—	38
Saga	33	36
Nagano	28	36
Ibaragi	19	35
Aomori	12	35
Shiga	—	34
Miyagi	12	32
Tochigi	6	31
Kochi	21	30
Miyazaki	—	29
Kagoshima	—	27
Iwate	11	24
Fukushima	5	22

*"Emigrant" prefectures
SOURCE: Hideichi Horie, "The Agricultural Structure of Japan in the period of Meiji Restoration (2)", *Kyoto University Economic Review* 32.1 (April 1962):15.

The final path chosen may have had more of a relationship with the type of thinking and initiative shown by later Japanese who emigrated abroad. Sumiya points out that a large number of young men left the farms to work in remote factories and mines.[31] These were the type of workers who would form the basis of the urban labor force. For our purposes, the formation of this group of workers represents an important step in the development of internal migration patterns in Japan.

Studies of villages in the Tokugawa period (1601 to 1867) have indicated the effects of permanent and temporary migration on fertility and population increases in the countryside.[32] It is important to note that temporary migration (*dekasegi rōdō*) of workers to towns and cities on a labor contract of a year or longer began in Tokugawa Japan.[33] This type of labor migration had other characteristics that would also be noticeable in emigration to Hawaii. Hanley and Yamamura have pointed out in *Economic and Demographic Change in Preindustrial Japan 1600-1868* that not only were these migrating workers young and single but it was not unusual for heads of families to leave their villages.[34]

Whereas in the Tokugawa period survivors of economic crisis occasionally traveled to find jobs, in the Meiji period there was an increase in the number of young workers leaving the countryside for work in the cities. In terms of later patterns, the important legacy of this internal migration is not that these workers were going to the cities but that they were willing to leave their villages and travel to a distant place to find work. Although it is impossible to prove that those who eventually left Japan to work in Hawaii had previously migrated to work in Japanese cities, it seems reasonable to assume that the rise of internal migration at least gave some legitimacy to this process. Thus, overseas migration, though certainly different in many ways from its predecessor, nevertheless would be acceptable as a means of temporarily solving specific economic problems in the countryside. There might have been in existence a type of "two-stage migration." Individuals who migrated internally may have been more apt to move overseas in later years because they would have understood the necessity of finding new jobs even if it meant traveling abroad.

Although this study does not deal with the effects of natural disasters and climate on the crops during this period, we might keep in mind that at crucial points in time, a series of crop disasters or a particularly devastating typhoon might have been sufficient to force farmers to leave their villages and seek their fortunes elsewhere. There is evidence to suggest that during the period from 1879 to 1888, the year 1884, just before the start of emigration to Hawaii, saw the worst crop harvests in a long time.[35] This is a generalization for harvests nationwide, and it is difficult to say exactly what influences it had on farmers deciding whether to go to Hawaii; but it is safe to say that it could have had some effect.

CONSCRIPTION AND EMIGRATION

Several writers, particularly Yamato Ichihashi, have alleged that a number of Japanese went abroad to evade the national conscription law.[36] Whether this was in fact a major factor in emigrating to Hawaii during this early period must be considered in detail.

Japan's national conscription law was promulgated on January 10, 1873 and went through changes in 1879, 1883, 1889, and 1906. The changes involved several different areas, but for our purposes the important one is that of exemptions in the conscription system. Gotaro Ogawa in *Conscription System in Japan*[37] has noted that these changes followed the pattern of progressively reducing the types of exemptions granted. Apparently, Japanese were taking advantage of every type of exemption in such numbers that changes had to be made to insure an adequate supply of men for the armed forces.

There were two important types of exemptions that may have affected emigrants. The first dealt with Japanese who were not in Japan at the time they were either to register for conscription or to be physically examined for enlistment. Since there were no emigrants abroad in 1873, those exempted were Japanese studying abroad. By 1879 this was extended to those living abroad for study or for business.

For emigrants, their staying abroad was, in fact, postponing or avoiding altogether their entry into the conscription system. Therefore, for men who for one reason or another did not want to be conscripted, the alternative was to go overseas and stay there until after the age of thirty-two, when they would be too old to be drafted.

There was another area of exemptions that may have influenced emigration. The earliest conscription law also excused from enrollment "heads of families," "heirs and lineal grandsons," and "the only son and grandson." This was intended to preserve the Japanese family system and to provide a labor supply for agriculture. As we will note elsewhere in this study, a large number of heads of families and first-born sons emigrated to Hawaii. The reasons for this phenomenon might lie in a desire to evade conscription by using the exemption system. For example, by sending abroad the first-born son who was of conscription age and designating a younger son as the heir to the family, it would have been possible to "protect" two sons from conscription.

Ogawa's study made two important points. First, as the needs of the military increased, the government was willing to cut the number and types of exemptions even if it meant hurting and breaking up the traditional Japanese family. Second, he saw several effects of the conscription system that might explain the attempts to evade conscription even in peacetime. First and foremost, conscription meant a serious loss of labor in the countryside. Further, during this time members of the Japanese army were getting such low wages that soldiers were receiving money from home in order to pay for daily expenses. It was estimated that this loss of labor and the amount of money sent to the average soldier represented a loss of about 200 yen per individual conscripted.

We can expect that the attitudes and subsequent attempts at evasion would change over time depending not only on international events but also on people's perceptions about the possibility of being called into active service. One might guess that this became more of a factor after 1894, when the Sino-Japanese War started. Whether large numbers of Japanese farming families were able to perceive the possibilities of using emigration abroad as a way of protecting an additional member of the family is difficult to say without more documentation. In any case there is no evidence to suggest that this was a major cause of overseas migration.

CONDITIONS IN THE PREFECTURES

A survey of national conditions would be sufficient for our purposes if it could be shown that those Japanese who chose to emigrate to Hawaii came randomly from various areas of Japan. The argument would be that the general conditions of the time may have had much to do with why people chose to emigrate. Figures show, however, that a large majority of emigrants came from specific prefectures in southwestern Japan.

Of the first shipment of government-sponsored emigrants to Hawaii in 1885, most came from Yamaguchi, Hiroshima, Kanagawa, Okayama, and Wakayama prefectures.[38] The majority of passengers on the second ship to Hawaii came from Hiroshima, Kumamoto, and Fukuoka prefectures.[39] Of 20,651 emigrants who traveled to Hawaii from 1889 to 1894, 36 percent were from Hiroshima prefecture.[40] Yamaguchi emigrants made up 34 percent of the emigrants, followed by Kumamoto with 20 percent and Fukuoka with 8 percent.[41] This trend continued throughout the government contract period and into the period of emigration company activity. By 1960, when the Japanese consulate conducted a survey in Hawaii of first-generation immigrants, it was found

Fig. 7.1
Four Emigrant Prefectures.

that 24 percent were from Hiroshima, 20 percent from Yamaguchi, 14 percent from Okinawa, 13 percent from Kumamoto, and 5 percent from Fukuoka.[42]

One of the fundamental questions in Japanese emigration history centers on this point. Why were the overwhelming majority of emigrants from a few selected prefectures in Japan? What was so special about those areas that induced, persuaded, pressured, or forced thousands of Japanese to emigrate overseas? We have seen earlier that these prefectures did not have the highest rate of tenancy. Were there other factors that set these prefectures apart? Although these areas in southwestern Japan were not industrial centers and were not agriculturally well developed, one cannot argue that, as a whole, this was the poorest area of Japan and, thus, emigrants left. During this period the prefectures in northern Japan, the Tōhoku region, suffered the most economically. The question is, If poor economic conditions have a correlation with the number of people emigrating, why did so few emigrants come from the Tōhoku area?

This question can be answered in several different ways. One might argue that those who tended to go abroad were not of the poorest classes. In other words, emigrating abroad was an investment spread over a period of at least three years, and there was not going to be an immediate windfall of money. Prospective emigrants were not paid for their labor before going abroad. What money that was sent back to their families was saved from individuals' pay each month. Thus, if a farming family could not survive economically for at least a year, when remittances were received, it would have been of little benefit to send someone to Hawaii.

Another way of examining this problem would be not to look at the prefectures in southwestern Japan but at those in the Tōhoku region. The question would be changed from, why did the emigrants come from Hiroshima, Yamaguchi, and Kumamoto prefectures? to why didn't emigrants come from Aomori, Yamagata, and Akita prefectures?

The problem has always been that the people of this region did not travel to Hawaii and North America. This does not mean that unlike farmers in southwestern Japan, these farmers in the Tōhoku region did not migrate elsewhere. Large numbers of these people, rather than traveling east, instead went north to the island of Hokkaido. The central government had tried to persuade more Japanese farmers to go to Hokkaido and take part in the development of this frontier area. Thus, an examination of the birthplaces of Japanese shows that in addition to the urban centers in the Kanto and the Kinki areas, only Hokkaido had a substantial proportion of its population born elsewhere.[43] Irene Taeuber found that according to the 1920 census, nine-tenths of the population of Hokkaido born in other prefectures were from the Tōhoku area, mainly from the prefectures of Aomori, Iwate, Miyagi, Akita, Yamagata, and Fukushima.[44] Others were from Niigata, Toyama, Ishikawa, Fukui, and Gifu prefectures in central Japan.

The question still remains, why did so many emigrants come from southwestern Japan? One important factor may have been the size of the landholdings in different prefectures. In a survey conducted by the Ministry of Agriculture and Commerce in 1888, it was noted that in terms of the average size of farmland owned and rented (tenancy), Hiroshima prefecture had the smallest amount of land per household and per individual.[45] Two other emigrant prefectures, Yamaguchi and Fukuoka, had landholdings at about the national average.

The same survey reported the percentage of large and small land-holders in different prefectures, dividing them into three categories: those who held more than 3.67 acres of land, those whose holdings ranged between 3.67 acres and 1.96 acres, and those whose landhold-ings were less than 1.96 acres.[46] The national average per category was 15 percent, 30 percent, and 55 percent, respectively. In Hiroshima 70 percent of the landholders fell into the category of the smallest farmers. Only one other prefecture, Hyōgo, which was principally urban, had a higher percentage. The size of average landholdings during this period could have played a significant role in influencing emigrants from Hiro-shima to travel abroad.

Another part of the answer may be found in the recruitment practices preceding the early shipments to Hawaii and in the three-cornered rela-tionship between Foreign Minister Inoue Kaoru; the head of Mitsui Bussan, Masuda Takashi; and R. W. Irwin, the Hawaiian consul in Japan. Beginning in 1876 Irwin served as an adviser to Mitsui Bussan, one of Japan's large trading companies.[47] After becoming consul in 1884 Irwin was put in charge of recruitment in Japan. He was advised where to recruit by his business associate, Masuda, and by his close personal friend, Inoue.[48] Both Inoue and Masuda were originally from Yamagu-chi prefecture, and both were concerned about the poor economic con-ditions there. Inoue suggested that the emphasis on recruitment be placed in the prefectures of Yamaguchi, Hiroshima, and Kumamoto.[49] According to the official history of Mitsui Bussan, Masuda directed some of his company employees to go to Yamaguchi, Hiroshima, Fuku-oka, and Kumamoto to help recruit emigrants.[50] This apparently fit the instructions sent to Irwin by the Hawaiian government, which specifi-cally asked that Irwin recruit Japanese workers from the countryside who had experience in farming.[51] The result was that Irwin went to those areas, and recruitment in the initial stages was conducted in southwestern Japan.

Although Inoue was the foreign minister at the time and both Mas-uda and Irwin had close ties with the central government, it does not seem that the emphasis on emigration from southwestern Japan was in any way a part of official government policy. One historian has charac-terized this process and the subsequent developments as follows:

In regard to recruiting emigrants the Japanese government made stren-uous efforts, first tentatively, to recruit from specific sections of the nation where living standards suffered from overpopulation. However, the result of the initial shipments to Hawaii was a predominance of

emigrants from prefectures . . . like Hiroshima, Yamaguchi, Kumamoto, and Niigata. Thus, the government proceeded to recruit entirely
from those prefectures.[52]

It is easier to understand how the situation continued throughout the
succeeding decades after the initial pattern of emigrant prefectures was
set. Letters and accounts of success abroad would be most noticeable in
the home villages of emigrants, and this in turn would lead to more
emigrants from the same areas. The following concerns an emigrant on
the first ship to Hawaii who sent a large amount of money back to
Japan:

> Iwase Kansuke, a forty-five year old resident of Ōshima in Yamaguchi
> prefecture, emigrated to Hawaii on the very first ship. On November
> 27, 1886 he sent back to his home the sum of 129 yen, 24 sen, 8 rin.
> This money was sent by way of the town office. . . . At that time rice
> sold for 3 yen 80 sen per 60 kilogram bag . . . and yet one man, in less
> than ten months, was able to send back almost 130 yen. This was an
> accomplishment beyond the imagination of the other people of the
> island. Rumors quickly spread throughout the island; everyone's imag-
> ination was seized with the idea of emigrating to Hawaii to make
> money.[53]

One study of emigration from a specific area of Wakayama prefecture
showed that out of a total of 432 prospective emigrants, 25 percent gave
as their reason for being attracted to emigration "being stimulated by
seeing neighbors who have emigrated, returning in affluent circumstances."[54] Another 19 percent mentioned the "prevailing tendency in
the village to emigrate," and 11 percent were "exhorted by emigrants
residing abroad and inland." The combination of these three categories
gives a total of 55 percent, far more than the 21 percent seeking wealth
or the 19 percent trying to better their lives.

Although these may be the major reasons that certain prefectures
had an overwhelmingly high percentage of emigrants who traveled to
Hawaii, another level of analysis must be undertaken in order to look at
who the emigrants were. This is best done on the local level — that of
the individual villages.

EMIGRATION AT THE VILLAGE LEVEL

From material gathered from one source on the local level, particularly that dealing with one village, it is not always possible to take data
and make credible generalizations about emigrants as a whole and the

local conditions from which they left. The following data may not be sufficient to make generalizations to the extent I had hoped, but they nevertheless offer a valuable picture of local conditions that gave rise to the phenomenon of emigration.

One study examined the village of Kuchida in Hiroshima prefecture in terms of early emigration to Hawaii.[55] Statistics show that this was very clearly an "emigrant village" not only because many, 288 persons, emigrated but also because the number of villagers abroad during the period from 1898 to 1916 averaged 10.2 percent of the village population. The village was agricultural: out of 388 households, 278 were primarily and 50 were partially involved in the raising of crops. In 1898, 60 of the households owned the land they farmed while the other 268 households both farmed their own land and worked as tenant farmers.

Most of the land was used for growing rice. Other crops included millet, jute, indigo, and sweet potatoes. Although jute and indigo decreased in importance to the village, this change took place only after 1900. Very few of the households were involved in cottage industries or handicrafts. Most of the farms were very small. In the period after 1887, 55.5 percent of the holdings were less than about 0.7 acres. This is low compared to the national average. In 1888 the survey taken by the Ministry of Agriculture and Commerce showed that the national average landholding per family was about 2.40 acres and the average holdings in Hiroshima prefecture about 1.42 acres.[56]

There was no tradition of internal migration from the village, but with so many of the village farmers close to the poverty line, any change in the village economic structure meant that people had to leave in order to survive. The problem in this particular area was that there was no way this surplus labor could be absorbed within the village or in nearby factories. For the villagers during this period the only option left was emigration to Hawaii.

Another study of the village of Jigozen, again in Hiroshima prefecture, reported similar results.[57] In this case, a 1925 survey found that 50.8 percent of the village population was overseas and that there was an average of two emigrants per household. Once again, the village was composed mostly of farmers, with a sizable number also involved in fishing. About half of the emigrants were primarily farmers before they left. Shedding some light on the causes of emigration is the fact that between 1880 and 1890 the amount of cultivated land decreased more than 50 percent, and the crop yield decreased about 75 percent. Crops grown in the village included rye, rice, and sweet potatoes. The number of tenant farmers was high, and in 1885 tenant farmers worked 53.5 percent of the land under cultivation. This was considerably higher than the national average of 31.75 percent, and among those other than landholders who decided to emigrate, most were tenant farmers who did not own any land.

A third study looked at the village of Kuga on the island of Ōshima in Yamaguchi prefecture.[58] This area was of particular importance for emigration to Hawaii between 1885 and 1894. Of the 945 emigrants on the first ship to Hawaii, almost a third were from the island of Ōshima, and 35 were from this very village. It was estimated in 1967 that between 10,000 and 15,000 descendants of Ōshima emigrants lived in Hawaii. The village tended to be agricultural, with 35 percent of its prospective emigrants primarily involved in farming and another 35 percent involved in both farming and various other types of work. A closer examination of the emigrants who left in 1885, 1886, and 1887 showed that the number of farmers increased, particularly in 1887, when they were 50 percent emigrants. Figures also show that most of those who emigrated were tenant farmers and did not own land.

These village studies offer more than a look at the local conditions that led people to emigrate. If emigrants tended to be farmers rather than wage laborers, young rather than old, men rather than women, the reasons for emigration become clearer.

As with other groups of Asian emigrants, the Japanese who went to Hawaii tended overwhelmingly to be male. The study of Jigozen shows that from 1885 to 1894, 75 percent of the emigrants were men. The data from the study of Kuchida reveals that during the same period 81 percent of the emigrants were male. The survey of Kuga is somewhat more restricted and has data only for the years 1885 to 1887, but those show that 73 percent of the emigrants were male. These were not isolated examples. The percentage of males in the entire first shipment of emigrants in 1885 was 71.[59] During the first eight years of emigration to Hawaii, males averaged 80 percent of emigrants, as can be seen in table 7.5.

There were several reasons so many were male. Many of the Japanese emigrants saw this travel overseas as a variation of internal migration patterns. Thus, emigration even as far away as Hawaii was seen as temporary. Most of these emigrants were young, and most were not yet married. Others, intending to return immediately after their three-year contracts were over, decided to leave their wives and families at home. The Hawaiian government and its recruiters in Japan made no special effort to recruit women because there were no specific jobs on sugar plantations that required large numbers of women.[60]

There were a number of effects from this predominance of males among the emigrants. It resulted in an unequal sex distribution pattern in the Japanese population in Hawaii. It took decades before the male-

TABLE 7.5
PERCENTAGE OF MALE EMIGRANTS GOING TO HAWAII, 1885 TO 1892

Year	Percentage of male emigrants
1885	83
1886	75
1887	80
1888	82
1889	82
1890	81
1891	73
1892	87

SOURCE: Yoshida, "Meiji shoki," pp. 258-259.

TABLE 7.6
POPULATION OF JAPANESE IN HAWAII

Year	Male	Female
1890	10,219	2,391
1896	19,212	5,195
1900	47,508	13,603
1910	54,784	24,891
1920	62,644	46,630
1930	75,008	64,623

SOURCE: Ichihashi, *Japanese*, pp. 31-32.

female ratio was balanced, as can be seen in table 7.6. During these years those Japanese emigrants who decided to stay abroad either returned to find brides willing to travel to Hawaii or they sent for "picture brides." From 1907 to 1923 over 14,000 picture brides entered Hawaii.[61] In the early years of emigration almost all of the women who went were accompanied by their husbands. Only later did others join their husbands. It was for this reason that the second generation of Japanese developed later than expected in Hawaii.

Another characteristic of this group of emigrants was their age range. From the different village studies it is clear that most of the men who emigrated abroad were young. The Kuchida data show that 41.4 percent of the men were in their twenties and 27 percent were in their thirties. Over 62 percent of the women were in their twenties. A few of the emigrants were in their late teens, and several were in their forties. As with women of all ages, there seemed to be no market for older male workers. The survey of emigrants from Jigozen revealed that 60 percent of the men were in their twenties and 25 percent were in their thirties. The women from that village tended to follow the same pattern

— 63 percent were in their twenties and 18 percent were in their thirties. Forty-five percent of the emigrant men from Kuga were in their twenties and 26 percent were in their thirties. Of the twenty-seven women who emigrated, only four were teenagers, and none was older than thirty-nine.

As with the case of the sex of the emigrants it is not difficult to understand why those who chose to emigrate tended to be young. The sugar planters in Hawaii obviously wanted young men who could work efficiently for the duration of the three-year contracts in the sugar fields. In addition, there is evidence that the age range of the emigrants might have been partially influenced by the recruitment methods carried on in certain parts of Japan. A recruitment announcement issued by the governor of Hiroshima prefecture in 1889 stated that the age of prospective emigrants was to be between twenty and thirty.[62] It is not difficult to see that more adventuresome younger men would be attracted to overseas emigration.

Another characteristic of these Japanese is the position of the emigrant within his family. In other words, was the emigrant a head of a family, an eldest son, or a second or third son? One theory of Japanese emigration has argued that those who went overseas tended to be "non-successors rather than successors."[63] The argument is that few emigrants would have been heads of families or even first sons. Rather, those who did not stand to inherit in a society based on primogeniture — second or third sons — would be released to travel overseas to work. This seems to be the general pattern of *dekasegi rōdō*. Heads of families and first sons continued to work on the farms and carry on the family name. Surplus workers, whether they were younger brothers or sisters, would be available to work elsewhere and remit money to the family.

Although this theory may be attractive, it does not hold true for the villages that have been studied. In Kuchida from 1885 to 1897, 37.1 percent of the emigrants were heads of families, 10.7 percent were wives of heads of families, and 21.5 percent were eldest sons. In this case the classic "non-successors" made up no more than 30 percent of the emigrant population.[64] In Jigozen, 30.1 percent were heads of families, 23.3 percent wives, and 20.8 percent eldest sons. Second, third, and fourth sons made up only 15 percent. For Kuga in Yamaguchi prefecture 38.9 percent were heads of families, 23.8 percent were wives, 15 percent were eldest sons, and only 6 percent were second, third, and fourth sons.

Although the number of villages studied is quite limited, the evidence thus far indicates that successors or established members of families went as emigrants to Hawaii. This does not necessarily negate the argument that emigration served as a release for surplus labor in the countryside. Families who could send members abroad were better off in terms of the number of mouths to feed at home and the prospect of money coming in from overseas. In that regard it may not matter which member of the family left. The large percentage of successors may indicate that overseas emigration was seen by the emigrants themselves as well as by the emigrant families to be a case of temporary work. It is probable that if these Japanese families had felt that the emigrants would be staying for longer than their initial contracts or perhaps never returning, there would have been a larger percentage of nonsuccessors sent from the villages. Heads of families and eldest sons would have been expected to return to the farms and carry on the family name.

One indication of the nature of this early emigration is seen in the number of emigrants who returned to Japan and when they came. Data from specific emigrant villages show that a small percentage of emigrants did, in fact, return. Of the 288 emigrants from Kuchida, 147 did not return at all. Several returned before their contracts were over, but most returned two or three years after the end of their initial three-year contracts. This trend held true for the 793 emigrants from Jigozen village, where 318 emigrants did not return. In terms of the 113 emigrants from Kuga, 53 did not return. A survey of 19,074 emigrants taken in 1894 found that in the period up to 1891, 34 percent or 6,652 emigrants returned to Japan.[65] A similar survey taken of 10,404 Hiroshima emigrants in 1941 found that 2,629 or 25 percent returned to Japan.[66] In both cases the majority of emigrants settled in Hawaii, and a small number, no more than 3 or 4 percent, went to the mainland United States.

The above data seem to suggest two things seemingly contradictory in their implications. It seems that most emigrants left their villages intending to return after a short stay overseas; yet a large number of them decided to settle in Hawaii. There can be two explanations for a phenomenon like this. One is that emigrants who had originally intended to return found that it was more difficult to save money in Hawaii than they had expected. Thus, they signed up for a second or third contract, moved into other jobs, or left for the mainland United States. The opposite explanation is that these emigrants found it extremely profitable to work in Hawaii. They were able to send money back to their families, and from the point of view of their own futures as well as the fortunes of their families in Japan, it was better to settle in Hawaii. An examination of wages and remittances offers some clues.

WAGES AND REMITTANCES

Given the type of economic conditions pointed out earlier in this paper, it does not seem unusual that emigrants from the Japanese countryside would be seeking a temporary form of economic relief by traveling overseas. There was of course another side to this issue. Japanese emigrants had to be attracted to working in Hawaii. Initially, only 600 emigrants were to be sent on the first ship to Hawaii. Because over 28,000 applications were received, however, 945 emigrants were sent on the first ship.[67] The reason for this enthusiasm was the wage difference between the sugar plantations in Hawaii and the Japanese countryside. The contracts of the sugar planters in the beginning stipulated wages of $9.00 a month. Later this was raised to $15.00 a month. The rate of exchange at the time was about 85¢ per yen.[68] Thus, at most the wages in Hawaii represented about 17.65 yen per month. Table 7.7 presents examples of the wages for several types of occupations in Japan at the time (1 yen equals 100 sen).

Japanese workers going to Hawaii used the phrase "400 yen in three years," meaning that they intended to save a total of 400 yen out of their wages and return to Japan.[69] Of course it was optimistic to think of saving 11 yen out of wages of less than 18 yen per month. Yet, it was certainly more realistic than accumulating 400 yen out of the wages cited in table 7.7. The day laborer would have to work almost seven years and the silk mill worker ten years without spending any of their wages to accumulate 400 yen.

Another example that illustrates the importance of this economic motive is the method used by emigrants to save money and benefit their home villages. Saving on all levels of society was a long-established tradition in Japan, and the accumulation of capital in the Meiji period was partially a result of wide-scale savings. For the emigrants, all the indications are that saving was an important part of their going abroad and their work in Hawaii. The contracts signed by the emigrants stipulated that 25 percent of their wages would be held by the Japanese consul in Honoulu until their time to return to Japan.[70] This not only guaranteed return fare home but also meant a sizable sum in what could best be termed "forced savings."

Most of the money sent to the Japanese villages was saved voluntarily by the emigrants. Remittances sent to the island of Ōshima in Yamaguchi prefecture from those who left on three ships to Hawaii are shown in table 7.8. These emigrants left from 1885 to 1887, so these sums represent money sent over a period of five to seven years. Of course not all of the emigrants may have been sending money back to their villages,

TABLE 7.7
JOBS AND WAGES IN JAPAN

Occupation	Sen/day	Yen/month
Roof tile maker	26	7.8
Carpenter	21	6.3
Printing typesetter	21	6.3
Day laborer	16	4.8
Silk mill worker (female)	11	3.3
Farmer (female)	10	3.0

SOURCE: Kaigai ijū jigyōdan, *Kaigai ijū jigyōdan jūnenshi* (Tokyo: Kaigai ijū jigyōdan, 1973), p. 5.

TABLE 7.8
REMITTANCES FROM HAWAII, 1885 TO 1892

Number of emigrants in specific villages	Total amount of remittances until 1892	Average per emigrant
7	250.274 yen	35.753 yen
48	4550.205	94.795
37	2238.328	60.495
27	914.495	33.870
58	3231.624	55.717
61	3224.320	52.857
133	7815.915	58.766
25	1594.450	63.778
6	309.393	51.565
15	2005.720	133.714
14	2068.523	147.751
3	128.353	42.784
24	2048.806	85.366
43	2130.233	49.540
72	3177.533	44.132
8	270.178	33.772
		Average 65.291

SOURCE: Doi, "Yamaguchi-ken," p. 808.

and a number of them may have returned to their homes during this period. Still, on an average these emigrants were sending back substantial sums of money.

This remitting of money took place for other areas of Japan, resulting in a significant amount of money being invested in Japan's rural areas. The total amount of money sent back from emigrants in Hawaii from 1892 to 1902 is shown in table 7.9.

TABLE 7.9
REMITTANCES FROM HAWAII, 1892 TO 1902

Year	Amount of remittances
1892	$ 125,629
1893	434,928
1894	532,163
1895	484,619
1896	660,950
1897	776,527
1898	841,637
1899	1,380,705
1900	1,846,042
1901	2,462,933
1902	2,582,728
Total	$12,128,861

SOURCE: Doi, "Yamaguchi-ken," p. 842.

The amounts of money sent back seem to suggest that of the two explanations for emigrants not returning to the Japanese villages, that of finding work in Hawaii too profitable to return even after their contracts were over seems to fit the case of a majority of emigrants in the early years.

CONCLUSION

In the early years of the Meiji period, government leaders pursued a policy of industrialization at the expense of the agricultural sector. With the severe deflationary period after 1881, a series of changes took place in the Japanese countryside. This led to smaller landholdings and increased dislocation in the rural areas. Some farmers turned to tenancy, others became wage laborers, and still others gave up farming altogether.

These economic changes in Japan, the beginning of recruitment by the Hawaiian sugar planters, and the perception of overseas emigration as a legitimate alternative to a life of tenancy resulted in overseas emigration. All of this came together in 1885, and those Japanese who chose to work in Hawaii became the first generation of Japanese in America.

NOTES

1. The events leading up to the signing of the labor convention are best summed up in Hilary Conroy, *The Japanese Frontier in Hawaii* (Berkeley and Los Angeles: University of California Press, 1953). A copy of the labor convention can be found in the same volume. For a brief summary of the needs of the sugar planters and the ways in which they recruited workers, see my article, "The 1909 and 1920 Strikes of Japanese Sugar Plantation Workers in Hawaii," Emma Gee, ed., *Counterpoint* (Los Angeles: UCLA Asian American Studies Center, 1976), pp. 169-180.

2. Samples of early labor contracts can be found in Conroy (1953) and in Doi Yatarō, "Yamaguchi-ken Ōshima-gun ni okeru Hawai imin-shi," *Yamaguchi daigaku nōgakubu gakujutsu hōkoku* 8 (1957): 773-849.

3. James Nakamura, *Agricultural Production and the Economic Development of Japan, 1873-1922* (Princeton: Princeton University Press, 1966), p. 160.

4. Nobutaka Ike, "Taxation and Landownership in the Westernization of Japan," *The Journal of Economic History* 7 (November 1947):164-165.

5. Henry Rosovsky, *Capital Formation in Japan, 1868-1940* (Glencoe: Free Press, 1961), p. 85.

6. Ibid.

7. See Motokazu Shindo, "The Inflation in the Early Meiji Era," *Kyoto University Economic Review* 24 (October 1954):41-46.

8. Giichi Ono, *War and Armament Expenditures of Japan* (New York: Oxford University Press, 1922), p. 263.

9. Kazushi Ohkawa and Henry Rosovsky, "A Century of Japanese Economic Growth," in William Lockwood, ed., *The State and Economic Enterprise in Japan* (Princeton: Princeton University Press, 1965), p. 63.

10. W. G. Beasley, *The Meiji Restoration* (Stanford: Stanford University Press, 1972), p. 381.

11. Ohkawa and Rosovsky, "A Century," p. 63.

12. Shindo, "The Inflation," pp. 51-56.

13. Ike, "Taxation," p. 175.

14. John Dower, *Origins of the Modern Japanese State: Selected Writings of E. H. Norman* (New York: Pantheon Books, 1975), p. 253. Original from E. H. Norman's *Japan's Emergence as a Modern State* (New York: Institute of Pacific Relations, 1940).

15. Ike, "Taxation," p. 177.

16. Ibid., p. 175.

17. Morris David Morris, "The Problem of the Peasant Agriculturalist in Meiji Japan," *Far Eastern Quarterly* 15 (May 1956):361.

18. Irene B. Taeuber, *The Population of Japan* (Princeton: Princeton University Press, 1958), p. 39.

19. Yasuzo Horie, "The Development of the Domestic Market in the Early Years of Meiji," *Kyoto University Economic Review* 15 (January 1940):51.

20. Ibid.

21. Keishi Ohara, ed., *Japanese Trade and Industry in the Meiji-Taisho Era*, Tamotsu Okata, trans. (Tokyo: Ōbunsha, 1957), pp. 327-340.

22. Mikio Sumiya, *Social Impact of Industrialization in Japan* (Tokyo: Japanese National Commission of UNESCO, 1963), pp. 12-13.

23. Ono, *War and Armament*, pp. 41-46.

24. Ibid., p. 277.

25. Ike, "Taxation," p. 176.

26. Ibid., p. 170.

27. Sumiya, *Social Impact*, pp. 24-25.

28. Ibid., p. 33.

29. Ōno Takeo, *Gendai Nihon bunmeishi, dai-kyūkan; nōsonshi* (Tokyo: Tōyō keizai shinpōsha, 1942), pp. 178-181.

30. Ibid.

31. Sumiya, *Social Impact*, pp. 24-25.

32. Susan B. Hanley and Kozo Yamamura, *Economic and Demographic Change in Preindustrial Japan 1600-1868* (Princeton: Princeton University Press, 1977), pp. 252-255.

33. Ibid., p. 254.

34. Ibid., pp. 254-255.

35. Nakamura, *Agricultural Production*, p. 72.

36. Yamato Ichihashi, *Japanese in the United States* (New York: Arno Press and New York Times, 1969), pp. 87-88.

37. Gotaro Ogawa, *Conscription System in Japan* (New York: Oxford University Press, 1921).

38. Irie Toraji, *Hōjin Kaigai hattenshi* (Tokyo: Ida Shoten, 1942), p. 57; and James Okahata, *A History of the Japanese of Hawaii* (Honolulu: The United Japanese Society of Hawaii, 1971), pp. 117-118.

39. Ibid.

40. Yoshida Hideo, "Meiji shoki no Hawai dekasegi," pt. 1, *Takushoku ronsō* 3 (1941):253-305; and part 2, *Takushoku ronsō* 3 (1941):260-264.

41. Ibid.

42. Hawai Nihonjin Iminshi Kanko Iinkai, *Hawai Nihonjin iminshi* (Honolulu: Hawai Nikkeijin Rengō Kyōkai, 1964), p. 124.

43. Taeuber, *Population*, p. 124.

44. Ibid., p. 174.

45. Tōgō Minoru, *Nihon shokuminron* (Tokyo: Bunbudō, 1906), pp. 141-143.

46. Information in this paragraph is from Tōgō, *Nihon,* pp. 137-139.

47. Kawazoe Zen'ichi, *Imin hyakunen no nenrin* (Honolulu: Imin hyakunen no nenrin kankō kai, 1968), p. 91.

48. Ibid.

49. Wakayama-ken, *Wakayama-ken iminshi* (Wakayama-shi: Wakayama-ken, 1957).

50. Kawazoe, *Hyakunen,* p. 93. See also Matsunaga, "Hawai imin."

51. Conroy, *Japanese Frontier,* pp. 82-83.

52. Kihara Ryūkichi, *Hawai Nihonjinshi* (Tokyo: Bunseisha, 1935), p. 439. My translation.

53. Kawazoe, *Hyakunen,* p. 93. I have shortened the passage in my translation.

54. Iwasaki Kenkichi, "Kii hanto minami kaigan ni okeru kaigai dekasegi imin no kenkyū," part 2, *Chirigaku hyōron* 13 (1937):200.

55. Ishikawa Tomonori, "Hiroshima-ken nambu kuchida-son keiyaku imin no shakai chirigakuteki kōsatsu," *Shigaku kenkyū* 99 (February 1967): 33-52.

56. Tōgō, *Shokuminron,* pp. 141-143.

57. Ishikawa Tomonori, "Hiroshima-wangan jigozen-son keiyaku imin no shakai chirigakuteki kōsatsu," *Jinbun chiri* 19 (February 1967): 75-91.

58. Ishikawa Tomonori, "Yamaguchi-ken Ōshima-gun kuga-son shoki Hawai keiyaku imin no shakai chirigakuteki kōsatsu," *Chiri kagaku* 7 (June 1967): 25-38.

59. Irie, *Hōjin kaigai,* p. 57; and Conroy, *Japanese Frontier,* p. 154.

60. According to Katherine Coman, "The History of Contract Labor in the Hawaiian Islands," *Publications of the American Economic Association,* 3d series, 4 (August 1903):42, when the Hawaiian government first tried to reopen emigration in 1879, its initial draft of the contracts stipulated that 40 percent of the emigrants were to be women. This was not put into later official contracts.

61. Okahata, *A History,* pp. 165-166.

62. Gaimushō ryōji ijūbu, *Kaigai iju hyakunen no ayumi* (n.p.:1968), p. 22.

63. Philip Staniford, "Nihon ni itemo sho ga nai: The Background, Strategies and Personalities of Rural Japanese Overseas Immigrants" (n.p., n.d.), mimeographed. While there is no date on this essay, it seems clear that it predates Philip Staniford, *Pioneers in the Tropics* (London: Athlone Press, 1973).

64. Ishikawa, "Kuchida-son," p. 41. If we do not include brothers, adopted children, and so on, the number is smaller. Second, third, fourth, and fifth sons made up only 22 percent of the total.

65. See Conroy, *Japanese Frontier*, p. 154 for the results of the first shipment of emigrants from Japan. Of those emigrants, about 700 returned to Japan by 1894.

66. Yoshida, "Meiji shoki," pp. 296-297.

67. Irie, *Hōjin kaigai*, p. 57.

68. Ishikawa, "Jigozen-son," p. 85.

69. Kaigai ijū jigyōdan, *Kaigai ijū jigyōdan jūnenshi* (Tokyo: Kaigai ijū jigyōdan, 1973.7), p. 5.

70. Doi, "Yamaguchi-ken," pp. 803-804.

References

Beasley, W. G.
  1972 The Meiji Restoration. Stanford: Stanford University Press.
Coman, Katherine
  1903 "The history of contract labor in the Hawaiian Islands." Publications of the American Economic Association 4, no. 3 (3d series).
Conroy, Hilary
  1953 The Japanese Frontier in Hawaii. Berkeley and Los Angeles: University of California Press.
Doi, Yataro
  1957 "Yamaguchi-ken Ōshima-gun ni okeru Hawai iminshi." Yamaguchi daigaku nōgakubu gakujutsu hōkoku 8: 773-849.
Dower, John
  1975 Origins of the Modern Japanese State: Selected Writings of E. H. Norman. New York: Pantheon Books.
Gaimushō ryōji ijūbu
  1968 Kaigai ijū hyakunen no ayumi. n.p.
Hanley, Susan B., and Kozo Yamamura
  1977 Economic and Demographic Change in Preindustrial Japan 1600-1868. Princeton: Princeton University Press.
Hawai Nihonjin Iminshi Iinkai
  1964 Hawai Nihonjin iminshi. Honolulu: Hawai Nikkeijin Rengō Kyōkai.
Horie, Yasuzo
  1940 "The development of the domestic market in the early years of Meiji." Kyoto University Economic Review 15, no. 1 (January):51.
Ichihashi, Yamato
  1969 Japanese in the United States. New York: Arno Press and New York Times.
Ike, Nobutaka
  1947 "Taxation and landownership in the westernization of Japan." The Journal of Economic History 7, no. 2 (November):164-165.
Irie, Toraji
  1942 Hōjin Kaigai hattenshi. Tokyo: Ida Shoten.
Ishikawa, Tomonori
  1967a "Hiroshima-ken nambu kuchida-son keiyaku imin no shakai chirigakuteki kōsatsu." Shigaku kenkyū 99 (February):33-52.
  1967b "Hiroshima-wangan jigozen-son keiyaku imin no shakai chirigakuteki kōsatsu." Jinbun chiri 19, no.1 (February):75-91.
  1967c "Yamaguchi-ken Ōshima-gun kuga-son shoki Hawai keiyaku imin no shakai chirigakuteki kōsatsu." Chiri kagaku 7 (June):25-38.
Iwasaki, Kenkichi
  1936 "Kii hanto minami kaigan ni okeru kaigai dekasegi imin no kenkyū," pt.2. Chirigaku hyōron 13, no. 3:200.
Kaigai ijū jigyōdan
  1973 Kaigai ijū jigyōdan jūnenshi. Tokyo: Kaigai ijū jigyōdan.

Kawazoe, Zen'ichi
    1968   Imin hyakunen no nenrin. Honolulu: Imin hyakunen no nenrin kankō kai.
Kihara, Ryūkichi
    1935   Hawai Nihonjinshi. Tokyo: Bunseisha.
Moriyama, Alan
    1976   "The 1909 and 1920 strikes of Japanese sugar plantation workers in Hawaii."
           Pp. 169-180 in Emma Gee, ed., Counterpoint. Los Angeles: UCLA Asian Amer-
           ican Studies Center.
Morris, Morris David
    1956   "The problem of the peasant agriculturalist in Meiji Japan." Far Eastern Quar-
           terly 15, no. 3 (May):361.
Nakamura, James
    1966   Agricultural Production and the Economic Development of Japan, 1873-1922.
           Princeton: Princeton University Press.
Ogawa, Gotaro
    1921   Conscription System in Japan. New York: Oxford University Press.
Ohara, Keishi,
    1957   Japanese Trade and Industry in the Meiji-Taisho Era, translated by Tamotsu
           Okata. Tokyo: Ōbunsha.
Ohkawa, Kazushi, and Henry Rosovsky
    1965   "A century of Japanese economic growth." In William Lockwood, ed., The State
           and Economic Enterprise in Japan. Princeton: Princeton University Press.
Okahata, James
    1971   A History of the Japanese in Hawaii. Honolulu: The United Japanese Society of
           Hawaii.
Ono, Giichi
    1922   War and Armament Expenditures of Japan. New York: Oxford University
           Press.
Ono, Takeo
    1942   Gendai Nihon bunmeishi, dai-kyūkan; nosonshi. Tokyo: Tōyō keizai shinpōsha.
Rosovsky, Henry
    1961   Capital Formation in Japan, 1868-1940. Glencoe: Free Press.
Shindo, Motokazu
    1954   "The inflation in the early Meiji Era." Kyoto University Economic Review 24,
           no. 2 (October):41-46.
Staniford, Philip
    n.d.   "Nihon ni itemo sho ga nai: The background, strategies and personalities of
           rural Japanese overseas immigrants." Mimeographed paper. n.p.
    1973   Pioneers in the Tropics. London: Athlone Press.
Sumiya, Mikio
    1963   Social Impact of Industrialization in Japan. Tokyo: Japanese National Commis-
           sion for UNESCO.
Taeuber, Irene B.
    1958   The Population of Japan. Princeton: Princeton University Press.
Tōgō, Minoru
    1906   Nihon shokuminron. Tokyo: Bunbudō.
Wakayama-ken
    1957   Wakayama-ken iminshi. Wakayama-shi: Wakayama-ken.
Yoshida, Hideo
    1941a "Meiji shoki no Hawai dekasegi," pt.1. Takushoku ronsō 3, no. 2:253-305.
    1941b "Meiji shoki no Hawai dekasegi," pt.2. Takushoku ronsō 3, no. 3:260-264.

8
The Background of Korean Emigration

Linda Pomerantz

THE KOREAN SETTING: IMPERIALISM AND THE DECLINE OF THE FEUDAL ORDER

Emigration has been an important feature of Korean life in the twentieth century. By the end of World War II, over 2 million Koreans had left their native land, mostly to go to Japan or northeast China. According to Grajdanzev (1944:81-83), the emigrants constituted at least 10 percent of the entire Korean population.[1]

Korean emigration to Hawaii and the United States represents a relatively minor aspect of this entire movement of Koreans abroad. At most, about 8,000 persons immigrated to Hawaii and the United States before World War II. This movement was in three main phases. The first was from the 1880s to 1902, during which a small number of merchants and students traveled there. The second phase was from 1903 to 1905, when over 7,000 workers were recruited to work on Hawaiian sugar plantations; and the third, 1906 to 1924, was composed of a small trickle of persons, mostly "picture brides" and intellectuals in exile. This chapter will focus on the second phase, with some attention to the third.

In general, the immigrants were members of social groups displaced from their livelihoods as a consequence of the decay and dissolution of the traditional feudal order, a process greatly exacerbated by the impact of imperialist penetration of Korean society and politics in the late nineteenth century. It is to these phenomena that we shall now turn.

The Decline of the Yi Dynasty

At the end of the nineteenth century, Korea was a weak, impoverished country showing signs of social upheaval, economic distress, and political instability. Powerful nations fought over the right to dominate its economy and political structure. As a result of its victory over Russia in 1905, Japan emerged as the sole power in Korea and established a protectorate over the Yi dynasty, gravely compromising Korea's independence. In 1907, Japan forced the Korean king to abdicate. After defeating the Korean resistance, Japan finally annexed Korea in 1910, and Korea remained a Japanese colony until liberation in August 1945. The loss of independence is the single most important event and issue in Korean history in the early twentieth century. (For surveys of modern Korean history see Kim and Kim 1967; Sohn 1970:229-247; Henderson 1968:57-112.)

The way was paved for Japanese aggression by the decline and disintegration of Korea's traditional order in the nineteenth century. Since 1392 Korea had been governed by the Yi family. The Yis ruled this country, largely composed of farming households, with the aid of a small group of officials, all of *yangban* or aristocratic background, and another even smaller group of officials of *chung'in* origin, a hereditary class of minor government officials, technical specialists, and managers (Kim and Kim 1967:5-7; Kim Hei Chu 1971:26-30; Henderson 1968:36-50).

In theory, Korean society consisted of four rigidly separated classes. At the top in power and prestige was the yangban, about 3 percent of the population.[2] Next was the tiny chung'in class, followed by the *sangmin*. The sangmin class consisted of farmers, and merchants, who were 75 to 85 percent and about 6 percent of the population, respectively. Last was the *ch'onmin*, a despised stratum composed of slaves, monks, entertainers, butchers, and certain other occupational groups (Chang 1974:59-60; Moore, 1898). Table 8.1 indicates social classes in Korea as estimated by the Japanese colonialists in 1910.

In reality, the class structure of Yi Korea seems to have been more complex than the structure outlined above and more fluid than previously realized. Henderson (1968:37-45) has suggested that it is erroneous to view the yangban as a single stratum. Although only yangban men could hold official posts or take the civil service examination, in fact only a small number of yangban were politically powerful. The latter was a "tight, Seoul-residing, intermarried clique" that constituted a miniscule proportion of the total yangban population. Another small stratum of yangban were those Henderson terms "middle yangban."

TABLE 8.1
SOCIAL CLASSES OF KOREA, 1910

Social Class	Percentage of households
Yangban, government employees, literati	3.3
Farmers	84.1
Fishermen	1.1
Merchants	6.2
Laborers	2.4
Unemployed	1.0
Others	1.9
	100.0%

SOURCE: Documents of the Government General of Chosen, vol. 12, Migration in Chosen, cited in An 1974:31.

These were members of lineages who had lost out in factional struggles and were deprived of political power or others who had chosen not to accept appointment, thereby retaining an independent stance as moral critics of the system.

According to Henderson, the largest group of yangban were the local yangban, or *hyangban* and *toban*, whom he calls "semi-yangban." This may have been a transitional group consisting of declining yangban families en route "down" to commoner status and wealthy farmers en route "up" toward status as local squires. The existence of this large and fluid group helps explain why so many Koreans claimed yangban status toward the end of the Yi period. In the eighteenth and nineteenth centuries, the number of ch'ŏnmin declined while the number of those claiming yangban status rose. This suggests some degree of upward mobility but also the decline of the yangban as a traditional class upholding traditions of elite status.[3]

In addition to office holding, the main economic basis of the yangban class was the system of tax farming developed by the Yi monarchs. In theory all land was owned by the king. Land was divided into two categories according to who held the right to collect the taxes on it. The taxes on public land were collected directly by the government, while private land was that on which taxes were collected by those to whom the land had been assigned by the Yi rulers. These persons included royal clansmen; officials according to rank, whether or not they actually held office; special "merit subjects"; and others to whom this privilege had been specially granted (Park 1975; Wagner 1974:20-21; Choe 1972:1-6).[4]

Some of these privileges were hereditary, while others were meant to last only the lifetime of the grantee; yet in practice the entire system became hereditary. At first the system was applied only to Kyŏnggi province, the area nearest Seoul, but as the shortage of land became acute, it was applied to most of the farmland of southern Korea. Efforts by the Yi monarchs to limit the privilege to actual officeholders were not successful, and by the eighteenth century, there was considerable pressure from the proliferating yangban class for more land from which to extract taxation. Various reform efforts by the government could not stem this demand. The government's regulation of the system of owner-ship and taxation became increasingly threatened and its financial basis more precarious, while the farmers found themselves increasingly squeezed by the demands of the yangban (Choe 1972:6-12).

From all accounts, there was considerable corruption within the yang-ban class in the nineteenth century. The use of public funds for private luxuries started at the top with the royal family and its inlaws and extended down to the local yangban. The prevalence of corruption resulted in the impoverishment of many farmers and contributed to the loss of legitimacy of the traditional order. A memorialist of 1893 noted this sad state of affairs and described Korea as an aged tree that had rotted within, leaving only a hollow bark shell (Kim and Kim 1967:75; *Han'guk sa* 1965, V:464-465, 940-945; Bishop 1897:87, 439).

At least three-fourths of the Korean population consisted of farmers, but little is known about strata within this large group. Rice agriculture was most prevalent in the rich valleys of the Naktong and Han rivers in the South and in the Taedong River valley in the North. Much of cen-tral and eastern Korea consisted of mountainous terrain where farming was more difficult. These areas were sparsely populated, and less farm-ing was attempted. Writing in 1905, Arthur J. Brown estimated that less than one-half of the arable land in the country was under cultivation (1905:493).

Yangban rule was strongest in the areas where agriculture was most highly developed, that is, in the area around Seoul and in the rich rice lands of the South. In these areas, most farmers were tenants on large estates where the yangban were *de facto* owners, although the latter frequently resided in Seoul and left the management of their estates to kinsmen or stewards. The farmers not only owed part of their crop to the state or yangban as tax and/or rent but also were subject to military and labor conscription. Both forms of conscription could be commuted for a fee, giving rise to opportunities for further squeezing by predatory yangban and officials (Choe 1972:6-12). A poor harvest could mean disaster for many farming households, leading some to move to less desirable areas where they might evade the exactions of landlord and government but where farming might be more difficult. By the late 1860s these conditions had led some northern Korean farmers to move northward into Siberia and establish farms on land under Russian control (Bishop 1897:215-219, 223-234).

These same conditions contributed to the rise of a new religious movement of "eastern learning" (*Tonghak*) in the 1860s. The movement provided a focus for the discontent of many poor farmers and eventually led to a massive peasant uprising in the 1890s, as discussed below (Weems 1964).

Given this situation, it is not surprising that Korean agriculture was not highly productive. The yangban were more interested in national politics than in the management of their estates. Little interest or capital was expended to develop agricultural technology, while the actual cultivators were probably largely concerned with survival and escaping the unwelcome attention of hyangban and local officials.

Similarly, commerce was not highly developed. There were two main forms of commercial activity in mid-nineteenth century Korea. The first consisted of the supply of grain and other goods for the royal family and the court in Seoul. Specially commissioned merchants controlled this commerce. Although the dimensions of this trade were substantial by the early nineteenth century, these merchants were unable to form themselves into an independent economic or political force. Their activities left the population at large virtually untouched (DPRK 1968:23-28).

The vast majority of the farming households were self-sufficient. What few needs they had for goods were supplied by traveling peddlers, or *pobusang*, who carried goods on a regular circuit that connected with periodic markets held in towns on a five-day pattern (Kim Mun-sik 1971:11-12; Lee 1975; Bishop 1897:27-28, 305-308). The pobusang had their own guild and were capable of some degree of organization to protect their own interests. In the Yi period they doubled as unofficial spies by reporting suspicious activities to the government (Henderson 1968:52; Shikata 1933:137-143).

In the nineteenth century there was some development of handicraft industries and agricultural side occupations such as fishing. Although there is disagreement among experts about whether or not capitalism was developing at an accelerated pace in nineteenth-century Korea,[5] the general impression of foreign visitors at that time was that Korea was a poor and "underdeveloped" country with a weak merchant class and a low level of handicraft production; in short, that it was ripe for "development" at the hands of a foreign nation (e.g., Bishop 1897; Brown 1905).

The formal ideology of the yangban was the orthodox Neo-Confucianism developed by Zhu Xi (Chu Hsi) in the Song dynasty in China in the eleventh century. Among the economic features of this orthodoxy was an emphasis upon thrift and self-sufficiency and the disparagement of commerce as a valuable activity. While the Korean elite did not necessarily live up to the ideals of Zhu Xi-ism, for its members spent lavishly on luxuries for their own consumption, they nonetheless looked down upon commercial activity and would not have considered engaging in it themselves. Agriculture remained the foundation of the social order. This outlook contributed to a kind of insularity among the Korean people. There was only marginal foreign trade in the form of tribute missions to the Qing (Ching) government at tribute market towns on the Korean-Chinese border and in a small-scale trade at Pusan with the Japanese *daimyo* of Tsushima. Trade and contact with foreigners was not viewed as desirable, and apparently there was little curiosity about conditions outside of Korea or China (Shikata 1933:127-135).

This, in general terms, was the situation in Korea on the eve of imperialist penetration of its society.

The "Opening" of Korea

Through much of the nineteenth century, Korea was able to avoid contact with the imperialist powers, in part through its own vigorous exclusionist policies and in part because the imperialists were more interested in China and Japan as fields for conquest. Under the regency of the Taewŏngŭn, King Kojŏng's father (1864-1873), the Korean government successfully rebuffed European incursions. But in the 1870s, the situation changed drastically (Choe 1972).

For many centuries, China had been the most powerful country in eastern Asia, and the Yi rulers viewed themselves as vassals of the Qing dynasty emperors. The Koreans called this policy *sadae*, serving the great, and did so by regularly sending tribute missions to China and by deferring to the greater authority of the Son of Heaven in Peking. In turn, the Chinese emperor was obligated to come to the assistance of the Korean king at the latter's request. This occurred most notably in 1592 when Korea was invaded by Japan.

By the 1860s, however, the enfeebled Qing dynasty was itself subject to imperialist aggression and increasingly unable to protect itself, let alone its vassals. Under these changed circumstances, Japan sought control over Korea after the Meiji Restoration of 1868. Japan's interest in Korea in part reflected the desire for a source of foodstuffs and other raw materials and eventually a market for manufactured goods. (But compare Conroy 1960, who discounts these motives for Japanese imperialism.)

As a result of Japanese pressure and hostile threats and China's inability to fulfill its traditional role in support of Korean isolationism, the Yi rulers were forced to sign the Kanghwa Treaty with Japan in 1876. This treaty opened Inchŏn and Wŏnsan to foreign trade and residence and expanded those privileges at Pusan. By prohibiting Korea from levying tariffs on imported goods, the treaty established unequal terms favoring Japan in the conduct of trade (Deuchler 1978:23-49). It should be noted that Japan's model in this venture was the Western imperialist nations in their relations with Japan itself.

The opening of trade had social consequences for Korean agriculture, quickly eroding the self-sufficient, self-contained household economy of many Korean farmers. The foreign merchants brought the farmers into a market economy. Japanese merchants bought their crops of rice and beans, selling them in Japan at great profit. Korean farmers in turn began to use their new supplies of cash to buy foreign goods, especially imported cotton piece goods, kerosene, and matches (Han'guk sa 1965, V:444-446; Bishop 1897:24-25, 75, 168, 293; Brown 1905:502).

Tables 8.2 and 8.3 show the structure of trade with Japan between 1877 and 1882. The total value of this trade was about 10 million yen. Eighty-five percent of the imports to Korea were textile goods, principally of British origin. Nearly half of Korea's exports were foodstuffs, with gold dust and cowhides being the other major items.

The activities of foreign missionaries, who entered Korea in the late 1880s, contributed to the demise of the farmers' self-sufficiency. Missionaries stimulated interest in foreign goods, and some United States missionaries engaged directly in commerce as agents for United States

TABLE 8.2

MAJOR IMPORTS TO KOREA, 1877 TO 1882

Product	Value in yen	Percentage
Cloth, piece goods and dyestuff	3,918,149	85.1
Metal or metal products	376,767	8.0
Foodstuff	45,447	1.0
Miscellaneous	272,074	5.9
Total	4,612,437	100.0%

SOURCE: Han'guk sa 1965, V:865.

TABLE 8.3
EXPORTS FROM KOREA TO JAPAN, 1877 TO 1882

Product	Value in yen	Percentage
Rice	1,529,636	29.9
Gold	972,242	19.0
Leather	829,131	16.2
Beans	557,057	10.9
Seaweed	178,016	3.5
Raw silk	174,019	3.4
Silver	87,056	1.7
Dried fish	86,620	1.6
Other	691,082	13.8
Total	5,104,859	100.0

SOURCE: Based on Conroy 1960:459.

trading companies. These "trading missionaries" believed, according to American diplomat Horace N. Allen, that they were providing a service to humanity by making "the benefits of western civilization" available to the Koreans (Harrington 1944:105; Sands 1930:94; Kim Hei Chu 1971:213).

By the 1880s a cycle of debt and dependency upon foreign — principally Japanese — merchants had been established. Because of the relatively low productivity of Korean agriculture, the survival margin was fragile and could be upset by one poor harvest. Many farmers accepted cash advances from Japanese merchants for sale of their crops after harvest. In bad years this meant severe food shortages in some regions. Foreseeing the problem of food shortages and the subsequent dire social consequences, the Korean government had insisted upon the right to prohibit food exports in famine years (Han'guk sa 1965, V:412).

In the so-called bean controversy of 1889, the governor of Hamgyŏng province in northeastern Korea placed a ban on exports of food from his province as a result of a severe famine. The Japanese government, claiming that the governor had not followed the correct procedures in proclaiming the ban, sued the Korean government for damages sustained by Japanese grain merchants. After lengthy negotiations, the Korean government was forced to pay the enormous sum of 110,000 yen to Japan (Kim and Kim 1967:71-72; Han'guk sa 1965, V:894-911).

Food shortages and spiraling debts, when added to the abuse of power by corrupt officials and yangban, resulted in virtually intolerable conditions for many farmers. In the 1880s many spontaneous uprisings occurred in the countryside as some farmers sought relief (Han'guk sa

1965, V:953-963); others were forced to leave their farms and migrate elsewhere. Migration to Siberia from Hamgyŏng province increased, and destitute farmers flocked to newly established treaty ports in hopes of work. Inchŏn and Wŏnsan, both of which had been villages in 1876, developed into cities of about 15,000 persons each by the 1890s. This new urban population provided the source of much of the emigration to Hawaii from 1903 to 1905 (Bishop 1897:176; Brown 1905:498).[6]

"A Shrimp Among Whales"

This expression is one that Koreans sometimes sardonically use to describe their nation's plight. The social changes described above contributed to the growing instability of Korean politics in the late nineteenth century. Imperialist rivalry compounded the factionalism that was endemic to Yi dynasty politics (Palais 1976).

The Kanghwa Treaty was followed by a treaty with the United States in 1882 and then by others with all the major European powers. By 1887, Korea had been brought into the network of imperialist relations that dominated eastern Asia in the late nineteenth century. Foreigners had the right to reside in Korean treaty ports (see table 8.4 and fig. 8.1) and to conduct trade on terms advantageous to them, were not subject to Korean laws, and had the right to proselytize people to Christianity. Foreign enclaves increased.

Japan monopolized Korea's foreign trade during the first six years after the signing of the Kanghwa Treaty and also persuaded the Korean

TABLE 8.4
KOREAN TREATY PORTS AND DATE OPENED TO TRADE, 1876 TO 1905

1876	Pusan
1880	Wŏnsan
1883	Inchŏn
1883	Yanghwajin
1883	Seoul
1888	Kyŏnghŭng
1897	Chinnampo
1897	Mokpo
1898	Pyŏngyang
1899	Kunsan
1899	Masan
1899	Songjin

SOURCE: Shikata 1933:160-161; Choe 1973:51.

Fig. 8.1

government to institute a number of modernizing reforms that increased Japanese influence in Korea. In 1882 these plans received a setback as Korean soldiers, discriminated against by Japanese-trained troops, rioted. This crisis resulted in Chinese intervention to maintain order, but China was too weak to assume its former role as suzerain.

A clash between China and Japan was averted for the time being but Korean officials and yangban polarized over the issues confronting them: reform versus tradition, alliance with Japan or with China. In December 1884 a group of pro-Japanese reformers were unsuccessful in their bloody revolt against the traditionalist faction headed by Queen Min (Cook 1972; DPRK 1968).

With the failure of the *coup*, China once again intervened to maintain order, and a crisis in international relations was at hand. It was averted with the signing of the Treaty of Tientsin in 1885 (Li-Ito Convention) in which China and Japan agreed to notify the other before dispatching troops to Korea.

The decade from 1885 to 1894 saw a rise in China's influence in Korea. Chinese merchants provided stiff competition for Japan. While Japan continued to monopolize exports from Korea (91 to 98 percent during this period), total imports from Japan decreased from 81 to 55 percent as Chinese merchants successfully undercut the Japanese in textile sales (Kim and Kim 1967:70; *Han'guk sa* 1965, V:862-871; Shikata 1933:176-183; Conroy 1960:460). Japan also faced competition from China in the shipping and fishing industries (*Han'guk sa* 1965, V:872-883).

The European imperialists and the United States did not pose a serious threat to Japan during this period. Russia's attempt to expand its influence into Korea in the mid-1880s brought a countermove from its archrival, Great Britain, in a demand to occupy Komundo (Port Hamilton). When the overextended Russians withdrew, Great Britain, too, gave up its occupation in 1887 (Deuchler 1978:109 ff.).

The Korean court proved ineffectual in meeting the crisis resulting from these encroachments. Under the domination of the Min family, national politics reached new lows of corruption and confusion. The Mins (the king's in-laws) and the royal family plundered the national treasury and irresponsibly contracted numerous debts to foreign banks and governments. Finances were a hopeless muddle (*Han'guk sa* 1965, V:946-948).[7]

To the farmers' complaints were added those of the Korean peddlers facing severe competition from Chinese and Japanese merchants (Kim and Kim 1967:67-68). Finally, in the 1890s, farmers rallied to the banner of the Tonghak religion and rose up against corrupt local officials and yangban and then the Japanese. By 1894 a full-scale rebellion was under way, posing to the Yi dynasty its severest threat. The king's decision to ask China for help maintaining order brought on the Sino-Japanese War.

China's loss to Japan in 1895 ended its influence in Korea. The war resulted in new forms of imperialist expansion: (1) financial control by foreigners, (2) sale of land to foreigners, (3) awarding of concessions to foreign industrialists, and (4) expansion of missionary influence. Although these phenomena overlapped, we shall consider them here separately.

Financial Control

The Japanese Dai Ichi Bank assumed a position of paramount influence by 1897. First established in Pusan in 1878, the bank rose to prominence handling the burgeoning Japanese-Korean trade, and its branches proliferated throughout Korea. Because of the cumbersome nature of Korean cash, the Japanese yen gradually came to be used as standard currency. By 1897 there were 3 million yen circulating in Korea, and in 1902 the bank issued additional notes for about 16 million yen for circulation there. As a result of reforms Japan forced upon the Yi dynasty during and immediately after the Sino-Japanese War, the Dai Ichi Bank came to assume the functions of a government bank. After a brief period of competition from Russian banking interests, the Dai Ichi Bank assumed financial hegemony over Korean finances and banking (Shikata 1933:44-125; Conroy 1960:450-451, 473-479).

Land Purchases

Japanese businessmen took advantage of their government's influence and bought large amounts of urban property at bargain prices. This resulted in an inflationary trend in urban rents. The purchases were especially noticeable in, but not limited to, the city of Pyŏngyang, where a major battle in the war had occurred. Most of the city's population fled the approaching troops, reducing its size from about 80,000 to a mere 15,000. Four-fifths of the houses were destroyed as Japanese soldiers used the wood and thatch for fuel or else just burned and looted the empty houses. Japanese military authorities appropriated food and supplies, leading to food shortages and a rise in prices for Koreans (Bishop 1897:312-328).

Japanese profiteers rushed into the area to buy up land, especially in a large area outside the city's south gate and in the path of the soon-to-be-constructed railway from Seoul to Sinŭiju. A missionary described these events as follows:

> The Japanese are buying property right and left in the city, and outside the city . . . where the railroad is to run. . . . The expectation is that a large city is to spring up there. The Japanese have staked off their purchases, marking the stakes as defining Japanese property. The railroad men have run the line for the road through growing crops and houses and on either side of it have marked off a large "concession" of hundreds of acres containing the best land and best houses in the Province. Within this concession, the land and 400 houses have been condemned and the people are ordered out by the Japanese and Korean officials and told to look to the Korean Government for pay. . . .
>
> The people are highly enraged and see no hope of redress. They do not understand what is being done, cannot trust their own officials, are driven out of house and land and lose their crops. (Brown 1905:549)

This "Japanese city" had about 7,000 inhabitants by 1907. Even pro-Japanese accounts acknowledge mistreatment of Koreans in this land grab, as the following account by a pro-Japanese American indicates:

> The original inhabitants of the Japanese city were by no means altogether of the class most creditable to Japan, or comfortable as neighbors for the Korean population. There were many adventurers, hangers-on and panderers to the army, who did not stop at either fraud or violence in their treatment of the native population of Pyeng-yang. (Ladd 1908:90)

Similar processes of land purchases or expropriations, accompanied by food shortages and inflation, occurred in other cities (Grajdanzev 1944:36; Bishop 1897:32-33; Brown 1905:549). Japanese-inspired land reform measures in 1898 further opened the way to foreign land purchases. This was but the opening wedge in the wholesale dispossession of Korean farmers from their land that later occurred under Japanese colonial rule (Shikata 1933:9-43).

Concessions

From 1895 to 1898 European and American companies competed with Japan for contracts and concessions. Japan's high-handedness had created a counterreaction among many Koreans, who especially opposed a number of reforms Japan promoted. Most notable of these was a decree for Korean men to cut off their topknots. Anti-Japanese sentiment was heightened further by the assassination of Queen Min by Japanese in 1896. With her murder the balance of power shifted radically as the king sought refuge in the Russian legation, thereby bringing a temporary setback to Japan.

Under these circumstances, King Kojŏng granted a number of concessions to European and American firms in hopes of countering Japan's
power (table 8.5). These concessions gave foreigners the right to exploit
railway, telegraph, mining, and timber rights. During this period, Korea's
major rail lines were laid, telegraph lines were installed, and foreign-
owned mining was developed. In general, however, Japan succeeded in
regaining control over most of these concessions by 1900 because of the
weakness of Russian and American capital and the greater commitment
of French, British, and German capital elsewhere (Kim and Kim
1967:97-99).

The United States was very active in this flurry of concession seeking
that followed the Sino-Japanese War. United States companies built
Korea's first electric facilities in the royal palace, its first gas plant,
street railways, and modern mines. Although Korea was never a major
area of United States investment in the late nineteenth and early twentieth centuries, American businessmen were prominent in Korea because
of the efforts of Horace N. Allen, who consistently sought to expand
the United States presence in the peninsula and who was willing to ally
temporarily with Russia against Japan toward that end (Harrington
1944:168-201). Allen was a major promoter of emigration to Hawaii.

The most successful of the United States concessions was mining in
the Unsan gold fields in North Pyŏngan province. During its years of
operation the Unsan mines yielded 9 million tons of ore and a net profit

TABLE 8.5

CONCESSIONS AWARDED BY KOREA TO FOREIGNERS, 1896 TO 1900

Year	Concession	Country
1896	Seoul-Inchŏn railway	United States*
1896	Mining rights, Kyŏngwŏn and Chongsong, N. Hamgyŏng Province	Russia
1896	Gold mines in Unsan, N. Pyŏngan Province	United States
1896	Seoul-Uiju railway	France
1896	Timber concession, Yalu River area and Ullendo	Russia
1896	Gold mines, Kangwŏn Province	Germany
1897	Electric street cars, Seoul	United States
1898	Seoul-Pusan railway	Japan
1899	Gold mines, S. Pyŏngan Province	Great Britain
1900	Gold mines, N. Chungchong Province	Japan

SOURCE: Choe 1973:61.

*This concession was sold to Japan in 1898.

of about $15 million to its owners (Palmer 1962:391). The United States mines resulted in the displacement of traditional miners. The concessionaires won the right to monopolize all gold mining in North Pyŏngan province. (King Kojŏng received one-fourth of the company's stock in return for this favor.) This evoked a protest from some miners who sought 6.6 million won from the United States government as compensation for their lost livelihood. To worsen their situation, the company hired cheaper labor from the treaty ports rather than local people. The miners' petitions were ignored (Harrington 1944:129-133, 144-167).

Missionary Influence

Christian converts figured prominently among the emigrants to Hawaii. Although Christian missionaries began working in Korea in the 1880s, only after the Sino-Japanese War did their efforts bring results. In particular, their greatest success was among the populace of Pyŏngyang and its environs and among migrants from that area to Inchŏn. The Protestant denominations with greatest success were the Presbyterians, centered in Pyŏngyang, and the Methodists, centered in Inchŏn and Seoul (Rhodes n.d.:143-172; Brown 1905:498; Paik 1929:253-278).

By 1904 Pyŏngyang was believed to have as many as 15,000 Christian adherents, which amounted to one-fourth of its population (Brown 1905:642). Smaller communities like Sorai and Haeju, located between Pyŏngyang and Inchŏn, had even larger proportions of Christians (Brown 1905:529-535).

Figure 8.2 shows the annual increase or decrease in membership for Presbyterians and Methodists from 1895 to 1911. Conversions increased among Presbyterians in the late 1890s and after a brief setback in 1901, increased dramatically, especially during the Russo-Japanese War (1904 to 1905) and the Great Revival of 1906 to 1907.

The popularity of Christianity in Korea may have reflected the ability of the missionaries to link its main tenets with some indigenous Korean religious concepts and the willingness of the missionaries to use *han'gŭl*, Korean alphabet script, in their writings. The egalitarianism of Christian doctrine appealed to outcast groups such as butchers (Paik 1929:193), while the personal heroism of missionaries of Pyŏngyang in the typhus epidemic after the Sino-Japanese War was inspiring to some Koreans (Brown 1905:570-571; Rhodes n.d.:148-149). But the popularity of Christianity also reflected the particular circumstances surrounding the collapse of the old order, especially the discrediting of Confucianism as the formal ideology of the corrupted yangban class and the widespread revulsion against Japanese imperialism (Palmer 1967:69-88).

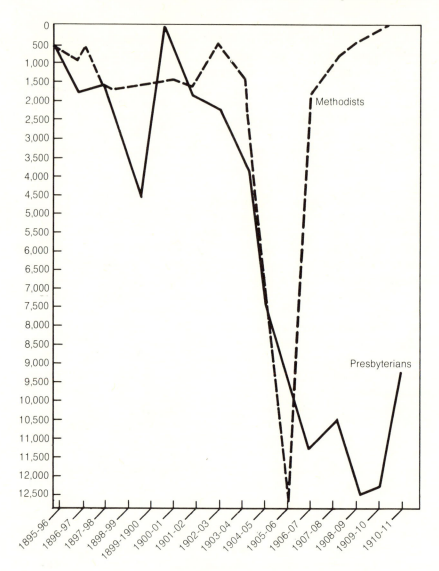

Fig. 8.2
Korean Protestant membership annual increases or decreases, 1895 to 1911.
Source: Palmer 1967: facing pp. 92-93.

In summary, the general background to the mass emigration of 1903 to 1905 is to be found in the transformation of Korean agriculture and the accompanying impoverishment of many Korean farmers because of the penetration of foreign capitalism in an increasingly corrupt and decadent feudal society. The penetration of foreign capitalism linked the farmers to the international market and a cash economy, thereby eroding their traditional self-sufficiency. These circumstances led to a growing number of bankruptcies among farmers and caused their migration across the border to Siberia and to treaty ports such as Wōnsan and Inchŏn. Their migration created a new labor supply for foreign-owned enterprises such as the Ūnsan mines and for emigration to Hawaii.

These trends occurred at the same time that the United States was rising as an imperialist power. With the acquisition of the Philippines in 1898, the United States became an Asian power, but the goals of United States capitalists at this stage were oriented more toward expanding trade with Asian nations and less toward investment. Given the relative weakness of United States capital in Asia, the United States was not in a position to play a major economic or political role in Korea. At the same time, however, Japan was unable to establish full control over Korea until 1905. For a brief interlude, then, it was possible for the United States, in consort with Russia, to exert some measure of influence in Korea, principally in the cultural realm, through the activities of missionaries and educators, and to a lesser degree in the economic realm, through the activities of businessmen. Let us now turn to the latter and examine the immediate circumstances surrounding the mass emigration of 1903 to 1905.

ORGANIZED EMIGRATION TO HAWAII, 1903 TO 1905

During the period from December 1902, when the first shipload of Korean workers left Inchŏn, to April 1905, when the Korean government banned further emigration, some 7,800 Koreans arrived in Honolulu for work on the sugar plantations of the Hawaiian islands.[8] In all, sixty-five shiploads came to Hawaii during this brief period in response to the covert activities by the Hawaiian Sugar Planters' Association (HSPA), the main organ of the plantation owners.

The planters' interest in Korean labor stemmed from their continuous need for fresh sources of cheap labor to work in the fields. At the turn of the century, Japanese comprised nearly 80 percent of the work force on the plantations. Japanese workers created problems for owners not only by frequently striking for higher pay and better conditions but also by migrating in growing numbers to the mainland in search of better jobs. While the planters did not plan to replace Japanese workers with Koreans, they hoped that the introduction of another ethnic group would help keep wages low. Toward this end, the HSPA set about to recruit Korean workers (Patterson 1977a:108-119, 146).

Emigration Organized

The planters' first attempt to recruit Korean workers in 1896 was unsuccessful (Patterson 1977b). In 1900, the United States passed the Organic Law prohibiting the planters from importing contract workers. The law stipulated that the planters could not prepay passage or assist the immigrant by paying passage, nor could employment be promised or workers signed up before they arrived in Hawaii. In 1902, however, the HSPA organized the emigration of Koreans in a manner that violated the spirit if not the letter of the law, making the entire enterprise of dubious legality.

The key figure in the HSPA's effort to recruit Koreans was Horace N. Allen, United States Minister to Korea. Allen was most eager to promote United States commercial interests in Korea and had vigorously assisted American companies seeking concessions (Harrington 1944). According to secret HSPA materials briefly examined by Wayne Patterson, the planters contacted Allen in 1902 while he was on leave in the United States and asked his support in obtaining the Korean government's approval for the emigration of Korean workers to Hawaii. Allen agreed and secretly met again with HSPA representatives while en route to Korea (Patterson 1977a:135-143).

Back in Korea, Allen selected David W. Deshler as the HSPA's agent in charge of recruitment. Deshler was a speculator and promoter who had lived in Asia for a number of years. Through his influential family in Ohio, Deshler had persuaded the McKinley administration to appoint Allen minister to Korea in 1896. In gratitude, Allen had aided Deshler on several occasions before the emigration plan arose. Thus Deshler established the Deshler Bank in Inchŏn to receive the HSPA monies and formed a company, the East-West Development Company, to handle the recruitment and shipment of Korean workers to Hawaii (Patterson 1977a:151-166).

With this mechanism established, the HSPA sent its representative, E. Faxon Bishop, to Korea and Japan to meet with Deshler. The Deshler Bank received $25,000 from the HSPA to begin its operations, and

Bishop drew up proposed regulations based on those used in Japan. He then left Korea to give Deshler and Allen a free hand in obtaining the Korean government's approval (Patterson 1977a:167-178).

Allen may have mentioned emigration to Hawaii to the king several times after his return from the United States, and in November 1902 he formally requested that a franchise to recruit workers be granted to Deshler. Deshler was introduced to the king as an official of the Territorial Bureau of Immigration from Hawaii. This was, in fact, a misrepresentation, apparently made to convince Kojŏng that the plan was sponsored by the United States government (Patterson 1977a:195, 201-202).

Allen described Hawaii to the king in glowing terms. Recounting the history of Chinese exclusion from the United States, he led the king to believe that it would bolster Korea's international prestige to have its nationals admitted where Chinese had been refused entry. He also suggested emigration as a solution to the pressing economic crisis that had developed during the past years (Hyŏn 1967, II:797).

In 1901 a severe drought in the northwestern region had brought famine and the migration of many people from that area. The government imported grain from Indochina and established a relief agency, but it is unlikely that these measures had much positive effect (Yun 1977:34-35, Hyŏn 1967, II:795).

In the belief that emigration could temporarily ease the situation for famine victims, would raise Korea's international prestige, and would increase United States involvement in Korea, King Kojŏng signed an edict on November 16, 1902 establishing the *Sumin wŏn* (or *Yumin wŏn*), Office of Emigration (literally: Bureau to Relieve the People) and authorizing Deshler to recruit workers for Hawaii. The bureau's regulations were those developed by Bishop.[9] Much to the disgust of some reformers, the bureau was placed directly under the royal household, with the two won passport fee to go to the royal family, rather than under the Foreign Ministry where it properly belonged (Patterson 1977a:208-209).

With this official approval, Deshler set about to recruit workers. From his office at the Deshler Bank in Inchŏn, he advertised for interpreters to recruit workers and accompany them to Hawaii. Announcements were posted throughout the cities and towns of Korea telling of the availability of jobs in Hawaii. Hawaii was described as having a mild climate, jobs for $16.00 per month, and free education. Since $16.00 (approximately 60 won) was well above prevailing wages in Korea,[10] the announcement attracted much attention. Moreover, the project seemed government sponsored to some, for the company's interpreters often worked with officials from the Sumin wŏn arranging passports, and the company's circulars appeared official (Hyŏn 1967, II:797-798; Seventy-Fifth Anniversary 1978:58-60; Kim 1937:80).

Even with the inducements offered, Deshler was unable to attract many recruits at first. With no tradition of overseas migration, most Koreans were dubious about the project. What was needed was someone to lend the project credibility and persuade people to go: in short, a promoter. This person was the Reverend George Heber Jones, an American missionary and pastor of a Methodist church in Inchŏn. Jones was apparently motivated by the belief that life would be better for Koreans in Hawaii as well as by the hope that mission work would be easier there than in Korea. Jones spoke so eloquently and persuasively that about fifty persons (half of his own congregation) decided to go. They were joined by about twenty dock workers from Inchŏn and a number of others from the Seoul-Inchŏn-Suwŏn area (Hyŏn 1967, II:799; Kim 1977:50; see also Paik 1929:135-136).

Thus the first group departed from Inchon on December 22, 1902 and arrived in Honolulu on January 13, 1903 after a brief stopover in Japan. Deshler's company advanced the money for passage, miscellaneous funds, and about $50 in pocket money. This last amount was necessary for the workers to be admitted to Hawaii. They were carefully coached to enable them to answer the immigration agents' questions. After their arrival in Honolulu, the $50 was collected by Deshler's agents. In all, the HSPA advanced a little over $100 as a loan to each emigrant via Deshler (Patterson 1977a:321-327).

The legality of the venture rested on the assertion that the monies advanced did not constitute prepayment of passage but rather a loan to be repaid by the worker. As Horace Allen wrote in a letter to the Hawaiian governor, Sanford B. Dole, the Koreans were too poor to save money for passage themselves, and the Korean government was in no position to assist them (reprinted in Kim and Patterson 1974:85-86). When this rationale was accepted by the immigration officials and the first shipload of Koreans was permitted to enter as legal immigrants, the HSPA and Deshler must have been relieved, and plans to step up the pace of recruitment were developed.

The HSPA apparently viewed the money as a loan to be repaid by the immigrants, but the immigrants themselves had different recollections of the facts surrounding their passage fees. Some immigrants viewed the money as a loan to be paid in ten monthly installments (Ko 1973:209-210), while others believed their passage to have been paid by Deshler (Lyu 1977:37). It is difficult to know whether the HSPA/Deshler operation varied from time to time or whether the immigrants' memories had become unclear by the time interviewers spoke with them. Whatever the situation, Deshler and the HSPA had considerable difficulty collecting from the Korean immigrants,[11] who believed that they had been misled by the recruiting agents. Instead of easy work in a tropical paradise, they were engaged in back-breaking work at bare subsistence wages.

The Course of Emigration, 1903 to 1905

The second shipload left Korea on February 10 with 90 persons on board, arriving at its destination on March 2. Deshler was then ordered to recruit at the rate of 500 men a month, and he opened branch offices in a number of Korean cities. By June 1903 there were about 600 Koreans working in Hawaii, but at this point, the project encountered difficulties leading to its temporary suspension (Patterson 1977a:242).

The Organic Law of 1900 was amended in March 1903 to provide for rewards to persons who uncovered instances of illegal immigration, and an opportunity soon presented itself. On April 30, 113 Koreans on the Nippon Maru were detained when the interpreter accompanying them revealed to the authorities that prior arrangements for their employment existed. On May 6 a special board ruled that the Koreans were legal immigrants and they were permitted to enter, but further immigration was temporarily suspended while the HSPA negotiated with the immigration commissioner (No 1965:4).

At this point a group of reward seekers brought suit against the HSPA charging that the 113 were illegal immigrants. In a trial marked by "dirty tricks" on both sides, the judge at first ruled against the HSPA and then later reversed his decision on a technicality. Not until October 1903 did the immigration commissioner agree to lift the suspension, and Koreans once more arrived in Honolulu (Patterson 1977a:336-368).

During the five months that emigration was halted, Deshler also encountered opposition from within the Korean government. News of the conditions on the sugar plantations had begun to trickle back to Korea, and rumors circulated about the poor conditions Koreans in Hawaii faced. Allen did his best to counteract these rumors and proposed that the Korean government establish a consulate in Honolulu to monitor the situation. Rather than legitimize the emigration project thusly, however, Yi Yong-ik, a powerful royal advisor, decided to move toward ending it. In October 1903 the Sumin wŏn was eliminated and its functions were given to the Foreign Ministry.[12] Thus the emigration project continued for a time but had little institutional approval and no legal regulations governing it (Hyŏn 1967, II:801; Patterson 1977a: 292-302).

While these events involving emigration were occurring, the international situation in Asia was rapidly worsening. Russia's refusal to withdraw its troops from northeastern China (Manchuria) and to agree to Japan's hegemony over Korea led to a Japanese declaration of war against Russia on February 10, 1904. The war had a profound effect upon Korea and upon Deshler's enterprises.

The Japanese First Army landed at Inchŏn in early February and marched north to the Chinese border, engaging in minor skirmishes with Russian scouts. The only major battle in Korea occurred at the Yalu River border town of Ŭiju in early May (Wood 1905:2-12). Although there was virtually no fighting in Korea, the fear of war resulted in floods of refugees fleeing northwestern Korea in anticipation of battle. Western journalists traveling with the Japanese forces from Seoul to Ŭiju reported large numbers of refugees, their houses stripped bare, carrying all their possessions as they fled south (McKenzie 1905:96-97, 117-120).

One of Japan's main objectives was to secure uncontested control over Korea. The presence of Japanese troops left the Korean court with little choice but to sign a protocol on February 23, 1904 putting Korea firmly under Japan's control. Under the terms of this agreement, Korea was to follow Japan's advice in instituting reforms, give Japan "full facilities" to promote its aims, and permit its forces to occupy areas as necessary. Korea also agreed that it would not conduct independent negotiations with other countries. Needless to say, these terms gravely compromised Korea's sovereignty and set the stage for Japan's assumption of a protectorate over Korea in 1905 (Asakawa 1970:367-368).

These conditions temporarily created a large pool of Koreans for emigration. First, the refugees from the North found themselves destitute in Inchŏn or Seoul. They were joined by others from the Vladivostok area who similarly fled the war zone (Morris Pang, "A Korean Immigrant," reprinted in Kim and Patterson 1974:116-118). Deshler moved to take advantage of the flow of refugees by opening a branch of his company in the northern city of Sŏngjin (Patterson 1977a:380).

Second, the general uncertainty that prevailed and the specter of Japanese domination made the emigration project seem attractive to persons who might not have considered it otherwise. This was especially true for a large number of Korean soldiers who found themselves supplanted by Japanese troops in their barracks. Drifting of soldiers and ex-soldiers from place to place was not uncommon, and eventually about 500 of these men went to Hawaii (Kim 1937:83).

Thus, the numbers of emigrants rose dramatically after the outbreak of the war. In 1903, a total of sixteen ships had brought 1,133 Koreans to Hawaii, with perhaps 600 of them arriving after September of that year. In 1904, however, thirty-three ships brought about 3,400 persons to Hawaii, or three times the number for 1903; and the first six months of 1905 brought 2,800 Koreans to Hawaii, with the peak in May of 1,003 persons. In all, sixty-five ships brought about 7,300 persons during the entire period of organized emigration, bringing the total of Koreans in Hawaii and on the mainland to about 7,800.[13]

Background and Motivation of the Emigrants

In spite of recent efforts by several scholars to obtain concrete data on the origins of the emigrants, our understanding unfortunately is still impressionistic. Kim (1937), Lyu (1977), Moon (1976), and Patterson (1977a) agree that the emigrants were heterogeneous in geographic origins and social class.

Many of the Korean migrants were probably city or town dwellers who had recently migrated from the countryside or whose families had done so. In a 1970 survey of elderly Korean immigrants conducted by students at the University of Hawaii, 37 percent of those interviewed stated that although their families had originally been farmers, they themselves were from towns and cities (cited in Patterson 1977a:416-417). This suggests the phenomenon noted above, namely, the movement of farmers to new urban areas as a result of economic dislocation. Similarly, Japanese documents identified most of the first group of travelers as being from regions with poor harvests the previous year, suggesting a similar pattern of dislocation and movement to urban areas (Patterson 1977a:275).

Contemporary Japanese documents estimated that about half of the emigrants came from the Seoul-Inchon-Suwon region, with the rest coming from all over Korea (Patterson 1977a:415). But impressions of immigrants themselves are that most of them were from Pyŏngan province in northwestern Korea. This discrepancy can be explained by viewing many of the emigrants or their families as farmers from the Northwest compelled to migrate south as a result of poor economic conditions and the dislocations of war; then, finding themselves jobless or only marginally employed, they decided to emigrate to Hawaii.

The emigrants were also of varied social backgrounds. Although perhaps half of those on the first shipload were originally of farming backgrounds, relatively few of the total number were themselves actual farmers. Bernice Kim estimated that only one-seventh of the total were farmers. The next largest group was composed of laborers working periodically in port cities and towns; then came ex-soldiers followed by minor government clerks, rural laborers, students, policemen, miners, woodcutters, household servants, and a few Buddhist monks (Kim 1937:85).

Hyung June Moon estimated that farmers, farm laborers, and urban laborers constituted about one-third of the total, with the remaining two-thirds a miscellaneous group comprised of ex-soldiers, scholars, students, miners, policemen, and a small group of actors and butchers, these last two being of ch'onmin caste (Moon 1976:58).

Whatever the precise composition of the emigrant groups, it is clear that there was a fairly large group of declassed persons from various social strata. Although the data do not permit meaningful analysis, this group was probably representative of the nonelite segment of Korea's urban population at the turn of the century, with former farmers, farm laborers, and craftsmen forming the nascent working class or prole-tariat and with a large "floating" population of declassed or lumpen proletariat, similar in essence to the population of London and other large cities in the early phases of industrialization and urbanization (see, e.g., Tobias 1967).

Another important characteristic of the emigrants is that they were mostly young men in their early twenties. Even though some of them were married, they went to Hawaii as single men and were sometimes able to return home and then to go back to Hawaii with the rest of their family. Of the 7,296 immigrants who arrived in Hawaii, 6,641 were males while only 613 were women. An additional 447 persons were under the age of fourteen. The sex ratio was more than 10 to 1 (Kim 1937:83).

This skewed sex ratio reflected the policies of the HSPA. Since women did less fieldwork than men, they were viewed as somewhat of a liability by the planters, as were children. But this had to be offset by the planters' belief that family units were a more stable work force than single men. In view of the large turnover in the fields and the large number of Japanese leaving for the mainland, some of the planters attempted to recruit entire families. But this policy was not applied consistently. In the case of Japanese workers, for example, at various times there were efforts to recruit 30 to 40 percent women. Yet the emigration companies received smaller commissions for women than for adult males, and around the turn of the century, the Japanese popu-lation in Hawaii was 80 percent male (Moriyama this volume).

Although the Korean migrants were overwhelmingly male, there were instances of entire families going to Hawaii. Some of the recruit-ing material encouraged families to emigrate (Patterson 1977a:384), but it is unclear whether Deshler received the same commission for men, women, and children. There were cases of families selling home, farm, furniture, and implements to move to Hawaii (Hwangsong Sinmun, May 22, 1903, cited in Patterson 1977a:278-292).

As the material presented earlier suggests, most of the emigrants were motivated by severe economic hardship, with many of them unable to find work in towns or cities, and migrated to Hawaii as sojourners with the expectation of returning in a few years (Sunoo 1977:155; Moon 1976:60-62; Patterson 1977a:424). The life of Ekpo Pyun may serve as an example: He was born in 1881 to a "teacher-farmer" (probably a hyangban) and housewife. His mother died when he was eight years old, and his father died when he was seventeen. His brothers later died in a cholera epidemic. He struggled to keep his farm going but finally gave up and migrated to Hawaii in 1904 (Seventy-Fifth Anniversary 1978:22-27).

Although economic hardship is the dominant theme, emigration as an outlet for personal dissatisfaction is a persistent undercurrent. Persons of varied social backgrounds who experienced injustice, who wanted to live in a more enlightened atmosphere, or who simply wanted adventure also went to Hawaii.

One example of this phenomenon is a woman of yangban status who was saddened by her husband's acquisition of a concubine, so she threatened to take her three children to Hawaii (Sunoo 1977:152-155). One of her children later recalled,

> My father laughed when mother announced that she was going to Hawaii with my seventeen year old brother as principal laborer. "How are you going to live? You never did a day's work in your life." But she was determined to leave him and his concubine, even if it meant working in the canefields. (Seventy-Fifth Anniversary 1978:40-43)

Others may have looked to Hawaii as a place with a more enlightened atmosphere than Korea. This may have been especially true of Christians desirous of religious freedom (Lee Tai Sung, "The Story of Korean Immigration," reprinted in Kim and Patterson 1974:106-108). There were several Christian households in northern Korea that emigrated, giving rise to fears among American missionaries that their work would be set back by these departures (Patterson 1977a:278-292).

Finally, some "wanderers" and "loafers" found themselves in Hawaii (Moon 1976:64-65; Seventy-Fifth Anniversary 1978:57), as did others in search of excitement or adventure. One such person, for example, was born in Pyŏngyang in 1880, the fifth child of seven. His father was a wealthy liquor manufacturer, who married him at the age of sixteen to a woman he disliked intensely. He attempted to run away from his unhappy domestic situation but failed and was forced to work for his father collecting funds from wine shops. Then he and his brother-in-law, a graduate of a military academy who knew some Chinese, Japanese, and English, decided to run away from Pyŏngyang and go to America. He accumulated 5,000 *yang* (ounces of silver), a substantial sum, and the two of them came to Inchŏn and Seoul. After several months of sight-seeing and visiting singing girls in Seoul, the money was gone and his family was on his trail, so he signed up to come to Hawaii (Yim 1979).

The diverse backgrounds and motives of the emigrants reflect the particular situation in Korea around the turn of the century. The decline of the traditional order combined with the effects of imperialism to create economic disorder and social instability. Bankrupt farmers and unemployed townspeople sought emigration, while others dissatisfied with their lives for various reasons found emigration an outlet for their frustrations.

The Ban on Emigration

On April 1, 1905 the Korean government suddenly issued a declaration halting all emigration of Korean workers. The circumstances surrounding this decision had been somewhat unclear, but Japanese archival materials recently made available to scholars have shed light on it.[14]

United States influence in Korea was drastically reduced in the weeks prior to the decision. In mid-March, United States Minister Horace Allen was recalled, and the American legation in Seoul closed down in deference to Japan's claims of hegemony, which had been strengthened by a second protocol signed by Japan and Korea in August 1904 allowing Japan to choose advisors for Korea's Foreign Affairs and Finance ministries. With Allen's departure, Deshler lost his most powerful promoter and backer.

Deshler also faced competition from the Japanese-owned Continental Settlement Company (Dairoku Shokumin Kaisha). This company was one of several private emigration companies recruiting and transporting Japanese workers to Hawaii and, in this case, to Mexico as well. (On the Japanese emigration companies, see Moriyama 1977.) Under circumstances that are somewhat unclear, the Continental Settlement Company began recruiting workers in Korea as contract laborers for large plantations in Mexico. From December 1904 until their departure at the beginning of April 1905, 1,033 persons were recruited for this enterprise (Yun 1977:40-42).

When the terms of their contracts became known, the Korean government decided to ban further emigration of this type. Indeed, the harsh fate awaiting these 1,033 persons became a national scandal. According to Deshler, the Japanese government persuaded the Korean government to extend the ban to include emigration to Hawaii, on the grounds that it was unfair to permit one but not the other. The king willingly complied, in part because stories had reached Korea of Koreans in Hawaii desirous of returning home but unable to raise money for the return passage. Further, the king was probably unwilling to resist Japanese pressure on this matter, in view of that country's power in Korea by that time (Hwangsong Sinmun, April 5, 1905, cited in Patterson 1977a:512-520; Deshler to H. Wilson, reprinted in Kim and Patterson 1974:87-89).

The Japanese government was, in fact, glad to see the ban on emigration to Hawaii and subsequently put pressure on the Korean government to ensure that it was implemented (Yun 1977:39-40). In part the attitude of the Japanese government resulted from pressure from the Continental Settlement Company. In a letter written to Japanese Foreign Minister Komura, the company asked the Japanese government to place a ban on Korean emigration to Hawaii. The company feared that Japanese interests would be shut out in the future if increasing numbers of Koreans went to Hawaii. There was a kernel of truth in this charge: the ratio of Japanese and Korean immigrants in Hawaii had shifted from 8:1 to 2:1 by 1904, but it is unclear whether this resulted in worsened conditions for Japanese and other plantation workers. Japanese workers in the plantation work force went from 70 to 62 percent by July 1905, while the percentage of Koreans rose from about 5 to 11 (Patterson 1977a:527-528, 378-379, 637).

The willingness of the Japanese government to act on behalf of the emigration companies reflected its larger political concerns. While the status of Japanese workers in Hawaii may have been seen as reflecting Japan's national honor, Japanese diplomats probably viewed Deshler's operation with concern for other reasons stemming from their desire to control Korea. First, Deshler was a United States citizen operating with support from what appeared to be high levels in his government. Moreover, the nationalist movement developing among Koreans in Hawaii was a potential nuisance. And perhaps, as Patterson suggests, the Japanese government was moving toward voluntary prohibition of Japanese immigration to the United States in anticipation of the effects of the anti-Japanese movement (Patterson 1977a:519-520). In view of these various factors, the Japanese government had ample reason to desire an end to the emigration of Koreans in Hawaii.

There were brief efforts to revive the emigration project. The Korean government dispatched its vice-foreign minister, Yun Ch'i-ho, on an inspection tour of Koreans in Hawaii, perhaps with a view toward establishing a consulate in Honolulu, as Koreans in Hawaii had requested. But Japanese pressure forced Yun to return to Korea, disheartened (Yun 1977:37; Patterson 1977a:582-611; Lyu 1977:58-61).

Deshler appealed to the Korean Foreign Ministry, and when his appeal failed, he sought assistance from American diplomats in Tokyo. His appeal was forwarded to the United States State Department, but the materials appended by Deshler revealed that he had misrepresented himself to King Kojong as an official of the Hawaiian Territorial Bureau of Immigration. This proved an embarrassment, and he was forced to drop his case (Patterson 1977a:638-660). Thus by the end of 1906 the emigration project had been completely buried.

EXILES, REFUGEES, AND BRIDES, 1905 TO 1924

Japanese Colonialism

In 1905 Japan established a protectorate over Korea. Armed resistance was easily crushed by Japan's military juggernaut, and the king's secret mission to The Hague Conference in 1907 was met only with disinterest. Finally Japan annexed Korea in 1910 following the assassination of Governor-General Ito Hirobumi in 1909 by a Korean patriot (Kim and Kim 1967).

Before annexation and even more so following it, the fate of Korean farmers worsened. Japanese businessmen and settlers flooded Korea, forming a new large ruling class (3,622 in 1882; 42,460 in 1905; 171,543 in 1910; 336,812 in 1918; and 708,448, or 3.2 percent of the population, in 1940) (Henderson 1968:75). Koreans were largely frozen out of administration and wealth-producing activities, while farmers were squeezed mercilessly.

The early colonial policies of Japan aimed at dispossessing Korean farmers to make way for Japanese settlers, especially those organized by the government-sponsored Oriental Development Company. As one Japanese official wrote in 1908, Koreans should migrate to "cold parts" such as Siberia and allow Japanese to farm their lands. Further, "Japanese people should emigrate to Korea and conversely we should bring Korean people to Japan. Only in this way can we secure our national defense and promote our national wealth" (Conroy 1960:471).

By the late 1920s the Oriental Development Company was the largest landowner in the country, owning perhaps one-fifth of all the arable land or one-half of the total land in Korea (Grajdanzev 1944:105-107).

Because the average size of a Korean farm was two acres and that of a Japanese farm was five to six acres, about three farm households had to move to make way for one Japanese settler. "There are many instances in South Kyungsang and North Chulla Provinces [the area of the largest emigration after 1905] in which a whole Korean village community is replaced by Japanese settlers invited by the company," wrote one investigator in the 1930s (Lee 1936:284).

The plight of Korean farmers became grave. High rents and an inadequate diet created misery for them. Many were forced off the land and became migrants or wanderers (Lee 1936:142-180, 274-280). Hence, about 1 million persons fled to northeastern China and another 200,000 to Siberia to establish farms, while about 1 million were forced to migrate to Japan as unskilled laborers (Grajdanzev 1944:81-83).

Moreover, Japanese colonialists in Korea ruled with an iron fist. The quality of life became harsh and oppressive, leading one writer to describe it as "colonial totalitarianism" (Henderson 1968:72-112; see also Grajdanzev 1944:47). Koreans of all social classes, with the exception of a small group of collaborators, found the oppressiveness of life loathsome and desired independence.

Japanese rule in Korea made the nearly 8,000 Koreans who had emigrated to Hawaii reconsider returning. In all, about 1,500 persons returned to Korea between 1905 and 1915, but the vast majority stayed abroad (Moon 1976:83). Thus the original community of migrants and sojourners was transformed into a community of exiles.

Toward a Permanent Community

In the years following Japan's domination of Korea, Koreans in Hawaii and the western continental United States moved toward the establishment of permanent communities of exiles and refugees. Leadership was provided by a small number of intellectuals and ministers, some of whom accompanied the original immigrants and others of whom left Korea by surreptitious means after 1910. In view of the situation in Korea and the interests of the leadership, the activities of the Korean independence movement were the main focus of the Korean communities in Hawaii until liberation in 1945 (Yang 1979).

While Hawaii was the area of greatest concentration, California also attracted many Koreans. A few went to the mainland in 1903 and 1904, but in 1905 over 600 left Hawaii for California. In March 1905 a Korean contractor for the Great Northern Railway went to Honolulu to recruit Korean railway workers. The company advanced the steamship fare to encourage recruitment, and, since plantation work was universally detested, the railway work seemed attractive (No 1965:15). Some

Koreans left the plantations on a moment's notice upon hearing of the opportunities on the continent, departing in secret to circumvent efforts by the plantation managers to hold them to their contracts (Kim 1937:167-168). In spite of legislation hampering the work of recruiters, the flow of persons to the continent continued (Patterson 1977a:632). From 1905 until 1907, the year the gentlemen's agreement put an end to Japanese and Korean immigration, about 1,000 Koreans migrated from Hawaii to the mainland, mainly to California. By 1907, Hawaii was left with about 6,000 Koreans.[15] Those on the mainland were later joined by a small number of persons who trickled over, and by 1916, 1,168 persons had left Hawaii for the mainland (Kim 1937:166).

As the Korean communities in Hawaii and the mainland shifted toward permanence, efforts were made to redress the skewed 10:1 sex ratio. Some male workers went for their wives, and about 600 picture brides were brought to Hawaii and the mainland between 1910 and 1924 as wives for the men who had immigrated earlier (Lyu 1977:26-27).

As with the male immigrants, the picture brides were from diverse geographic areas; but whereas the men were mostly from northwestern Korea, most of their brides-to-be were from Kyŏngsang province in southern Korea. They were mostly young, between the ages of eighteen and twenty-four (Kim 1937:121; but see Lyu 1977:27). Most were illiterate (Lyu 1977:27).

It cost the husband $300 to $400 to bring over a wife. Since most were unable to save this sum, it was usually borrowed, often through credit-loan associations formed among workers toward this end (Kim 1937:122). Go-betweens made the arrangements and took a commission for their efforts, on occasion cheating their clients. According to Lyu (1977:27-28) the main go-between in Seoul and the central part of Korea was a returnee who started in this line by arranging marriages for his friends who were still in Hawaii and then expanding to include others. In the North, the main go-between started by finding spouses for some of his relatives in Hawaii and then included others. In Kyŏngsang province, the area from which most of the picture brides came, networks of kinship and friendship were similarly employed in arranging marriages.

Most of the brides were from poor rural families, and in some cases poverty alone motivated the women to accept these marriages. One bride, for example, later told her children that she had been so poor in Korea that on two occasions she had nearly starved to death. When her cousin wrote proposing a match with a man in Hawaii, her family agreed to send her abroad (University of Hawaii 1977; II:32-33).

In addition to poverty, however, some of the wives seem to have been motivated by a desire for personal and political freedom or by a spirit of adventurousness. In one survey of twenty-four women who left Korea between 1910 and 1924, all gave Japanese oppression as the primary reason for their decision to leave Korea (Sunoo 1977:158). Others wanted a greater degree of personal freedom. One former picture bride recalled that fabulous stories circulated in her tiny, very poor village in Kyŏngsang about Hawaii: "Hawaii's a free place, everybody living well. Hawaii had freedom, so if you like talk, you can talk; you like work, you can work. I wanted to come, so, I sent my picture" (Chai n.d.:2). Since she had little freedom of movement, she used subterfuge to visit an aunt in Pusan who made the marriage arrangements. Deception was necessary, she said, because "going to Hawaii alone is just like girl selling."

Another woman recalled how she bridled against the restrictions imposed on her and then heard of the picture brides:

> Ah, marriage! Then I could get to America! That land of freedom with streets paved of gold! . . . Since I became ten, I've been forbidden to step outside our gates, just like all the rest of the girls of my days . . . [so] becoming a picture bride, whatever that was, would be my answer and release. (Sunoo 1977:149).

Perhaps because of their independence and high-spirited qualities, these women were sometimes disappointed with their husbands and with life in Hawaii. Occasionally, the grooms had engaged in deception in order to attract a wife. The photos were sometimes of the groom as a young man, while he had since aged considerably. In other cases, plantation workers did not reveal their true economic status. The dismay at the first meeting is well known:

> I saw him for the first time at the Immigration Station. He didn't look like his picture. He was really old, odd looking. So my heart stuck. My cousin in Honolulu arranged the marriage, and I was very angry at her. I'm so disappointed, I cry for eight days and don't come out of my room. But I knew that if I don't get married, I have to go back to Korea on the next ship. So on the ninth day I came out and married him. But I don't talk to him for three months. Later on, it was all right. (Seventy-Fifth Anniversary 1978:50; see also Lyu 1977:29)

A few of these women went to plantations with their new husbands, there to join the handful of women who had come with the original group, to cook and do laundry for other Korean workers. In spite of the traditional seclusion of Korean women, some of them were apparently not too reluctant to run boarding houses on the plantations. Most newly married couples stayed in Honolulu, however (Kim 1937:122, 132, 180-186).

TABLE 8.6

MOST POPULAR OCCUPATIONS OF KOREAN WOMEN IN HAWAII, 1930

Occupation	Number	Percent
Servants	37	16.8
Home laundresses	23	10.4
Dressmakers (not in factories)	18	8.2
Trained nurses	17	7.7
Clothing industry operatives	13	5.9
Teachers	12	5.4
Tailors	12	5.4
Agricultural laborers	12	5.4
Other	76	34.8
Total	220	100.0

SOURCE: Kim 1937:160-161

In a 1930 survey of Koreans who had lived in Hawaii for over ten years and who were gainfully employed, 2,137 men and 220 women were listed by occupation. Of the men, approximately half (1,110) were employed in agriculture. There were about 1,200 Korean women in Hawaii, of whom about 16 percent were employed outside the home for wages, mostly in urban occupations. Eight occupations accounted for close to two-thirds of the 220 women (see table 8.6).

In addition to raising children and caring for their families, then, many women found work as servants and launderers or in garment making and tailoring. They were noted for a continued spirit of independence and frequent marital unhappiness (Kim 1937:207-209) and became the backbone of the Korean communities in Hawaii and the mainland United States (Lyu 1977:29), their presence and work making possible the flourishing of exiled Korean communities.

CONCLUSION

The dislocations caused by the decline of the old order in Korea and the effects of foreign imperialism created conditions leading to the organized emigration of Korean workers to Hawaii. The disruption of agriculture, the development of the cash economy, the dislocations of war, and the establishment of colonial rule combined to create a group of impoverished, bankrupt farmers who became city dwellers facing unemployment or marginal unemployment. This group contained many who were willing to consider temporary emigration as a solution to their situation. They were joined by others for whom emigration was an outlet for frustrations engendered by the feudal order.

Organized emigration was made possible by a particular series of circumstances leading the Korean king to approve it in hopes of offsetting strong Japanese influence in Korea. When the United States presence proved too threatening to Korea's new rulers, pressure was exerted to halt the flow of persons to Hawaii.

In view of the later mass migration of 2 million Koreans to Japan, northern China, and Siberia, the United States episode should be seen as a brief interlude reflecting imperialist rivalry for domination of Korea. Imperialists seek control of the resources of the nations they colonize, and for many Third World peoples, the labor power of their masses constitutes their most precious resource. Although the United States was a relatively weak imperialist power in Korea in the early twentieth century, Japan sought to exclude it from Korea partly as a means of controlling the flow of labor power in its new colony. As a case of abortive immigration, then, the Korean episode reflects the mechanisms of imperialist rivalry.

NOTES

1. Grajdanzev estimated there were about 1,000,000 Koreans in Manchuria, about 1,000,000 in Japan, 200,000 in the Soviet Union, and about 100,000 in other countries, mostly other areas of China. But Hyŏn (1967, I:2) estimates there were 2,160,000 Koreans in Manchuria in 1945. This figure appears to be too high.

2. Considerable confusion exists about the size of the yangban population in the later Yi period and its proportion to the rest of the population. The 3.3 percent of total households for yangban, government employees, and literati for 1910 (table 8.1) may be too small, reflecting changes during the Japanese protectorate. Further, since yangban households were probably larger than those of commoners, they may include a larger percentage of the total population than 3.3 percent. At the other end of the scale, some estimates of yangban population are around 18 percent or even higher (Henderson 1968:39-42, 388-390).

3. Shikata Hiroshi's (1933) studies of selected districts in the Yi period indicate that the number of slaves fell from 43.1 percent of the population in 1690 to 31.3 percent in 1858, while commoners declined from 49.5 percent to 20.1 percent. Yangban (or those claiming that status) rose from 7.4 percent to an enormous 48.6 percent (Henderson 1968:41-42).

4. Although the principle of the monarch's ownership of all land existed throughout the Yi period, in practice the existence of private ownership was acknowledged in the law by the eighteenth century (Park 1975).

5. Some Marxist historians in North Korea believe that the pace of economic transformation was quickening in eighteenth-century Korea and might have led to capitalism had not foreign imperialism intervened (DPRK 1968:23 ff.). On the other side, Japanese economic historians have traced the introduction of capitalism to Japanese colonialism (Shikata 1933; Deuchler 1978:67).

6. In 1910 Korea had eleven cities with a population of 14,000 or more, with an aggregate population of 566,000, or 14 percent of the total population (Grajdanzev 1944:80). The population of Seoul was around 220,000 at the turn of the century, Pyongyang around 60,000 to 75,000, Taegu about 75,000, and Kaesŏng about 60,000 (Henderson 1968:99; Bishop 1897:34, 176; Brown 1905:498).

7. Kim and Kim (1967:68-69) estimate that Korea probably owed 1.3 to 1.5 million yen to all foreigners by 1892 in addition to a 200,000 *tael* loan from China. Han'guk sa (1965, V:951) estimates a total of 710,877 won outstanding debts by the outbreak of the Sino-Japanese War. In 1896 the total income for the Korean government from taxes, customs revenues, and government-owned gold mines was about 5 million won ("The Budget for 1896," *Korean Repository* 1896, III:33).

8. The following works deal entirely or in part with the early wave of Korean immigrants: Houchins 1976; Hyon 1967; Kim and Patterson 1974; Kim 1959, 1977; Ko 1973; Lyu 1977; Moon 1976; No 1965; Patterson 1977*a*; Seventy-Fifth Anniversary 1978; Yang 1979; Yun 1977. Of these various works, Patterson 1977*a* has been most useful.

9. The Sumin wŏn (or Yumin wŏn) was given a modern organizational form and was headed by the noted reformer, Min Yŏng-hwan. For an organizational chart see Patterson 1977*a*:Appendix. See also Hyŏn 1967, II:797.

10. Data on wages in Korea in the early twentieth century are scarce. One contemporary estimate was 5¢ to 10¢ a day (which was about $1.50 to $3.00 per month). The Hawaiian Commission on Labor estimated Korean wages to be $4.00 to $5.00 per month, while Korean workers in Japan in 1897 were earning 40¢ a day (or about $12.00 per month). The wage labor system seems to have been poorly developed at that time: workers probably received meals, board, and incidentals from the employer, and perhaps gifts or a small stipend in addition. Hence the surprise of many Korean workers to discover that the wages of $16.00 in Hawaii did not include food or other expenses (Patterson 1977*a*: 321-322).

11. In 1904, A.W. Teller, said to be representing Deshler, tried to collect money from Korean workers on Oahu. An altercation resulted and Teller was unable to collect. The Sin Min Hoe, or New People's

Society, organized opposition to Deshler's efforts to collect money from the immigrants (No 1965:10; Patterson 1977a:577).

12. Deshler and Allen apparently believed that the *kamni* or leading local official of Inchon opposed the emigration project because he hadn't been bribed sufficiently by the Americans. Allen also believed that Yi Yong-ik opposed the project because of his antiforeignism (Patterson 1977a:292-297).

13. The figures on immigrants vary somewhat. No Chae-yon estimated that 7,226 immigrants, of which 755 were women and children, arrived (No 1965; I:1-28). Bernice Kim, citing Hawaiian Bureau of Immigration data, gives the figure of 7,296 (6,641 men, 613 women, and 44 under the age of 14) (1937:83).

14. These materials are *Kankoku serfu Hawai oyobi Mokoshika yuki Kankoku imin kinshi Ikken-tsuki hogo itaku Kankoku no ken* (The Matter of the Prohibition of Emigration to Hawaii and Mexico by the Korean Government— The Matter of Recommendation and Protection), 1905 (Meiji 38), *Gaimusho Gaiko Shiryo Kan* (Diplomatic Records Office), Tokyo, Japan. They are discussed by Patterson 1977a:511-550.

15. The 1930 Hawaii census revealed a total of 6,461 persons of Korean origin, of whom 2,932 or 45.3 percent were aged 14 or younger (Kim 1937:202).

References

An Pyong-jik
    1974   "Socio-economics of the nationalist movement in the early twentieth century." Korea Journal 14 (September):30-36.
Asakawa, K.
    1970   The Russo-Japanese Conflict: Its Causes and Issues. Port Washington, N. Y.:
    [1904] Kennikat Press.
Bishop, Isabella Bird
    1897   Korea and Her Neighbors. New York: Revell.
Brown, Arthur J.
    1905   "A reading journey through Korea." Chautauquan 41:491-578.
Chai, Alice
    n.d.   "A picture bride from Korea: The life history of a Korean-American woman in Hawaii." Unpub. paper, Women's Studies Program, University of Hawaii.
Chang Dae-hong
    1974   "A study of Korean cultural minority: The Paekchong," Pp. 55-88 in Andrew C. Nahm, ed., Traditional Korea: Theory and Practice. Kalamazoo: Center for Korean Studies, Western Michigan University.
Choe Ching Young
    1972   The Rule of the Taewongun, 1864-1873. Cambridge: Harvard University Press.
Choe Ho-jin
    1973   Kŭndae Han'guk kyŏngjesa. Seoul: Chaemundang.
Chung, Henry
    1921   The Case of Korea. New York: Revell.
Conroy, Hilary
    1960   The Japanese Seizure of Korea, 1868-1873: A Study of Realism and Idealism in International Relations. Philadelphia: University of Pennsylvania Press.
Cook, Harold F.
    1972   Korea's 1884 Incident: Its Background and Kim Ok-kyun's Elusive Dream. Seoul: Royal Asiatic Society, Korea Branch.
Deuchler, Martina
    1978   Confucian Gentlemen and Barbarian Envoys: The Opening of Korea, 1875-1885. Seattle: University of Washington Press.
DPRK: Choson Minju Chuui Inmin Konghwaguk, Hwahakwon, Yoksa Yonguso [Center for Historical Studies, Academy of Sciences, Democratic People's Republic of Korea].
    1968   Kin gyokukin no kenkyu. Ed. and tr. by Nihon Chosen kenkyuso [Research on Kim Ok-kyun]. Tokyo: Nihon Chosen kenkyuso.
Grajdanzev, Andrew J.
    1944   Modern Korea. New York: Institute of Pacific Relations.
Han'guk sa
    1965   Chindan Hakhoe, ed. 3d ed. 5 vols. Seoul: Il munhwa sa.

Harrington, Fred Harvey
1944 God, Mammon and the Japanese: Dr. Horace N. Allen and Korean-American Relations, 1884-1905. Madison: University of Wisconsin Press.
Henderson, Gregory
1968 Korea: The Politics of the Vortex. Cambridge: Harvard University Press.
Houchins, Lee, and Chang-su Houchins
1976 "The Korean experience in America, 1903-1924." Pp. 129-156 in Norris Hundley, Jr., ed., The Asian American: The Historical Experience. Santa Barbara: ABC-Clio.
Hyŏn Kyu-hwan (Hyun Kyoo Whan)
1967 Han'guk yu imin sa [A History of Korean Emigrants]. 2 vols. Seoul: Ōmungak.
Japan. Gaimusho Gaiko Shiryo Kan (Diplomatic Records Office) Tokyo
1905 Kankoku Seifu Hawai oyobi Mokushika yuki Kankoku imin kinshi ikken-tsuki hogo itaku Kankoku no ken [The Matter of the Prohibition of Emigration to Hawaii and Mexico by the Korean Government — The Matter of Recommendations and Protection].
Kim, Bernice B. H.
1937 The Koreans in Hawaii. Master's thesis, University of Hawaii.
Kim, C. I. Eugene, and Han-kyo Kim
1967 Korea and the Politics of Imperialism, 1876-1910. Berkeley, Los Angeles: University of California Press.
Kim Hei Chu
1971 "The role of religious belief and social structure in Korea's breakthrough into modernity." Ph.D. diss., New School for Social Research.
Kim Hyung-chan
1977 "The history and role of the church in the Korean American community." Pp. 47-63 in Kim Hyung-chan, ed., The Korean Diaspora: Historical and Sociological Studies of Korean Immigration and Assimilation in North America. Santa Barbara: ABC-Clio.
Kim Hyung-chan, and Wayne Patterson
1974 The Koreans in America, 1882-1974: a Chronology and a Fact Book. Dobbs Ferry, N. Y.: Oceana Publishers.
Kim Mun-sik
1971 "Il-je ha ui nŏngo" [Agriculture under Japanese Imperialism]. Pp. 3-109 in Asia munje yongu so, Il-je ha ui kyŏngje ch' imtal sa [History of Economic Aggression under Japanese Imperialism]. Seoul: Minjong.
Kim Wŏn-yong (Warren Y. Kim)
1959 ChaeMi Hanin Osimnyon sa [A Fifty Year History of the States]. Reedley, Calif.
Ko Sung-je
1973 Han'guk imin sa yongu [Research on the History of Korean Emigration]. Seoul: Changmunkak.
Korean Repository. 1-5, 1892-1898.
Ladd, George Trumbell
1908 In Korea with Marquis Ito. London: Longmans.
Lee, Chong-sik
1963 The Politics of Korean Nationalism. Berkeley and Los Angeles: University of California Press.
Lee, Hoon K.
1936 Land Utilization and Rural Economy in Korea. Chicago: University of Chicago Press.

Lee Hyoun-young (Yi Hyŏn-yŏng)
    1975   "A geographic study of the Korean periodic markets." Korea Journal 15 (August):12-24.
Lyu, Kingsley K.
    1977   "Korean nationalist activities in Hawaii and the continental United States, 1900-1945. Part I: 1900-1919." Amerasia Journal 4 (January):23-90.
McKenzie, Frederick Arthur
    1905   From Tokyo to Tiflis: Uncensored Letters from the War. London: Hurst and Blackett.
Moon, Hyung June
    1976   "The Korean immigrants in America: The quest for identity in the formative years, 1903-1918." Ph.D. diss., University of Nevada.
Moore, S. F.
    1898   "The butchers of Korea." Korean Repository 5:127-132.
Moriyama, Alan T.
    1977   "Japanese emigration companies and Hawaii." Unpub. paper.
No Chae-yon
    1965   Chae Mi Hanin sa ryok [Outline History of Koreans in America]. Los Angeles.
Paik, L. George
    1929   The History of Protestant Missions in Korea, 1832-1910. Pyongyang: Union Christian College Press.
Palais, James B.
    1976   "Political leadership in the Yi Dynasty." Pp. 3-38 in Suh Dae-sook and Chae-jin Lee, eds. Political Leadership in Korea. Seattle: University of Washington Press.
Palmer, Spencer J.
    1962   "American gold mining in Korea's Unsan district." Pacific Historical Review 31 (November):379-391.
    1967   Korea and Christianity: The Problem of Identification. Seoul: Hollym Corp.
Park Byoung-ho (Pak Pyong-ho)
    1975   "The legal nature of land ownership in the Yi Dynasty." Korea Journal 15 (October):4-10.
Patterson, Wayne
    1977a The Korean Frontier in America: Immigration to Hawaii, 1896-1910. Ph.D. diss., University of Pennsylvania.
    1977b "The first attempt to obtain Korean laborers for Hawaii, 1896-1897." Pp. 9-31 in Hyung-chan Kim, ed., The Korean Diaspora. Santa Barbara: ABC-Clio.
Rhodes, Harry A.
    n.d.   History of the Korea Mission, Presbyterian Church, USA, 1884-1934. Seoul: Chosen Mission Presbyterian Church, USA.
Sands, William Franklin
    1930   Undiplomatic Memories. New York: McGraw Hill.
Seventy-Fifth Anniversary of Korean Immigration to Hawaii.
    1978   1905-1978. Honolulu: 75th Anniversary of Korean Immigration to Hawaii Committee.
Shikata Hiroshi
    1933   "Chōsen ni okeru kindai Shihonshugi no seiritsu katei" [The process of formation of modern capitalism in Korea]. Pp. 1-226 in Chosen shakai keizai shi kenkyu [Research on Korean Socio-economic History]. Seoul: Hogakkai, Keijo Teikoku Daigaku.
Sohn Pow-key, Kim Chol-choon, and Hong Yi-sup
    1970   The History of Korea. Seoul: Korean National Commission for UNESCO.

Sunoo, Harold Hakwon, and Sonia Shinn Sunoo
1977 "The heritage of the first Korean women immigrants in the United States, 1903-1924." Pp. 124-171 in Kim Byong-suh et al., Koreans in America. Memphis, Tenn.: Korean Christian Scholars Publication no. 2.
Tobias, J. J.
1967 Crime and Industrial Society in the Nineteenth Century. New York: Schocken Books.
University of Hawaii at Manoa
1977 Waialua and Haleiwa: The People Tell Their Story [Transcripts of Oral History Interviews]. Ethnic Studies Oral History Project.
Wagner, Edward Willett
1974 The Literati Purges: Political Conflict in Early Yi Korea. Cambridge: East Asian Research Center, Harvard University.
Weems, Benjamin B.
1964 Reform, Rebellion, and the Heavenly Way. Tucson: University of Arizona Press for the Association of Asian Studies.
Wood, Oliver Ellsworth
1905 From the Yalu to Port Arthur: An Epitome of the First Period of the Russo-Japanese War. Tokyo; Kansas City, Mo.: F. Hudson.
Yang Eun-sik
1979 "Korean community, 1903-1970's: Identity to economic prosperity." Unpub. paper. Los Angeles: Koryo Research Institute, Project on Koreans in America: Problems and Issues in Settlement.
Yim Sun-bin
1979 Interview data.
Yun Yo-jun
1977 "Early history of Korean immigration to America." Pp. 33-46 in Hyung-chan Kim, ed., The Korean Diaspora. Santa Barbara: ABC-Clio.

9
Colonial Impact and Punjabi Emigration to the United States

Sucheta Mazumdar

While the large-scale emigrations of the nineteenth and twentieth centuries must necessarily be seen within the broad framework of the development of the world capitalist system, micro studies focusing on specific regional patterns of emigration can aid our understanding of the dynamics of emigration. Historically, definite patterns of emigration have evolved, with emigration from specific geographical areas being directed toward certain other equally specific destinations. Thus the majority of Chinese emigrants to the Americas originated in the district of Taishan, and Hiroshima-ken on Honshu provided the majority of Japanese emigrants. In the case of India, emigrants to the Pacific Coast of North America came from the state of Punjab and five contiguous districts in particular. These were the districts of Jullunder, Hoshiarpur, Gurdaspur, Amritsar, and Ludhiana (fig. 9.1); and to this day most Punjabi emigrants to the United Kingdom, Canada, and California are primarily from the Hoshiarpur and Jullunder districts. The development of such patterns of emigration is the result of specific historical phenomena and the response of the local population to them.

This study will examine the emigration of the Punjabis to North America during the first two decades of the twentieth century and offer an explanation of how and why 99 percent of the Indian emigrants to the Pacific Coast came from so localized an area. For this purpose, I will use the conceptual framework presented at the beginning of this volume. The central idea is that capitalist development leads to imperialism, which in turn distorts the development of colonized territories.

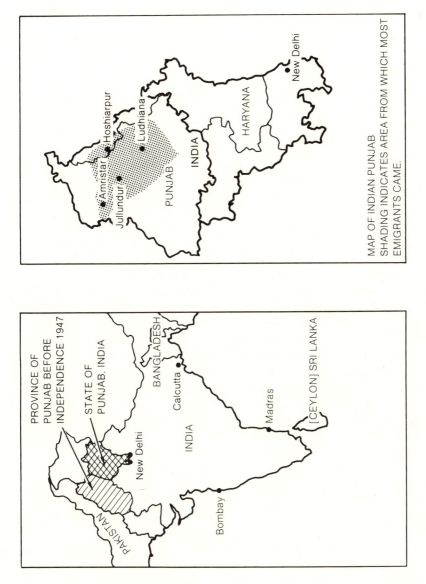

MAP OF INDIAN PUNJAB

SHADING INDICATES AREA FROM WHICH MOST
EMIGRANTS CAME.

Fig. 9.1

Consequently many people are displaced from their traditional economic systems, becoming available for emigration. They then provide the labor force necessary in the developed capitalist society for further development.

ORIGINS OF INDIAN EMIGRATION

Organized emigration from India that was of any numerical significance did not exist prior to the establishment of British colonial rule. Reasons for this varied. A fundamental reason may have been that Hinduism, the predominant religion, had certain taboos against sea travel. More importantly, the unfree nature of labor relations in the settled agricultural regions of India, where the agricultural workers were bound to the land they worked, precluded the possibility of individual emigration. By the end of the eighteenth century, however, because of increased overseas contacts under British rule, Indian laborers were to be found in most of the ports of southeast Asia. On the sugarcane estates of Mauritius there were at least 6,000 Indian slaves, and thousands of others were brought to Réunion, in what was but "a modified form of the slave trade" (Tinker 1974:44). These were primarily individuals from the coastal areas, often kidnapped and sold by both Indian and non-Indian traders. The role of the British colonial government in these earliest instances of mass labor movements cannot be determined, and private profiteers seem to have controlled the trade.

Officially sanctioned emigration dates from 1842, when three centers or ports were established in Calcutta, Madras, and Bombay under government auspices for the purpose of facilitating labor emigration. Expanding colonial industries, such as sugarcane in Mauritius and the West Indies and capitalist ventures into railroad building in East Africa, created a need for an inexhaustible source of cheap labor. With the abolition of slavery in the British Empire in 1834 and the refusal of the liberated slaves to work on the sugar plantations of Trinidad, Jamaica, British Guiana, and Mauritius, the sugar planters became actively interested in searching out new areas of labor recruitment. India, a British colony with a large population, was the obvious choice. During the nineteenth century, nearly 700,000 Indians were taken to the West Indies, British Guiana, and Mauritius as indentured laborers (Saha 1970:1).

During the first thirty years of organized emigration, almost to 1870, the main point of embarkation for the laborers was Calcutta, the center of British power in India. Emigrants were drawn from an ever-widening circle around Calcutta, a circle which progressively reached for supplies of new recruits into northern India and, by the 1870s, into Punjab. Initially, most recruits were hill tribal people, but the developing colonial tea industry in eastern India set up its own demands for labor and began to draw from the same sources. Recruiters, searching for indentured laborers to take overseas, then expanded operations into the Indo-Gangetic plain, and agricultural laborers were drawn into emigration. Changes initiated by the British legal system and land reforms in Bengal and Bihar had transformed the class of revenue collectors into landlords, who had acquired enormous power over the rural population. Because of the extractions of this landlord class, many of the lower class agriculturists had lost their lands and had been reduced to the status of indentured serfs, a condition that would last for generations to come. Recruiters from emigration firms found these laborers quite willing to emigrate for terms of servitude lasting five to seven years, which seemed light in comparison to the condition they were in. By the turn of the century indentured labor emigration, by which the laborer was indentured to the company or plantation that acquired the services of the laborer, had been gradually replaced by emigration under contract to labor contractors. Officially, indentured labor emigration did not cease until 1922 (Tinker 1974:368).

In one form of emigration a labor contractor recruited semiserf, debt-bonded agricultural workers, whom he sponsored by paying their debts to the village landlords and moneylenders and transferring these debts to himself. The labor contractor then made the workers pay their debts to him, primarily through the process of cuts from the wages received by the worker employed in estates or plantations with which the labor contractor had connections. The vast majority of Indian laborers emigrating to Malaya and Ceylon in the twentieth century emigrated under contract labor obligations. By the beginning of the twentieth century there was also a very small percentage of laborers emigrating independently. These individuals provided for their own passage and were not bound by labor obligations to employers prior to emigration. Punjabi emigration to North America falls largely in the category of independent emigration, though instances of labor contract emigration are also known.

PRECOLONIAL PUNJAB

Since major emigration of labor began only after British colonization of India, it is an implicit assumption that the socioeconomic changes brought about by colonization fostered this emigration. In order to examine this premise somewhat more closely, it is necessary briefly to state the conditions prevailing in Punjab prior to colonization.

Punjab (literally, the "land of five rivers") is a rectangular-shaped province on the northwestern perimeter of India. It is essentially agricultural, with deserts and semiarid regions on three sides. The province itself has four geographically distinct areas, but we are primarily concerned with the area of the plains, for most of the emigrants came from this densely populated, fertile region (see fig. 9.1). Though there had been roads connecting this part of the province to the principal trade routes of India since the seventeenth century, transportation was difficult and there were few all-weather roads. Given that there are several major rivers in the area, it is indeed surprising that river transportation was not better developed in the Punjab. The explanation seems to be that the economy did not warrant a more advanced system of transportation. The few urban centers that existed were primarily religious or administrative centers and had little relevance to the lives of the majority of the people. The economy was localized, predominantly agricultural, and not tied into any national structure. It remained primarily agricultural even after the British annexation of Punjab in 1849, but certain fundamental administrative and economic changes transformed the precapitalist nature of Punjab society.

Before proceeding further, however, terms such as *Punjabi*, *Jat* and *Sikh*, which are used frequently and interchangeably to refer to those who have emigrated to North America and to the United Kingdom, need to be clarified. *Punjabi* refers to all individuals, regardless of religion, who come from the state of Punjab, divided since independence in 1947 into the province of Punjab in Pakistan and the states of Punjab and Haryana in India. *Jat* refers to the tribal ethnic origin of many of the emigrants who are from this area.

The term *Sikh* indicates the religion of most of the emigrants, which began as a reform religion in the late fifteenth century. Sikhism tried to reconcile Islam and Hinduism and develop a syncretic creed that preached equal dignity for all and thus challenged the Hindu caste system and the dominance of the Hindu priestly class. In response to persecutions by the Muslim rulers, the leaders (gurus) of the Sikh transformed the believers into a military theocracy. This marked the beginning of a military tradition that is followed to this day and that has also had an impact on the pattern of emigration to North America. To emphasize religious identity, a distinctive appearance was also adopted by the Sikh males, namely, never shaving off the beard or cutting the hair. Once baptized, it is a disgrace for the Sikh to cut his hair, which is regarded as a symbol of his commitment. Often a turban is worn over the hair, and a man is not allowed to enter the Sikh temple without covering his head.

Since most of the emigrants to the Pacific Coast were Sikhs, this adherence to wearing turbans got them branded as "ragheads" in both Canada and California.

Punjab was part of the Muslim Mogul empire (centered in Delhi); but by the late eighteenth century Mogul power was on the decline, and local Sikh feudal lords had acquired political power. In order to understand the patterns of land ownership and consequent land alienation that preceded large-scale emigration, a brief mention of property rights in precolonial Punjab is appropriate. Individual ownership of land was not recognized, nor did the feudal chieftains have direct ownership of the agricultural land. They only had the right to collect revenue from people in the areas under their control. Land was controlled and cultivated in perpetuity by proprietary groups, whose functions and origins were somewhat similar to those of the lineage groups in southern China. Later under British rule, when these agricultural units, which were dominated by one or two lineage groups, became synonymous with the unit of revenue collection (the village), these lineages became even more powerful politically. The village itself came to be identified by the caste[1] of the dominant lineages within it, and even 100 years later the number and composition of these lineages within a village remained an influential factor affecting migration.

This description should not suggest that the rural settlements in precolonial Punjab were homogeneous and lacked socioeconomic inequalities. There were property groups that controlled large tracts of land and other property groups that had only a few acres. There were also a small tenant population and agricultural workers who were traditionally employed by individual households. Further, the caste system meant that artisans or leather workers could never hope to cultivate land and had to depend on the mutual patronage system of the village cultivating castes for their supplies of grain in exchange for services rather than cash. But, in general, unless warfare intervened or the armies of the local chieftains needed replenishing, the economic *status quo* was maintained with little opportunity for mobility or change.

COLONIAL PUNJAB

With the British annexation of Punjab in 1849, much that has been described above changed. Land tenure patterns were particularly affected. By this time, the first stage of colonialism, which is typically marked by direct plunder and seizure of economic surplus (Chandra 1980:273), was past. Instead, British colonial policy became directed toward making the Indian colony productive by developing capitalist agriculture, which would enable it to complement, by supplying raw materials, the metropolitan British economy (Chandra 1980:278). For this purpose land tenure systems had to be altered, and a cash economy had to be sponsored. The ultimate result of these policies was that small holders were forced off the land and had to become agricultural laborers in order to survive. Some of these laborers, when provided with the option of emigration, were the first to apply and thus became completely disengaged from the existing political economy.

British law and concepts of property rights as introduced in the Punjab (and elsewhere in India) gave a landlord full authority to sell and transfer land. Land revenue laws further demanded that the revenue be paid by a certain date; failure to pay the revenue tax made the land or a part of it liable to sale. A *landlord*, according to these laws, was defined as the person responsible for paying the revenue on a particular plot of land. Application of these concepts to Punjab created immediate dislocation, for, as seen, very different concepts of land tenure prevailed, and land as private property had not been recognized in the precolonial period.

When the first land settlement was made in Punjab, the British government recognized as landlords/landowners only those who were willing to take the responsibility of meeting revenue demands by the specified date. Smaller property groups or families who had cultivated certain plots of land for generations and had retained the harvest as owners in the preannexation period suddenly found themselves unable to come up with the required cash for revenue payments on the date stipulated by the British authorities. For many the only solution seemed to be to enter on the revenue records the names of more prosperous fellow villagers as proprietors of land and then continue to cultivate the land as "occupancy tenants" who could not be dispossessed without a court order (Sharma 1971:17). In a static economy such arrangements may have been viable. In the boom in commercial agriculture that followed the colonization of Punjab, however, land became a valuable commodity to be bought, sold, and mortgaged for credit, leaving those who had entrusted land to larger proprietors perpetually in the position of tenants.

ECONOMIC TRANSFORMATION

Immediately after British annexation a noticeable change occurred in the realm of transportation. British interest in Punjab had stemmed as much from a conscious recognition of the agricultural wealth of the area as from a fear of the expansionist motives of Imperial Russia. The British, therefore, sought to secure both Punjab and Afghanistan and improved those transportation facilities that were necessary for troop movements. By the end of the nineteenth century over 2,000 miles of metaled roads, connecting the larger cities of the North with border military outposts, had been constructed. A flurry of railway construction resulted in the Punjab heartland being linked to all major Indian cities and ports, with close to 2,000 miles of railway laid in the province itself. By the early twentieth century, a former British administrator could boast that there were very few areas in the province that were more than 25 miles from a railway line (Calvert 1936:109).

After annexation, the agricultural potential of this newly acquired territory was fully exploited by the British. Several canals were built, and land reclamation and irrigation projects increased the total land under cultivation by over 3 million acres between 1869 and 1879 (Calvert 1936:121). Besides the traditional crops of wheat and sugarcane, recently introduced crops such as New Orleans cotton, flax, and tobacco began to be extensively cultivated. A veritable economic revolution occurred in the Punjab.

The growth of a money economy, improved transportation, and the feasibility of selling surplus grain in distant areas brought about a rapid commercialization of agriculture in the 1860s and 1870s. Prior to annexation, for example, there had been practically no export of agricultural products outside the province. But following annexation and the land settlement, export of food products increased dramatically. From 1871 to 1873, wheat export alone was valued at Rs 500,000 and forty years later it was valued at well over Rs 100 million (Calvert 1936:157). In order to survive in an increasingly cash-based economy, those with small holdings found it necessary to cultivate such cash crops as tobacco, fruit, or legumes, though this inevitably tied them to the larger provincial or national markets and left them extremely vulnerable to changes in the market prices of commodities.

In an expanding economy and with private ownership of land, land prices began to rise steadily. At the time of annexation, land had no recognized sale value, since it was collectively owned, and transfer or alienation were impossible. In 1862-1863, the average price per acre was 8 rupees. By the early 1870s it had risen to over 50 rupees per acre, and by 1917-1918 the price of an average acre of land was between 250 and 400 rupees (Calvert 1936:155). Under such circumstances class distinctions in the countryside became further polarized. Rich peasant entrepreneurs constantly sought to expand their holdings, since agriculture was the most profitable of all business ventures besides money lending.

MORTGAGING OF LAND AND LAND ALIENATION

Mortgaging of land and the consequent alienation of land had become a major problem in Punjab by 1900. The typical form of mortgage usually had a sale clause attached stating that if redemption did not take place by a certain date, the pledged asset would pass into the hands of the creditor (Calvert 1936:266). Since most of the moneylenders were also land-hungry agricultural entrepreneurs, the illiterate peasant who mortgaged an acre or two of land would seldom be informed of this clause by the moneylender and would ultimately lose his land. The rate of interest was also prohibitive, varying from 18 to 36 percent per annum and making it certain that the mortgagee would be unable to redeem his land unless he had sudden access to a large amount of money. This was the typical manner in which land was accumulated by moneylenders in India.

There were several reasons for mortgaging land. The revenue demand in itself was between 50 and 65 percent of the net income of the farmer (O'Donnell 1908:112). Though this was apparently lower than precolonial feudal revenue dues, it was nevertheless a severe imposition. Moreover, the inflexibility of revenue collection in Punjab, irrespective of local calamities and problems, drove numerous people into debt. A study made in the 1880s found that 12 percent of rural debt resulted from loans made for the purpose of paying land revenue taxes (Calvert 1936:251). In addition, land was often mortgaged for unproductive purposes like bride price, weddings, and litigation.

Natural disasters further aided those who were in a position to lend money and expand their holdings at the cost of those who lived more tenuously. In 1869 there was a severe famine, and 600,000 head of cattle were lost in four districts alone (Singh 1966:151). Extensive shortages again occurred in 1877, and yet another long and severe famine affected Punjab between 1899 and 1902. In fact, some feel that this last famine was one of the chief causes for emigration to North America (Bagai 1968:28). The Punjabi peasant depended on his cattle for survival almost as much as he did on his land, and these famines, causing immense cattle mortality, drove the small holders into debt. As much as 11 percent of all mortgages resulted from loans for buying cattle. Mortgaging was so widespread that it has been calculated that by 1920, 80 percent of all the peasant proprietors in Punjab were in debt (Darling 1925:4). Though the extent and frequency of debt bondage in Punjab are unknown, debt was used by the moneylender-capitalist to control what the peasant produced and the price at which he sold to his creditor.

POPULATION GROWTH

Rural indebtedness and pressure on land were also increased by a dramatic rise in population. The economic opportunities provided by the opening up of the canal colonies were exhausted, and frequent subdivisions of land in an area where primogeniture was not followed resulted in uneconomical small landholdings. Between 1855 and 1881, the population had increased between 18 and 20 percent in some of these fertile districts not only because of the lowered death rates of peacetimes but also because of internal migration from drought-affected areas (Darling 1925:261; Singh 1966:153). The consequent land hunger and inability of a large segment of the population to eke out an existence from their limited landholdings further accentuated the polarization of the rural class structure.

RURAL CLASS STRUCTURE IN COLONIAL PUNJAB

By the turn of the century, the class structure that emerged reflected the economic and social changes of the preceding decades. In the fertile districts of the plains area that we are concerned with, fourteen acres was regarded as the limit that an average man could hope to cultivate alone if he had a pair of oxen. Detailed statistics are unavailable for the nineteenth century, but studies from the early twentieth century show that gross maldistribution of land had certainly occurred: 17.9 percent of the peasants owned less than one acre of land, and 40.4 percent owned between one and five acres (Calvert 1936:172). Since five acres of land was judged adequate for a family only if the land was very fertile and well irrigated, the above averages indicate that 60 percent of the population did not own enough land to make ends meet. But 8.7 percent of the population held 25.7 percent of the land; and these rich landlords, along with those who owned more than fifteen acres, controlled 61 percent of the total arable land. Tenancy had also increased proportionately, and by the 1920s fully half the cultivated area of the province was being worked by tenants (Calvert 1936:221). In an era of rising prices for agricultural products, rents were typically paid in kind and were often as high as 50 percent of the produce. The landlord invested nothing in the land and was a rent receiver, pure and simple. Needless to say, then, a vast majority of the population led a precarious existence at best; and, under such circumstances, if opportunities for emigration could be found, they would be readily seized.

COLONIAL IMPACT ON THE MANUFACTURING SECTOR

One may well ask why, with surplus money seeking investment and being used for lending and the buying of land, industry did not develop in the Punjab. The development of industry would have provided employment for many and eventually would have brought in a high rate of return on the investment. The underdevelopment of industry in Punjab may be explained by examining several factors. Punjab had entered the phase of commercial agriculture relatively late. Long staple cotton and tobacco were therefore new crops at a time when they had been known in other parts of India for a much longer period. By the end of the nineteenth century, there were already some Indian-owned mills and factories in western India that produced for the home market. These textile mills faced stiff competition from Lancashire and Manchester cotton mills, which, under the British, had cornered the home market in India (Harnetty 1972:7-35). The market demand for raw cotton and cotton yarn from Punjab was, therefore, well established, most of it going to mills in Bombay. It would have been necessary to create a market for Punjabi textiles, a venture that did not promise the easy returns of money lending.

The industrial sector of precolonial Punjab was only nominally developed. Three-fourths of the items manufactured were in the category of luxury handicrafts and involved artisans specializing in the making of fine muslins, jewelry, luxury clothing, decorative swords, and furniture inlaid with ivory. Export trade from the area primarily consisted of these same articles. British colonization wiped out the main consumers of these goods, namely the Mogul aristocracy in Delhi and the innumerable warlords and chieftains who had dominated the Punjab.

Other local Punjabi industries, such as woollen shawl making, carpet weaving, and silk making, which also produced luxury items for the ruling class and for export, definitely declined in the late nineteenth century from a combination of such factors as the changes in fashion tastes and the availability of foreign imports. The *pashmina* shawl industry of Amritsar, for example, produced clothing for the Sikh nobility and for the aristocracy of Delhi, Hyderabad, and Lucknow.* After annexation, the industry flourished for a period because European exporting firms found profitable markets for these shawls in Paris and London. The collapse of the industry came when, at the end of the nineteenth century, fashions in Paris changed and shawls were no longer worn (*Amritsar District Gazetteer* in Research Society of Pakistan

---

*Pashmina is a particularly soft and fine wool from a breed of Himalayan goats.

1978:36). By the twentieth century, very few weavers were employed, and 60 to 70 percent of the shawls were being imported ready-made from Germany and only embroidered locally as a handicraft industry for the Indian market. Similar circumstances prevailed in the carpet industry in the districts of Amritsar and Gurdaspur, where changes in taste and fashion patterns in the export market dramatically reduced sales. In the nineteenth century the silk industry of Amritsar and Gurdaspur was primarily concerned with yarn dyeing and weaving. Most of the raw silk came from Shanghai via Bombay and Karachi. It was then dyed, woven, and sold in lengths. This trade, too, was disrupted by the importation of machine-made silk lengths from Japan and France (*Amritsar District Gazetteer* in Research Society of Pakistan 1978:37).

More fundamentally, however, the cotton textile manufacturing sector, which was geared to providing a wide range of cloths and yarns to the general populace, was also affected by British colonial policies. The Punjabi cotton weaving and dyeing industries suffered a setback from British imports. Factory-made cloth and yarn from England were sold at a lower price than the locally made products because of special taxes attached to such goods by the British and the indigenous yarn spinning industry was almost eliminated. But the thesis stating that the entire Indian cotton industry including the weaving sector was ruined by British imports needs to be examined more closely; for it has been found that the durable "country cloth" or *khadi* continued to be preferred by the poorer segments of society while the superior cotton cloths, used extensively by the well-to-do, were totally replaced by imports (*Jullunder District Gazetteer* in Research Society of Pakistan 1978:526).

Thus it is seen that the manufacturing sectors most severely affected by British colonization in the Punjab were those that produced luxury items. These goods had a narrow base and a limited internal market. The precapitalist structure kept the industries from expanding, and the sudden availability of cheaper, foreign-made goods left the domestic product unable to compete. The organization of labor in these precapitalist workshops, however, made it unlikely that they could have competed with capitalist production of any sort. The artisans from these industries were not a free labor force but were entirely dependent on the "master artisan" or entrepreneur who owned and operated the workshop. In the Amritsar carpet-weaving industry, for example, all artisans owed 300 to 1,000 rupees to their employers, debts which were incurred not only as part of their apprenticeship but also from minor emergencies afterward (Calvert 1936:309). If the artisan wanted to leave or join another employer, the entire amount of the debt would first have to be paid. This sort of debt bondage restricted the artisan class, and when conditions worsened because of foreign imports, the artisans became even more rapidly impoverished than the small landholders. What followed is a classic case of debt bondage migration (Omvedt 1980:186).

EARLIEST EMIGRATION FROM PUNJAB

Although detailed archival research would be necessary to establish a direct relationship between artisanal displacement in the particular manufacturing industries discussed above and emigration to East Africa, available materials indicate that the earliest emigrants from Punjab were predominantly indentured laborers from the artisan class (Tinker 1977:6). The most massive emigration of this type took place in 1896, when 19,000 Indians, more than half of them from Punjab, were recruited for the construction of the railway in Uganda (Tinker 1974:278). Most of the laborers had been enlisted by contractors of "gangers," employed by the emigration agents for each of the British colonies seeking labor (Saha 1970:82). The workers on the Uganda Railway were considered to have a "high paying" job — 30 shillings per month, compared to Indian laborers in sugarcane estates in Mauritius, paid 11 shillings a month (Tinker 1974:185). But the hard work damaged their health, and of the few who could return to India, most brought back nothing (Tinker 1974:175). Some Punjabi indentured workers were also sent to Fiji, but the humid climate and work conditions brought strong objections from the workers, and plantation management decided South Indian coolies more used to the humidity were the preferred labor force.

Initial emigration to North America from Punjab occurred via the Pacific Ocean. Later, however, with the ban on Indian immigration to the United States in the 1920s, individuals and small groups went to Central America via the Atlantic route and smuggled themselves across the Mexican border. The predominantly Sikh Punjabi composition of the North American emigrants does raise the question of why Punjabis, rather than any other ethnic/linguistic group from India, first came to the United States and Canada.

PUNJABI EMIGRATION TO NORTH AMERICA

The British Indian army became the single most important employer of Punjabis outside their native area. In 1920, Sikhs formed one-fifth of the British Army in India though the Sikh population was only 1 percent of the Indian population (DeWitt 1969:18). From the 1870s, the army may have provided an alternative to indentured labor emigration from the Punjab (Nijjar 1974:170). It was as soldiers in the British army that significant numbers of Sikhs first went to Hong Kong, Shanghai, and later Canada. As part of a contingent of soldiers sent to England to participate in the Jubilee Celebrations for Queen Victoria in 1897, some Sikhs were sent back to India via Canada and the Pacific. This apparently first made Sikhs aware of the possibility of emigration to Canada (Das 1923:4).

The Sikhs sent to China undoubtedly became aware of the extensive Chinese emigration to the Pacific Coast. The Twenty-fourth Punjab Infantry and the First Sikhs were among the Allied forces taken to Peking during the Boxer Movement (O'Connor 1974:125), and hundreds of others were employed as policemen in Hong Kong. A Sikh veteran of the Tianjing (Tienstin) operation reported to an interviewer in California that participation in the Allied maneuvers during this period first brought him into contact with Americans, and he felt concerned about political freedom (Jacoby 1982:23). Others came into contact with men of other nationalities who had worked in America and who "gave them rosy pictures of economic opportunities" in Canada and the United States (Jacoby 1982:23). The testimony of David E. Brown, who lived in Hong Kong for fourteen years, also supports the hypothesis that Sikh emigrants to the North American Pacific Coast came via Hong Kong. As the general superintendent of the Canadian Trans-Pacific Railway, Brown participated in an investigation of Indian emigration, reporting that "Indians were employed very largely as policemen in Hong Kong and that it was from their number that the movement [to emigrate] has started in the first instance" (U. S. Government Immigration Records 1910:75). It is difficult to establish exactly how many Punjabis nationwide came via Hong Kong; but this trend seemed to continue until the early 1920s, when Indian emigration to Canada and the United States virtually stopped. Records, such as naturalization petitions from southern California, showed that two out of three Punjabis entering the United States between 1913 and 1923 gave Hong Kong as their place of emigration (Federal Immigration Petitions 1948-1950). Above all, as has been pointed out, Sikhs working in Hong Kong, Shanghai, or Canton, while not receiving generous salaries in the British army, probably found it far more feasible than did those in India to accumulate the $50 necessary at that time for passage money from Hong Kong to Vancouver or San Francisco (Jacoby 1982:25).

Sikhs coming to the United States or Canada seldom came alone and typically traveled in groups of at least five to ten people in the initial period. While it is difficult to trace the routes taken by the very earliest

emigrants, some information can be gathered from the highly publicized case of the ship *Komagata Maru*, which was chartered from Hong
Kong to Vancouver in 1914 as a test of Canadian immigration laws. It
showed a high degree of organization and a well-developed network of
companies and individuals involved in emigration as well as the despera-
tion of the emigrants who had staked everything on getting to America.
By this time (1914), there were a number of Sikhs in Hong Kong,
Shanghai, and Manila waiting for a way to get to North America
because the "white Australian policy," inaugurated in 1901, had terminated the earlier and fairly large Sikh emigration to Australia. Many,
perhaps thousands, had left Punjab planning to enter the United States
through the Philippines but had been stranded when a California district court ruled that Indians were ineligible to enter the United States
even though they came from an American territorial possession (Johnston 1979:23). The urgency felt by these emigrants to get to North
America is vividly recorded in a letter that came to the attention of
Daniel Keefe, a former chief of the American Immigration Service, in
1914. The letter was prepared on behalf of 600 Sikhs in Hong Kong and
was addressed to their friends in America:

> For God's sake, help us to get to the United States or Canada. The new
> Canadian law will go into effect on 5 March 1914 [this was not quite
> true but close enough] after which time a few Hindus[2] will be admitted
> into Canada. It has been much more difficult for the past six months to
> get into Manila than heretofore. We are shut out of Australia and New
> Zealand. For God's sake, come to our assistance so that we will be able
> to get into the United States or Canada. (cited in Johnston 1979:23)

Hong Kong had a large Sikh community made up of soldiers, policemen, watchmen, and businessmen. Though more precise information
on this community awaits further research, the Gurdwara (i.e., Sikh
temple) in Hong Kong was a well-established point of contact. Arrangements for the travel of emigrants to North America were made by
businessmen operating with Gurdwara contacts, and at least some of
these operators had contacts all over Asia. Gurdit Singh, for example,
the man who chartered the *Komagata Maru*, had associates in Malaya,
Manila, Shanghai, Nagasaki, and Moji, and Sikh passengers were picked
up at each of these ports. All Sikh emigrants coming to Vancouver on
another ship carried tax receipts, time cards, receipts of money orders,
and so on to prove to the Canadian immigration authorities that they
had been residents in Canada before, though in reality they were new
immigrants and had picked up these documents in Hong Kong and

Calcutta (Johnston 1979:17). The Sikh emigration network also had access to substantial funds, it would seem; for, again, though the *Komagata Maru* was a special case, the fact remains that the community and the individuals involved with it could come up with most of the funds necessary for chartering the ship (HK$11,000 per month for six months, of which HK$44,000 had to be paid within the first month) and could also pay for fuel and provisions costing approximately another HK$20,000 (Johnston 1979:27). The breadth of these operations raises the question of how much profit the investors hoped to make through the Sikh emigration.

Interviews[3] and other sources indicate that those emigrating to North America typically were not utterly destitute individuals but came from the class of peasant proprietors owning less than ten acres of land. Internal and overseas migrations not only were seen as ways of ensuring financial solvency but also represented the hope that the family would be able to acquire more land through earnings abroad. But travel, particularly to the Pacific Coast of North America, was an expensive proposition. Those coming directly, without a sojourn in southeast Asia or China, had to mortgage an acre or two of land to raise the fare of about $65 for a trip to Vancouver (Johnston 1979:2) or, as interviewees recalled, 400 rupees or the price of 1.5 acres of land in the fertile and prosperous districts.

The decision to emigrate was seldom made privately. As a shareholder or coparcener in the land the decision was made jointly by the property group. Often the father made the decision to send either the second or the youngest son overseas as an emigrant (Kessinger 1974:169; DeWitt 1969:15). Almost all the emigrants were men who planned to go back to their villages, where some had left wives. They were considered successes only if they managed to send back money and add to the family fortunes. Having mortgaged family property to leave, even those waiting in Hong Kong or Manila to get to North America could not consider returning unless they had a chance to earn good money (Johnston 1979:25). Remittances by emigrants were used for buying land, building brick houses, and even money lending (Darling 1930:33, 162, 166), thus continuing the cycle of impoverishment through usury, which would ultimately increase the number of potential immigrants.

Though the majority of the Sikh emigrants came from the small landowning class, some did come as contract laborers. Among those trying to enter the United States (probably at Seattle and San Francisco) between 1907 and 1920, a total of 133 individuals were debarred from entering because they had come under a contract labor system (Das 1923:3). This seems a surprisingly low figure, particularly in view of the fact that many more Punjabi emigrants came to Canada as laborers under contract. There may well have been many more who came under verbal contracts but were forewarned that if word of the contract got out they would be barred from entering the United States.

An investigation by the Royal Commission into "the methods by which oriental laborers have been induced to come to Canada" reported in 1908 that there were three main causes of immigration from India: the activities of steamship companies and agents; the distribution of literature in some of the provinces of India, advertising the opportunities of making a fortune in British Columbia; and the bringing in of Indians by residents of British Columbia under agreements to work for hire (Immigration Commission 1911:329). The third category included Indian middlemen, for the commissioner in charge of the investigation mentioned the following:

> A Brahmin named Davichand and certain of his relatives, who induced a number of the natives of India to come to Canada under actual or verbal agreements to work for hire, the purpose being that of assisting one or two industrial concerns to obtain a class of unskilled labor at a price below the current rate and at the same time exploiting their fellow subjects to their own advantage. (Immigration Commission 1911:329)

The Canadian Pacific Railway was under construction, and certain firms like Messrs. Gillanders and Arbuthnot, acting as agents for the railway company, recruited Sikhs in the Punjab. Approximately 1,200 tickets for travel were sold to the Sikhs, who were promised jobs at $2 to $3 a day (Huttenback 1976:178). The Calcutta branch of this same firm, along with plantation interests in Mauritius, had been involved in transporting 25,000 Indians as indentured laborers to Mauritius between 1835 and 1838 (Tinker 1974:63). The Hong Kong agents of the Canadian Pacific Railway were also involved in bringing Sikhs to Canada, particularly after the lowered volume of Chinese emigration when the Chinese head tax was raised by the Canadian government (Johnston 1979:2).

The emigration of Punjabis to the United States was really a "spill-over" from that to Canada and occurred after immigration laws prevented Indians from entering that country. It appears that the movement of Punjabis to Canada was not spontaneous or simply a matter of casual coincidence. It was induced by Canadian capital in collaboration with middlemen, such as steamship companies and local labor contractors, who advertised opportunities in Canada and facilitated the arrival of the earliest Sikh emigrants.

This may also explain, to some extent, why the emigrants came from Punjab rather than from any other region of India. Canadian capitalists, at this juncture, required laborers who could do heavy work in mills and lumberyards (Johnston 1979:3). Since open recruiting of contract labor was frowned upon and then banned by the Canadian government, the emigrants had to be from a class potentially able to provide for their own transportation. At the turn of the century, when Canadian recruiters were searching for new sources of labor, internal conditions in Punjab had created a large labor force of potential emigrants. The other regions in India from which emigrants and indentured laborers were available were, to a certain extent, already monopolized by the demands of plantations and estates in Malaya, Ceylon (Sri Lanka), Fiji, and Mauritius. The Patidars, a western Indian community of rural traders and manufacturers, who also entered the emigrant labor market in large numbers after a severe famine in Kaira (Gujarat) in 1900, were obviously unsuitable for the needs of the Canadian mill owners and fruit growers who required agriculturists. The Sikhs were better suited to working in the cold Canadian weather than any other group of potential emigrants from India, and furthermore they were familiar with farming. Their employment in the British army and their connections in Hong Kong facilitated their arrival in Canada and, once initiated, the immigration process acquired its own momentum. Between 1905 and 1920, official statistics show that approximately 12,200 Indian immigrants arrived in Canada and the United States (Das 1923:5, 11) in response to preexisting needs of the Canadian and American economy. Therefore, in the final analysis it must be understood that the very nature of the local economy along the Pacific Coast of North America, dependent upon resource extraction and food production in the form of mining, lumber, agriculture, and the fishing and canning industries, has historically determined the need for a cheap wage labor force. Punjabi immigrants, among many other diverse ethnic groups, simply fulfilled this need for cheap labor at a particular juncture in time.

NOTES

1. Though the term *caste* has numerous religious and social ramifications, for our study it is adequate to understand it as a nonlocalized endogamous unit, comprised of numerous subcastes (Kessinger 1974:35).

2. All Indians coming to North America were called "Hindus" by immigration authorities, Hinduism being the predominant religion in India. But, in fact, most of the Indians coming to the United States and Canada were Sikhs, not Hindus.

3. During 1978, I interviewed nineteen immigrants who arrived between 1920 and 1924 in Los Angeles, Yuba City, and Stockton and three individuals who were sons of these early immigrants.

References

Bagai, Leona
  1968   The East-Indians and the Pakistanis in America. Minneapolis: Lerner Publications.
Bal, Sarjit Singh
  1971   British Policy Towards the Punjab. Calcutta: New Age Publishers.
Calvert, H.
  1936   The Wealth and Welfare of the Punjab. Lahore: Civil and Military Gazette Press.
Chandra, Bipan
  1980   "Colonialism, Stages of Colonialism and the Colonial State." Journal of Contemporary Asia 10, 3:272-285.
Darling, Malcom L.
  1925   The Punjab Peasant in Prosperity and Debt. London: Oxford University Press.
  1930   Rusticus Loquitar. London: Oxford University Press.
  1934   Wisdom and Waste in the Punjab Village. London: Oxford University Press.
Das, Rajani K.
  1923   Hindustani Workers on the Pacific Coast. Berlin: W. de Gruyter.
DeWitt, John Jr.
  1969   Indian Workers Associations in Britain. London: Oxford University Press.
Federal Immigration Petitions
  1948-   Naturalization Petitions, Volumes 600-636. Laguna-Nigel: National Archives.
  1950
Harnetty, Peter
  1972   Imperialism and Free Trade: Lancashire and India in the Mid-Nineteenth Century. Vancouver: University of British Columbia Press.
Helweg, Arthur W.
  1979   Sikhs in England. Delhi: Oxford University Press.
Huttenback, Robert A.
  1976   Racism and Empire. Ithaca: Cornell University Press.
Immigration Commission
  1911   Reports. Vols. 23 and 25. Washington, D. C.: U. S. Government Printing Office.
Jacoby, Harold S.
  1982   East Indians in the United States. Unpub. manuscript.
Johnston, Hugh
  1979   The Voyage of the Komagata Maru. Delhi: Oxford University Press.
Kessinger, Tom G.
  1974   Viliyatpur 1848-1968. Berkeley, Los Angeles, London: University of California Press.
Manchanda, Mohinder K.
  1972   "Early Indian Emigration to America." In Proceedings of Punjab History Conference. Seventh Session Annual Number. Patiala: Punjab University.
Nijjar, Bakhshish S.
  1974   Punjab Under British Rule. 3 vols. New Delhi: K. B. Publications.

O'Connor, Richard
    1974   The Boxer Rebellion. London: Hale.
O'Donnell, C. J.
    1908   The Causes of Present Discontent in India. London: Fisher Unwin.
Omvedt, Gail
    1980   "Migration in colonial India: The articulation of feudalism and capitalism by the
           colonial state." Journal of Peasant Studies 7 (January):185-212.
Research Society of Pakistan, University of the Punjab
    1978   Extracts from the District and State Gazetteers of the Punjab. Lahore:
           Research Society.
Saha, Panchanan
    1970   Emigration of Indian Labor 1834-1900. Delhi: Peoples Publishing House.
Sharma, Sri Ram
    1971   Punjab in Ferment. New Delhi: S. Chand and Co.
Singh, Kushwant
    1966   A History of the Sikhs. 2 vols. Princeton: Princeton University Press.
Tinker, Hugh
    1974   A New System of Slavery. London: Oxford University Press.
    1977   The Banyan Tree. London: Oxford University Press.
U. S. Government Immigration Records
    1910   Annual Reports of the Commissioner General of Immigration to the Secretary
           of Commerce and Labor. Washington, D. C.: U. S. Government Printing Office.

10
The Philippines: A Case of Migration to Hawaii, 1906 to 1946

Miriam Sharma

Between 1906 and 1946 over 125,000 Filipinos, predominantly single men, came to labor on the sugar plantations of Hawaii (see table 10.1). Most of this emigration had occurred by 1932, and only small numbers were admitted during the next two years. When the Tydings-McDuffie Act was passed in 1934, granting commonwealth status and eventual independence to the Philippines, annual entry to the United States was limited to 50. Some 7,000 more Filipinos were allowed into Hawaii in 1946, expressly recruited to break the sugar strike organized by the "one big union" (International Longshoremen's & Warehousemen's Union, ILWU) of all plantation workers.[1] Of the many thousands who came, more than half were from the Ilocos region — that narrow coastal band of rugged terrain bordering on the China Sea and stretching along the northwest corner of Luzon, largest of the Philippine islands. It contains Ilocos Norte, Ilocos Sur, La Union, and Abra (see table 10.2 and fig. 10.1).

The Ilocos region has a long history as the most densely populated area in the country. Since the last decades of the nineteenth century, it has had the more dubious distinction of having become one of the most economically backward areas as well. This small and rugged land mass does not easily lend itself to the production of large-scale cash crops, and the region has remained predominantly rural. Its peasants engage primarily in small-scale rice production (and occasionally tobacco raising) for home consumption. A readiness to migrate, combined with a reputation for being sturdy, thrifty, and industrious, are further characteristics of the Ilocano.

337

Fig. 10.1

Source: Philippines (Republic).
        Department of Commerce and Industry. Bureau of the Census and Statistics.
        Census of the Philippines 1960 Population and Housing Summary, vol. 2:vii.

TABLE 10.1

FILIPINOS COMING TO HAWAII THROUGH HSPA FROM 1909 TO 1946

Year	Men	Women	Children	Total
1909	554	57	28	639
1910	2,653	169	93	2,915
1911	1,363	173	74	1,610
1912	4,319	553	362	5,234
1913	3,258	573	351	4,182
1914	1,848	360	228	2,436
1915	1,363	238	185	1,786
1916	1,674	141	134	1,949
1917	2,536	182	210	2,928
1918	2,196	298	395	2,889
1919	2,642	312	278	3,232
1920	3,030	232	181	3,443
1921	3,982	434	240	4,656
1922	8,513	704	457	9,674
1923	4,830	1,482	787	7,099
1924	4,915	1,414	648	6,977
1925	9,934	459	252	10,645
1926	3,960	121	96	4,177
1927	8,976	95	88	9,159
1928	10,508	193	156	10,857
1929	6,971	152	186	7,309
1930	6,904	177	291	7,372
1931	5,597	217	200	6,014
1932	953	151	122	1,226
1933	9	22	10	41
1934	25	43	39	107
1946	6,000	446	915	7,361
Total	109,513	9,398	7,006	125,917

SOURCE: Hawaiian Sugar Planters' Association Files, quoted in Dorita, *Filipino Immigration to Hawaii* 1954:131.

Stemming from my earlier work on the Filipinos in Hawaii between 1906 and 1946 (Sharma 1979, 1980), this paper concentrates on the same time frame, but instead of looking at the labor needs and plantation environment of Hawaiian sugar, it examines conditions in the labor-exporting country. The discussion revolves around economic changes in the Philippines, especially under American colonial rule, and the forces propelling emigration. This work is both an exploratory attempt to apply a theory of international labor migration under capitalism to certain facts and an attempt to go beyond the Ilocano stereotype as the reason for their migration. It looks at conditions in the Philippines and the northern Ilocos region during the general period under

TABLE 10.2
NUMBER AND PROPORTIONS OF FILIPINO LABORERS MIGRATING FROM THE
PHILIPPINE ISLANDS TO HAWAII FROM DIFFERENT PROVINCES, 1919 TO 1928

Province	Number of emigrants	Percentage
Abra	1,476	2.22
Bohol	4,592	6.91
Cebu	9,121	13.73
Ilocos Norte	21,400	32.21
Ilocos Sur	11,307	17.02
La Union	3,031	4.56
Leyte	1,317	1.98
Oriental Negros	2,769	4.17
Pangasinan	6,296	9.48
Tarlac	2,229	3.36
35 other provinces	2,898	4.36
Total	66,436	100.00

SOURCE: Lasker 1931:167.

study and discusses the manner in which the interests of United States
and Filipino capital, the Filipino political elite, and Filipino labor converged to influence migration. The following section presents an overview of general changes that occurred in the Philippine economy, with
the legacy of over three centuries of Spanish rule forming the basis of
the United States colonial regime. It is followed by a discussion of
aspects of socioeconomic change in the Ilocos region affecting migration.

THE PHILIPPINE COLONIAL ECONOMY

Changes that occurred in the Philippine economy under United States
rule were basically continuations of the policies previously initiated by
the Spanish. Over three centuries of Spanish rule brought about a
transformation of economic life in the sphere of foreign trade and made
it an agricultural export region, while changes in production and technology appear to have been minimal (Legarda y Fernandez 1967:1).[2] The
implementation of a tobacco monopoly, the growth of an agricultural
export economy between 1820 and 1870, and the changing tide of
imports that made the Philippines dependent upon outside sources for
rice and textiles after 1870 were most significant. They continued to
influence the direction of the economy under United States colonial rule
and laid the basis for the need to emigrate during the United States
period.

The tobacco monopoly (effective from 1782 to 1882) was the first major attempt by the Spaniards to foster an export crop, and it proved to be the major source of government revenue. Its imposition restricted the planting of tobacco to certain specified regions and limited the manufacture of tobacco products to government agents. Although grown in Ilocos Norte, Ilocos Sur, and elsewhere, tobacco was produced mostly in Cagayan, joined later by Isabela Province (Census of the Philippine Islands 1903, IV:34-35). There is evidence that the government forced the natives to produce specified amounts of the crop, as well as to migrate to the Cagayan region from the Ilocos (Barrows in Census of the Philippine Islands 1903, I:449; Valdepeñas and Bautista 1977:78-79; Legarda y Fernandez 1967:8; see also below).

Roughly coinciding with the second half-century of the tobacco monopoly was the growth of the Philippine agricultural export economy between 1820 and 1870. This marked a critical shift, not so much in the deployment of old resources,[3] as in the channeling of new resources and land that opened to export production (e.g., the island of Negros). From the early 1820s to the mid-thirties indigo, rice, sugar, cotton, and *sibucano* (sappenwood) were major export commodities. While sugar maintained its ascendancy for the rest of the century, the other products were displaced by abaca, tobacco, and coffee. At the end of the century, coffee was replaced by copra as a leading export, while foreign trade (imports and exports) rose from 2.8 million pesos in 1825 to 62 million pesos by 1895 (Legarda y Fernandez 1967:10-11; Valdepeñas and Bautista 1977:103). Larkin points out that by mid-century, sugar, abaca, coffee, and tobacco accounted for 70 to 80 percent of Philippine exports, while the first two products accounted for two-thirds of the total (1972:65).

This shift to an agricultural export economy also caused significant changes and dislocations in the native economy. The immediate effect could be seen in the case of rice and textiles — food and clothing basic to the sustenance of the masses. After the 1870s the Philippines, previously an exporter of rice, became consistently a rice-importing country and remained so throughout the period of United States rule. The inability of the country to feed itself was a result of colonial policies (Hernando 1969:26-27; Valdepeñas and Bautista 1977:103). Nor could it clothe itself.[4] By the 1840s, textiles already accounted for one-half of all imports. Its decline to 30 to 40 percent by the 1890s is not a secular decline but only reflects the increased importation of other foodstuffs, machinery, kerosene, and so on (Legarda y Fernandez 1967:11; see also Legarda 1955).

United States colonial rule continued this basic policy of exporting agricultural products and natural resources. From 1899 until 1937, sugar, abaca, copra, coconut oil, and — to a lesser extent — tobacco remained overwhelmingly the major export commodities (Valdepeñas and Bautista 1977:114, 117). The free-trade and tariff policies of the United States government bound the economic fate of the Philippine islands ever closer to their imperial overlords, even while the latter were speaking of political independence. American private investment in agricultural exports continued, especially in sugar, and involved Hawaiian capital as well. Because of restrictions placed by the United States on foreign ownership of Philippine land, however, foreign capital and control were relegated mainly to the processing of sugar at the mills (Gilbert 1967:78-79), while land concentration under the rule of local *caciques** and increasing tenancy and landlessness among the rural poor continued unabated.

Before discussing these main aspects of the economy under the United States flag, I must mention the "interlude" in Philippine history —its wars of independence from 1896 to 1902 — which marked the transference of colonial power from Spain to the United States. The specific effects of the prolonged warfare that are of interest here were the devastation of agriculture and the enormous loss of lives and, hence, manpower. The effect of the latter on subsequent labor needs within the country has not been investigated and will surely be important to an understanding of population pressures, regional imbalances, and emigration.

The devastation of agriculture is reflected in the severe drop in sugar exports, for example, from 341.47 million kilos in 1895 to 8.47 million kilos in the last five months of 1898 (Valdepeñas and Bautista 1977:97). The most serious dislocation to agriculture and the national economy, however, was caused by the Philippine-United States war, lasting from the beginning of 1899 until 1902. Sugar exports were consistently low throughout these years (see table 10.3). The major areas affected by the war were central and southern Luzon and the richest sugar lands in the Visayan islands of Panay, Negros, and Cebu (Kalaw 1969:247-250; Storey and Lichauco 1926:104; Taylor 1971, II:359ff).[5] Elsewhere, people were unable to sell their agricultural products because of the war, and the decimation of their cattle made them unable to cultivate their fields (Taylor 1971, I:363). The total loss of life from famine, pestilence, and disease has been variously estimated as being from 200,000 for the entire country (Blount 1913:596-599) to 600,000 for Luzon alone, espe-

---

*Local political bosses and powerful landholders.

TABLE 10.3
QUANTITY AND DESTINATION OF PHILIPPINE SUGAR

	To all countries			To United States, including Hawaii and Puerto Rico	
Fiscal years	Quantity (metric tons)	Value in U.S. currency	Percentage of total exports	Quantity (metric tons)	Value in U.S. currency
1899	57,447	$ 2,333,851	15.9	2,340	$ 143,500
1900	78,306	3,000,501	12.3	143	21,000
1901	56,582	2,293,058	8.6	2,153	93,472
1902	67,795	2,761,432	10.0	5,225	293,354
1903	111,647	3,955,828	9.9	34,433	1,335,826
1904	75,161	2,668,507	7.2	11,626	354,144
1905	113,640	4,977,026	13.4	57,859	2,618,487
1906	125,794	4,863,865	14.8	7,302	260,104
1907	120,289	3,934,460	11.5	6,610	234,074
1908	151,712	5,664,666	17.2	48,476	2,036,697
1909	112,380	4,373,338	14.0	21,285	881,218
1910	127,717	7,040,690	17.6	94,156	5,495,797
1911	149,376	8,014,360	20.1	128,926	7,144,755
1912	186,016	10,400,575	20.6	161,783	9,142,833
1913	212,540	9,491,540	17.8	83,951	3,989,665

SOURCE: Worcester 1914:899.

cially central Luzon and the areas around Manila (Bell quoted in Storey and Lichauco 1926:121; see also Hernando 1969:28-29 for general effects of the war).[6] Even after the war was over, mass fatalities continued. In March 1902 a devastating cholera epidemic broke out and killed some 200,000 people before it ended in 1904. Another factor affecting loss of lives was the "retaliatory practice of throwing recalcitrant Filipinos into concentration camps" carried out during the early years of United States administration in the Philippines, from 1902 (Mahajani 1971:192).

United States colonial interests stepped into a war-torn economy marked by a depletion of the population in specific areas of the country. For the next four decades, American economic involvement was concerned with governmental policies on tariff and trade agreements and private United States investments, especially in sugar. This involvement bolstered both the agricultural export economy of the Philippines as well as its complete economic dependence on the United States. The lack of any colonial agrarian policy and the obstruction of any such possible reforms by the Filipino elite, who invested heavily in agricultural exports, aggravated tenancy and landlessness in central and southern Luzon and endemic peasant unrest until the 1920s.

Tariffs and subsequent free-trade policies enacted by the United States government ensured the continued orientation of the economy toward agricultural exports. Between 1902 and 1909, the sale of United States products in the Philippines was encouraged by low tariff schedules erected for the country by the United States Congress. The Payne-Aldrich Tariff Act of 1909 (Section 5) "instituted virtual reciprocal free trade between the two countries" (Jenkins 1954:32; see also May 1980:158; Owen 1971:157). Limitations were placed on Philippine sugar and tobacco products that could enter the United States duty-free, but the quotas were set high, beyond the actual production capabilities of 1909 (May 1980:158). An additional tariff in 1913 removed even these restrictions and allowed rice to move free of duty, but it retained the 20 percent maximum limit on the content of non-Philippine or non-American materials allowed in duty-free Philippine manufactures (Jenkins 1954:33; Reyes 1923:119).

The effect of this tariff policy after 1909 was to discourage potential investment in Philippine industry. Owen notes that "the free entry of American goods into the Philippine market left the local entrepreneurs with only shipping costs as a comparative advantage against greater experience and capital of established American firms" (1971:107-108). Jenkins, writing earlier, puts it more succinctly: "Twenty-five years of free trade had tailored the economy of the islands to fit the American market" (1954:34). She further concludes that

> the nature and extent of prewar Philippine foreign trade illustrates, with some variations, the pattern of colonial development familiar throughout southeast Asia. To the United States came agricultural raw materials and products needed for manufacture in this country, and from this nation went industrial goods and commodities vital to an underdeveloped economy. (1954:38)

Although the total United States investment in the Philippines was miniscule, representing only 1 percent of its total foreign investment, it meant disproportionately more for the colonized society. The Philippines depended almost exclusively on the United States for its imports and exports, which reached 65 percent and 83 percent, respectively, for the period from 1930 to 1935 (Valdepeñas and Bautista 1977:113).

The interests of the Filipino elite also coincided with, and indeed fostered, those of the United States in keeping the Philippines an unindustrialized export economy. It was not only a preoccupation with political and parliamentary struggles to achieve independence that made it inattentive to pressing agrarian and economic problems. This elite also benefited most from a policy favorable to its control of large tracts of land. Members of this elite simply "settled for a subsidy protecting their agrarian interests" (Valdepeñas and Bautista 1977:141; see also Bauzon 1975:11; May 1980:160). The link between political power and landlord power was rooted in a politicoeconomic structure that had evolved during more than three centuries of Spanish rule and that the United States was reluctant to change (Hernando 1969:138).

Free trade encouraged concentration on a few export crops and the continuation of a dependent and predominantly agricultural economy. Jenkins notes that the discouragement of industrialization did not require deliberate United States policy; it flowed naturally from trade preferences for sugar, copra, and hemp that channeled investment into areas of unskilled labor and low wages. She further observes,

> Dependence on plantation products and overspecialized unmechanized agriculture have produced the same evils the world over: low wages, poor living conditions, and lack of impetus for rationalization of production and modernization of techniques. Displaced agricultural workers have not been able to turn to an expanding industrial system for employment, but have remained a burden on an already exhausted land economy. Similarly, promotion of home industries, such as needlework and embroidery, has not meant raising of levels, but rather has taken advantage of existing low wages. (1954:41).

One other "evil" that Jenkins might have mentioned is the compulsion of these displaced agricultural workers to emigrate from their home countries.

The major agricultural export throughout the United States colonial period was sugar (see table 10.4). Sugar production in the Philippines in general expanded rapidly after the mid-1850s and even earlier in the Pampangan region (Larkin 1972:59). Rice-growing areas were converted to the growing of sugar for export, and much of central Luzon and the Visayas followed that crop. By the 1890s Negros had taken the lead from Pampanga (Valdepeñas and Bautista 1977:96). On the eve of the initial entrance of United States capital into sugar production, however, the industry was nearly destitute (Gilbert 1967:3; Larkin 1972:216).

The 1909 tariff regulations reversed the trend of hard times for sugar and encouraged the infusion of United States capital and technology. The industry made a rapid recovery. One thing it could not so quickly recover from, however, was the chronic shortage of labor and the vast demand for a large seasonal (i.e., migrant) work force. To drain labor from central and southern Luzon or the Visayas to the Hawaiian Islands would have meant competing with the needs of the sugar-growing areas, some of which suffered from underpopulation.[7] The extent of

TABLE 10.4

PHILIPPINE SUGAR EXPORT, 1908 TO 1921

(in long tons)

Year	Total export	Percentage of 1908 export*	Export to U.S.	Percentage of total to U.S.
1908	142,448	100	45,969	32
1909	127,284	89	52,234	41
1910	119,552	84	99,109	82
1911	205,741	144	184,694	89
1912	193,962	136	131,763	67
1913	154,848	109	30,232	19
1914	232,761	163	166,851	71
1915	207,678	146	81,532	39
1916	332,157	233	129,801	39
1917	202,654	142	61,392	30
1918	268,940	189	104,405	39
1919	133,910	94	31,651	23
1920	177,491	125	121,979	68
1921	285,295	200	148,101	51

SOURCE: Larkin 1972:271.

*The base year 1908 was both the last full year of production before the Payne Act and the best year of sugar export since 1898.

specifically Hawaiian, and generally American, investment in Philippine sugar would also have put pressure on the Hawaiian Sugar Planters Association (HSPA) not to divert thousands of these needed laborers overseas. That would have meant going directly against its own interests. Further, there is some evidence that Filipino sugar investors wanted a sort of "trade-off" between aid to their impoverished industry, via United States capital investment, and the continued remittance of human resources to Hawaii (see below). It appears to have been the articulation of all these interests, rather than a reality conforming to the stereotype of the efficiency of Ilocano laborers and their propensity to migrate, that prompted the HSPA to focus its recruitment efforts on the Ilocos region. There, conditions made men willing to leave.

Sugar production was concentrated in three major areas in the Philippines: the islands of Panay and Negros (where several large Hawaiian-owned sugar *centrals** were located); the provinces of Pangasinan, Bataan, Tarlac, and especially Pampanga in the central plains of Luzon; and the provinces of Batangas and Laguna, south of Manila. Together, these three areas produced 90 percent of all sugar (Glago 1966:15; see also

*These were the highly capitalized centrifugal mills which contracted with large and small landowners to process their cane harvests.

Gilbert 1967:preface, 13). Three mills were started specifically by Hawaiian capital. In 1912, the San Carlos Milling Company on Negros Occidental was incorporated by J. D. Cooke (president and manager of Alexander & Baldwin), A. D. Cooper (a Honolulu stockbroker), R. Ivers (secretary of C. Brewer & Company), M. P. Robinson (vice-president of First National Bank of Hawaii), S. M. Swanzey (managing director of Theo H. Davies & Company), and E. D. Penney (occupation unknown). They entered into a contract with the principal private planters to process all sugarcane for thirty years. The company received 40 percent of the manufactured sugar as its compensation and continued to profit, throughout the twenties, until the depression (Glago 1966:18-23).

The next Hawaiian venture appears to have come about after a committee of businessmen, prominent in the sugar industry, left Honolulu for the Philippines at the end of 1917 with the express purpose of "canvassing the island" to establish a modern factory (Hawaiian-Philippine Co., *First Report for the Two Fiscal Years Ending September 30, 1922*:14-15, quoted in Glago 1966:32-33; Gilbert 1967:60). The search was prompted by the fear that leaders of the Philippine sugar interests would become hostile and thus endanger further emigration of laborers to Hawaii unless the Philippine sugar industry was helped (Glago 1966:31). After their visit and return home, however, they could hardly have been blind to the investment opportunities in the Philippines (Gilbert 1967:60-61). All HSPA members subsequently subscribed to stock and expressed their confidence in Philippine sugar and their appreciation for the assistance that the Hawaiian industry had received from Filipino labor (Hawaiian-Philippine Co., *First Report*, quoted in Glago 1966:30). The HSPA representative in Manila, W. A. Babbitt, became president of the Hawaiian-Philippine Co. in June 1918. The principal investors were the vice-presidents of Hawaii sugar factors Castle and Cooke (Atherton) and C. Brewer Co. (Gartley). The site finally chosen was at Siley, Negros Occidental, and the mill was built by two Hawaiian companies (Glago 1966:31-32). The last company founded by Hawaiian capital was the Cebu Sugar Co. at Talisay (in 1927) with another small associated mill founded the following year at Bogo, Cebu. Theo Davies, another Hawaiian sugar factor, financed this operation (Gilbert 1967:69; cf. Glago 1966:38 ff.).

At the bottom of the structure of the Philippine sugar industry were the migratory workers coming at the harvest and milling time — those called *sacadas* in Negros. They formed the broad lower base along with tenant farmers producing the cane. A 1927 report by Hermenegildo Cruz,[8] the director of labor in the Philippines, notes that "the planting and milling season in Occidental Negros, the sugar district, draws thousands of laborers from the *neighboring provinces*. Laborers from Antique,

Iloilo, and Cebu are *recruited* to work in the sugar centrals and plantations . . . [and stay] there during the milling season, generally from
November to April. . . . About 15,000 go to the place during the milling season" (Cruz 1927:31, quoted in Gilbert 1967:83, my emphasis).

It is also significant that continued efforts were made by American
and European businessmen—as well as Filipino planters—to introduce
much cheaper Chinese labor into the country from the time the Chinese
exclusion law was implemented in the Philippines (1902). The wage
levels of Filipino workers had been raised because of the overall increase
in national trade and the rise in material standards of living. Production
costs for sugar were therefore higher than they were in Java, for example (Hernando 1969:99). One way to arrest the declining competitiveness of Philippine sugar (and to increase profits) would be to use Chinese workers in the field. While Governor Taft's testimony before the
Philippine Commission in 1902 advised against the importation of Chinese, he did state, "The very great increase in the foreign commerce and
coastwide trade in the islands, together with the needs of the army and
insular government, has caused a corresponding increase in the demand
for all kinds of labor in and about commerce, so that the increase in
wages and failure of the local labor supply are easily understood" (U.S.
Philippine Commission 1902; see also Jensen 1956:89).

From 1902 on—and especially after the 1909 preferential sugar tariff
was enacted—local Filipino sugar interests joined with those of the
foreigners to petition for coolie labor, despite the overwhelming protest
of Filipino leaders and workers against the admission of the Chinese
(Foncier 1932:27; Jensen 1956:51, 85 ff.). Filipino planters made a concerted effort to agitate for Chinese agricultural laborers. While nothing
came of this, it remains an important expression of a perceived labor
shortage by capitalists in the Philippines. Such a situation existed even
under Spanish colonialism. Valdepeñas and Bautista note that the establishment of sugar plantations in Luzon, less striking than that on Negros
from 1861, "was deterred by the shortage of labor" (1977:98). The
extent to which labor shortages were subsequently corrected by the
process of progressive land consolidation and dispossession of peasants,
thus making them "free" to enter the labor market, needs to be
determined.

By 1919 the HSPA had shifted active recruiting to the Ilocos in
response to a number of events. Political hegemony earlier had passed
to a new political overlord, the United States, and so the Philippines and
Hawaii were under the same government. Second, the expansion of a
national export economy, built upon the legacy of Spanish policies, was
fostered by United States tariff regulations and consequent free trade

between the two countries. Third and most important, sugar emerged as the major export crop, and its development was confined to specific regions—generally in central and southern Luzon and certain Visayan islands. Finally, along with the phenomenal recovery and growth of the industry, there existed a constant hedge on its expansion because of a shortage of labor. To some extent this was overcome by mass migratory movements from the neighboring provinces.[9] While this combination of growth, investment, and labor shortage was characteristic of certain regions of the Philippines, what may be said of conditions in the Ilocos region?

ASPECTS OF SOCIOECONOMIC CHANGE IN THE ILOCOS

This section will point to a number of areas that appear to be significant in determining why the Ilocos region was the main supplier of Filipino human capital to Hawaiian sugar between 1906 and 1946. A major purpose here is to go beyond the stereotypic views of the Ilocano as willing to migrate because of severe population pressure and as being the favored laborer because he is hardworking and thrifty—the "Yankee(s) of the Philippines" (Blount 1913:247).[10] A paucity of available material on the region necessitates a briefer and more tentative treatment than that in the preceding section.[11] The major question here is, Why was the Ilocano the preferred agricultural laborer for Hawaii's plantations?

Geographically, the Ilocos region is a narrow stretch along the coastline on the northeastern part of Luzon. Administratively, it consists of the provinces of the Ilocos Norte, Ilocos Sur, La Union, and the inland valley province of Abra. It contains only 3.1 percent of the country's total land mass (Smith 1981:2) and has been the most densely populated until at least the first quarter of this century (Census of the Philippine Islands 1903, I:27; 1918, II:29; 1939, II:47, map). Despite all its outflow of human capital and inflow of material capital from dollar remittances, the region remains the "least developed in the country" (Smith 1981:27). This was not always the case, although admittedly the evidence is not abundant. During the early Spanish period when Chinese junks frequented its ports, Ilocanos exported tobacco, fish, and primarily, textiles (Bello 1956:121; Census of the Philippine Islands 1903, I:465). Cotton became its most important product and was grown in great quantities. For example, from 1785 to 1795 the production of blankets (the major textile product) more than doubled, and an interisland trade also flourished. Indigo and rice (produced in surplus in the Ilocos) were also part of the domestic trade (Valdepeñas and Bautista 1977:75, 87).

By the late eighteenth century, a marked population expansion was met by an equally marked urban development (Keesing 1962:161). A half-century later a Spanish writer noted the economic basis of urban development in Ilocos Norte:

> A network of roads and trails threaded particularly its south and central sections. The rural zones trade rice, maize, sugar cane, tobacco, and other crops into the towns, and sustained large horse and cattle ranches. . . . The town households, too, notably swelled commerce by manufacturing cotton, fiber, and silk goods often of "magnificent quality," which were much in demand through the Philippines and even overseas. The ocean, together with plentiful lakes and waterways, supplied fish foods; salt was extracted along the shores; palm and sugar-cane wines were manufactured. . . . Currimao, southwest of Paoay, served as the principal port from which goods of the area were traded extensively by sea. Not least among exports, as noted already, were surplus people. (Summarized in Keesing 1962:162)

Tobacco also has been grown as a commercial crop on the Ilocos coast since Spanish times. In the late eighteenth century a peasant revolt against imposition of the tobacco monopoly was narrowly averted in the North. While some rice lands were also converted into tobacco fields during the last twenty years of the monopoly, 1862 to 1882 (Valdepeñas and Bautista 1977:87), the major tobacco-producing regions were east of the Ilocos. There, in the Cagayan Valley, the Spaniards appear to have established tobacco haciendas that constituted government *estanco* (monopoly) as early as the late sixteenth century. Barrows, writing in the *Census of the Philippine Islands* for 1903, states that even at this time the migration of Ilocanos eastward was "fostered, encouraged, and *impelled* by the Spanish to supply colonists and laborers for the tobacco haciendas" (I:449, my emphasis). The suggestion that early Ilocano migration could have been coerced may put subsequent migration in a new light.

With the onset of the Spanish shift to an agricultural export trade in the last quarter of the nineteenth century and the destruction of the important textile industry in the Ilocos (discussed above), the stage was set for the region to slip into being a neglected economic backwater. No attempts were made by the Spaniards, the Americans, or the local elite (*baknang*) to implement technological advances that could improve rice productivity in the region. The possibility of investing in other manufactured exports to take the place of textiles was not considered. All of the investment and concern was channeled into the leading agricultural exports of sugar, copra, hemp, and abaca, none of which could be grown profitably in the Ilocos. The main industry in the area then became the production, reproduction, and subsequent export of human resources.

Yet it is curious to note that despite all the foreign exchange earned in return, in the form of an enormous amount of dollars remitted from 1906 to 1946, the Ilocos remained a backward region. If, in fact, remittances can be shown to have contributed even further to the maintenance of regional backwardness, then a strong case could be made for the conclusion that migration is no demographic solution for what are ultimately political and economic problems.

Further consideration of population pressure and migration as a solution needs to examine the nature of rice production and land tenure in the Ilocos. Rice is not grown generally as a plantation crop; it can be produced on small areas and is seasonally labor intensive. Family holdings that have been reduced to the point where exchange or contract labor is no longer needed or desired are sufficient for this crop (Lewis 1971:57). Large, extensive landlord holdings, as are found in the sugar areas, are absent in the Ilocos, as are the large number of landless laborers. All along the coast the "very measure and worth of land is in terms of how much rice it produces; the worth and measure of a man is in terms of how much rice-producing land he owns" (Lewis 1971:51).

Coincident with a crop that can be grown on small areas of land and the absence of large estates is the central importance of land inheritance to the maintenance of family ties and wider alliance systems. Most of the Philippines follows the general southeast Asian custom of partible inheritance, and Ilocano custom ideally prescribes equal inheritance of property. The unique *sabong*, or male land dowry, abrogates the local custom and national law "by the act (or promise) of giving land to one male heir or more. The *sabong* is considered necessary for a 'proper' marriage" (Lewis 1971:87, 89; see also Bello 1956:1716). An effect of this custom has been to reinforce the critical importance of land ownership to maintaining even kin ties and, perhaps, to make ownership of land much more widespread throughout the area (vis-à-vis central and southern Luzon and parts of the Visayas). Many of those who migrated to Hawaii left with the express intent of earning enough money to return to their homeland and buy land (Sharma 1980:96). One consequence of such emigration, however, was to inflate the price of land increasingly as migrants and remittances flowed past each other.

Another result of the nature of rice production, land scarcity, and the male dowry in the Ilocos was that landholding tended to be more diffuse and a person was often an owner-operator and tenant at the same time. This configuration of practices, I suggest, made the Ilocano more closely approximate the ideal of an independent peasant-proprietor than happened elsewhere in the Philippines, where greater numbers of landlords, large estates, tenants, and landless laborers appear much more common. The characteristics of any group of peasant-proprietors the world over are industriousness and perhaps, the disinclination to make trouble. I am suggesting that the stereotype of the Ilocano has less to do with a certain cultural or psychological mystique than it has to do with the more general nature of his relation to obtaining the means of subsistence.

It would be this factor that also fostered the views of the HSPA and others about the hardworking Ilocano, but it would not account for why he was the preferred laborer. He was preferred, as I tried to indicate in discussing the competing needs of Philippine sugar, because he was superfluous for the development of the Ilocos. He was also, perhaps, less willing to migrate in large numbers to sugar areas in the country where conditions and wages were poor (Runes 1939).[12] He was, at the same time, the cheapest laborer available in the Philippines, consistently receiving lower wages than workers in any other area, and the least involved in the peasant unrest that swept through the country in the twenties and thirties (Sturtevant 1976, Kerkvliet 1977, Larkin 1972:240 ff.).

The loss to the country of exporting so many of its human resources was also perceived in the Philippines. The director of labor, Hermenegildo Cruz, outlined these effects in a paper prepared for the Institute of Pacific Relations. He stated,

> In this country where surplus labor is not so plentiful, this constant drain of Filipino manpower cannot but produce a retarding influence on the economic development of the Islands. Public lands which are lying idle can be had for the taking and yet our laborers are emigrating abroad and spending their energies for the benefit of other nations. Local conditions seem to offer no encouragement and our laborers' increasing wants must be met by better incentives from some other quarter. (Cruz 1931:4)

Yet the export continues, fostered today by the political elite as a way to contain seething problems at home, and the Philippines increasingly sends its own labor to subsidize the development of other nations.

CONCLUDING REMARKS

This chapter has described those significant changes in the Philippine national economy under Spanish rule that were continued by the United States. Foremost among these were the turn to an agricultural export economy, with sugar in the lead, and the growing dependence upon imports for the basic necessities of rice and textiles. The United

States fostered this export/import policy by its tariff regulations and by subsequent free trade between the two countries. With the growth of sugar production in central and southern Luzon and part of the Visayas, the labor shortage became a significant obstacle to expansion of production. There was a futile yet continued attempt by American and other foreign businessmen and Filipino planters to engage the cheaper Chinese labor for agricultural work.

Parallel to the uneven development of capitalism on a world scale, which put the Philippines in an increasingly dependent position, was the uneven development of capitalism on a regional basis within the nation. With admittedly scanty data, I attempted a closer look at why it was the Ilocanos who migrated in large numbers to Hawaii (and the rest of the mainland) and why they became the preferred workers. Neither the stereotypic views of the industrious and migratory Ilocano nor demographic models suffice as explanations of this phenomenon. An examination of the historical factors that led to the region's slip into the backwater of economic development appears to provide better clues. Until the last decades of Spanish rule, the Ilocos was a thriving agricultural and textile-manufacturing area. The decision to transform the national economy to provision of agricultural exports for the world market and the continuation of this policy under the United States adversely affected the region. By 1910, when labor recruitment for the sugar fields of Hawaii began in earnest, severe economic displacements and dislocations had led to a crisis of "surplus" population. Yet the ultimate decision to recruit labor mostly from the Ilocos did not result from pressures of demography or poverty alone. Other areas of the Philippines were in dire straits as well. Rather, it was because of the particular way in which the interests of Hawaiian planters, foreign and indigenous capital, the Philippine national elite, and the peasants of the Ilocos were articulated and converged upon the common need for migration.

ACKNOWLEDGMENTS

This paper could not have been written without the knowledge gained during a valuable year spent as a research affiliate in the economics department of the New School for Social Research (New York, 1979 to 1980). Mahalo also to friends in the sociology department for stimulating discussions and especially to Jim Matson, for his perceptive comments, and to Ninotchka Rosca, who helped "translate" this into English. Thanks also to Ed Beechert who alerted me to some valuable documents.

NOTES

1. Several Filipino union members managed to join on as crew members aboard the vessel that transported these workers. On the return voyage, they succeeded in signing up everyone as union members. These new recruits then joined their fellow countrymen on the picket line after reaching Honolulu.

2. One of the early innovations of the Spanish friars in the Ilocan plain appears to have been the irrigation canals that crossed the region (Blair and Robertson xxiii:247, 276-279, in Keesing 1962:27).

3. This general statement may not be entirely true in the case of central Luzon—the "rice bowl" of the Philippines—which was transformed into a sugar-exporting area. This occurred as early as 1838 for Pampanga (Valdepeñas and Bautista 1977:97; Larkin 1972:45 ff.). Valdepeñas and Bautista also state that"when sugar emerged as a commercial commodity, missionaries in Negros persuaded the farmers to shift from rice to sugar culture" (1977:52).

4. Much earlier, the galleon trade, which drew Chinese traders to the Philippines to exchange their goods (including cheap textiles) for Mexican silver, had ruined some early textile centers.

5. The United States also fought the Filipinos in Mindoro, Samar, and Bohol (Storey and Lichauco 1926:119).

6. The population of the Philippines was estimated to be 9,703,311 in 1898 and reported as 6,987,686 in the 1903 census I:15,18; cf. figures in Smith 1981).

7. *Underpopulation* is defined vis-à-vis labor needs in production.

8. Many Filipinos who were repatriated in 1932 and 1933 "complained bitterly that both Cruz and Cayetano Ligot, appointed Resident Commissioner of Labor in Hawaii, were HSPA 'stooges'" (Sharma 1980:100-101).

9. The writer of the *Commercial Handbook of the Philippine Islands 1924* (Philippine Islands, Bureau of Commerce and Industry, 1924) states:

> Statistics show that the Ilocanos, Visayans, Tagalogs, and Bicols are the *most migratory* [!]. The inhabitants of such overpopulated islands as Cebu, Bohol and Panay leave their original homes and settle in the vast unoccupied areas of Mindano and Mindoro. The Ilocanos are spreading from the crowded regions of Ilocos Norte and Ilocos Sur toward the northeastern and central parts of Luzon, establishing themselves in the fertile valleys of the Cagayan, Agno, and Pampanga rivers, and in the virgin fields of Mindano. A stream of Ilocano settlers continue to pour into Cagayan, Isabela, the Mountain Province, Nueva Ecija, Nueva Vizcaya, Tarlac, and Zambales. The Tagalogs and Pampangans are expanding chiefly into underdeveloped local territory and into Tarlac, Neuva

Ecija, and Mindoro. The Bicols have a *tendency to migrate* to Samar and Masbate. Local crop conditions constitute also a factor in the migration of labor. Laborers from Panay and Cebu go to Negros Occidental during the sugar-planting and milling seasons. The coconut growers of Laguna and Tayabas obtain their additional work-men from the more thickly populated provinces of Central and Northern Luzon. During the rice harvest time in the Central Plain of Luzon, the Ilocos provinces send laborers to help in gathering the the the crop. (168-169, my emphasis)

10. These views on the Ilocano also prompted the work of such writers as Lewis (1971) and are repeated with some interesting variations in Amina (1976:8-9).

11. I have not had sufficient time to carefully analyze the important data collected by the *Census of the Philippines Islands* for 1903, 1918, and 1939. They contain a wealth of information about demographic patterns as well as about land, agricultural holdings, the nature of land tenure, industrial activities, occupations, wages, and so on. Owen provides a cautionary note, however, on the comparability of data for all censuses (1971:117-118).

12. Runes also notes:

The Ilocanos are growing in number in Tarlac and Pampanga and their willingness to accept compensation *lower* than what the local laborers have been asking has been the root of the continuous troubles in the plantations of Central Luzon. When *replacing* the workers and the tenants with those coming from the Ilocos provinces, the *planters argue that the Ilocano is more hard working and efficient as a farmhand.* The procedure has aroused indignation among the local laborers, not so much on the willingness of the Ilocanos to accept lower wages as on their obstruction to movements for higher wages through organized labor unions. (1939:7-8, my emphasis)

References

Amina, Nid
1976   Ilocandia: Land of contrasts and contradictions. Quezon City.
Bauzon, Leslie
1975   "Philippine agrarian reform, 1800-1965. The revolution that never was." Institute of Southeast Asian Studies (Singapore), Occasional Paper no. 31.
Bello, Moises C.
1956   "The Ilokano." Pp. 1695-1728 in Fred Eggan et. al., eds., Area Handbook on the Philippines. Human Relations Area Files (HRAF), no. 16, vol. IV.
Blount, James H.
1913   The American Occupation of the Philippines, 1898-1912. New York: G. P. Putnam's Sons.
Census of the Philippine Islands
1903   United States Bureau of the Census, Washington, D.C. 4 vols. (pub. 1905).
1918   Census Office of the Philippines, Manila. 4 vols. (pub. 1921).
1939   Commission of the Census, Manila. 3 vols. (pub. 1941).
Cruz, Hermenegildo
1931   "Emigration of Filipinos to Hawaii and the United States." In Institute of Pacific Relations, Papers on Philippine Progress, Manila.
Dorita, Sister Mary
1954   "Filipino immigration to Hawaii." Master's thesis, University of Hawaii.
Foncier, Tomás A.
1932   "The Chinese in the Philippines during the American administration." Ph.D. diss., Stanford University.
Gilbert, Richard John
1967   "The introduction of American capital into the sugar industry of the Philippines and its import on the pre-existing patterns of land." Master's thesis, University of Hawaii.
Glago, Mark Aaron
1966   "American private capital in the Philippines, 1898-1941." Master's thesis, University of Hawaii.
Hernando, Milagros Bulan
1969   "American colonial economic policy in the Philippines." Master's thesis, University of Hawaii.
Jenkins, Shirley
1954   American Economic Policy Towards the Philippines. Stanford: American Institute of Pacific Relations, Stanford University Press.
Jensen, Irene Khin Khin Myint
1956   "The Chinese in the Philippines during the American regime, 1898-1946." Master's thesis, University of Wisconsin.
Kalaw, Teodoro M.
1969   The Philippine Revolution. Quezon City: R. P. Garcia Pub. Co.
Keesing, Felix M.
1962   The Ethnohistory of Northern Luzon. Stanford: Stanford University Press.

Kerkvliet, Benedict J.
    1977   The Huk Rebellion. A Study of Peasant Revolt in the Philippines. Berkeley, Los
           Angeles, London: University of California Press.
Larkin, John A.
    1972   The Pampangans. Colonial Society in a Philippine Province. Berkeley, Los
           Angeles, London: University of California Press.
Lasker, Bruno
    1931   Filipino Immigration, to Continental United States and to Hawaii. Chicago:
           Institute of Pacific Relations, University of Chicago Press.
Legarda, Benito Fernandez Jr.
    1955   "Foreign trade, economic change and entrepreneurship in the nineteenth-
           century Philippines." Ph.D. diss., Harvard University.
Legarda y Fernandez, Benito
    1967   "The Philippine economy under Spanish rule." Solidarity 2 (November-
           December):1-21.
Lewis, Henry T.
    1971   Ilocano Rice Farmers. A Comparative Study of Two Philippine Barrios. Hono-
           lulu: University of Hawaii Press.
Mahajani, Usha
    1971   Philippine Nationalism: External Challenge and Filipino Response, 1565-1946.
           St. Lucia, Queensland: University of Queensland Press.
Maldonado-Denis, Manuel
    1972   Puerto Rico: A Socio-historic Interpretation. (trans. Elena Vialo). 1st American
           ed. New York: Random House.
    1980   The Emigration Dialectic. Puerto Rico and the U.S.A. (translated from the
           Spanish edn., 1976). New York: International Publishers.
May, Glenn Anthony
    1980   Social Engineering in the Philippines. The Aims, Execution, and Impact of
           American Colonial Policy, 1900-1913. London: Greenwood Press.
Owen, Norman G.
    1971   "Philippine economic development and American policy: A reappraisal." Pp.
           103-128 in Norman G. Owen, ed., Compadre Colonialism. Studies on the Phi-
           lippines Under American Rule. Michigan Papers on South and Southeast Asia,
           no. 3.
Petras, Elizabeth McLean
    1980   "Towards a Theory of International Migration: The New Division of Labor."
           Pp. 439-449 in Roy Bryce-Laporte, ed., Sourcebook on the New Immigration.
           New Brunswick, N. J.: Transaction Books.
Philippine Islands, Bureau of Commerce and Industry
    1924   Commercial Handbook of the Philippine Islands. Bureau of Commerce and
           Industry. Manila: Bureau of Printing.
Pido, Antonio J. A.
    1980   "Some macro-dimensions of immigration: The case of the Philipinos." Paper
           presented at the Annual Meeting of the American Sociological Association,
           New York, August 27-30, 37 p.
Portes, Alejandro
    1978   "Migration and underdevelopment." Politics and Society 8 (1):1-48.
Reyes, Jose S.
    1923   Legislative History of America's Economic Policy Toward the Philippines. New
           York: Columbia University Press.

Runes, I. T.
1939   General Standards of Living and Wages of Workers in the Philippine Sugar Industry. Philippine Council, Institute of Pacific Relations, Philippines.
Sharma, Miriam
1979   "An overview of Filipino immigration to Hawaii: The 'old' plantation and the 'new.'" Pp. 49-72 in Tomas C. Hernandez, ed., Sadino ti Papanam: Selected Issues Affecting Filipinos in Hawaii. Honolulu: Hawaii Filipino-American Community Foundation and Philippine Studies Program, University of Hawaii.
1980   "Pinoy in paradise: Environment and adaptation of Filipinos in Hawaii, 1906-1946." Amerasia VII (Fall-Winter):91-117.
Smith, Peter C.
1981   Population Pressure and Social Response on the Ilocos Coast in the Philippines. Honolulu: East-West Center Population Institute, Working Papers, no. 2.
Storey, Moorfield, and Marcial P. Lichauco
1926   The Conquest of the Philippines by the United States, 1898-1925. New York: G. P. Putnam's Sons.
Sturtevant, David C.
1976   Popular Uprisings in the Philippines, 1840-1940. Ithaca: Cornell University Press.
Taft, William Howard
1902   Testimony before the Philippine Commission. In Report of the U.S. Philippine Commission to the President, October 1, 1902.
Taylor, John R. M.
1971   The Philippine Insurrection Against the United States. A Compilation of Documents with Notes and Introduction. 5 vols. Pasay City: Eugenio Lopez Foundation.
U.S. Philippine Commission, 1900-1916
1902   Report of the Philippine Commission to the President, Oct. 1, 1902. Bureau of Insular Affairs, War Department. Washington, D. C.: Govt. Printing Office.
Valdepeñas, Vicente B. Jr., and Gemelino M. Bautista
1977   The Emergence of the Philippine Economy. Manila: Papyrus Press.
Worcester, Dean C.
1914   Commercial Possibilities of the Philippines. New York: Macmillan Company.

PART III
Asian Immigrant Workers and Communities

In this section we turn to the Asian immigrant workers themselves, examining what happened to them after they arrived in the United States. We have included at least one chapter on each of the five major Asian groups, each covering the experiences of that group differently. Some chapters are regionally confined, others limit themselves to a particular historical period, and still others concentrate on a single occupation. Of course, a thorough analysis of each group's experience would require at least a volume apiece. Our purpose, therefore, is to illustrate the kinds of studies our framework can generate rather than giving a comprehensive account.

All the essays are concerned with issues of both race and class. Racial or national oppression was experienced by all Asian immigrants, since all were marked off by their origins as a specially stigmatized group. Unlike other immigrants, they were legally defined as "aliens ineligible for citizenship." The reasons for this special treatment are complex, and prominent among them is the fact that Asian countries had been, to varying degrees, subdued by western European and, later, American imperialism. Their nationals could thus be seen as "inferior" and "unfit" to join a society of "free men." This special oppression can be seen as "racial" to the extent that all Asians were treated as a single category, and "national" to the extent that the immigrants from each country faced unique attacks. Both forms of oppression set Asians apart from the rest of society.

Racial and national oppression set the context for the Asian immigrant experience. It limited their occupational choices, affected their ability to form workers' organizations, and hindered the possibility of forming a united interracial working-class movement. Asians occupied the position of cheap labor. To the extent that they were recruited by United States capitalists, they were sought because they were cheap. And employers were determined to bind them to this status for as long as possible. Racial and national oppression were mechanisms for achieving a pool of cheap labor.

In general, Asian immigrants occupied a peculiar class position in the economy of the United States. They were the lowest stratum of the proletariat, assigned to the dirtiest work for the lowest wages under the worst conditions. Making up an especially oppressed segment of the working class, they contributed more than their share to the accumulation of capital, enabling United States capitalists to earn larger profits, which stimulated the country's economic development.

The peculiar position of Asian immigrants as cheap labor put them in conflict, to some extent, with the local working class, which found their presence threatening. Local workers feared that capitalists would use Asian labor to displace them and formed political movements to push for an end to Asian immigration. There were exceptions to this general pattern, with some local workers' groups supporting the organization of the immigrants rather than their exclusion, but these were rare. Thus Asian workers not only had to face the special oppression of their employers but also the antagonism of the local working class.

The exclusionary practices of local workers were not limited to efforts to cut off immigration from Asia. They also made efforts to exclude Asians from certain sections within the United States economy. For instance, local workers sometimes used their trade unions to force employers not to hire Asian workers. Several incidents of violence against Asians took this form in an effort to push Asian workers out of the labor market. Thus confinement of the immigrants to the poorest, lowest-paying jobs was a product of local working-class efforts as well.

Given this double layer of oppression, the options of Asian immigrants were severely limited. They were forced to turn inward to their own communities for aid and often for employment. Communal and even national solidarity held out more hope than did cross-national class solidarity. While there were important internal sources of nationalism in Asian immigrant communities, ethnic solidarity was fostered by these external constraints as well, with important consequences for the internal class development of these communities.

As an especially disadvantaged segment of the working class, Asian immigrants were hampered in their labor organizing. Not only were they typically excluded from white trade unions but as immigrants and noncitizens, they were also subject to punitive retaliations by their employers. They might, for instance, face deportation for striking. In addition, their exclusion from many manufacturing jobs pushed them into the occupations where labor organizing was most backward and difficult. For instance, in agriculture the system of migrant labor combined with the tremendous political power of agribusiness capital to severely retard labor organizing. Similarly, work as household servants was detrimental to the formation of unionism.

Nevertheless Asians did join together to struggle against their oppression, provided with ample motivation by the particularly intense levels of exploitation many of them experienced. They truly had "nothing to lose but their chains." Some of the chapters in this section document instances of such struggle, revealing that the immigrants were not as docile as their employers may have wished.

While Asian immigrants mainly joined the proletariat, owning no productive property and living by selling their labor power for a wage, some of them were able to move out of this class. Several of the chapters in this section are thus concerned with describing class formation and differentiation within the Asian immigrant communities.

In some of the communities a small bourgeoisie developed, but compared to U.S. capitalists they generally had little capital and employed relatively few workers. One might categorize Asian immigrant capitalists, with a few notable exceptions, as being in the competitive sector of U.S. capitalism. They never joined the ranks of the dominant class in the society. Those who were especially successful were likely to be dealing with a protected market, such as importing goods from Asia to be sold to an Asian clientele or importing luxury goods through special connections in Asia.

A much more numerically important class was the petite bourgeoisie. Asian immigrants revealed a tendency to become farmers, gardeners, and shopkeepers whenever they had the opportunity. Despite their formal independence from a wage-earning status, however, many of these occupations closely resembled common labor. The Chinese laundry owner or Japanese farmer and gardener worked very hard, for long hours, earning low "wages" (or profit margin, which was the equivalent of wages). He often employed unpaid family labor, thus raising the ratio of work to earnings still higher. In other words, the Asian small business or farm was really a form of cheap labor, too. As such, it was useful to U.S. capitalism, in part because it produced goods and services cheaply.

The apparent independence of Asian small business contributed to its cheapness. As an entrepreneur, the immigrant worker felt that he was not really a worker at all, but an independent business owner. This made it more difficult for such workers to see their common oppression and to organize. They were more likely to compete with one another, driving the earnings of each still lower.

Even when Asian-owned businesses and farms employed wage-earners, they were useful to U.S. capitalists because they performed an important labor-control function. The Asian entrepreneur served as a kind of middleman between big capital and the immigrant workers, supplying the former with a group of workers that they helped to control and absorbing most of the antagonism the workers felt toward their employers. The most obvious example of this was the labor contractor. But even Asian farm or factory owners who employed their own workers were often a small link in a chain of capital accumulation. For example, garment manufacturers were likely to have their products retailed by much larger, non-Asian stores that could mark up the prices and earn huge profits on the basis of cheap Asian labor. Similarly, large shipper-growers could benefit from buying cheaply grown (and often higher quality) produce.

Even if no U.S. capitalist intervened directly, Asian business still redounded to his benefit by decreasing consumer costs and, ultimately, wages. Note that Asian capitalists and petite bourgeoisie concentrated heavily in the production, distribution, and servicing of consumer items, clothing, and food in particular. Laundries, restaurants, garment and shoe factories, grocery stores, and even produce farms fit this mold. Because Asian immigrant labor was cheap, these consumer items could be reduced in price, enabling capitalists to lower their workers' wages.

The ability of Asian entrepreneurs to exercise a labor-control function was, in part, a function of racial and national oppression. Because of the discrimination they experienced at the hands of both employers and workers in the surrounding society, the immigrants were often driven into the hands of the wealthier members of their ethnic communities. This class could then take advantage of the fact that their employees (or clients, in the case of labor contractors) had few options and were forced to accept low wages. Given that the Asian entrepreneur himself was often operating in a highly competitive market with limited profits, the opportunity to employ very low-wage labor was eagerly seized upon. Of course some Asian entrepreneurs took advantage of their "captive" labor force not only by cheating the workers but also by earning excessively high profits.

In a sense, the small business and farming class occupied an ambiguous intermediate position between Asian immigrant workers proper and U.S. capitalists. On the one hand, they were often virtually laborers themselves and could at times identify with the problems and demands of other Asian immigrants who were strictly wage earners. On the other hand, they could be exploiters of Asian labor, acting to suppress immigrant workers' struggles to improve wages, work, and living conditions. In the latter capacity, Asian entrepreneurs often served the interests of U.S. capitalists as well as their own, by controlling the workers. Even those small business owners who did not exploit other immigrants would sometimes oppose workers' struggles, since their own precarious position between capitalist and laborer would make them eager not to rock the boat. The conflicting interests of this class made them unreliable allies for the workers, since sometimes their claims to lead the community in struggles against national or racial oppression could also be used in efforts to suppress workers' demands.

Another numerically important class in the emerging Asian communities was the household servant. The large number of Japanese American gardeners can be seen as a segment of this class, even though they were able to transform the occupation from strictly wage-earning to an independent small business. Chinese laundry owners can be viewed in a similar light. This underclass of servants did not contribute to capital accumulation but rather was a consequence of successful accumulation, an index of consumption by the wealthy, who could afford to enhance their lives by employing people to cater to their needs.

The emergence of a servant class among an exploited racial minority is, of course, not unique to Asians. It arose among blacks in the U.S. South, among Africans wherever colonial rulers established themselves, and probably in every colonized territory of the world. There seems to be a link between colonial labor systems having coercive elements, and the creation of a life-style by capitalists, and even by some segments of the colonizing nation's working class, which depend heavily upon the use of domestic servants. One reason for this link is that excessive profits can be earned from coerced labor, making money available for such a luxury. Another reason is that, under coerced and semicoerced labor systems, technical development is stalled, which carries over into the tools of consumption as well: fewer household machines are available. And given the cheapness of coerced labor, there is little incentive to mechanize household chores.

In the Asian immigrant case in the United States, the high ratio of men to women during the settling of the Pacific Coast contributed to the concentration of Asian workers in domestic chores. That is, the absence of female domestic workers (including wives) among the whites created a vacuum that could be filled by Asian immigrants. But, as in the American South, the servant role was by no means contingent on the absence of women and continued long after the sex ratio equalized. So, while the special legal disabilities of Asian immigrants (for example, their ineligibility for citizenship) permitted some U.S. workers to benefit by being able to employ servants, it also had the effect of liberating some white women from domestic work.

Asian immigrants also entered the criminal classes to a certain extent. Some of the crime was simply another form of small business, providing services which the populace was willing or eager to buy. Gambling, prostitution, liquor, and drugs are all cases in point. Again, Asian immigrants are not unique in these roles; various groups of European immigrants have similarly entered the "vice" trade.

There are important reasons why immigrants would cluster in these businesses. They have the characteristic of being marginal, and, since immigrants are continually squeezed out of, or denied access to mainstream businesses, they are more likely to cluster in fringe occupations. The difference between operating a liquor store and operating a gambling establishment is minimal. The legal distinctions themselves are frequently arbitrary. Immigrants tend to concentrate in marginal industries because of difficult or barred access elsewhere, and some of these industries are likely to be defined as illegal. A definition of illegality can, however, have other important consequences. In particular, illegal enterprises require special protection, from the police or their underworld rivals. They may therefore require a network of connections that are unnecessary in legitimate enterprise.

Workers in marginal illegal enterprises are, in many ways, like any other workers. Their labor is used to earn surplus value for employers; they are engaged in exchanging their time for a wage. The particular content of the work they do matters little to the workers. Similarly, from the employer's point of view, the "vice trade" is strictly a profit-making venture. And, as in other businesses, bigger capitalists in the society may be able to drain off some of their profits through unequal exchange and the like. Further, the legal distinction between marginal and legitimate may be used as basis for extortion.

Asian immigrant communities also spawned criminal activities that cannot be seen as marginal enterprises, namely, thugs and extortionists, or "lumpen," described in chapter 11. Again there are important reasons why these elements would proliferate among immigrant workers in capitalist societies, especially in immigrant communities that suffer special legal disabilities. As suggested above, the inadequacy of work opportunities in the legitimate economy may have driven some people to pursue any available means of survival. More important, because Asians were not permitted citizenship, they already existed in a sense "outside the law." Their communities did not receive adequate police protection and, therefore, had to police themselves. The use of extralegal violence can be seen as an alternative mechanism for establishing social order.

Asian immigrant communities thus became progressively diverse as time passed. Increasing class differentiation within the community led to an increase in the basis of class conflict. Yet their common experience of racial and national oppression still tended to bond the different classes together in self-defense and served to delay the emergence of class identification and class struggle. This, in turn, made it even harder for cross-national class alliances to form. Asian workers often identified themselves first as Japanese, Chinese, Filipino, Korean, or Indian and only second as workers. Pan-Asian workers' movements were difficult to form, let alone interracial organizations, a fact that could be taken advantage of by employers. In large measure this difficulty arose from the special circumstances under which Asian immigrant workers were brought to the United States.

Two of the essays in this section, chapters 12 and 14, deal with Asian immigrant women. The immigrant experience is somewhat different for women because of their dual role: responsibility for reproduction as well as for production in the economy. Women are typically held responsible for the domestic sphere, often under patriarchal conditions, where their chastity (among other things) is controlled to ensure the male lineage. This responsibility for the domestic sphere limits women's role in production. And they are often likely to be the cheapest labor since they are susceptible to male domination in the workplace and are typically assumed to be merely supplementing the income earned by the chief male breadwinner.

Women made up a small proportion of immigrant labor in the early phases of Asian immigration to the United States, though later on, especially in some communities, women joined the men in larger numbers and helped to establish families. The migration of single males, leaving women behind in the home village, was a product of conditions both in the homeland and in the United States. In the home countries of the emigrants, capitalist development and imperialism led to the erosion of peasant agriculture and craft production, but many of these precapitalist features were retained. An important motive for emigration was the reestablishment on a sounder footing of a precapitalist way of life. Emigrants from Asia had no intention of permanently leaving their villages and towns. Thus it made sense to leave most of the family behind, sending only the most able-bodied workers abroad. These tended to be males because they could probably earn the needed money faster, since men are generally paid higher wages than women. Men were also more likely to emigrate because of long-standing patriarchal traditions in Asian societies: it was virtually unthinkable to permit a single woman to travel abroad. Selectivity in favor of single males was exercised by employers in the United States, as well, since they could avoid having to pay a family wage, and reproduction costs would be borne by the homeland villages.

Within the immigrant communities this pattern of predominantly male migration meant there was a severe shortage of women to perform the domestic labor functions typically performed by women, especially in the early phases of capitalist development. As a result, these functions became commoditized, reflected in the large numbers of laundries and restaurants, household servants and prostitutes. In the Asian case at least some of these functions were performed by male migrants.

A small number of women did accompany the male migrants, however, and they were especially likely to perform the role of commoditized domestic labor. In so doing they inadvertently helped support the system of single male migration (to the benefit of local capitalists) by making it unnecessary for the migrants to bring their families or marry in the new country. The unmarried male workers continued not to require a family wage. At the same time, these female immigrants could be used to help perpetuate the patriarchal family back home by preventing defections by the male immigrants, by providing for their immediate "family" needs. Prostitutes, for example, played this role. Such defections did occur on occasion anyway.

Single male migration, while providing cheap labor, is not always the cheapest way to acquire workers. Under certain conditions it is more profitable to bring in whole families. Rather than pay a family wage, which would indeed be more costly, female immigrants can also be employed directly or work indirectly as unpaid family labor. In virtually every known human society female labor is cheaper than male labor. Since immigrant labor is typically cheaper than local labor, immigrant women tend to be among the lowest paid of all sources of labor power. Thus it remains highly profitable for capitalists to encourage female immigration.

Asian immigrant women tended to have a higher participation in the labor force than local women. Even so the statistics mask the amount of work they actually performed. Not only did immigrant women remain responsible for reproduction and domestic chores but they also often worked as unpaid family labor in the businesses or farms of their husbands or relatives. It seems plausible that these women had to work much harder in the United States than they ever had to work in their homelands. One reason for this assessment is the loss of support of their extended families, which typically shared at least some of the domestic workload. Thus, by permitting women to come to the United States in the later phases of immigration, capitalists could reap the benefits of a heavy work effort with very little compensation to the workers.

Immigrant women posed special problems to labor organizing. Their dual responsibilities of reproduction and production limited the time and energy they had available for organizing. Similarly, because women resided in patriarchal families, men could exert pressure on them not to be active in male-dominated unions, assuming that such unions ever showed an interest in organizing women. Husbands also probably preferred their wives to spend any spare time on domestic chores rather than participating in external organizations. These problems are faced by all women, immigrant and nonimmigrant.

More peculiar to Asian immigrant women was the high incidence of unpaid family labor. In this circumstance women were not only employees but were also in a sense in the "employ" of that person most likely to exercise the highest level of personal power over them — their husbands. Given their cultural training, it was virtually impossible for Asian married women to rebel against their husband-employers or even to perceive a conflict of interests between them. Since both husband and wife were working excessively hard to eke out a living, and the benefits of much of their labor were siphoned off by those higher up in the economic system, in a sense there was no conflict of interests between spouses. But given the added burden of domestic responsibilities and patriarchal traditions, women were often the more stressed members of the "partnership."

In sum, Asian immigrant women were likely to suffer multiple layers of oppression. They suffered all the usual forms of exploitation as workers, as immigrants, and as members of a stigmatized racial or national minority. And they also suffered all the usual disadvantages of being women. These two sets of disadvantages combined to make the status of immigrant women particularly oppressed, producing such roles as semienslaved prostitutes, highly exploited sweatshop, restaurant, and laundry workers, and unpaid family workers on farms and in shops.

Throughout most of this volume we have emphasized similarities among the various Asian nationalities and disregarded differences. The latter certainly exist. For instance, the Japanese immigrants who accumulated enough capital to become small business owners were much more likely to purchase farms than were the Chinese, who concentrated more in urban trades. Of all the groups, Filipinos were much less likely than the others to move into the petite bourgeoisie and, in later years, they became more active in the labor movement than other Asian immigrant groups. There are other important differences as well, some of which emerged especially clearly in the decades after World War II, when many of the severe legal restrictions against Asians were lifted.

Although the topic of differentiation has not been developed in these essays, we believe our theoretical orientation would aid in such analysis. For example, the ability of a particular group to pursue economic opportunity in the United States would appear to be partially related to the degree of imperialist domination of its homeland. The two ends of the scale for Asian immigrants are Japan and the Philippines, with Japan the least, and the Philippines the most thoroughly colonized of the territories. This history not only affected the terms home governments could negotiate for their emigrant nationals but also left a lasting impact on cultural forms.

Another factor which may have played a part in differentiating the Asian groups from one another is the time of their arrival in the United States. Each group arrived at a different phase in the development of United States capitalism and its local variants, with accompanying differences in the opportunities for immigrant workers. The Chinese and Japanese both arrived in California during a period of early growth and development, while the later arrival of the Filipinos coincided with more restricted opportunities for unskilled labor. The Filipino and Mexican immigrations to California overlap substantially, and it would be interesting to compare these two groups to assess the degree to which the political economy of the receiving area molded the experience of both, irrespective of culture and origin.

Apart from conditions in the surrounding society, each Asian group provided an environment for succeeding groups. The fact that the Chinese became established in small urban businesses in both Hawaii and California before the arrival of other Asians may have limited access to the later arrivals. The Japanese dominance in agriculture in California may reflect this limitation far more than it does a positive cultural value for farming. Similarly, the concentration of Chinese in San Francisco and the accompanying rise of an anti-Chinese movement there may have played a significant role in a Japanese preference for Los Angeles. Competition among Asian immigrant groups (and, one might add, between Asians and others) has not been developed in this volume, but it is clearly a topic worthy of further study.

Despite differences among the Asian groups, there were considerable similarities in their experiences in the United States and Hawaii prior to World War II. As we have said, they were all treated as aliens ineligible for citizenship, a category unique to Asians. They concentrated in the same region and in similar sectors of the economy. They tended to be more exploited than other workers, as shown in generally lower wages than whites received. They were all discriminated against by the white labor movement, the leaders of which sometimes dug up their old speeches against an earlier immigrant group to use against a newer immigrant nationality. And they were all subjected to exclusionary efforts that eventually succeeded. These are profound similarities that breathe reality into the category "Asian American" and justify their treatment in a single volume.

Each chapter in this section deals with a single Asian nationality. The chapters are arranged in order of arrival of the groups, starting with the Chinese and ending with the Filipinos. Our original goal was to have one essay on each group, with another entire section on women. However, given an already lengthy volume and the paucity of information on Asian women for most groups, we present only two essays on women, one on Chinese and the other on Japanese women workers.

Generally the chapters in this section aim at opening new ways of thinking about the Asian American experience. In most cases they also uncover some new sources of data. But their chief goal is less the amassing of new information than the demonstration of how our framework raises important questions for investigation. Issues of class development and class conflict, both within Asian communities and between Asians and others, receive special attention in all of these essays. We do not aspire to prove that a class approach is scientifically valid, but we certainly hope to have demonstrated that it raises important, and largely neglected, questions for investigation.

In conclusion, there is considerably more to be uncovered about the history of class formation and development in Asian immigrant communities and about their relations across ethnic lines. Most research has ignored these questions. Instead, it has focused heavily on the adjustment problems of immigrants, their changing self-definitions and identifications, and the stages of assimilation they have passed through. Few studies have considered the issue of class at all, except as a kind of status scale (or hierarchy of evaluations of occupations). We believe that class, as understood within a Marxist framework, with its emphasis on potential bases for conflict and struggle, can introduce a dynamic element into an interpretation of the Asian immigrant experience.

11

Socioeconomic Developments among the Chinese in San Francisco, 1848-1906

June Mei

The Chinese communities in the United States were often described by nineteenth-century writers as "little Chinas," meaning that Chinese-Americans of the period preserved intact the dress, foods, religions, and life-styles of China. While it is true that the majority of Chinese in America still had immediate family members in their homeland and that they culturally assimilated more slowly than did European immigrants, there were nevertheless important changes afoot that created a Chinese American community very different from the society in China at this time. Many factors affected the pattern of change among California Chinese, such as laws against immigration and naturalization. This essay will examine the interaction of some of these factors, with emphasis on the emergence of new class formations and their interaction with classes in white society. It is an effort to draw new conclusions from information already available rather than to introduce new source materials, although some are used. Specifically, it covers the Chinese in San Francisco from the first years of large-scale immigration until 1906, when "old Chinatown" was physically leveled by the great San Francisco earthquake.

San Francisco was the chief port of entry for Chinese in the nineteenth century. Within a few years, it also became the largest Chinese community in the country. The special place held by San Francisco's Chinatown was reflected in the popular name by which the immigrants knew it: *dafu*, or "the Big Town." Throughout the nineteenth and twentieth centuries, it housed the national headquarters of the principal overseas Chinese organizations in the United States, and in many ways it was the center of their activities. Developments in San Francisco also affected Chinese living elsewhere in the United States. For example, the anti-Chinese movement, which was directed primarily against Chinese workers in the city of San Francisco, contributed to the passage of the Exclusion Act of 1882, a law, which along with its later continuations, severely restricted the immigration of Chinese for over half a century.

The term "Chinatown" suggests only an amorphous, faceless mass of people living in a definable part of town. Limited contact with whites in the United States and politically motivated distortions often made "Chinatown" into a fantastic blend of truth and wild rumor in the press and popular literature. In reality, Chinatown was the social center for virtually all Chinese in San Francisco. Even those whose jobs required them to live elsewhere, such as domestic servants, generally spent their leisure hours in Chinatown. During periods of anti-Chinese violence, it became a refuge for Chinese and a target for their enemies. Thus, "Chinatown" in this paper is virtually a synonym for Chinese in San Francisco. In some respects, it was a place of transition. Some left San Francisco's Chinatown to settle elsewhere in the United States, some stayed in Chinatown permanently, whereas others returned to China. At all times, Chinatown was affected by changes in both California and China. Therefore, rather than seeing Chinatown as a fixed, rigid entity, it is probably more accurate to describe it as a constantly changing structure of social relations.

Before the 1906 earthquake, the historical development of San Francisco's Chinatown went through several distinct periods, each characterized by new social and economic developments. These include the early formative years, 1848-1850; the years 1850-1870, when it was a way-station for Chinese going elsewhere in the state; the boom years, 1870-1882, when its population and businesses were at their peak; and the years of decline, 1882-1906.

OCCUPATIONAL TRENDS

1848-1850

Some of the first Chinese to settle in San Francisco were engaged in trades directly related to various scarcities and needs of that city. For example, many houses were prefabricated in China, transported across the Pacific, and assembled in San Francisco, sometimes by Chinese contract laborers. Other Chinese were involved in building houses out of materials available locally.[1] Even laundry was sometimes sent to Canton for washing because of exorbitant costs in San Francisco, and Chinese businessmen may have been involved in this business.[2]

In these early years, there were also a few Chinese cooks, tailors, shoemakers, and general laborers in California.[3] However, the majority of San Francisco's Chinese, at least until 1850-1852, were merchants. One contemporary writer observed that in late 1849, "most of the Chinese who came here were men of means enough to pay their own way and here they mainly embarked on mercantiles or trading pursuits."[4] At least some of them went into the restaurant business, where they became formidable competitors because of the low prices they charged.[5] Some Chinese merchants were probably involved in the importation of buildings, while others were in the grocery business.

1850-1870

There were only 3,000 or fewer Chinese living in San Francisco in the mid-1850s, but they operated some thirty-three general merchandise stores, fifteen apothecaries, and various other businesses.[6] Since the ratio of general merchandise stores to residents was rather high, it seems likely that a substantial portion of the business activity was aimed at supplying Chinese miners and others who worked inland.

Chinese workers first entered the local laundry trade when they joined the work force at Washerwoman's Lagoon in 1850 and caused the price for washing a dozen shirts to drop from $8 to $5.[7] Since most of their patrons were non-Chinese, Chinese laundries soon multiplied and spread to various parts of the city. Most of these laundries were small, employing an average of five men each.[8] Often the same premises would be shared by two different laundries, one using it by day, the other by night. This enabled them to lower their overhead costs by halving the rent and other expenses. As they proliferated, prices fell even more sharply, to as low as $2 per dozen shirts.

By the mid-1850s, Chinese were also involved in the fish and abalone businesses.[9] Their fisheries multiplied and apparently thrived, as more fishing camps were set up at various points along the California coast. Abalone fishing, in particular, flourished after 1860 owing to the popularity of abalone shells as ornamental materials; moreover, the flesh could be exported to China, where it was prized as a delicacy.

By 1859-60, there were at least forty stores in Chinatown selling foodstuffs, general goods, fancy wares, and herbal medicines.[10] Restaurants and other small trades also increased slightly in numbers. Most of the wholesale and retail merchants sold their provisions and general goods primarily to other Chinese. This was also true of the apothecaries and craftsmen who plied their trade in Chinatown. The only businesses that catered to significant numbers of whites were restaurants and those stores that sold fancy goods such as silks and lacquers to tourists. These, however, were also patronized by wealthy Chinese, and they were by no means entirely dependent on tourists. Gambling houses and brothels were established in Chinatown from 1848 to 1860.[11] The former had an almost exclusively Chinese clientele, while the latter were "graded" according to the nationality of their patrons. Both were subsequently to grow in numbers and significance. Table 11.1 gives the occupational distribution of Chinese in San Francisco for 1860.

The single most important economic development in Chinatown and San Francisco between 1860 and 1870 was the growth of manufacturing enterprises (see table 11.2). Chinese labor was drawn to specific industries, notably the production of cigars, slippers and woolens.[12] Before this time, the majority of the Chinese in San Francisco were merchants, independent small producers, or small tradesmen, craftsmen and "professionals" (e.g., druggists and interpreters). Although these categories continued to grow — if only because Chinatown itself was growing — their ratio to the total Chinese populace declined.

Another field that absorbed large numbers of Chinese was domestic service. It is not known exactly when the Chinese "houseboy" became a familiar sight in San Francisco, but this apparently occurred in the 1860s. It was then that large, wealthy families generated the demand, and Chinese leaving the mines and railroads provided a supply. The Manuscript Census of 1870 lists 989 Chinese servants, indicating that by then this form of employment had probably already existed for at least several years.

The number of stores in Chinatown grew as rapidly as the population. A directory of 1868-69 lists ninety-nine "principal" Chinese merchants, most of whom sold imported foodstuffs, fresh meats and groceries, general goods, fancy wares, and medicinal herbs.[13] Some of the larger restaurants offered expensive banquets and imported delicacies for a largely Chinese clientele. This was a shift from the days when these restaurants offered cheap and hearty but simple meals for white miners (see table 11.1).

1870-1882

As Chinatown continued to expand after the completion of the transcontinental railroad, so too did the industries of San Francisco. Two industries in particular came to rely heavily on Chinese labor: boot and

TABLE 11.1
OCCUPATIONAL DISTRIBUTION OF CHINESE IN SAN FRANCISCO

Occupation	1860	1870	1880
Merchants/proprietors	136	165	692
Laundry workers	127	1,279	2,992
Food peddlers			241
Peddlers		223	948
Fishermen	428	143	
Miners		544	
Servants		989	2,471
Gardeners		122	
Factory workers		206	
Clothing manufacturers		7	874
Cigar makers		1,610	2,724
Laborers	625	2,014	
Porters		79	142
Shoemakers		105	1,746
Tailors	43	183	721
Woolen makers		118	
Waiters		22	
Gamblers	263	222	
Prostitutes		1,404	435
Actors	9	87	
Musicians		21	
Bookkeepers		28	119
Clerks		96	
Opium dealers	12		
Druggists	34	28	
Interpreters		13	
Physicians		27	
Students		32	
Painters		26	
Cooks	56		
Carpenters	45	59	109
Other craftsmen		328	
"At home" workers			1,505
Miscellaneous	187	1,254	6,794
Unlisted/illegible	728	275	
Total	2,693	11,989	22,513

SOURCE: Based on a more detailed compilation of the 1860, 1870, and 1880 Manu-script Census, by Paul Nakatsuka, made for a research project on Asian American female labor sponsored by the Asian American Studies Center, UCLA.
NOTES: 1. Only larger occupational groupings are given in this table.
2. Absence of any category in any year does not necessarily mean that no Chinese were engaged in that occupation at that time. For example, no gamblers are listed for 1880, and yet gambling dens in Chinatown were flourishing at this time. Either respondents gave different answers to avoid legal troubles, or else the census preferred to list them as "miscellaneous."

shoemaking, and machine sewing. Chinese also accounted for much of the local shrimping business. Meanwhile, previously established enterprises such as the import-export business, laundries, cigar-making, and domestic service continued to flourish throughout the decade.

As early as 1869, Chinese workers were sewing pantaloons, vests, shirts, drawers, and overalls.[14] However, it was not until 1875-76 that the clothing industry in San Francisco reached its zenith and labor costs bottomed and allowed it to stand up against Eastern competition. During this period, Chinese were hired because they were cheap, easily trained, and available.[15] Most of these Chinese clothing workers manufactured overalls, underwear, shirts, and men's clothing, and many worked in Chinese-owned sweatshops (see table 11.2). In addition, there were also tailors and seamstresses who custom-made both Chinese and Western-style garments for their clients. By 1880, as many as 500 people worked in this area.

Chinese shoemakers were first introduced into San Francisco shoe factories in 1869 as strikebreakers.[16] Their availability and skill made them desirable workers; moreover, the relatively low initial capital costs enabled some Chinese to establish their own sweatshops. In 1870, Chinese accounted for 19 percent of all San Francisco shoemakers; by 1877 they represented over 60 percent (see table 11.2). In a roundabout way, one reason for this increase was an anti-Chinese movement in the industry which started in 1872 but did not crest until 1875. This movement, initiated by the Knights of Saint Crispin, demanded, among other things, the expulsion of Chinese from the industry. By 1873, however, there were already signs of Chinese dissatisfaction with working condi-

TABLE 11-1 NOTES (continued)

3. This table is based on the U.S. Manuscript Census, which offers relatively detailed information not available elsewhere. However, these census figures tend to be consistently lower than the probable actual numbers, for several reasons: seasonal fluctuation of the Chinese population; underreporting (Chinese often shied away from contact with officials, particularly after anti-Chinese sentiment increased); errors resulting from a language gap (surnames were often omitted, and under the name of "Ah X" it would be possible for several people named X to be mistaken for the same person). Hence although the absolute numbers of the census may be in error, the percentages of people in the occupations are probably close to being correct. Other sources citing the size and distribution of Chinese population vary from the census figures to differing degrees. James Rogers, police officer responsible for San Francisco's Chinatown, testified to the California State Senate in its 1876 hearings that the Chinese population that year was 20,000 to 25,000, but his figures were all rounded off to the nearest hundred or thousand. Otis Gibson estimated the Chinese population in 1877 to be 32,488, but again his figures were rounded off, and his categories are at times rather vague. The great difference between Gibson's estimate and those of Rogers and the Manuscript Census may have resulted from seasonal fluctuations. Since Gibson was raising money for his missionary efforts, there may also have been reason for him to err on the high side.

TABLE 11.2
CHINESE IN MANUFACTURING INDUSTRIES

Industry	Year	1867	1868-9	1870	1873	1876	1877	1878-9	1880
Cigars		450 (90%)*		1,657 (91+%)		3,300	5,500	4,000	
Woolens			400-500 (55-66%)						
Slippers				191 (90.5%)					
Sewing					2,000	2000-2500			1,692
Shoes				296 (.19%)			2000-3000 (66-75%)		

SOURCE: Chinn 1969; Chiu 1963; Coolidge 1909.
*Percentage of total work force in this industry. Given where data available.

tions in white-owned firms. As a consequence, by 1875 many Chinese shoemakers had resigned or been fired from their jobs. To absorb and utilize this pool of skilled workers, some of these firms were set up by men who had gone to work in white-owned companies with the primary purpose of learning the shoemaking business. Chinese owners almost exclusively hired Chinese workers. Thus, they were able to accommodate and even slightly expand the Chinese work force in the industry.

During the 1870s, the California shrimping industry, which was centered in San Francisco, was dominated by the Chinese. There may have been as many as several hundred Chinese shrimpers in 1875-76, operating out of camps on San Francisco Bay.[17]

As the Chinese population of San Francisco increased, so did the number of Chinese working outside Chinatown. The number of Chinese-owned laundries grew to around 300 by 1876, employing some 1,500 workers. Another 1,500 or so Chinese worked in white-owned laundries.[18] In addition, one writer estimated that there were some 4,500 Chinese domestic servants in 1877, and approximately 300 Chinese peddlers.[19] Besides selling fruits, vegetables, and fish, as they had been doing for at least a decade, some of the peddlers also sold sundries such as tape, pins, matches, and cigars. Others entered the luxuries trade on a small scale, selling imported brocades and porcelains to wealthy socialite families. There were also some who sold sundries in the downtown business district. To a large extent, this increase in the number of Chinese employed outside Chinatown was made possible by the growth of San Francisco itself: by 1880, its total population had exceeded 230,000, an increase of some 50 percent in a decade.

The Chinese role in the cigar industry also continued to grow. By 1877 over half the city's cigar makers were Chinese (see table 11.2), but in 1878-79, partly because of anti-Chinese agitation, some white-owned factories discharged a number of Chinese workers. Subsequently, Chinese-owned factories proliferated, and in 1878 there were 49 cigar manufacturers, wholesalers, and retailers in Chinatown. Many used Spanish names to avoid hostility from the anti-Chinese movement.

Other Chinatown businesses also flourished. In 1878, there were over 150 wholesalers and retailers of fresh and preserved foods, 12 restaurants, 25 apothecaries, 35 fancy goods stores, 10 jewelry stores, 10 tinsmithies and over a dozen small craftsmen and artisans. The sharp increase in stores selling groceries and general goods was necessitated by the growth of Chinatown, which had over 20,000 inhabitants. Chinatown had become a well-established tourist attraction, and many of its fancy goods stores sold silks, lacquers, and porcelains to visitors and rich San Franciscans.

Houses of gambling and prostitution also could be found in large numbers during the 1870s. There were at least 40 to 60 of the former, and as many as 150 to 200 of the latter. Opium-oriented businesses also thrived. At least 8 stores sold opium, which was offered to Chinese in restaurants, opium dens, and private homes. By 1876, at least 8 dens were established which catered to whites and Chinese alike, but this alarmed the authorities, who quickly suppressed them.[20]

Two industries employing substantial numbers of Chinese declined in the mid-1870s. An economic recession in 1875-76, coupled with a wave of anti-Chinese agitation, forced owners of woolen mills to reduce their Chinese work force.[21] The slipper industry also encountered difficulties during this period. After 1876-1878, the business became increasingly unprofitable, and although there were still 14 Chinese factories in 1878, their product value per worker decreased continuously until it was halved by 1880.[22]

1882-1906

The effects of the growing anti-Chinese movement could already be felt during in the 1870s in the shoe, cigar, and woolen industries. Passage of the Chinese Exclusion Act and continued hostility toward Chinese during the 1880s further affected their employment opportunities, particularly in white-owned businesses. Moreover, most of the industries employing many Chinese workers, especially cigar making and the sewing trades, went into a general decline in the face of competition from the East Coast. Hence, there was a reversal of previous occupational and business trends. The number of Chinese in manufacturing decreased, as did the number of Chinese-owned firms. At the same time, there was a temporary increase in the number of Chinatown businesses and laundries, which lasted until the Chinese population declined as a result of the Exclusion Act and job scarcity.

By the turn of the century, less than one-quarter of the Chinese in San Francisco were engaged in industrial manufacturing, these being primarily in the sewing trades. Almost two-thirds worked in laundries or as domestic servants.[23] The remainder either worked in Chinatown businesses or were unemployed. In addition, in the two decades after the Exclusion Act, criminal activity was on the rise. Full- or part-time professional toughs knows as "highbinders" increased in numbers, probably as a result of spreading joblessness in Chinatown. This unemployment forced people into extortion or bloodshed in order to make money, and promoted gambling, both as a means of earning and as a way of killing time. In turn the increased gambling revenues fostered criminal interest in controlling gambling dens.

SOCIAL CLASSES

Although Chinese could be found in a wide and constantly changing variety of occupations between 1848 and 1906, it is possible to detect the growth and decline of four broad social classes during this time: capitalists, wage workers, petite bourgeoisie, and "lumpen." Of course, the exact status of every business cannot be easily determined. For example, some small retailers and owners of large laundries fall in the gray area between capitalists and petite bourgeoisie, while workers in some small enterprises such as barbershops may have been either wage workers or independent businessmen. The following observations, then, are generalizations about a majority of people in various occupations.

Capitalists

Broadly speaking, there were two types of Chinese capitalists in nineteenth-century San Francisco: mercantile and industrial. The former were engaged primarily in the import-export business and marketing within Chinatown, where capital was used for trade rather than for production. The latter's investments were in the manufacture of such commodities as cigars, shoes, and clothing. Although both hired wage workers, only the industrial capitalists were actually involved in producing goods. The mercantile capitalists only bought and sold goods. Paralleling this dichotomy was the difference in their markets. The products of the industrial capitalists were mostly intended for the general American market, while the mercantile capitalists sold their wares mainly to other Chinese and to an occasional tourist. Of course, both groups included wholesalers and retailers, individual enterprises, and partnerships, but these distinctions were less important.

One of the most significant differences between the mercantile and industrial capitalists was the size of their assets. Wholesalers of items such as tea, rice, and herbs were among the richest men in Chinatown, and their worth is suggested by their tax assessments. In 1876, when both types of capitalists were flourishing, tax assessments on twenty-five firms and individuals ranged from $5,000 to $25,000 for personal property alone. Almost all of these successful businesses imported goods from China and Japan to sell in Chinatown. One contemporary writer noted that "several of the leading Chinese merchants are reputed to be worth from two to five hundred thousand dollars."[24] In describing a group of Chinese merchants at the turn of the century, one Chinese source states that two successful men, who were forced by legal harassment to return to China abruptly, managed by selling their businesses at a great loss to net only $1,000 and $7,000, respectively. Three other businessmen liquidated their firms at their own pace: one who was a partner in several companies cleared $150,000; a garment firm brought $80,000, and a restaurant $30,000.[25] Even by their own peers, these businessmen were regarded as successful, so it is clear that large fortunes could be made by mercantile capitalists. Their businesses also had the longest survival rates of all Chinatown stores,[26] which is another measure of their financial success.

In contrast, most of the Chinese-owned manufacturing firms had very little capital. Ping Chiu noted that two Chinese cigar firms reported capital of $300 each, and only 23 to 28 of the city's 70 to 90 Chinese companies reported a capitalization of $1,000 or more.[27] Similarly, he observed that Chinese shoe factories all were modestly capitalized. The Chinese factories in the marginally profitable slipper trade had an average capital of $1,500. Likewise, only a small amount of capital was needed to enter the sewing trades; in fact, Chinese could "serve as apprentice and journeyman at $6 to $20 per month for a short period to acquire the necessary skill and capital to open his own shop."[28] In this manner, many Chinese industrial capitalists established their own businesses. In the cigar, shoe and slipper manufacturing businesses many Chinese could work in white-owned firms just long enough to learn the trade and accumulate enough capital to get started on their own. One feature shared by all of the Chinese industrial capitalists of this period was the small amount of capital needed to start their own shop. In fact, Chinese investment was almost exclusively in those industries where ease of entry was outstanding.[29]

The mercantile capitalists, on the contrary, appear to have brought their capital, or at least their starting capital, with them from China.[30] They probably came from merchant families, and apparently few diversified by investing extensively in industries. There were, however, two other important sources of income for mercantile capitalists. Some of the largest import-export firms were also involved in labor contracting and supplying Chinese workers outside San Francisco with foodstuffs and other commodities.[31] They were particularly well suited for this trade because they sold goods that were part of their usual business. At the same time, at least a few leading merchants also invested in brothels, gambling parlors, and opium dens in Chinatown. However, when police crackdowns on Chinatown rackets and tong wars proved to be bad for business, most of the wealthiest merchants expressed an eagerness for a return to law and order. This suggests either that only a minority were heavily involved in these illegitimate operations, or that income from their regular business operations was so substantial that it was not worth getting involved in illegal activities and subsequent police action.

Though the source and size of capital differed considerably, mercantile and industrial capitalism did not constitute mutually exclusive categories for it was possible for the same person to be involved in several different businesses. For example, the notorious racketeer Fung Ching Doy ("Little Pete") was the proprietor of a shoe factory while also investing in gambling houses and fixed horse races. The $100,000 or so in profits he derived from the races were, in turn, invested in various Chinatown businesses and fish hatcheries.[32] Thus, he diversified his sources of income and combined features of both mercantile and industrial capitalism, as well as racketeering. There were reasons for legal and illegal enterprises to overlap in ownership. Each could generate capital for the other, and while regular businesses provided respectability, the rackets were more lucrative and beyond the reach of tax collectors.

Wage Workers

After the 1850s, wage workers constituted the single largest class of the Chinese population. As a group, these workers were primarily employed as laborers in the manufacturing industries, or as shop attendants in Chinatown, or as domestic servants. Since job competition and wage levels were the key issues of the anti-Chinese movement, the Chinese wage workers became its chief target. According to data on the average wages received by Chinese workers in some of the major industries in 1870 (table 11.3), relatively few factory workers made over $300 a year, which was less than the average income of white males in the

TABLE 11.3
ANNUAL WAGES OF CHINESE AND WHITES IN CERTAIN INDUSTRIES, 1870

	Chinese	Whites
Cigars	$200-300	$250-400+
Slippers	200-250	(Too few whites to estimate)
Shoes	200-350	700-900
Shirts	200-300	300 (women, children)
		460 (men)
Clothing	300-400	600-900 (women)
		900-1200 (men)
Woolens	330-500	600-1000

SOURCE: Chiu 1963: chaps. VI-VII.
NOTES: 1. Unless otherwise indicated, all wages given are for male workers.
2. If data is available only for daily wages, annual wages are computed based on a 300-day working year.
3. Ranges given are very approximate, since there was great variation according to a worker's skill, job description, number of days worked, labor/job shortages, and other factors.

same job. Domestic servants, by contrast, were paid more than whites, and received as much as $40 to $60 per month.[33] There were several reasons for their high wages. First, their pay was not linked to the market prices of commodities that they made. Second, they were hired as "luxuries" or "conveniences" by wealthy families and were not expected to generate income for their employers. Finally, there was no East Coast competition in their line of work. By the same token, however, a factory employee could hope to quit and establish his own business, having gained some training in that line of work, which for the domestic servant was not possible. The wages of workers in Chinatown stores are not recorded, but they were probably comparable to the pay of Chinese industrial workers.

Petite Bourgeoisie

The category of petite bourgeoisie probably included the broadest assortment of occupations: independent small businessmen and partnerships, professionals with special skills such as physicians and interpreters, plus craftsmen and artisans. The largest of all these occupational groups was the laundrymen, followed next by the fishermen and shrimpers. Most seem to have had small partnerships with an average of five members each. Incomes were also comparable: about $1 per day, or slightly more than the average income of a factory worker. Although whole or part ownership of a business may have enhanced feelings of financial security, the work was hard and not especially lucrative.

Some members of the Chinese petite bourgeoisie, especially the professionals, managed to amass considerable fortunes and exercise a great deal of influence in the community. For example, interpreters could wield power over others because of their importance in legal matters. Virtually all Chinese who had to appear in court relied on interpreters, and the latter could therefore affect the outcome of most cases. Hence, some were offered fees and bribes if they would produce the desired testimony, while others were occasionally threatened with reprisals if they did not say the right things in court.

Most wage workers who saved enough to establish their own businesses probably became, at least initially, petite bourgeois small businessmen who relied more on themselves than on employees in their operations. If they prospered, they could become capitalists; if they failed, they might revert to working for others. Because of this, the composition of the petite bourgeoisie was probably the most fluid of all classes among the Chinese. Although it had fewer members than the wage worker class, most workers regarded it as a more desirable category, since the income for the petite bourgeoisie was potentially greater than that for wage earners. Mercantile capitalists were, as a group, the wealthiest Chinese, but few workers could realistically hope to acquire the capital or the business connections needed to become a successful merchant. It was not very difficult, however, for an industrious and thrifty worker to save enough money to start a small enterprise or partnership, and many industrial capitalists did indeed start their businesses in this manner. In this sense, entry into the petite bourgeoisie was the next step up the socioeconomic ladder for most Chinese workers.

"Lumpen"

"Lumpen" refers to those who provided neither capital nor labor, and who did not produce goods or services, but whose incomes were derived primarily from appropriation of others' wealth, usually by the use of real or threatened violence. In the case of Chinese in San Francisco, the lumpen were professional toughs popularly known as "highbinders." Some of them received regular salaries to act as bodyguards. Others were paid fixed fees for specific tasks on a "piece-work" basis, and still others "free-lanced" by living off income from extortion and blackmail. Most of their operations were related to gambling or prostitution,[34] yet it is useful to distinguish these men from the owners or proprietors of gambling dens and brothels. These establishments, seldom owned by highbinders, were conducted like regular businesses, where capital was invested in expectation of profit. Highbinders, however, were often employed by the capitalists in gambling and prostitution.

As early as the 1850s, the lumpen included some professional fighters in Chinatown,[35] but their heyday was from 1882 to 1906. As suggested earlier, it seems likely that some had once been workers who had turned to violence when they lost their jobs. Besides coming from the ranks of the unemployed, some "hatchet men" were also sent for specific jobs from places as distant as Hong Kong or from other Chinese communities. This method was particularly useful if an unrecognized assassin was needed, or if local talent was not up to the job. Still, even in the peak years of highbinder activity, it is doubtful that there were more than 1,000 such men, and it is probable that there were fewer than 500 hard-core toughs in Chinatown.

The lumpen elements existed on the economic fringes of society, preying on those who had no answer to their use of violence. Although they resembled wage workers in being paid for specific services, they were different because they had the option of doing the same work for themselves whenever they pleased. At the same time, they differed from independent petite bourgeois entrepreneurs because their business required no capital. Some lumpen became extremely wealthy by investing their proceeds from blackmail and extortion operations in gambling dens and brothels.[36] Since these lumpen capitalists did not have legitimate businesses, they had nothing to gain but everything to lose if rackets were suppressed, so it is possible that they led the opposition to the mercantile capitalists during the disputes over control of Chinatown during the period of tong violence.

CLASS ORGANIZATIONS

Capitalists

The competitive nature of capitalism generally discourages capitalists from organizing among themselves, and the San Francisco Chinese were no exception. It is thus not surprising that Chinese capitalists had fewer organizations than did the other social classes. In fact, there was seldom any need for collective action on their part, since they were rarely threatened by other forces. There were, however, some Chinese businessmen's associations. The earliest one soon split into two groups because of hometown differences among its members.[37] Both were established to fix prices and prevent unbridled competition. In this respect, they resembled traditional Chinese guilds.[38] Generally, when Chinese capitalists had to take action through an institutional channel, they worked through family associations or through the Six Companies,[39] which were dominated by merchants. Although the highbinders were, theoretically, members of the Six Companies, there was hostility between the lumpen elements and the leading merchants, and the position taken by the Six Companies generally reflected the interests of the merchants. This is most evident in the struggle to break the power of the highbinders in the last two decades of the nineteenth century. The conflict between the lumpen and the merchants, however, was sometimes complicated by the fact that many merchants belonged to the Sam Yup Association, while many highbinders were members of the See Yup and Ning Yeung Associations.[40] Hence, what was in reality a conflict of classes often appeared to be a clash between district associations.

To complicate matters, Chinese resistance to racism and national oppression also made for strained alliances within the associations. Chinese workers and capitalists alike often encountered hostility and discrimination from whites, and Chinese businessmen were often active in resisting unequal treatment. In the mid-1870s, for example, the Six

Companies sent a memorial to President Grant rebutting some of the charges made against the Chinese in the United States. Nowhere in the document did they suggest that Chinese cheap labor was undemocratic and therefore wrong. Instead, they merely blamed white capitalists for welcoming Chinese cheap labor into the country.[41] Some went so far as to defend cheap labor because it made development of new territories possible (the same argument presented by the U.S. capitalists who opposed Exclusion). They also reasoned that some non-Chinese were paid wages equally low or even lower, and therefore Chinese workers should not be singled out as "cheap labor."[42] In light of the fact that some Chinese businesses were also dependent on inexpensive Chinese workers, this line of argument was quite understandable. However, the position advanced by Chinese capitalists regarding Chinese cheap labor was very different from that of Chinese workers who struck for equal pay.[43] Because the Six Companies professed to speak for all Chinese, including Chinese workers, in their common struggle against racism and unequal treatment, the probusiness slant of the Six Companies has often been overlooked.

Wage Workers

Various factors such as trade-union narrowness, racism, and cultural differences made it difficult for Chinese workers to join white trade unions. They did, however, establish their own organizations (see table 11.4), which had many unionlike functions. In form, they resembled traditional Chinese guilds, but their goals and contents were different. Their principal functions generally included bargaining over wages,

TABLE 11.4
CHINESE WORKERS' ORGANIZATIONS

Industry	Name of Organization[1]
Men's clothing, tailors[2]	Tung Yip Tong ("Hall of Common Occupation")
Women's clothing, shirts, underwear[2]	Gwing Yi Hong ("Guild of Bright Clothing")
Work clothes, overalls[2]	Gum Yi Hong ("Guild of Brocaded Clothing")
Shoemakers	Lei-Shing Tong ("Hall for Treading the New")
Cigar makers	Tung Dak Tong ("Hall of Common Virtue")

SOURCE: Chinn 1969:49-54.
1. These are only the principal trade guilds. There were probably other, smaller ones.
2. Among the garment sewing trades, the fine distinctions between trades may have been caused by the fact that workers in each of these three areas generally came from different districts in China.

investigating grievances, arbitrating disputes, and organizing strikes. Strikes were conducted against both Chinese and non-Chinese employers. Disputes between workers and employers were sometimes handled by more extreme measures, as in the case during the 1890s when a guild offered to pay for the assassination of an overalls factory owner.

Chinese workers formed their own guilds for a variety of reasons. It was common in China for members of the same profession to belong to an occupational association. In the United States, the reluctance of white unions to accept Chinese made it difficult for Chinese workers to join those organizations that already existed. Moreover, Chinese were often segregated on work sites in separate living and working quarters,[44] which impeded assimilation into the general work force. Wage differentials also fostered white worker antagonism toward the Chinese because their cheap labor threatened to undercut the higher priced labor of the white workers. Thus, the traditional guilds of China were transformed by Chinese workers in the United States to meet some of their new needs. Initially these associations retained a narrow orientation, as illustrated by the fine subdivisions within the sewing trades;[45] as the workers' guilds developed, however, they began to perform entirely new functions such as calling for strikes and bargaining for wages. This suggests that regardless of their origins, the main purpose of workers' guilds became the resolution of problems in a capitalistic society. The fact that employers also formed guilds is another indication of how new wine could be put in the old bottle of a traditional social organization.

Petite Bourgeoisie

Chinatown's craftsmen and professionals were, for the most part, too few in number to organize. There were, however, enough laundries to form a Chinese Wash-house Society, which functioned as a guild of laundrymen.[46] This group established rules on territorial rights, including the stipulation that no laundry was to open within ten doors of another guild member. It also fixed prices, and members joined together to undercut an outside competitor, but they were forbidden to undercut each other. Before the advent of steam laundries in California, the guild charged an entrance fee of $30, but it also paid dividends. After 1882, white competition and a decline in the total number of Chinese seriously affected the prosperity of the guild.[47] Not reluctant to use force, the Wash-house Society put out contracts on those who violated its rules, especially regarding territorial rights. It also attempted to assassinate a white printer who tried to collect a rather large debt from the society.[48]

Lumpen

The organizations most closely identified with the lumpen class were the so-called tongs. The term is misleading because it was also in the name of many trade guilds. In popular usage, however, tongs refer exclusively to fighting societies and those involved in racketeering activities. Most of these secret or semisecret societies were spinoffs of the Triad Society, which was formed in China centuries earlier to overthrow the Qing dynasty. Transplanted to the urban United States, however, their original political goal soon became a secondary and oft-forgotten feature of the tongs,[49] although they did in fact assist Sun Yat-sen in some of his revolutionary undertakings. Nevertheless, their goals changed, and many tongs became organizers of the gambling and prostitution rackets, while others extorted money from brothels and small merchants in Chinatown.

Membership in the tongs, particularly in their heyday from 1882 to 1906, was deceptively large. Many men joined, but only a minority were really active. People who were not highbinders or racketeers joined a tong for several reasons. First, it gave them some insurance against attack by highbinders. Second, they may have sympathized with the political goals of the association. And finally, they may have been invited to join by friends or relatives who were already members. It must be remembered that most Chinese were automatically members of their district associations and family associations, and workers probably belonged to a trade guild. Hence, joining another organization would not have been an unusual step, and membership in a tong did not preclude membership in other non-tong groups. Dues were minimal, and there was no social stigma attached to membership. Professional highbinders, of course, joined tongs because tong activities were the source of their livelihood. Their personal economic interests were closely intertwined with the tongs, and hence they were the most active members.

BETWEEN CHINA AND THE UNITED STATES

Like most immigrants to the United States, Chinese in San Francisco retained a number of ties to their homeland. Most Chinese immigrants had immediate families remaining in China, and some owned property there. Many were interested in Chinese political developments, and most Chinese-language newspapers in San Francisco devoted considerable space to major news items from China. At times, differences over politics in China also found expression in San Francisco's Chinatown.

Many leading import-export merchants came from the urban, commercialized area around Guangzhou, while the majority of Chinese immigrant laborers tended to come from poorer families in rural areas.[50] Thus, there existed not only an economic gap but also cultural and linguistic differences between many of Chinatown's wealthiest merchants and the far more numerous wage workers. The merchants' social values were closer to those of China's scholar-gentry class than to those of the peasantry, and their preference for traditional signs of authority and prestige was reflected in some of their actions. The Six Companies, for example, regularly brought men from China with traditional civil service degrees to act as titular leaders, even though they knew little about the affairs of Chinese in America.

Chinese wage workers, in contrast, were more sympathetic to reform and revolution in China. They were quite aware of the weakness of the Qing dynasty in foreign affairs because they were victimized by it. Moreover, their prospects for upward social mobility in China were thwarted by the traditional social system, which could exclude them from the elite even if they returned home rich. Finally, they were exposed to concepts of democracy and popular government during their stay in the United States. In contrast, most wealthy merchants took a different political stand. Even though they were aware of the Qing government's weaknesses abroad and hoped for a stronger homeland, they owned too much in China to support a total overthrow of the dynastic system. Hence, while they favored the "Self-strengthening Movement" and the Reform Movement of 1898, many merchants opposed republicanism. After the failure of the 1898 reforms, these political differences became apparent in San Francisco's Chinatown. Many affluent merchants backed the more conservative Baohuanghui (Society for the Preservation of the Emperor), while less wealthy Chinese generally supported Sun Yat-sen's revolutionary Tongmenghui (United League).[51]

The impact of continued ties to China can also be seen in the many traditional forms of social grouping in Chinatown. Besides class organizations, there were district and family associations. On the whole, the family associations in San Francisco were exclusively benevolent organizations for mutual aid. District associations were far more complex. The Six Companies, for instance were district associations, but their functions were far broader than those of most "hometown clubs," associations based on place of origin. At the same time, geographical divisions sometimes paralleled economic ones. As previously mentioned, the leading merchants were mostly from the vicinity of Guangzhou and were therefore part of the Sam Yup Association. Many workers were members of the See Yup Association, which represented a more rural area with its own subdialect. In the 1890s, a feud between the Sam Yup and See Yup Associations led to a boycott of stores owned by Sam Yup merchants. Since there were more See Yup people in Chinatown, the boycott succeeded in hurting the business of the major Sam Yup firms. At first glance, this might seem to have been no more than a quarrel based on place of origin. It is worth noting, however, that owners of smaller Chinatown stores, who were primarily See Yup men, managed to expand their businesses at the expense of the Sam Yup import-export companies. Thus, the boycott also represented a successful effort by minor merchants to break the relative monopoly of the Sam Yup mercantile capitalists in Chinatown.

As compared to all this activity related to differences in China, there was little interest in political developments in the United States. Many Chinese saw themselves as only temporary immigrants whose ultimate goal was to return to their homeland. Hence, they did not concern themselves with U.S. politics unless the issues affected them directly. At the same time, the various restrictions placed on Chinese naturalization made it difficult for many Chinese to become U.S. citizens, so that even those who might have had an interest in U.S. political developments were not legally qualified to participate in the political process. Furthermore, as anti-Chinese sentiment grew, Chinese in San Francisco tended to stay within the confines of Chinatown for protection, and this isolation increased their ignorance of broader developments in the United States.

Economically, most Chinese were also limited to jobs where they had little contact with whites. Even when both Chinese and white workers were employed at the same place, they were usually deliberately segregated. Domestic servants, of course, worked for white employers, but their work allowed them no chance to associate with whites as peers. The majority of Chinese wage workers were employed by other Chinese, thus reinforcing the psychological and cultural isolation that other factors had already created.

RACISM AND ASSIMILATION

The earliest classes to appear in San Francisco Chinatown were mercantile capitalists, some petite bourgeoisie, and a few shop workers. Industrial capitalists and workers did not exist in significant numbers until after the completion of the transcontinental railroad. Before their advent, the class that grew most rapidly was the petite bourgeoisie, which expanded as laundries and fishing flourished. The money needed to establish some of these small businesses probably came from miners, who also were independent small producers and petite bourgeoisie who returned to the city. Although small numbers of lumpen existed even by the 1850s, they did not become significant as a class until immediately after Exclusion, when economic pressures on the Chinese were intense. The one factor that seemed most decisive in affecting the rise and fall of these classes was the condition of the U.S. economy. The condition of the mining and railroad industries had a direct bearing on the number of Chinese seeking work in San Francisco. The condition of the various manufacturing industries also influenced both Chinese ownership and Chinese employment in them. Generally, Chinese capital was able to establish itself in industries that were marginally profitable. Because of their low levels of profit, such industries required cheap labor, which was supplied by Chinese workers. Thus, while Chinese capitalists were probably not averse to playing on workers' nationalism and identification with other Chinese in order to hire them for low wages, they were also forced to do so by the nature of the industries in which they had invested.

Chinese capitalists were caught in a bind that was partially a result of anti-Chinese sentiments. If they were to assimilate into the U.S. economic mainstream by investing in a wide variety of businesses, they would have to compete with white capital, which was much greater than Chinese capital. Chinese companies that tried to enter major fields of business dominated by white capital and compete on equal terms usually failed;[52] for to increase their assets to the magnitude of white capital, they had to win acceptance from white consumers for their products, and anti-Chinese feelings generally discouraged potential customers from buying Chinese-made goods. This sentiment was most evident in the cigar trade, where a boycott against Chinese cigars caused many Chinese companies to adopt Hispanic names. Thus, if Chinese capitalists were to stay in business while their products were being rejected by the general public, then the only alternative was to cultivate the Chinese market.

As mentioned earlier, most successful Chinese businessmen sold their goods primarily to other Chinese. This captive market was not subject to white boycotts, as were the goods manufactured by the industrial capitalists. This phenomenon strengthened the economic position of those whose ties to China and to Chinese culture were strongest, which in turn may well have encouraged the growth of a narrow nationalism among the most successful merchants. The wealthier merchants were quite aware of this. One experienced merchant in a contemporary novella noted that "when you bring Chinese goods to sell in America, nothing is suited for use there, so you are still selling to sojourning Chinese." Another commented, "In recent years, most of the work done by Chinese workers has been done in Chinese factories, and most of the goods shipped to America by Chinese merchants have been sold to Chinese. It's still Chinese doing business among themselves, not Chinese doing business with Americans."[53] Nevertheless, there were limits to their success. The size of the Chinese population in the United States was restricted by factors such as Exclusion, and their businesses could not cater to many non-Chinese. Moreover, most merchants re- mitted at least a portion of their profits back to China, instead of reinvest- ing the entire amount in the United States. As a result, the Chinese mercantile capitalist class as a whole was slow to grow.

The narrow nationalism of mercantile capitalists was fairly selective. They benefited from the integration of Chinese workers into main- stream areas such as agriculture, since they could act as both labor contractors and food suppliers. That is, they could profit from Chinese economic assimilation as long as it occurred through channels they could control. Conversely, cultural assimilation would have reduced the demand for their imported goods. It is worth noting that while the merchant-controlled Six Companies established and supported schools to teach Chinese to children born in the United States, they made few efforts to teach English to adult immigrants from China.

If Chinese capitalists were at a disadvantage in competing with white capital, then Chinese workers were even worse off in their relationship with white workers, at least those involved in unions. The principal accusation leveled against them was that they were "cheap labor" which depressed the wages of all workers. The Chinese workers could not effectively refute this charge. If they demanded equal pay from white employers, they would probably negate the reason for their being hired in the first place, and would be fired or perhaps even deported. More- over, many worked in industries that were so marginally profitable that higher wages would have caused the firm to close down. Thus, bur- dened with debts incurred in coming to the United States and faced with the task of supporting families in China, most Chinese workers had no choice but to accept the wages they were offered.

It was basically the capitalistic system that pitted Chinese capital against white capital and Chinese workers against white workers, in the incessant competition for profits and jobs. It was racism, however, that drove Chinese capitalists and workers together for self-protection. Although the Six Companies rebutted anti-Chinese charges only when doing so did not undercut their own capitalist position as merchants and businessmen, and although it is also possible that they put up less re- sistance than they might have against Exclusion because it affected low-paid laborers far more than merchants, when the Geary Act required all Chinese to register with the government, the Six Companies went so far as to defy the law by advocating noncompliance. This action was stronger than any they took against the Exclusion Act. Similarly, when harassment began to affect merchants as well as laborers, many agitated merchants sent messages urging the Chinese government to intervene on their behalf.[54] Such activity was unprecedented, probably because no previous measures had so threatened the merchant capitalists as a class.

The social class that experienced the greatest expansion over time was the petite bourgeoisie and independent, nonindustrial wage workers, especially domestic servants. In many respects, this was due to the fact that all other classes had constraints on their growth. The Chinese industrial proletariat was hampered because the big Chinese capitalists were in trade rather than manufactures, while U.S. capitalists were under pressure to refrain from hiring Chinese. The areas of industry with substantial Chinese investment were too marginally profitable to grow greatly and could only absorb a limited number of Chinese workers. Mercantile capitalists were financially very successful, but as a class, their numbers were limited because their business depended on patronage from Chinatown, which was itself limited in size by Exclusion and other factors such as the inability of workers to find jobs outside Chinatown. Furthermore, some of the wealth of the mercantile capitalists was remitted to China rather than reinvested. The Chinese industrial capitalists did not grow because few industries existed that could be started with their limited capital, whereas those with more capital generally put it in trade. Like the mercantile capitalists, the lumpen depended on Chinatown for a living, albeit in a somewhat different way. Hence, there were limits as to how many of them could be sustained by a community that had ceased to grow. Furthermore, competition between tongs, legal constraints, and conflicts with some of the big merchants all held down the growth of the lumpen element.

Thus, almost by the process of elimination, the only classes that could expand were the petite bourgeoisie and nonproduction wage workers. After Exclusion, there were signs that Chinese workers began to demand equal pay with white workers.[55] This development was attributed to the drop in the number of Chinese workers, suggesting that one reason Chinese labor was cheap was because Chinese were competing among themselves as well as with non-Chinese. Just as white workers who demanded higher pay could be threatened with replacement by Chinese, so too could Chinese be threatened with replacement by other Chinese, as long as immigration was unchecked. In any case, white-owned firms were generally unwilling to hire higher priced Chinese, and one alternative for those workers who rejected discriminatory wages was to enter small business themselves. This would contribute to the growth of the petite bourgeoisie but slow the growth of the Chinese working class.

The characteristics of the different social classes also affected their ability to assimilate, culturally and economically, into American society. For instance, because the business of mercantile capitalists was based on an adherence to Chinese cultural patterns, both on their part and on the part of their customers, they had little reason to encourage assimilation. The industrial capitalists and proletariat, which would have been the most likely to assimilate, were prevented by the anti-Chinese movement and trade-union chauvinism from doing so. Lumpen activities were frowned on by U.S. law, and so they would not have been eager to enter the mainstream of American society. In any case, their closed, secretive organizations were resistant to assimilation. Again, the most likely classes to assimilate were the petite bourgeoisie, especially those in the laundry trade, and domestic servants. Their businesses were dispersed around the city and depended on white patronage. Hence they had the greatest incentive to look beyond Chinatown and to learn English.

As immigration from China declined after Exclusion and a new generation of American-born Chinese began to play an active role in Chinatown, old class lines were somewhat altered. The earthquake also contributed to this change, destroying many establishments and particularly affecting the power of the tongs. After 1906, therefore, development of San Francisco's Chinese community was somewhat different than described here. Until 1906, however, certain features of Chinatown made it highly distinctive even in a society as varied as that of California. Immigration patterns created a predominantly male population or "bachelor society," which was atypical of both China and California after the 1850s. During the latter half of the nineteenth century, the United States was a rapidly developing capitalist country, while China was still a largely agrarian, semifeudal society. The percentage of wage workers among Chinese in San Francisco during this period was much higher than that in China, reflecting the fact that many Chinese were employed in manufacturing. By the same token, the position of these Chinese workers was rather precarious, since they worked in marginally profitable enterprises and were also the targets of anti-Chinese hostility. It was difficult for them to assimilate, either culturally or economically, into American society.

Chinatown was also different because few of its capitalists were heavily involved in major industries, unlike their American counterparts. Instead, they put their money into the safer import-export business. And even though they had somewhat more opportunity to prosper than did merchants in China, who were politically dominated by the scholar-gentry class, they were still excluded from the most lucrative industries that were developing in late nineteenth-century United States. Nevertheless Chinese capitalists flourished because they had found a niche that was outside both the Chinese and U.S. economic mainstreams but which was essential for the daily existence of the 50,000 to 100,000 Chinese living in the United States.

The political activities of the Chinese in San Francisco extended to affairs in both countries if their own interests were affected. Generally, because a majority planned to return to China, all major changes and developments there were a matter of concern. Since few were U.S. citizens, however, there was little interest in American politics except when issues like Exclusion directly threatened them. Among some groups, particularly the lumpen, there was even outright aversion to any unnecessary contact with U.S. authorities. In fact, law enforcement agencies frequently were bribed to stay out of Chinese affairs, partly owing to distrust of justice in a society that was at times overtly anti-Chinese, and partly owing to a desire to keep illegitimate activities operating. Thus, the political and cultural isolation of Chinatown was a result both of external circumstances and also of pressures from certain groups within the community itself.

Because social conditions in China and the United States were so different, many Chinese who had lived for many years in the United States had difficulty readjusting to China when they returned to their homeland. Some even chose to return with their families to settle permanently in the United States, though most were prevented from doing so by restrictive immigration rules. Those who did settle in the United States, whether by choice or circumstance, usually lived in or around Chinatown. This is another indicator of how Chinatown had become something different from both China and the United States, while still home to a large number of immigrants.

As mentioned earlier, throughout most of the nineteenth century, the proletariat was the single largest class among the Chinese in San Francisco. It is important to note that the majority of Chinese wage workers were employed by white capitalists, both large (railroad companies) and small (woolen mills, cigar factories, etc.). This economic relationship was ultimately the catalyst for the anti-Chinese Exclusion Act of 1882. Chinese workers were increasingly portrayed as cheap labor that undercut the wages of white workers, although most Chinese workers undoubtedly would have welcomed higher wages. Their ability to fight for a better living was severly hampered by two factors.

First, and most important, most Chinese immigrants were men who had borrowed money to travel to the United States. They had to send money back to China regularly to repay their debts and to support their families — in short, their very existence in the United States was predicated on a sort of "installment plan." Hence, any interruption of earnings threatened them and their kin with foreclosure or, in extreme circumstances, with starvation. Under such circumstances, a strike (which is the most effective weapon available to labor organizations in fighting for wage increases) was unacceptable to many Chinese workers, even if they recognized and sympathized with its aims. Their short-term financial pressures were too great for them to take the risk that a strike for long-term improvements would require. Workers who cannot or will not strike are of little use to a labor movement, and given the already formidable racial, linguistic, and cultural barriers between Chinese and white workers, it is not surprising that relatively few efforts were made to organize them. The second factor was that in most cases, Chinese were barred from becoming naturalized U.S. citizens. This discouraged them from seeing any long-term future for themselves in American society and made membership in labor organizations seem rather pointless. Thus, racism on the part of white workers and the personal financial constraints coupled with being barred from becoming naturalized U.S. citizens contributed to keeping Chinese out of the labor movement.

It must be pointed out that anti-Chinese legislation was being passed well before there were strong labor unions in California. In fact, initial agitation for laws discriminating against Chinese miners came primarily from independent white miners, that is, from the white petite bourgeoisie trying to prevent competition from the Chinese petite bourgeoisie. Likewise, white owners of small manufacturing companies failed to protest strongly against the presence of Chinese (who, after all, were working for them at very low wages) until Chinese entrepreneurs began to establish similar businesses that undercut them. At this point they joined the white workers in the drive for Exclusion.

There is a rough parallel here with the experience of the Chinese in Hawaii, where "agitation among the *Haoles* became more strident when the Chinese began moving from the plantations and rural occupations into the town and urban occupations, and began competing with them for jobs. . . . 'Cheap labor' became 'unfair competition' when the Chinese moved into the kinds of work *Haoles* had been doing."[56] In this case the urban white petite bourgeoisie recognized the usefulness of Chinese as plantation workers in the labor-short rural economy, but resented efforts by the Chinese to leave the working class and enter petite bourgeois occupations themselves. Thus, both in Hawaii and in California, the white petite bourgeoisie actually was in the forefront (chronologically) of legislative activity against the Chinese, although because of their smaller numbers they have received less attention than the white workers.

The development of classes among the Chinese in San Francisco was constricted in many ways by racial competition. The Chinese bourgeoisie lacked the capital to compete with the large, white-owned corporations and was tolerated precisely because it posed no threat to the white bourgeoisie. The Chinese petite bourgeoisie aroused opposition from the white petite bourgeoisie when it attempted to expand into white-dominated occupations. The Chinese working class, under pressure not to interrupt the flow of remittances to China, was perceived by white workers as "cheap labor" and "scabs" who refused to strike for higher wages. The only possible form of development left was the one that actually took place: the greatest growth came in the ranks of Chinese who were *not* in occupations with significant numbers of whites, namely in laundry and restaurant work. This explains the big shift that took place by the turn of the century: the predominantly working class Chinese population of the 1870s and 1880s had turned into a predominantly petite bourgeois population. The Chinese bourgeoisie remained stable within its limits but incapable of significant growth while the Chinese working class that remained was comprised primarily of those hired by Chinese employers. Although white capitalists probably would have been glad to continue hiring Chinese workers for lower wages, opposition from white labor made this impossible, and given the limited Chinese capital in San Francisco, there was no way for the Chinese working class to maintain its former size, let alone grow.

This essay is not an attempt to give exhaustive socioeconomic data about the Chinese in San Francisco. Rather, it is an effort to interpret some long-established facts about them and to explore how each class's special characteristics influenced its relations with other classes and in turn how this affected Chinese adaptation to life in the United States, as well as attitudes toward politics in China. For too long the Chinese in the United States have been treated by both Chinese and non-Chinese writers as a monolithic bloc, with much attention paid to relations between the bloc and "outside society" but little attention paid to differences, conflicts, and nuances within the bloc itself. While the question of how Chinese reacted to American society (and vice versa) is undoubtedly an important one, even this cannot be properly understood without taking into account changes within the community itself, for some of these changes in turn affected the way the community related to the American society at large.

It surely would be too simplistic to speak of "the white response to Chinese immigration," for the white capitalists behaved very differently from the white workers, and even the white workers differed among themselves. Such differences among whites produced forces that both advocated and opposed Chinese Exclusion. Yet, very few works go beyond a discussion of "the Chinese response to white racism," which is an equally simplistic approach. Further studies will yield more raw data on the Chinese in the United States, and new findings may require reinterpretations and new conclusions. However, it is the author's belief that new information will only confirm that the Chinese community was a complex society with its own conflicts and dynamics.

NOTES

1. Chinn 1969:43; Bancroft (1888a:168n) also refers to Chinese engaged in dismantling beached vessels that obstructed the harbor.

2. Taylor (1949:85) notes that a vessel from Canton returned with 250 dozen pieces of linen which had been sent out a few months before for washing.

3. Chinn 1969:9,43.

4. O'Meara 1884.

5. Taylor 1949:89.

6. Chinn 1969, from *The Oriental,* Feb. 1856, Chinese Directory.

7. Chinn 1969, from the *Daily Alta California,* 1850.

8. Bancroft 1888b:348.

9. For more detailed information on Chinese in fishing, see Chinn 1969:40ff. Also, Bancroft mentions Chinese gathering abalones for the local and China markets (1888b).

10. From the 1859 and 1860 editions of *The San Francisco Directory,* Henry G. Langley, comp. Only the names of the stores are given, and not the nature of their business. However, by comparing them with names in later directories which do indicate the type of merchandise sold, it is possible to deduce the principal types of wares.

11. Details on a mid-1850s gambling house are given in Capron 1854:150-151.

12. Specific information on the cigar, slipper and woolens industries can be found in Chiu 1963, U.S. Congress 1911 and Chinn 1969.

13. Pacific Union Express Company, "Address of Principal Chinese Merchants of San Francisco," 1868-69.

14. Loomis 1869.

15. Chiu 1963:95-96.

16. Chiu 1963:106.

17. Chinn 1969:38-40; Bancroft 1888*b*:349-350.

18. Bancroft 1888*b*:348; also Coolidge 1909:151.

19. Gibson 1877:59; also in U.S. Congress 1877:151.

20. U.S. Congress 1877:152.

21. Chiu 1963:91-92.

22. Chiu 1963:117-118. Chiu finds the slipper industry to be a basically unprofitable one, and he sees 1870-74 and 1875-76 to be atypical boom years.

23. California Bureau of Labor Statistics 1904:75-76.

24. Lloyd 1876:253. Bancroft 1888*b*:342 indicates that merchants often formed partnerships of up to a dozen men. Bancroft also observes that the major commodities handled by these large firms were rice, tea, opium, silk, clothing, and fancy goods. One sign of the scale of their operations is the fact that in 1877, the customs duties alone on their imports amounted to $1,756,000. Some wholesale firms also operated retail outlets. U.S. Congress 1877 also contains testimony from many witnesses on the wealth of Chinese merchants.

25. "The Bitter Society" n.d.:42, 50, 64.

26. Based on a comparison of Wells Fargo Co. Chinese business directories, 1876, 1878, 1882.

27. Chiu 1963:123.

28. Chiu 1963:94-95.

29. Chiu 1963: chaps 6, 7.

30. See n. 4; also Mei 1979:475-476.

31. See, e.g., Saxton 1971:7-9; Liu 1976:275; Chiu 1963:46.

32. Liu 1976:209.

33. According to the 1902-1904 report of the California Bureau of Statistics, these incomes had not changed greatly even by 1903.

34. For more details on tong activities, see Dobie 1936: chap. 7; and Liu 1976: chap. 6.

35. Dobie (1936) notes that the Hip Ye Tong was founded in 1852, and that some of the fighting tongs may have been established as a result of the interdistrict feuds between Chinese in the mining areas. See also Liu 1976:205.

36. Dobie 1936:174; Liu 1976: chaps. 5-6; Hirata, this volume.

37. Liang 1941:113-114. More details are given in the records of the Chinese Chamber of Commerce of San Francisco, portions of which are cited in Liu 1976:213-214.

38. Further details on trade guilds can be found in Morse 1932.

39. The "Six Companies" was a federation of the major district associations in Chinatown. It provided a form of self-government within the community and also represented Chinatown in dealings with outside institutions.

40. The Sam Yup Association was an organization of people from three counties in and around Guangzhou; the See Yup and Ning Yeung Associations represented people from the four counties of Taishan, Kaiping, Enping, and Xinhui.

41. Chinese Six Companies 1877.

42. "The Bitter Society," p. 65.

43. Chinn 1969:46; also in Chiu 1963:47; and Saxton 1971:9-10, 215-218.

44. The Immigration Commission report (U.S. Congress 1911:429) describes conditions of the Chinese working in powder factories.

45. Chinese guilds have been divided along very clearly defined trade lines at least since the Tang dynasty (618-907 A.D.).

46. U.S. Congress 1877:123

47. Coolidge 1909:406-407.

48. U.S. Congress 1877:147-148.

49. Liang 1941:118; Dobie 1936:145-147.

50. Mei 1979:464, 475-476; Liu 1976:213.

51. Lai 1976.

52. Liu 1976:344-352.

53. "Ku shehui" ("The Bitter Society"), anonymous, in Qian Xingcun 1966:82, 111.

54. McKee 1977:104-105.

55. California Bureau of Labor Statistics 1895-96:101.

56. Glick 1981:9. Glick (1980:16) also makes the following remarks: "It was the nonagricultural Chinese workers, men seeking positions above those of domestic service and manual labor in the towns, who were likely to compete directly with Caucasian artisans and tradesmen and to be regarded as a threat to the latter's occupational security. What irritated their Caucasian competitors was that the Chinese who worked cheaply on the plantations were still willing to work cheaply in other occupations. It was fair enough for Chinese to do this on menial jobs; it was 'unfair competition' when Chinese accepted lower pay for work Caucasians and others wanted for themselves." This description of why both Chinese wage workers and self-employed workers had trouble getting more desirable petite bourgeois jobs was basically also true on the mainland.

References

Bancroft, Hubert H.
   1888a History of California, 6:1848-1859. Vol. 23 of Works. San Francisco:
      A. L. Bancroft.
   1888b "Mongolianism in America." Chap. 13, Vol. 28 of Works. San Francisco: A. L.
      Bancroft.
"The Bitter Society"
   n.d. Anonymous work, trans. June Mei, Jean Pang Yip, with Russell Leong. Amer-
      asia 8, 1 (1981):42, 50, 64.
California Bureau of Labor Statistics
   1895- Seventh Biennial Report of the California Bureau of Labor. Sacramento.
   1896
   1904 Eleventh Biennial Report of the California Bureau of Labor. Sacramento.
Capron, E. S.
   1854 History of California. Boston: J. P. Jewett.
Chinese Six Companies
   1877 Memorial. San Francisco: Chinese Six Companies.
Chinn, Thomas W.
   1969 A History of the Chinese Labor in California: A Syllabus. San Francisco: Chi-
      nese Historical Society of America.
Chiu, Ping
   1963 Chinese Labor in California. Madison, Wisc.: State Historical society of Wis-
      consin for the University of Wisconsin.
Coolidge, Mary R.
   1909 Chinese Immigration. New York: Henry Holt & Co.
Dobie, Charles
   1936 San Francisco's Chinatown. New York: D. Appleton-Century.
Gibson, Otis
   1877 The Chinese in America. Cincinnati: Hitchcock and Walden.
Glick, Clarence E.
   1980 Sojourners and Settlers. Honolulu: University Press of Hawaii.
   1981 "The Chinese in Hawaii." Gum Saan Journal 5, 1(December). Los
      Angeles: Chinese Historical Society of Southern California.
Lai, H. Mark
   1976 "China politics and U.S. Chinese communities." Pp. 152-159 in Emma Gee, ed.,
      Counterpoint. Los Angeles: Asian American Studies Center, University of
      California, Los Angeles.
Liang Qichao
   1941 "Xindalu yuji jielu." Yinbingshi heji (Cafe Collections). Shanghai: Zhongna
      Book Company.
Liu Boji
   1976 Meiguo huaqiaoshi (A history of Chinese in America). Taibei: Liming Cultural
      Work Company.

Lloyd, Benjamin E.
    1876 Lights and Shades in San Francisco. San Francisco: A. L. Bancroft.
Loomis, A.
    1869 "How our Chinamen are employed." Overland Monthly 2:231-240.
McKee, Delber
    1977 Chinese Exclusion vs. the Open Door Policy. Detroit: Wayne State University Press.
Mei, June
    1979 "Socio-economic origins of emigration from Guangdong to California, 1850-1882." Modern China 5, 4 (October).
Morse, Hosea B.
    1932 The Gilds of China. Shanghai: Kelley and Walsh.
O'Meara, James
    1884 "The Chinese in early days." Overland Monthly, n.s. 3 (May): 477-481.
Qian Xingcun [A Ying], ed.
    1966 Fan Mei huagong jinyue wenxueji (Collected writings of opposition to the U.S. Chinese Exclusion Act). Beijing: Zhonghua Book Company.
Saxton, Alexander
    1971 The Indispensable Enemy. Berkeley, Los Angeles, London: University of California Press.
Taylor, Bayard
    1949 Eldorado. New York: A. A. Knopf.
U.S. Congress
    1877 Report of the Joint Special Committee to Investigate Chinese Immigration. 44th Congress, 2d session. Senate Report 689. Washington, D. C.: Government Printing Office.
U.S. Congress
    1911 Reports of the Immigration Commission, 61st Congress, 2d session, pt. 25. Washington, D. C.

12
Free, Indentured, Enslaved: Chinese Prostitutes in Nineteenth-Century America

Lucie Cheng

In societies undergoing rapid industrialization, prostitution serves a double economic function. It helps to maintain the labor force of single young men, which is in the interest of the capitalists who would otherwise have to pay higher wages to laborers with families to support. In addition, prostitution enables entrepreneurs to extract large profits from the work of women under their control and thus accumulate considerable capital for other investments. Further, in multiracial areas, prostitutes of minority or colonized groups can also provide cheap labor themselves. Chinese prostitutes in the nineteenth-century American West performed all three functions as free agents and as enslaved and indentured workers.

After the formal abolition of black slavery, the capitalist mode of production predominated in nineteenth-century America. However, aspects of slavery persisted in varying degrees among racial minorities, for example, in contract labor and in Chinese prostitution in California. White prostitution on the American frontier quickly moved from a precapitalist form of organization to one characterized by either a partnership between madam and prostitutes or a relationship of employer and wage worker. Chinese prostitution, in contrast, remained a semifeudal organization until the twentieth century. While sexual prejudice obscured the exploitative nature of prostitution as a business, a sense of racial superiority at first led whites to condone Chinese female slavery.[1] In addition, the linkages between the emigrant societies in China and the

Chinese community in California helped to perpetuate the precapitalist relations in prostitution. Chinese prostitution also provided Chinese entrepreneurs one of the few opportunities to accumulate capital in a hostile society.

This chapter will examine the social history of Chinese prostitution within the context of conditions in nineteenth-century China and the economic development of California. It will focus on Chinese prostitution as an economic institution and on the Chinese prostitute as a particular class of labor, earning direct or indirect profits for a complex web of individuals. Furthermore, it will seek to explicate the double oppression by race and sex and the lethal exploitation of Chinese prostitutes both as part of the working class in America and as sacrificial victims for the maintenance of patriarchy in semifeudal China.

CONDITIONS LEADING TO THE IMPORTATION OF WOMEN FOR PROSTITUTION

Victimized by population pressure, landlord oppression, and foreign imperialism, many peasant families in nineteenth-century China lived on the edge of subsistence.[2] In a number of communities, particularly in Fujian and Guangdong, where emigration to distant lands was feasible, a large proportion of the male population left home in search of employment.[3]

In times of natural disaster and war, families often resorted to infanticide, abandonment, mortgaging, or selling of children.[4] Females, whose labor was less valuable than that of males, were frequently the first victims of extreme poverty. Furthermore, in patriarchal and patrilineal Chinese society, the family that raised a girl would not benefit from her labor and she could never carry on the ancestral line.

One remunerative solution for relieving the family of its female members was prostitution: the family did not have to provide for the girl's upkeep and her sale or part of her earnings could help support the family. The importance of this for the survival of the family is seen in the report of a Qing dynasty official that ten family members were dependent for their sustenance upon every prostitute in Canton.[5]

The discovery of gold in 1848 along the American River brought thousands of immigrants from many countries to California.[6] Mining was an exclusively male activity; few of the men brought families with them because, among other reasons, mining involved moving from place to place seeking the most productive site. Among the first female arrivals were prostitutes of varying racial and national origins.[7] In San

Francisco, where miners from nearby sites congregated during the winter and where immigrants gathered before they went into the mining areas, prostitution became a lucrative business. It was not uncommon for successful prostitutes to use their earnings to finance the miners or to invest in other pursuits.[8] The tremendous sexual imbalance (shown in table 12.1) and the lack of alternative employment made prostitution a major occupation for women. This relationship between a surplus of males, limited employment opportunities for women, and the demand for prostitution in developing areas is well documented by Boserup.[9]

The demand for prostitution in San Francisco was partially met by Chinese women from Hong Kong, Canton, and its surrounding areas. Canton, opened up as a treaty port under the guns of Western imperialism, and Hong Kong, ceded to the British after the Opium War, were the first cities where a large number of foreigners arrived, and from them the early Chinese prostitutes came.[10]

Only a few women crossed the Pacific on their own in search of better compensation for their labor in prostitution. Usually the family, not the girls, arranged the sale. Girls often accepted their sale, however reluctantly, out of filial loyalty, and most of them were not in a position to

TABLE 12.1
SEX RATIO OF CHINESE AND TOTAL POPULATION IN CALIFORNIA, 1850-1970

	Chinese*	Total*
1850	39,450†	1,228.6
1860	1,858.1	255.1
1870	1,172.3	165.4
1880	1,832.4	149.3
1890	2,245.4	137.6
1900	1,223.9	123.5
1910	1,017.0	125.4
1920	528.8	112.5
1930	298.6	107.6
1940	223.6	103.7
1950	161.9	100.1
1960	127.8	99.5
1970	107.0	96.9

SOURCE: Ratio for Chinese from 1860 to 1960 based on California Department of Industrial Relations, *Californians of Japanese, Chinese, and Filipino Ancestry* (San Francisco State Office, 1965); 1970 data based on U.S. Bureau of the Census, *Historical Census of the United States,* Bicentennial ed. (Washington, D.C.; Government Printing Office, 1975).
*Males per 100 females.
†There were only two Chinese women in 1850.

oppose their families' decision. In addition, the sheltered and secluded lives that women were forced to live made them particularly vulnerable to manipulation, and many were tricked or lured into prostitution.

An important but unexplored facet of the relationship between patriarchy and prostitution in the Chinese case is its role in perpetuating Chinese sojourning abroad and its support of the migrant labor system in America. The Chinese patriarchal family system discouraged or even forbade "decent" women from traveling abroad. In addition, the anti-Chinese sentiment and violence in California was often cited by immigrant Chinese merchants as a major reason for not bringing their families.[11] These two factors discouraged the emigration of Chinese women, who would have made possible a stable Chinese community in America. The failure of the Chinese to form families that would reproduce the work force locally prolonged the use of the Chinese by American employers as a migrant labor force.

Further, the patriarchal system required the preservation of the relationship between the men who went abroad to seek work and the families they left behind. It was common practice for the emigrant male to marry before his departure to insure that a wife be at home to fulfill his filial duties and with luck to give him a male descendant. These married women in the emigrant communities of China and Hong Kong, as noted by Chen Ta and Watson, were under more watchful eyes than their counterparts in nonemigrant communities.[12] The relatives were charged with the duty of keeping the women of the emigrants "pure," and in return the emigrants were obliged to send their earnings to support their families. This arrangement permitted the preservation of the Chinese family at home and the perpetuation of the Chinese emigrant laborer's sojourning role in America. The emigrants, whenever they could afford it, returned to China to sire a child. If the child was a boy, he eventually joined his father in America. This arrangement recirculated Chinese labor in the migrant labor system; and the home villages of China reproduced the labor force, in terms of procreation and child rearing, for work in America.

Chinese prostitution was an integral part of that arrangement. While patriarchy prohibited the emigration of "decent" women, it did not forbid the emigration of prostitutes. The emigration of Chinese prostitutes helped to stabilize and preserve the family because Chinese emigrant males could thereby avoid liaisons that might lead to permanent relationships with foreign women. Moreover, the earnings of Chinese prostitutes in America helped to support their families in China. One such prostitute sent back as much as $200 or $300 after seven months in San Francisco.[13]

The phenomenon of Chinese sojourning and the use of Chinese as migrant labor could not be attributed to poverty, patriarchy, and prostitution alone. Equally, if not more important, was the racist hostility of white society. In addition, like the European colonists who often made sure that the African laborer's wife and children did not follow the man to his new workplace,[14] American capitalists paid low wages to Chinese men to deter their women from crossing the Pacific. (The same phenomenon is observed in Western Europe today.)[15] Some whites in California advocated the importation of more Chinese laborers and not their women so they would not establish a permanent population here; others advocated the importation of more Chinese prostitutes who could meet the sexual demands of Chinese men and thus lessen the threat they perceived to white womanhood.[16] Similar arguments were later advanced by whites in Australia vis-à-vis Japanese prostitutes.[17]

Despite these mutual economic and social advantages, profit was undoubtedly the major reason for the creation and maintenance of the traffic in prostitution. Two distinct periods of Chinese prostitution in California corresponded with two types of relations in profit making: (a) the initial period of free competition, during which the prostitute was also the owner of her body service; and (b) a period of organized trade, during which the prostitute was a semislave and other individuals shared the benefits of her exploitation.

Period of Free Competition: The Self-employed Prostitutes and Small Entrepreneurs

The brief period of free competition (ca. 1849-1854) was characterized by individual initiative and enterprise. Like their white counterparts, a number of Chinese prostitutes during this period were able to accumulate sufficient capital to leave the profession. Some returned to China as relatively affluent members of the business community. Others remained in America and either continued in prostitution as brothel owners or invested in other businesses.

Among the first Chinese female residents in America allegedly was a twenty-year-old prostitute from Hong Kong who landed in San Francisco late in 1848.[18] A free agent serving a predominantly non-Chinese clientele during a period of affluence, she accumulated enough money to buy a brothel within two years and retired the widow of a wealthy Chinese man.[19]

Other free-agent prostitutes during this initial period emigrated under different circumstances. A popular social novel in the late Qing dynasty period told of a Cantonese prostitute brought to San Francisco by her American paramour when she was eighteen. After seven years, she returned to Hong Kong with approximately $16,300, married a Chinese laborer, and opened a store specializing in foreign goods.[20]

This period of free competition among owner-prostitutes did not last long. Few Chinese prostitutes could afford the transportation expenses or had the business know-how to take advantage of the situation. Still, the affluence of the male residents and the extreme imbalance of the sexes suggested that a considerable sum of money could be made in the business. That prospect attracted Chinese entrepreneurs, who organized various aspects of the business; specialization occurred, and a monopoly developed by 1854 under the control of the Chinese secret societies.

The Period of Organized Trade

In contrast to the first phase, the second period of Chinese prostitution in California (ca. 1854-1925) was characterized by a widespread organization of the trade with a network of specialized functions extending across the Pacific to Canton and Hong Kong. The persons chiefly responsible for this trade were the procurers who kidnapped, enticed, or bought Chinese women; the importers who brought them into America; the brothel owners who lived by their exploitation; the Chinese highbinders who collected fees for protecting them from other highbinders; the police who collected monies for keeping them from being arrested; and the white Chinatown property owners who leased their land and buildings for exorbitant rents.

The process by which brothels in San Francisco obtained their inmates was complex. The owner of a brothel recruited workers either by taking a trip to Canton or Hong Kong or by securing them through an agent or importer. A West Coast newspaper reported that agents of California brothels regularly went about China buying girls and young women. These agents received a regular circular or "price current" from San Francisco, which gave them information concerning the state of the market and the maximum prices that could be paid to derive an acceptable profit.[21]

Luring and kidnapping were the most frequent methods of procurement, particularly after 1870. When the agents did not find enough females to fill their orders, they sent subagents into rural districts to lure or kidnap girls and young women and forward the victims to them at the shipping ports.[22] Quite frequently those individuals who did the luring were returned emigrants from that community. The baits used included promises of gold, marriage, jobs, or education.[23] Sometimes the victims were invited to see the big American steamer anchored at the docks, and while they were enjoying the tour, the boat would sail off to San Francisco.[24] More often, kidnapping was carried out by force, and the victims were sometimes daughters of relatively well-to-do families.[25]

A number of women came to San Francisco under a contractual arrangement similar to that described in the Chinese contract coolie system.[26] The contract involved body service for a specified time, and if the prostitute succeeded in fulfilling the terms of service, she could, theoretically, get out of the business. Families, rather than women themselves, arranged these contracts. Most Chinese women, who could not read or write, could easily be duped into affixing their thumbprint to any document by the agent or party who was the beneficiary of the contract.

In the organization of the trade, importation was a separate activity from that of procurement. Importers received the women from the recruiting agents, arranged for their passage, and handed them over to the brothel owners upon arrival in the United States. Although other secret societies were known to have engaged in the traffic of women,[27] the Hip Yee Tong was clearly the predominant importer during the third quarter of the nineteenth century. It was estimated that between 1852 and 1873, the Hip Yee Tong alone imported 6,000 women,[28] or about 87 percent of the total number of Chinese women who arrived during that period. The Hip Yee Tong charged a $40 fee to each buyer, $10 of which were said to have gone to white policemen.[29] The Hip Yee netted an estimated $200,000 between 1852 and 1873 from the import business.[30]

The traffic in women became more difficult after the passage of the code that allowed the commissioner of immigration to prevent certain classes of people, including "lewd or debauched" women, from immigrating to California,[31] and after the enactment of the Page Act of 1875. The immediate effectiveness of these laws in reducing the number of female arrivals is unclear, but the statutes did subject women to close scrutiny both in Hong Kong and San Francisco and eventually made it more expensive to import women. These added expenses took the form of bribes that had to be paid to various U.S. consulate and customs officals.

The American consulate in Hong Kong was charged with the initial examination of Chinese women to determine if they were "lewd or debauched." If the consul's office was convinced of their good character, it would stamp the women's arms and send them to the harbor master, who would do the same. Only then would the women be allowed to purchase tickets and board the steamer.[32] The certificate with the woman's photograph issued by the consulate was mailed to the collector of customs at San Francisco. Women without appropriate documentation were refused landing and often had to wait more than twenty-four hours before they were cleared.[33] This procedure was subject to abuse by corrupt consular officials, who could be convinced of a woman's good character with money or could refuse to certify a woman's good character without money. It was discovered in 1879 that Consul Bailey's office received $10 to $15 for every woman shipped to the United States during his tenure in Hong Kong.[34]

Americans on this side of the Pacific also benefited materially from these new statutes. As noted by the U.S. Supreme Court, the 1873 code was subject to a variety of abuses: "It is hardly possible to conceive a statute more skillfully framed, to place in the hands of a single man the power to prevent, entirely, the vessels engaged in a foreign trade, say with China, from carrying passengers, or to compel them to submit to systematic extortion of the grossest kind." The commissioner, noted the Court, could arbitrarily designate immigrants as paupers, idiots, convicted criminals, or prostitutes and deny them entrance on that basis.[35]

These regulations benefited white lawyers as well as the customs inspector. Some lawyers colluded with the Chinese importers in obtaining habeas corpus decrees to allow the landing of Chinese women headed for the brothels.[36] Although a number of these women were legal immigrants, some probably sought the help of American lawyers because U.S. customs officers were dissatisfied with their documentation.

The Chinese Exclusion Act of 1882 allowed only women who were native born, married, or born overseas to domiciled merchants to immigrate to the United States. Accordingly, enterprising Chinese developed elaborate arrangements to continue the traffic in women. Chinese agents in the United States instructed agents in China to coach the emigrant women in responding to questions by the immigration authorities. These coaching papers, circulated in Hong Kong and Canton, included eighty-one questions on subjects ranging from standard personal details to the geography of San Francisco.[37]

Each successive law placing additional restrictions on Chinese immigration provided more opportunities for corruption. People soon found that U.S. immigration inspectors and interpreters could easily be persuaded to accept bribes to render favorable decisions and interpretations of the law.[38] As the rules became more severe, the investigation of the immigrants' status took longer to complete, and the immigrants were subjected to greater indignities, pain, and suffering. Beginning in 1891 and particularly after 1910, Chinese men and women were detained at Angel Island while waiting to be cleared. Most stayed at least three or four weeks, while others waited under very austere living conditions for months or even years while their cases were being fought in the courts.[39]

As importation became increasingly complex and expensive, the Hip Yee Tong gradually lost its monopolistic control over the traffic. Because of the increasing complexity and costs of importing prostitutes, the price for their delivery skyrocketed. After 1870, for example, girls who originally sold for $50 in Canton now brought $1,000 in San Francisco.[40] And in the 1890s it was reported that as much as $3,000 in gold was paid for a single Chinese female in San Francisco.[41]

Still, the importation of women continued primarily because it provided large profits. In the 1890s a shoe manufacturer and tong leader, Fong Ching, alias Little Pete, was well known for, among other things, his ingenuity in importing women for prostitution. Besides bribing customs officials and paying both white and Chinese men $30 each for bearing false character witnesses, he used fairs and expositions held in Chicago, Atlanta, and San Francisco to import women. For example, during the Midwinter Fair in Golden Gate Park he imported over a hundred women ostensibly to perform at the fair. They ended up in brothels after spending only a brief time at the fair. San Francisco newspapers reported that Little Pete netted $50,000 through his female imports.[42]

Other methods employed by the tongs to land Chinese women were smuggling in women attired as boys, hiding them in buckets of coal, and concealing them in padded crates billed as dishware.[43] The cost of smuggling a woman into the United States may have been as high as $2,500.[44] When customs officials at San Francisco began enforcing the law, women were brought in through Portland, Oregon, Canada, or Mexico.[45]

Eventually, however, faced with the dwindling supply of females in China,[46] the nearly prohibitive costs and difficulties of procurement and importation, and the loss of prostitutes from brothels in San Francisco to other cities and mining towns, the tongs were forced to look for their supply locally. Whereas local Chinese women were supplementary to overseas recruitment previously, after 1882 they became the major source of new supply.[47] It was reported that, in just one week in February 1898, eight women were kidnapped for prostitution.[48]

THE LIFE AND ECONOMICS OF PROSTITUTION

After the women had been transported to Chinatown, they were housed in temporary quarters known as "barracoons" to await their distribution. One barracoon reputedly held up to 100 women.[49] Those who had been imported for specific customers left when their owners paid the passage fare and the $40 fee. The others were carefully dressed and displayed before the bidding.[50] Well-to-do Chinese in San Francisco purchased the cream of this lot as concubines or mistresses. The remainder fell into two categories: the best went into higher-class brothels reserved only for the Chinese, while the rest were sold to inferior dens of prostitution which served a racially mixed clientele.[51]

The distinction between higher- and lower-grade brothels was one of both class and race. Chinese men generally felt that the most degrading thing a Chinese woman could do was to have sexual relations with a white man.[52] However, because of their comparatively low fees of twenty-five to fifty cents, the lower-class prostitutes were visited by whites and Chinese alike, while higher-class prostitutes had an exclusively Chinese clientele. Thus, the lower-grade prostitutes tended to attract the poorest laborers, teenage boys, sailors, and drunkards. They were often mistreated by their owners as well as their customers. A few brothel owners, for example, occasionally even beat some of them to death,[53] and white men often forced them to engage in aberrant sexual acts.[54] Prostitutes in mining camps served both Chinese and white clients and were often more harshly treated than their counterparts in San Francisco.[55]

The lower-grade prostitutes lived in rooms usually not larger than 4 x 6 feet, often facing a dimly lit alley.[56] "Bright cotton hangings hung in the doorways leading off from the main room or were sometimes used to break a larger room up into smaller compartments."[57] These rooms were sparsely furnished, usually with only a bamboo chair or two, a washbowl, and hard bunks of shelves covered with matting and set against the wall. The door, normally the only opening to the outside, was invariably covered with bars or a heavy screen behind which the woman would stand and call to passersby.[58]

The prostitutes who only served Chinese generally lived in upstairs apartments and had more or less long-term, regular customers. Very often the prostitute's client was also her owner. It is not always accurate to characterize them as prostitutes, for some may have been concubines while others may have lived in polyandry.[59] These higher-class prostitutes were often attractive and expensively adorned. Although they may have appeared to be well treated, they were nevertheless chattel, "one day loaded with jewels, the next day to be stripped and sold to the highest bidder, if it were the desire of their masters."[60]

Neither lower- nor higher-class prostitutes received regular wages, but the latter were sometimes asked to entertain at parties given by tong leaders and Chinese merchants, and they were permitted to keep the jewelry, silk, and cash gifts given to them by their customers. This is perhaps how some prostitutes were able to send money to their parents in China.[61]

The exploitative relations between the prostitute-worker and the procurer and brothel owner are clear. The capital outlay — kidnapper's fee, passage, bribes, legal fees — was miniscule compared with the profits from the woman's labor as a prostitute. For example, the cost of her passage would have been around $50 if she traveled in the same manner as the Chinese male laborers, and at the most $150 if she had comfortable accommodations, no doubt extremely rare.[62] The kidnapper's fee was once reported at $185.[63] And although we do not have data on the exact amount of bribes and legal fees, it seems safe to say that these did not usually exceed $100, although they became increasingly larger as restrictions on Chinese immigration grew.

The most profitable way of importing a woman, from the procurer's point of view, was to lure the woman to go with him or her voluntarily to America. In one such case, the procurer, after painting a glowing picture of life in California and paying $98, obtained the consent of a girl's mother to permit her daughter to emigrate. Upon arrival, the procurer sold the girl for $1,950, a net profit of at least $1,700. This girl continued to bring in profits for her owner by laboring two years and averaging no less than $290 per month. At the end of the two years she was resold for $2,100.[64] The brothel owner's gross income from her labor as a prostitute and from her resale was about $9,060; even if she was kept at a higher standard of living and if we deduct the cost of her purchase, the brothel owner's net profit was no less than $5,000 in two years.

Besides by being kidnapped and lured, Chinese women entered American brothels under a system of contract mentioned before. Although this was, on the surface, the least exploitative form of Chinese prostitution, it was in fact devised to mask those features that permitted the procurers, importers, and brothel owners to derive considerable profits without any real advantage to the prostitute or indentured worker. The contracts were drawn up in appealing terms: they offered the contractee free passage to America, an advance of over $400, and a limited period of labor of about four and a half years. The contract system seemed all the more attractive considering that females were often sold for about $400 at the time.

In reality, though, the contract system offered very little advantage over the outright sale or slave system and was, in a number of ways, more brutal because it raised false hopes. First, the length of a prostitute's career, as noted before, was about four or five years. Thus, as far as the brothel owner was concerned, a prostitute was useful only for about four years, the period of the contract. Second, the terms of the contract specified that the person must work a minimum of 320 days, failing which the contract period could be extended to one additional year. Third, the contract prostitute would have less incentive to run away because of her limited period of labor. Fourth, her family was discouraged from redeeming her because the repurchase price included an exorbitant interest.[65] And finally, even after a woman had served out her contract, there were cases in which she continued in servitude and was not released.[66] The following is a translation of one such contract:[67]

> The contractee Xin Jin is indebted to her master/mistress for passage from China to San Francisco and will voluntarily work as a prostitute at Tan Fu's place for four and one-half years for an advance of 1,205 yuan (US$524) to pay this debt.[68] There shall be no interest on the money, and Xin Jin shall receive no wages. At the expiration of the contract, Xin Jin shall be free to do as she pleases. Until then, she shall first secure the master/mistress's permission if a customer asks to take her out. If she has the four loathsome diseases, she shall be returned within 100 days; beyond that time the procurer has no responsibility. Menstruation disorder is limited to one month's rest only. If Xin Jin becomes sick at any time for more than fifteen days, she shall work one month extra; if she becomes pregnant, she shall work one year extra. Should Xin Jin run away before her term is out, she shall pay whatever expense is incurred in finding and returning her to the brothel. This is a contract to be retained by the master/mistress as evidence of the agreement. Receipt of 1,205 yuan ($524) by Ah Yo. Thumb print of Xin Jin the contractee. Eighth month 11th day of the 12th year of Guang-zu (1886).

Thus far, a total of four such contracts have been discovered, the earliest dated 1873 and the latest 1899.[69]

A fourth way in which Chinese women entered San Francisco brothels was through outright purchase; in this case the women were no more than slaves. Initially, the average capital outlay for a woman brought over in this way amounted to no more than $600: the purchase price, the cost of passage, and the expenses associated with importation. But as immigration restrictions became more severe and the complexity of the importation system grew, the cost of buying and importing a prostitute likewise increased. The purchase and importation of a seventeen-year-old named Tsoi Ye illustrates this process. Tsoi Ye was sold in Hong Kong in the 1880s for a little over $400. She was resold by the procuress to a tong man for $882, who in turn entrusted a Chinese sailor to bring her over. After she was landed successfully, she was resold to a brothel for $1,800 in gold.[70] Despite the high cost, it is clear that brothel owners found it profitable to purchase women at such prices on account of their potential earnings as computed above.

If the kidnapped woman was sold during the later decades of the nineteenth century, the importer could receive between $1,000 and $3,000. If, however, the importer was also a brothel owner, the kidnapped woman would labor in his or her brothel. From the information on hand, one can venture some conservative estimates of her earnings. The lowest grade of prostitutes received 25¢ to 50¢ per customer. According to the literature on prostitution in general, an average full-time prostitute-worker receives four to ten customers per day,[71] and the average career life of such a prostitute is estimated at four to five years.[72] This means that, at an average of 38¢ per customer and seven customers per day, a lower-grade prostitute would earn about $850 per year and $3,400 after four years.[73] Since women in lower-class brothels were generally kept at subsistence levels,[74] the cost of maintaining them probably did not exceed $8 per month or $96 per person each year.[75] The profits for the owner of a prostitute, then, even one of the lower grade, were considerable.

If a lower-grade prostitute earned an average of $850 a year, and if we assume that the average brothel in 1870 contained nine prostitutes (see table 12.2), the owner's gross annual income would have been about $7,650. In 1873, Chinese owned only 7 percent of the 153 major pieces of property in Chinatown, and as late as 1904, they owned only 8 percent of the 316 major parcels listed.[76] White landlords, many of whom were prominent citizens of San Francisco, owned most of the real estate in Chinatown, and they extracted high rents from brothel owners, often double or treble the rent they received from whites.[77] According to the Bureau of Labor Statistics, the average rental per month of a flat consisting of three to six rooms in San Francisco was $14.[78] The Chinese brothel owners probably had to pay no less than $28 per month or $336 a year. If the rent and maintenance of the women are deducted from the gross income, the owner would still have received an annual profit of no less than $6,000. Even if we added other expenses such as protection fees paid to the police and taxes extorted by the tongs from brothels not owned by their members, the profit that the brothel owner received would still compare very favorably with the less than $500 average annual income of other occupations in which he or she might engage.[79] Other commentators' estimates of the income of brothel owners make this look conservative. For instance, Cameron, a contemporary San Francisco reformer, stated that the average Chinese prostitute usually made between $5 and $6 per day; one prostitute estimated that she made $278 per month, while another claimed to have made $318 per month.[80]

TABLE 12.2
NUMBER AND SIZE OF CHINESE BROTHELS IN SAN FRANCISCO, 1860-1880

Size	1860	1870	1880
1	3	2	13
2	13	2	19
3	9	4	29
4	20	12	14
5	7	18	7
6	13	13	3
7	6	10	6
8	6	20	1
9	8	15	0
10	3	10	2
11	2	15	1
12	1	12	1
13	0	7	0
14	0	2	0
15	0	5	1
16-20	0	10	3
21-25	1	2	0
26-30	1	0	1
31-35	1	0	0
Total	94	159	101
$\overline{M}$ size of brothel	5.9	9.0	4.3

SOURCE: Computed from unpublished census manuscripts for San Francisco for 1860, 1870, and 1880 (available from the National Archives).

The exploitation of Chinese prostitutes was not limited to sex alone but also included their labor as semiskilled workers. Many sources indicate that in the daytime, when business was slack, women in the brothels sewed buttonholes and pantaloons and worked on shirts, slippers, men's clothing, and women's underwear.[81] The work was farmed out by sweatshops which subcontracted with the manufacturers. Since these female operatives probably did not receive payment for this extra work, the brothel owners and sweatshop owners reaped a handsome profit.[82]

There were still other forms of exploitation. Besides the tax levied on brothel owners who were not tong members, the tongs imposed a weekly tax of 25¢ on every Chinese prostitute. If any woman refused to pay, they promised to use "harsh measures" to collect.[83] These harsh measures included whipping, torture by fire, banishment to brothels in the mining regions, and finally, shooting and killing the victim.[84]

Blackmailing Chinese prostitutes was another method employed by the tongs to extort money. Members of a tong, noted one report, "went around among Chinese prostitutes and told them that a new chief of police had come in, and unless he received a handsome present, would shut up the houses. They collected from one and a half to five dollars from each one, and it was divided among the members of that society."[85]

Owners of brothels sometimes also owned opium dens and gambling joints.[86] A number of prostitutes were addicted to opium and/or gambled excessively.[87] The owners often encouraged these addictions so that the loans needed to feed them would increase the prostitutes' debts.[88] Desperate women committed suicide by swallowing raw opium or drowning themselves in the bay.[89]

The best thing that could happen to these women was to be redeemed and married. Occasionally a white male fell in love with a brothel inmate and married her after having paid the owner.[90] However, most of the men who married prostitutes were Chinese laborers. Chinese working people did not attach the same stigma to prostitution as whites did. One reason might have been that prostitutes in China were generally not seen as "fallen women" but as daughters who obeyed the wishes of the family. Although prostitution was not considered an honorable profession, particularly among the gentry, women who were able to get out of it were usually accepted in working-class society. Furthermore, the fact that there was such a shortage of Chinese women in San Francisco during this period would have tended to relax the sex mores that men might have held.

Apparently, quite a few women in San Francisco were able to leave the brothels, although not without struggle and often at tremendous risk. Throughout the mid-nineteenth and the early twentieth centuries, reports of such instances abound.[91] Typically, a woman ran away to a mission, the police station, or her lover, with hired tong soldiers in pursuit. The lengths to which the tongs would go in recapturing a runaway prostitute indicated her value to her owner. The tongs often kidnapped the escaped woman or even used the American courts to get her back by filing a charge of theft, claiming the woman had absconded with some clothes or jewelry. After the police had located the woman, the tongs would hire white lawyers to arrange for her bail and then return her to the brothel.[92] If that tactic failed, they placed public announcements on Chinatown walls, warning others who might assist her escape and offering rewards for her capture.

The tongs also offered rewards for the capture of the prostitute's male accomplice; sometimes such rewards ran into the thousands, depending on the value of the woman. If the male accomplice paid the sum asked for the woman's redemption, then the couple was left alone, but very often the man could not pay the exorbitant amount that the tong required. There are stories that tell of such men and women fleeing the San Francisco area in disguise or hidden in wooden boxes.[93] However, the tong network of informers reached even into rural communities. Telegraphs between Chinese men in Marysville, Downieville, San Francisco, and other places reveal that such a system operated at least during the 1870s.[94]

As further insurance against the escape of a prostitute, tongs gave the local police a retainer fee. Until 1877, a Special Police Force was engaged in a quasi-official capacity as peace officers in Chinatown. They received no set wages but derived their income from the Chinese residents. Normally, the "Chinatown Specials" collected fifty cents a week from each prostitute,[95] and they admitted that whenever there was a crackdown on prostitution, their income was reduced.[96] Tongs also made payments to City Hall to secure its agreement not to interfere.[97]

As mentioned before, a prostitute's work life in the brothels was normally four to five years, not surprising in the absence of sound medical care. The abundance of Chinese advertisements of "secret formulas" for curing syphilis and gonorrhea during the period testifies to the prevalence of such diseases.[98] Although some doctors blamed the Chinese prostitutes for spreading the diseases to the white population, it was pointed out by other physicians that these illnesses were equally, if not more, prevalent among white prostitutes in San Francisco.[99]

When a woman was no longer profitable as a prostitute, she might work as a cook or a laundry woman for the brothel.[100] If she was hopelessly ill, she would be left to die by the brothel.[101] Although, in general, the remains of the Chinese male laborers were shipped back to their place of nativity for burial, few cared about the remains of these working women. The *Alta* reported in 1870 that the bodies of Chinese women were discarded and left on the streets of Chinatown.[102]

Chinese prostitutes were mostly young women between the ages of sixteen and twenty-five. The year 1870 stood out as a watershed in that there were proportionately more younger prostitutes in that period than in either 1860 or 1880. Table 12.3 shows that close to 46 percent of the women were under twenty years of age in 1870, which was 12 and 23 percentage points higher than the 1880 and the 1860 aggregates, respectively. Since a great majority of the Chinese prostitutes were of child-bearing age, a natural question arises as to the mobility of their children.

TABLE 12.3
AGE AND NATIVITY OF CHINESE PROSTITUTES IN SAN FRANCISCO, 1860-80

	1860			1870			1880			
	Foreign born	U.S. born	%	Foreign born	U.S. born	%	Foreign born	U.S. born	Total	%
15 and under	8	0	1.4	16	1	1.1	18	4	22	5.0
16-20	122	0	21.9	637	0	44.7	125	2	127	29.2
21-25	105	0	18.9	416	0	29.2	129	1	130	29.9
26-30	165	0	29.7	215	0	15.1	86	0	86	19.8
31-35	64	0	11.5	70	0	4.9	32	0	32	7.4
36-40	64	0	11.5	34	0	2.4	20	0	20	4.6
41-45	19	0	3.4	14	0	1.0	8	0	8	1.8
46-50	6	0	1.1	18	0	1.2	8	0	8	1.8
51 and over	3	0	.6	5	0	.3	2	0	2	.5
Total	556	0	100.0	1,425	1	100.0	428	7	435	100.0

SOURCE: See table 12.2.

TABLE 12.4
CHINESE CHILDREN IN SAN FRANCISCO BY SEX, NATIVITY,
AND PLACE OF RESIDENCE, 1860-80

	Live in Brothels			Live Outside		
	Male	Female	Total	Male	Female	Total
1860:						
U.S. born	5	23	28	0	0	0
Foreign born	3	12	15	7	2	9
Total	8	35	43	7	2	9
1870:						
U.S. born	98	74	172	71	57	128
Foreign born	34	48	82	79	34	113
Total	132	122	254	150	91	241
1880:						
U.S. born	24	26	50	203	198	401
Foreign born	11	27	38	89	114	203
Total	35	53	88	292	312	604

SOURCE: See table 12.2.

The children of prostitutes, particularly female ones, were likewise exploited by the brothel owners. Table 12.4 shows the number, place of nativity, and residence of Chinese children living in San Francisco. The data reveal a significant trend: in the 1860 census, proportionately more children lived in brothels than outside brothels; in 1870, an almost equal number of children lived in brothels and outside; and finally, in 1880, the situation was reversed with many more children living outside than inside. The overrepresentation of girls over boys in the brothels for all three decades was probably due to the owner's practice of retaining girls to do household chores and his or her intention to recruit them into prostitution. It is probably safe to say that native-born children living in brothels were almost invariably the children of prostitutes. But most of the children of prostitutes somehow managed to escape the clutches of the brothel. In 1880, nearly thirty years after the first large-scale importation of prostitutes, only 7 of the 435 prostitutes in San Francisco were native born (table 12.3). In general, children moved away from the brothels and into the wider society (table 12.4).

Some of these children were placed into mission homes and with families of Chinese Christians.[103] Others might have returned to China or moved to the American interior. For those who remained in San Francisco, the occupational distribution of native-born Chinese females in the 1880 manuscript census gives a clue as to their destinations. Of the 250 U.S.-born women who were not classified as prostitutes, 227 were housewives, while the rest were students, apprentices, house-keepers, and seamstresses. Although certainly not all native-born women were offspring of prostitutes, a number of them clearly were. It is not incorrect to say, therefore, that the daughters of some indentured and slave prostitute-workers managed to become wage laborers and housewives.

EXTENT AND DISTRIBUTION OF CHINESE PROSTITUTES IN SAN FRANCISCO

The exact number of Chinese prostitutes in California and San Francisco during the nineteenth century is not known. Although several contemporary estimates are available, their tremendous variation indicates low reliability. Fortunately, we are not solely dependent on impressionistic accounts. The recently released manuscript census for 1860, 1870, and 1880 contain social and demographic information on individuals that makes it possible to estimate the numbers and to construct a statistical profile of Chinese prostitutes for these decades.

A tabulation of the census schedules of 1860 reveals that there were 2,693 Chinese residents in San Francisco, 654 or 24 percent of whom were women. Eight of these were laundry/washerwomen; five, gardeners; five, fisherwomen; three, laborers; four, storekeepers; two, clerks; and one, a tailoress; the remainder had no occupation listed. Eliminating from the last category (a) those women living in households with a man with or without children, (b) those living in households with more than one man, and (c) girls under twelve years old, we have 556 women whose occupations might be said to have been prostitution. This figure represents 85 percent of the Chinese female population in San Francisco, and it is probably a reasonable estimate.

Since "prostitution" was used as an occupational category in the 1870 and 1880 census manuscripts, we have simply followed the designation of the census taker to identify Chinese women engaged in prostitution during those two decades. Obvious distortions may arise from this procedure. Although the census enumerator was instructed to record what was reported to him or her by the interviewee, a language problem could lead to guessing by the census worker. It is also reasonable to assume that the census taker was probably biased toward designating a woman a prostitute because of popular racist beliefs or an inability to distinguish between concubinage and prostitution. Conversely, the interviewee was probably inclined not to state that she worked as a prostitute even if she really did. Since these biases run in opposite directions, they tend to neutralize each other.

A tabulation from the 1870 census schedules yielded 2,018 Chinese women in San Francisco, of whom 1,426, or 71 percent, were recorded as prostitutes. From these figures, we can see that while the percentage of women in San Francisco engaged in prostitution declined relative to the total Chinese female population, the actual number of prostitutes more than doubled.

Between 1870 and 1880, Chinese prostitution became one of the salient issues in the anti-Chinese movement in California. During the two legislative hearings on Chinese immigration, one conducted by the California State Senate in April 1876 and the other by the U.S. Congress in October of the same year, numerous individuals testified on the extent of Chinese prostitution in San Francisco.[104] These estimates contradicted one another and revealed the witnesses' political biases and self-interests. Because of those contrasting interests, the estimates of Chinese prostitutes in San Francisco differed widely, ranging from 200 to 2,700. In neither hearing did witnesses or legislators cite the census figures.

A tabulation of the manuscript census for San Francisco in 1880 yielded 2,058 Chinese women, of whom 435, or 21 percent, were recorded as prostitutes. Although this figure was probably an underestimate, other sources suggest that it was not too far afield. The San Francisco police testified in the congressional hearings of 1876 that, as a result of several raids on Chinese prostitution a few months before the hearings, many prostitutes left the city for inland towns.[105] Later, in 1885, the San Francisco Board of Supervisors reported that there were 567 professional prostitutes in Chinatown.[106]

From the statistics presented, we see the dramatic increase in the number of prostitutes between 1860 and 1870, and the dramatic decrease in both the number and percentage of prostitutes between 1870 and 1880. These figures suggest that the heydey of Chinese prostitution in San Francisco was around 1870, and its precipitous decline occurred just before 1880.

Although Chinese prostitutes served a racially mixed clientele, they were physically concentrated in a few blocks in Ward Four, where Chinatown was located. Outside of Chinatown, in 1860, some brothels were found in three other wards, but in 1870, Chinese brothels were found in only one other ward. Data on the distribution and size of brothels (table 12.2) clearly confirms that the years around 1870 were the heydey of organized prostitution. There were more prostitutes, more and larger brothels, and a heavier concentration of brothels in a very small area. The data also suggest the idea that this was the period when small businesses were consolidated or liquidated by big enterprises.

DECLINE OF ORGANIZED PROSTITUTION

Several converging factors account for the decline of organized prostitution in San Francisco. First, the female supply in South China dwindled, making families less willing to sell or mortgage their daughters and increasing the difficulty of procuring prostitutes. Second, the Chinese Exclusion Act of 1882 greatly reduced the number of prospective prostitutes and made their importation harder. The decline in the annual number of Chinese women immigrants—from an average of 304.6 between 1854 and 1882 to an average of 107.6 between 1883 and 1904—testifies to the effectiveness of the Exclusion Act,[107] despite the ingenious evasive methods devised by the importers, tongs, and brothel owners. The skyrocketing value of prostitutes in America and the increase in kidnapping in California after the 1880s also reflect the decline in Chinese women entering the United States for the purpose of prostitution.

Local conditions in San Francisco and California after the 1880s similarly led to the decline and eventual demise of this organized phase of prostitution. These included the more balanced sex ratio of the California population (see table 12.1); the availability of other sources of supply; the move of Chinese labor from migrant to stationary industries; the desire of capital to maintain a stable, cheap labor force; the change from sojourning to settlement or return; the increased alternatives for women's labor;[108] intra-tong conflicts and the struggle between the tongs and the allied forces of the Chinese consulate and the Six Companies; the enforcement of codes directed against Chinese prostitution; the arrival of white Victorian women and the establishment of white families in California; and finally, the crusade of the white missionaries for the abolition of Chinese prostitution.

The Six Companies, led by Chinese merchants, had their financial basis in Chinese laborers and trade. They supplied labor, collected membership fees, served as bankers for the immigrants, and sold provisions to the laborers.[109] The secret societies, which controlled the gambling, opium, and prostitution businesses, challenged the traditional authority of the Six Companies and competed with the merchants for the laborers' dollars. Their opposition sharpened during the 1880s, partly because the increase in local kidnapping related to prostitution alienated the Chinatown elites, who had families with them.[110] The more money laborers spent in San Francisco tong-controlled businesses, the less they had to spend in the merchants' shops or to send home to their families.[111] Since many emigrant communities in China depended on remittances, the Chinese consulate and the Qing government were also concerned.[112] In addition, the merchants knew that American families would not patronize the growing number of legitimate restaurants, stores, and curio shops in Chinatown if it was seen as a vice district.[113] The fierce competition among secret societies for the control of gambling, opium, and prostitution during the last few decades of the nineteenth century also contributed to their decline.[114]

Moreover, the heyday of Chinese prostitution in San Francisco corresponded with the period of mounting agitation against Chinese labor in general. And although prostitutes consisted of no more than 6 percent of the Chinese population in California, they were singled out for attack by the politicians. Chinese prostitution not only threatened the health of white men, claimed those politicians, but Chinese prostitutes serving as slave labor took away sewing and other jobs from white women.[115] Between 1866 and 1905, at least eight California codes were passed, all aimed at restricting the importation of Chinese women for prostitution and suppressing the Chinese brothels. Although white prostitution was equally if not more prevalent, these were additional and specific laws directed only against the Chinese. Chinese prostitutes, if caught, were sentenced to a fine of $25 to $50 and a jail term of at least five days.[116]

Both the Chinese consulate and the Six Companies saw prostitution as one of the major causes for the anti-Chinese movement in California. Further, both were concerned about the economic loss and image of the Chinese, so they actively collaborated with the American authorities in identifying and deporting Chinese prostitutes.[117] In reality, however, since Chinese prostitution was not the reason for the anti-Chinese movement, their action did not thwart the hostility; but their efforts did bring about a temporary decline in the organized traffic.

The arrival of increasing numbers of white women immigrants to San Francisco throughout the second half of the nineteenth century transformed the city from a frontier society with a fluid, predominantly male population to a more stable society with families. Smith accurately pointed out that the status of prostitutes declined with the advent of the Victorian ladies from the East Coast. These women were concerned with the preservation of the family, and their Puritan morality led them to crusade against prostitution in general and Chinese prostitution in particular.[118] In 1873, the interests of the Victorian ladies in San Francisco found expression in the Women's Occidental Board. Reportedly alarmed by the immorality of the traffic in women and the sinfulness of the prostitute's sexual activity, Margaret Culbertson and her successor, Donaldina Cameron, set out to rescue the Chinese slaves.[119] Although clergymen like Gibson and Loomis also crusaded against prostitution, Cameron was always singled out as the bravest and cleverest savior of Chinese females. She was said to have rescued approximately 3,000 girls during her forty-year career,[120] although Cameron herself testified in 1898 that, twenty-three years after the establishment of the Mission Home, about 600 girls had been rescued.[121]

Missionaries thought that every slave girl or prostitute would rather live at 920 Sacramento Street, but Chinese women did not always prefer this alternative, particularly if the brothel owner did not mistreat them too badly.[122] Most women who ran away from brothels to seek the protection of the Mission or the police cited cruelty, such as flogging and beating, as the reason for their escape.[123] The Mission established strict rules for the activities and behavior of the runaways and trained them in "motherhood" and "industrial skills." The rule against idle hands extended to cooking, cleaning, and maintaining the Mission, and even to the use of the women in hard labor. Cameron was known to have contracted with fruit growers in Northern California for the labor of Mission residents. She often sent twenty or thirty Chinese women from the home to work from four to eight weeks in the fields. It is not difficult to see why many prostitutes refused to run away to the Mission Home, or why a number of women who had been "rescued" by the missionaries later escaped from their saviors.[124]

There can be no doubt, however, that as a result of the efforts of Cameron and others like her, many prostitutes became wives and lived normal family lives. A few of these women became Christians and joined in missionary work. Many white women, perhaps including Cameron herself, were motivated by a sense of moral superiority. The more they saw Chinese women as helpless, weak, depraved, and victimized, the more aroused was their missionary zeal. Saving the Chinese slave girls seemed to have become the "white woman's burden."[125]

CONCLUSION

Rotenberg observed that "the heavy emphasis on the 'sinful' nature of the prostitute's sexual activity has obscured her role as a worker."[126] I have argued here that prostitution is a form of labor. In the case of the individual owner-prostitute, she is a free agent, in possession of her own sexuality, offering it in the market in exchange for a fee from her clients. But the prostitute can be ruthlessly exploited by others who own her sexuality and/or expropriate her earnings. The institution of Chinese prostitution was characterized by many layers of exploitative relations. Men and women, Chinese and white, reaped benefits from their oppression. The development of Chinese prostitution as a large enterprise in nineteenth-century California was related to both material and ideological conditions in the two countries; to the need for cheap labor in California and the economic underdevelopment of China; and to white racism and Chinese patriarchy.

NOTES

This paper is part of a research project on "Asian American Labor before World War II" organized by the Asian American Studies Center at UCLA. I am indebted to Edna Bonacich, Alex Saxton, Gerald Surh, Peg Strobel, Don Nakanishi, and three anonymous reviewers for their helpful comments on an earlier draft. Special thanks to Gary Okihiro, who gave editorial assistance; to Paul Nakatsuka, who extracted part of the data from the census manuscripts; and to the Mormon Temple Library in Los Angeles, the Bancroft Library, the Library of Congress, and the National Archives for permission to use their collections. I wish also to acknowledge a grant from the UCLA Academic Senate which made this research possible. Parts of this essay are summarized and incorporated in my "Chinese Immigrant Women in Nineteenth-Century California," in *Women of America,* ed. C. Berkin and M. B. Norton (Boston: Houghton Mifflin Co., 1979).

1. Later on, when anti-Chinese sentiment grew into a widespread movement, the slavery aspect of Chinese prostitution was emphasized in anti-Chinese rhetoric (see, e.g., California Senate, *Chinese Immigration* [Sacramento: State Office, 1878] [hereafter known as California Senate]).

2. F. Wakeman, *Strangers at the Gate* (Berkeley and Los Angeles: University of California Press, 1966), pp. 117-156; K. Hsiao, *Rural China* (Seattle: University of Washington Press, 1967).

3. T. Chen, *Emigrant Communities in South China* (New York: Institute of Pacific Relations, 1940); Hsiao.

4. Hsiao, pp. 311-411; A. Smith, *Village Life in China* (New York: Greenwood Press, 1899), pp. 258-316; P. Ho, *Studies on the Population of China* (Cambridge, Mass.: Harvard University Press, 1959), pp. 58-62.

5. D. Chen, *Zhong-guo fu-nü sheng-huo-shi* (Shanghai: Shang-wu, 1928), p. 296.

6. J. Borthwick, *The Gold Hunters* (New York: Book League, 1929).

7. D. Smith, *Rocky Mountain Mining Camps* (Lincoln: University of Nebraska Press, 1967).

8. Ibid.

9. E. Boserup, *Women's Role in Economic Development* (London: Allen & Unwin, 1970).

10. Y. Wu, *Er-shi-nian mu-du guai-xian-zhuang* (Hong Kong: Guang-zhi, 1903), pp. 248-243; X. Chen, *Dan-min di yan-jiu* (Shanghai: Shang-wu, 1946), pp. 124-128; U.S. Congress, Joint Special Committee to Investigate Chinese Immigration, *Report* (Washington, D.C.: Government Printing Office, 1877), p. 286 (hereafter cited as U.S. Congress); O. Gibson, *Chinese in America* (Cincinnati: Hitchcock Printers, 1877), p. 134.

11. Zhong-guo ko-shang hui-guan, "Letter," *Tung-ngai san-luk* (February 8, 1855).

12. T. Chen; J. Watson, *Emigration and the Chinese Lineage* (Berkeley, Los Angeles, London: University of California Press, 1975).

13. Wang Ah-so's letter to her mother in *Orientals and Their Cultural Adjustment*, ed. Fisk University, Social Science Institute (Nashville, Tenn.: Fisk University Social Science Institute, 1946), p. 34 (hereafter cited as Fisk University).

14. Boserup, p. 76.

15. S. Castles and G. Kosack, *Immigrant Workers and Class Structure in Western Europe* (London: Oxford University Press, 1973).

16. "Editorial," *Out West* (1911), pp. 355-356; U.S. Congress, pp. 141, 652.

17. R. Evans, "'Soiled Doves': Prostitution and Society in Colonial Queensland," *Hecate* 1 (July 1975): 6-24.

18. C. Gentry, *Madams of San Francisco* (New York: Doubleday & Co., 1964).

19. S. Wu, *Mei-guo Hua-qiao bai-nian ji-shi* (Hong Kong: by the author, 1954); Gentry; C. Lee, *Days of the Tong Wars* (New York: Ballantine Books, 1974); Borthwick.

20. Y. Wu, pp. 238-243.

21. *Eureka West Coast Signal* (January 6, 1875).

22. C. Holder, "Chinese Slavery in America," *North American Review* 165 (1897):285-294.

23. C. Shepherd, "Chinese Girl Slavery in America," *Missionary Review* 46 (1923):893-898; Fisk University, pp. 31-35; U.S. Industrial Commission, *Report*, 21 vols. (Washington, D.C.: Government Printing Office, 1901), 15:783-790 (hereafter cited as U.S. Industrial Commission).

24. Shepherd, pp. 896-897.

25. C. Dobie, *San Francisco's Chinatown* (New York: Appleton-Century Publishers, 1936), p. 69.

26. Z. Chen, "Shi-jiu shi-ji sheng-xing di qi-yue Hua-gong-zhi," *Li-shi Yan-jiu* (1963): 161-179.

27. R. Park and H. Miller, *Old World Traits Transplanted* (New York: Harper & Bros., 1921), p. 164; R. Lee, *The Chinese in the United States of America* (Hong Kong: Hong Kong University, 1960).

28. Gibson (n. 10).

29. *Alta California* (December 14, 1869).

30. Gibson.

31. *Statutes of California and Amendments, 1873-74* (Sacramento: State Office, 1875).

32. *Alta California* (August 27, 1873).

33. U.S. Congress, pp. 387-920.

34. M. Coolidge, *Chinese Immigration* (New York: Henry Holt & Co., 1909), p. 419.

35. U.S. Congress, p. 1165.

36. U.S. Industrial Commission, p. 762; Gibson, pp. 146-154.

37. U.S. Senate, *Chinese Exclusion* (Washington, D.C.: Government Printing Office, 1902), pp. 470-472 (hereafter cited as U.S. Senate).

38. H. Lai, "The Chinese Experience at Angel Island," *East/West* 10 (1976):7-9; R. Dillon, *The Hatchet Men* (New York: Coward-McCann, 1962), p. 290.

39. Lai.

40. A. McLeod, *Pigtails and Gold Dust* (Caldwell, Idaho: Caxton Printers, 1948), p. 18.

41. U.S. Industrial Commission, p. 763.

42. Dillon, pp. 319-321.

43. U.S. Congress, p. 599; C. Wilson, *Chinatown Quest* (Stanford, Calif.: Stanford University Press, 1950), p. 87; D. Gray, *Women of the West* (Millbrae, Calif.: Les Femmes Publishing, 1976), p. 69.

44. U.S. Senate, p. 124.

45. Holder (n. 22).

46. The establishment of orphanages and children's welfare organizations was partly responsible for the decline (see Ho [n. 4], pp. 58-62).

47. *Alta California* (January 31, 1875); *San Francisco Bulletin* (March 28, 1876); Y. Zhang, *San-zhou ri-ji* (n.p., 1896), chap. 5.

48. Dillon.

49. McLeod, p. 178.

50. Holder (n. 22), p. 292.

51. Dobie (n. 25), p. 195.

52. Ibid., pp. 242-243; California Senate, p. 213.

53. Dobie, p. 61; A. Genthe, *Pictures of Old Chinatown* (New York: Moffat, Inc., 1909), p. 52.

54. California Senate, pp. 28, 99, 176; Dillon, p. 46.

55. *Sacramento Bee* (June 5, 1876); S. Lyman, *Chinese Americans* (New York: Random House, 1974), p. 94.

56. U.S. Congress, p. 192.

57. Dobie, p. 243.

58. McLeod, pp. 182-183; U.S. Congress, p. 192.

59. Cases of polyandry among the Chinese in San Francisco and Californian interior towns were reported by Henry K. Sienkiewicz, "The Chinese in California," *California Historical Society Quarterly* 34 (1953): 307.

60. McLeod, p. 183.

61. Fisk University, p. 34.

62. J. Kemble, "Andrew Wilson's Jottings on Civil War California," *California Historical Society Quarterly* 32 (1953): 209-224, 303-312.

63. Holder (n. 22), p. 292.

64. U.S. Industrial Commission, p. 783; Shepherd (n. 23), pp. 892-895; Fisk University, pp. 31-35.

65. U.S. Industrial Commission, p. 783; G. Leong, *Chinatown Inside Out* (New York: Barrows Mussey, 1936), p. 231; Wilson (n. 43).

66. *Alta California* (April 14, 1870); California Senate, p. 99.

67. S. Wu (n. 19), p. 92; McLeod (n. 40), p. 177.

68. Although not specified in the contract, I suspect that the currency used was Mexican silver dollars. One Mexican dollar was equivalent to approximately US$0.48 in the mid-nineteenth century.

69. The other three contracts can be found in California Senate, 1877, p. 128 and 135, and U.S. Industrial Commission, p. 771.

70. U.S. Senate, pp. 227-228.

71. K. Sie, *Mai-yin zhi-du yu Tai-wan chang-ji wen-ti* (Taipei: Da-feng, 1972), p. 352.

72. W. Sanger, *The History of Prostitution* (New York: Eugenics, 1939); McLeod, p. 183.

73. The contracts examined indicate that a prostitute had to work a minimum of 320 days per year. An absence of more than fifteen days would subject her to a penalty of having to work one additional month, and menstruation disorder was limited to one month's rest per year.

74. Dobie (n. 25), p. 243.

75. B. Lloyd, *Lights and Shades of San Francisco* (San Francisco, 1876).

76. Dillon (n. 38).

77. E. Robbins, "Chinese Slave Girls," *Overland Monthly*, n.s., 51 (1908):100-102; California Senate, pp. 106, 155, 197.

78. California Bureau of Labor Statistics, *Biennial Reports, 1887-1888* (Sacramento: State Office, 1888), p. 104.

79. U.S. Bureau of the Census, *Historical Statistics of the United States: Colonial Times to 1970* (Washington, D.C.: Government Printing Office, 1975), p. 165.

80. U.S. Industrial Commission, p. 786; Leong (n. 65); Fisk University, p. 36.

81. California Senate, pp. 146, 154; U.S. Congress, pp. 211, 1169; Dobie (n. 25), p. 243.

82. U.S. Congress, p. 1170.

83. *Alta California* (March 26, 1873).

84. Ibid. (December 4, 1870); U.S. Congress, pp. 110, 211.

85. California Senate, p. 213.

86. Ibid., pp. 164-166.

87. M. Stabler, "A Bit of Blue China," *Out West,* n.s., 3 (1911): 256-259; U.S. Congress, p. 96.

88. U.S. Congress, p. 96; California Senate, p. 99.

89. California Senate, pp. 99, 180; *Alta California* (July 6, 1876); Y. Fu, *You-li Mei-li-jia guo tu-jing You-ji-lei*, vol. 5 (n.p., 1889).

90. *San Francisco Chronicle* (April 1, 1877).

91. "Bancroft Scraps," an unpublished collection of newspaper clippings (Bancroft Library, University of California, Berkeley), vols. 6-9 (1862-1881); Wilson (n. 23).

92. California Senate, p. 120.

93. *San Francisco Bulletin* (June 11, 1878).

94. *California Chinese Chatter* (San Francisco: Dressler, Inc., 1927).

95. California Senate, p. 166.

96. Ibid., p. 158.

97. Ibid., p. 113.

98. Bancroft Library has in its collection of Chinese immigration pamphlets advertisements for such secret formulae ("Chinese Immigration Miscellaneous," unnumbered boxes, Bancroft Library, University of California, Berkeley).

99. U.S. Congress, p. 142.

100. U.S. Industrial Commission, p. 778; Gray (n. 43), p. 69.

101. *San Francisco Chronicle* (December 5, 1869).

102. *Alta California* (October 9, 1870).

103. M. Slingerland, *Child Welfare Work in California* (New York, 1915), pp. 98-99.

104. California Senate; U.S. Congress.

105. U.S. Congress, p. 192.

106. San Francisco Board of Supervisors, *Special Committee Report on Chinatown* (San Francisco, 1885), p. 9; California Bureau of Labor Statistics, *Biennial Reports, 1887-1888* (Sacramento: State Office, 1888), p. 108.

107. Coolidge (n. 34), p. 502.

108. V. Nee and B. Nee, *Longtime Californ'* (New York: Pantheon Books, 1973); J. Hooks, *Women's Occupations through Seven Decades* (Washington,

D.C.: Women's Bureau, 1947); B. Liu, *Mei-guo Hua-qiao shi* (Taipei: Li-ming, 1976).

109. S. Lyman, "Conflict and the Web of Group Affiliation in San Francisco's Chinatown, 1880-1910," *Pacific Historical Review* 43 (1974): 473-499.

110. Dillon (n. 38); I. Light, "From Vice District to Tourist Attraction," *Pacific Historical Review* 43 (1974): 367-394; Liu; Lyman, "Conflict and the Web of Group Affiliation."

111. Q. Liang, *Xin-da-lu you-ji jie-lu* (Shanghai: Zhong-hua, 1936), p. 110.

112. T. Chen (n. 3); Hsiao (n. 2); G. Li, *Huan-you di-qiu xin-lu* (n.p., 1877); D. Li, "Zao-qi Hua-ren yi-Mei ji An-ji-li tiao-yue qian-ding," *Lien-ho Shu-Yuan Xue-bao* 3 (1964): 1-29; Liu.

113. Light.

114. E. Gong and B. Grant, *Tong War!* (New York: Brown, Inc., 1930); Dillon (n. 38); C. Reynolds, "Chinese Tongs," *American Journal of Sociology* 40 (1935): 610-623; C. Lee (n. 19).

115. California Senate; U.S. Congress; U.S. Senate.

116. California Senate, p. 163.

117. Gibson (n. 10); Liu (n. 108).

118. D. Smith (n. 7).

119. Robbins (n. 77); Wilson (n. 23); Gray (n. 43), pp. 67-74.

120. Gray, p. 74.

121. U.S. Industrial Commission, p. 788.

122. Wilson.

123. *Alta California* (July 31, 1873).

124. Wilson, pp. 85, 125; *Alta* (May 28, 1876).

125. Gray (n. 43).

126. L. Rotenberg, "The Wayward Worker: Toronto's Prostitute at the Turn of the Century," in *Women at Work,* ed. J. Acton, P. Goldsmith, and R. Shepherd (Toronto: Canadian Women, 1974), pp. 33-69.

References

Alta California. December 14, 1869; April 14, 1870; December 4, 1870; March 26, 1873; July 31, 1873; August 27, 1873; January 31, 1875; May 28, 1876; July 6, 1876.

"Bancroft Scraps"
1862- Unpublished collection of newspaper clippings. Bancroft Library, University of
1881 California, Berkeley.

Borthwick, J.
1929 The Gold Hunters. New York: Book League.

Boserup, E.
1970 Women's Role in Economic Development. London: Allen and Unwin.

California
1875 Statutes of California and Amendments, 1873-74. Sacramento: State Office.

California Bureau of Labor Statistics
1888 Biennial Reports, 1887-1888. Sacramento: State Office.

California Chinese Chatter
1927 San Francisco: Dressler, Inc.

California Senate
1878 Chinese Immigration. Sacramento: State Office.

Castles, S., and G. Kosack
1973 Immigrant Workers and Class Structure in Western Europe. London: Oxford University Press.

Chen, D.
1928 Zhong-guo fu-nu sheng-huo-shi. Shanghai: Shang-wu.

Chen, T.
1940 Emigrant Communities in South China. New York: Institute of Pacific Relations.

Chen, X.
1946 Dan-min di yan-jiu. Shanghai: Shang-wu.

Chen, Z.
1963 "Shi-jiu shi-ji sheng-xing di qi-yue Hua-gong-zhi." Li-shi Yang-jiu 79: 161-179.

"Chinese immigration miscellaneous" (collection of Chinese immigration pamphlets, advertisements, unnumbered boxes). Bancroft Library, University of California, Berkeley.

Coolidge, M.
1909 Chinese Immigration. New York: Henry Holt and Company.

Dillon, R.
1962 Hatchet Men. New York: Coward-McCann.

Dobie, C.
1936 San Francisco's Chinatown. New York: Appleton-Century Publishers.

Eureka West Coast Signal. January 6, 1875.

Evans, R.
1975 "'Soiled doves': Prostitution and society in colonial Queensland." Hecate 1 (July):6-24.

Fu, Y.
1889 You-li Mei-li-jia guo tu-jing You-ji-lei. Vol. 5, n.p.
Genthe, A.
1909 Pictures of Old Chinatown. New York: Moffat, Inc.
Gentry, C.
1964 Madams of San Francisco. New York: Doubleday and Company.
Gibson, O.
1877 Chinese in America. Cincinnati: Hitchcock Printers.
Gong, E., and B. Grant
1930 Tong War! New York: Brown, Inc.
Gray, D.
1976 Women of the West. Millbrae, Calif.: Les Femmes Publishing.
Holder, C.
1897 "Chinese slavery in America." North American Review 165: 285-294.
Ho, P.
1959 Studies on the Population of China. Cambridge, Mass.: Harvard University Press.
Hooks, J.
1947 Women's Occupations through Seven Decades. Washington, D.C.: Women's Bureau.
Hsiao, K.
1967 Rural China. Seattle: University of Washington Press.
Kemble, J.
1953 "Andrew Wilson's jottings on Civil War California." California Historical Society Quarterly 32: 209-224, 303-312.
Lai, H. Mark
1962 "The Chinese experience at Angel Island." East/West 10: 7-9.
Lee, C.
1974 Days of the Tong Wars. New York: Ballantine Books.
Lee, R.
1960 The Chinese in the United States of America. Hong Kong: Hong Kong University.
Leong, G.
1936 Chinatown Inside Out. New York: Barrows Mussey.
Li, D.
1964 "Zao-qi Hua-ren yi-Mei ji An-ji-li tiao-yue qian-ding." Lien-ho Shu-Yuan Xue-bao 3: 1-29.
Li, G.
1877 Huan-you di-qiu xin-lu.
Liang, Q.
1936 Xin-da-lu you-ji jie-lu. Shanghai: Zhong hua.
Light, I.
1974 "From vice district to tourist attraction." Pacific Historical Review 43: 367-394.
Liu, B.
1976 Mei-guo Hua-qiao shi. Taipei: Li-ming.
Lloyd, B.
1876 Lights and Shades of San Francisco. San Francisco. A. L. Bancroft.
Lyman, S.
1974 Chinese Americans. New York: Random House.
1974 "Conflict and the web of group affiliation in San Francisco's Chinatown, 1880-1910." Pacific Historical Review 43: 473-499.

McLeod, A.
1948 Pigtails and Gold Dust. Caldwell, Idaho: Caxton Printers.
Nee, V., and B. Nee
1973 Longtime Californ'. New York: Pantheon Books.
Out West
1911 "Editorial."
Park, R., and H. Miller
1921 Old World Traits Transplanted. New York: Harper & Brothers.
Reynolds, C.
1935 "Chinese tongs." American Journal of Sociology 40: 610-623.
Robbins, E.
1908 "Chinese slave girls." Overland Monthly, n.s., 51: 100-102.
Rotenberg, L.
1974 "The wayward worker: Toronto's prostitute at the turn of the century." Pp. 33-69 in Women at Work, edited by J. Acton, P. Goldsmith, and R. Shepherd. Toronto: Canadian Women.
Sacramento Bee. June 5, 1876.
San Francisco Board of Supervisors
1885 Special Committee Report on Chinatown. San Francisco.
San Francisco Bulletin. March 28, 1876; June 11, 1878.
San Francisco Chronicle. December 5, 1869; April 1, 1877.
Sanger, W.
1939 The History of Prostitution. New York: Eugenics.
Shepherd, C.
1923 "Chinese girl slavery in America." Missionary Review 46: 893-898.
Sienkiewicz, Henry K.
1953 "The Chinese in California." California Historical Society Quarterly 32:307.
Slingerland, M.
1915 Child Welfare Work in California. New York: Russell Sage Foundation.
Smith, A.
1899 Village Life in China. New York: Greenwood Press.
Smith, D.
1967 Rocky Mountain Mining Camps. Lincoln: University of Nebraska Press.
Stabler, M.
1911 "A bit of blue China." Out West, n.s., 3: 256-259.
U.S. Bureau of the Census
1975 Historical Statistics of the United States: Colonial Times to 1970. Washington, D.C.: Government Printing Office.
U.S. Congress, 44th Congress 2d session.
1877 Report of the Joint Special Committee to Investigate Chinese Immigration. Senate Report 689. Washington, D.C.: Government Printing Office.
U.S. Industrial Commission
1901 Report, Vol. 15. Washington, D.C.: Government Printing Office.
U.S. Senate
1902 Chinese Exclusion. Washington, D.C.: Government Printing Office.
Wakeman, F.
1966 Strangers at the Gate. Berkeley and Los Angeles: University of California Press.
Wang, Ah-so
1946 "Letter to her mother." In Orientals and Their Cultural Adjustment, edited by Fisk University, Social Science Institute. Nashville, Tenn.: Fisk University Social Science Institute.

Watson, J.
  1975 Emigration and the Chinese Lineage. Berkeley and Los Angeles: University of California Press.
Wilson, C.
  1950 Chinatown Quest. Stanford, Calif.: Stanford University Press.
Wu, S.
  1954 Mei-guo Huo-qiao bai-nian ji-shi. Hong Kong: by the author.
Wu, Y.
  1903 Er-shi-nian mu-du guai-xian-zhuang. Hong Kong: Guang-zhi.
Xie, K.
  1972 Mai-yin zhi-du yu Tai-wan chang-ji wen-ti. Taipei: Da-feng.
Zhang, Y.
  1896 San-zhou ri-ji. n.p.
Zhong-guo ko-shang hui-guan
  1855 "Letter." Tung-ngai san-luk (February 8).

13

Japanese Gardeners in Southern California, 1900-1941

Nobuya Tsuchida

If one should ask what kinds of people have contributed most to the development of the Japanese community in America, we would be able to answer proudly that it is us gardeners. In spite of the important role that we have played, our fellow countrymen somehow tend to slight us. The only time they think of us is when they want to raise money for this and that. Japanese American history books and the like always have the same old stuff. First of all, these publications deal with Little Tokyo in Los Angeles and then dwell on big farmers and wealthy fishermen, namely so called "successful immigrants." . . .Therefore, whether we gardeners make significant contributions or become rich, those community leaders and Japanese government officials think nothing of it.[1]

Since the turn of the twentieth century, gardening has been one of the most important urban occupations among the Japanese in Southern California. The area's hot, dry climate, coupled with the rapid growth of greater Los Angeles into a huge population center, created an ever increasing need for gardeners. Many Japanese Americans, spurred on by job discrimination, the profitability of this trade, and their familiarity with plants, thus turned to gardening in quest of a secure means of livelihood.

Japanese gardeners formed a unique petite bourgeoisie with something of a proletarian consciousness. Theoretically they were self-employed independent contractors. In actuality, however, they were manual laborers, doing work that could be described as both an extension and mixture of farming and domestic work, two of the major occupations pursued by earlier immigrants.

Known as a typical Japanese trade since the 1920s, yard maintenance has always been one of the economic mainstays of the Japanese in the Southland. In the postwar period, this line of business not only enabled many Japanese Americans to accumulate sufficient capital for going into other small businesses, but it also helped the gardeners provide their children with higher education.

Even today, gardening continues to play a very important role in the economic life of Japanese Americans. Numbering approximately 8,000 as of 1970, gardeners were still the principal breadwinners for roughly 20 to 25 percent of the Japanese American households in Southern California.[2] Although gardening has constituted an integral part of the Japanese experience in California, to date no serious study has been made of these workers. Such studies as *People in Motion: The Postwar Adjustments of the Evacuated Japanese Americans* (War Liquidation Unit, U.S Department of Commerce, 1947), *Removal and Return: The Socio-Economic Effects of the War on Japanese Americans* (Leonard Bloom and Ruth Riemer, 1949), and *Changing Occupance of the Japanese in Los Angeles County, 1940-1950* (Midori Nishi 1955) are very limited in scope, dealing only with Japanese American gardeners as one of many other occupational groups, mainly in terms of the postwar resettlement of the Japanese on the West Coast.

This chapter will present an overall history of issei (first-generation Japanese) gardeners before World War II, analyzing the emergence of this petite bourgeois occupation in the wake of California's systematic efforts to exclude the Japanese from agriculture. In the process, attention will be focused on the following points: (1) the various factors that caused Japanese immigrants to turn to this trade; (2) the background of issei who became gardeners; (3) the gardeners' (prolabor) predilection, as demonstrated during the 1936 Venice lettuce strike; and (4) the mechanisms by which the Japanese gardeners tried to protect their interests. I will attempt to show how vulnerable this ethnic petite bourgeoisie was to racism and economic fluctuations in the United States.

Data for the present study were derived from interviews with many issei and nisei gardeners, both active and retired; from such primary sources as autobiographies, Japanese vernacular newspapers and the *Gadena no Tomo* (Gardeners Monthly) published by the Southern California Japanese Gardeners Federation; and from Japanese-language secondary sources consisting of Japanese history books compiled by various community organizations.

A BRIEF HISTORY

Gardening was one of the oldest urban occupations taken up by issei pioneers. In Southern California, this line of business dates back to around 1900, when several domestic workers began to take care of their employers' yards. Because lawn mowing turned out to be quite profitable, many Japanese immigrants entered into contracts to cut lawns for affluent American families. Gardening yielded over $2 per day, as compared with the prevailing daily wages of $1.35 for railroad workers in the Pacific Northwest[3] or $1.75 for day laborers in Los Angeles.[4] Furthermore, the patron usually provided his gardener with lunch. As word of the relatively lucrative nature of this job spread among the issei, a growing number of Japanese gardeners were seen operating in Hollywood, in the Crenshaw district, and in uptown Los Angeles.[5] These laborers moved from one house to another by cart or by bicycle, carrying hoses across their shoulders in the latter case.[6] On New Year's Day, some issei gardeners worked their routes in swallow-tailed coats.[7]

In its 31 December 1905 issue, the *Nichibei Shimbun* of San Francisco published demographic and occupational data on the Japanese in Southern California (see table 13.1). According to the report, as of that year 3,387 Japanese resided in Los Angeles, including 277 women and 70 children. Of the 3,040 issei men, 179 made their living on garden maintenance, comprising 5.9 percent of the male labor force. Since table 13.1 fails to differentiate between hotelkeepers and guests, it would be safe to assume that gardening was the fourth most important trade among the Los Angeles Japanese in the early 1900s.[8]

It was not long before the Japanese earned a reputation as the finest in garden maintenance for they not only had experience with plants but they worked hard and conscientiously. As their reputation increased, so did the demand for their expertise. By 1918, the number of issei gardeners in the greater Los Angeles area had increased to 558. Since approximately 80 percent, or roughly 446, of them are believed to have resided within the city limits, one out of every ten of the able-bodied members of the Los Angeles Japanese community was engaged in this trade. Still ranked fourth in order of numerical strength, the gardeners (10.4 percent) were preceded by 760 farm laborers (17.8 percent), 697 domestics (16.3 percent), and 477 fishermen (11.2 percent), while being followed closely behind by 429 cannery workers (10.0 percent) (see table 13.2). However inaccurate the estimated number of Japanese gardeners in Los Angeles may have been, it is no doubt clear that by the second decade of the twentieth century, gardening had become one of the major pursuits among the urban Japanese.

TABLE 13.1
OCCUPATIONS OF THE JAPANESE IN LOS ANGELES, 1905

Occupations	Number of persons	Percentage
Hotel owners and patrons*	931	30.6
Domestic workers	650	21.4
Restaurant owners and employees	273	9.0
Store owners and employees	246	8.1
Gardeners	179	5.9
Schoolboys**	75	2.5
Guests at organizational dormitories***	70	2.3
Bathhouse owners and barbers	67	2.2
Pool hall owners	60	2.0
Employment agents	44	1.4
Clerical workers	40	1.3
Nurserymen	35	1.2
Journalists	27	0.9
Laundrymen	22	0.7
Tailors	17	0.5
Teachers	13	0.4
Miscellaneous workers	291	9.6
Total	3,040	100.0

SOURCE: Nanka Nikkeijin Shogyo Kaigisho, *Nankashu Nihonjinshi* (Los Angeles: Nanka Nikkeijin Shogyo Kaigisho, 1956), pp. 94-95.
*Hotel patrons were temporarily unemployed men who were in the process of finding new jobs.
**Among the Japanese, a "schoolboy" meant a young immigrant who attended school while working as a domestic, receiving room and board in addition to a small salary.
***Several community organizations, such as churches, had facilities in which to accommodate newcomers from Japan and out-of-town members.

Around this time, however, gardeners were not included among those considered affluent or influential in the affairs of the Japanese community. In the Who's Who section of *Nanka no Nihonjin* (The Japanese in Southern California) published in 1919, coauthors Shinzo Toda and Hisato Horie listed 559 prominent issei men, selected from among 15,000 Japanese residents[9] on the basis of one or a combination of the following qualifications: officeholding in community organizations, higher education, annual income of over $2,000, and ownership of landed property. The great majority of the 559 so-called eminent members of the community were farmers and merchants; none were gardeners. Shigezo Nishida, a wholesale nurseryman, was the only person listed who had been engaged in garden maintenance prior to under-

TABLE 13.2
OCCUPATIONS OF THE JAPANESE IN LOS ANGELES, 1918

Occupations	Number of persons	Percentage
Farm workers	760	17.8
Domestic workers	697	16.3
Fishermen	477	11.2
Gardeners	446	10.4
Fish cannery wokers	429	10.0
Store employees	384	9.0
Operatives	160	3.8
Clerical workers	74	1.7
Cooks	55	1.3
Drivers	45	1.1
Journalists	37	0.9
Nurses and midwives	32	0.8
Photographers	27	0.6
Small manufacturers	22	0.5
Clergymen	22	0.5
Physicians	17	0.4
Insurance agents	17	0.4
Movie actors and actresses	14	0.3
Dentists	13	0.3
Lawyers and interpreters	13	0.3
Teachers	9	0.2
Miscellaneous workers	521	12.2
Total	4,271	100.0

SOURCE: Computed from Shinzo Toda and Hisato Horie, *Nanka no Nihonjin* (Tokyo: Hakubunkan, 1919), pp. 41-44.
*The number of gardeners is a rough estimate. The original chart classified them under the category of "miscellaneous and unknown occupations." Since the compilers of the occupational data maintained that approximately 80 percent of the 556 Japanese gardeners in the greater Los Angeles area resided within the municipal limits, the author estimated that 446 issei engaged in gardening in the city of Los Angeles.

taking a business venture. Arriving in Los Angeles in 1902, he worked as a live-in gardener for nine years. In 1911, Nishida quit the job and opened a 2.5-acre nursery on West Adams Boulevard.[10] Although several other nurserymen were also included on the roster of "successful immigrants," none of them had used gardening as a stepping-stone to achieve economic mobility. As far as officeholding was concerned, throughout the 1910s, no gardeners are known to have assumed any leadership positions in the numerous Japanese and prefectural associations.

By 1920, the number of issei gardeners in Southern California[11] soared to 1,000. With the introduction of Ford pickups, many of them were able to expand their routes to other cities in the vicinity of Los Angeles. Within a decade, the Japanese gardening population exceeded 3,000.[12] As of December 1934, almost a third of the Japanese labor force in Los Angeles consisted of gardeners. Of the 5,125 Japanese whose occupations were reported to the Japanese Association of Los Angeles, gardening claimed 1,500 (29.3 percent), while the produce industry and farming accounted for 790 (15.4 percent) and 615 (12.0 percent), respectively (see table 13.3)

The rising popularity of this trade among the issei is attributable to several factors. First, because of California's Alien Land Laws of 1913, 1920, and 1923, many Japanese were pushed out of agriculture. Second, during the post-World War I housing boom, the Los Angeles area rapidly expanded both physically and demographically, thereby generating more jobs for gardeners. Third, the climate of Southern California was such that yards needed constant, year-round maintenance, except

TABLE 13.3
OCCUPATIONS OF THE JAPANESE IN LOS ANGELES, 1934

Occupations	Number of persons*	Percentage
Gardeners	1,500	29.3
Produce retailers and wholesalers	790	15.4
Farmers	615	12.0
Grocery stores, owners/employees	470	9.2
Hotels and apartments, owners/employees	305	5.9
Restaurants and bars, owners/employees	232	4.5
Nurseries and flower farms, owners/employees	210	4.1
Barbers	162	3.2
Florists	105	2.0
Laundrymen	96	1.9
Doctors, dentists, and pharmacists	74	1.4
Insurance agents	55	1.1
General stores, owners/employees	45	0.9
Trading firms, owners/employees	45	0.9
Others	421	8.2
Total**	5,125	100.0

SOURCE: Compiled from the *Kashu Mainichi* (December 11, 1934).
*Includes both employers and employees.
**When the Japanese Association of Los Angeles took a census in December, 1934, there were 30,000 Japanese residents in the city of Los Angeles, of whom 8,135 were gainfully employed. However, the census identified the occupations of only 5,125 people.

during a few winter months. Fourth, since most Japanese had farming experience, gardening was relatively easy for them. Finally, this line of business yielded a comfortable income while requiring only a small initial investment.

On the whole, the Great Depression played less havoc with Japanese immigrants than it did with the American people at large, for few of the issei owned stocks or had significant bank savings. Moreover, the majority of the issei were farmers, agricultural laborers,[13] gardeners, or domestics; factory workers, who were hurt the most, constituted only a very small percentage of the Japanese labor force. Of the hundreds of Japanese flower farmers in California, for example, not a single one went bankrupt throughout the depression era.[14] Still, even though relatively less affected, many members of the Japanese community, in both its urban and rural sectors, came to feel the negative impact of the depression.

By late 1931, the number of jobless Japanese reached 600 in Los Angeles alone.[15] Many of these people were farm hands who had lost their jobs to cheaper Mexican and Filipino labor. Since the majority of unemployed agricultural laborers stayed at issei-owned boarding houses without paying their rent, the proprietors also found themselves on the brink of bankruptcy.[16] The predicament, however, was not restricted to farm workers and boarding house operators. When a Japanese lease farmer growing potatoes in La Puente defaulted on his rent in the spring of 1931, his white landlord claimed the tenant's entire crop in lieu of the arrears.[17] Many other issei tenant farmers who failed to pay their rent on time either lost their lease or had the fruits of their labor confiscated.

As a means of coping with the rising unemployment rate among the issei, in April 1932, the Japanese Association of Los Angeles appealed to Japanese farmers and businessmen to hire their compatriots. At the same time, the association leaders requested that Japanese doctors and dentists treat needy countrymen gratuitously.[18] A month later, the Japanese Medical Association agreed to provide free medical services and to lower hospital fees for the poor.[19] In May 1932, two Japanese hotel owners set up camps in San Gabriel to accommodate forty jobless agricultural workers. Two issei farmers provided land, while as many grocers donated provisions. These laborers were offered occasional farm jobs whenever they were available.[20]

Seeing no signs of economic recovery on the horizon, both the issei and nisei in the urban area felt increasingly desperate. When Hori & Company of Los Angeles wanted to hire a shipping clerk in April 1933, it was inundated by forty well-qualified nisei women applicants. In the same month, as many as thirty-six men applied for a single salesman's job at a Little Tokyo store.[21] Throughout the Depression era, several Japanese vernacular newspapers in California ran occasional articles on issei immigrants who committed suicide out of despair.

Surprisingly, gardening was not one of the hardest hit occupations at the time of the financial crisis, suggesting that the Depression had an unequal impact on the wealthy who could afford the luxury of employing gardeners. Far from bearing the brunt of economic stagnation, Japanese gardeners remained relatively unscathed and fared rather well in the 1930s. Immediately following the collapse of the New York Stock Exchange, however, many gardeners in Los Angeles lost customers. Some gardeners' monthly incomes dropped from $200 to $150, while others were halved from $120 to $60. Even so, Los Angeles gardeners' earnings were by no means meager, particularly in comparison, for instance, with the lot of some 800 issei restaurant workers who received only a dollar and free meals for a twelve-hour work day. And the gardeners did not suffer adversity for long. Gradually, their income rose again, surpassing the pre-Depression level by the mid-1930s. Around this time, an average gardener had approximately twenty customers and worked ten to twelve hours daily six days a week. Each customer paid him $10 per month for maintaining the yard twice a week, for an average income of $200 a month. (The monthly fee was dropped to $5 per month if the homeowner wanted only one day a week maintenance.)[22] During the same period, farm laborers could earn barely $12 per week.[23] It is estimated that by the eve of World War II, the 3,000 Japanese gardeners in California south of Santa Barbara earned, in the aggregate, $5,400,000 per annum.[24] Hence, their annual income averaged $1,800 per person. Compared with the incomes of Japanese businessmen, however, the gardeners' earnings were less than impressive. In 1939, for example, over 200 nurserymen reportedly earned $1,500,000 or $7,500 per person, whereas some 600 Japanese grocery stores and markets had total annual sales of over $10,000,000, or $16,700 per establishment.[25]

With respect to individual wages, gardening compared very favorably with many other types of jobs held by Japanese immigrants — or by white workers, for that matter. In the late 1930s, a gardener could collect $150 to $200 a month, or $37.50 to $50 a week.[26] By contrast, a produceman was paid $20 per week for sixty hours of labor. As of 1940, the union wage paid at major supermarkets in Los Angeles was $22.50 a week. When Japanese American produce workers joined the AFL in 1941, their working conditions were improved to $25 for a forty-eight-hour week. The highest monthly salary that a nisei produceman could draw was $130.[27] Even by the War Agency Liquidation Unit's more conservative estimate of $125 for an average gardener's monthly income,[28] gardeners would still have been better off than the 4,000 Japanese American produce workers.

Although it was an exhausting job, gardening could be undertaken without much capital, knowledge of English, or special skills. Once a good reputation was established by Japanese gardeners, issei from agricultural backgrounds could easily go into this trade. Garden maintenance was indeed a very convenient and remunerative occupation for those who lacked capital or the experience to engage in small business or independent farming, as well as for those who had failed in them. Recollecting the bygone days, a former gardener wrote, "No one can deny that gardening was a respectable occupation which saved the Japanese from poverty."[29] Undoubtedly, during the Great Depression, yard maintenance did provide thousands of Japanese immigrants and their dependents with an adequate livelihood. Furthermore, a considerable amount of money derived from gardening was eventually funneled to many of the Japanese-owned business establishments patronized by the gardeners.

The Japanese dominated Southern California gardening during the two decades preceding the wartime evacuation, comprising roughly 70 to 80 percent of the total gardening population in this region.[30] Issei gardeners encountered little competition from white workers, in part because the rapid growth of the Los Angeles basin always created a sufficient demand for horticultural care. Moreover, it was the Japanese immigrants who were largely responsible for developing gardening into a viable occupation. At the least, it was not one of those predominantly white trades that Asian immigrants threatened to invade. Most Caucasian workers shunned yard maintenance as too strenuous, especially since they had more attractive alternatives. It was only at the height of the Depression, when jobs became scarce for white workers, that competition in the field of gardening emerged.

GARDENERS' BACKGROUNDS

Before the war, gardening was more of an issei than a nisei occupation. Even among the immigrants, however, few took up gardening as their first occupation on arrival in the United States. Most gardeners had initially been engaged in some kind of agricultural work, while some had worked as domestics or "schoolboys" before going into garden maintenance.[31]

Based on autobiographies, personal interviews, and articles in *Gadena no Tomo*, it appears that most issei gardeners were relative latecomers to the United States. The passage of the Alien Land Laws proved to be more of a handicap to these later immigrants, who could not establish a foothold in agriculture. They were restricted to hiring themselves out as farm hands, or becoming sharecroppers for established Japanese growers. Forseeing little future in agriculture, many of the later Japanese immigrants sought more stable and rewarding jobs in the city. Had they not been restricted in agriculture, however, many of the gardeners would undoubtedly have pursued farming.

In terms of educational background, most issei gardeners had finished primary or junior high school in their mother country. Shoji Nagumo, a leader in the Japanese Gardeners' Association of Hollywood, who received sixteen years of formal education prior to immigration, was definitely an exception, not only among the gardeners but in the Japanese community as a whole. Perusal of the *Gadena no Tomo* reveals that a significant number of issei had professional horticultural knowledge, as well as a keen literary interest, especially in the composition of haiku (seventeen-syllable verse) and senryu (satirical poetry). This suggests that, on the whole, issei gardeners were underemployed relative to their talents and training.

To enter the field of gardening, a Japanese immigrant often received help from issei who had previously entered this occupation. In his autobiography, *Gadena Goroku* (A Gardener's Essays), Shoji Nagumo describes how, when he was penniless after a string of bad luck, an old friend, Takao Yamada, who was a gardener, hired him as a helper for $5 a day. Through Yamada's recommendation, Nagumo also worked for other gardeners. Finally, when some gardeners gave Nagumo their excess customers, he could begin gardening on his own.

Another issei revealed in an interview that after having worked in agriculture, he entered gardening by living in a Japanese-owned boarding house in Los Angeles and hiring out as a houseboy on a daily basis. Owners of boarding houses typically acted as employment agents. In this case, the job entailed gardening as well as house cleaning, and the issei soon transferred to working full-time as a gardener's helper. Through the recommendation of his gardener friends, current customers, and families for whom he had previously worked as a houseboy, this issei was eventually able to establish himself as an independent gardener.

In contrast to the nisei, the issei had to face more stringent job discrimination because of their ineligibility for U.S. citizenship and their inadequate knowledge of English. Since the Japanese immigrants fully understood that their employment opportunities were severely limited in the host society, however, they tended to view gardening in a more positive light than did their American-born children. Generally speaking, those issei who became gardeners stuck to their new occupation throughout the prewar period. Deriving an adequate income, many of them could afford to own a house, a pickup truck, and a passenger car. One gardener in West Los Angeles reportedly netted as much as $1,000 per month in the late 1930s, using several Mexican helpers who were paid $4 to $5 a day,[32] though the majority of Japanese gardeners did not earn as much. A small number of issei gardeners, however, were able to accumulate sufficient capital to move on to more substantial small businesses, such as nurseries, grocery stores, lawn mower shops, garages, restaurants, and boarding houses. These commercial establishments in turn could count on patronage by their owners' former fellow gardeners. For the majority, though, gardening was a sufficiently satisfying and remunerative occupation for them not to desire change. One gardener put it this way:

> As was the case with most of us, I became a gardener to avoid starvation. Coming from an agricultural background, I was always interested in plants and fond of manual labor. The longer I gardened, the more I came to enjoy this occupation.[33]

This seems to have been a common attitude.

Japanese exclusion from California's agriculture coincided with the remarkable economic and demographic growth of the Los Angeles basin. The population of the city of Los Angeles swelled from 576,673 in 1920 to 1,238,048 in 1930, while that of Los Angeles County grew from 936,455 to 2,208,492 during the same period.[34] The concomitant construction boom provided the issei with plenty of employment opportunities in garden maintenance. Coming from rural Japan, most immigrants were able to handle, or could pretend to handle, horticultural work. Their farming experience in Japan or America on the one hand, and the good reputation of Japanese gardeners established by hundreds of precursors, on the other, facilitated Japanese penetration into the gardening industry of California's Sunbelt.

Another illustration comes from the autobiography of Shoji Nagumo. During the housing boom of the mid 1920s, Nagumo entered into a contract with the Borman Construction Company to build gardens for its newly constructed homes. He hired several Mexican helpers for landscaping. As many of the buyers of these houses asked Nagumo to maintain their yards, he was able to earn two to three times more than his fellow gardeners. His knowledge of Spanish proved to be very useful in utilizing Mexican laborers efficiently for both gardening and land-scaping. Nagumo faithfully stuck to his motto, "Make more money than middle-class Americans, but spend less than an average Japanese family," so that his children could all go to college. He believed that the nisei would survive in a racist society only by obtaining a better education than that given to white Americans. Although Nagumo lost the lucrative landscaping contract in 1931 when the Great Depression caused the Borman Construction Company to go bankrupt, he did not lose any of his gardening customers, for most of them were propertied people who did not have to work to make a living.[35]

Another reason why gardening attracted thousands of issei was that they did not need much capital to enter this line of business. During the first two decades of the twentieth century, one could go into this trade with only a hose, a rake, a manual lawn mower, and a bicycle. Even if the gardener did not have a lawn mower, most homeowners owned one he could use. In those days, a gardener's route was concentrated in a single area. Some gardeners had an entire block to themselves. Newcomers could often expand their operation without purchasing an additional route, for their clients' friends and neighbors also hired them. Although the mechanization of gardening proceeded rapidly in the 1930s, initial investment ranged widely from a few hundred dollars to $1,000, depending on how many customers and how much new equipment one wanted.[36] Because of this feature, former farm laborers and domestic workers with little savings, as well as those who did not do well in business, turned to this promising urban occupation.

For example, in another interview, an issei who entered the field of gardening as late as 1938 said that at the time a newcomer needed to spend $300 on tools, $850 to $900 on a pickup, and $300 to obtain a route, provided that he wanted new equipment and all the customers he could handle. Secondhand trucks and tools were available at much lower prices, of course. Generally speaking, a new gardener could acquire a contract for a yard from an established gardener for a price equivalent to its two-month fee. In other words, if the departing gardener was making $150 a month, he could sell his route to the new gardener for $300. This particular issei's total initial investment was not very great, for he bought an old pickup, a minimum number of used tools, and a small route. He gradually acquired new equipment and customers. Charging each family a monthly fee of $10 for servicing their yard three times a week, this immigrant could make approximately $200 a month by 1940.

Issei attitudes toward gardening are captured in Nagumo's autobiography. For him, yard maintenance was the most ideal urban job for the following three reasons. First, gardening paid well and brought in a steady income because no gardener would lose all of his customers at one time. It was one of the few occupations hardly affected by depression. Second, working outdoors with nature every day, the gardener could stay healthy for a long time. Moreover, gardening could be very creative and challenging because the plants faithfully reflected the quality of his work. Third, the gardener was his own boss. The absence of occupational stress arising from relational problems was naturally good for his mental health. After starting garden work, Nagumo himself never fell ill again, nor did he even catch cold.

While admitting that gardeners often became narrow-minded owing to the nature of their work, Nagumo was convinced that gardening was the best available employment for the Japanese immigrants in the urban area. His perception of this trade was apparently based on his thirty-five years of experience as a gardener. The most decisive factor seemed to be the stability and profitability of this occupation. In 1939, he mentioned in one of his essays that he could easily earn $150 a month. Although Nagumo had several children, his family never wanted for anything. When his father became disabled in 1931, Nagumo sent him 500 yen ($250). This issei gardener also built three houses for rent in Tokyo, in order to provide his aging parents with a secure source of income for the rest of their lives.[37] Granted that Nagumo worked at least sixty hours per week and led a very frugal life, there is still no doubt that he could always draw a considerable income from garden maintenance.

Gardening was less often an occupation of the nisei, in part because many of the American-born Japanese were too young to enter the labor market before the War. As of July 1935, the average age of the nisei was fourteen and a half.[38] Still, even among those nisei old enough to join the labor force, gardening was not a preferred occupation. Based on a 20 percent sample taken in 1941, Bloom and Riemer found that fewer than 30 percent of the Japanese contract gardeners in Los Angeles County were nisei, the majority of whom were kibei.[39]

According to the survey, two-thirds of the nisei gardeners had not finished high school,[40] suggesting that those second-generation Japanese who had become gardeners generally had lower levels of educational attainment than those who took up other urban occupations. It thus appears that those nisei who entered yard maintenance mainly did so in the absence of more desirable alternatives.

Indicative of the unfavorable attitude toward gardening among the second generation is the fact that, despite the unemployment of 1,200 adult nisei in Los Angeles and 4,500 in the whole of Southern California in late 1939,[41] they still did not turn to gardening. Unemployment was apparently preferable. Two factors might account for this phenomenon.

In the first place, better educated than the issei, the nisei tended to consider gardening too menial to pursue. These second-generation Japanese demonstrated conspicuous preference for produce market jobs, perhaps in the hope of becoming an owner. Secondly, those issei gardeners who had more customers than they could handle themselves generally hired Mexican helpers,[42] for nisei labor was more expensive and less compliant. While in high school, many nisei sons helped their fathers with gardening over the weekend and during the vacations. After graduation, however, the nisei felt, and their parents concurred, that they were qualified to pursue better careers. Thus gardening remained largely in the hands of issei and kibei.

The prewar issei gardeners liked the idea of being self-employed, independent contractors. They lived modestly and did not exert much influence in the community establishment. But they worked hard and meticulously for many years for the same customers. Before the outbreak of war between Japan and the United States disrupted their socioeconomic life, the Japanese had established and solidified the reputation that they were the best in the trade.

GARDENERS' ASSOCIATIONS AND FEDERATION

During the Great Depression, some issei came to consider the idea of forming a gardeners' union. A number of gardeners' associations had appeared before the financial panic, but they were often nothing more than social clubs. Such organizations either remained inactive or disappeared quickly. In the 1930s, however, the situation was drastically different. The nationwide unemployment rate was going up, while economic stagnation persisted. Farm labor disputes broke out one after another. Clouds of uncertainty about the recovery of the U.S. economy hovered over the Japanese community. As for the gardeners, they faced the threat of losing some customers. To make matters worse, growing numbers of displaced white workers began taking up yard maintenance as a stopgap measure. In an effort to expand their routes, many of these impromptu gardeners underbid their Japanese counterparts. The non-Japanese gardening population jumped from several hundred in the mid-1920s to 2,000 in 1933, further saturating the already shrinking market.[43] It was in the face of this new competition that issei gardeners began seriously to organize themselves.

The incident that precipitated the formation of the first gardeners' association was an attempt to establish discriminatory employment practices against Japanese gardeners in Beverly Hills. On May 16, 1932, the Community Employment Agency of Beverly Hills made an appeal to the residents for their cooperation in hiring U.S. citizens for domestic and gardening jobs, in preference to aliens. With unqualified endorsement from the Beverly Hills Chamber of Commerce, E. J. McGuire, director of the Employment Agency, initiated a campaign to register jobless residents as well as to have homeowners notify the agency of job openings.[44] Under the veil of saving unemployed Americans, the measure actually sought to replace Japanese gardeners with whites.

With the object of ascertaining the true motive behind this relief program, on May 20, Sei Fujii, president of the *Kashu Mainichi*, met with Ellis Wales, executive secretary of the Beverly Hills Chamber of Commerce. Wales lauded the Japanese as excellent gardeners, well liked by white property owners, and assured Fujii that the campaign was by no means intended to squeeze the Japanese out of the gardening industry in Beverly Hills.[45] However, concerned gardeners who conducted their own investigation came up with a very different picture. They sent their representative, Heimatsu Nagai, to the Beverly Hills City Hall to verify a rumor that the City Council had passed a resolution to exclude the Japanese gardeners. Even though a city official denied the rumor, he revealed his attitude by saying to Nagai, "Since Mexicans are going back to Mexico, why don't you Japanese go back to Manchuria?" When Nagai visited a women's society to find out what housewives thought of this issue, one of the officers told him bluntly, "If the wife of an unemployed U.S. citizen is hired as a domestic, her husband will also be employed as a gardener, thereby displacing their employer's Japanese gardener." In the course of his inquiry, Nagai also discovered that some women's social clubs in Beverly Hills had passed a resolution to boycott Japanese goods.[46]

On May 21, some thirty representatives of gardeners in Los Angeles County met in the Japanese School of Hollywood to deliberate on how to deal with the alarming development in Beverly Hills. When Heimatsu Nagai reported on the findings of his investigation, the delegates understood the seriousness of the situation. Disturbed by the gloomy implication of such a discriminatory campaign, these representatives reached a consensus that they had to organize a gardeners' federation to cope with this threat to their livelihood.[47]

The emergence of anti-Japanese sentiments in Beverly Hills may have been touched off by two factors. First, Japan's increasingly bellicose foreign policy in the early 1930s antagonized many Americans. Following the Manchurian Incident of September 1931, Japan extended hostilities to Shanghai in January 1932, and established Manchuko with a puppet emperor in March 1932. Second, two white-owned nurseries in

Beverly Hills, which did not generate any business from issei gardeners, allegedly played a significant role in instigating the exclusion movement. These nurserymen are believed to have conspired to drive out the Japanese in order to bring in white gardeners who, they hoped, would patronize their nurseries.[48] The underlying cause, however, was undoubtedly the fact that the Depression drove unemployed whites into this field in competition with the Japanese. Denied citizenship rights, the Japanese were easily singled out by white workers and their supporters as "foreigners" who were taking over "their" jobs.

In the end, the discriminatory campaign and the boycott of Japanese imports proved quite ineffective. Nevertheless, these hostile actions and threats, coupled with serious competition from white gardeners, were largely responsible for creating the milieu in which issei gardeners finally organized themselves.

At the initiative of Shoji Nagumo, Japanese gardeners' associations were established in 1933 in Hollywood, uptown Los Angeles, and West Los Angeles. Member gardeners paid a dollar each in annual dues and were able to purchase fertilizers, plants, and tools at discount rates through their respective organization.[49] The Hollywood group issued a monthly bulletin to disseminate useful information among its members. It is interesting to note that this particular association was originally created as the Japanese division of a predominantly white gardeners' organization. The racially mixed coalition came into being in July 1933, when sixty-two whites and thirteen Japanese attended a gardeners' conference at the hall of the Arden Milk Company in Hollywood to exchange ideas on how to stabilize gardening fees.[50] By the late 1930s, however, since most of the Caucasian members had switched to more remunerative jobs in the defense industry, the multi-ethnic gardeners' association was reduced to its Japanese membership only.

In 1937, the three Japanese gardeners' associations jointly founded the Southern California Gardeners Federation. The federation published a monthly newsletter entitled *Gadena Shimbun*, which was upgraded to a journal form under the title of *Gadena no Tomo*, beginning in April 1940. As of that year, there were 350 members in West Los Angeles, 300 in uptown Los Angeles, and 250 in Hollywood, or a total of 900 in the umbrella organization. This membership comprised somewhat less than a third of all the Japanese gardeners in Southern California.[51]

Functions of the Associations and the Federation

The functions of each member association overlapped those of the federation in many respects. Generally speaking, however, the association ministered to its members' social and economic needs at a more personal level, whereas the federation protected the interests of all the membership in a more official capacity. Once a month, each association held a meeting to accomplish the following: (1) to promote friendship among the members; (2) to have a guest lecture on horticulture; (3) to discuss issues and problems affecting the gardener; and (4) to hold *tanomoshiko* (rotating credit system) meetings.

Socializing and *tanomoshiko* were the two most important aspects of these association activities. In addition to picnics and parties, the monthly meetings allowed the gardeners to get to know one another so that "route grabbing" would be inhibited, at least among the members of the same association. As the market became saturated in the 1930s, many Japanese gardeners resorted to stealing clients from their own compatriots.[52] By offering to do the same job for a lower fee, a route snatcher enticed the homeowner to fire his gardener. In one of the boarding houses on Sawtelle Boulevard, West Los Angeles, a group of issei gardeners beat up a nisei and broke his leg because he had taken away a customer from one of the tenants. Some of the "unethical" gardeners were nisei, for route grabbing involved a lot of "smooth talk" in English.[53]

It is not that association members never stole customers from other gardeners, but when they did, they refrained from victimizing their own association members. While cultivating comradeship among its members through various social and recreational programs, the gardeners' association also implemented social sanctions against deviants. When the perpetrator and the victim belonged to different associations, the officials of the two organizations negotiated a solution.

Tanomoshiko is an old Asian institution in which a group of trusted friends forms a small mutual credit association, extending loans to the highest bidder within the group. Every month *tanomoshiko* members pay a fixed sum, and the pooled money is made available on a monthly basis to the individual who offers to pay the highest interest. Among the Japanese in America, this rotating credit system had been popular since the early 1900s, as neither American nor Japan-based banks provided adequate financing. In the uptown Los Angeles Gardeners' Association three *tanomoshiko* groups were created in 1935, with each member paying $5 per month. Within two years, the number of groups increased to eight, while the monthly payment was raised to $10. Through this device, the association pooled $960 a month or $11,520 per year, to be loaned at low interest to whomever needed to borrow.[54] The West Los Angeles and Hollywood Gardeners Associations operated five and six *tanomoshiko* groups, respectively, with a monthly payment of $5.[55] In comparison with Japanese flower farmers, who transacted $150,000 annually in their *tanomoshiko*,[56] the gardeners' mutual credit associations were conducted on a rather modest scale. For many issei gardeners who could not obtain a bank loan or did not wish to go to a usurer, however, the *tanomoshiko* was a convenient and safe way to take care of large or unexpected expenses.

In addition to publishing a monthly journal, the Southern California Gardeners' Federation (as opposed to its member associations) organized field trips in an effort to improve the members' gardening techniques. Both the magazine and lectures dealt with how to landscape a garden, take care of the lawn, grow seasonal plants, and apply fertilizers and insecticides. The field trips, by contrast, provided the gardeners with an opportunity to supplement book learning. Thanks to their incessant efforts to advance their horticultural expertise, the Japanese not only maintained a high professional standard but successfully warded off competition from other racial groups.

The federation's most important role was in the area of protecting the members' livelihood. The organization had two main functions: (1) settlement of the difficult cases of route grabbing that could not be solved at the association level; and (2) collection of overdue maintenance fees. If a nonmember stole a client from a member gardener, there was little the local associations could do. In such a case, the most common solution was for the federation officials to pressure the snatcher into paying the victim a sum equivalent to the two-month fee for the yard in question, in exchange for keeping it. Since the federation was big enough and could even, if need be, expose the perpetrator's wrongdoing in its monthly organ, the invader usually agreed to "buy" the route. Were he to refuse, the federation would send its members to steal his clients. More often than not, the mere suggestion of such retaliatory action was sufficient.[57]

There were also numerous instances of abuse by customers. For instance, many homeowners would take advantage of complaisance on the part of issei gardeners and ask them to perform extra tasks at no additional charge.[58] The most serious malfeasance a gardener had to face was a client's default on his monthly payment. Most delinquent customers got away without paying the overdue fees, however, since the Japanese gardeners were helpless against this type of exploitation, inasmuch as it would have cost them more to sue the clients or to retain a lawyer. As for the homeowners, they could easily find a replacement. Such misfortunes often befell gardeners when homeowners wanted to improve their yards before selling their houses.[59]

The federation was sometimes effective in helping its unfortunate members recover their losses. In several instances, the federation leaders succeeded in making delinquent clients believe that the gardeners belonged to the CIO, with the result that the homeowners complied to avoid trouble with the "union." The following anecdote indicates the effectiveness of the federation in debt collection. In 1941, Torajiro Watanabe acquired a new customer, an Italian woman, through a Japanese-language paper. Her yard, having been neglected for a few months, needed extensive gardening. When the place became beautiful in three months, the client fired Watanabe and refused to pay the last month's bill. After several futile attempts to collect the debt, Watanabe, who did not belong to any gardeners' association then, bluffed that he would report the matter to the Gardeners' Federation. He lied that his union had white members as well. It worked, and he got his money. Shortly thereafter, Watanabe joined one of the gardeners' associations.[60]

By 1940, the federation had acquired a legal counselor by the name of L. M. Weinberg. He handled some automobile accidents involving member gardeners but mainly took on difficult back-pay collection cases that the individual gardeners and their associations had been unable to solve. At first, Weinberg either wrote or called delinquent customers.[61] If that did not work, he would take those cases to court, settle them out of court, or send them to a collection agency. Of the thirty-six cases that Weinberg took care of during 1940, five were settled successfully and the customers paid the aggregate sum of $212; eighteen were sent to the United States Credit Bureau, a collection agency; six were abandoned as hopeless; one went to court; and five were still pending as of January 1941.[62]

Weinberg charged $2.50 for damages under $25; $5 for a settlement involving $25 to $50; and a third of the money recovered in larger cases. Initially, the federation advanced legal fees for the claimants.[63] When the number of cases multiplied, the umbrella organization discontinued this practice, with the result that the lawyer began to handle the gardeners' cases with less enthusiasm. The federation leaders blamed the low success rate on the fact that only seven clients, or 20 percent of the total, paid lawyer's fees in advance.[64]

It should be noted that a far greater number of gardeners did not even bother to bring their problems to the attention of the federation. The collecting of arrears was simply so costly and vexatious that it often did not pay to pursue the matter. The United States Credit Bureau took half the fees collected, although it did not charge any commission if no money was recovered.[65] And even if a gardener won his case through the legal system, he would be left with little money after deducting the lawyer's fees and trial cost.

Small Claims Court might have been an alternative option, since the cost was only a dollar and the decision was handed down immediately.[66]

But most Japanese gardeners were not likely to utilize this institution, for they were not fluent in English. Besides, the amount of money involved was not large enough to warrant such an action.

In spite of the costly and time-consuming process of collecting arrears, Nobuyoshi Nakamura, director of public relations of the federation, strongly urged the victims not to give up but to get what was due them at any cost. Nakamura's rationale was that the most effective way to prevent such abuse from recurring was to establish the fact that no Japanese gardeners would tolerate default on the part of homeowners. Nakamura also proposed that delinquent customers be blacklisted so that they might not take advantage of other gardeners in the future. The Japanese Gardeners Association of West Los Angeles in fact compiled a list of "undesirable clients."[67]

Limitations of the Federation

There were two areas in which the federation had little success. The first concerned the raising of gardening fees. After Japanese producemen won a substantial pay increase by joining the AFL in 1940, some federation leaders proposed that Japanese gardeners also become members of the white union and that the federation print form letters requesting homeowners to raise their gardeners' wages.[68] Because most yards were not uniform in the amount and quality of horticultural care required, it was extremely difficult to standardize maintenance fees. Furthermore, since many unemployed people were constantly moving into this trade, charging merely $3 to $5 instead of the prevailing monthly rate of $10,[69] the Japanese found it hard to negotiate a raise from a position of strength. Indeed, the mere mention of a raise might have cost the gardener a customer. Moreover, fewer than a quarter of the 4,000 gardeners of all racial backgrounds in Southern California were organized. And the majority of the 900 members of the Japanese Gardeners Federation not only considered themselves as independent contractors but also were unwilling to cooperate with the white working class. When Nobuo Noda, executive secretary of the federation, called on his fellow members to join forces with the whites to form a mixed union,[70] his appeal went unheeded by the Japanese gardeners who distrusted the white union because of its discriminatory practices toward racial minorities. Besides, the rank and file of the federation believed that, given the nature of their trade, no union could help them improve their working conditions.

The very nature of gardening as an occupation made labor organizing among gardeners difficult. Although they were, in a sense, laborers, and certainly worked hard for long hours, the conditions of their labor acted against their perceiving themselves as workers, or sharing together their grievances as workers. Not only did they not work together in the same place, but they also lacked a common employer against whom to unite. Besides, the fact that they were able to accumulate a small amount of property, in the form of gardening equipment, gave them a sense of being independent businessmen. Thus, the way in which the occupation functioned ran counter to efforts to form a labor union. Needless to say, these features benefited employers who could use the competition between gardeners, both within and between different ethnic groups, to keep fees low.

The disposal of cuttings, trimmings, and fallen leaves was the second area in which the Japanese Gardeners Federation failed to produce any tangible results. In the prewar period, merely a handful of Southern California cities, such as Beverly Hills and Santa Monica, collected both garbage and rubbish. Most municipal governments, including Los Angeles, collected only garbage.[71] It was customary, therefore, for the majority of gardeners to remove rubbish from their customers' yards. In order to get rid of the rubbish collected, the gardener would do one of three things: take the rubbish home and burn it in an incinerator installed in his own backyard; dump the rubbish in a vacant lot; or transport it to a commercial hauler who in turn disposed of it at a dump site. In Los Angeles County there were several city-operated burning dumps in such places as Venice, Marina del Rey, and Santa Monica. A gardener was charged $2 for disposing of a pickup-load of rubbish, whereas a commercial hauler paid $5 to $8 per truck. Furthermore, the CIO sometimes harassed Japanese gardeners by ordering dump workers not to accept rubbish from nonunion members.[72] As for throwing away rubbish steathily at night in a vacant lot, it was of course illegal, and not a few issei gardeners were fined $50 and jailed a few days for doing so.[73] For these reasons, 80 to 90 percent of gardeners burned rubbish in their backyard incinerators, with the rest utilizing the services of haulers who charged upwards of $2 per month.[74]

In the late 1930s, the Japanese Gardeners' Association of Hollywood entered into a contract with rubbish hauler Tanzo Toyofuku to provide an inexpensive hauling service. Those who wished to avail themselves of this program became "rubbish members" by paying the minimum of $2.50 a month and progressively more, depending on the number of clients. But this system met an early demise, owing to irresponsible acts on the part of some of the participants. Some gardeners dumped more rubbish than they paid for. One such individual had a route actually worth $180 per month, but he claimed his monthly income to be $120. Although he paid a lower fee, he brought to the collection site more rubbish than he was entitled to dispose of. Other gardeners dumped rubbish for their friends who were not participants in the hauling program. In addition, many nonmembers took advantage of the absence of a guard in Toyofuku's rubbish collection yard to get rid of their loads.[75] As a result, the hauling service had to be discontinued in December 1940. Since Toyofuku suffered considerable losses, former rubbish members were required to pay an additional 50¢ each, or a total of $15, as a token of compensation.[76]

The disposal of rubbish continued to inconvenience Japanese gardeners, whether they incinerated it themselves or took it to a hauler. In April 1941, therefore, the leaders of the Japanese Gardeners Federation met with four Los Angeles city officials in Kawafuku Restaurant of Little Tokyo in order to request that the city collect rubbish. Sympathetic as they were to the gardeners, the bureaucrats made it clear that City Hall lacked funds to provide this kind of service.[77] Because the officials recommended that the gardeners submit to the city a petition regarding this matter, Shoji Nagumo, president of the federation, drew up a letter in which he proposed the following:

1. If the City was unable to collect rubbish because of a budgetary constraint, a law should be enacted prohibiting nonhaulers from collecting rubbish. The measure would free gardeners from this burden.
2. In the event that the above proposal could not be implemented, the City should construct more dumps on city-owned land so that gardeners could easily dispose of their rubbish. Existing disposal sites were too few and too far away.[78]

The federation leadership felt that gardeners should not be required to collect rubbish and that they ought to be paid additional fees if their customers wanted them to do so. As a matter of fact, however, large numbers of gardeners were willing to take care of rubbish to retain their customers or to steal routes from other gardeners. Given this situation, it was almost impossible for gardeners to be relieved of this task.[79]

In an effort to deal with this problem, an attempt was made to join forces with white gardeners. In May 1941, several representatives of the federation established contact with a white gardeners' association by attending their monthly meeting held at a clubhouse in North Hollywood Park. Established two months earlier, this organization consisted of twenty-six members who did gardening in North Hollywood. These white gardeners were willing to cooperate with their Japanese counterparts in solving their common problems, such as the stabilization of fees and the prevention of route grabbing. In June, the white gardeners' association and the federation reached a basic agreement that they should strive to establish a mixed union in the future. To begin with, the federation consented to send its representatives to the Caucasian gardeners' monthly meeting with the object of maintaining communication between the two organizations. It was also decided that those Japanese gardeners in North Hollywood who refused to join with the white organization should be encouraged to belong to one of the three existing Japanese gardeners' associations.[80]

Some of the federation leaders were staunch supporters of interracial cooperation. Nubuo Noda, for one, was of the opinion that a united front formed by both Japanese and Caucasian gardeners would be able to bring pressure to bear upon City Hall. He advocated, therefore, that the Japanese should work with the white gardeners' association in North Hollywood for the purpose of organizing approximately 1,000 non-Japanese gardeners in the Los Angeles area. The ultimate goal, Noda stressed, should be to create a huge union composed of all gardeners regardless of their racial background.[81] Another leader of the federation, Nobuyoshi Nakamura, asserted that the Japanese ought to join the AFL as a means of solving the rubbish problem. He maintained:

> We have to understand that a union's problems can be solved only by the union. . . . After all, what really counts is citizenship and franchise. The white union is powerful not because it has large membership, but because its members are U.S. citizens and have the right to vote.[82]

Although a small number of the officers in the federation expressed these kinds of views on the direction their organization should take, the concept of unionism was still alien to the rank and file. An essay written by federation president Shoji Nagumo reveals how apathetic the majority of member gardeners were to their leaders' endeavor to cooperate with non-Japanese gardeners and to join the white union. He lamented:

> One of the weaknesses of the Japanese is that they are not only interested in their own individual well-being but preoccupied by a desire to monopolize profits. In other words, they feel no qualms about tripping their competitors. The Japanese are ignorant of an economic theory that a nation's socio-economic factors affect all the people in the same trade. Therefore, our countrymen tend to jump to a conclusion that those who advocate the unity of gardeners or the organizing of all the working class are communists.[83]

Owing to indifference on the part of the rank and file, the leadership of the federation was unable to achieve any noteworthy progress in their efforts to deal with the problems of gardening fees and rubbish disposal.

The federation members' apathy can be attributed to several factors. First of all, despite the fact that gardening was a highly competititve industry in the 1930s, Japanese gardeners could still derive a good income so long as they did not lose their customers. In the second place, although some federation officers insisted that homeowners should be responsible for the disposal of rubbish, many Issei traditionally took it for granted that gardeners should get rid of trash. Third, neither the stabilizing of gardening fees nor the dumping of rubbish constituted such an overriding issue that the Japanese were willing to set aside their long-standing distrust of the whites and their union, a distrust based upon a long history of racist practices by white unions. Finally, as suggested earlier, the structure of gardening as an occupation made the concept of a labor union seem inappropriate. Inasmuch as gardeners conceived of themselves more as businessmen than as laborers, effective competition against the whites seemed more desirable than interracial cooperation as workers. In the end, the outbreak of war between Japan and the United States stifled any move in this direction by the Japanese gardeners.

THE VENICE CELERY STRIKE

Despite their difficulties in forming or joining a genuine labor union, the gardeners' role as part-laborers affected their consciousness such that they did not always identify with business interests. An instance of this was the position they took during an important farm labor strike in 1936 in Venice.

Excluded from the AFL, Japanese farm laborers in Los Angeles organized their own association in June 1935. Called the California Farm Laborers Association, this group was headed by Tokijiro Saisho, a socialist from Saga.[84] Led by this organization and the Federation of Farm Workers of America, some 1,000 Mexican, Japanese, and Filipino celery pickers struck, on April 17, against Japanese growers in Venice.[85] The strikers made two demands:

1. Hourly wages should be increased from 22.5 to 35 cents for a field worker and to 40 cents for a celery picker.
2. The growers should recognize the California Farm Laborers Association as a bargaining body.[86]

The Southern California Farm Federation, composed of 800 Japanese farmers, flatly rejected the demands. By April 20, the strike spread to Lomita, San Pedro, Dominguez Hills, Norwalk, Montebello, San Gabriel, and Oxnard, affecting other crops grown by Japanese farmers.[87] Aimed at the harvest season, the walkout not only hurt the growers but also caused extensive bloodshed between Japanese scabs and the pickets.[88] The farm federation received full support and cooperation from the Los Angeles Sheriff's Department, the Los Angeles and Culver City Police Departments, the U.S. Immigration Service, and the Japanese Consulate. For fear that the Japanese community might ultimately suffer severe economic losses, major community organizations, such as the Central Japanese Association of Southern California, the Japanese Association of Los Angeles, the Little Tokyo Businessmen's Association, and the Orange County and Los Angeles chapters of the Japanese American Citizens' League, all endorsed the position of the growers.[89]

Intent on crushing the strike, the Japanese Association of Los Angeles raised over $2,400 in emergency funds, donated by local Japanese associations, the Yokohama Specie Bank, the Sumitomo Bank, the Japan Mail Steamship Company, and Mitsui & Company.[90] The leadership of the Japanese community, including the *Rafu Shimpo*, was definitely on the side of the farmers. Against these formidable odds, the gardeners' associations, in conjunction with the Rodo Kyoyukai (Laborers Cooperative and Friendly Society),[91] expressed their support for the strikers. In an attempt to present the perspective and predicament of the farm laborers, the two organizations held a public forum on May 26, 1936, at the Union Church, under the sponsorship of the *Kashu Mainichi*. With Kentaro Abe of the Kyoyukai in the chair, representatives from the gardeners' associations, the AFL, and the California Farm Laborers Association, as well as a lawyer and spokesman for the striking Filipino and Mexican laborers, defended the legitimacy of the strikers' demands in front of a packed audience.[92]

The six-week old labor dispute came to an abrupt end in an anticlimactic manner on June 8, when 1,500 Mexican workers unilaterally accepted hourly rates ten cents lower than the strikers' request, and dropped the demand for the growers' recognition of the laborers' right to collective bargaining. On behalf of the farm federation, Central Japanese Association President Yaemon Minami and Los Angeles Japanese Association President Gongoro Nakamura signed a pact with David Benites, who represented the Mexican workers.[93]

It is noteworthy that the leaders of the issei gardeners took such a seemingly inexpedient stand in a losing battle. While it is possible that these leaders did not reflect the dominant view among the rank and file of gardeners on the labor dispute, still they publicly challenged and defied the authority of the powerful community establishment. Perhaps one reason the gardeners could afford to take such a stance was the fact that they depended almost exclusively on a white clientele for their livelihood and were thus less dependent on the goodwill of community leaders than those who served Japanese patrons. But more importantly, the ambiguous class position of gardeners, between labor and the petite bourgeoisie, seems in this instance to have led to their identification with, and support of, the workers.

Considering the background of the majority of gardeners, it is perhaps not surprising that many of them identified with the striking farm laborers. Many of them probably resented the high-handed attitude of the big farmers, rich merchants, and a small number of intellectuals, who reigned over the Japanese community. Commenting on a big picnic held by the Gardeners Federation, Masaru Matsudaira, an issei gardener, stated that he had had a good time because none of those arrogant merchants, who would usually attend a prefectural association picnic, attended.[94] At any rate, the 1936 labor conflict disclosed that thousands of gardeners were not only alienated from the community leadership but were also capable of opposing certain decisions of the community establishment without fearing retaliation.

CONCLUSION

At the turn of the twentieth century, a growing number of Japanese immigrants, attracted by higher wages, came to specialize in gardening on a contractual basis. Since many issei had worked as farm laborers or domestic servants upon arrival in America, it was relatively easy to go into this trade. When the 1923 Alien Land Law finally prohibited the Japanese from engaging in agriculture in any capacity other than as farm hands, many issei agricultural workers and tenant farmers turned to yard maintenance in the urban areas. The Japanese exclusion from California agriculture coincided with the rapid urbanization of Los Angeles, which provided displaced Japanese immigrants with gardening routes. Advantages such as small capital requirements, good remuneration, and the sense of being one's own boss made this occupation increasingly popular among the issei. Because the Japanese had already been recognized as skilled horticulturists by the early 1920s, yard maintenance helped thousands of Japanese Americans survive the Great Depression.

The majority of prewar Japanese gardeners were issei who had migrated to this country so late that they were excluded from independent farming following the passage of the Alien Land Laws. These gardeners constituted a stratum of the petite bourgeoisie that differed

from small businessmen or landed farmers in terms of class consciousness. Yard maintenance was a variation of farm labor and domestic
work combined, although the gardeners were self-employed and generally derived a higher income than laborers. Because of the nature of the
work they performed, the gardeners were treated as manual laborers
and were not highly regarded by the Japanese community leadership,
which consisted of big farmers and successful merchants. While forming an intermediate class between the proletariat and big business
owners, the Japanese gardeners felt antagonistic toward the community
establishment and identified more with the working class. The 1936
Venice farm labor strike revealed the gardeners' prolabor stance.

Most prewar Japanese gardeners clung to this trade as though it were
their lifetime calling. In view of the profitability of their work, it would
have been possible for a considerable number of gardeners to move on
to other types of economic activities, but such mobility was uncommon.
Few of the issei gardeners were ashamed of their occupation. As a
matter of fact, the majority of them had a positive attitude toward
horticultural work and made the most of it. At least for thousands of
urban issei residents, of all the available jobs in the prewar period, yard
maintenance was the best thing they could find in terms of income and
the nature of work involved.

During the Great Depression, the influx of unemployed workers into
the gardening industry, coupled with a threatened exclusion movement
in Beverly Hills, caused the issei gardeners to form three associations,
which were later organized into a federation. Although the associations'
primary function was strictly social, these institutions played a significant role in protecting their members' interests. The associations operated *tanomoshiko* to provide low-interest loans, sponsored lectures and
field trips to raise the professional standard of Japanese gardeners, and
occasionally interceded for their members in cases of route grabbing.
Because of the fragmented structure of gardening as an occupation, the
associations were more like trade guilds than labor unions. Although
they proved quite effective in solving such internal problems as route
snatching among their members, small-scale financing, and improve-
ment of gardening skills, their most important contribution was to give
their members a strong sense of security and group solidarity.

The Southern California Japanese Gardeners Federation, by contrast,
was entrusted with the task of dealing with external problems that
were beyond the power of the member associations. The federation
undertook the collection of arrears with the assistance of a legal coun-
sel, negotiated with municipal authorities to have the city of Los Angeles
collect rubbish, and made a feeble attempt to stabilize gardening fees.

While attaining some success in the area of retrieving overdue wages, the umbrella organization had no control over City Hall's policy on rubbish disposal, nor over the fixing of maintenance fees which were determined basically by the law of supply and demand. Outnumbered by unorganized gardeners at a ratio of three to one, the federation members were never numerous enough to exert any influence on municipal politics or to make nonmembers honor the prevailing monthly rate. Undoubtedly, the fact that Japanese immigrants were "aliens ineligible for citizenship" contributed to their political impotence.

Since neither the associations nor the federation were labor unions in the conventional sense, the Japanese gardeners' organizations were in no position to negotiate a pay raise with property owners. Furthermore, because gardening was actually an individual contracting business, there existed no labor-capital relationship between the gardeners and their customers. To make matters more complicated, it was virtually impossible to standardize gardening fees owing to the great variety of yards and gardens in terms of size, terrain, and extent of maintenance required. The fact that each gardener worked separately for a different set of owners meant that the owners themselves were not organized, while the gardeners each experienced a unique set of work conditions. For these reasons, the federation was hardly successful in coping with the external issues affecting the gardening population. Nonetheless, considering its structure and the resultant limitations, it was obvious that there was little this umbrella organization could do to transform the gardeners into a genuine labor union.

The federation was headed by several able Issei immigrants who provided the rank and file with progressive leadership. Some of the objectives these leaders attempted to achieve, such as forming a coalition with white gardeners and joining the AFL or CIO, were certainly way ahead of their time. As the Venice celery strike of 1936 illustrated, the influential representatives of Issei gardeners were not only prolabor but were also able to take an independent stand in defiance of the community establishment. Because the gardeners depended little on the Japanese community for their livelihood, they were relatively immune from intimidation and sanction by the community hierarchy. Before the majority of the federation members came to fully understand the farsighted views expressed by their leaders, this institution was forced to dissolve in the wake of the Pearl Harbor attack. The policies promoted by the leadership, however, survived the war years and served as a guiding principle when Japanese gardeners in the mid-1950s founded a powerful federation based on the prewar prototype.

NOTES

1. Torajiro Watanabe, "Doho Hatten to Gadena," *Gadena no Tomo*, no. 39 (July 1940):6.

2. According to the 1970 census, this region had 123,327 Japanese American residents, who comprised 33,881 households. Since almost every gardener was the head of a household, gardening families constituted roughly 23 percent of the total Japanese American households in Southern California. See U.S. Bureau of the Census, *1970 Census of Population: Japanese, Chinese, and Filipinos in the United States* (Washington, D.C., 1973), pp. 40, 50.

3. Enclosure, Japan. Gaimusho, *Nihon Gaiko Bunsho*, 32 (Tokyo, 1955), p. 655.

4. Nanka Nikkeijin Shogyo Kaigisho (hereafter NNSK), *Nankashu Nihonjin Shichijunenshi* (Los Angeles, 1960), p. 186.

5. Among the Japanese in Southern California, "uptown Los Angeles" referred to the area surrounded by Ninth Street on the north, Pico Boulevard on the south, Vermont Avenue on the east, and Western Avenue on the west.

6. Personal interview.

7. Personal interview.

8. NNSK, *Nankashu Nihonjinshi* (Los Angeles, 1956), pp. 93-95.

9. A survey conducted by the Japanese Association of Los Angeles revealed that, as of August 1918, 15,320 Japanese Americans resided in Southern California. See NNSK, *Nankashu Nihonjinshi*, p. 368.

10. Shinzo Toda and Hisato Horie, *Hanka no Nihonjin* (Tokyo, 1919), p. 55.

11. Shiro Fujioka, *Ayumi no Ato* (Los Angeles, 1957), p. 528.

12. Shoji Nagumo, *Gadena Goroku* (Los Angeles, 1970), p. 186.

13. In 1935, Japanese farmers and farm laborers numbered 8,000 and 18,000, respectively. See the *Shinsekai Asahi Shimbun* (August 3, 1935).

14. Shinichi Kato, *Beikoku Nikkeijin Hyakunenshi* (Los Angeles, 1961), p. 49.

15. *Shinsekai Asahi Shimbun* (November 20, 1931).

16. *Rafu Shimpo* (October 22, 1931).

17. *Kashu Mainichi* (May 22, 1932).

18. *Rafu Shimpo* (April 19, 1932).

19. *Rafu Nichibei* (May 14, 1932).

20. *Kashu Mainichi* (May 28, 1932).

21. *Rafu Shimpo* (April 12, 1933).

22. Personal interview. Karl Yoneda, *Zaibei Nihonjin Rodosha no Rekishi* (Tokyo, 1967), pp. 87-88, 101-102.

23. *Rafu Shimpo* (March 26, 1936).

24. Zaibei Nihonjinkai, *Zaibei Nihonjinshi* (San Francisco, 1940), p. 859.

25. Mizuchi Murai, *Zaibei Nihonjin Sangyo Soran* (Los Angeles, 1940), p. 576.

26. Personal interview. Leonard Bloom and Ruth Riemer found that in 1941, Japanese gardeners earned $100 to $300 per month depending on their skills and experience. See Leonard Bloom and Ruth Riemer, *Removal and Return: The Socio-Economic Effects of the War on Japanese Americans* (Berkeley and Los Angeles, 1949), p. 116.

27. James Oda, *Aru Nikkei Beihei no Shuki* (Tokyo, 1973), pp. 40, 44, 66-67.

28. U.S. Department of the Interior, War Agency Liquidation Unit, *People in Motion: The Postwar Adjustment of the Evacuated Japanese Americans* (Washington, D.C., 1974), p. 94.

29. Akira Kotobuki, "Teien Gyosha no Kako Genzai to Shorai," *Gadena no Tomo* 22, no. 2 (March 1977):8.

30. Nagumo, *Gadena Goroku*, p. 89; Nobuo Noda, "Chingin Neage Mondai to Nippakujin Kumiai Teikei," *Gadena no Tomo*, no. 51 (July 1941):10.

31. Kenichi Fujioka, "Schoolboy," *Gadena no Tomo*, no. 53 (September 1941):9.

32. Personal interview and interview with Bay Cities Gardeners Association.

33. Nagumo, *Gadena Goroku*, p. 85.

34. U.S. Bureau of the Census, *Fifteenth Census of the United States, 1930: Population*, I (Washington, D.C., 1931), pp. 128, 133.

35. Nagumo, *Hokujin Nagumo Shoji no Iko: Ichi Paionia no Jijo* (Los Angeles, 1978), pp. 11-95, passim.

36. Personal interview. Bloom and Riemer established that prior to World War II, a gardener's initial investment averaged approximately $400. See Bloom and Riemer, *Removal and Return*, p. 117.

37. Nagumo, *Gadena Goroku*, pp. 11-15, 86, 115, 525, 568, 584.

38. *The Shinsekai Asahi Shimbun* (August 3, 1935).

39. The "kibei" are the American-born children of Japanese immigrants, who were sent to Japan in their infancy or childhood in order to receive Japanese education, and who later returned to the United States, speaking Japanese as their primary language.

40. Bloom and Riemer, *Removal and Return*, pp. 117-118.

41. Rafu Shimpo, *Rafu Nenkan* (Los Angeles, 1939), p. 58.

42. Tsugio Fujimoto, "Seirin Mitamama Kiitamama," *Gadena no Tomo*, no. 39 (July 1940):8.

43. Yoneda, *Zaibei Nihonjin*, p. 106.

44. *Rafu Shimpo* (May 18 & 19, 1932).

45. *Kashu Mainichi* (May 20 & 21, 1932).

46. *Rafu Shimpo* (May 24, 1932).

47. Ibid. (May 23, 1932).

48. *Rafu Nichibei* (May 23, 1932).

49. Nagumo, *Gadena Goroku*, p. 83.

50. Tanzo Toyofuku, "Nento Shokan," *Gadena no Tomo*, no. 45 (January 1941):3.

51. Personal interview.

52. *Gadena no Tomo*, no. 47 (March 1941), 11-12. Some informed Japanese sources estimated that by the early 1930s, the number of Japanese gardeners rose to 4,000. See *Shinsekai Asahi Shimbun* (October 20, 1931) and *Kashu Mainichi* (April 18, 1933).

53. Personal interview; *Gadena no Tomo*, no. 40 (August 1940):16.

54. *Gadena no Tomo*, no. 40 (August 1940):10.

55. *Gadena no Tomo*, no. 47 (March 1941): 11; Ibid., no. 48 (April 1941):10; Ibid., no. 49 (May 1941):12.

56. Kinji Inoue, *Kashu Nihonjin Kaengyo Hattenshi* (San Francisco, 1929), p. 127.

57. Personal interview.

58. *Gadena no Tomo*, no. 53 (September 1941):10.

59. Personal interview.

60. Watanabe, "Gadena Kumiai no Na o Riyoshita Jiken," *Gadena no Tomo*, no. 40 (August 1940):6.

61. Nobuyoshi Nakamura, "Gochui Onegai," *Gadena no Tomo*, no. 37 (May 1940): 14; Nagumo, "Komon Bengoshi Riyoseyo," Ibid., no. 41 (September 1940): 8-9.

62. Nakamura, "Jinjibu Hokoku narabini Kongo no Hoshin," *Gadena no Tomo*, no. 46 (February 1941):15.

63. Nakamura, "Gochui Onegai," *Gadena no Tomo*, no. 38 (June 1940):14.

64. Nakamura, "Jinjibu Hokoku narabini Kongo no Hoshin," *Gadena no Tomo*, no. 46 (February 1941):15.

65. Nakamura, "Jinjibu Hokoku," *Gadena no Tomo*, no. 41 (September 1940):15.

66. Nakamura, "Gochui Onegai," *Gadena no Tomo*, no. 38 (June 1940):14.

67. Nakamura, "Jinjibu Hokoku," *Gadena no Tomo*, no. 41 (September 1940): 15; Nakamura, "Jinji Seiji," Ibid., no. 42 (October 1940):15; Nakamura, "Nishi Rafu Kumiai Iho," Ibid., no. 47. (March, 1941):11.

68. Nakamura, "Jinji Seiji," *Gadena no Tomo*, no. 44 (December 1940):8; Shinsei Yukichi, "Chingin Neage ni Tsuite," Ibid., no. 54. (October 1941):1.

69. *Gadena no Tomo*, no. 36 (April 1940):1.

70. Noda, "Chingin Neage," p. 10.

71. Nagumo, "Rabishi Mondai ni Kansuru Ikensho," *Gadena no Tomo,* no. 49 (May 1941):2.

72. Personal interview.

73. Nagumo, "Rabishi Mondai no Nariyuki," *Gadena no Tomo,* no. 52 (August 1941):1. In June 1941, one gardener was fined and jailed, because he had picked up an old newspaper on the lawn of one of his customers and had thrown it into an adjacent vacant lot. See "Uwamachi Kembunki," *Gadena no Tomo,* no. 51 (July 1941):8.

74. Personal interview; *Gadena no Tomo,* no. 41 (September 1940):10.

75. "Seirin Kumiai Iho," *Gadena no Tomo,* no. 38 (June 1940):8; "Seirin-ran," Ibid., no. 42 (October 1940):8; Fujimoto, "Seirin Mitamama Kiitamama," Ibid., no. 47 (March 1941): 13.

76. "Seirin Kumiai Iho," *Gadena no Tomo,* no. 45 (January 1941):12; Hariuddo Kumiai Iho," Ibid., no. 46 (February 1941):12.

77. Iwakichi Hayashida, "Rabishi Mondai ni Tsuite," *Gadena no Tomo,* no. 49 (May 1941):1; "Shiyakusho Tokyokusha to no Kondankai," Ibid., p. 15.

78. "Rabishi Mondai ni Kansuru Ikensho," *Gadena no Tomo,* no. 49 (May 1941):2.

79. Nakamura, "Ware Ware no Mondai." *Gadena no Tomo,* no. 52 (August 1941):15.

80. Hayashida, "Kita Seirin Hakujin Kumiai Shukai ni Shussekishite," *Gadena no Tomo,* no. 50 (June 1941):1; Nagumo, "Kyodo Sensen," Ibid., no. 51 (July 1941):8.

81. Noda, "Chingin Neage," p. 10.

82. Nakamura, "Ware Ware no Mondai," *Gadena no Tomo,* no. 53 (September 1941):15.

83. Nagumo, "Keikirai," *Gadena no Tomo,* no. 53 (September 1941):1.

84. Some of the objectives of the California Farm Laborers Association were as follows: (1) To improve the working conditions of farm laborers. (2) To establish the right to collective bargaining. (3) To abolish all anti-Japanese laws. (4) To join the American Federation of Labor. Boasting a membership of 1,000, the association published a monthly organ entitled, "Noen Rodosha (Farm Laborers)." See Yoneda, *Zaibei Nihonjin,* p.94.

85. *Kashu Mainichi* (April 17, 1936).

86. *Rafu Shimpo* (March 27 & April 18, 1936).

87. *Kashu Mainichi* (April 20, 1936).

88. Ibid. (April 25, May 24, 26, & 27, 1936).

89. *Rafu Shimpo* (April 27, 1936).

90. Ibid. (May 11, 1936); *Kashu Mainichi* (May 26 & 29, 1936); Yoneda, *Zaibei Nihonjin,* p. 96.

91. The Rodo Kyoyukai dates back to 1906, when Japanese domestic workers in San Francisco and Richmond established, respectively, the Kyorokai (Cooperative Labor Society) and the Koyukai (Friendship Society), with a view to coping with the mounting anti-Japanese movement. In 1910, the two organizations merged to form the Rodo Kyoyukai, which later spread out to other major Japanese communities. See Yoneda, *Zaibei Nihonjin,* p. 59.

92. *Kashu Mainichi* (May 25 & 26, 1936). Shoji Nagumo, Nobuyoshi Nakamura, and Shigemori Tamashiro spoke at the forum on behalf of the Japanese gardeners.

93. *Rafu Shimpo* (June 8, 1936).

94. *Gadena no Tomo,* no. 53 (September 1941):10.

References

Bloom, Leonard, and Ruth Riemer
    1949   Removal and Return: The Socio-Economic Effects of the War on Japanese Americans. Berkeley and Los Angeles: University of California Press.
Fujimoto, Tsugio
    1940   "Seirin mitamama kiitamama." Gadena no Tomo 39 (July):8.
    1941   "Seirin mitamama kiitamama." Gadena no Tomo 47 (March):13.
Fujioka, Kenichi
    1941   "Schoolboy." Gadena no Tomo 53 (September):9.
Fujioka, Shiro
    1957   Ayumi no Ato. Los Angeles.
Gadena no Tomo. April 1940, June 1940, August 1940, September 1940, October 1940, January 1941, February 1941, March 1941, April 1941, May 1941, July 1941, September 1941.
Gaimusho
    1955   Nihon Gaiko Bunsho. Vol. 32. Tokyo.
Hayashida, Iwakichi
    1941a   "Rabishi mondai ni tsuite." Gadena no Tomo 49 (May):1.
    1941b   "Kita seirin hakujin kumiai shukai ni shussekishite." Gadena no Tomo 50 (June):1.
Inoue, Kinji
    1929   Kashu Nihonjin Kaengyo Hattenshi. San Francisco.
Kashu Mainichi. May 22, 1932; May 28, 1932; April 17, 1936; April 20, 1936; April 25, 1936; May 24, 1936; May 25, 1936; May 26, 1936; May 27, 1936; May 29, 1936.
Kato, Shinichi
    1961   Beikoku Nikkeijin Hyakunenshi. Los Angeles.
Kotobuki, Akira
    1977   "Teien Gyosha no Kako genzai to shorai." Gadena no Tomo 22, no. 2 (March):8.
Murai, Mizuchi
    1940   Zaibei Nihonjin Sangyo Soran. Los Angeles.
Nagumo, Shoji
    1940   "Komon bengoshi riyoseyo." Gadena no Tomo 41 (September):8-9.
    1941a   "Rabishi mondai ni kansuru ikensho." Gadena no Tomo 49 (May):2.
    1941b   "Kyodo sensen." Gadena no Tomo 51 (July):8.
    1941c   "Rabishi mondai no nariyuki." Gadena no Tomo 52 (August):1.
    1941d   "Keikirai." Gadena no Tomo 53 (September):1.
    1970   Gadena Goroku. Los Angeles.
    1978   Hokujin Nagumo Shoji no Iko: Ichi Paionia no Jijo. Los Angeles.
Nakamura, Nobuyoshi
    1940a   "Gochui onegai." Gadena no Tomo 37 (May):14.
    1940b   "Gochui onegai." Gadena no Tomo 38 (June):14.
    1940c   "Jinjibu hokoku." Gadena no Tomo 41 (September):15.
    1940d   "Jinji seiji." Gadena no Tomo 42 (October):15.
    1940e   "Jinji seiji." Gadena no Tomo 44 (December):8.

1941a "Jinjibu hokoku narabini kongo no hoshin." Gadena no Tomo 46 (February):15.
1941b "Nishi rafu kumiai iho." Gadena no Tomo 47 (March):11.
1941c "Ware ware no mondai." Gadena no Tomo 52 (August):15.
1941d "Ware ware no mondai." Gadena no Tomo 53 (September):15.
Nanka Nikkeijin Shogyo Kaigisho
1956   Nankashu Nihonjinshi. Los Angeles.
1960   Nankashu Nihonjin Shichijunenshi. Los Angeles.
Noda, Nobuo
1941   "Chingin neage mondai to Nippakujin kumiai teikei." Gadena no Tomo 51 (July):10.
Oda, James
1973   Aru Nikkei Beihei no Shuki. Tokyo.
Rafu Nichibei. May 14, 1932.
Rafu Shimpo. March 3, 1926; October 22, 1931; April 19, 1932; April 12, 1933; March 27, 1936; April 18, 1936; April 27, 1936; June 8, 1936.
1939   Rafu Nenkan. Los Angeles.
Shinsekai Asahi Shimbun. November 20, 1931; August 3, 1935.
Toda, Shinzo, and Hisato Horie
1919   Nanka no Nihonjin. Tokyo.
Toyofuku, Tanzo
1943   "Nento Shokan." Gadena no Tomo 45 (January):3.
U.S. Bureau of the Census
1931   Fifteenth Census of the United States, 1930: Population, I. Washington, D.C.: Government Printing Office.
1973   1970 Census of Population: Japanese, Chinese, and Filipinos in the United States. Washington, D.C.: Government Printing Office.
U.S. Department of the Interior, War Agency Liquidation Unit.
1974   People in Motion: The Postwar Adjustment of the Evacuated Japanese Americans. Washington, D.C.: Government Printing Office.
Watanabe, Torajiro
1940a "Doho hatten to Gadena." Gadena no Tomo 39 (July):6.
1940b "Gadena Kumiai no na o riyoshita jiken." Gadena no Tomo 40 (August):6.
Yoneda, Karl
1967   Zaibei Nihonjin Rodosha no Rekishi. Tokyo.
Yukichi, Shinsei
1941   "Chingin neage ni tsuite." Gadena no Tomo 54 (October):1.
Zaibei Nihonjinkai
1940   Zaibei Nihonjinshi. San Francisco.

14

The Dialectics of Wage Work: Japanese-American Women and Domestic Service, 1905-1940

Evelyn Nakano Glenn

INTRODUCTION

The work of women has been a much neglected topic in the economic and social history of Japanese Americans. Yet, from the moment they arrived, Japanese-American women labored alongside the men to secure their own and their families' livelihood.[1] Although much of their work took the form of unpaid labor on family farms and businesses, many women turned to wage work to supplement family income. Until World War II, the most common form of nonagricultural employment for the immigrant women (*issei*) and their American-born daughters (*nisei*) was domestic service.

As was true for immigrant women from other rural societies, domestic work served as a port of entry into the urban labor force.[2] The demand for domestic help among urban middle-class families ensured a constant pool of jobs, but the occupation's low status and unfavorable working conditions made it unattractive to those who could secure other kinds of jobs. Thus, the field was left open to the newcomer and the minority woman.[3]

For European immigrants, domestic service was a temporary way station. By the second generation, they had moved into the expanding, white collar clerical and sales occupations.[4] The Japanese, however, like blacks and other minorities, were barred from most industrial and office settings.[5] Thus, Japanese women remained heavily concentrated in domestic work even into the second generation. Only after World War II did institutional racism diminish sufficiently to enable the nisei and their children to move into other occupations. Involvement in domestic service was thus an important shared experience for Japanese women in the prewar years, serving as one basis for ethnic and gender solidarity.[6]

This chapter examines that experience, using the case of issei women in the San Francisco Bay Area in the period from 1905 to 1940. The account is based primarily on interviews with domestic workers and community informants.[7] The first three sections describe the historical context in which issei women's specialization in domestic work evolved: the development of Bay Area Japanese communities, the arrival of issei women, and the labor market structure they confronted. The next five sections give a detailed account of domestic workers' experiences: the circumstances leading to involvement in domestic work, the entry socialization process, the conditions of work, relations with employers, and the interaction between the women's wage work and their unpaid work in the family.

What is highlighted in this account is the contradiction between the multiple forms of oppression to which the women were subjected and the resilience that they developed.[8] Issei domestic workers were subjugated by institutional racism, by conditions of work in domestic employment, and by the structure of issei family life; yet, they were not passive victims, but active participants shaping their own lives. Faced with oppression, issei women strived, often in covert and indirect ways, to gain control over their work and other aspects of their lives. Out of this effort, I argue, grew a sense of autonomy and self-reliance that enabled them to transcend the limitations of their circumstances and gain a measure of satisfaction from essentially menial work.

HISTORY OF BAY AREA JAPANESE COMMUNITIES

I begin by examining the historical context in which Japanese women's involvement in domestic work developed. The pre-World War II history of Japanese communities in the San Francisco Bay Area can be divided into three periods: frontier, settlement, and stabilization, each demarcated by specific historical events that shaped the immigrants' lives.[9]

The frontier period, roughly 1890 to 1910, was when the first wave of immigrants arrived. The issei were remarkably homogeneous, and most of the immigrants were young single males from rural villages in southern Japan, with an average of eight years of education.[10] They came as sojourners, expecting to work a few years to amass sufficient capital to establish themselves in Japan. They started out as unskilled wage laborers in agriculture, railroading, mining, and lumbering, or in domestic service.[11] Later, as they accumulated capital and know-how, many launched small enterprises, usually laundries or stores. In place of their old kin ties, the issei men formed mutual aid associations with others from the same prefecture (*Kenjinkai*) and organized rotating credit associations (*tanomoshi*) to raise capital.[12]

Up until 1907, San Francisco, as a port city, was one of three main centers of Japanese population. [13] The Japanese congregated in a section of the Western Addition, a district of low-rent rundown housing that became known as Little Osake. From San Francisco, the issei spread to other cities in the East Bay. By 1910, the Japanese populations of the four main cities were: San Francisco, 4,518; Oakland, 1,520; Berkeley, 710; and Alameda, 499.[14]

Growing anti-Japanese agitation led to a series of legal measures designed to reduce immigration and to discourage permanent settlement. The 1907 "Gentlemen's Agreement" between Japan and the United States closed entry to laborers. Between 1910 and 1929, more men returned to Japan than entered.[15] However, those who remained began to think in terms of a longer stay. The "Gentlemen's Agreement" contained a loophole: it permitted the entry of wives and relatives. The issei began returning to Japan to marry and bring back wives or began sending for picture brides.

The arrival of issei women marks the beginning of the settlement period. Between 1909 and 1923, over 33,000 issei wives immigrated.[16] During this period of family and community building, the sex ratio became less skewed, and the population came to include children as well as adults. Extensive infrastructures developed with the establishment of ethnic churches, newspapers, language schools, and business and service establishments.[17] Ethnic enclaves formed in San Francisco's Western Addition, on the borders of Chinatown in downtown Oakland, and around City Hall in Alameda. Except for jobs, the issei could fulfill most of their social and material wants within the ethnic community. According to one observer, "Very few Japanese ventured beyond those comfortable environs."[18]

Meanwhile, partly in response to more permanent settlement, anti-Japanese sentiment grew. An Alien Land Law was passed in California in 1913, prohibiting the issei, who were ineligible for citizenship, from owning land or leasing it for more than three years. Finally, the Immigration Act of 1924 cut off all further immigration from Asia.[19]

The end of immigration marks the start of the stabilization period, 1924 to 1940. Henceforth, the growth of population depended entirely on births. There was little room for expansion of ethnic enterprises serving a largely Japanese clientele. Thus, the issei found their opportunities shrinking and began to pin their hopes for the future on their children, who by virtue of American citizenship had rights denied their parents.[20]

The restriction on immigration also created distinct generational cohorts. The majority of issei were born between 1870 and 1900, and their children, the nisei, were born mainly between 1910 and 1940. By the mid-1930s, the issei were primarily middle-aged, while the eldest nisei were just reaching maturity and entering the labor force. Despite American citizenship and education, the nisei confronted the same racist restrictions as their parents; they were still barred from union jobs and employment in white-run offices and stores. It is unclear what course ethnic assimilation would have taken over the next decade under normal circumstances, for the Japanese community was shattered almost overnight by the commencement of World War II. The Japanese were evacuated and incarcerated in concentration camps. Those who returned to the Bay Area after the war settled in scattered areas, rather than concentrating in the old enclaves, so the old physical communities were never fully reconstituted.

ISSEI WOMEN

Most of the issei women who arrived in the United States between 1907 and 1924 were from the same southern rural backgrounds as the male immigrants. They had levels of education comparable to the men: the fifteen issei domestics in the study averaged six years of education, with two having no schooling and two having completed ten years, the equivalent of high school. The typical issei woman was in her early twenties and was married to a man ten years her senior who had lived for some years in the United States, working as a wage laborer or small entrepreneur.[21]

Following Japanese custom, the marriages were arranged by the families of the bride and groom through a go-between (baishakunin). Many issei men managed to save or borrow money to return to Japan to meet their prospective brides and to get married. In such cases, the match was arranged by the go-between through an exchange of photographs, hence the term "picture marriage." The union was legalized by registering it in the husband's home prefecture.

For the most part, the women felt they had little say in the selection of a husband; daughters were expected to go along with their parents' judgment. Yet, the extent to which women felt forced or manipulated by their parents and by circumstances varied.[22]

At one extreme is Mrs. Takagi,[23] who recalls that her father tricked her into going to stay with her adopted grandfather on the pretext that she would receive training to become a midwife:

> Otherwise, I wouldn't have gone, you see. I knew my mother needed help. . . . I stayed one week and helped my uncle [a doctor]. I was thinking I would stay to help him. Pretty soon, they took me to see this man. I'd never seen or heard of him. He was my second cousin. You don't know the Japanese system: they just pick out your husband and tell you what to do. So, I just did it, that's all. . . . I never gave my parents a fight.

Another issei, Mrs. Nishimura, falls somewhere in the middle of the continuum. She was only fifteen when she was persuaded by her father to marry Mr. Nishimura:

> In the Japanese style, we used a go-between and the husband would come to Japan to pick up his bride. My father was rather new in his thinking, so he told me that rather than stay in Japan to attend school, I should come to the U.S. My mother told me even then that I was too young. But, it's something that had to be done so. . . . I was rather big for my age, and . . . but I cried at the time, and I'll always remember that. My parents felt a little guilty about it, almost as if they had forced me to come, and apparently they kept asking about me, about how I was doing, until they died.

At the other extreme, we have Mrs. Shinoda who claims she dreamed of going to the United States even as a child:

> I told my father that I wouldn't get married unless I could come to the United States. [Did your parents oppose you?] Yes, they were all against me. [How did you know you wanted to come to the United States?] I don't know. When I was small, in elementary school, we had to write an essay on "What I Wish For." I wrote in that essay that I'd like to go to America. My friends read and told what I had written. That's funny, huh?

Mrs. Shinoda was stubborn enough to hold out until her father gave in. She didn't marry until she was twenty-eight, but she got her way.

In leaving their families and going to the United States, the issei women were following usual Japanese practice. Custom dictated that a woman leave her parents' household or village to live in her husband's home. The issei were simply traveling a much greater geographic and cultural distance.[24] Despite the pain of separation and fear of the unknown, the majority of the women said they left Japan with positive expectations. Just as the men came to the United States to better their lot, issei women came with their own hopes: to further their education, to help their families economically, to seek a happier home life, and to experience new adventures.

The boat trip to the United States, usually from Yokohama to Seattle or San Francisco, normally took over a month. The women report feelings of homesickness and physical illness, although they also recall fondly the friendships they developed with other women during the voyage. Upon arrival; the women confronted many new and strange experiences. The first shock for the picture brides was meeting their new spouses. Mrs. Yoshida, who traveled with a number of other picture brides, recalls the responses of some of her companions upon catching glimpses of their husbands:

> A lot of people that I came together with said, "I'm going back on this very boat." I told them, "You can't do that; you should go ashore once. If you really don't like him, and you feel like going back, then you have to have a meeting and then go back. . . ." Many times, the picture was taken twenty years earlier and they had changed. Many of the husbands had gone to the country to work as farmers, so they had aged and became quite wrinkled. And very young girls came expecting more and it was natural.

As for herself, Mrs. Yoshida says she was disappointed that her husband (sixteen years her senior) looked much older than a neighbor at home the same age. However, many people from her village in Hiroshima had traveled to Hawaii and to the mainland United States, and she wanted to go too: "I didn't care what the man looked like."

The second shock was having to discard the comfort of kimonos and slippers for constricting dresses and shoes. The women were generally taken straight off after clearing immigration to be completely outfitted. Mrs. Nomura, who arrived in Seattle in 1919, said:

> At that time, ships were coming into Seattle every week from Japan, carrying one or two hundred Japanese brides. So, there was a store set up especially for these new arrivals. There was a hotel run by a Japanese and also Japanese food available. The Japanese wouldn't go to the stores run by whites, so there were stores run by Japanese to deal with Japanese customers. We did all of our shopping there. The lady there would show us how to use a corset—since we had never used one in Japan. And how to wear stockings and shoes.

Mrs. Okamura, who came in 1917, laughs when she remembers her first dress:

> It felt very tight. I couldn't even move my arms. That was the first time I had ever worn Western clothes, so I thought they were supposed to be like that. . . . Later, Mrs. S. taught me to sew my own clothes. She had a pattern that we all used to make the same dress in different materials. So I found out that first dress was too small.

As Mrs. Okamura's account indicates, earlier immigrants taught new arrivals "the ropes," and living quarters were usually secured within the ghetto. Many couples rented rooms in a house and shared kitchen and bathroom facilities with several other Japanese families. Thus, help and comfort were close at hand. Mrs. Horiuchi says the best time in her life was when she was a new bride, just after arriving in the United States. All her husband's friends dropped in to welcome her and bring gifts. Sometimes, husbands who had worked as "schoolboys" or domestics taught their wives how to shop, cook, and clean. Community agencies such as the YWCA, and the public schools, sponsored housekeeping and English courses for newcomers. Most of the women in the study took some of these classes but claimed that they were unable to continue their studies once children arrived. Partly for this reason, most never fully mastered English. Another reason was that the women rarely ventured outside the confines of their ethnic community, except to do domestic work for wages. The ethnic community provided for most of their needs and insulated them from the hostility of the larger society.

The issei women arrived at a time of accelerating anti-Japanese agitation. Their arrival was itself a focus of attack because it signaled an intention on the part of the issei to settle on a long-term basis. Anti-Japanese propaganda depicted the practice of picture marriages as immoral and a ruse to contravene the Gentlemen's Agreement. As a result of mounting pressure, the Japanese government stopped issuing passports to picture brides in 1921.[25]

Mrs. Takagi was outspoken about the racism of the period, saying:

> I think all the [Japanese] people at that age had a real hard time. [They had to work hard, you mean?] Not only that, they were all thinking we were slaves, you know, sleeping in the stable upstairs. And even when we'd get on a streetcar, they'd say, "Jap, get away." Even me, they always threw stuff from up above. [They did? What do you mean?] I don't know why they did that. I was so scared. . . . One man, he was going on a bicycle and someone threw cement. That night he lost an

eye. But they never sued, they never reported it because they didn't
speak English. . . . I don't know what other people think, but we didn't
have very much fun. We didn't have very many jobs. A lot of people
graduated from college and still no job, before the war.

The issei downplay personal difficulties they encountered as a result
of racism. Although they were able to avoid hostile encounters by
remaining within their own world, it is clear nevertheless that their
lives were affected in a variety of ways, especially economically. Furthermore, discrimination reinforced the issei's sojourner orientation.
Mrs. Adachi notes that because of discrimination, her husband always
opposed putting down permanent roots, and they always rented apartments rather than buying a house, even after they could afford to do so.
Her husband also became increasingly nationalistic, keenly following
the political and military developments in Japan.

ECONOMIC ACTIVITIES OF ISSEI WOMEN

Issei women had little time to brood about their situations. Whether
rural or urban, they found they were expected to be full economic
contributors almost immediately upon arrival. Like other working-class
women of that era, they manufactured many basic household necessities, such as foodstuffs and clothing, as well as performed the maintenance and childcare tasks.[26] In addition, according to an early observer
of the issei:

> The great majority of wives of farmers, barbers and small shopkeepers
> take a more or less regular place in the fields or shops of their hus-
> bands, while a smaller number accept places in domestic service, or in
> laundries or other places of employment. Thus, a larger percentage of
> those admitted find a place in the "labor supply."[27]

According to U.S. census figures, 20.8 percent of all Japanese women
over age fifteen were gainfully employed in 1920. This proportion is
similar to the proportion of women employed in the overall population
(23.3 percent). However, because virtually all Japanese women over
fifteen were married, the issei rate of employment was remarkably
high. In the population at large, only 9.0 percent of all married women
were in the labor force.[28] Also, because Japanese men were concentrated in agriculture and small businesses, which relied on wives' unpaid
help, the extent of issei women's gainful activity is probably underestimated.

TABLE 14.1

OCCUPATIONS OF EMPLOYED JAPANESE WOMEN IN THE UNITED STATES, 1900-1940[a]

	1900		1920		1930		1940[b]	
	985		25,432		36,693		6,693	
Total females 10 years of age or older	Number	Percent	Number	Percent	Number	Percent	Number	Percent
Total females in gainful occupations	266	100.0	5,289	99.9[c]	6,741	100.0	6,693	100.0
Occupations								
Agricultural, including farm and nursery labor	13	4.9	1,797	34.0	2,041	30.3	2,525	37.7
Domestic service, including cooks, chambermaids, some waitresses and other servants	151	56.8	1,409	26.6	1,195	17.7	690	10.3
Other personal services, including barbers, waitresses, lodging house keepers, laundry operatives, etc.	57	21.4	951	18.0	1,463	21.7	1,579[d]	23.6
Trade, including saleswomen, clerks, etc.	9	3.4	369	7.0	946	14.0	683[e]	10.2
Dressmaking, seamstresses, tailors	23	8.6	124	2.3	121	1.8	NAp[f]	NAp
Other manufacturing, mechanical pursuits	8	3.0	378	7.1	348	5.2	810[g]	12.0
Professional services (teachers, nurses)	5	1.9	145	2.7	329	4.9	214	3.2
Clerical occupations	NAp.	NAp.	75	1.4	271	4.0	NAp[h]	NAp
Other	NAp	NAp	41	.8	27	.4	201	3.0

SOURCES: For 1900: U.S. Department of Commerce, Bureau of the Census Special Reports, *Occupations of the Twelfth Census* (Washington, D.C.: U.S. Government Printing Office, 1904), table 35: Distribution, by Specified Occupations, of Males and of Females in the Chinese, Japanese, and Indian Population Gainfully Employed, 1900.

For 1920: U.S. Department of Commerce, Bureau of the Census, *Fourteenth Census of the United States Taken in the Year 1920*, vol. 4, *Population, Occupations* (Washington, D.C.: Government Printing Office, 1923), table 5: Total Persons of 10 Years of Age and Over Engaged in Each Specified Occupation: Classified by Sex, Color, or Race, Nativity, and Parentage, for the United States, 1920.

For 1930: U.S. Department of Commerce, Bureau of the Census, *Fifteenth Census of the United States*, vol. 5, *Population*, General Report on Occupations (Washington, D.C.: Government Printing Office, 1933), table 6: Chinese and Japanese Gainful Workers 10 Years Old and Over by Occupation and Sex, for the United States and Selected States, 1930.

For 1940: U.S. Department of Commerce, Bureau of the Census, *Sixteenth Census of the Population, 1940. Population Characteristics of the Non-White Population by Race* (Washington, D.C.: Government Printing Office, 1943), table 8: Non-White Employed Persons 14 Years Old and Over, By Major Occupation Group, Race, and Sex, for the United States, by Regions, Urban and Rural, 1940.

[a] Data for 1910 are omitted because occupational figures for Japanese and Chinese were combined in the census report.

[b] Only foreign-born (issei) women are included in the figures for 1940. The 1940 census for the first time separated out native and foreign born. The figures for 1930 contain some native born (nisei), but they probably constitute only a small proportion of the total. Because of immigration patterns, most Nisei were born after 1910.

[c] Due to rounding.

[d] Consists of two categories, "Proprietors, managers, and officials, farm" and "Service workers, exc. domestic."

[e] The category is named "Clerical, sales and kindred workers" in the 1940 census.

[f] This category is no longer separately reported; presumably these occupations are included under manufacturing.

[g] This category is named "Operatives and kindred workers" in the 1940 census.

[h] Included in trade category, see also[e].

It is difficult to specify the occupational distribution of issei women, for the women frequently divided their time between housework, unpaid work in family farms and businesses, and paid employment. In these cases, the main occupation cannot be pinpointed. However, there are data that indicate the range of their activities. Edward K. Strong surveyed 1,716 issei women in a 1933 study of Japanese-American occupations. He classified 998 (58 percent) as housewives, 438 (26 percent) as full-time assistants, and 227 (13 percent) as engaged in independent occupations. He noted, however,

> Undoubtedly, the last two figures are too low and the first figures too high. Accuracy in this connection was very difficult to secure because many of these women speak very little English and are unaccustomed to talk to strangers, and in some cases the Japanese men prevented or interfered in the interviewing of their wives.[29]

There are similar limitations in the U.S. census data.[30] The figures in table 14.1, which show the occupational distributions for 1900, 1920, 1930 and 1940,[31] should be seen as a rough estimate of the proportion of women engaged in various fields. As table 14.1 shows, agricultural work, including work in plant nurseries (which was an early Japanese specialty), was the largest field of employment.[32] The figures also show that domestic service was by far the most common form of nonagricultural employment. In 1900, over one-half of all women were so employed; however, the numbers are so small as to make the data inconclusive. By 1920, domestic service accounted for 40.3 percent of all women engaged in nonagricultural occupations. Overall, there seems to have been a trend away from concentration in domestic work between 1920 and 1940.[33]

During this period, there was increased employment in personal service (which in the Bay Area was primarily laundry work) and in retail trade. The growth of employment in service and trade reflects the move of Japanese men away from wage labor into small enterprises, which employed women as paid and unpaid sales, service, and clerical workers. A small but steady percentage of women found work in manufacturing, primarily in food processing and garment manufacturing. With the establishment of ethnic community institutions, there was a small demand for professionals, such as teachers in Japanese language schools.

The occupations in which Japanese women specialized shared several characteristics. The work could be fit in around family responsibilities (for example, children could be taken to work, or the hours were flexible); they were an extension of women's work in the home (such as food preparation, laundry, and sewing); they were in low-technology, labor-intensive fields in which low wages and long hours reduced competition from white women; they took place in family-owned or ethnic enterprises in which language or racial discrimination did not constitute barriers to employment. Domestic service included the first three characteristics and was, therefore, consistent with the general run of occupations open to Japanese women. Because of the common characteristics of the occupations, one would expect the jobs to be highly substitutable. The job histories of the women support this expectation, for the women in the study moved easily between these occupations, although never outside them. The eleven women with experience in nondomestic employment had worked in one or more of the following fields: farming, hand laundry at home, embroidery at home, midwifery, and assisting in family-owned cleaning store, hotel, or nursery work. Domestic service, thus, can be seen as belonging to a set of occupations that constitute a distinct and narrow labor market for Japanese women.

Evidence from the 1940 census indicates that the labor market in the Bay Area was particularly restricted. A comparison of the proportion of issei women engaged in domestic work in four cities with substantial Japanese populations shows that domestic work was a specialty among issei women only in the Bay Area. Over one-fourth (26.8 percent) of all employed issei women in Oakland and over one-half (50.4) in San Francisco were found in domestic work. By contrast, only 6.4 percent of issei women in Los Angeles and 3.3 percent in Seattle were so employed. A comparison of the occupational distributions for women in Seattle and San Francisco, cities with comparable Japanese populations, is instructive. Nearly two-thirds of the Seattle women were employed as proprietors, service, and clerical workers (table 14.2). These figures reflect the

TABLE 14.2
MAIN OCCUPATIONS OF ISSEI WOMEN
IN SAN FRANCISCO AND SEATTLE, 1940

	Seattle		San Francisco	
	Number	Percent	Number	Percent
Total employed	611	100.0	367	100.0
Proprietors	11	18.2	41	11.2
Clerical	112	18.3	21	5.7
Operatives	143	23.4	58	15.8
Domestic	20	3.3	185	50.4
Service	167	27.3	28	7.6

SOURCE: U.S. Department of Commerce, Bureau of the Census, *Sixteenth Census of the Population: 1940. Population Characteristics of the Non-white Population by Race* (Washington, D.C.: Government Printing Office, 1943), table 38: Japanese Employed Persons 14 Years Old and Over, by Major Occupation, Group, City and Sex for Selected States, Urban and Rural, and for Selected Cities.

opportunities for small entrepreneurs in Seattle, where the issei ran hotels, restaurants, and shops catering to transient male laborers in lumbering and canning. Such opportunities were more limited in the Bay Area, leaving domestic work as the main employment for women and gardening as the main occupation for men.

ISSEI WOMEN'S ENTRY INTO DOMESTIC WORK

Having described the historical and economic context of issei women's wage labor in the Bay Area, I now turn to an analysis of the circumstances that came together in the lives of issei women to lead them into domestic service.

Unlike other immigrant groups that specialized in domestic service, these women did not have a prior tradition of service in their homelands. Generally, only indigent and unattached women became servants in Japan. Most of the immigrants who came to California were better off economically than the average rural peasant. They had sufficient resources to pay their fares and as much cash on hand as immigrants from northern Europe.[34] Thus, becoming a domestic worker meant a drop in status as well as a break with tradition. Given the lack of previous experience in wage labor generally, and a cultural prejudice against domestic service, the explanation for issei women's involvement in domestic work must lie in the situations they confronted in the United States.

One unusual historical circumstance was that the path into domestic work was paved by issei men starting in the early days of immigration. Many had gained their first footholds in the United States as "Japanese schoolboys." This designation was reportedly coined in the 1880s by a Mrs. Reid, who enrolled a few Japanese students in her boarding school in Belmont, California. These students earned their tuition and board by doing chores and kitchen work.[35] The term came to refer to any Japanese apprentice servant, whether or not he had any involvement in formal schooling. The job itself was the education: it provided the new immigrant with an opportunity to learn English and become familiar with American customs. In return for his services, the schoolboy received token wages of about $1.50 a week in 1900 ($2.00 a week by 1909), in addition to room and board, compared with the $15.00 to $40.00 a month earned by trained servants. It has been estimated that at the height of male immigration (1904 to 1907), over 4,000 Japanese were employed as schoolboys in San Francisco.[36]

Still other immigrants earned their first wages in the United States as dayworkers; they hired out to do yard chores and housecleaning on a daily or hourly basis. Groups of men from the same prefecture sometimes took lodgings together and advertised their services. Newcomers were invited to join the household and were quickly initiated into the work. H. A. Millis found 163 Japanese daywork firms listed in the 1913 San Francisco City Directory.[37] In addition, issei who had their own businesses sometimes acted as agents for dayworkers. Ads for a Japanese nursery included notices such as the following, which appeared in the *Alameda Daily Argus* in 1900: "Japanese Help. Also, first class Japanese help for cooking, general housework, or gardening, by day, week or month, furnished on short notice."

Both forms of domestic service were temporary stopgaps. Schoolboy jobs and daywork were frequent first occupations for new arrivals; after a short time, the issei moved on to agricultural or city trades.[38] In the Bay Area, many dayworkers graduated into a specialized branch of domestic service—gardening. The Japanese gardener became a status symbol, but the indoor male domestic had largely disappeared by 1930. The early association of men with domestic service, however, established the stereotype of the Japanese domestic—a stereotype inherited by the issei women when they arrived. The situations wanted columns in Bay Area newspapers, which before 1908 had been dominated by ads for Japanese schoolboys, now began to include ads for women, such as "Japanese girl wants situation to assist in general housework and taking care of baby. Address, Japanese Girl, 1973 P . . . Street."

The path into domestic service was, thus, clearly marked. The issue remains, what were the personal circumstances that launched many issei women on the journey?

The case of Mrs. Yoshida is a good place to begin. Ninety-one years old at the time of the interview, she arrived in 1909 as a picture bride. Her husband, sixteen years her senior, had lived in the United States for almost twenty years and had managed to acquire a laundry in Alameda, which the couple ran together. Because they had one of the few telephones in the Japanese community, they began acting as agents for dayworkers. Employers called to request help for cleaning or other jobs, and the Yoshidas referred the requests to the issei men who dropped by. By 1912, Mrs. Yoshida had two small children, and she felt that they needed extra income. She explains:

> I started to work because everyone went on vacation and the summer was very hard for us. The cleaning business declined during the summer. . . . I bought a second-hand bicycle from a friend who had used it for five years. I paid $3 for it. So, at night I went to the beach and practiced on that bicycle. At night nobody was at the beach, so even if I fell down, I didn't feel embarrassed. And then I went to work. I worked half a day and was paid $1. . . . We didn't know the first thing

about housework, but the ladies of the house didn't mind. They taught us how at the beginning: "This is a broom; this is a dustpan." And we worked hard for them. We always thought America was a wonderful country. At the time, we were thinking of working three years in America and then going back to Japan to help our parents lead a comfortable life. . . . But, we had babies almost every year, and so we had to give up that idea. [She had 10 children between 1910 and 1923.]

Although the specific details are unique, Mrs. Yoshida's account reveals several elements common to the lives of issei women who entered domestic work. First, the Yoshidas' intention of accumulating a nest egg and returning to Japan was shared by other immigrants during this period. The women in the study all claimed that they expected to return to Japan eventually. Many were sending remittances to support parents or other relatives in Japan. Because the sacrifice was seen as short term, the immigrants were willing to work long hours and in menial jobs. In this context, wage work could be viewed as a temporary expedient which, therefore, did not reflect on the family's social standing.

A second common element was the economic squeeze experienced by many issei families, especially after children arrived. Some families managed to accumulate enough capital to return to Japan.[39] Those who were less well off postponed their return and continued to struggle for day-to-day survival. The majority of women in the study were married to gardeners, whose earnings fluctuated. As Mrs. Yoshida's case illustrates, even those who owned small businesses found their marginal enterprises did not generate sufficient income to support a family. Some women were in even more dire straits: a husband who was ill, who refused to turn over his earnings, or who died and left children to support. Three women facing this situation took or sent their children to Japan to be cared for by relatives so they could work full-time.

Mrs. Shinoda was part of this group. Her husband, a college graduate, was killed in an accident in 1928. She was thirty-nine and had two young sons:

I started work after my husband died. I went to Japan to take my children to my mother. Then, I came back alone and started to work. . . . My sons were ten and eight . . . and I worked in a family. At that time, I stayed in the home of a professor at the University of California as a live-in maid. . . . I got the job through another Japanese person. She was going back to Japan, so I took her place. [What kind of things did you do?] Cleaned house, and cooking, and serving food. [Did you know how to cook and things like that?] No, I didn't at first. The lady told me.

Given the factors pushing the issei to seek wage work, what factors drew them particularly into domestic work? The basic limiting factor was the labor market situation described earlier. Race segregation, family responsibilities, and the lack of English and job skills severely limited job options. Given limited choices, domestic work offered some desirable features. Its main attraction was flexibility; those with heavy family responsibilities could work part-time, yet during times of financial pressure, they could work extra days or hours, as needed. A further pull was the demand for domestic labor. Dayworkers were sought by the growing number of middle-class urban families who could not afford regular servants. The demand was great enough so that, as Mrs. Yoshida and Mrs. Shinoda noted, employers were willing to take on someone with no experience and provide on-the-job training.

ENTRY AND SOCIALIZATION PROCESS

The know-how for obtaining and working in domestic jobs was widespread in the community as a result of the early experience of issei men in schoolboy jobs and in daywork. The women sometimes resorted to advertisements, but primarily they found employment through informal job networks. They heard about jobs through friends or acquaintances working as gardeners or domestics, and sometimes they inherited a position from another issei who was taking another job or returning to Japan. As the Japanese gained a reputation in domestic work, employers began to make requests through Japanese churches, businesses, and social organizations. Once one job was secured, other jobs were easily obtained through employer referrals.

Among the women in the study, two patterns of entry emerged. One pattern was to begin as an apprentice just as the Japanese schoolboys had done; in fact, some women used the term schoolgirl to refer to these positions. A schoolgirl job was typically entered soon after the woman's arrival and before she had children; she was more or less thrust into the position without a specific intention of beginning a career of domestic service. The job was arranged by a husband, relative, or friend. Wages were nominal, and in return, the employer provided training in housekeeping and cooking. Many of the issei women actually attended classes part-time to learn English. The job was, thus, intended as part of the socialization of the newcomer. However, in many cases, it portended the beginning of a career in domestic service.

The experience of Mrs. Takagi, who arrived as a nineteen-year-old in 1920, illustrates the entry into domestic service by way of a schoolgirl job. Mrs. Takagi's husband's parents had immigrated with him, and the couple lived with them in Oakland:

I was here 28 days, and my mother-in-law took me to the first job on the 29th day. So I didn't even know "yes or no." I was so scared to go out then. [She took the trolley.] I got off at — Street. I just did it the same way, counting "one, two, three stops." If I lost my way home, I couldn't ask anybody. . . . I couldn't hardly sleep at night. . . . The first time I went, she [employer] taught me all the things I said . . . they had a coal stove, a big one. Burned coal just like a Japanese hibachi. It has a pipe inside and heats the water from down below. I had to bring the coal up, all the time I went up and down. Then I had to wash diapers. Me, I grew up on a farm, so I never had to do that. When I came to America, I didn't know anything. So I just had to cry. She said, "What happened to your eyes?" Then she gave me $5.00 and gave me a note and said to take it home. . . . My mother [in-law] and father [in-law] said, "Oh, that's big money." They thought it was supposed to be $5.00 a month.

Mrs. Takagi was fortunate in having an employer who treated her as an apprentice and who encouraged her to attend English classes: "She put a hat on me, put a book in my hand, and gave me carfare. She said, 'Go to school.' " After six months, Mrs. Takagi went on to a general housekeeping job with a banker, and then with a widow, before finally settling into daywork.

The second pattern was to enter into daywork on a part-time basis after the arrival of children, when family expenses began to outrun income. Mrs Yoshida, who was discussed earlier, followed this path. In these cases, the women entered into domestic work deliberately. They initiated the job search themselves, after deciding that they needed to work to make ends meet. The example of other issei women working as domestics provided both the impetus and the means to secure employment. Mrs. Yoshida's account indicates that her husband attempted to discourage her employment; yet she persisted in her resolve. The conflicting wishes of husband and wife are even more apparent in the case of Mrs. Adachi. She began daywork in her mid-thirties after several years of taking in home laundry.

When the kids got to be in junior high school, Mrs. S. said, "Why don't you go out to work?" Other people with small children did go out to work but Mr. Adachi was sickly when he was young, so he didn't want the children left alone. He said, "What if the children got hurt. You couldn't get their lives back. The children are worth more than a few dollars. Just as long as we have enough to eat, that's enough." So, I went out secretly to work in one place. And that one became two and that became three. By three, I stopped [adding more jobs] because by that time, my husband found out, and, of course, there was still work at home, because I was still taking in home laundry.

Mrs. Adachi's decision to secretly defy her husband is interesting and illustrates the contradictory nature of issei women's involvement in domestic labor. On the one hand, circumstances beyond their control appear to have ruled these women's lives. They were forced to seek employment because of economic deprivation, husbands' inability to provide adequate support, and the needs of parents and other relatives in Japan. They had to travel in unfamiliar neighborhoods and enter strange households without any experience or knowledge of English. Some confessed that they felt fearful and helpless in the beginning. Yet, on the other hand, some women actively sought out employment, even in the face of opposition from husbands. And, among those who took schoolgirl jobs more or less passively, many continued in domestic work even without great financial pressure. These latter instances suggest that employment, even in a menial capacity, provided some resources the women desired but lacked when they worked exclusively within the family.

The most obvious resource provided by wage work was an independent source of income. Although the women put most of their wages into a common family pool, their contribution was more evident when it was in the form of money than when it was in the form of unpaid labor. Moreover, because of informal pay arrangements and flexible work hours, the women could hide the amount of their earnings. (Some women reported keeping their own bank accounts.) They could use some of their earnings to purchase things for their children or themselves without having to ask their husbands. It is also important to note that some women were largely self-supporting and/or were supporting others. This was a source of considerable pride and an option that married women did not have in traditional Japanese society. This was pointed out by Mrs. Takagi. After describing "killing" herself working forty to sixty hours a week as a domestic to support herself and her children and helping her mother and her brothers, who were able to attend high school because of her, she concluded: "I'm glad to be able to do that. I'm so lucky to be in the United States. In Japan, I wouldn't have had the chance as a woman."

Going out to work also took women outside the confines of the family, away from the direct control of their husbands. They could form outside relationships with employers, and at the very least, these relationships expanded the issei women's store of knowledge and experience. Some employers provided material and emotional support. Mrs. Takagi's employer visited her in the hospital when she was sick and gave her the money to return to Japan to retrieve her son. She also credits this employer with helping her weather many personal crises. For women who were cut off from kin, the ties with employers could be a valuable resource. If we recall Strong's remark that issei men prevented interviewers from talking to their wives, we can see the significance of outside alliances to internal family power relationships. Thus, it is not surprising that some issei men opposed their wives' employment, even when the extra wages were needed, and that some issei women persisted in working, despite their husband's opposition and in the absence of overwhelming financial need. Domestic service offered a compromise resolution. It permitted women to work and form relationships outside the family, yet it kept them within a female sphere in which they were supervised by other women.

CONDITIONS OF WORK

Domestic service encompasses a variety of specific situations. The jobs that the issei women entered were of three types: live-in service, full-time nonresidential jobs, and daywork.

For most of its history, domestic service was a live-in occupation, and until World War I, this was the most common pattern in the United States. This merging of residence and workplace stood as a marked exception to the increasing separation of production from the household and the accompanying segregation of work and nonwork life brought about by industrialization. For the live-in domestic, there was no clear delineation between work and nonwork time. Work hours were open-ended, with the domestic "on call" most of her waking hours, and with little time to devote to family and outside social relationships. As other forms of wage work that gave workers greater autonomy expanded, the confinement and isolation of domestic service grew more onerous. Observers noted that women preferred factory or shop employment even though wages and physical amenities were frequently inferior.[40] Two issei in the study had worked as live-in servants; a widow who needed a home as well as a job, and a woman who arrived as an adolescent with her parents and worked as a live-in schoolgirl before marriage.[41]

Their situations were unusual for issei women. Unlike European immigrant domestics, who were primarily young and single, almost all issei domestics were married and had children. Their circumstances were similar to those of black women in the South, and like them, the issei turned to nonresidential work. Until the 1930s, full-time positions with one employer were fairly common. Some issei women worked as general household help for middle-class families, performing a wide range of tasks from laundry to cooking to cleaning. Other issei worked as "second girls" in multiservant households, where they carried out a variety of tasks under the direction of a paid housekeeper.

The nonresidential jobs gave workers stable employment, set hours, and a chance for a private life. However, for the worker to provide all-around services, she had to put in an extended day, which typically began with breakfast cleanup and ended only after supper cleanup. The day was broken up by an afternoon break of one to three hours, during which the women returned home to prepare meals or do chores. Mrs. Kayahara described her workday, which began at 6:30 in the morning when she left home to catch a trolley. She arrived at work before 8:00. Then, "Wash the breakfast dishes, clean the rooms, make lunch and clean up. Go home. Back at 5:00 to help with cooking dinner and then do the dishes. Come, go, and back again. It was very hard. I had to take the trolley four times."

Partly because of the extended hours in full-time domestic jobs and partly because of the greater availability of day jobs, all the women in the study eventually turned to daywork. They worked in several different households for a day or half-day each week and were paid on an hourly or daily basis. The workday ended before dinner, and schedules could be fitted around family responsibilities. Many women worked part-time, but some women pieced together a forty- or forty-eight-hour week out of a combination of full and half-day jobs.

The duties of the dayworker generally consisted of housecleaning and laundry. Sometimes the worker did both, but many employers hired different workers for the two sets of tasks. Laundry was viewed as less skilled and more menial and was often assigned to minority women, such as the Japanese.[42] Both cleaning and laundry were physically demanding, because of low-level household technology. Ruth Cowan suggests that the availability of household help slowed the adoption of labor-saving appliances by middle-class housewives.[43] Moreover, employers felt that hand labor produced superior results. Workers were expected to scrub floors on hands and knees and to apply a lot of elbow grease to waxing and polishing. Some sense of the work is conveyed by Mrs. Tanabe's description of her routine, when she began to work in 1921.[44]

> When we first started, people wanted you to boil the white clothes. They had a gas burner in the laundry room. I guess you don't see those things any more — an oval shaped boiler. When you did daywork, you did the washing first. And, if you were there eight hours, you dried and then brought them in and ironed them. In between, you cleaned the house from top to bottom. But, when you go to two places, one in the morning and one in the afternoon, you do the ironing and a little housework.

The issei express contradictory attitudes toward the demands of the work. On the one hand, they acknowledge that the work was menial, that it consisted largely of unskilled physical labor. As one put it, "You use your body, not your mind." The women also say that the reason they were satisfied with the work is that they lacked qualifications; for example, "I'm just a country person." Yet, on the other hand, one is also aware that the women are telling stories of their own prowess when they describe the arduousness of the work. What emerges out of their descriptions is a sense of pride in their physical strength and endurance, a determination to accomplish whatever was asked, and a devotion to doing a good job. Mrs. Yoshida explains that she never found housework difficult; even today she can work for hours in her garden without being aware of it, because

> From the time I was a little girl, I was used to working hard. I was born a farmer and did farm work all along. Farm work is very hard. My body was trained so nothing was hard for me. If you take work at a hakujin [Caucasian] place, you have to work hard. There was a place where the lady asked me to wash the ceilings. So I took a table and stood up on it. It was strenuous, but I washed the whole ceiling. So the lady said: "That was hard work, but next time it won't be so hard." She gave me vegetables, fruits and extra money and I went home.

This kind of pride in physical strength is talked about in relation to men in manual occupations but is rarely seen as relevant to women. Similarly, an orientation toward completing a task is seen as more evident among skilled craftsworkers than among those engaged in devalued work. Yet, there is evidence of both among this group of older women engaged in what has been called "the lowest rung of legitimate employment."[45]

The evolution from live-in service to nonresidential jobs to daywork can be viewed as a modernizing trend that has brought domestic work closer to industrialized wage work. First, work and nonwork life became clearly separated. Second, the basis for employment became more clearly contractual; that is, the worker sold a given amount of labor time for an agreed-upon wage. Yet, as long as the work took place in the household, it remained fundamentally preindustrial. While industrial workers produced surplus value that was taken as profit by the employer, the domestic workers produced only simple use value.[46] In a society based on a market economy, work that produces no exchange value is devalued.[47] Whereas the work process in socially organized production is subjected to division of labor, task specialization, and standardization of output, domestic labor remained diffuse and nonspecialized. The work consisted essentially of whatever tasks were assigned by the employer. While industrial workers were integrated into a socially organized system of production, the domestic worker remained atomized. Each domestic performed her tasks in isolation and her work was unrelated to the activities of other workers.

Because of its atomization, domestic work remained invisible and was not subject to regulation. Domestic workers were excluded from protections won by industrial workers in the 1930s, such as social security and minimum wages.[48] Although sporadic attempts to organize domestics were made in large cities, such efforts rarely succeeded in reaching more than a small minority. The issei in the study appear never to have been included in organizing efforts. Thus, there was no collectivity representing their interests, and, of course, the issei received none of the benefits accorded more privileged workers, such as sick days or paid vacations. In fact, when the employer went out of town, the worker was put on unpaid leave. The issei claimed, in any case, that they never took vacations before World War II.

It also follows that wages depended on idiosyncratic factors. Informants and subjects reported that the rate for dayworkers around 1915 ranged from $0.15 to $0.25 an hour. The top rate rose to around $0.50 an hour by the late 1930s. Full-time domestics earned from $20.00 to $45.00 a month in 1915, while schoolgirls earned from $2.00 to $5.00 a week. I was unable to find wage data on other semiskilled occupations in the Bay Area, but other studies have found that domestic wages during this period compared favorably with those of factory, sales, or other low-level female occupations.[49]

Some of the variation in wages can be attributed to market factors. Wealthier households were expected to pay more. The rate in some communities was higher than in others, probably because of the balance of labor supply and demand. Alameda had a higher proportion of Japanese seeking domestic work and had among the lowest wages. Still, what is striking is the seeming arbitrariness of wages. Some workers were willing to work for less than the average rate, and some employers were willing to pay more than they had to to get a worker.

It may be useful to examine the process by which wages were set in individual cases. Generally, the employer made an offer, and the worker either accepted it or looked for another job at a higher wage. Although the shortage of workers may have maintained a minimum level for wages, the effect was not uniform. What employers offered depended a great deal on personalistic factors. Sometimes, the worker benefited, if the employer especially wanted to keep her for personal reasons. At other times, employers used their knowledge of the workers' personal situation to push wages down. Both these elements are evident in Mrs. Takagi's story. Her employers liked her and paid her more than the average rate. However, during the depression, employers cut back on help and Mrs. Takagi couldn't find enough work to fill the week. One employer knew about her situation and offered her an extra day's work if she would take a cut in pay.

> She said to me, "I tried another girl, because you get the highest wages. I tried a cheaper one, but she wasn't good. She never put the clothes away and never finished the ironing. . . . What do you think—take $4.50 and I'll keep you? I'll give you two days a week." I wanted the money—Iwas trying to save money to get r y son [from Japan]. So I said, "fine." She said, "I'll never tell anybody." Here, a month later, she told every friend. . . . Everybody said, "You're working for so and so for $3.50 and here you're getting $4.00." See, that's the way all the jobs were. A lot of people worked for $2.50, so I was just crying.

Mrs. Takagi weathered this crisis and did not have to take cuts from the others, but she felt humiliated at being found out.

EMPLOYER-EMPLOYEE RELATIONS

As this incident illustrates, the relationship between employer and employee was, perhaps, the most distinctly preindustrial, as well as the most problematic, aspect of domestic service. The relationship has been described as feudal[50] or premodern.[51] According to Lewis Coser, the traditional servant role was

> rooted in a premodern type of relationship in which particularism prevails over universalism and ascription over achievement. . . . While post-medieval man is typically enmeshed in a web of group affiliations and hence subject to pushes and pulls of many claims to his commitment, the traditional servant . . . is supposed to be entirely committed and loyal to a particular employer. . . . Moreover, while in other occupational roles, the incumbent's duties are largely independent of personal relationships with this or that client or employer, particularistic elements loom very large in the master-servant relationship.[52]

Although the totalism of the traditional master-servant relationship was much reduced under conditions of daywork, relations between white employers and issei domestics retained two essential and interrelated characteristics of the earlier period, personalism and asymmetry.

Personalism pervaded all aspects of the employer-employee relationship. Employers were concerned with the worker's total person—her moral character and personality—not just her work skills. The issei domestics in the study in turn judged their employers on moral and characterological grounds; for example, whether they were good Christians and clean and neat in their habits. The importance of the personal can also be seen in the issei's preference for personal referrals for job placement. Compatibility and mutual trust were important because employer and employee were thrown together in a situation with little mutual privacy. The worker had access to the most intimate regions of the household where she might become privy to family secrets. The worker in turn was open to constant scrutiny by her employer.

A sense of mutual obligation, a carry-over of feudal values, also colored the tie between employer and employee. The domestic was expected to demonstrate loyalty, and the employer was expected to concern herself with the worker's welfare. This mutuality was viewed as a positive feature by some of the issei. Mrs. Shinoda recalls her first employer's concern fondly: "That lady was really nice. She would turn on the light and the heat in my room and stay up waiting for me to return. Usually, she would go to sleep early, but even if I returned late at night, she would wait up for me with the room heated up."

For some women, the tie with the employer became an extension of familial relationships. Mrs. Takagi described her second employer, Mrs. Cox, in these terms: "She was a Christian. Anytime I came down with a sickness, she said, 'Call a doctor.' If I go to the hospital, she came every day. She was almost a second mother. If I didn't have her help, I would have been badly off. I went to Japan and she gave me help with that."

Despite the intimacy, there remained a not quite surmountable barrier of status, which was reinforced by cultural and racial differences. Thus, the familiar attitude of the employer usually took the form of benevolent maternalism. Even Mrs. Takagi, who formed close and longlasting ties with her employers, recognized the employer's need to perform acts of *noblesse oblige*. She said she had learned to accept gifts, including old clothes and furnishings, even when she didn't want them. Otherwise, the employer was apt to feel the worker was "too proud," and would withhold further gifts and bonuses.

Thus, the second main feature of the relationship was its asymmetry. The traditional mistress-servant relationship exhibited in pure form the relation of superior to inferior. This aspect, though modified with the advent of daywork, continued to stigmatize the domestic as a menial and "unfree" worker. In extreme cases, the domestic was treated as a "nonperson." Mrs. Takagi recalls being offered a lunch consisting of asparagus stalks whose tips had been eaten off by the employer's son. This kind of treatment was probably rare, at least according to the women in the study. However, less direct expressions of asymmetry were common. For example, in an asymmetric relationship, the lower status person has to be attuned to the feelings and moods of the higher status person. Mrs. Nakashima provided an insight into this aspect when she described her approach to domestic work:

> At first, since I hadn't had much chance to enter Caucasian homes, I was a little frightened. But, after I got used to it, it became very easy. And I concluded, after working for a while, that the most important thing in this type of job is to think of and be able to predict the feelings of the lady in the house. She would teach me how to do certain things in the beginning, but after a month or two, I gradually came to learn that person's likes, tastes, and ideas. So I try to fulfill her wishes— this is only my way of doing it, of course, and so, for example, I'll change the water in the vase when it's dirty or rearrange wilting flowers while I'm cleaning house. In that way, I can become more intimate with the lady of the house in a natural way and the job itself becomes more interesting. . . . Sometimes, I plant flowers in the garden without being asked . . . so, then I'll start to feel affection even for that garden.

Although her employers may have appreciated Mrs. Nakashima's aesthetic sensibilities, it is doubtful they were as aware of and responsive to her thoughts and feelings as she was to theirs.

The personalism and asymmetry in the employer-employee relation were complementary. The supposed inferiority and differentness of the domestic made it easy for the employer to be generous and to confide in her. The domestic was not in a position to harm her or make excessive demands, and secrets were safe with someone from a different social world. An informant suggested that the language barrier, though it hampered communication, may have contributed to the smoothness of relationships. The issei could not "hear" insulting or denigrating comments. One worker confirmed this by saying she had never minded being a domestic but added that had she understood English, she might have gotten into quarrels with her employers.

Ultimately, however, the personalism and asymmetry created contradictions in the employer-employee relationship. As Coser put it: "The dialectic of conflict between inferior and superior within the household could never be fully resolved, and hence the fear of betrayal always lurked behind even the most amicable relationship between master and servant."[53] The fear is evident in issei women's complaints about employers who distrusted them. Mrs. Takagi once found money left under the corner of a rug. She carefully replaced the rug without touching the money or saying anything about it; she had been warned by her father-in-law that employers sometimes tested the domestic's honesty by leaving valuables about. Mrs. Nakashima indignantly reported an incident in which she was suspected of dishonesty:

> There was a place I was working temporarily. They asked me whether I had seen a ring. I didn't know what kind of ring they meant, so I just told them no. I hadn't seen any ring while I was vacuuming. They sounded a little skeptical, saying it's strange I hadn't seen it. I felt insulted then, as though they were accusing me of something.

The conflict took its most concrete form in a power struggle between employer and employee over control of the work process. On one side, the employer attempted to exercise as much control as possible. Mrs. Noda echoes the sentiments of many of the issei, when she said that her greatest dislike was an employer who was *yakamashi* (noisy, critical): "Indeed, where they don't say too many things, the work is better. If they ask, 'Have you done this? Have you done that? Do you understand?' There is that sort of place. Most people don't say such things because they know [better]."

Some employers seemed to assume the worker would load or cut corners if she were not watched. Mrs. Nakashima said she quit one job because her employer spied on her. She said most of her employers left the house while she worked; if they returned, they announced themselves loudly. In this case: "The Mrs. would come in very quietly without warning, so it made me feel as if she were spying on me to make sure I wasn't doing anything wrong. I disliked that a great deal."

Another area of conflict was over the amount and pace of the work. Employers sometimes engaged in the household equivalent of work "speedup." If the worker accomplished the agreed-upon tasks within a designated period, the employer added more tasks. To finish everything, the worker was forced to "do everything fast." Employers were thus able to exploit the issei worker's conscientiousness.

The issei had only limited resources to resist employer's attempts to control their work and the conditions of employment. Yet, within their capabilities, they strove to wrest some degree of control over their work and their lives. The choice to shift to daywork can be seen as one means to gain greater autonomy.[54] By working for several families, the domestics became less dependent on one employer. Work hours could be adjusted to fit in with the workers' other interests and responsibilities.

As Mrs. Tanabe said about her change from full-time work with one employer to daywork, "You're freer to yourself."

Within the structure of daywork, the issei maneuvered the situation to increase control over the work process. One way was to minimize contact with employers. Mrs. Adachi deliberately chose employers who went out during the day:

> I liked it best when nobody was there. The places I worked, they went out. The children were in school, and I was all by myself, so I could do what I wanted. If the woman was at home, she generally went out shopping. I liked it when they didn't complain or ask you to do this or that. The places I worked, I was on my own. It was just like being in my own home, and I could do what I wanted.

Her sentiments were seconded by Mrs. Noda: "I don't like it when people stay home. I like nobody home. It's more easy to work — everything is smooth."

Mrs. Adachi retained her autonomy by adopting a utilitarian orientation toward her employers. She "picked up and dropped" jobs on the basis of convenience, rather than become attached to particular employers:

> Sometimes I gave the job to someone else and looked for something else. I changed from this job to that job. If I had to walk too far to the bus, or the people were too messy, I kept the job until I found a better one, and then I changed. [How did you find the other job?] When they're playing cards, they talked about the help. If someone knew who is a good worker, they would give the other ladies my name, and they would call me. Then I'd go and see. If I like it better than the other places, I'd quit the other and move to the new one.

Some women maintained control over the work by defining and enforcing their own standards; they insisted on working on the basis of tasks rather than time. The job was done when the tasks were accomplished to their own satisfaction. If they worked extra time, they did not want to be paid; if they accomplished it in less time, they reserved the right to leave.

The last recourse in the face of a recalcitrant or unreasonable employer was to quit. This was a difficult step for the issei. They felt it was a loss of face to complain about mistreatment, and furthermore, they felt employers should know how to act properly without being told. Thus, when they quit, they did so in a way that was designed to maintain both the employer's and their own dignity. If an employer asked why they were leaving, the issei usually made up an excuse that avoided any criticism of the employer. Mrs. Adachi was typical when she said, "I wouldn't say I didn't like it, so I would say I was tired or sick." Yet, their own pride was also important. Mrs. Yoshida reported this incident when she quit: "There was one place that no matter how much you do, that person would let you do more. So I thought I would quit. That day I did a lot of work — more than usual — and finished up everything she gave me." By meeting the challenge, no matter how unreasonable, Mrs. Yoshida was able to leave with her self-respect intact.

WORK AND FAMILY LIFE

Issei women's experiences in domestic employment cannot be understood without also considering the relationship between wage work and family roles. Some of the connections between work and family life have been alluded to in earlier sections, but I would like now to examine the dialectics of this relationship more systematically.

To do so, we must refer back to the family system of the society from which the immigrants came. In late nineteenth- and early twentieth-century southern, rural Japan, the basic social and economic unit was the *ie* (household), which typically included husband, wife, unmarried children, and in the case of an eldest son, the husband's parents. The *ie* served as the basic unit of production and as a corporate economic body. Ownership and authority were vested in the male head of household. Members were graded by gender, age, and insider-outsider.[55]

Most households were engaged in small-scale farming and petty manufacturing and trade, the economy of which relied on the unpaid labor of all members, including women and children.[56] Most of what was produced was directly consumed, and any income generated was corporate rather than individual. There was no separation of work and family life because production, consumption, maintenance, and child-care were carried on more or less simultaneously. Women's work was thus incorporated into the overall work of the household and did not differ organizationally from men's work. There was, of course, a clear division of labor by sex. Women were assigned most domestic chores, as well as certain female-typed agricultural and manufacturing tasks; men supervised the household work and represented the family in relation to the larger community.

When they came to the United States, the issei were entering an industrialized economy in which wage labor was becoming the predominant mode. The majority of issei families found "preindustrial" niches in farming and small business enterprises. In these families, the traditional system of household labor, as well as the old role relationships, were transplanted, more or less intact.[57] Many issei families, however —especially those in Bay Area cities — adapted to the urban economy by turning to multiple wage earning. Husband and wife and older children were individually employed, mostly in marginal, low-paying jobs. Each worker's earnings were small, but the pooled income was sufficient to support a household and to generate some surplus for savings, remittances, and consumer goods.

This strategy was in many ways consistent with the values of the *ie* system. Because multiple wages were needed, the economic interdependence of family members was preserved. Moreover, the employment of women was consistent with the assumption that women were full economic contributors. In other ways, however, the strategy was inconsistent with the traditional *ie* structure. Wage work represented a form of economic organization in which the individual, rather than the family, was the unit of production, and in which work and family life were separated rather than integrated. Women working outside the home violated the principle that men had exclusive rights to, and control over, their wives' labor.

Perhaps because of this duality, issei men were divided in their attitudes toward their wives' participation in the labor force. As noted earlier, some men opposed their wives' employment on the grounds that their services were needed at home. In contrast, other men expected their wives to pull their full weight by being employed, regardless of the women's own inclinations. Thus, while Mrs. Adachi said she was defying her husband's wishes by going out to work, Mrs. Uematsu indicated that she felt compelled to seek wage work:

> My husband didn't bring in enough money, so I went out to work. I didn't even think twice about it. If I didn't take a job, people would have started to call me "Madam" [i.e., accusing her of thinking she was too much of a lady to work]. . . . It was like a race; we all had to work as hard as possible.

The duality is further mirrored in the contradictory impacts of wage work on women's position in the family. On the one hand, to the extent that the traditional division of labor and the structure of male privilege persisted, wage work added to the burdens and difficulties experienced by women. On the other hand, to the extent that wage work reduced women's economic dependence and male control over their labor, it helped the women transcend the limitations of traditional role relationships. Evidence of both tendencies emerge from the women's accounts; the increased burdens are greater and more obvious.

Among the women in the study, the major share of housework and childcare remained with them even if they were employed. All but two women claimed their husbands did no work "inside" the house. Mrs. Nishimura explained:

> No, my husband was like a child. He couldn't even make tea. He couldn't do anything by himself. He was really Japan-style. Sometimes, I had too much to do, so although I would always iron his shirts, I might ask him to wait a while on the underwear, but he'd say no. He'd wait there until I would iron them. People used to say he was spoiled. He was completely a Japanese man. Some people divorce their husbands for not helping around the house, but that never entered my mind. I thought it was natural for a Japanese.

Although Mr. Nishimura might be viewed as extreme, even by other issei, there was unanimous agreement among the women that Japanese men expected to be waited upon by their wives.

The result was that the women experienced considerable overload. The men worked long hours, often at physically exhausting jobs, but the women's days were longer. Their days began earlier with the preparation of a morning meal and ended later with the preparation and cleanup of the evening meal; in between, they had to fit in laundry and cleaning. Some women were endowed with natural vitality. They could maintain an immaculate household and do extras, such as making clothes for children. Mrs. Nishimura described her schedule during the years she was doing seasonal garment work:

> Since I had so many children, I asked my mother-in-law to take care of the children. I would get up at 5 o'clock and do the laundry. In those days—we'd do it by hand—hang up the laundry, then go to Oakland. I would come home and since my husband didn't have much work then, he'd get drunk and bring the children home. I would cook and eat, and then go to sleep. They all asked me how long I slept at night. But, since I was in my twenties, it didn't affect me too much.

Others, like Mrs. Uematsu, were exhausted at the end of the day and had to let things slide. She exclaimed: "My house was a mess. I went to work in the morning and when I came back from work, I'd cook a little and then go to sleep and that's about all."

As Mrs. Nishimura's account indicates, an additional problem was created by wage work that did not exist under the family work system— the need for separate childcare. Employers sometimes allowed domestics to bring a young child to work, but as more children arrived, other arrangements had to be made. Friends, neighbors, older children, and husbands were recruited to baby-sit. Women with older children often set their work hours to correspond with school schedules. When no other means were available, and employment was a necessity, the issei sometimes resorted to sending their children to Japan to be raised by relatives, as three of the women in the study did. They planned to return to Japan and rejoin their children. In all three cases, the women stayed in the United States, and the children returned as adolescents or adults.[58]

Despite the prevalence of male privilege, role relationships sometimes underwent change in response to new circumstances. The most common adjustment was for husbands to take on some childcare responsibilities. Even Mr. Nishimura, the "completely Japanese man," took on transporting and minding children when he was out of work. One woman, Mrs. Nomura, claimed that her husband did quite a lot around the house, including drying dishes. She explained:

> He was considerably Americanized. He was young when he came over and he was a schoolboy, so he was used to the American way of doing things. Even when we quarreled, he wouldn't hit me, saying it's bad in this country for a man to hit a woman, unlike Japan. In Japan, the man would be head of the family without any question. "Japan is a man's country; America is a woman's country," he often used to say.

Some respondents and informants reported cases of role reversal between husband and wife (although not among the women in the study). Role reversals occurred most often when the husband was considerably older than the wife. Because many issei men married late in life to much younger women, they were in their fifties by the time their children reached school age. As laborers, their employment prospects were poor, while their wives could easily find domestic jobs. Mrs. Tanabe, a nisei raised in Alameda, recalls that her husband was "retired" while she was still a young girl:

> The Hiroshima men in Alameda were the laziest men. Their wives did all the work. My dad raised me while my mother went out and did domestic work. He did the cooking and kept the house and did the shopping and took me when I went to work. So, he didn't do much really. But, in Alameda, they're known for being the lazy ones — most Hiroshima men are — so no one's rich.

One reason for this pattern may be that domesticity was considered appropriate for older men. Mrs. Yamashita, another nisei, reported that her father, a widower, acted as a housekeeper and baby-sitter while she and her husband both went out to work.

In addition to the division of labor by sex, the traditional Japanese family was characterized by what Elizabeth Bott[59] has called segregated conjugal role relationships; that is, husband and wife had a considerable number of separate interests and activities. This pattern seems to have been maintained by the issei to a marked degree.[60] Leisure time was rarely spent in joint activities. Women's orbit was restricted to the home and the domestic world of women; men engaged in a wider range of formal church and community activities. Informal socializing, including drinking and gambling, were common male activities. The men's drinking seems to have been a source of conflict in many families. Two women's lives were tragically affected by their husband's drinking. Mrs. Takagi's husband got into frequent accidents and spent much of his earnings on alcohol. Mrs. Shinoda's husband was killed in a judo mishap that occurred while he was intoxicated. Perhaps a more typical story is Mrs. Kayahara's, who described her husband in these terms:

> Not so much nice, but not so bad. [Was he old-fashioned?] Just like a japan boy! So, I did everything — cook, wash, keep house. My husband drank. He drank so much, his stomach went bad. Once we were married, he would have five or six drinks every day — sake. All his life, he did that. But, he did work hard.

The extent of drinking among issei men can be gauged by the fact that women whose husbands did not drink thought it worthy of comment. Mrs. Nomura feels her life was much easier than other women's because her husband was straitlaced:

> Yes, I've been lucky. I worked, of course, and encountered social problems [discrimination], but . . . I didn't suffer at all with regard to my husband. He didn't smoke, drink or gamble. . . . Very serious Christian with no faults. Everyone else was drinking and gambling. Part Street was full of liquor stores, and so they'd all go there; but my husband led such a clean life, so I was lucky.

Overwork and poverty exacerbated conflicts generated by gender division in the family: the discrepancy in power and privilege, the unequal division of household labor, and the separation of female and male emotional spheres. Far from being passive, the women actively fought with their husbands. Mrs. Nakashima had to send her three children back to Japan and work in a laundry to support herself because her husband was sickly. She reports: "My life in the U.S. was very hard in the beginning because my husband was ill so much and we had such totally different personalities. We were both selfish so we had many problems. But, after I started going to church, I became more gentle. So we had fewer quarrels. I think that is a gift from God." Mrs. Nishimura also reported that she and her husband quarreled a great deal. She explained: "Well, he was rather short-tempered . . . there were times when I thought he was stubborn, but we were far apart in age, so I would attribute our differences to that. Being apart in age does create quite a lot of differences. . . . But, I bore it all." Thus, while the issei women express the traditional Japanese attitude that women must bear up under hardship, it is evident that they did not always do so quietly!

Given these additional strains imposed by employment, what did the women gain in the family through domestic employment? There was, of course, the tangible benefit of income, part of which could be retained for individual saving or spending. A less tangible, but perhaps more significant, gain was increased control over their economic circumstances. In Japan, women were ultimately at the mercy of their husband's ability or willingness to provide support. Mrs. Takagi's mother suffered extreme poverty as a result of her father's irresponsibility and drinking. He ran up debts that led to the loss of their farm in Japan. Her own husband proved to be similarly unreliable. However, Mrs. Takagi felt less victimized than her mother because she could work to support herself and her children. As she put it, "I killed myself, but did it all, myself." The sense of self-sufficiency is clearly important to the women, for they maintain an independence, even in later life, from their children. About one-half of the women worked into their seventies and even eighties, and all the women worked into their sixties.

In addition to working for their own independence, the issei worked for their children. They gained a sense of purpose by seeing their work as contributing to their children's future. Although most women agreed that the present was the best (that is, easiest) period of their lives, many looked back nostalgically to the days when their children were growing up. Mrs. Nishimura spoke for this group when she said: "This is my best time, but my happiest time was then, when my children were small. I was poor and busy then, but that might have been the best time. It was good to think about my children—how they'd go through high school and college and afterwards."

It is difficult to document the extent of special consideration or deference the women received as a result of their sacrifices. However, the long-term respect they earned is strikingly evident. The daughters and sons of these women were uniform in their expressions of respect toward their mothers. They were eager to do whatever possible to make life comfortable for them. A few spoke ruefully about their mothers' "stubbornness" or "independence," which prevented them from doing more.

The very difficulty of the issei's circumstances and their ability to "bear it all" gave them added respect. Looking back, the women expressed amazement at their own capacities: Mrs. Nishimura concluded it was because she was young; while Mrs. Yoshida cited her early conditioning in farm work. The hard work of the issei women has become legendary within the Japanese community. Several nisei domestics claimed that even now they are unable to match the endurance of issei women in their seventies.

The good opinion of others was important in the close-knit Japanese community. The camaraderie and common frame of reference eased some of the hardships and counteracted the isolating conditions of their work. Sharing their experiences with others in the same situation, they found sympathy and understanding. Mrs. Kayahara recalled:

> In Alameda, the Japanese were living in five or six houses near the City Hall—all of them from Fukuoka were living together. That was so enjoyable. Myself, I never thought to be ashamed of doing domestic work. We had to do any sort of work that was available. Also our friends were doing the same sort of work, and we used to talk about it. . . . Sometimes, things that were worrying us, we'd talk about it. That helped us. If you don't talk to anyone, your heart gets heavy. So we told each other things right away.

CONCLUSIONS

This chapter has analyzed the contradictions in issei women's involvement in domestic work in the pre-World War II period. The approach taken here has highlighted several aspects of these contradictions.

First, it draws attention to conflict as an underlying dynamic in women's relationship to paid and unpaid work. The focus on conflict makes it possible to see issei women as actors striving to gain control and self-respect rather than as passive targets of oppression. The contest was obviously uneven: issei women had few resources for direct resistance, and they lacked collective strength in the form of worker organizations or female kin networks. Thus, there is no evidence that they directly confronted their employers or their husbands, that they were militant, or engaged in collective action. If these are the criteria, it is easy to overlook the women's resistance to control by employers and husbands. The strategies the issei adopted reflected their relative lack of power; they engaged in indirect forms of resistance, such as evasion. The issei maximized autonomy in employment by choosing work situations in which employers were absent or inactive. In the family, they went out to work secretly or withheld part of their wages as a means of gaining control over disposable income. Another strategy women used in both employment and family life was to define their own standards and goals. The issei had internalized criteria for what constituted a good day's work; some women defined their jobs in terms of tasks accomplished, rather than hours, for example. They also set their own priorities in relation to housekeeping, education for their children, and the family's standard of living. There is evidence that the women gained satisfaction from meeting their own standards, irrespective of their employers' or their husbands' evaluations.

Second, as the previous discussion indicates, the analysis highlights the interconnectedness of different aspects of the women's experiences, particularly between paid and unpaid work. In both employment and family life, women were in a subordinate position in which their role was defined as service to another. The content of activities in both spheres was also similar, and the structures of employment and family life were, therefore, mutually reinforcing. The parallel structures in turn contributed to a similarity in the strategies used to cope with subordination. The reliance on indirect strategies in conflicts with employers, for example, can be related in part to issei women's experience of subordination in the household and the community and to their inability to directly confront their husbands' authority. In contrast, black women domestics resisted or defied their employers more openly and were also less subordinate in the family.[61]

Coping strategies are usually conceptualized as situationally specific; that is, as growing out of and being confined to a particular setting.[62] In this case, at least, the strategies appear to form a coherent whole. This is to be expected in part because of structural parallels in women's positions in work, family, and community life and in part because of internalized cultural attitudes, such as the value of hard work, which carried across situations. Perhaps, more important, the process of striving in one area developed orientations that carried over into other arenas. Thus, the theme of self-sufficiency pervaded all aspects of the women's life and has persisted over time.

Finally, the analysis points to the contradictory implications of employment for issei women's status. The issue has often been framed in either/or terms. Some theorists, including some Marxists, have viewed employment as a liberating force, arguing that women would gain status in society by becoming producers in the market economy, rather than remaining nonproductive household workers. By contributing to family income and by gaining a role outside the family, women would increase their power in the family. More recently, analysts have argued that employment, far from contributing to equality, actually reinforces women's oppression. They point out that women are relegated to low-status, routine, and low-paying jobs; that women remain responsible for unpaid domestic work and are, thereby, saddled with a double burden; that in both realms, women are subjugated by male authority.[63] Although the present account shares this recent perspective and documents the multiple forms of oppression faced by issei domestic workers, the focus on contradictions makes it possible to see oppressive and liberating consequences as interrelated. Issei women were constrained by the larger economic and political system that forced them to seek employment but limited them to the most marginal jobs. The conditions of domestic work subjected them to further oppression. But, out of these conditions, issei women gained advantages that enabled them to achieve certain goals (such as helping their families in Japan and providing extras for their children), to become less dependent on the ability or willingness of husbands to provide support, and to form ties outside the immediate family group. And, despite the menial nature of employment, the issei achieved a sense of their own strength, and in some cases, superiority to employer and husband within their own area of competence.

NOTES

The research for this paper was supported in part by a faculty grant from the Graduate School, Boston University. The author is grateful to Jean Twomey for assistance in organizing the data; Haru Nakano for help in arranging interviews; Peter Langer for detailed suggestions during writing; Murray Melbin for clarifying issues in an earlier version; and Edna Bonacich and Lucie Cheng for encouraging me to explore the topic. Special thanks are also owed to the Women and Work Group, Chris Bose, Carol Brown, Peggy Crull, Roz Feldberg, Myra Ferree, Heidi Hartmann, Alice Kessler-Harris, Dorothy Remy, Natalie Sokoloff, and Carole Turbin. Our meetings were supported by a grant from the Problems of the Discipline Programs, American Sociological Association; and our discussions helped crystallize some key conceptual issues.

1. H. A. Millis, *The Japanese Problem in the United States* (New York: The Macmillan Co., 1915); and Edward K. Strong, *Japanese in California* (Stanford, Calif.: Stanford University Press, 1933).

2. David Chaplin, "Domestic Service and Industrialization," *Comparative Studies in Sociology* 1 (1978): 98-127; and Janet M. Hooks, *Women's Occupations Through Seven Decades*, Bulletin no. 218, U.S. Department of Labor, Women's Bureau (Washington, D.C., 1947).

3. Lewis Coser, "Domestic Servants: The Obsolescence of a Social Role," *Social Forces* 52 (1973): 31-40.

4. George J. Stigler, *Domestic Servants in the United States, 1900-1940* (New York: National Bureau of Economic Research, 1946).

5. See Gerda Lerner, *Black Women in White America: A Documentary History* (New York: Vintage Books, 1973).

6. William L. Yancey, Eugene P. Ericksen, and Richard N. Julian, "Emergent Ethnicity: A Review and Reformulation," *American Sociological Review* 41 (June 1976): 391-403.

7. The material for this paper is drawn from several sources. Information on the economic context and historical background was obtained from census material, a few early surveys, and secondary accounts. Newspaper files and documents furnished by community members provided valuable details; these sources included the files of the *Alameda Daily Argus* from the 1880s to 1920; surviving copies of the *Nichi-Bei Times* annual directories, 1910, 1914 and 1941; and privately printed church histories, *Eighty-fifth Anniversary of Protestant Work Among Japanese in North America* (1975) and *Buddhist Churches of America* (1976), which included the chronologies of individual churches and temples in the Bay Area. Overall, however, documentary evidence was scanty. Japanese community directories, organizational records, and newspaper files were lost during World War II, or they were destroyed by their owners prior to evacuation because they feared the material would be used as evidence of subversive activities.

The heart of the data for this paper was derived from in-depth interviews of fifteen issei women who worked as domestics, and for comparison, twelve nisei (American-born) and seven kibei (American-born, Japan-educated) domestics. These interviews were supplemented by informant interviews of thirty older issei and nisei who had lived in the prewar communities of San Francisco, Oakland, Alameda, Berkeley, and San Leandro. Interviews were semistructured; particular topics were systematically covered, but new ideas were explored if subject's remarks provided new insights. Topics covered included individual work histories, work attitudes, work experiences, and nonwork areas such as health, ethnic identity, and social and family life. Initial interviews took from one to two and one-half hours with a follow-up of twenty minutes to one hour. With a few exceptions, interviews were taped, translated (if necessary), and transcribed verbatim. Only a small part of the information is reported in the present paper.

The analysis of the interview data was primarily qualitative. The aim was to identify patterns in the women's experiences and to generate hypotheses, rather than to test prior ones; see Barney G. Glaser and Anselm L. Strauss, *The Discovery of Grounded Theory* (Chicago: Aldine Publishing Company, 1967).

8. Cf. Bonnie Dill, "The Dialectics of Black Womanhood," *Signs* 4 (Spring 1979): 543-555, for a similar argument regarding black women.

9. Frank Miyamoto, "Social Solidarity Among the Japanese in Seattle," *University of Washington Publications in the Social Sciences* 11 (1939): 57-130, first designated these three time periods in his study of the prewar Seattle, Washington, Japanese community. I have adopted his chronology, substituting the term "stabilization period" to designate the third period, which Miyamoto called the "second generation period." For a discussion of the social characteristics of frontier situations, for example, the preponderance of males, see Murray Melbin, "Night as Frontier," *American Sociological Review* 43 (1978): 3-22.

10. Edward K. Strong, *The Second-Generation Japanese Problem* (Stanford, Calif.: Stanford University Press, 1934).

11. See Yamato Ichihashi, *Japanese Immigration* (San Francisco: The Marshall Press, 1915) and his more detailed *Japanese in the United States* (Stanford, Calif.: Stanford University Press, 1932); also Roger Daniels, *The Politics of Prejudice* (New York: Atheneum, 1973).

12. For an account of the immigrant associations, see Ivan H. Light, *Ethnic Enterprise in America* (Berkeley, Los Angeles, London: University of California Press, 1972).

13. The other areas of concentration were around Sacramento and the upper San Joaquin Valley (Daniels, *Politics of Prejudice*).

14. Strong, *Second-Generation Japanese Problem*.

15. Ichihashi, *Japanese in the United States*.

16. Census figures for 1900 show only 985 Japanese women over age fifteen. By 1910, the number had jumped to 9,087. Sidney Gulick compiled data showing that 45,706 Japanese females were admitted to the continental United States between 1909 and 1923, of whom 33,628 were listed as wives (reprinted in Ichihashi, *Japanese in the United States*, as appendix C).

17. *1914 Yearbook of the Nichi-Bei Times* is a directory of residents, associations, and businesses in the Bay Area. Most Christian churches were founded in the 1890s with the aid of white Protestant churches. The

Buddhist churches, which were ethnically supported, were founded and developed between 1900 and 1915. Oakland, 1901, was the earliest, followed by Berkeley, 1908, and Alameda, 1912. Japanese language schools were usually attached to the churches (see *Buddhist Churches of America*, and *Eighty-fifth Anniversary of Protestant Work*).

18. Harry H. L. Kitano, "Housing of Japanese Americans in the San Francisco Bay Area," in *Studies in Housing and Minority Groups*, ed. Nathan Glazer and D. McEntire (Berkeley and Los Angeles: University of California Press, 1960), pp. 178-197.

19. Daniels, *Politics of Prejudice*.

20. Miyamoto, "Social Solidarity."

21. Strong, *Japanese in California*.

22. Although the women spoke of the decision as their parents', it appears to be the father as head of the household who had the power. See beginning of section on the Japanese family. The full range of attitudes among the women did not necessarily fall in one dimension; however, roughly scaling the women's attitudes from "most reluctant" to "most eager," the following attitudes can be identified: (1) felt tricked, went reluctantly; (2) was persuaded, inveigled by promises for the future by parents; (3) felt "carefree," thought it would be a new experience; (4) felt that this mate or going to the United States was better than another alternative, (5) aspired to come to the United States and parents concurred; and (6) aspired to come to the United States but had to overcome parents' opposition.

23. This and all other names in the text are pseudonyms. Other identifying details have been disguised to ensure anonymity.

24. During this period, many Japanese women had to marry men who were emigrating for demographic reasons. This was a time of Japanese expansionism. Young men were colonizing Manchuria and Korea, as well as seeking their fortunes in Hawaii and the mainland United States. Among the various destinations, the United States was viewed as offering the easiest situation for women. Mrs. Nomura reported: "I was among the lucky ones, coming to the U.S. as I did. I almost wound up in Manchuria, you know. In Japan, the woman doesn't go out hunting for a husband. We used a go-between. The marriage arrangement offer from Mr. Nomura came a week before the one from the person going to Manchuria. So my father rejected the latter offer."

25. Ichihashi, *Japanese in the United States*.

26. Robert W. Smuts, *Women and Work in America* (New York: Columbia University Press, 1959).

27. Millis, *Japanese Problem*, p. 27.

28. U.S. Department of Commerce, Bureau of the Census, *Fourteenth Census of the United States Taken in the Year 1920*, vol. 4, *Population, Occupations*

(Washington, D.C.: Government Printing Office, 1923); Joseph A. Hill, *Women in Gainful Occupations, 1870 to 1920,* Census Monographs 9, U.S. Department of Commerce, Bureau of the Census (Washington, D.C.: U.S. Government Printing Office, 1929).

29. Strong, *Japanese in California,* p. 109.

30. Unless special instructions were given to enumerators (as occurred in 1910) to count the unpaid work of women and children, such labor was likely to be overlooked. (See Hill, *Women in Gainful Occupations.*) Because the Japanese faced legal harassment, they were suspicious of outsiders and feared giving out personal information. Finally, the women's inability to communicate in English undoubtedly hampered accuracy in reporting. Despite these shortcomings, the census remains the best source of detailed occupational information.

31. Unfortunately, data for a key census, 1910, are missing because compilers aggregated occupational data for Chinese and Japanese, and so no separate figures exist for Japanese alone. Extrapolating from population and employment trends for the Japanese and Chinese, I would estimate that about 30 percent of all gainfully employed and about 45 percent of all nonagriculturally employed issei women were employed in domestic service in 1910. Because the Chinese female labor force grew very little between the 1900 and 1920 censuses, the distributions for the Japanese for 1910 can be estimated in the following way. We assume that the 1910 figures for the Chinese were the same as they were in 1900 and then subtract the 1900 Chinese figures from each 1910 combined total. The remainder in each case should be a rough approximation of the 1910 Japanese total. Using this method, I estimate that gainfully employed Japanese women numbered 1,800, of whom about 540, or 30 percent, were employed as "servants."

32. This figure is lower than would be expected from geographic distributions. During the period between 1900 and 1930, slightly more than one-half of the Japanese (56 percent) lived in rural areas, according to a survey conducted by the Japanese consulate (Strong, *Japanese in California*). There appears to have been an undercount of unpaid agricultural labor among women.

33. If data for issei and nisei are combined, however, the percentage in domestic work actually goes up slightly in 1940. This is because the nisei were even more heavily concentrated in domestic work than the issei.

34. Ichihashi, *Japanese in the United States.*

35. Ibid.

36. Daniels, *Politics of Prejudice.*

37. Millis, *Japanese Problem.*

38. Strong, *Japanese in California.*

39. An old-time resident of Alameda recalled that the early stores and businesses were owned by a succession of different families. The owners sold their businesses to other families and returned to Japan.

40. Lucy M. Salmon, *Domestic Service* (New York: Macmillan Co., 1897); and Amy Watson, "Domestic Service," in *Encyclopedia of the Social Sciences* 5 (New York: Macmillan Co., 1937), pp. 198-206.

41. Some other women later worked as live-in help right after World War II in order to have a place to live after returning from internment camp.

42. Cf. Lerner, *Black Women in White America*; and David M. Katzman, *Seven Days a Week: Women and Domestic Service in Industrializing America* (New York: Oxford University Press, 1978).

43. Ruth S. Cowan, "The Industrial Revolution in the Home: Household Technology and Social Change in the Twentieth Century," *Technology and Culture* 17 (January 1976):1-23.

44. Mrs. Tanabe is counted as one of the nisei, even though she is technically an issei, having arrived in Hawaii as an infant and later coming to California when she was five. She is one of the oldest nisei however, having been born in 1898, and her work experience overlaps with those of the issei.

45. Theodore Caplow, *The Sociology of Work* (New York: McGraw-Hill, 1954), p. 233.

46. Perhaps, the point is made clearer by Braverman's remark that although the work of a cleaner employed by a firm that sells cleaning services generates profit and thereby increases the employer's capital, the work of the private domestic actually reduces the wealth of the employer. Harry Braverman, *Labor and Monopoly Capital* (New York and London: Monthly Review Press, 1974).

47. Margaret Benston, "The Political Economy of Women's Liberation," in *From Feminism to Liberation,* ed. Edith H. Altbach (Cambridge, Mass. and London: Shenkman Publishing Company, 1971), pp. 199-210.

48. Social security coverage was extended to domestics in the 1950s, and federal minimum wage laws in the 1970s. See U.S. Department of Labor, Women's Bureau, *Handbook of Women Workers* (Washington, D.C.: Government Printing Office, 1975); and David M. Katzman, "Domestic Service: Woman's Work," in *Women Working,* ed. Ann H. Stromberg and Shirley Harkess (Palo Alto, Calif.: Mayfield Publishing Company, 1978), pp. 377-391).

49. For example, studies by Katzman, *Seven Days a Week,* and Stigler, *Domestic Servants in the United States.*

50. Jane Addams, "A Belated Industry," *American Journal of Sociology* 1 (March 1896): 536-50.

51. Coser, "Domestic Servants."

52. Ibid., p. 32.

53. Ibid., p. 36.

54. Katzman, *Seven Days a Week,* points out that employers preferred live-in help and deplored the trend toward living out, because they preferred the control they could exert over the time and behavior of the domestic who lived in.

55. Chie Nakane, *Kinship and Economic Organization in Rural Japan,* London School of Economics Monographs on Social Anthropology, no. 32 (London: The Athlone Press, 1967).

56. Sylvia J. Yanagisako, "Two Processes of Change in Japanese-American Kinship," *Journal of Anthropological Research* 31 (1975): 196-224.

57. Ibid.

58. These kibei children (American born, Japanese educated) frequently encountered the same difficulties as their parents. Language and cultural barriers handicapped them in the labor market. Mrs. Nishimura's three older children raised in Japan, for example, ended up in farming and domestic work, and the three younger children became white-collar workers.

59. Elizabeth Bott, *Family and Social Network: Roles, Norms and External Relationships in Ordinary Urban Families* (London: Tavistock Publications, 1957).

60. This is in contrast to the Azorean immigrant families described by Louise Lamphere, Filomena Silva, and John Sousa, in "Kin Networks and Family Strategies: Working-Class Families in New England" (unpublished paper). These families also adjusted to the urban economy through multiple wage earning. Traditional division of household labor by gender was maintained, but social activities were joint, and centered around the extended family.

61. See Dill, "Dialectics of Black Womanhood"; and Lerner, *Black Women in White America.*

62. For example, Erving Goffman, in *Asylums* (Garden City, N.Y.: Anchor Books, 1961) identifies several situationally specific strategies that patients develop for coping with conditions in total institutions.

63. Heidi Hartmann. "Capitalism, Patriarchy, and Job Segregation by Sex," *Signs* 1 (Spring 1976): 137-169; and Natalie Sokoloff, "A Theoretical Analysis of Women in the Labor Market," paper presented at the meetings of the Society for the Study of Social Problems, San Francisco, 1978.

References

Addams, Jane
    1896   "A belated industry." American Journal of Sociology 1 (March): 536-550.
Benston, Margaret
    1971   "The political economy of women's liberation." Pp. 199-210 in Edith H. Altbach, ed., From Feminism to Liberation. Cambridge, Mass. and London: Shenkman Publishing Company.
Bott, Elizabeth
    1957   Family and Social Network: Roles, Norms and External Relationships in Ordinary Urban Families. London: Tavistock Publications.
Braverman, Harry
    1974   Labor and Monopoly Capital. New York and London: Monthly Review Press.
Buddhist Churches of America
    1974   Seventy-Five Anniversary of the Buddhist Churches of America. Chicago: Nobart Publications.
Caplow, Theodore
    1954   The Sociology of Work. New York: McGraw-Hill.
Chaplin, David
    1978   "Domestic service and industrialization." Comparative Studies in Sociology 1:98-127.
Coser, Lewis
    1973   "Domestic servants: The obsolescence of a social role." Social Forces 52:31-40.
Cowan, Ruth S.
    1976   "The industrial revolution in the home: Household technology and social change in the twentieth century." Technology and Culture 17 (January):1-23.
Daniels, Roger
    1973   The Politics of Prejudice. New York: Atheneum.
Dill, Bonnie
    1979   "The dialectics of Black womanhood." Signs 4 (Spring):543-555.
Glaser, Barney G., and Anselm L. Strauss
    1967   The Discovery of Grounded Theory. Chicago: Aldine Publishing Co.
Goffman, Erving
    1961   Asylums. Garden City, N.Y.: Anchor Books.
Hartmann, Heidi
    1976   "Capitalism, patriarchy, and job segregation by sex." Signs 1 (Spring):137-169.
Hill, Joseph A.
    1929   Women in Gainful Occupations, 1870-1920. Census Monographs 9. Washington, D. C.: U.S. Department of Commerce, Bureau of the Census.
Hooks, Janet
    1947   Women's Occupations Through Seven Decades. Bulletin no. 218. Washington, D.C.: U.S. Department of Labor, Women's Bureau.
Ichihashi, Yamato
    1915   Japanese Immigration. San Francisco: The Marshall Press.
    1932   Japanese in the United States. Stanford, Calif.: Stanford University Press.

Katzman, David M.

1978*a* "Domestic service: Woman's work." Pp. 377-391 in Ann H. Stromberg and Shirley Harkess, eds., Women Working. Palo Alto, Calif.: Mayfield Publishing Company.

1978*b* Seven Days a Week: Women and Domestic Service in Industrializing America. New York: Oxford University Press.

Kitano, Harry H. L.

1960 "Housing of Japanese Americans in the San Francisco Bay Area." Pp. 178-197 in Nathan Glazer and D. McEntire, eds., Studies in Housing and Minority Groups. Berkeley and Los Angeles: University of California Press.

Lerner, Gerda

1973 Black Women In White America: A Documentary History. New York: Vintage Books.

Light, Ivan H.

1972 Ethnic Enterprise in America. Berkeley, Los Angeles, London: University of California Press.

Melbin, Murray

1978 "Night as frontier." American Sociological Review 43:3-22.

Millis, H. A.

1915 The Japanese Problem in the United States. New York: The Macmillan Co.

Miyamoto, Frank

1939 "Social solidarity among the Japanese in Seattle." University of Washington Publications in the Social Sciences 11:57-130.

Nakane, Chie

1967 Kinship and Economic Organization in Rural Japan. London School of Economics Monographs on Social Anthropology, no. 32. London: The Athlone Press.

Omi, Frank, ed.

1975 Eighty-Fifth Anniversary of Protestant Work among Japanese in North America. n.p.

Salmon, Lucy M.

1897 Domestic Service. New York: Macmillan Co.

Smuts, Robert W.

1959 Women and Work in America. New York: Columbia University Press.

Sokoloff, Natalie

1978 "A theoretical analysis of women in the labor market." Paper presented at the Society for the Study of Social Problems meetings, San Francisco.

Stigler, George J.

1946 Domestic Servants in the United States, 1900-1940. New York: National Bureau of Economic Research.

Strong, Edward K.

1933 Japanese in California. Stanford, Calif.: Stanford University Press.

1934 The Second-Generation Japanese Problem. Stanford, Calif.: Stanford University Press.

U.S. Department of Commerce, Bureau of the Census

1923 Fourteenth Census of the United States Taken in the Year 1920. vol. 4. Population, Occupations. Washington, D.C.: Government Printing Office.

U.S. Department of Labor, Women's Bureau

1975 Handbook of Women Workers. Washington, D.C.: Government Printing Office.

Watson, Amy

1937 "Domestic service." Encyclopedia of the Social Sciences 5:198-206.

Yanagisako, Sylvia J.
    1975   "Two processes of change in Japanese-American kinship." Journal of Anthropological Research 31:196-224.
Yancey, William L., Eugene P. Ericksen, and Richard N. Julian
    1976   "Emergent ethnicity: A review and refomulation." American Sociological Review 41 (June):391-403.

15

The Social Structure of Korean Communities in California, 1903-1920*

Sun Bin Yim

The objective of this chapter is to analyze the nature and consequences of class structure and class relations among Korean immigrants as well as to examine their work relationships with non-Koreans in California during the period 1903 to 1920.[1] While a number of studies have been made of Korean communities in California from this period,[2] generally the role of class in the social structure of these communities has not been considered.

The present study differs not only analytically from previous contributions, but also methodologically. Three primary sources were used extensively: the files of the *New Korea* between 1903 and 1920,[3] personal documents and interviews,[4] and the city directories of Los Angeles.[5] Since no study of Koreans can ignore the background issue of immigration, the first section of the chapter will discuss trends in the volume and characteristics of Korean immigrants, based on census data.

IMMIGRATION AND RESIDENCE

The immigration of Koreans to the United States and Hawaii has fluctuated noticeably since it was first officially recorded in 1899.[6] In the initial years, from 1899 to 1902, there were 168 Korean immigrants, or an average of 42 per year. It was not long, however, before there was a

*This paper could not have been written without the generous cooperation and effort of the interviewees, many of whom were quite elderly. The author would also like to express her gratitude to *New Korea* for making its files freely available.

515

dramatic increase in the annual number of immigrants, from 28 in the fiscal year ending in 1902, to 564 in 1903, 1,907 in 1904, and reaching a peak of 4,929 in 1905 (see table 15.1). Most of this mass migration was directed to Hawaii in part because of the recruitment activities in Korea by representatives of Hawaiian sugar plantation owners. While somewhat different figures are given in other sources, trends are comparable.[7]

The number of immigrants dropped sharply to 127 in the fiscal year ending in 1906, to 39 in 1907, 26 in 1908, and 11 in 1909. Most likely, this abrupt decline resulted from the legislation adopted by the Korean government in April 1905 banning emigration (Hyun 1976:805). In July of the following year an edict made it virtually impossible for Koreans to emigrate directly to the United States without the consent of the Japanese authorities (Hyun 1976:807); in order to come to the United States, Koreans first had to flee to Shanghai, Siberia, or Europe. Though numerous interpretations of the reasons behind such legislation have been offered, none are conclusive. One interpretation suggests that Japanese companies in charge of emigration were unable to send Japanese workers to Hawaii during the Russo-Japanese war of 1903-1905,

TABLE 15.1

KOREAN ALIENS AND MIGRANT ALIENS ADMITTED AND DEPARTING, UNITED STATES,
1899 TO 1920

Year	Immigrants	Emigrants	Net Immigration
1899	22		
1900	71		
1901	47		
1902	28		
1903	564		
1904	1,907		
1905	4,929		
1906	127		
1907	39		
1908	26	188	-162
1909	11	114	-103
1910	19	137	-118
1911	8	41	- 33
1912	33	55	- 22
1913	64	44	+ 20
1914	152	43	+109
1915	146	47	+ 99
1916	154	29	+125
1917	194	45	+149
1918	149	77	+ 72
1919	77	23	+ 54
1920	72	14	+ 58

SOURCE: U.S Commissioner General of Immigration (1899-1919).

and as a consequence Korean workers were used as substitutes until the war was over, when they were no longer needed (Ko 1973:212). It is interesting to note that during the sharp rise of Korean immigration to the United States from 1903 to 1905, Japanese immigration declined markedly—from 20,041 to 11,021. Then, during the steep decline of Korean immigration, Japanese immigration increased—from 11,021 in 1905 to 30,824 in 1907 (U.S. Immigration Commission 1911a). Another interpretation is that, despite the Japanese government's claim that Korean immigration should be halted because there was no official Korean representative to protect Korean immigrant workers, their main concern was to protect Japanese workers in Hawaii from competition (Hyun 1976:807).

The distribution of Koreans varied from the initial concentration in Hawaii to a more dispersed pattern (see table 15.2). From 1910 to 1920 there was some redistribution of the Korean population from Hawaii to California, so that the percent of Koreans who resided in California increased from 6.4 to 14.6. The Middle Atlantic and the North Central regions (comprising New York and Chicago, respectively) also gained in numbers between 1910 and 1920.

According to emigration data, the return movement back to Korea appears to have been quite substantial until 1910. In the six years from 1905 to 1910 some 1,133 Koreans emigrated (B. Kim 1937). Faced with such a large exodus, Korean American leaders tried to stem this out-

TABLE 15.2

DISTRIBUTION OF KOREANS BY REGIONS ON THE MAINLAND AND IN HAWAII, 1910 AND 1920

Regions	Korean population		Percent distribution	
	1910	1920	1910	1920
Pacific	318	901	6.4	14.6
(California)	(304)	(772)	(6.1)	(12.5)
New England	0	7	0.0	0.1
Middle Atlantic	4	40	0.1	0.7
South Atlantic	0	15	0.0	0.2
North Central	26	111	0.5	1.8
South Central	2	6	0.0	0.1
Mountain	112	144	2.3	2.3
Mainland Total	462	1,224	9.3	19.8
Hawaii	4,533	4,950	91.7	80.2
Total (Mainland & Hawaii)	4,955	6,174	100.0	100.0

SOURCE: U.S. Bureau of the Census 1933.

flow, which could weaken their new community. Editorials and articles in the *New Korea* (1 Dec. 1909, 4 May 1910; and passim), published by the Korean National Association, pointed to the problems emigrants would face when they went back, hoping this would discourage prospective emigrants:

> Usually those who don't study and don't make enough money tend to return. . . . Those who returned today included 2 by Korean ship, 10 by Mongolian ship, and 20-30 by Manchurian ship. . . . If this continues, not only will we not be able to find Koreans in America within a year, but also associations like the Korean National Association can't function anymore. . . . If you wish to return with a very limited knowledge of English and with less than $1,000, don't come back to the States. . . . Don't disappoint Koreans in Korea by returning without money and study. . . At first, after you return, you'll be busy and happy with families and friends, etc. for 10 days, and later you will be upset by many things: you will spend all the money you brought back from America, and then you will take your watch, glasses, clothes, etc. to pawn shops. Afterwards, you will ask yourself: "Why did I come back?". . . So, think two or three times before leaving. I myself went to Korea for a half a year after being in Hawaii and the U.S. I went through the same experiences that I described, and so did other returnees. . . . Don't return unless you achieve and become successful. (Editorial, 1 Dec. 1909)

Some of the emigrants, however, went back to Korea because of sickness and poverty, and this was generally accepted (*New Korea*, 8 Jan. 1908; 15 Jan. 1908; and passim). In fact, other Koreans voluntarily collected money to help pay their passage home.

Following the Japanese annexation of Korea in 1910, there was a sharp reduction in the number of emigrants, from 137 in 1910 to 41 in 1911. In the whole period of 1911 to 1920, there were altogether 418 emigrants, or an annual mean of 42 (see table 15.1). Letters to the *New Korea* suggest that Koreans who went back after the annexation found themselves mistreated by the Japanese police and felt dehumanized:

> Let Koreans in America know that America is heaven. . . . Let them know not to go back where it is like hell now. . . . I returned without knowing what was going on in Korea. . . . Please don't let any Koreans return to Korea from now on. (2 June 1910)

> A Korean who went to Korea because of sickness wrote a letter to his friend in America saying: How could I get out of this lion's den and manage to go to heavenly America again? (23 April 1910)

RESIDENTIAL DISTRIBUTION IN CALIFORNIA

The residential distribution of Koreans in California was essentially determined by the type of work they did. As long as Koreans worked mainly in agriculture, their residential distribution was determined by the nature of the demand for agricultural labor. A large share of California's agriculture was devoted to the cultivation of intensive crops such as vegetables, fruits, and citrus fruits. Most communities or farm areas in California specialized in only one or a few crops which matured at different times. During the harvest, a large pool of labor was required, and farmers depended heavily on migratory labor. For instance, in a survey of 316 Japanese farm laborers in 1910, it was found that more than half had been in two or more localities within a year, and some of them in as many as six or seven (U.S. Immigration Commission 1911a:15). Therefore it is likely that many Koreans traveled extensively in California and changed their residences frequently.

In a survey of farm workers carried out in 1909 (U.S. Immigration Commission 1911a), Koreans were mentioned as pickers in the citrus groves of the Pomona-Riverside-Redlands areas. They were also working in the fruit and vegetable canneries where the work was equally seasonal. Interviewee K states:

> About ten days after I arrived in San Francisco (in 1916), I went to Stockton, and through a Korean contractor I went to work on a Caucasian-owned bean farm. There were about 20 other Koreans working there. . . . We were hoeing the bean fields and when we finished we went to another bean farm for hoeing. It was hard work. . . . Then we went to Dinuba picking grapes. I was flocking with other Koreans, and I went wherever they went for available farm jobs.

According to news items in the *New Korea*, "there are not many Koreans in Dinuba, but when it is grape picking time, many Koreans will come," and "Sacramento is a stopping place for Koreans who go back and forth to work on farms and on the railroad . . . and there are always 30-40 Koreans in town." A few years later, in 1917, it was asserted that "Dinuba had to establish vigilantes because 200-300 Koreans were moving in every year during grape picking season and 40-50 Koreans were always living there" (15 Nov. 1917). Table 15.3 shows the estimated size of various California Korean communities at various points in time, suggesting shifts over relatively short periods.

The opening or closing of a branch office of the Korean National Association gives some measure of the fluctuations of an area's Korean population. When a community had 20 or more Koreans, the association

TABLE 15.3
ESTIMATES OF THE RESIDENT KOREAN POPULATION FOR VARIOUS PLACES,
1911 TO 1918

	Southern California			Northern California	
Place	Population	Date of Article	Place	Population	Date of Article
Claremont	40	1/25/11	Lompoc	30	1/01/11
Claremont	20	4/30/14	Lompoc	20	4/30/14
Redlands	10	4/30/14	Sacramento	30-40	6/07/11
Upland	40	4/30/14	Sacramento	50	9/02/15
Upland	70	4/29/15	Dinuba	20	6/14/14
Los Angeles	40-50	4/30/14	Dinuba	40-50	11/15/17
Imperial Valley	60	7/08/15	Manteca	60	5/26/16
Riverside	45	1/23/18	Idria	10	7/27/16

SOURCE: *New Korea*, 1911 to 1918.

approved the establishment of a branch; if a community fell below 20 Korean residents, it was likely to lose the branch. Between 1911 and 1918, Dinuba gained a branch, and Idria and Redlands lost theirs.

Unfortunately, most of these places have no census data since their populations number less than 100,000. However, census data are available for Koreans residing in San Francisco, Los Angeles, Oakland, San Diego, and Long Beach. (It should be noted that in 1910, about 83 percent of Koreans in California resided outside these cities.) There is some disagreement between census figures and estimates published by the *New Korea*. Specifically, the *New Korea* estimated the Korean population of Los Angeles to be around 60 in 1911-1913 and that of California in 1913 between 700 and 800. By contrast the census of 1910 figures the Korean populations of Los Angeles and California to be 14 and 304, respectively. It is possible that there was a marked undercount at that census because of the seasonal migration of most Koreans in 1910 in search of work. Yet, there is no doubt that the vast majority of Koreans resided in rural centers and smaller towns. In view of the boom in agriculture during World War I, the situation probably did not change drastically between 1910 and 1920. Indeed, the percentage of Koreans living in the five biggest cities of the state only increased slightly from 17.3 to 21.1 during those years, although the share in Los Angeles increased rapidly, from 4.6 percent in 1910 to 10.8 percent in 1920. Los Angeles, in fact, displaced San Francisco as the city with the largest Korean population during this decade. Los Angeles became the one metropolis with a strong attraction for Koreans, in part because many of them resided in the agricultural towns and communities close to Los

Angeles, such as Upland, Oxnard, Riverside, and Redlands. San Francisco, the other center of Korean population concentration, assumed an early importance as a port of entry for Koreans coming from Hawaii and abroad, including Korea. Oakland, San Diego, and Long Beach had little attraction for Koreans, and the few Koreans who were in Oakland may have come from San Francisco.

City directories are the only systematic and quantifiable primary source materials on the residential segregation of Koreans. As a way of assessing the extent of this segregation before 1920, I examined the directories of San Francisco and Los Angeles for Korean names.

I started with the two uniquely Korean names of Kim and Ahn and found that the directories of San Francisco (Crocker-Langley San Francisco Directory, 1908-1917) proved useless for my purpose. A search of the volumes from 1908-1909 to 1916-1917 yielded only two entries with these names. As early as 1910, however, there were four Kim entries in the Los Angeles directory (Los Angeles City Directory, 1910-1920). I decided, therefore, to focus my analysis on Los Angeles. Two other common Korean names are Lee and Park, but unlike Kim and Ahn, they are also found among Caucasians and Chinese. The task of differentiating between Korean and non-Korean Lees and Parks requires a consideration of given names and addresses. For the present analysis, only the extensive listings of Lees were examined to identify the ones that could be considered Korean. For the period 1910-1920, there were 25 unduplicated Kim and Ahn entries and 7 presumed Korean Lees. The directories prior to 1910 were not used, because they had fewer than four Kims, all of whom appeared in the 1910 directory.[8]

The spatial distribution of addresses of the 32 Kims, Ahns, and Lees is shown in figure 15.1.[9] These were two areas of Korean concentration: around Macy and Alameda Streets in the present location of Union Station and the Post Office, and in the Bunker Hill area, around 1st and Figueroa. But several addresses were scattered away from these two centers, suggesting that the segregation of Koreans in Los Angeles was not extreme during the years 1910 to 1920.

MAJOR SOCIAL CLASSES

This discussion will focus on the three major social classes, capitalists, petite bourgeoisie, and working class or proletariat. Among Koreans in California, many individuals experienced extensive job mobility and "circulated" among the various social classes. For instance, interviewee Y started as a laborer and then became a labor contractor for grape pickers and railroad workers in the Fresno area around 1906. After

DISTRIBUTiON OF ADDRESSES OF KIM, AHN, AND RELEVANT
LEE ENTRIES IN THE 1910-1920 LOS ANGELES CITY DIRECTORIES
(1916 Map of Los Angeles) *

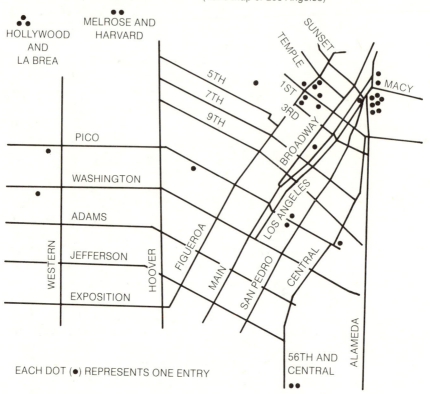

EACH DOT (●) REPRESENTS ONE ENTRY

Fig. 15.1

marriage, he and his wife went into the restaurant and hotel business in and out of the state. They became very successful and accumulated $35,000 in savings, which they invested in a 150-acre rice farm in 1919. But after World War I, rice prices dropped rapidly and they lost everything they had. Y became a laborer again, and at one point, when he was a janitor in an oil company, he even joined a labor strike. In the end, however, he became a successful owner of a restaurant. Other Koreans faced similar successes and failures as small capitalists and had to join the ranks of the proletariat at various times in their lives.

The following cites another example of job mobility, as told by interviewee G about his father:

During the years that my father was working as a farm laborer, he made up his mind that he had to own his own business in order to make money. So, he and a group of friends got together and formed a company and pooled their money together. They were making great profits in potato farming in Stockton. Then the Depression came, and we couldn't sell the potatoes and lost everything. Afterwards, we went to Colusa where my father and mother washed and ironed. . . . After that we went to Idria where my father worked for four years in the mercury smelting furnaces.

Working Class

The working class comprises all laborers on farms, in mines, and in industry, irrespective of the nature of wage payments. In agriculture, payments could be on a daily or an hourly basis, as piece work, or by a flat rate for a specific job (*do-geup*), such as hoeing a piece of land. Small scale sharecroppers probably belong to this class since they did not own the means of production and had little control over investments. The working class also included wage workers in the service industry, such as domestic servants and porters, and white-collar employees such as clerks, typists, and sales workers.

The size, composition, and components of the Korean proletariat are difficult to assess. Presumably it was the largest class and was composed mainly of farm laborers in the early days of Korean settlement in California. Evidence to support this statement, however, is only indirect and partial. Because about 98 percent of Korean immigrants with reported occupations on entry declared themselves to be farm laborers, it is likely that many of them remained for a while in that line of work. In addition, the *New Korea* (24 Oct. 1913) asserted that most Koreans in California were laborers but provided no direct evidence. It is possible, nevertheless, to piece together various bits of information to estimate the relative magnitude of the farm proletariat. According to one survey of 10,692 agricultural laborers in California in 1909, 122 were Koreans, only 2 of whom were women (U.S. Immigration Commission 1911a). While it is important to relate this number to the potential labor force, only a rough estimate of percentage of population can be obtained, since the requisite data are not available from the 1910 census. On the basis of a number of assumptions about age-sex distribution,[10] it was estimated that about 62 percent of Korean males age fifteen and over were in agricultural labor. This may be too low an estimate of the relative significance of farm labor. The same report states that "during the busiest season when the raisin grapes are being picked (in Fresno county) . . . there are . . . some 200-300 Koreans, who ordinarily work with Japanese and can not be distinguished from them" (U.S. Immigration Commission 1911a:22). While this figure seems somewhat high, other unpublished sources suggest that the number of Korean grape pickers in Fresno in 1907-1908 must have been somewhere around 100 or higher.[11] Indeed the *New Korea* announced that one Korean had contracted for 30 to 40 workers in the Fresno area in 1907 and for 100 workers in 1908 (26 Nov. 1907). Furthermore, there were 60 Koreans working in citrus groves (U.S. Immigration Commission 1911a:217). Consequently, there must have been many more than 122 Korean farm laborers in California in 1910, but the exact number is impossible to determine. There is no doubt, however, that the agricultural proletariat was the most numerous element in the Korean population of California around 1910.

In addition to the substantial agricultural proletariat, there was a small industrial working class. The size of the latter group is even more difficult to estimate, particularly because many Koreans shifted back and forth from agriculture to industry as required by the demand for cheap labor. Railroad work was the most important source of industrial employment in California. The following figures are for Koreans working in industry in Western states in 1909: 74 men working for nine railroad companies in maintenance-of-way, the lowest paid and least skilled railroad work; 3 in railroad shops; 2 in streetcar maintenance-of-way; and 13 in the coal and coke industry of Southern Colorado, Wyoming, and Washington (U.S. Immigration Commission 1911b). Information from the *New Korea* implies that those numbers are too low. There were reports of 20 to 30 Koreans working in Kismilia and of 23 Koreans in Serino in California in 1909 (23 June and 17 Nov. 1909).[12]

A number of Koreans were also employed as workers in fruit and vegetable canneries, but the tabulations of a 1909 survey do not distinguish between Japanese and Koreans. Finally, some life histories prove that a few Koreans were employed in mining and other industries in California. As stated by one old-timer (interviewee G): "I had news about year-around work in quicksilver mines in Idria. My family lived there about four years. We worked in mercury melting furnaces, worked steady the year around, and we had enough money to support the family. . . . Then, I got sick from mercury vapors." In 1915, 34 Korean workers were employed in Idria by the quicksilver mine company (*New Korea*, 16 Sept. 1915).

The relative size of the Korean agricultural proletariat was just as great in the decade following 1910 as it had been previously, partly because of the great demand for food and the need for agricultural manpower during World War I. This was reflected in the increase of *New Korea* announcements for farm labor and in the continued high rural concentration of the Korean population of California. The percent living outside of the big cities, and mostly in farm areas and small towns, declined only slightly from 83 percent in 1910 to 79 percent in 1920.

Occupational data would be needed to establish with any certainty the composition of the Korean working class during this period, but unfortunately, these are not available from the pertinent censuses. Some estimates of the working class, however, could be obtained from the analysis of city directories. As was indicated earlier, there were 25 Kims and Ahns in the Los Angeles city directories of 1910 to 1920. There were an additional 7 Lees, thus making a total of 32 persons. Of these, 3 were students, 3 had no occupation, and 26 reported their occupation as shown in table 15.4. Blue-collar workers were the only working class element and constituted about 27 percent of the total.

Conditions of work and wages varied by occupation. The following considers the conditions in two industries: agriculture and railroads.

Agriculture

In California, the particular conditions of farm work were related to the nature and structure of agriculture. As observed earlier, the scale and intensity of agriculture, particularly with respect to citrus and other fruits, and vegetables, required an abundant and cheap supply of labor during the fairly short period of harvest time. The varying climate of California meant that the labor that was needed had to shift from one location to another. One way in which a grower or farm owner could assure a reliable supply of workers was to contract with certain individuals who would insure that the labor would be available when needed. This system of "gangs" and labor "bosses" was introduced by the Chinese and practiced by Koreans. The bosses or labor contractors secured ranch work for their men and carried out all the negotiations with the ranchers pertaining to conditions and rate of pay. The bosses were also in charge of paying the men from the funds made available by the ranchers.

Again, it is difficult to estimate the population of Koreans who worked in gangs under Korean contractors. The U.S. Immigration Commission (1911a:18) reported in 1909: "The 'gang' system still obtains among Chinese, also among the more recently arrived and less numerous Koreans." From November 1905 to September 1910 there were 18 announcements by Korean contractors in the *New Korea*, most of which indicated the numbers of workers wanted. Comparing these numbers

TABLE 15.4

OCCUPATIONAL DISTRIBUTION OF ALL UNDUPLICATED ENTRIES WITH THE NAMES OF
KIM AND AHN AND A FEW ENTRIES WITH THE NAME OF LEE, 1910-1920

Occupation	Numbers	Percent distribution
Professional and semi-professional		
President, Korean Nat. Assoc.	1	
Secretary, Korean Nat. Assoc.	1	
Total	2	7.6
Small business		
Grocer, general and Chinese merchandise	7	
Wholesale produce	1	
Horse market	1	
Fish counter	1	
Cigars	1	
Restaurant	1	
Florist	1	
Barber	1	
Brewer	1	
Laundry	1	
Jeweler	1	
Total	17	65.4
Blue collar		
Houseman, elevator operator, porter, domestic	6	
Cook	1	
	7	26.9
Total with occupation	26	100.0
No occupation given	3	—
Students	3	—
Total	32	

SOURCE: Los Angeles City Directories.

to the estimated 122 farm laborers in California, it appears that labor
contracts were the most common organization of farm work among
Koreans in this early period.[13]

The most extensive information on wages is available from a 1909
survey of California agriculture, although Koreans were included with
and not differentiated from the Japanese. A distinction in the tabulation
was made between earnings with or without board. About 80 percent of
the Chinese received earnings with board as compared with about 10
percent for Japanese and Koreans combined. If the data were available
separately for Koreans, they would show a much higher proportion of

earnings with board. Indeed, five of the 18 announcements in the *New Korea* indicated the availability of boarding provided by Korean contractors. Furthermore, according to the U.S. Immigration Commission, Asian farm laborers "are never boarded by white employers unless employed as domestics. . . . Where 'gangs' of Orientals are employed through a 'boss,' the 'boss' usually boards the men either on a cooperative basis at the actual cost, or as is often the case he charges a fixed rate (usually between 25-30¢ a day)" (1911*a*:20). For 92 percent of 863 Japanese and Korean workers surveyed, the most common wages without board were between $1.50 and $1.75 a day. Of the 93 Japanese and Korean workers who received wages with board, 67 percent earned either $1.30 to $1.50 a day (U.S. Immigration Commission 1911*a*:35). Japanese and Korean workers were paid less than white farm laborers. Many more of the latter than the former received wages of $2.00 or more a day (48 percent as compared to 3 percent). While all farm laborers were exploited, Asians were exploited even more.

More specific data on prevailing wages and modes of payment for Koreans working in California agriculture are derived from the *New Korea* and personal interviews. A farm laborer could be paid on a daily or monthly basis, for the amount of work done (piecework), or by a flat rate for a specific job (*do-geup*). Piecework was mentioned in 5 of the 18 relevant announcements in the newspaper and "job assigned" in only two. Daily wages, mentioned 11 times, must have been the most common form of payment. It is possible, however, that the figures on daily earnings were based on average piecework rates.

Types and rates of pay for various crops for the period 1905 to 1910 include the following:
1. Vineyards (in Redlands and Riverside).
   Daily wages between $1.75 and $2.50. One announcement of piecework stated that workers could earn up to $4.00 to $5.00 a day.
2. Oranges (in Riverside and Redlands).
   Mostly $2.50 a day although one announcement in 1905 mentioned 60 to 75¢ a day.
3. Sugar beets (in Oxnard and Lompoc).
   Ranged from $1.80 to $3.00-$4.00 for a ten-hour day.

Wages seemed to be higher for sugar beet cultivation than for other crops or even for manufacturing. Moreover, the greater prevalence of piecework for sugar beets made it possible for workers to earn more by working more hours. It should be noted that the cultivation of sugar beets requires intensive labor for short periods during the thinning of new plants in the spring, for the first and second hoeing of weeds, and finally during the harvest.

Agricultural rates and hours of work began to increase in 1916-1917 when the United States entered the war. There was an increasing demand for food, combined with the shortage of manpower (W. Kim 1971, and personal interviews). In 1917, farm labor wages increased to $2.50, $3.00, or even $4.00 a day (*New Korea*, 24 May 1917). In Upland, according to interviewee C, wages for picking oranges were 25 to 35¢ an hour for a nine-hour day or $4.20 for a twelve-hour day, as compared with $2.50 a day a few years earlier.

Railroad

During the early years, 1905 to 1910, the Korean industrial proletariat of California worked mainly on the railroad, especially during the slack agricultural months. Unfortunately this industrial/agricultural combination still did not provide steady employment for Korean laborers, who must have experienced periods of unemployment and underemployment. Just as in agriculture, railroad workers were organized as "gangs" under a "boss" or contractor:

> After talking with the foreman of a railroad company, I entered into a contract with him to provide a "gang" of Korean workers. The conditions were that we worked repairing railroad tracks, ate and slept in wagons. (Interviewee W)

For the period of 1906 to 1910, there were about four or five announcements by Korean contractors in the *New Korea* for work on the railroad.[14] Because of the nature of railroad work, wages for this type of employment were lower than for farm labor. Data from a 1909 survey show that all 74 Korean maintenance-of-way workers were paid between $1.25 and $1.50 a day (U.S. Immigration Commission 1911*b*:471). From 1908 to 1910, wages were in the range of $1.40 to $1.60 a day, mostly for maintenance-of-way work on railroads near Los Angeles and Fresno and for the Ocean Shore Railroad and the West Pacific Railroad (*New Korea*, 15 Jan. 1908; 27 May 1908; 14 April 1909; 10 May 1918).

Most Korean workers were apparently recruited through personal contacts with relatives and friends:

> My parents could not find work in San Francisco after we arrived, and some friends down in Southern California told us about work available on extra gangs on the railroad in Reedley. . . . We lived there for a period of months. Then we had connections in Redlands, and moved over there. . . . From Redlands we moved to Riverside where we had some Korean friends. There was a group of Koreans there with one man as a labor boss. . . . (Interviewee P)

The two major Korean associations, the Dai-Dong and the United Korean Association (which were combined in 1909 and called the Korean National Association), recruited Koreans as members and then tried to find them jobs. For instance, in 1908, the United Korean Association organized a committee to welcome Koreans arriving in San Francisco "in order to get them to join the Association and provide them with jobs and free room and board until they could pay" (*New Korea*, 19 March 1908). Sometimes, the associations found the work first and then asked them to join. A member of the Dai-Dong said that his organization did this. Their method was to go to the port, or railroad station, and, as quickly as possible, attach the cards of their association to the suitcases of newly arrived Koreans, who were then guided to a boarding house owned by the association and given free board. The association found jobs for them in order to get them to join and pay the dues. In many cases, members of the associations entered into contracts to provide work for Koreans, and this was announced in the *New Korea*. Newspaper advertisements about possible work were another way in which Koreans were recruited to work on farms or on the railroad. Finally, Koreans flocked together wherever jobs were available, or they looked for employment in areas where other Koreans were already working.

From 1900 to 1920, it was almost impossible for Koreans to get any skilled work or white-collar jobs in Caucasian-owned enterprises. Evidence for this is found in the tabulation of occupations of persons with the names of Kim, Ahn, and Lee in the Los Angeles city directories (table 15.4) which shows the absence of white-collar or skilled blue-collar occupations. It is possible that a lack of knowledge of English was one factor that forced Koreans into unskilled labor both in agriculture and industry. It was, in fact, cited as one of the reasons why so few Koreans were employed in the more skilled and better paid railroad shop jobs (U.S. Immigration Commission 1911*b*). A more salient factor, however, was the discrimination that all Asians experienced in California and which in one way or another had an impact on their opportunity for employment. The pervasive nature of this discrimination is illustrated by the passage of the California Alien Land Act in 1913. This law was viewed by many Koreans as a restriction of their opportunities for becoming independent farmers:

The reason we left California, in the first place, was because they passed the anti-alien exclusion law. . . . You couldn't control your farm. . . . When we went to Washington where it was possible for Orientals to have farm land. . . . After we lived there for a few years, Washington passed an anti-alien exclusion farm law, so we went to Utah where they did not have such a law. . . . (Interviewee K)

Sometimes Caucasians hostile to Asians physically prevented Koreans from working. For example, thirteen Koreans and their labor contractor were surrounded and stopped from working in a farm in Hemet, California, by five hundred residents and white workers (*New Korea*, 14 July 1913).

Around 1910, women constituted a very small proportion of the Korean farm work force. This was inevitable, considering the imbalanced sex ratio of nearly 1,300 males per 100 females in the Korean population of the United States. While the evidence from a 1909 survey of California agriculture is suspect with respect to the number of Korean farm laborers, the ratio of 1 woman per 60 Korean farm workers is not too far from the truth (U.S. Immigration Commission 1911*a*). Another reason for this near absence of women from the fields is that they were more likely to be working in the kitchen cooking for work gangs of Korean men:

> When we were in the citrus orchards in Redlands, I was in the kitchen cooking food, Korean foods. I was one of the cooks for Korean farm workers. A hundred workers needed a lot of women cooking in the kitchen. . . . In Colusa, there were fifteen to twenty Koreans working, and I cooked their meals. At the same time, I had to raise ten children. Oh, it was pretty hard, but what could you do? (Interviewee M)

As in rural areas, women in urban areas undertook wage work that was compatible with their roles as wives and mothers. Interviewee Mrs. P, residing near Sacramento where her husband was a laborer, said: "I did the laundry for Caucasians and Korean bachelors. I had to wash by hand and to iron. I got paid about 80¢ or $1.00 per day in 1916." She continued this work for about eight years and was able to save a lot of money. Meanwhile, she had to look after her old husband and their seven young children: "I never went to bed before 1:00 A.M. and had to get up at 4:00 A.M. to cook for my husband who had stomach trouble."

Petite Bourgeoisie

The size and composition of both the petite bourgeoisie and the capitalists were influenced by restrictive and discriminatory legislation and by citizenship requirements for different professions and businesses. Were it not for the Alien Land Law, for instance, a greater proportion of these two classes would have been made up of farm owners, judging from the number of Koreans who owned farms before 1913. Some Koreans, however, married American-born women and bought land in their wives' or their American-born children's names. Some Koreans owned or operated farms varying in size from a few acres to several hundred acres. Generally, if the farm was relatively small, the Korean owner or tenant would operate it by himself with the help of his family. In this case, he could be considered a member of the petite bourgeoisie, even though he might have hired some seasonal workers during the harvest. By contrast, the owners or tenants of very large farms that required an extensive use of farm labor should be viewed as capitalists. The distribution of the number of farms and number of partners in 1917 by areas is given in table 15.5.

In one year, Korean owners or tenants, in partnership or alone, cultivated at least twenty-seven parcels or farms totaling 6,200 acres. Four of the individual tenants of the biggest parcels accounted for 36 percent of the total acreage. While there is no doubt that these four were capitalists, the others constituted a mixed group of capitalists and petite bourgeoisie. The rural petite bourgeoisie included not only some of these farm owners or tenants but also contractors and a few of the more successful sharecroppers. The urban petite bourgeoisie comprised owners of small businesses such as grocery stores, barber shops, hotels, restaurants, and some professional and semiprofessional persons.

In the early days of Korean settlement, around 1910, the petite bourgeoisie was quite small, composed mostly of labor contractors, farm tenants, a few farm owners, owners of inns and boarding houses and

TABLE 15.5

NUMBER AND ACREAGE OF FARMS CULTIVATED BY KOREANS ALONE OR IN PARTNERSHIP IN SELECTED CALIFORNIA AREAS FOR SELECTED CROPS, 1917

Manteca (sugar beets)		Stockton (sugar beets)		Delevan (rice)		Willows (rice)		Sacramento (rice)	
No. of partners	Acres	No. of partners	Acres	No. of partners	Acres	No. of partners	Acres	No. of partners	Acres
1	600	10	800	1	1,030	1	250	1	100
4	300	6	700	1	240	1	100	1	60
2	160	2	400	1	150	1	80	1	40
2	100	1	300	1	80			1	35
1	70	1	300	1	80			1	35
1	50	3	300	1	75				
1	40								
Total 12	1,320	23	2,600	6	1,580	3	430	5	270

SOURCE: File of the *New Korea*, 8 March 1917, 26 April 1917, 3 May 1917.

other small businesses. There were few professionals in this period since the newly arrived Korean immigrants did not have the necessary training to engage in a profession. It is difficult to assess the relative importance of the various components of the petite bourgeoisie. However, since the Korean population was overwhelmingly rural around 1910, it may be surmised that farm labor contractors, small farm owners, or tenants, and owners or operators of boarding houses and farm labor camps made up most of this class.

Advertisements of businesses in the *New Korea* suggest that for the period 1915 to 1919, the main elements of the urban petite bourgeoisie were owners or operators of small establishments such as barbershops, laundries, restaurants, and boardinghouses or inns, all of which required only modest capital. These advertisements, listed in table 15.6, provide

TABLE 15.6

NUMBER AND TYPES OF BUSINESSES IN VARIOUS CALIFORNIA CITIES AND TOWNS,
1915-1919

Types of businesses	Cities and Towns			
	San Francisco	Los Angeles	Oakland, Sacramento, Stockton	Small Towns (Marysville, Tracy, and Manteca)
Hotels, inns, boarding houses	3	1	3	5
Restaurants, cafes	1	2	1	1
Cigarette stands	2	1	—	—
Grocery stores	2	3	—	—
Barber shops and/or pool rooms	2	4	5	—
Laundries	3	—	—	1
Clothing, tailoring establishments	2	1	—	—
Bookstores	2	—	—	—
Other (export-import shops, photo studios, wholesale food stores, employment agencies)	4	1	—	—
Total	21	13	9	7

SOURCE: Advertisements in the *New Korea*.

some minimum data on the range and number of small businesses in various urban areas of California. Many of the businesses listed had a very short "life" and experienced substantial turnover.

Judging from these advertisements, hotels and inns were almost the only establishments owned by Koreans in rural market towns like Marysville and Tracy. This implies that the Korean petite bourgeoisie in these towns must have been oriented toward the rural population. That is to say, these inns were needed by farm labor contractors for themselves and for their workers. By contrast, in San Francisco, the urban center for Koreans in this earlier period, the petite bourgeoisie was much more diversified.

A few of the advertisements indicate that some Koreans owned fairly large establishments involving more than small amounts of capital. For example, two Koreans in San Francisco bought a grocery store from a Caucasian for $8,000, and another Korean spent $6,000 for a restaurant. Since they employed very few or no workers, they are still considered to be petite bourgeois even though they might also be classified as small capitalists.

The Los Angeles city directory data offer some additional clues about the size of the urban petite bourgeoisie in 1910 to 1920. Combining the occupational categories of small business, professional, and semiprofessional, I estimate that this class accounted for nearly three-quarters of the heads of households in Los Angeles in the late 1910s (see table 15.4). The preponderance of the petite bourgeoisie in Los Angeles suggests that its growth was partly a consequence of the process of urbanization. Not only did it grow at the expense of the farm and urban proletariat but it also experienced a change in internal composition with a decline in the importance of small farmers.

Advertisements in the *New Korea* for the period 1915 to 1920 yield some data on the extent of turnover in ownership. Of the thirteen business establishments in Los Angeles that had advertised in this period, four closed after an average period of a little over a year, one was for sale, and one had been sold to another Korean. The cigarette stand, the barbershops, and the poolroom had the shortest life. Businesses in San Francisco, by comparison, seemed somewhat more stable. Out of twenty-two that advertised, only one closed approximately a year after opening, and three others had been bought or sold recently. It is intriguing to note that while these transactions of ownership almost exclusively involved Koreans, the customers of the businesses were not always all Koreans. For some types of business and in some locations, the customers were a mixture of Koreans and non-Koreans, including

Mexicans, Caucasians, and Chinese. For instance, a Korean-owned hotel and poolroom in Sacramento had many Mexican customers (Diary of Mr. B), and the Chinese were often seen in a Korean barber shop near Chinatown in San Francisco (Interviewee O).

Many Korean small businesses exacted long hours of work from the owners and their families and yet yielded limited income. Some of the bigger businesses were more lucrative, which made it possible to hire some help. Still other Koreans made their income and accumulated capital by purchasing and selling business properties. As indicated above, one Korean businessman made a $6,500 profit by buying and selling a large hotel within a year in Marysville. He then moved to Stockton, bought a poolroom from a Japanese for $1,000, and after repairing and remodeling it, sold it to three Koreans for $7,500. This budding capitalist had accumulated $35,000 by 1919, which he invested and lost in rice farming. It is clear, therefore, that at least a few members of the Korean petite bourgeoisie saved enough capital to allow them to venture into capitalist enterprises.

Conditions of work and the income of one small business were reported by the owner's wife:

> He owned a barbershop with four chairs, and he hired three barbers: Korean, Filipino, and Chinese, because it was located in Chinatown. . . . Each barber had his own customers and for every dollar that he made, he gave 30 cents to my husband. He owned it for eighteen years, and we could save money and send our children to school. . . . He worked in the barbershop until 8:00 P.M., and at night he worked as a cook and as a night clerk. (Interviewee O)

The petite bourgeoisie primarily included workers who had accumulated sufficient funds to acquire a small business. As delineated in a number of editorials in the *New Korea,* the prevailing ideology of the Korean community was petit bourgeois. The newspaper exhorted workers "to save little by little through work" and then "they will be able to start a small business" (16 Sept. 1908). In 1910 the newspaper admonished Koreans to work hard "in agriculture or in industry" in order to set a good example for other Koreans. Many Korean workers took the first opportunity to go into business, no matter how small.

Capitalists

In spite of the discriminatory legislation and practices that hindered the growth of both the petite bourgeoisie and the capitalist class, economic conditions in California facilitated the emergence of a Korean capitalist class. At first, this class was predominantly agrarian and mercantile, though it became more mercantile and industrial in later years. Compared to their white counterparts, however, Korean capitalists had modest wealth and power. While a few individuals raised capital by themselves or in partnership with a few others, most capital was generated by corporations (see the following section for a discussion of corporations). One example of an individual Korean capitalist is the owner of the Oriental Food Products of California, a company that specialized in the production of canned and freshly prepared Oriental foods. The following description of this capitalist was given by one of his employees:

> I got a job as a shipping clerk for a company owned by a Korean.
> . . . The owner made a lot of money and made good profits but took the
> blood out of the poor people. He always had a Packard car, the most
> expensive car. . . . There were about thirty people working for him
> (Japanese, Mexicans, and Koreans). . . . He was a slave driver.
> . . . Sometimes I worked from 4:00 A.M. till late at night. . . . (Interviewee P)

Similarly some Koreans—such as Jong-Lim Kim, known as the rice king—made a great deal of money growing rice on leased land during 1916-1917 only to lose most of it when rice prices collapsed at the end of World War I. In 1917-1918, Kim was leasing up to 3,000 acres and made $18,400 in profits. Other Korean rice farmers in the Willows and Marysville areas earned profits of $1,113 per acre on 60 acres, $437 per acre on 80 acres. Using size of farm or amount of profits as criteria, there may have been at least fifteen agricultural capitalists in the rice and sugar beet fields in the same period (*New Korea*, 27 April 1917, 29 Dec. 1917, and passim). By the same token, some Korean agricultural capitalists lost money in rice ventures.

The favorite methods of raising capital were the pooling of funds and incorporation; only a few individuals managed to accumulate sufficient money alone to start a capitalist enterprise. Interviewee L was one of these few. He had made $35,000 in profits in business and invested it by leasing 100 acres for rice farming in 1919. He hired fifteen experienced Korean workers to do the farming. As a result of the precipitous drop of rice prices at the end of World War I, however, he lost his entire investment. As indicated by the tabulation of size of farms (see table 15.5), at least a few Koreans owned or leased very large farms that must have required substantial capitalization.

There were many more examples of Koreans who combined their savings to start an enterprise, especially in agriculture (see table 15.5). This practice was described by interviewee S:

> I joined a group of friends who pooled their money together to start
> potato farming in the Stockton area. They were making great profits,
> but when I joined to put in 1,200 acres of potatoes, we couldn't sell the
> potatoes. . . . It was a dead loss.

Similar cases of loss with rice planting in 1918-1919 imply that Korean
capitalists were particularly vulnerable to economic depressions or
adverse climatic conditions. They did not have enough capital to cushion
their losses.

For economic and political reasons, incorporation became a fairly
common method of raising capital among Koreans to finance projects
both in the United States and in Korea. Incorporation thus increased the
influence of capitalism and facilitated the expression of nationalistic
sentiments or unity.

The files of the *New Korea* (1908-1911) provide the following descriptions of corporations started in that period:

a) Asian Industrial Corporation: Established in 1908 by thirty-one
   Koreans, all whom were members of the United Association of
   California. The purpose was to develop industry in Korea and help
   to liberate Korea from Japanese rule. The capital was $20,000,
   raised by selling 800 shares at $25 each.
b) Kwon-Up Industrial League Corporation: Set up in 1908 by several
   Koreans in Los Angeles to purchase land in Korea for agricultural
   and industrial purposes. There were thirty-six stockholders in 1908,
   and the capital was $2,200. By 1911 the capital had increased to
   $6,000. They bought some land in Korea.
c) Tae-Dong (Great Eastern) Industrial Corporation: Established in
   San Francisco in 1909 with $25,000 in capital. A year later there was
   still a balance of $5,000 to be raised.
d) Hung-Up Corporation: Started in Redlands in 1909 to purchase
   land for cultivation. The corporation raised $4,000 from fifty
   Koreans. Work was started on orange fields, but the corporation
   went out of business in 1911.
e) The Korean American Trading Company: Started in San Francisco
   in 1910 to import Korean paintings and antiques and to export
   American goods. The shares were priced at $15.
f) The Industrial League: Organized in 1911 in Los Angeles for agricultural and industrial purposes. By 1914, $33,000 was raised by
   thirty-three shareholders, each of whom contributed $1,000. The
   league planned to open businesses in trees, vegetables, restaurants,
   stores, hotels, and the like.

g) Buk-Mi (North American) Industrial Company: Started in 1912 in Los Angeles with a focus on agriculture. Originally a total capital of $45,000 was to be raised with 150 shares at $300 each, and 120 Koreans had already subscribed. The amount raised reached $4,000 in 1917 and $15,000 in 1918.

h) Shin-Han Sang Hoe Company: Organized in 1911 in San Francisco by the headquarters of the Korean National Association. The objectives were (1) selling farm products (potatoes) in the Stockton area, where the corporation owned a general store; and (2) entering into partnership with Koreans who wanted to farm. Bankruptcy of the bank where this corporation had its funds forced the company to close. It lost most of its capital.

The majority of stockholders in these corporations owned only a few shares and were mainly workers and petit bourgeois who invested their small savings. At least two of the eight corporations had direct links to the Korean National Association, and the other six may have been linked indirectly to it through joint membership. Capitalism among Koreans thus had a political as well as an economic role. Many stockholders hoped that, by financing development projects in Korea, they would hasten the day when independence would be won.

There were more failures than successes among Korean agricultural capitalists, particularly in the early years. The reasons for such failure were detailed in a lengthy *New Korea* editorial in 1913. First, Koreans did not have enough capital, borrowing money from friends or acquaintances when they started a farm. If they did not make sufficient profits to pay back the landowner, everything was repossessed. Furthermore, when the landlords anticipated that the price of crops would rise, they had their Korean tenants sell their crops in order to benefit from this increase. Second, when the crops failed because of rain or wind, Koreans lost everything and lacked the capital to begin again the next year. Third, since they did not usually own all the means of agricultural production (such as horses or tools), they had to rent them out of their income. Fourth, Koreans did not have adequate experience in leasing or buying agricultural land. They usually acquired land that was poorer than an American would take. Besides, they planted poor quality rice that had a lower yield, or they hired too many workers. Finally, they started farming on a large scale when they had no experience. If they failed the first year, they had difficulty in continuing. The newspaper advised its readers, "If you start with a small tract of land and get some experience, you will be able to keep your land in the following year even if you fail the first year, and if you keep your land for several years, you

will start to get some profits" (12 Dec. 1913). After failures for ten
years, Koreans were to become successful in rice production, and by
1918, "they had enough experience in agriculture and owned needed
agricultural tools and equipments" (*New Korea*, 20 June 1918). Unfortunately, their success was short-lived, for the collapse of agricultural
prices after the end of World War I dealt a heavy blow to nascent
Korean agricultural capitalism.

LIVING CONDITIONS

Most Koreans in California were single, particularly during the period
between 1910 and 1920, and resided in boarding houses, inns, and labor
camps. This housing was located in areas where Korean farm and industrial workers were concentrated and was well suited to their changing
needs. Boarding houses, inns, and labor camps were owned not only by
individual Koreans but also by organizations such as the Korean National
Association. On some farms and on the railroads, the camps were
owned by the white employer and leased or provided free of charge to
the Korean labor contractors. Some Korean contractors owned inns or
boarding houses or arranged to use Korean-owned facilities for their
workers. Where board was provided, cooking was usually done by married Korean women or by the wives of contractors.

Inns and boarding houses fulfilled an important function for the
newly arrived immigrants. They provided them with job information
and readily available space where they could stay until they became
settled. For example, a Korean who arrived in San Francisco from
Hawaii in 1903 stated that he "knew nobody in that city, so he went to a
hotel owned by and for Koreans where there were also ten other
Koreans" (Diary of Mr. B). About ten years later, when his picture bride
arrived in San Francisco, they spent a few days in a Korean hotel where
there were both families and bachelors. It was a convenient place to stay
until they could find a residence of their own. On arriving from
Shanghai, Interviewee K stayed for ten days in a San Francisco Korean
inn until he found a job in Stockton.

Descriptions of inns, boarding houses, and labor camps suggest that
they were often overcrowded, substandard, and very inadequate. Around
1910, some San Francisco inns had as many as ten to thirty single men
sharing one big room as sleeping quarters. In the same period, "old
dilapidated buildings or small rough quarters or camps" were provided
by California ranch owners to Chinese, Japanese, Korean, and Indian
farm workers, housing that was much worse than what was available to
whites (U.S. Immigration Commission 1911a:19). At about the same
time, railroad companies provided "broken-down box cars fitted with

wooden bunks," which were sufficient for two families or sheltered from six to twelve or even more single men (U.S. Immigration Commission 1911*b*:23). In the late 1910s, one picture bride who had a cottage provided by a farm owner described it as a "barn" with no kitchen facilities. She and her husband had to build a Korean "firepit" for cooking. They had no mattress, only straw, on which to sleep (Interviewee C).

Throughout the period, some urban Koreans took jobs as houseboys in Caucasian-owned homes, working as live-in domestic servants while they were going to school. Interviewee H took such a position between 1915 and 1918, and here he was given his own living quarters for performing a variety of household tasks. He was well treated and ate the same food as the owner. In contrast, Interviewee L, who did the same kind of work, was not so well treated, and he and his wife had to eat leftovers.

With an increase in the number of families, the hotels and inns became less popular, and there was increasing demand for houses and apartments. But throughout the period, it was very difficult for many Koreans to reside in the better, more desirable neighborhoods because of anti-Asian feelings and discrimination. Restrictive covenants made it almost impossible for them to become homeowners. One couple had "a hard time finding a good house in San Francisco," because "whites did not want to rent a clean and nice house to Orientals." Unavoidably, many workers and small business owners lived in small and inadequate quarters located in older, less desirable neighborhoods. An exception was the capitalist owner of the Oriental Food Products Company who had a "palatial home."

The low wages earned by the Korean proletariat and the modest income of the petite bourgeoisie provided quite a low standard of living, and much of the meager family income was spent on food and lodgings. The standard of living of one Korean family in California in the 1910s was pictured as follows:

> We went to Willows, California, north of Sacramento in the wilderness, lived there over a year. . . . All we ate was *Mulchee Guk*, dried little fish soup and flour noodles. That was all we could afford to buy . . . one year of real hardship. . . . (Interviewee P)

While contractors usually earned more than workers, they tended to save portions of their income for later use (for education of their children, investments, and so on). Also, they had other expenses, such as donations, or sending money to Korea. Judging from interviews, the amount of money remaining for food, lodging, and other necessary items could not have been much higher than that of the workers.

At the opposite end of the economic scale, there was the Korean "rice king" of California who spent $5,000 on his wedding in 1918 (*New Korea*, 7 March 1918). Obviously, there was a wide gulf separating the standard of living of the few Korean capitalists and the majority of wage workers and petite bourgeoisie.

RELATIONS BETWEEN CLASSES

Korean capitalists used any labor available, Korean or not. Like other capitalists, they maximized their profits, and one way to achieve this was to pay the lowest possible wages. There was a report in the *New Korea* (12 Feb. 1912) of Korean partners who owned 500 acres and who employed Korean as well as twenty to thirty Indian workers. Unfortunately, no information is available on wages paid.

As mentioned earlier, most Korean agricultural or railroad laborers worked under Korean foremen or contractors. Being Korean, and often having been laborers themselves, these contractors or foremen understood the problems faced by their workers and frequently tried to help them in many different ways. Some contractors assisted in raising the necessary funds to pay their workers' expenses, and some defended the interests of their workers and tried to secure wages that were due them. In one case, "two Korean contractors arranged to pay Korean railroad workers who did not get paid due to the financial difficulties of the railroad company, and for this purpose they took railroad equipment owned by the company and sold it" (*New Korea*, 8 May 1912). Some Korean contractors, according to interviews, negotiated with farm owners and were able to obtain better wages for the workers they were going to recruit.

Since contractors were in charge of disbursing the wages, a few of the less scrupulous ones would appropriate some of these wages. More specifically, "one Korean boss who was picking hops with 20-30 Koreans ran away with $600 of wages for these workers" (*New Korea*, 22 Sept. 1910). The *New Korea* accused a Korean contractor in Manteca of absconding with $3,550 of the workers' money and of spending it on gambling and women in Stockton (9 Aug. 1916).

Inevitably, foremen and contractors were sometimes caught between the workers and the capitalists. Obviously, the capitalists preferred "reliable" contractors sympathetic to their views—those who would accept worker exploitation rather than support the workers. Contractors who favored the workers over the capitalists often had a hard time securing contracts. By the same token however, if they did not favor the workers they would have difficulty in recruiting them.

To obtain a contract or become a foreman, some Koreans had to develop a personal relation with the Caucasian bosses. There were a number of instances in which contractors were chosen by white farm owners after having worked hard for them as laborers and having gotten their special attention. Interviewee A "had worked so hard in an American farm owner's house that the farmer allowed him to use 200 acres to cultivate radishes on his own." More often, however, the Koreans had to compete with other contractors and were forced to lower wages to win a contract. In Stockton, a Korean who offered to provide workers at 40 cents an hour lost the contract to a Filipino who paid only 35 cents an hour (*New Korea*, 27 May 1918).

INTERETHNIC RELATIONS

During the early days of Korean settlement in California, Koreans often worked in "gangs" with Japanese workers, partly because in this period many of the bosses were Japanese (U.S. Immigration Commission 1911*a*). Conflict arose between Korean and Japanese workers because of strong nationalistic feelings among the former. The Japanese workers on the Pacific Railroad irritated the Korean workers by saying that the "Korean gang is no good, so join the Japanese gang," and the Korean workers in the Japanese gang were not allowed to visit other Korean workers (*New Korea*, 27 Oct. 1909). The newspaper concluded from this story that Koreans should get out of Japanese gangs and work with Koreans only. According to several interviews, Korean contractors often warned that if not enough Koreans showed up for work, their place would be taken by the Japanese. In general, however, Korean workers related well with non-Korean workers, especially the Chinese. In fact, some Chinese collected money among themselves to donate to Korean coworkers who were sick or in need of help.

In addition to the animosity between Korean and Japanese workers, there was also a strong hostility toward all Asian laborers among white workers. The following incident in Hemet, California, in 1913 shows not only the strength of anti-Asian feelings and agitation but also the feelings of the Koreans toward the Japanese:

> Thirteen Korean workers went to work to pick cherries under a Korean boss, but they were kicked out by American workers. After a white owner made a contract with a Korean boss and the workers were ready to start working, they were surrounded by 600 white workers and businessmen who asked the Korean workers: "What are you doing here?" The workers answered: "We came to pick cherries on Samson's

farm." Then the crowd said: "This town doesn't want any Koreans, Chinese, Japanese or Orientals. Leave now." So the Korean workers were forced to leave. Afterwards, the Korean boss met with the white farm owner to ask for compensation for the loss of money for travel. The farm owner said that he came to this town from London not so long ago, and did not know about people in this town, and apologized. He gave the workers travel expenses. When the Japanese consulate offered help to the Koreans in this matter, they refused. (*New Korea*, 14 July 1913)

Undoubtedly, an important factor in the hostility among white workers was the fear that Asian workers would take their jobs away or would drive wages down. While in the Hemet incident the white farm owner was sympathetic to Koreans, in other cases white capitalists did not object to hostility expressed by white workers. Conflict or competition between workers could bring down the price of labor and hence benefit the capitalist.

SUMMARY AND CONCLUSION

The Korean population of California, which probably did not exceed 100 in 1903, grew rapidly to at least 304 in 1910, and to 772 in 1920. While natural increase accounted for some of this growth, particularly in the decade from 1910 to 1920, immigration was responsible for most of it. Some newcomers came directly from Korea or, after its annexation by Japan, came indirectly via China and other foreign countries. Others were in-migrants from Hawaii who had only recently emigrated from Korea but who sought a better fate in California. Until 1907, Korean migration to California originated mainly from Hawaii. Restrictive legislation greatly reduced this stream after 1907, and as a consequence, direct immigration became the most important source of the movement of Koreans to the mainland. The accelerated pace of immigration between 1910 and 1920, involving a substantial number of picture brides, more than doubled California's Korean population. Even though San Francisco was their main port of entry, this city, as well as other large cities of the state, did not grow much more rapidly than rural areas and small towns. In 1920, as many as nine out of every ten Koreans resided outside of these large cities, and the Korean population was still predominantly rural.

Irrespective of their class or regional origin, most of the Koreans who came to California initially could not escape a proletarian status, the fate of most Asian immigrants. Until the early 1910s, Koreans were overwhelmingly farm laborers in the citrus orchards, beet farms, vineyards, and other farms and orchards. In order to survive they had to follow the crops. Thus, the Korean population of communities such as Upland, Dinuba, or Lompoc ebbed and flowed with the demand for labor.

During the slack agricultural season, needed employment was found in the railroads, but this was not sufficient to prevent seasonal unemployment. The Korean nonfarm proletariat was relatively small and consisted mainly of railroad workers, miners, and personal service workers.

The nature of the capitalist mode of production is the key determinant of class formation and class relations. Therefore, this factor, coupled with discrimination against Asians, explains in large part the living conditions of Koreans and their relations to each other and to whites. White capitalists relied almost exclusively on contractors to provide them with the needed supply of cheap labor. Inevitably, a petit bourgeois class of Korean contractors emerged almost simultaneously with the growth of the rural proletariat. Korean workers were organized into "gangs" under the supervision or leadership of one or more contractors. It was the contractor who negotiated an agreement with the railroad companies and the farm owners to offer laborers at specified wages, and who actively recruited workers through personal contacts, the Korean associations, and announcements in newspapers. The contractor needed the workers as much as they needed him, and a pattern of interdependence developed between Korean laborers and contractors.

As long as there was a large reserve of cheap labor that was not organized to bargain collectively, wages were very low and housing and other facilities for workers were extremely inadequate. For Asians the situation was worse than average. They received lower wages than those paid to whites and lived under more adverse conditions.

Again, discrimination reinforced the dependence of the Korean proletariat on the mercantile segments of the petite bourgeoisie and contributed to the further growth of the latter class. These segments included mostly small, and somewhat marginal businesses (restaurants, barbershops, and cigar stands). Professional and semiprofessional elements of this class were almost totally absent. The Koreans who became members of the petite bourgeoisie were initially in the agricultural or industrial proletariat of California. They were never too far from this class and would easily rejoin it in the face of economic adversity (such as crop failure or a decline in agricultural prices).

The same structural conditions that gave rise to the petite bourgeoisie also facilitated the emergence of a small capitalist class among Koreans. However, discrimination and the problems of securing capital limited the growth of this class and made it more vulnerable to economic crises than was its white counterpart. Before the restrictive Alien Land Act was passed in 1913, only a few Koreans had the funds necessary to acquire farms and become rural capitalists. After 1913, they could only go into tenancy or sharecropping, which often had to be done in partnership with other Koreans. A few capitalistic corporations were launched during this period, mostly in agriculture, but with an increasing focus on trade. Since most of the capital had to be raised among Koreans, it seldom was adequate enough to insure success.

World War I brought with it a rapid rise in the demand for food and an increase in agricultural prices, which contributed to the growth of a rural capitalist class. Many Koreans, often in partnership or as corporations, went into large-scale farming and were able to make substantial profits. When agricultural prices collapsed at the end of the war, however, many of these budding capitalists were ruined. They rejoined the ranks of the rural proletariat or petite bourgeoisie. Some of them drifted into cities where they contributed to the expansion of the urban petite bourgeoisie. The small Korean capitalist class became even smaller by 1920, and commerce rather than agriculture was its main source of profits.

The story of Koreans in America, like that of other Asians, did not correspond to the "American dream" of economic success. The prosperity of the war years was short-lived. With the exception of the very few capitalists who managed to survive economically, the Koreans were not much better off in 1920 than they had been a decade earlier. Moreover, they were subject to extensive racism and discrimination which limited their opportunities for upward mobility and affected the quality of their lives.

NOTES

1. The year 1903 was chosen as a starting point for this study because it was the first year that Koreans immigrated in large numbers to the United States. The period of study terminates with 1920 because the immediate post–World War I years consitituted a turning point in the social and economic history of Koreans in California.

2. W.Y. Kim (1971); Moon (1976); No (1951); Ko (1973); H. C. Kim and Patterson (1974); Houchins and Houchins (1974); Yun (1974); Hyun (1976); Melendy (1977); Lyu (1977); and Choy (1979).

3. The *New Korea* (*Shin-Han Minbo*) was originally called the *United Korea* (*Kong-Lip Shinbo*) and was established in San Francisco in 1905. The name *New Korea* was adopted in February 1909. It has been published ever since then by the Korean National Association and has mostly

appeared weekly, although there were periods of financial difficulty when publication was less frequent. The *New Korea* is the only newspaper written in Korean that has such a long history. The author translated pertinent articles for this research.

4. Includes a diary of Mr. B who was born in 1881 and came to the U.S. in 1903. There were altogether nine women and six men who were interviewed between January and April 1978. In order to protect their anonymity, I assigned a code letter to each one of them. The interviews differ greatly in terms of their length, richness of information, and wealth of details. Korean was used with all interviewees except for members of the second generation and those who came to the States when they were children, with whom English was spoken. All the persons interviewed were over 65 years old, and one of them was as old as 100 years.

5. The directories offer an alphabetical list of names with a residential and/or a business address, and, quite frequently, an occupation or type of business. They were used to describe the residential and occupational distribution of persons with selected names.

6. All immigration figures are for fiscal years ending June 30 of the given year. Thus, 1899 refers to the period July 1, 1898, to June 30, 1899.

7. There is some confusion in the literature about the exact number of immigrants to the mainland and Hawaii. Figures of 1,133 in 1903, 3,434 in 1904, and 2,659 in 1905 are given by W.Y. Kim (1971) and Hyun (1976). Kim obtained his information from a report of the Korean Hap-Sung Association, while Hyun secured his data from the Hawaii Bureau of Immigration. No (1951) and Ko (1973) also present immigration figures different from the above. Part of the problem is that some authors might have referred to calendar years and others to fiscal years. Published official immigration figures were on a fiscal-year basis.

8. The number of Kim, Ahn, and Lee entries in the 1910-1920 directories constituted two-thirds of the average census figures for the Korean population in Los Angeles during this period (i.e., 49). Even without an allowance for additional persons at each address, this ratio suggests that the census of 1910 and 1920 must have undercounted Koreans. In any event, it appears that these entries represent a substantial proportion of the Korean population of Los Angeles.

9. Since some of the streets where Koreans resided in the 1910s no longer exist, it was necessary to use an early map of Los Angeles. A 1916 map included all these streets.

10. The following assumptions were made: (1) the proportion of the Korean population of California fifteen years old and over in 1910 is equal to the proportion of the California Korean population thirty-five

years old and over in 1930; and (2) the proportion of the California Korean population that was male in 1910 is the same as the proportion of males in the U.S. Korean population 10 years old and over in 1910.

11. The diary of Mr. B stated that he had made an agreement to provide ninety Korean workers in Fresno at about the same time. Interviewee H also corroborated these numbers.

12. The names of Kismilia and Serino are transliterations from Korean.

13. From this comparison, it is possible to infer that Korean farm laborers worked mainly for Korean rather than other contractors.

14. Since there were ten farm contractors for every one railroad contractor, railroad work must have been a much less significant source of employment for Koreans than agriculture was. This assumes that the announcements by contractors are proportional to the number of jobs.

References

Choy, Bong-Youn
  1979 Koreans in America: Nelson-Hall Publishers.
Crocker-Langley
  1908- San Francisco Directory. San Francisco: H. S. Crocker Co.
  1917
Houchins, Lee, and Chang-su Houchins
  1974 "The Korean experience in America, 1903-1924." Pacific Historical Review 18.
Hyun, Kyoo Whan
  1976 A History of Korean Wanderers and Emigrants. Vol. II. Korea: Samwha Publishers, Inc.
Kim, Bernice B. H.
  1937 The Koreans in Hawaii. Master's thesis, University of Hawaii, Honolulu.
Kim, Hyung-chan, and Wayne Patterson, eds.
  1974 The Koreans in America, 1882-1974. New York: Oceana Publications.
Kim, Warren Y.
  1971 Koreans in America. Korea: Po-Chin.
Ko, Sung Jae
  1973 Hanguk Iminsa Yeonku (A Study of Korean Emigration History). Korea: Jang Moon Kak.
Los Angeles City Directory
  1919- Los Angeles: Los Angeles Directory Co.
  1920
Lyu, Kingsley K.
  1977 "Korean nationalist activities in Hawaii and the continental United States, 1900-1945. Part I: 1900-1919." Amerasia Journal 4.
Melendy, H. Brett
  1977 Asians in America: Filipinos, Koreans and East Indians. Boston: Twayne Publishers.
Moon, Hyung June.
  1976 The Korean Immigrants in America: The Quest for Identity in the Formative Years, 1903-1918. Ph.D. dissertation, University of Nevada, Reno.
No, Jae-Yun
  1951 Chae-Mi Hanin Sa Ryok (A Short History of Koreans in America). Los Angeles.
Nordyke, Eleanor C.
  1977 The Peopling of Hawaii. Honolulu, University of Hawaii.
U.S. Bureau of the Census
  1933 Fifteenth Census of the United States: 1930. Population. Vol. II. General Report, Statistics by Subjects. Washington, D. C.: Government Printing Office.
U.S. Commissioner General of Immigration
  1899- Annual Reports. Fiscal Year Ended June 30, 1899 to Fiscal Year Ended June 30,
  1919   1919. Washington, D. C.: Government Printing Office.

U.S. Congress, Senate. Immigration Commission Reports
    1911a Immigrants in Industries. Part 25: Japanese and Other Immigrant Races in the
          Pacific Coast and Rocky Mountain States. Vol. II: Agriculture. Washington,
          D. C.: Government Printing Office.
    1911b Immigrants in Industries. Part 25: Japanese and Other Immigrant Races in the
          Pacific Coast and Rocky Mountain States. Vol. III: Diversified Industries. Wash-
          ington, D. C.: Government Printing Office.
Yun, Yo-Jin
    1974 "Early history of Korean emigration to America (1)." Korean Journal 14.

16

Punjabi Agricultural Workers In California, 1905-1945

Sucheta Mazumdar

Research on the Indian immigrants in California prior to World War II, while not extensive, is fairly substantial in volume. Most of the published literature on this subject (e.g., Hess 1974; Melendy 1977), however, either deals with the group as a whole and is therefore more in the nature of general surveys, or discusses Indian immigrants as a phenomenon in isolation, without reference to other immigrant groups in California. Also in this literature, class distinctions within the Indian community are generally neglected while anti-British nationalist activities of the educated immigrants receive far more attention than do the activities of the more numerous working class immigrants. Thus, this paper focuses primarily on the working class immigrants and agricultural workers in particular and tries to provide some perspective on their role in California agribusiness.

While drawing heavily on secondary and primary source materials, both published and unpublished, research for this paper is also based on a series of interviews carried out in 1978. During that year, I interviewed nineteen immigrants who arrived in California between 1920 and 1924, and also three individuals who were sons of these early immigrants. I stayed at the Sikh temples in both Yuba City and Stockton, and, with the help of community social workers, located several of my informants. Practically all the informants had worked as field hands immediately after their arrival, though later some had moved into urban occupations. The recollections of these informants, often men in their late eighties and nineties, provided valuable insights into the daily lives of immigrant agricultural workers in California.

ARRIVAL

The immigration of laborers from India began at the turn of the century. The first laborers arrived in the United States in 1898, but they were not a numerically significant group. The 1900 census reported 2,050 persons born in India, though not necessarily Indian, residing in the United States, excluding Alaska and Hawaii (U.S. Immigration Commission 1911:325). The group included mostly businessmen, students, and swamis, none of whom encountered any notable opposition (Das 1923:9).

It was not until 1904 that Indian immigration to the United States involved more than a hundred persons per year. However, the majority of Indians arriving between the years 1904 and 1909 entered the United States via British Columbia. Table 16.1 shows the proportion of immigrants reporting Canada or India as their last permanent residence. Although these figures should not be taken too literally—according to the Immigration Commission "most of those giving India as their last place of residence came via British Columbia" (U.S. Immigration Commission 1911:328)—the table does reveal the years in which indirect immigration was important and shows its demise in 1910.

TABLE 16.1

NUMBER AND PERCENT OF INDIANS ARRIVING IN THE UNITED STATES
WHOSE LAST PERMANENT RESIDENCE WAS INDIA AND CANADA, 1901-1910

Year	Number of arrivals	Number from India	Number from Canada	Percent from India	Percent from Canada
1901	20	20	0	100	0
1902	84	84	0	100	0
1903	83	83	0	100	0
1904	258	224	0	87	0
1905	145	70	17	48	12
1906	271	155	6	57	2
1907	1,072	833	89	78	8
1908	1,710	999	593	58	35
1909	337*	138	129	41	38
1910	1,782	1,615	23	91	1
Total	5,762	4,221	857	73	15

SOURCE: U.S. Immigration Commission 1911:327.

*In 1908 a distinction was first made between "immigrants" and "nonimmigrants" (e.g., students, merchants). From 1908 the table only presents immigrants.

Since the Canadian route carried significant numbers of immigrants and Indian immigration to the United States is sometimes thought of as a spillover from Canada, I shall briefly trace the movement to Canada and from there to the United States. The Indians who first came to Canada were apparently soldiers or policemen employed by the British government in Hong Kong, Shanghai, and other parts of China. During the Boxer War, many Sikhs were employed by the British in China, and it is entirely possible that it was through Chinese connections that some traveled to the Pacific Coast (Das 1923:4). Still others, traveling through Canada after participating as British Indian soldiers in the Diamond Jubilee Celebrations in Britain in 1897, became aware of immigration opportunities in British Columbia. Indian immigration even to Canada, however, was nominal until 1905.

Once in Canada, however, the Punjabis ran into bitter antagonism from the local residents of British Columbia who were opposed to Asian immigration in general, despite the continuation of acute labor short-ages. The chief concern was over immigrants from Japan. Because of the Anglo-Japanese Alliance of 1902 and the extension of commercial advantages received by Canada under the terms of the Anglo-Japanese Convention of 1905, it was not possible for the Dominion government to take too stringent a stand on Japanese immigration. Anti-Asian para-noia in British Columbia was therefore considerably exacerbated when, in addition to large numbers of Japanese, between 1905 and 1907 some 2,693 Indians entered British Columbia, followed by another 2,623 who arrived in 1908. The general feeling toward Indian immigration was aptly reflected in an article in the Vancouver *World*, which proclaimed in 1906: "British Columbians are proud of India . . . proud of East Indians as boys of the flag. But an East Indian in Canada is out of place" (Hut-tenback 1976:174-177). The local white work force felt their position would be undermined and sought exclusion: "To protect the white workingmen, whose standard of comfort is of a higher order, and who, as citizens with family and civic obligations, have expenditures to meet and a status to maintain, which the Hindu laborer is in a position to wholly ignore" (Millis 1912:380).

By 1908 there were 5,179 Indians in British Columbia, located primar-ily in Vancouver (Das 1923:4). While they did not constitute a very large group, they were deemed numerous enough by the Dominion govern-ment for, unlike the Japanese, Punjabis sought to "engage in the same class of work as the white laborers do, viz., mill work and street work. They will not engage in domestic labor, gardening or agricultural work that white men leave untouched, but seek the same line of work usually followed by the white laborer" (Huttenback 1976:176). The government of Canada subsequently succeeded in essentially terminating Indian emigration to Canada by stringently enforcing a provision in the Immigration Act that denied entrance to those immigrants who came to Canada other than by continuous journey from their country of origin or citizenship. This provision effectively kept out Indians, for there was no way they could travel to Canada by continuous journey (Timlin 1960:529). Another deterrent was provided by a ruling of the Canadian Immigration Council in 1908 which declared that, henceforth, the minimum amount of money required by each Indian for admittance was $200 (U.S. Immigration Commission, 1911:329-330). The result was that, between 1909 and 1920, only 118 Indians managed to enter Canada.

Arrival in the United States

While anti-Indian sentiments continued to mount in Canada in 1907-1908, immigrants found employment opportunities across the border in Washington lumber mills, where they could earn $1.60 per day compared with $0.80 to $1.25 in British Columbia (U.S. Immigration Commission 1911:676). Later in this chapter we shall return to the subject of high wages received by Indian immigrants in the lumber industry, but at present it will suffice to note that their employment in this industry marked the beginning of substantial immigration of Indians into the United States via Canada. After immigration to Canada was virtually terminated in 1909, Indians came to the United States directly, the great majority of them entering at San Francisco (U.S. Immigration Commission 1911:677).

Before proceeding further, however, it is necessary to examine the question of why Indian immigration to the United States was permitted initially at all and then why, within a decade, it was drastically curtailed by official fiat. Though it is not possible to document any direct attempts made by United States capitalists to encourage Indian immigration to the Pacific Coast, it is clear that the need for labor made certain sectors at first quite willing to accept Indian immigration. Indeed, as the Gentlemen's Agreement made the curtailment of unskilled laborers from Japan imminent, California fruit growers seem to have experienced considerable panic. For example, the *California Fruit Grower* (August 1907:4) reports:

> Now that the first harvesting season is at its height and practically all plants are in operation the labor problem, which has been predicted all along would be troublesome, is proving extremely so. Few if any plants

are able to secure an adequate force of hands to run the plants to capacity. And everything that could be accomplished to make the workers as comfortable as possible, and wages [have been] raised to a higher plane than before, but still the necessary help cannot be secured.

The editorial then goes on to discuss the "problem" of Japanese labor:

In the past Japanese labor has been depended on to a large extent, especially in the raisin and grape sections, but ranchers have been for some time dissatisfied with Japanese labor, and it can hardly longer be called "cheap" in anything but quality.

Then, however, there follows a section most relevant to the discussion here:

Someone has suggested that efforts be made to induce Indian laborers to come here. Not long ago a small colony of full-blooded Sikhs arrived from India some of whom are now working in Fresno vineyards. These people are said to have a degree of education and culture in many cases, but are handicapped by their lack of knowledge of the English language.... A report is current that a scheme is on foot to railroad these people into the United States by hordes by having them become naturalized British subjects and as such escape the immigration requirements governing Asians.

It is most revealing to contrast these descriptions, written at a time when Indians were obviously welcome, with later negative descriptions given when they were no longer a desirable immigrant labor force.

In addition to agribusiness, there were other industrial concerns eager to hire Indians. "In 1910, a demand for construction workers on the Western Pacific Railroad led to a relaxation of immigration restrictions" (Hess 1974:580). Consequently, 1,782 Indians were admitted that year, mostly at San Francisco. Many of these immigrants secured railroad construction jobs near San Francisco almost immediately, "giving rise to a widespread belief that there was organized traffic in this labor" (Millis 1912:381).

Table 16.2 shows the fate of Indian immigration. As can be seen, an increasing proportion of Indians were debarred from admittance, and immigration on the whole fell off considerably after 1911. How can this phenomenon be understood in view of the demand for Indian labor? The underlying causes seem to have been manifold. To some extent, the Indian immigrants were affected by a preemptive exclusion policy. The Asiatic Exclusion League began to warn against an Indian "menace" as

TABLE 16.2

NUMBER OF INDIANS ADMITTED AS IMMIGRANTS, DEBARRED FROM
ENTERING AS IMMIGRANTS, AND WHO LEFT THE UNITED STATES, 1908-1920

Year	Admitted	Debarred	Departed
1908	1,710	606	124
1909	337	329	48
1910	1,782	409	80
1911	517	861	75
1912	165	99	164
1913	188	234	213
1914	172	157	143
1915	82	300	162
1916	80	44	91
1917	69	24	136
1918	61	17	154
1919	68	18	106
1920	160	28	162
Total	5,391	3,126	1,658

SOURCE: Das 1923:10-14.

early as 1908. The popular press (general newspapers, not special interest newspapers like the *California Fruit Grower* quoted above) augmented
this campaign using exaggerated Exclusion League reports on the number of Indian immigrants arriving in the United States (*The Survey*
1910:2-3). It is entirely possible that immigration officials, responding
to pressures from the Exclusion League, denied admission to many
Indians (Hess 1974:580), but there were other factors involved as well.
The *California Fruit Grower*, in the article quoted at length above, also
indicated interest in Mexican workers as a possible source of labor
supply. As the Japanese abandoned harvest labor in the post-1910
period, Mexicans and Mexican-Americans became the major labor force
in the citrus belt, the cotton areas of the San Joaquin Valley, and the
Imperial Valley (Jelinek 1979:69-70). Indians, however, as we shall see,
began to lease land extensively after 1911 and demanded "as high
wages as were being paid to other Asiatics" (Millis 1912:384). This
made them far less desirable as immigrants, particularly in comparison
to Mexican laborers who "gained employer acceptance because of their
apparent docility and ability to appear and disappear as needed" (Jelinek
1979:70).

Indian immigration to the United States before World War II can be
divided into three, fairly distinct periods. Though various scholars have
chosen different years as demarcation points, I feel that 1904 to 1917

can be treated as the years when the majority of Indian immigrants came to the United States through legal channels. This period ended in 1917, when India was included among the countries labeled as a "barred zone" in an American immigration act that excluded all immigrants and exempted only such nonimmigrant classes as students, travelers and officials (Das 1923:16).

The second period is marked by the arrival of over 1,000 Indians who came in as students, primarily between 1920 and 1924, and approximately 3,000 Indians who came in as illegal immigrants between 1920 and 1930 (Jacoby 1956:7-8).

The last period of immigration that we are concerned with, 1930 to 1945, saw only a marginal number of Indian immigrants or students come into the United States. Several hundreds of the earlier immigrants had departed by this time, so that the total Indian population of the United States stood at 3,130 in 1930 and at 2,405 in 1940 (Hess 1974:592).

Of the 5,424 Indians shown by the census to be living in the United States in 1910, over 2,742 were in California (Das 1923:17-20). In fact, throughout the pre-World War II period, in spite of fluctuations in the size of the total Indian population in the United States, the majority (50-60 percent) were living in that state. Though official records suggest a lower figure, informed estimates from fairly dependable accounts, such as Carey McWilliams (1942:119), suggest that there may have been as many as 10,000 Indian workers in California before World War I. Other trends, too, remained fairly constant. The immigrant population, as table 16.3 indicates, was disproportionately male between the ages of fourteen and forty-four. Literacy levels were generally low (approximately 50 percent), but were relatively high when compared even with present-day Indian standards.

OCCUPATIONS

One can divide Indian immigrants into two broad categories: professionals, students, and businessmen on one hand, and agricultural workers and laborers on the other. As can be seen from the Indian occupational distribution in 1910 (table 16.4), agricultural workers and unskilled laborers constituted well over three-quarters of the immigrants. Most immigrants, particularly those from the agricultural worker class, intended to return to India after accumulating some money,

TABLE 16.3
SEX RATIO, AGE, AND LITERACY OF INDIAN IMMIGRANTS DURING
FIRST PHASE OF IMMIGRATION, 1904-1917

Year	Total admitted	Percent male	Percent ages 14-44	Percent can't read or write
1904	258	93.4	85.7	29.5
1905	145	94.5	84.1	11.7
1906	271	93.0	*	*
1907	1,072	98.5	98.4	45.4
1908	1,710	99.5	98.0	57.6
1909	337	97.0	92.6	29.1
1910	1,782	99.2	98.9	52.5
1911	517	98.8	97.5	49.7
1912	165	92.7	95.2	5.5
1913	188	97.9	96.3	12.2
1914	172	94.8	93.6	13.4
1915	82	85.4	91.5	4.9
1916	80	87.5	88.8	*
1917	69	92.8	*	*
Total	6,848	97.8	92.0	42.6

SOURCE: Annual Reports of Commissioner General of Immigration.
*Figures unavailable for certain years.

TABLE 16.4
OCCUPATIONS OF INDIAN IMMIGRANTS, 1910

Professional occupations	6.6%
Small trade, business, manufacturers etc.	13.3
Skilled workers	1.7
Agricultural workers	11.7
Laborers	66.8
Total	100.0%

SOURCE: Misrow 1915:20.

$2,000 being most often quoted as the desired amount (U.S. Immigration Commission 1911:677). Another study, also cited by the Immigration Commission, found that 85 percent reported having been farmers and farm laborers (1911:677). Though it is possible that, in a large percentage of the cases, occupation in British Columbia may have been cited rather than occupation in India, table 16.4 nevertheless does provide an indication of the class composition of the immigrants.

Professionals, Students and Businessmen

Before 1904 and after 1917, the immigrants primarily derived from either the landlord class or the urban bourgeoisie in India. They came to the United States for professional reasons or out of political considerations such as their involvement in the developing struggle for Indian independence. Most of them settled in the major urban centers on the East Coast, though some lived on the Pacific Coast, mainly in California.

Quite a few of these upper class immigrants in California were students at the University of California, Berkeley, but worked as agricultural laborers during their summer vacations. It is my impression, acquired through interviews, that, despite the differences in class background, these students in California were more closely affiliated with agricultural workers than they would have been if they had been attending a university elsewhere. Though most of them came from the landlord class, particularly from families that owned over a hundred acres, they were not from urban backgrounds (interviews with Sharma, Ram, and Teja). Their familiarity with the rural scene enabled them to find temporary work more easily in agriculture, and later, in spite of their professional training, a few chose to become farm operators. At times these students were even financially supported by Indian agricultural workers living in the Sacramento Valley.

The nonacademic professionals and businessmen were also located in the urban centers, though numerically they were almost an insignificant group. Because of their socioeconomic status and their command of English, however, they and the students became the spokesmen for the rest of the community, thereby enjoying a position of respect and power. It is difficult to establish exactly how many such individuals lived in this country, or where they were located, since records are available only for the more prominent or active members. Using these assorted sketches, one can nonetheless suggest in broad outline the general situation in California. It seems there were three businessmen living in the Los Angeles area engaged primarily in the import-export business. They ran individually operated enterprises, and only one of them ever became successful enough to be affiliated with a national corporation (interview with Ram). In the 1930s a couple of professionals moved to the Los Angeles area from Berkeley, including D. S. Saund, who later became a congressman from the Imperial Valley, and a biochemist who became a prominent researcher in the agricultural industry. In addition, there were a few academicians, including a professor of history who taught at the University of Southern California, and a lecturer at Stanford University. There were also a few religious teachers, a journalist who worked on the staff of the *San Francisco Examiner*, a lawyer who lived in Los Angeles, a couple of salesmen, a veterinarian, and a chiropractor. Some individuals from this group also bought urban real estate and owned hotels and apartments in the Stockton and San Francisco area.

Personal interviews revealed that most members of this class came with some money, often as much as $1,000 to $2,000. They usually had more than a high school education, and in some instances, had had a few years of university training as well. The approximately 70 Indians who had become U.S. citizens between 1914 and 1923 primarily came from this class, for the criterion applied in granting them citizenship was that they be "high caste Hindus of the Aryan race" (*The Calcutta Review* 1925:41). The United States Supreme Court decisions granted Indians citizenship on the grounds that they were Caucasians and thus entitled under the naturalization legislation of 1790 and 1875 to be considered "white persons" eligible for citizenship (Hess 1974:590). However, in 1923 the Supreme Court, in the case of the *United States* v. *Bhaghat Singh Thind,* ruled that Thind was not a "white person" in the "understanding of the common man." High caste Hindus were judged not to be "free white persons" and as such were ineligible for citizenship (Hess 1974:591). The ramifications of the Thind case were extensive. Besides establishing a precedent for the denial of citizenship requests by Indians, it also provided a basis for the annulment of citizenships previously granted (Hess 1974:591). The most negative impact of this case was felt by the Indian farm operators in California, for it made them subject to the restrictions of the California Alien Land Law which prohibited the sale or lease of land to aliens ineligible for citizenship (Hess 1974:592).

The relationship of these professionals and businessmen to the agricultural workers' community was, in most instances, somewhat paternalistic. After 1930, when most of the "oldtimers" (those who came before 1917) returned home, contact between the two groups became almost perfunctory. Most of the professionals married Caucasian women from urban backgrounds, and this too led to their further isolation from the majority of the Indian immigrants, who had very few social dealings with Caucasians. For the agricultural workers, religious activities and the Sikh temple were focal points of group identity; those who married urban Caucasian women very seldom participated in these activities. It was thus simply a matter of time before the two groups lost contact totally.

Agricultural and Other Laborers

As mentioned earlier, about 75 to 80 percent of the Indian immigrants were unskilled workers and agricultural laborers. Most of them eventually came to live in California, but before joining the agricultural ranks, many worked for the railroads or in lumber mills. The following is perhaps a typical story of arrival and subsequent employment in the United States, based on a informant's account of his life given to an anthropologist:

> At the age of seventeen, while still beardless, he [Munshi Singh Thiara] joined a cousin and seven other Sikhs from his home town on his trip to this country. His father gave him 400 rupees for the trip. Together with 500 other Sikhs he departed from Hong Kong on the *Empress of Canada*. They arrived in Vancouver on October 14, 1907. Munshi stayed six days in Canada, but he found it too cold, and so, at the suggestion of some Sikhs who had arrived in 1905, he left for Seattle. His cousin remained in Canada, being unable to pass the physical examination required for U.S. entry. At Seattle, Munshi and fourteen other Sikhs rode the freight cars to Chico. None could speak English, and Munshi recalls the strange looks they received as people peered at their turbans and beards and listened to their Hindustani language. At Chico, the eighteen Sikhs (who were now without money) befriended two Sikhs who had arrived in 1905. They were taken to a Sikh camp for three or four days but, as they had no work, they moved on to Sacramento. There they found a Sikh who owned a hotel, and for seventy-five cents a night they moved into his basement. For two weeks they were unemployed, but finally they were hired by the Western-Pacific Railroad for a period of two and a half months.
>
> On April 15, 1908, Munshi returned to Chico with ten of his countrymen to work in the sugarbeet fields. . . . (Miller 1950:79-80)

Thirteen different railroad companies on the Pacific Coast employed Indians in construction gangs. Because this was not the preferred form of employment, Indian workers left as soon as they could find other jobs. Most railroad jobs involved temporary construction work; only occasionally were jobs for section hands available. Since railroad work was usually the first job found by immigrants, the available figures provided by the Immigration Commission from the years 1910-1911 do not accurately reflect how many Indians may have worked for the railroads over the years. These figures show that by 1909 there were only 73 Indians working on the railroads of the Western Division and that by 1910 the number had fallen to 54 (U.S. Immigration Commission 1911:677). An eyewitness account, however, states that 700 Indians were employed in the construction of the Three-Mile Spring Garden Tunnel of the Western Pacific Railroad (Samra 1940:5). Elsewhere 33 Indians were employed by the Western Division as section hands on the lines west of Albuquerque (U.S. Immigration Commission 1911:683).

Indians were not popular among other ethnic groups working on the railroads because of their previous employment in Tacoma (Washington) as replacements for some striking Italians. The antagonism they faced undoubtedly contributed to the fact that whenever possible they chose not to work in railroad construction. Indians were paid less than the Italians and Greeks, but there are no detailed records indicating how their wages compared with those of Japanese and Korean workers. One source suggests, however, that Indians were paid on the same scale as Japanese workers, namely $1.25 per day; and "in several instances" they were replaced by Mexicans who were paid $1.00 per day, the lowest wage paid to any ethnic group (U.S. Immigration Commission 1911:683). The employment patterns of the railroad companies were repeated in California agriculture.

Initially some Indians were also employed in the lumber mills of Washington and Oregon. Again, it is difficult to determine exactly how many were employed by this industry before 1910, for by then agriculture had become the primary source of employment for most Indians. However, in 1910 some 200 Indians were employed in Oregon around Astoria, Linnton, and Bridal Veil, while others were also employed by sawmills in Washington, in the towns of Bellingham and Tacoma (U.S. Immigration Commission 1911:678).

The wages paid to the Indians in mill work were, on the average, higher than those received by the Japanese, this being the only line of employment where this occurred. The wages of Indians were, therefore, only slightly lower than those of Scandinavians and Germans, and sometimes even the same. These high wages, $1.67 to $1.87, and even to $2.00 per day, were paid to the Indians because employers feared that the white workers might go on strike if Indians were brought in as a source of cheap labor (U.S. Immigration Commission 1911:331).

A study of six lumber mills employing some 53 Indians in 1910 shows that, on the whole, they were much better off than the Indians employed solely in agriculture. The lumber mill workers could spend an average of $12.00 per month on food and drink, compared with less than $7.50 per month even among the relatively well-to-do agricultural workers. Housing was often provided, with three people usually sharing a room. Those who had to pay rent were less well off since rent was an expensive item in their budget. Rented accommodations were typically small rooms in the basement of buildings in the poorer parts of the city (Das 1923:21).

Given the comparatively better working conditions, it might seem surprising that more Indians did not seek work in the lumber mills. When one examines the underlying reasons for this higher wage level, however, it becomes clear why Indians were not hired more extensively in the lumber industry. Bellingham and Tacoma were areas that experienced considerable labor conflict, and the Indians' higher wages were a by-product of a class struggle between white workers and employers, rather than the price Indians were able to command in terms of their bargaining power. Employers, therefore, became reluctant to hire Indians, for they felt they were being coerced by the white workers into paying higher wages than they had to in view of the fact that Indians were new immigrants to the area, unfamiliar with the machinery, and often unable to understand English. White workers, however, threatened to go on strike if Indians were brought in as a source of cheap labor in the lumber industry. Two incidents occurred in 1907 that clearly indicated the resentment felt by the white workers toward this new immigrant group. In September a mob raided the Indian living quarters in Bellingham, forcing about 750 Indians to cross back into Canada (Wynne 1966: 174). In November, the Indians were driven out of the city of Everett by 500 workers (Hess 1974:579). A similar situation seems to have occurred in Saint John, Oregon, in 1910 (Das 1923:112). With the decline of employment opportunities in Washington and Oregon, Indian immigrants moved southward into California agriculture.

BEGINNING OF AGRICULTURAL WORK BY PUNJABI INDIAN WORKERS

Indian entrance into California agriculture coincides with the Gentleman's Agreement of 1907–1908, which restricted the immigration of laborers from Japan. Indians first found work in California's orchards, vineyards, and sugar beet farms in 1908, and in the large farms specializing in various vegetables (Millis 1912:384). The relationship between Indians and earlier Asian immigrants is made clear by Millis (1912:384) in a series of somewhat contradictory statements. First he points out that Indians had found employment "because of the diminishing number of Chinese and Japanese available as wage laborers for seasonal work." Then he states it was "because of a widespread desire to break the monopoly control of the labor supply by the Japanese, or because of the higher wages than formerly commanded by other Asiatics." And finally he points out that in "1908 their [Indians'] wages varied from twenty-five to fifty cents per day less than was paid to Chinese and Japanese." The composite picture that emerges is that agribusiness had found another souce of cheap labor with which to displace not only white labor, but other, increasingly expensive, Asian labor. Another factor of importance, not mentioned by Millis but of considerable alarm to the growers, was that Japanese farm-laborers had begun to develop "a sort of spontaneous organization that made them not quite so tractable as the Chinese" (McWilliams 1942:114). An organized labor force that actually carried out strikes soon meant that Japanese labor could not be hired at the low wages they had previously earned.

The first of the Indian immigrants in agriculture were located near Marysville and Chico, north of Sacramento. They apparently found their first job on a farm in Chico owned by an Englishman who was familiar with Indians and thought them good workers (Samra 1940:6). In the summer of 1908, about 500 of them were employed in the New-castle fruit district, east of Sacramento, where "the orchardists, being short of help and being thoroughly tired of the Japanese because of their monopoly control of labor supply were glad to hire them" (U.S. Immi-gration Commission 1911:333). It is important to note that, at this point, Indians were willing to work for any wage offered and in general averaged about $.50 less than the minimum rate for the Japanese. A similar example can be found in the Vaca Valley, an area comprised of some 15,000 acres, approximately half of which were farmed by Japa-nese tenants. In the summer of 1908, a large shipper/grower employed 300 Indian fruit pickers at wages of $.25 less than those paid to other ethnic groups in an effort to break the Japanese monopoly of the labor supply (U.S. Immigration Commission 1911:333).

Since most of the crops being cultivated commercially were labor intensive, it is not surprising that, initially, Indians were found in prac-tically every sphere where the Japanese were employed. There were three main areas of concentration: the Sacramento Valley, the San Joa-quin Valley, and the Imperial Valley. In the Sacramento Valley, Indians worked in the deciduous fruit growing areas or in the rice growing areas such as Marysville, Tudor, Willows, Chico, and Butte City. In 1909 they also worked in the sugar beet fields near Hamilton, where it had been difficult to get workers; three-quarters of the hand-workers employed that year were Indians (U.S. Immigration Commission 1911:334).

In the San Joaquin Valley, Indians worked in the grape and celery fields. Celery cultivation apparently required workers to sit cross-legged on the ground for long periods, a position that Indians could easily adapt to because it was their usual sitting posture. One interviewee men-tioned that they preferred working in celery fields because the pay scales were better as a compensation for the physical discomfort (inter-view with Makkhan Singh). Indians also helped open up new lands in the vicinity of Fresno, near Mendota, clearing poison oak, and according to an eyewitness account, "killed hundreds of rattlesnakes daily" (Samra

1940:15). Wages were relatively high for this dangerous work, but there are no records indicating how many workers may have suffered working under these conditions.

Somewhat to the south, Indians also found work in the Tulare citrus belt. The citrus industry was rapidly expanding around 1910 and faced a shortage of seasonal labor. Approximately 600 Indians worked there on a fairly regular basis (Misrow 1915:15). After 1915, however, Mexicans and Mexican Americans became the major labor force in the citrus belt (Jelinek 1979:70).

After 1910, a large percentage of the Indian agricultural workers were found in the Imperial Valley. They were considered better suited to working in the intense heat than were other groups, and though some of them came down from the San Joaquin Valley to work in the cantaloupe fields, it was primarily cotton which brought them to the Imperial Valley in large numbers. They apparently helped "pick the first cotton harvest of any great commercial importance" (Taylor 1930:6). Eventually some workers developed a seasonal migration pattern, moving back and forth between the San Joaquin Valley and the Imperial Valley following the harvests.

It is difficult to find information about active protests made by one group of workers against another unless such an incident turned violent and involved the police. One such occasion was a riot that broke out in Live Oak, California (near Marysville), where on January 26, 1908, a mob of unknown ethnic composition marched to a camp of Indian workers. They burned the camp, beat and terrorized the hundred or more Indians in the camp, drove them out of the community, and robbed them of about $2,500 (McWilliams 1942:139). When the governor ordered an investigation, the local district attorney came to the defense of the rioters and accused the Indians of robbing "hen roosts" and of being guilty of "indecent exposure" (the latter charge was never fully explained). After a while, however, the Indians seem to have returned to that area. This seems to be the only well recorded case of large scale violence against Indian workers in agriculture, though there may have been other minor skirmishes.

Among the Indian agricultural laborer groups there were some individuals who worked permanently as labor contractors, while others became farm operators and dropped out of the migrant circuit. The majority, however, were migratory workers who made most of their money during the harvest season. Some of the laborers developed a pattern of migration that limited their period of unemployment to about two months in the year. They worked as pruners in December and January, on irrigation canals through March, April, and May, and as fruit pickers in July, August, September and October (Das 1923:26).

The basic organization of the Indian agricultural workers was, like that of other ethnic groups, the "gang." Each gang consisted of three to fifty members, under a team leader/contractor usually referred to as the "boss." The boss would find employment and make all the business arrangements for the group since usually he was the person most fluent in English. The Immigration Commission Reports indicate that Indian contractors, unlike their Japanese counterparts, did not charge a commission from their gangs and only received a higher pay from the employer. However, personal interviews and other sources suggest that this was not entirely true (Misrow 1915:33; interviews with Johl, Khan). It seems that the boss did receive a commission from workers in the gang, as well as higher pay from the employer. Since he also made arrangements for food and since Indians are rather particular about their food, it is probable that the contractor made quite a comfortable living. Some of the interviewees who had worked as labor contractors said that they were bosses not only for Indian workers but also for Mexicans, and after the Depression, for white workers as well. They said that in the 1920s, contracting for large groups, such as fifty to sixty people, usually made them a profit of at least $200 to $300 from each job—and even more in the late 1930s. Often, especially in the initial period of immigration, an individual could be elected to the position of boss by his coworkers because of his knowledge of English and his ability to deal with employers.

Once the individual became bossman over even ten or twelve people, the next step was easier, and he could become the contractor for a large gang. The success of a bossman depended on his ability to satisfy both the employer and the men under him. If a bossman was caught cheating the gang, he would be deposed and perhaps even have legal suits brought against him. One study shows that 25 percent of the civil suits on record in the Sutter County Court House are concerned with the failure of Indian bossmen to pay their workers (Miller 1950:23). The frequency of these cases suggests that many bossmen probably did cheat their illiterate compatriots and get away with it.

On the more positive side, the bossman was also the caretaker of his gang, the one who removed the wine bottle from a drunk gang member, bailed out those who landed in jail, or settled an argument that threatened to get out of hand. My own interviews as well as studies made by others suggest that those who remained contractors made more money than their workers but also were lonely men who had few friends because they were obliged to keep their distance from the men who worked for them in order to maintain discipline within the gang (Miller 1950:83).

Poverty can induce people to offer their services for a bare subsistence, being that individuals in such circumstances are in a very poor bargaining position, unable to hold out for higher wages. An immigrant group is therefore willing to work at wages unacceptable to those who have a slightly higher margin of survival. Indian immigrants, especially those in agriculture, generally provided the cheapest labor available. Wage comparisons for Indians, Japanese, and whites in some California districts (see table 16.5) indicate that Indians were cheaper than both the other groups. These data, compiled by the U.S. Immigration Commission on the basis of information provided by 103 Indian workers in the Vaca Valley, are probably fairly reliable.

Elsewhere, in areas other than those indicated in table 16.5, wages must have been even lower, for the same source indicates that the average wage of Indian workers was $1.00 to $1.50 per day. The length of their working day was anywhere from ten to fourteen hours, depending on the season and the type of crop. By all accounts it was backbreaking work even for those who were accustomed to working hard. One individual recalled that he went to work in the asparagus fields at 3:30 A.M., long before it was light, and worked until after dark at night picking asparagus for a few cents a box (McWilliams 1942:119). Indians preferred to work on a time/hour basis rather than on a piecework basis, especially when it came to crops they were not familiar with, such as hops, sugarbeets, and grapes.

As table 16.5 also indicates, Japanese workers initially made $.25 to $.50 more per day than the Indians. But later, by the 1920s, this pay differential disappeared. By that time Indians were demanding, and receiving, the same wages as white workers. Eventually this resulted in a much reduced demand for Indian agricultural workers.

Agricultural wages had risen in the intervening decade, and by 1921 the average wage for an Indian agricultural worker was $3.00 per day or slightly more—approximately the same pay as received by Indian work-

TABLE 16.5
DAILY WAGES WITHOUT BOARD IN CALIFORNIA AGRICULTURE, 1908–1909

Location	Indians	Japanese	Whites
Newcastle Fruit District	$1.25–1.60	1.50–1.80	1.50–2.00
Vaca Valley Orchards	1.25–1.50	1.50	1.50
Sacramento Valley			
Vegetable Farm	1.50–1.60	1.65–1.75	
Highgrove Orange Orchards	1.50	1.75	2.00

SOURCE: U.S. Immigration Commission 1911:333–335.

ers in mills at that time. Agricultural wages were usually paid on a monthly basis, but there were instances when Indians received their wages once or twice a year in a large sum (Samra 1940:10). I have no further information regarding those individuals who were paid so infrequently, and I do not know who provided for their board in the intervening months; one can only wonder how they managed to survive.

Das, in his *Hindustani Workers on the Pacific Coast*, calculated that the average earnings for an Indian agricultural worker in 1921 were around $900 per year. This is almost double the figure ($451) given by the U.S. Immigration Commission Reports in 1909 (Das 1923:61). Whether or not the standard of living of the Indians went up substantially with the increase in wages, however, is another matter. Food prices also went up during this period so that, while an individual was spending $7 to $14 per month for food in 1909 (U.S. Immigration Commission 1911:341), he/she had to spend $25 to $35 for food in 1921 (Das 1923:68). Tortilla-like whole wheat unleavened bread, rice, potatoes, and dried peas formed the staple diet of Indian workers. Often the laborers cultivated their own vegetables near the camps, and occasionally they raised chickens for their own consumption. Cultural and religious taboos regarding the eating of pork and beef were strictly maintained.

Most likely, some immigrants saved money, especially after they had become familiar enough with the agricultural cycle to keep months of unemployment to a minimum. About 50 percent of the immigrants sent money to India fairly regularly, especially before 1925. Most of the remittances were sent to family members. After the 1920s, however, fewer and fewer of those remaining in the United States sent money home. This may have been a survival practice adopted during the Depression, but it continued into the 1940s (Miller 1950:106).

It is not possible to estimate what the average yearly savings for an Indian may have been. Though savings of $21 per month is recorded for a seasonal agricultural worker in 1910, this tabulation does not take into account incidental expenses or expenses incurred during months of unemployment (U.S. Immigration Commission 1911:347). Undoubtedly, some individuals managed to save a little. Though 1908 may have been an unusually good year, records show that $34,000 (a sum almost too large to be credible) was remitted from the Marysville post office alone to India (U.S. Immigration Commission 1911:347). In nine savings banks in California and Oregon, 779 Indians had a total deposit of $238,630 in 1921, or $306 per capita (Das 1923:101). Though these may not have been typical individuals, some, it would seem, were able to make financial gains as immigrants.

Agricultural workers loaned money to friends fairly frequently, but these were in the nature of personal loans within the community. Apparently no interest was charged in such cases (Wenzel 1968:252). After a few farmers had become markedly successful, such as Jawala and Bisaka Singh, who were known as the "Potato Kings" in Holtville, many of their less successful compatriots would send all their money home and depend on the charity of these richer individuals for their survival (interview with Samra). On the whole, the majority either managed to make ends meet or were able to save around $100 a year. Only about 8 to 10 percent could not make enough money to survive from year to year (U.S. Immigration Commission 1911:345).

Since most of the Indians were working in agriculture, "housing" usually meant work-camp accommodations. Migrant workers simply slept out of doors or in tents. Long-term workers were provided with bunkhouses, barns, or woodsheds, typically without kitchen facilities or indoor plumbing (California Board of Control 1922:110). The Indians, like the Japanese, were rather particular about their baths, and farmers hiring them often had to provide bathing facilities at the very least. Agricultural workers, such as the Indians, usually did not own any furniture and slept on the floor with only a blanket for their bed. Living conditions were very congested, with twelve to thirteen people crowded into each room.

In urban areas such as Stockton and Fresno, depending on the season, there might be as many as a thousand Indians, most of whom lived in Japanese-owned rooming houses. Whether Indians chose to stay in Japanese rooming houses because they were working for Japanese farmers or simply because these houses were convenient is not known (California Board of Control 1922:109). Regardless of the reason, however, it is not likely that conditions in these rooming houses were any better than those found in the labor camps.

Farm Owners and Operators

By 1920 there were two fairly distinct groups of agricultural workers among the Indians in California: those who had become farm owners (a small minority), renters or sharecroppers, and who worked as agricultural laborers only in their spare time; and those later immigrants who worked entirely as agricultural laborers. There was also an intermediary group which might be considered part of the petite bourgeoisie, consisting of those who worked as foremen or contractors for the laborers, and agricultural workers-turned-storemen, who depended on their connections with agricultural workers for their business. Such store owners often also functioned as moneylenders, running the store on a credit basis (Miller 1950:102).

It is difficult to determine whether those who became tenant farmers or owners did so by climbing through the ranks of agricultural laborers and contractors finally to become tenant farmers, or whether they had become bossmen or contractors fairly early in their careers and therefore could save enough to become farm operators. Of course, there were also those from landlord class backgrounds who came to this country between 1920 and 1924 with quite a bit of money, acquired professional training, and later became farm operators, but here I am only concerned with the earlier group of farm owners. There is some evidence to suggest that those who became farm owners and operators were in a somewhat advantageous position vis-à-vis the agricultural workers, did often function as their gang leaders, had had some education, and could speak English. Typically they had also been in the country longer than the group working under them (interviews with Johl and Sikander; Miller 1950:80-81).

There are no records indicating that Indians either leased or owned land in California prior to 1910. By 1919, however, official records show that Indians in California had leased some 86,335 acres and owned 2,197 acres (California Board of Control 1922:48). Another source suggests that, if informal arrangements are taken into consideration, Indians cultivated 100,000 acres by 1919-1920 (Samra 1940:14). They also leased over 46,000 acres in the Sacramento Valley area, especially around Butte and Colusa Counties, and owned some 13,000 acres in that same area. In the Imperial Valley, Indians leased 3,200 acres, though in 1922 they seem not to have bought land there. There were also some smaller concentrations of Indian leaseholdings and owned property in the San Joaquin Valley, especially around Fresno and Mendota, but judging from the acreage given, these were probably isolated instances of two or three farmers operating small farms of around 40 acres each (Das 1923:23). After 1920, with the passage of the revised Alien Land Law, these patterns were considerably affected, for the Oriental Exclusion Act included the Indians as well. After 1920, landowners often registered land in the name of their children or sometimes entrusted an American with a "dummyship," that is, they registered property in the name of a citizen for legal purposes. However, this proved to be quite dangerous and led to numerous defaulted civil suits (Miller 1950:27).

Because Indians were already familiar with rice and cotton cultivation, these were the two major crops they initially cultivated in California. Both were "boom" crops. Rice profits went up during 1911-1920 and then plummeted; the demand for cotton decreased after the war, and the changing pattern of farming in the Imperial Valley after the 1920s eliminated many Indians. In the intervening years, however, many Indians devoted their energies to these two crops. Several Indians apparently even migrated to the United States specifically to become rice cultivators in California (Stark 1976:38). A few were quite successful, while others went bankrupt.

Indians first leased land for rice cultivation in Colusa County. By 1919, out of 59,000 acres owned and leased in the Sacramento Valley area by Indians, 45,000 acres were devoted to rice. Indeed, Indian rice growers accounted for 20 percent of the rice crop in California in 1919, and by 1925 they accounted for 25 percent of the total yield of the state. The year 1919 is generally thought to have been the best one for Indian farmers, especially those who were involved in rice cultivation (Samra 1940:12; Miller 1950:101).

Rice cultivation required the purchase of heavy machinery, including a thrasher, a tractor, and other rice-harvesting equipment (Miller 1950:101). Industrialized agriculture also made large-scale farming the norm, and records from 1923 show that operating farms ranged in size from 500 to 1,000 acres (Das 1923:24). These heavy financial liabilities meant, however, that in a bad year such as 1920, recent immigrants like the Indians, with precarious financial solvency, quickly went under. When the bottom fell out of the rice market in 1920 and much of the crop was washed away in torrential rains, Indians reportedly lost $7 to 9 million, and many were forced to declare bankruptcy (Samra 1940:17).

Those Indians involved in cotton cultivation in the Imperial Valley ultimately were also phased out of direct cultivation, but the process was less abrupt. The average size of farms leased by Indians in the Imperial Valley in 1923 was around 160 acres, though some were as large as 320 acres (Das 1923:24). Since they did not own the land they operated, rents constituted a major portion of their expense. This was particularly true during the "boom" years of cotton cultivation. Before World War I, rents for cotton fields had been as low as $4 per acre. During the war this rose to $35 an acre, decreasing only in 1921, and stabilizing at about $12 an acre (Das 1923:24). In addition to this, the specialized equipment required for spraying and harvesting the crop, and the scale at which these operations had to be run in order to remain competitive, eventually made it impossible for Indian farmers to continue cotton cultivation in the Imperial Valley. With the ideology of agribusiness and industrialized agriculture being firmly established in California by this time, land became increasingly concentrated on large farms, until there was a clear polarization between very small and very large farms (Jelinek 1979:63). Under these circumstances, during the 1920s, Indian farmers found they could find only one viable alternative, namely, to turn to small-scale, labor-intensive orchard farming.

Butte, Sutter, and Yuba Counties are particularly suitable for growing peaches, walnuts, almonds, and prunes. There were already several Indian leaseholders and owners in this area, and the pattern of cultivation allowed individuals to make a comfortable living if they could operate over 20 to 30 acres. Even in 1968-1972, only 8 acres in cling peaches were sufficient to gross $10,000 annually (La Brack 1975:26). Another aspect of orchard agriculture that proved attractive to the Indians was that it was possible to work as a hired hand during the day and work on one's own leaseholding during the evenings. This made it a suitable venture for those who did not have any accumulated capital. Eventually, by the 1940s, orchard farming had become the primary form of farming for Indians in California, and the pattern holds to this day.

Practically all the farms operated by Indians between 1910 and 1946 were leased and worked by partnerships, usually involving two or three people but sometimes as many as eight. The individuals in a partnership were equal shareholders, though the actual management of the farm was often left to one person. The money for such a venture was primarily borrowed by mortgaging crops, since individual savings were nominal and most people, even when working as agricultural laborers, were obliged to send money home. Interest rates varied between 7 and 10 percent across the state for these loans. Indians apparently were not charged higher interest than were other communities in similar circumstances.

Land was rented on either a share or cash tenancy basis, and the lessee also had to pay for the use of water. In cases of crop tenancy, one third of the crop and half of the price of water used had to be paid as rent to the owner. But, as Ichihashi has pointed out in the case of the Japanese tenants, if an individual could command the confidence of a landlord or a merchant, it was not difficult to get the advance needed to become a cash or share tenant, especially if the lease had the additional security of being a joint venture involving several partners (Ichihashi 1932:182). Similar circumstances seem to have been true for Indians. They were in demand for growing rice and cotton, and the rice growers' associations freely gave cash advances to them (California Board of Control 1922:80). The Bank of Italy (later named Bank of America) also played a major role in financing the start of cotton cultivation (Jelinek 1979:65). In general, land was leased to aliens far more readily during the First World War period, when there was a boom in agricultural prices and owners could circumvent the problem of labor shortage by leasing the land. (This allowed owners a share of the profits without the problems.) Indians were therefore able to move into the ranks of owner/ tenants within about ten years of arrival, more rapidly than other communities, because they were seeking leaseholdings at a particularly favorable time.

SOCIAL LIFE IN THE COMMUNITY

Family

Indians in California, and elsewhere in the United States, typically had no family, for practically none had managed to bring over their wives or children. Before 1914, only about a dozen women of Indian origin resided in California (Bagai 1968:23). In 1940, the sex ratio among Indians in California was 460 males to 100 females (Dadabhay 1954:140). Approximately one-third to half of the Indian immigrants coming in each year were married but had left their families in India, intending either to send for them or return to India after they had made some money. Most of the Indians acquired passage money by mortgaging their land, and under such conditions it was obviously unthinkable for the family to mortgage even more of their property for the purpose of sending a wife or child. By the time some of the Indian immigrants were in a position to send for their families, however, the Immigration Act of 1917 had become law, placing all Indians within the "barred zone," with exemptions only for travelers, students, and officials.

Like other Asians, many Indians did not plan to live here permanently but came instead with the intention of saving $2,000 or so and then returning home to the life of a comfortable landlord/farmer, the land being purchased with the money made abroad. This group, too, for obvious reasons, did not bring their families. After 1917, therefore, those who had left their families in India, had no means of bringing them here, and could save the money to return, went back to the Punjab. There were also scores of women, however, who waited until 1946 to see their husbands again, and dozens of others whose husbands never sent for them (Miller 1950:106).

Research on the subject has not yet been extensive enough to draw conclusions about Indian immigrant marriage patterns, but it is apparent that those from the educated professional class and the bourgeoisie usually married Caucasian women, and those from the agricultural working class usually married Mexican women; some in the Imperial Valley apparently even married Japanese women (Taylor 1930:6; Dadabhay 1954:139). In general, however, Indians did not have a family life here and often said in interviews, "If we had our women here, our whole life would be different" (Miller 1950:90).

Some researchers, such as Das, have suggested that the absence of a family in the United States was the main reason why Indian agricultural workers were able to save money. There may be some truth to this. Strict religious taboos and group pressure further inhibited Indian men from spending their money on gambling or visiting dance halls, common outlets for other immigrants that prevented the accumulation of even meager resources. But visiting prostitutes was far from uncommon, and, as Yuba County death certificates show, syphilis and chronic alcoholism were common killers among Indian immigrants from the earlier period (Leonard, personal communication, January 1981).

Although drinking alcohol is permitted by Sikh religion, excessive drinking is not condoned. It is taboo under Islamic law. The immigrants' tensions and problems and their lack of other outlets, however, seem to have broken down these traditional restrictions. Several individuals drank quite heavily, which limited their capacity to save (U.S. Immigration Commission 1911:343). Chronic alcoholism also proved to be a problem for many. For the period 1930-1947, the jail records of Yuba and Sutter Counties show that out of 461 crimes attributed to Indians, 227 were alcohol related (Miller 1950:42). Alcohol further contributed to the large number of murders arising out of drunken brawls involving Indian immigrants. Carey McWilliams recalls 49 murders in Sacramento County alone, while Miller's list from Yuba and Sutter Counties show 22 murders in the community (McWilliams 1942:144; Miller 1950:42).

This problem with alcohol undoubtedly resulted from tensions arising out of the immigrants' pattern of life. Like other ethnic groups, Indians kept very much to themselves, with an intense clannishness. Social ostracism, linguistic barriers, and hiring practices which usually treated them as a racial group or unit all contributed to their isolation, which, in turn, heightened intragroup fighting and squabbling. Those who became employers and farm operators developed some contacts outside of their own group, but for the majority, fellow gang members and coworkers formed the limits of social interaction.

Community Organizations

The focal point of group activities of the Indian agricultural workers was their religious center, the Sikh Temple or Gurdwara. A 1920 study shows that of the 2,600 Indians residing in California, 2,000 were Sikh,

500 were Muslim, and 100 were Hindu. There were numerous Gurd-waras. The earliest establishment was the Kalsa Diwan Society of Stockton, set up in 1914. A Hindustani Welfare and Reform Society was established soon after in El Centro. Besides celebrating religious festivals, which helped the immigrants feel that they still had ties with the homeland, these temples also functioned as community centers, even resolving litigations and quarrels among their members. Individuals would gather there on Sundays, often coming from as far as 50 miles away, simply to socialize with fellow countrymen or to exchange information about available jobs. Gurdwaras also provided newcomers with food and lodging until they could find some means of income.

There were some nondenominational organizations in California, notably those founded by the Gadar Revolution Party (Barrier 1979:2; Das 1923:91). This party gradually emerged as the most prominent, but originally it was one of several similar "patriotic associations." The unifying motive of all these organizations was the ouster of the British from India. Some of the associations published newspapers, and the leadership, predictably, was in the hands of the educated professional elite. The funds for the establishment and operation of the associations, however, came from the immigrant farm workers. Samples of Gadar Party literature, printed in Stockton, show that some effort was made to educate the agricultural workers about British imperialism in India. Compilations of patriotic songs were also made, though it is not known whether they were sung as part of typical Gadar Party meetings (Chandra 1916). But while there is a suggestion in their publications that an independent India could assist in protecting the rights of Indian immigrants in the United States, local issues more directly pertinent to the lives of agricultural workers were not focused on. After an abortive Gadar uprising in India, the party went into a general decline and virtually collapsed after 1917. The India League of America, based on the East Coast and supported by Indian intellectuals and businessmen, had little to do with farm workers in California and made no efforts to utilize them in their political campaigns (Hess 1974:594).

The Gadar Party, by virtue of its base in California and its Communist-sympathizing leadership, had, at least in the abstract, some interest in worker's issues. After its demise, Indian agricultural workers, owing to their isolation and the migratory nature of their work, ceased to be involved in any statewide or national organizations. Trade unions made some efforts to organize Indians and others working in the hop fields of California, but with little success (Das 1923:32). There were apparently some Indians among the foreign laborers involved in the Wheatland Riot of August 1913, where the anarchist-syndicalist International

Workers of the World had tried to unionize the harvest laborers (McWilliams 1942:160). Other than this one instance, however, Indians do not seem to have been involved in other strikes. Their contact with workers from other communities was minimal, and even among themselves religious and caste barriers persisted, as in matters of eating together (U.S. Immigration Commission 1911:342). These factors undoubtedly inhibited their ability to organize as workers.

When the living conditions or terms of employment proved unsatisfactory to an entirely Indian group or gang, they would sometimes move off a job silently if the employer refused to meet their demands. Occasionally, if the foreman was also Indian, he would be sent to the employer with a strike threat on behalf of the laborers. In other cases, if a rancher who thought the Indian workers were too slow provided pace setters to work with the Indians, the workers threatened the pace setter with violence unless he slowed down (U.S. Immigration Commission 1911:334). It appears, however, that Indians never carried out a strike by themselves before the 1930s. Perhaps there was no need, given the shortage of labor in the years 1908-1920 (when Japanese were no longer immigrating in large numbers), since employers were willing to negotiate terms and wages when faced with the threat of a strike.

Although there were far fewer Indians in California after the Depression, they seem to have become more effectively organized. Carey McWilliams tells of a conversation with a foreman of a large farm in the San Joaquin Valley around 1937 who reported: "Last year our Hindu workers struck. So this year we mixed half Mexicans in with them, and we aren't having any labor trouble" (McWilliams 1942:118). This is not only a typical example from the annals of labor history in California, but it also illustrates that farm labor organizations were severely handicapped by the presence of so many diverse ethnic groups who could be played off against one another to the advantage of the employer.

CONCLUSION

In conclusion, let me briefly sum up the Indian experience in California. Those who stayed on, either through choice or force of circumstances, usually state that they were economically more successful in the United States than they would have been in India. The general consensus among those I interviewed, however, is that life was happier in the Punjab, and they still feel, like most first generation immigrants, that America is not "home."

The majority of Indians have remained, to a great extent, an isolated group, venturing into direct contact with other ethnic groups only to the extent necessary for survival or economic success. (The one or two individuals who have held public office in the last twenty-five years are exceptions in the fullest sense of the word: they came from educated, professional backgrounds and had, in fact, more in common with white, middle-class U.S. citizens than they had with their illiterate rural compatriots.) The Indian's cultural isolation was reinforced by the fact that agricultural workers and farmers seldom had the opportunity to lead normal domestic lives; that is, many had wives and children still in India, while many others remained bachelors. Usually, the problems facing families, such as housing, education, and health, forced immigrant families to develop some contact with other groups, especially if the immigrant community was not very large. As single men, however, the Indians could function quite well within a limited frame of reference, making it unnecessary for them to break out of their isolation.

Indians came to the United States, and to California in particular, at a time when there was a demand for agricultural laborers in an expanding industry. The very shortage of labor that made them welcome and permitted economic survival initially, however, also made it possible for them to enter the ranks of leaseholding farmers more rapidly than other groups. During the years of World War I, when agricultural prices were rising, white farm owners were willing to lease land to various ethnic groups rather than let the land lie fallow. This process removed the Indians from the labor market; thus, rather than being supplies of labor, they became employers looking for workers.

Their sudden prosperity, and their use of Mexican, black, and even white labor, made them unwelcome rivals and, as such, "unnecessary" immigrants in rural California. The relatively few Indians who were still available as agricultural workers were often co-opted by their own countrymen, who offered other Indians higher wages than did white farmers. Das found Indian cotton growers in the Imperial Valley and rice growers in Sacramento Valley paying wages of $3.00 per day to Indians but only $2.00 a day to Mexicans and $2.25 to white laborers (Das 1923:58-59).

Later, Indian orchardists invariably hired exclusively Indian labor, usually from their original work gangs. Few Indians became farm hands to white farmers, as they preferred to move in groups with other Indians from orchard to orchard (Miller 1950:22). These maneuvers, which ultimately controlled the availability of Indian laborers for non-Indian farmers, surely did not help make Indians popular with agricultural interest groups.

When legal Indian immigration was ultimately curtailed in 1917, Indians were regarded as workers who had proved themselves to be less than the ideal solution to the labor shortage problem. Moreover, by this time, the potential of Mexican labor had been discovered. Mexicans were "good workers" but unorganized until the late 1920s. Best of all, Mexican labor could be brought over easily when necessary and just as easily deported when unwanted (McWilliams 1942:127-128). Thus, with the California farmer's labor shortage problems so conveniently solved, the Indian immigrants were no longer needed.

References

Annual Reports of the Commission General of Immigration to the Secretary of
    Commerce and Labor
  1911- Washington, D.C.: Government Printing Office.
  1920

Bagai, L.
  1968 The East Indians and the Pakistanis in America. Minneapolis: Lerner Pub-
    lications.

Barrier, G.
  1979 "The Hindustan Ghadar: Identity and organization among Indians in the West
    Coast of the U.S." Unpublished paper.

Calcutta Review, The
  1925 July 16, pp. 40-46.

California Board of Control
  1922 California and the Oriental. Sacramento.

California Fruit Grower
  1907 Vol. 36. August 24. Sacramento.

Chandra, R.
  1916 Deshbhakti ke Geet (Patriotic Songs). Stockton.

Dadabhay, Y.
  1954 "Circuitous assimilation among rural Hindustanis in California." Social Forces
    33:138-141.

Das, R. K.
  1923 Hindustani Workers on the Pacific Coast. Berlin: W. de Gruyter.

Hess, G. R.
  1974 "The forgotten Asian Americans: The East Indian community in the United
    States." Pacific Historical Review 43: 576-596.

Huttenback, R.
  1976 Racism and Empire. Ithaca, N.Y.: Cornell University Press.

Ichihashi, Y.
  1932 Japanese in the United States. Stanford: Stanford University Press.

Jacoby, H. S.
  1956 A Half Century Appraisal of East Indians in the United States. Stockton:
    College of the Pacific.

Jelinek, L.
  1979 Harvest Empire. San Francisco: Boyd & Fraser.

La Brack, B.
  1975 "Occupational specialization among California Sikhs." Unpublished paper.
    Stockton.

McWilliams, C.
  1942 Factories in the Field. Boston: Little, Brown & Son.

Melendy, H. B.
  1977 Asians in America. Boston: G. K. Hall.

Miller, A. P.
   1950   An ethnographic report on the Sikh (East) Indians of the Sacramento Valley.
          Unpublished paper. University of California, Berkeley.
Millis, H. A.
   1912   "East Indian immigration to British Columbia and the Pacific Coast states."
          American Economic Review 1: 72-76.
Misrow, J. C.
   1915   East Indian Immigration on the Pacific Coast. Stanford: Stanford University
          Press.
Samra, K. R.
   1940   Hindus in the United States. Unpublished paper. Carey McWilliams Collection,
          University of California, Los Angeles.
Stark, C.
   1976   Harvest of Sadness; Race, Nationality and Caste in California Agriculture
          1900-1930. Ph.D. dissertation, University of California, Berkeley.
Survey, The
   1910   "The Hindu, the newest immigration problem." No. 25, pp. 2-3.
Taylor, P. S.
   1930   Mexican Labor in the United States. Berkeley: University of California Press.
Timlin, M. F.
   1960   "Canada's immigration policy, 1896-1910." Canadian Journal of Economics and
          Political Science 24, no. 4.
U.S. Immigration Commission
   1911   Reports. Vol. 23 and Vol. 25. Washington, D.C.: Government Printing Office.
Wenzel, L. A.
   1968   "The Rural Punjabis of California: A Religion-Ethnic Group." Phylon 29: 245-256.
Wynne, R. E.
   1966   "American labor leaders and the Vancouver anti-Oriental riot." Pacific North-
          west Quarterly 58: 172-179.

Interviews, held in 1978
   Bagai, K. Los Angeles.   Samra, I. Stockton.
   Chandra, M. Los Angeles.   Sharma, J. Los Angeles.
   Everest, Hari Singh. Yuba City.   Singh, Gurbachan. Yuba City.
   Gill, M. Stockton.   Singh, Makkhan. Stockton.
   Gupta, K. San Francisco.   Teja, S. Yuba City.
   Gurdial, Paul Singh. Los Angeles.   Thind, V. Los Angeles.
   Heir, Gandasingh. Yuba City.   Two interviews, anonymous.
   Johl, G. S. Yuba City.   Sikh Temple, Yuba City. (Interviewees
   Kahn, Sikandar. Stockton.   would not give names; old men, prob-
   Ram, A. Los Angeles.   ably illegal entry; thought I was from
                                                   the Immigration Office.)

17

Labor Migration and Class Formation Among the Filipinos in Hawaii, 1906-1946

Miriam Sharma

The migration of Filipino workers to Hawaii, from 1906 to 1946, took place within the context of an ever-increasing capitalist penetration of the islands and Hawaii's concomitant absorption into the world capitalist economy (Kent, forthcoming; Lind 1938). A plantation-type sugar economy had evolved in Hawaii from the 1860s and by 1880 had become the dominant factor in the islands' political economy. Meeting the growing demand for cheap agricultural wage labor was critical for expansion of the industry, but constant labor shortages plagued the early planters. The attempt to use indigenous workers was not successful. Decimated by Western-imported diseases, alcohol, and a "loss of will to live," the indigenous population had plummeted from approximately 300,000 to 400,000 persons at the time of Western contact (1778), to just 40,000 a century later. Also, Hawaiians still had access to the land for meeting their subsistence needs, and no immediate imperative forced them to sell their labor for plantation wages. Thus confronted with an inadequate supply of local labor, the planters were compelled to look abroad to fulfill their needs.

During the latter part of the nineteenth century and continuing into the early years of the twentieth, the most divisive issue facing the *haole* ("white man") elite in Hawaii was the controversy over importing labor. Planters were continually at odds with the merchants, professional men, and government of the Territory over this issue. Ultimately, the planters succeeded in sponsoring a mass worldwide migration to meet the needs of the rapidly expanding sugar economy that came to rule the islands (Fuchs 1961:51, 90 ff. Gov. Files:Carter, Terr. Depts., Indus. and Labor Situation, 7 Jan. 1905; Immig., Bd. of, Carter to Cooke, 3 Jan. 1906; Kim 1937:104).

This chapter proposes to describe the migration of Filipino plantation laborers to Hawaii and to analyze the migration pattern's effect on the process of class formation and differentiation within this ethnic group.[1] The majority of these more than 125,000 predominantly male immigrants were landless tenants or petty landholders from *barrios* who came to be the major agri-industrial proletariat that lived and worked on sugar plantations through the Second World War. As Hawaii's last major immigrant group, following waves of others, the Filipinos faced more circumscribed economic opportunities (Lind 1938:266ff; 1967:78) and ultimately controlled less of the wealth of Hawaii than any other important group (Fuchs 1961:440). This served to reinforce their dominant class position as an agri-industrial proletariat. By 1946, only a barely nascent process of class differentiation had begun among the Filipinos, and the beginnings of a petit bourgeois class—engaged mostly in small businesses but including a few professionals—emerged as the basis for the subsequent postwar development of a *kamaaina illustrado* ("oldtimer elite") class.

The first part of this chapter outlines the migration pattern of Filipinos to Hawaii, the occupations they entered, their wages, and their general working and living conditions. The focus is on the plantation laborer, as 70 percent of all Filipinos in Hawaii were so engaged by 1932. The second part discusses Filipino workers' organizations and struggles for a better life, their relations with other workers, and the nature of class differentiation within the ethnic group. A final section deals with the impact of U.S. national oppression of Filipinos through its colonial rule in the Philippines and the direct link that oppression had to the status of Filipino labor in Hawaii. The conclusion draws together the main points of the discussion and suggests that the process of class formation among Filipino workers proceeded quite quickly. This was accompanied by a low level of differentiation, which has as much to do with their colonial status as with the timing of their entry into Hawaii's labor market.

FILIPINO LABOR MIGRATION TO HAWAII

Migration Patterns

Before the Organic Act of 1900, which made U.S. federal laws applicable to the Territory of Hawaii, laborers in Hawaii were indentured and subject to criminal prosecution if they attempted to depart before their contract expired. No doubt the impending restriction of Japanese laborers to the United States and its territories, culminating in the Gentlemen's Agreement of 1907, prompted planters to look to the Philippines, but it was the 1909 strike that sparked their concerted efforts. In that year the Japanese, well organized and no longer docile, staged the first big strike. This strike enhanced the already-existing fears of the Hawaiian Sugar Planters' Association (hereafter HSPA) regarding Japanese domination and intensified the search for Filipino labor. By the time Filipino laborers started to arrive in great numbers, the dominant society (represented by the planters and politicians) had already formulated definite ideas and policies regarding the treatment of immigrant workers. These applied to this last major ethnic group as well and formed the context within which their working conditions and class formation can be understood.

The attitudes of the dominant elite were predicated upon a firm belief in the superiority of the haole over the "Asiatic." Because these attitudes were reinforced by the need for a cheap labor force that would be compliant and easy to control, immigrant labor was viewed solely as an economic commodity; the planters had no concern for the social adjustments that each group brought to the islands would have to make. It was believed, in fact, that the best way to deal with the immigrants was to foster an environment that would encourage each ethnic group to remain separate and, in essence, not to adjust to living with one another. Although Filipinos did not come as bound indentured laborers, there is little evidence to suggest that the planters' attitudes toward "free" labor and its treatment were substantially different from their attitudes under the old system. The statements of the HSPA, government officials, and U.S. Commissioner of Labor Statistics illustrate several of these views.

First, the planters were concerned primarily with providing a constant flow of cheap labor, and they regarded the increasing aggressiveness of "Asiatics" as a serious threat to the continued prosperity of the sugar industry. For this reason they adopted the policy of employing as many different ethnic groups as they could and of setting one group against another (Bouslog 1948:11). They imported laborers (in this specific case, Chinese) in order to

> break up the race solidarity of the present plantation labor supply, destroy the monopoly now held by the Japanese, temper their aggressiveness, and very much simplify the problem of plantation discipline and plantation management. (U.S. Bureau of Labor Statistics [USBLS] 1906:45)

The planters were not at all concerned with the internal adjustments that each ethnic group would have to make. For them,

> The Asiatic has had only an economic value in the social equation. So far as the institutions, laws, customs and language of the permanent population go, his presence is no more felt than is that of the cattle upon the mountain ranges. (USBLS 1903:37-38).

> Nor was it uncommon to discriminate against immigrant laborers. The old customs and habit of regarding Japanese and other Orientals as people of inferior civil status as compared with whites still prevail in Hawaii and manifest themselves in a hundred unconscious acts on the part of managers and overseers, who have never considered that in the strict letter of the law residents of foreign countries . . . have the same rights to protection of person and property and to privacy and respect as ourselves. (USBLS 1906:141)

The ruling haole elite hardly questioned the wisdom and propriety of their right to dominate the islands. During the Congressional hearings to determine whether Hawaii should be exempt from Chinese exclusion (1921), the secretary of the HSPA said:

> The Territory of Hawaii is now and is going to be American; it is going to remain American under any condition and we are going to control the situation out there. . . . The white race, the white people, the Americans in Hawaii are going to dominate and will continue to dominate—there is no question about it. (U.S. Congress 1921:300-301).

Finally, regarding the ethics of Filipino immigration in particular and the effects that it might have on society in Hawaii, the president of the HSPA wrote: "From a strictly ethical standpoint, I can see little difference between the importation of foreign laborers and the importation of jute bags from India" (*Honolulu Star Bulletin*, 24 July 1930). In either case, human labor or jute bags, both were commodities for Hawaii's planters to deal with as they liked.

Filipino migration to Hawaii was largely a private HSPA undertaking, although it had strong government support (Lind 1938:193). Initially the Philippine government tried to discourage recruitment, as labor was needed for its own growing sugar industry. Legislation was passed to regulate this business and provide for free return of laborers after a three-year contract (Act No. 2486, quoted in Lasker 1931:392-393; USBLS 1916:27). Subsequently the HSPA embarked on an aggressive and well-organized recruiting program that capitalized on the inducements of free passage in both directions. Active recruitment and pecuniary inducements were discontinued after 1926 because migration had achieved a satisfactory momentum of its own, although movement was still carefully supervised. From 1926 to 1928 unsolicited boatloads of workers arrived, and in 1931 the HSPA ceased recruiting altogether. They subsidized sending 3,448 indigent former plantation workers back to the Philippines after major protests from Filipino labor leaders (Dorita 1954:64-65; Lasker 1931:164, 283, 286, 392-393; Lind 1938:208; Quezon Papers: W. A. Babbitt to Quezon, 1 Jan. 1923, W. A. Babbitt to Cruz, 23 Sept. 1929).

The planters' policy from the beginning was to recruit single men as transient laborers, a policy that the *Report of the Commissioner of Labor* reveals as being clear-cut. Writing in 1916, six years after emigration from the Philippines had begun, the commissioner stated: "Plantations have to view laborers primarily as instruments of production. Their business interests require cheap, not too intelligent, docile unmarried men" (USBLS 1916:40).[2] Table 17.1 shows the results of this policy.

The 1915 legislation passed in the Philippines, making it mandatory for the HSPA to provide free return passage, underscored this policy. Even the sudden increase of women in the early 1920s (after two big strikes) does not represent a significant change in orientation. The economic loss from labor instability, believed due to the lack of women, temporarily outweighed the gains from a transient, noncitizen work force. The planters seem singlemindedly to have attributed labor agitation to the paucity of females and family life among the Filipinos; with the increase of the latter, they reasoned, discontent would appear (Gov. Files: Frear, Terr. Depts., Immig., Bd. of, 1907-1909, Atkinson to Ivers, 23-24 Aug. 1909, Lasker 1931:32-136; Moe 1929:38-52).

This policy of recruiting single men was to prove a thorn in the side of the planters. While on the one hand, a transient male labor supply was more economic and allayed the problems of large numbers of nativeborn, on the other hand, the abnormal sex ratio and large numbers of unmarried men constituted a social problem for the dominant society. At no time during this first period of Filipino history in Hawaii did the ratio of men to women go lower than approximately 3.5 to 1 in 1940; at its highest, in 1910, there were more than ten men for every woman.

The abnormal sex ratio led to large numbers of men remaining single and to females marrying at an early age. This was a natural result of an imbalance in the population whereby approximately 65 percent of the females were under the age of twenty and more than 75 percent of the

TABLE 17.1

FILIPINOS COMING TO HAWAII THROUGH HSPA FROM 1909 TO 1946

Year	Men	Women	Children	Total
1909	554	57	28	639
1910	2,653	169	93	2,915
1911	1,363	173	74	1,610
1912	4,319	553	362	5,234
1913	3,258	573	351	4,182
1914	1,848	360	228	2,436
1915	1,363	238	185	1,786
1916	1,674	141	134	1,949
1917	2,536	182	210	2,928
1918	2,196	298	395	2,889
1919	2,642	312	278	3,232
1920	3,060	232	181	3,473
1921	3,982	434	240	4,656
1922	8,513	704	457	9,674
1923	4,830	1,482	787	7,099
1924	4,915	1,414	648	6,977
1925	9,934	459	252	10,645
1926	3,060	121	96	4,177
1927	8,976	95	88	9,157
1928	10,508	193	156	10,857
1929	6,971	152	186	7,309
1930	6,904	177	201	7,372
1931	5,597	217	200	6,014
1932	953	151	122	1,226
1933	9	22	10	41
1934	25	43	39	107
1946	6,000	446	915	7,361
Total	109,544	9,398	7,006	125,947

SOURCE: Amended from Dorita, 1967:29.

men were over that age. The percentage of Filipino men who were married increased with age and an early precedent seems to have been set, born of demographic necessity, for a youthful woman-older man marriage pattern. There was also an accompanying shift away from an extended family to a primarily nuclear one. To a great extent these families were emancipated from the control of elders and a wider network of kin. While this was especially true in urban areas, where there was considerable laxness in conforming to traditional standards of behavior, it was much less so in the rural areas. Here, people knew each other well and public opinion developed into strong community control over behavior (Cariaga 1936:110-113, 124; also Fuchs 1961-147; Luis and Sensano 1937:66).

Filipino women enjoyed a high status in their home country as important decision makers with control over the family funds. In Hawaii their position was enhanced owing to their small numbers. They were often the chief cause of disagreements and fights between men, and a stable family and home life was inhibited by instances of common-law marriages, considerable shifting of partners, and easy divorce. The incidence of intermarriage also may have contributed to a certain instability of family life and community organization (Luis and Sensano 1937; Menor 1949; Wentworth 1941:55; Cariaga 1936:142, 147).

Single men, and those who had left their families behind, made a number of adaptations to ease the difficulties of living as men without women. In some instances several men would live together, creating an artificial family patterned along lines of the ideal one. Position and status within such a "family" depended upon age and the occupation held. On the plantations the majority of bachelor Filipino houses were arranged in special parts of the village "to avoid disturbances or sexual irregularities" (Luis and Sensano 1937; also Cariaga 1936:142, 147). A certain amount of violence over sex, prostitution, and instances of *coboy-coboy* ("wife abduction") was, however, inevitable (Alcantara 1973:58; Fuchs 1961:147).

In lieu of the rich family life and associations they had known in the Philippines, the laborers found their major sources of social interaction on the plantation in organized sports and entertainment. Baseball, boxing, volleyball, and billiards, Filipino movies, activities in the Filipino club house, cockfights, and gambling were augmented by taxi-dance halls in town. The need for physical as well as mental distance from the grim monotony of fieldwork must have contributed strongly to the reported emphasis on personal care and to Filipino stereotyping. They were seen after work "in the latest Hollywood-style white suit, colorful silk shirt, handrolled hankerchief, carefully polished shoes and oiled hair" (Cariaga 1936:35; also Alcantara 1973:86; Clark 1947:152-154; Lord and Lee 1937:46-49; Wentworth 1941:174).

In addition to a skewed sex ratio, the Filipino population was also characterized by high illiteracy. Recruited specifically from the rural areas, migrants with calloused palms had an advantage in provincial and Manila recruiting stations; pens in a shirt pocket were enough to disqualify a prospective laborer. In 1920, some 48.7 percent of all Filipinos ten years old and over were illiterate. By 1930 the number had dropped only to 38.5 percent (U.S. Census 1930; literacy was not reported in subsequent censuses).

A large proportion of first-generation immigrants did, however, return to their barrios and there was a large outmigration from Hawaii. By 1935, 58,281 workers had returned home, while 18,574 (many as families) moved on to the U.S. mainland. The Filipino population in the territory reached its peak in 1931 when, at more than 63,000, it represented 17.1 percent of the islands' people. It was difficult, however, for the "failures" to return, and they formed the nucleus of an unemployed and destitute group of men congregating in the poorer sections of Honolulu. There were countless others who collectively sent enormous sums home but who were unable to save for their return passage.

Life and Labor in Sugarlandia

Once the Filipinos arrived in Hawaii, they were assigned to one of more than thirty HSPA-affiliated plantations located on the islands of Maui, Oahu, Kauai, and Hawaii—the latter having the greatest number (HSPA 1949:40-41). The ethnic composition on the plantations changed drastically with their coming. In 1915, Filipinos constituted only 19 percent of the work force, and the Japanese formed 54 percent; by 1932 it was the Japanese who were only 19 percent of plantation employees and 70 percent were Filipino (see table 17.2; Lind 1938:320, 325; USBLS 1916:18).

The conditions of life and labor on these plantations have been represented by as many different views as there were interests involved. Many Filipino journals and newspapers in Hawaii were overwhelmingly pro-HSPA (e.g., *The Filipino Outlook; Philippine Press of Hilo; Wagayway*). These publications seem to have walked a tightrope between not dis-

TABLE 17.2
SUGAR PLANTATION EMPLOYEES BY RACE

	1882	1902	Percent 1922	1932	1942
Hawaiian and Part-Hawaiian	25.1	3.5	4.4	1.2	2.4
Portuguese	6.2	6.4	5.7	4.0	6.8
Puerto Rican		4.8	3.9	1.6	1.9
Other Caucasian	8.1		2.1	1.8	2.7
Chinese	49.2	9.3	3.4	1.4	.9
Japanese	.1	73.5	38.3	18.8	30.6
Korean			2.6	.9	
Filipino			41.0	69.9	53.4
All others	11.2	2.5	.9	.3	1.3
Total Number	10,243	42,242	44,402	49,947	33,946

SOURCE: Lind 1967:75.

turbing the status quo of plantation life or invoking the displeasure of planters, and attempting to wrest certain benefits for their community from the government in the Philippines. The HSPA and allied writings on the subject of the conditions of plantation life also present a roseate view, as do most investigations made by representatives of the American colonial government in the Philippines. Filipinos were "satisfied, happy and contented" with the general living conditions and wages of $20 a month for ten hours a day, twenty days a month (Balmori 1912:46). In the 1920s it was found that "Filipinos get a square deal" and "Hawaii is the veritable promised land" (Duckworth-Ford 1926:1; Cruz 1926:16; Lasker 1931:340; Manzon 1938:12; Quezon Papers: Cruz to Quezon, 10 Jan. 1923).

There is, however, another, more realistic view of the system to which the Filipinos migrated, which comes through in the numerous works of the sociologist Andrew Lind and others, based on their own observations. Lind conceives of the plantation as being much like a political sovereignty—an estate in which the manager or proprietor exercises widespread political as well as economic and moral control over its labor force (Lind 1935:2-5; 1938:213; 1967:7, 74). The divide-and-rule policy of the planters was augmented by a system of residential segregation of ethnic groups, racial stratification, and differential pay and occupations for ethnic groups. Filipinos were invariably the lowest on the scale in these last two categories—the last hired and the first fired. Despite the planters' cry about a continual labor shortage, their creation of a labor surplus remained the most effective insurance against strikes (Aller 1957:34; Liebes 1938:70; USBLS 1916: table A).

The plantations also exercised control through the paternalism of perquisites and so-called welfare benefits. Even a series of articles that lauded plantation life relates that there were charges for all these benefits (Smith 1924:120). Similarly, an investigator from the Philippines noted that some workers had 15¢ deducted monthly from their paychecks for "quota" or hospital fees. He also found that hospital treatment, especially for operations, was not free and that permission even to see the doctor depended upon the overseer (Remigio 1919; see Wentworth 1941:54, 64, 192). The "free" housing provided to laborers remained one of the most effective ways a plantation could control labor and get rid of any "troublemaker," "agitator," or "striker." His belongings were set out on the street and the worker was evicted (bodily if need be) from the area; he could not return. For this reason, the planters consistently rejected the idea of home ownership as a means to upgrade and stabilize labor. Housing was used instead as a means of reward and punishment (Aller 1957:32; Lind 1938:231-232; 1967:5)

People who wished to enter the plantation needed passes. This was supposedly to protect the "gullible" and "childlike" workers from confidence men, extortionists, and others of that ilk. Epifanio Toak, president of the Filipino Labor Union, presented a memorandum to the Territorial Legislature to redress the "pitiful" condition of the Filipino worker. It protested the "Trespassing Law," among other things, for causing "great Injustice and Discrimination" against them and for arrests and prosecutions under this law that fell more heavily upon the Filipinos than upon other ethnic groups. The protest memorial cites the fact that relatives or friends of the workers were not allowed on plantation premises. If they challenged this, they were arrested, charged, and prosecuted for trespassing. While businessmen of other nationalities could enter the plantations without question, "the Filipino Laundry of Waipahu, Oahu, the Filipino Store at Honouliuli, Ewa, Oahu, some Filipino Vegetable pedlers, Filipino Fish men dealers or other Filipino business men were prohibited to enter the plantation" (*Philippine News Tribune*, 6 Nov. 1933). Even the voluntary dues collected for membership in the Filipino Club had to be petitioned from the American personnel director for use in club celebrations. Close supervision of other Filipino activities by the management enabled it to "circumvent activities regarded as 'subversive'" (Wentworth 1941:174-175).

By far the most detailed picture of the plantation system is given in Prudencio A. Remigio's 1919 report to the Philippine government. Written in Spanish and buried in the Quezon Papers, it seems (unlike other reports) not to have been either translated into English or published. Remigio's findings were highly critical of the treatment and conditions of Filipino workers. He found that they suffered from hard, monotonous work, lacked adequate recreation, and that—despite a bonus system meant to provide profit-sharing incentives—they received only a bare subsistence wage. Such a wage took into account neither the need to support dependents nor the ultimate satisfaction of economic gain (Remigio 1919; see also Lasker 1931:296; Wentworth 1941:91).

Payroll deductions left workers precious little to spend on their own. Deductions included such items as: the plantation store, electricity, dues and bills of the Filipino Club, charges at the health center and kindergarten, meat bills at the independent meat market, purchase of large-framed photos, auto licenses, plantation fines, insurance, school lunches, and garnished wages. Contributions to the United Welfare Fund of Honolulu were also deducted from the workers' wages, and the percentage of the salaries deducted depended upon the decision of the manager. Cariaga points out that, although housing was considered a "free" perquisite, in effect the management itemized this and other services so that "the net result is as if the laborer was paid with a house as part of his wage" (1936:101; also Wentworth 1941:54, 64, 192).

Filipinos were kept as unskilled laborers for the most part and were employed on either a daily wage or a contract basis. In 1915, 92 percent of their work force had this status, and by 1930 it had only dropped to 85 percent. Filipino workers carried out the arduous and monotonous tasks of hoeing, planting, and weeding during the cultivation of cane, and of cutting, hauling, loading, and fluming during the harvest. Their ten- to twelve-hour work day was rigorous, and their lives became attuned to the dictates of the factory mill whistle (Cariaga 1936:51 ff.; Lind 1938:252, fig. 17). The most typical reaction to the first day of plantation work was to shed tears at night (e.g., the life history in Interchurch Federation of Honolulu 1936:xi-11).[3] Two observers of the period have recorded the daily schedule of a plantation worker, based on their observations in the mid-1930s (Cariaga 1936:15; Wentworth 1941:53). The following is a composite view:

> 3-4 A.M.: Field workers arise to cook and pack their breakfast and lunch.
> 5 A.M.: The warning whistle blows to announce the arrival of buses or cane trains that will take the previously gathered men to the fields.
> 6 A.M.: Work begins
> 7:45-8 A.M.: Breakfast
> 11-11:30 A.M.: Lunch
> 3-4 P.M.: Work ceases and the laborers wait for transportation back to their houses.
> (Workers in the mill and shops have a twelve-hour schedule.)

After returning from the fields, workers first sought the bathhouses (one for each block or camp of workers). Married men in individual cottages frequently heated water in empty oil kegs set over wood in the yard. Dinner was usually eaten between 4:30 and 6 P.M., when members of the family often gathered together for the first time all day. Single men either cooked in their own cottages and barrack rooms or ate in one of the boarding houses run by enterprising Filipinas. By 7:30 or 8 P.M., most were in bed again (Cariaga 1936:53).

Under the different types of contracts that Filipinos signed with the HSPA, the basic wage for this type of labor remained at $18 to $20 a month from 1915 to 1933 (with perquisites and return passage stipulated). Remuneration for women was $12 to $14 a month. Not only did wages remain stable despite the enormous postwar inflation but in

1920, they were actually reduced. Before that, $18 was the minimum pay for a twenty-day working month; when the wage went up to $20 in 1920, the expected number of work days was extended to twenty-six. Hence the daily wage really decreased (Cruz, 1926:23 ff.; contracts in Quezon Papers; Wentworth 1941:91). After 1933, when a labor surplus was finally admitted to exist, contracts were no longer signed. Increasing mechanization and the corresponding demand for skilled labor to handle machinery decreased the need for unskilled laborers, and between 1939 and 1947 Filipinos were dropped from the payrolls in large numbers (Aller 1957:12).

The sugar companies maintained a complicated and arbitrary system of piecework and contract methods of payment, and a fluctuating bonus system. The complexity and diversity of wages often led to misunderstandings, and the arbitrary nature of determining payment led to abuses of power. Complaints against the whole system were widespread. While living conditions improved somewhat over the decades, especially after the strikes, wages remained insufficient, and paternalism and control were plantation policy until the unionization of cane and pineapple workers in 1946 (Alexander 1937:143 ff.; Aller 1957:12). Despite harsh living conditions and an inadequate wage, however, Filipinos were able to accumulate substantial savings and to send money to the Philippines. Relatives came to depend greatly upon their Hawaii emigres for support. Figures available reveal the following for the period 1915-1922:

(a) the HSPA Manila Office disbursed ₱3,743,700 (1 ₱ = 50¢) in the Philippines:[4]

(b) ₱814,780 were deposited for saving in their Honolulu office; and

(c) from 1920 to 1922 an average of ₱1,000,000 was annually sent directly to the Philippines through postal money orders.

Between 1926 to 1929:

(a) money order remittances to the Philippines totaled $8,727,719.96;

(b) returning laborers to the Philippines during 1927 to 1928 (8,416 in all) had sent to relatives and/or brought back with them $3,973,158; and

(c) as of June 30, 1928, the savings banks in Honolulu reported 9,069 depositors with savings amounting to $2,083,518 (presumably representing urban workers too).

In 1936,

(a) postal money orders to the Philippines exceeded $4,000,000, and an additional $1,000,000 was sent through other agencies; and

(b) the nearly 20,000 Filipino savings depositors had about $4,000,000 in their accounts in Hawaii (Cariaga 1936:83, 86-87; Lasker 1931:252; Quezon Papers: W. A. Babbitt to Faustino Aguilar, 11 Jan. 1923, W. A. Babbitt to Cruz, 25 Sept. 1929; cf. Norbeck 1959:85).

Lind reports that Filipino per-capita savings deposits for 1930, 1932 and 1934 (including nonplantation workers) were higher than those of the Japanese. This seems to indicate that by this time Hawaii was "home" for the Japanese, who were employing their savings in capital investment, whereas Filipinos were still saving for that bit of paradise in the barrio. Real property investment remained insignificant among Filipinos during this period (Lind 1938:266-267, tables 29, 30). For those with families in Hawaii, however, it was difficult to save. The single man or the married one who had left his family behind had a greater chance to accumulate money. Perhaps it was because the unattached men were overwhelmingly Ilocanos while the Visayans came as family groups, that the stereotypes of the thrifty Ilocano and the wasteful Visayan were carried over into Filipino life in Hawaii.

In any event, remittances to the Philippines from workers in Hawaii were often so great that they overwhelmed the Philippine provincial treasuries. The gain from work in Hawaii was particularly noticeable in the Ilocos region by the large number and increased size of land holdings belonging to "Hawaiianos" or their relatives. Throughout the 1930s Filipinos unflaggingly continued to invest their money in the Philippines, predominantly in land, and this had far-reaching effects within their homeland society (Gorospe 1933:246; see also Griffiths 1978). Their ability to save was commented upon even by W. A. Babbitt of the HSPA (Quezon Papers: W. A. Babbitt to Cruz, 25 Sept. 1929).

Movement and Occupations off the Plantations

Throughout the period under study (1906-1946), the vast majority of Filipinos in Hawaii remained on plantations. In 1930, 80 percent of all Filipinos were still engaged in plantation work, with several thousand also working on pineapple plantations or for independent planters in sugar, coffee, or taro (Lasker 1931:160; Robinson 1935; Fuchs 1961:146). There was a marked increase in the numbers working in the coffee fields after the 1924 strike—some 700 by 1933—as many strikers gravitated toward these jobs. There were extremely few independent Filipino planters because the Japanese did not allow encroachment on their domain (Lind 1938:146). Fewer than 300 (by 1933) were working on rice-taro-vegetable farms; not many of these were independent owner/farmers.

Following the 1920 and 1924 strikes, there was some movement to the urban centers of Hilo and Honolulu, especially the latter. The slow pace of this prewar migration to the city is reflected in the census data presented in table 17.3. Ten percent of the total Filipino population were in the urban areas in 1920; by 1940 this had risen only to 13

percent. In Honolulu, where the overwhelming majority of urban Filipinos lived, most of them congregated in several distinct slum districts
during the years 1920 to 1950. The largest concentration was around
the intersection of King and Liliha Streets. Others lived near the pineapple canneries where many worked, around Aala Park bounded by
Beretania and King Streets, or in quarters near the hospitals (Leahi,
Home for Tuberculosis, and Queens) or Waikiki hotels where they were
employed (Lind 1967:57).[5] The Royal Hawaiian and Moana hotels provided quarters for 200 of their single employees. Other hotels followed
suit, and by 1935 Cariaga found that about 400 Filipinos were housed in
cottages of eight to twelve rooms—with three to five boys in a room—
at the height of the tourist season (Cariaga 1935:43).

Filipino migration to the city was prompted by dissatisfaction and
disappointment with plantation life—with the lack of racial equality,
opportunity, and adequate medical care, with poor living conditions and
conflicts with employers over the bonus or during strikes (Cariaga
1935; 1936:103). Several hundred found employment in Honolulu as
stevedores, truck drivers, cannery workers, yard "boys," bootblacks,
construction workers, and as restaurant, hotel, or hospital employees. A
few hundred worked in retail jobs as sales clerks or found employment
in tailor, barber, and printing enterprises (Lasker 1931:160; HSPA Report
of 1933, quoted in Robinson 1935). Some worked as civilians for the
Army and Navy. Finally, there was work in the pool halls and dance
halls. Employment was primarily seasonal, and unemployment for most
of the year was a chronic problem.

Filipino workers in Honolulu also suffered from low wages. Work for
two or three months of the year during the pineapple canning season
paid 20¢ an hour for men and 10¢ an hour for women. Work as domes-

TABLE 17.3
FILIPINOS IN URBAN CENTERS

	1910	1920	1930	1940
Total Filipino population	2,361	21,031	63,052	52,569
Filipinos in urban centers	163	2,598	6,821	6,887
(Honolulu)	(87)	(2,113)	(4,776)	(6,834)
Percentage of total Filipino population in urban centers	—	10%	11%	13%
Percentage of Filipinos in total population	1.2%	8.2%	17.1%	12.4%
Filipinos as percentage of total urban population	0.31%	3.1%	3.5%	3.8%

SOURCE: U.S. Census 1910, 1920, 1930, 1940.

tics in hotels and as dishwashers and waiters paid $45 a month. The youngest of all Filipino workers (literally "boys") were found in the hotel industry, where they constituted up to 75 percent of all waiters. These young men, at the bottom of the scale, earned room and board and $34 to $40 per month. The temporary nature of their work turned Filipinos into urban migrants with no real home, only a place to sleep and cook. They changed residence often and would board with other Filipinos, as many as six to ten sharing a single cottage or apartment (Yamamura 1935; Cariaga 1935; 1936:103).

The Depression, along with subsequent mechanization on the plantations, was another major cause for migration to the city, and Filipinos were hardest hit during this period. Plantation cutbacks from 1930 to 1940 forced them to move to urban areas. Some plantations suffered a much more rapid depletion of labor than others. Grove Farm plantation, for example, lost 137 single men to Honolulu during six months in 1936. The following year, changes were implemented to keep men on the plantation. Activity programs were stepped up, including the establishment of boxing, baseball, soccer, and football teams. Workers were allowed to set up their own vegetable gardens, and the first Filipino restaurant opened in the village. While workers were frozen to their jobs and prohibited to travel to Honolulu during World War II, there was an immediate exodus from Grove Farm after the war (Krauss and Alexander 1965:339-340).

A new class of drifters emerged during the Depression period, unemployed and living mostly in slums centering around King and Liliha Streets. The problem of urban unemployment for Filipinos had loomed large as early as the mid-1920s, for the planters had worked to create a labor surplus (despite constant cries of a shortage) that would keep wages low. Serafin E. Macaraig, a professor of sociology at the University of the Philippines, made a study of the situation in 1926. He estimated the number of unemployed Filipinos in Honolulu to be about 300; this would represent approximately 14 to 20 percent (or even higher), depending upon the number of women and children out of the work force. His estimate included those who signed contracts for plantation work but went to the city instead; those found unfit for agricultural work ("lazy, shiftless, and unmanageable"); blacklisted workers from the 1920 and 1924 strikes; former U.S. government and Navy employees discharged because of a ruling against aliens in government employ; casual workers in canneries, docks, and personal homes; and a class of unemployed tricksters and parasites who preyed upon their countrymen (in Lasker 1931:186; cf. Quezon Papers; Butler to Babbitt, 10 Aug. 1926, who reports a figure of 1,000 or more unemployed in Honolulu for Macaraig).

Pablo Manlapit of the Hawaii Labor Federation, and Epifanio Toak, the president of the Filipino Labor Union, attempted to grapple with the problem of unemployment. In November of 1933, Toak addressed a long memorandum to the Territorial Legislature proposing some form of relief for the "several thousands Filipinos unemployed" by then. Barred from securing certain positions, they received only 2 percent of the relief distributed by the newly created Unemployment Bureau. Toak requested monies for the repatriation of Filipinos and asked that the HSPA send the unemployed back home (*Philippine News Tribune*, 6 Nov. 1933). In March of 1934, Manlapit sent a petition to President Roosevelt and a copy to Manuel Quezon, President of the Philippines. It pointed to the HSPA's recruitment policies and its creation of a labor surplus, as the basic cause of unemployment. This situation was abetted by the discrimination Filipinos faced in obtaining government positions. Manlapit requested massive voluntary repatriation of some 20,000 Filipinos, to be financed by the HSPA, and cited the cost-effective advantages that would accrue to the United States. The petition also exposed the purpose of the Honolulu Police Department in "rounding up the unemployed Filipinos" as a collaborating effort with the HSPA to "hide the existence of unemployment from the attention of the public in order to support the contention of the HSPA that there is no unemployment in Hawaii" (Quezon Papers: Manlapit to the U.S. President, 28 March 1934).

In summary, from 1906 to 1946, the vast majority of Filipinos in Hawaii remained dependent for their livelihood on either plantation jobs or other positions of unskilled labor. The slow rate of urban migration and upward occupational mobility accounts for the quickened pace of class formation among Filipino workers and, conversely, for the slow rate of internal differentiation. Both combined to equate the class position of Filipinos in Hawaiian society almost totally with that of the agri-industrial proletariat.

PROCESS OF CLASS FORMATION AND DIFFERENTIATION

The organization of work and the labor relationships of an agri-industrial proletariat are qualitatively different from those of a barrio peasant. In the Philippines, the latter was known as a *tao*, who was usually a tenant farmer who raised whatever crops he needed for home consumption and would sell only when he had a surplus or needed money. The tao's lot was in some respects a nonregimented life in which a fair amount of contentment and satisfaction was gained from seeing the results of one's labor in fruition. Family teamwork was important; women worked with men in the fields, and children were an economic asset. The tao, however, did not own the land, and his relationship with the landlord was usually sealed by indebtedness. A generalized model of patron-client ties held true for most of the Philippines.[6] The relationship was characterized by its basis in inequality and its flexibility as a system of exchange. In return for his client's labor, talents, and support, the landlord maintained a highly individualistic and personal interest in the well-being of his client-dependent. He ideally (often not realized in practice) was a protector and, like a father, advanced credit and assured the tao and his family of a minimum subsistence, regardless of work performed or harvest obtained.

The plantation system in Hawaii converted peasants into wage earning proletarians and in the process deprived many workers of the little security they had found in traditional relationships. "They labored from factory whistle to factory whistle, their hours mechanically regulated by the clock, their days by the calendar" (Cariaga 1936:54). Jobs were uniform and demanded less initiative than sheer stamina. A given line of work was followed to the exact specifications of the manager under the minute direction of the overseer (luna). There was no guaranteed subsistence without work, and layoffs, illness, incurring the displeasure of the management, being involved in labor organization, striking, or any number of reasons could cause loss of livelihood. Achievements were measured in terms of money alone, and personal satisfactions were gained from material possessions or accumulated savings. Women made an economic contribution by selling Filipino wares and taking in laundry or boarders; children became a liability. In the new system, haoles knew Filipinos not as individuals but only as laborers, and haole paternalism was, in effect, a supplementary wage whereby perquisites were paid for by labor. No individual intimacy existed between the workers and management, as they were separated and isolated by the use of overseers (Cariaga 1936:36-37, 55 ff.; Fuchs 1961:49; Lind 1938:237; Norbeck 1959:144; Wentworth 1941:66).[7]

Filipinos struggled to achieve a better life and better working conditions by means of militant organization of labor. The history of the Filipino role in labor in Hawaii is a crucial and neglected aspect of their history and one that is integral to their class formation. The outline presented here concentrates on their involvement in three main strikes.

Filipino Labor Organization and Workers' Struggles

Although the policies of control used in the plantation system included violence, intimidation, union-smashing, and divide-and-rule (which provided a ready supply of strikebreakers), work stoppages and full-blown strikes were not averted. Following the 1909 Japanese strike, and until 1925, there were at least nine labor strikes involving Filipinos, including the big ones of 1920 and 1924 (Reinecke n.d.). The prime mover behind the Filipino labor struggles was Pablo Manlapit, the controversial leader of the Filipino "fight for justice." A sympathetic commentator writes: "An eloquent agitator, but an incapable administrator, irresolute and untrustworthy in a crisis, and not overburdened with consistent principles, Manlapit for all his faults had charisma, and elderly Filipinos still speak of him with respect" (Reinecke n.d.:101). Events of the time prove this to be a fair assessment.

Born in Lipa City, Batangas, on January 17, 1891, Manlapit had an intermediate school education. He states that he came to Hawaii in 1910 through the HSPA. He was soon dismissed from plantation work and went to Hilo (Manlapit 1959). Subsequently, he started two papers, ran a pool hall, and worked as a salesman and stevedore in Honolulu. In the 1916 waterfront strike, some Filipinos beat him up as a strikebreaker. He then worked as an interpreter and also as a janitor in a lawyer's office, while studying law. He qualified as a District Court Practitioner, mostly acting as a troubleshooter for his countrymen.

In August, 1919, Manlapit organized the Filipino Labor Union (or Filipino Federation of Labor) after at least four months of agitation. The union's sphere of influence was limited to Oahu. Unlike the Federation of Japanese Labor, a grass-roots organization with strong community, professional, business, and monetary support, the Filipino union developed from the top down and lacked any middle-class support. After founding the union, Manlapit conducted a vigorous drive to organize Filipinos in the cane fields. He also hoped to discourage further immigration and to inform those back home of the true conditions in the islands (Polk-Husted Directory Co. 1913-1920; Probasco 1965-1966:9; Reinecke n.d.:101).

By 1920 the basic labor issue was that of wages. Postwar inflation had set prices 40 to 50 percent higher but prewar wages of 77¢ a day still prevailed. Changes in wages, the bonus system, and working conditions were demanded. On January 19, 1920, after HSPA rejection of their demands, Manlapit called his union out on strike on five plantations. Some 2,600 workers (and 300 more of other nationalities) struck at Aiea, Waipahu, Ewa, Waialua, and Kahuku. Manlapit had previously asked for support from the Japanese union, which had been making similar protests to the HSPA. On February 2, the entire Japanese work force of these five plantations, in addition to Waimanalo, joined the striking Filipinos.

There were internal quarrels, however, among the leaders in the Filipino Labor Union. Further, Manlapit's meeting with Acting-Governor Iaunka, together with his turning against the Japanese, led him to call off the strike on February 7, only to call for it back again a week later. Accusations of indecision and bribery were made against Manlapit. It was too late to continue the strike, however, for most Filipinos had already returned to work. The Japanese held out until April. At the height of the strike, 12,010 workers were evicted from plantation houses (1,472 Filipinos and the rest Japanese). Some 5,000 went to Honolulu where an influenza epidemic raged and more than 20 percent became ill. Fifty-six died (Fuchs 1961:215 ff.; Gov Files; McCarthy, Misc. File, Strike Data, 1920; Wakukawa 1938:238, 250-251; Probasco 1965-1966; Reinecke n.d.).

The strike had four main results. First, the HSPA, with strong government support, attempted to import Chinese labor through the establishment of a Hawaii Emergency Labor Commission delegated to Washington, which actually claimed that a labor shortage existed. Second, immigration from the Philippines was drastically stepped up, and new Filipino arrivals, along with other nationalities, were used as strikebreakers. The HSPA viewed the strike solely as a Japanese attempt to seize control of the industry, and the *Advertiser* and *Star Bulletin*, too, ignored the Filipino role (Liebes 1938:38; Probasco 1965-1966:24; Reinecke n.d.:107, 116 ff.; Wakukawa 1938:26). Then, though no wage concessions were made, extensive improvements in housing, sanitation, and water systems on the plantations were initiated. Sums in excess of one million dollars were spent on such improvements between 1921 and 1924. Lastly, the Japanese, perhaps realizing the futility of racial strikes at a time when intimidation and feelings against them were rising, withdrew from militant labor struggles for the next twenty years (*Honolulu Record*, 6 Sept. 1953; Johannessen 1956:70). Laborers continued to be housed in racially segregated camps, and there is ample evidence that the "planters and their agencies deliberately segregated racial groups to prevent 'labor collusion'" (Robert McElrath of the ILWU, quoted in *Star Bulletin*, 26 Feb. 1975, pt. 3:1).

After the 1920 defeat, Manlapit started to build up a new labor organization with the help of George Wright (later the English editor of the *Hawaii Hochi*). When the Higher Wages Movement petitioned the HSPA for $2 a day, forty hours a week, and abolition of the bonus in early 1923, they were ignored. Workers, who simultaneously had been requesting the Philippine government to send a Labor Commissioner who would mediate between them and the planters, were sent Cayetano Ligot as an ally. He had served a term as an elected governor of Ilocos Norte, been a schoolteacher and an organizer of cooperatives. However, he "actively worked hand in glove with the HSPA and was exposed for accepting money from employers," although he said that the money was only a "loan" (*Honolulu Record*, 6 Aug. 1953:7; *Star Bulletin*, 13 Oct. 1923). Ligot managed to hold up the strike for a year. He also widened the division within the Filipino community between Ilocanos and Tagalogs, as he and Manlapit belonged to different groups. To this day Ligot is ill-remembered by elderly Filipinos.

When the next strike started on Oahu in 1924, it also spread to Kohala (Hawaii) and even Kauai. Once again, the laborers were defeated by their leaders' lack of organization, the HSPA's employment of new (Ilocano) immigrants, and elaborate spy networks in the plantation camps. The most shocking incident of the strike occurred at Hanapepe, Kauai, on September 9, 1924. The sheriff and police attempted to gain the release of two Filipino strikebreakers who were being held by strikers. A struggle arose while the two were being led away from the camp; in the end, sixteen strikers and four policemen were murdered and many more were wounded.

Manlapit and another prominent strike leader, Cecil Basan, were convicted of subornation of perjury and sentenced to two years in prison. Manlapit was later exiled from the islands (but returned again in 1932). Resident Commissioner Ligot had meanwhile issued a manifesto condemning the strikers and urging the men to return to work after the Kauai tragedy. With the leaders jailed and the organization shattered, the strike continued ineffectively for another three months (Bottomley 1924; Fuchs 1961:233 ff.; Gov. Files: Farrington, Misc., 1924 Strike; Johanessen 1956:70-71; Liebes 1938:41 ff.; Quezon Papers, correspondence 1924-1925).

> The end of the 1924 strike was followed by several years of quiet on the plantation. The labor policy was one of thoroughgoing paternalism; clubhouses, athletic facilities, radio programs and other forms of company entertainment were employed in keeping the laborers contented. The growing pineapple industry also needed cheap labor, and the Hawaiian Pineapple Packers' Association was contributing to the cost of Filipino importation. At the annual meetings of the H.S.P.A. in 1926, 1927 and 1928, the fact was stressed that the labor situation was most satisfactory. (Liebes 1938:45)

Labor activity gradually declined until 1933, when a new Filipino Labor Union was formed by Manlapit, Antonio Fagel, and Epifanio Toak. The HSPA managed to put Toak in jail and to banish Manlapit permanently to the Philippine Islands in 1935. Fagel took the union underground and renamed it *Vibora Luviminda* (the first part is the name of a Filipino patriot, while the second refers to the main division in the Philippines into Luzon, the Visayas, and Mindanao). After campaigning to get laborers to join, Fagel brought it out into the open in June of 1936 and started a strike at Puunene plantation, Maui. Strikebreakers were again hired, and the Philippine Commissioner in Washington urged the workers to return to their jobs, as did President Quezon. The HSPA ultimately negotiated for the first time with the union, eighty-five days after the strike had begun, and workers won a 15 percent pay increase.[8]

Fagel could not complete the negotiations, for in May he was charged with conspiracy to kidnap a fellow Filipino during the strike. His trial dragged on past the strike, and he, along with seven other Filipino labor leaders, was found guilty and incarcerated. The Vibora Luviminda, the last of the racial unions, then fell into eclipse, making the Puunene strike the last racial strike in Hawaii. Perhaps the most significant outcome, besides the fact that the HSPA finally acknowledged the existence of a union and agreed to negotiate with it, was the haole labor support that Fagel received. He had filed a complaint with the National Labor Relations Board representative, E. J. Eagen, who conducted an official investigation. Eagen was brought to Hawaii through the efforts of Ed Berman (editor of the *Voice of Labor*) and gave the strikers support. Jack Hall, who was organizing Hawaii's waterfront workers, and William Bailey, the assistant editor of the *Voice of Labor*, also helped Fagel to organize (Felipe 1970; see also Johannessen 1956:71-73; Quezon Papers: J. K. Butler to Quezon, 27 Nov. 1933, 2 Dec. 1933, M. de Lonais to Gov. Gen. Murphy, 10 Oct. 1934, Fagel "Appeal to the Public," 1935).

The attempt to characterize Filipino labor organization from 1919 to 1937 simply as "blood unionism" is not useful. Felipe is quite correct in noting of the 1937 strike that, "True, it was exclusively Filipino. But it was not only because of blood or genetic identity or racial cliqueness. Racial unity was an inevitable manifestation of management's divide-and-rule policies" (1970:29).

During World War II and martial law in Hawaii, union organizing was practically outlawed. In early 1944, the International Longshoremen's & Warehousemen's Union began an organizing drive of plantation workers who were frozen to their jobs for as little as $1.50 per day while defense workers earned that much in an hour! The first territory-wide strike involving all nationalities occurred in September 1946, when 28,000 sugar workers walked off their jobs. The 6,000 Filipinos who had been imported by the HSPA on the eve of the strike had been signed up as union members aboard ship. In the strike that took place several days later, they stood fast (*Honolulu Record*, 6 Aug. 1953; Johannessen 1956:100-101). The strike ended with the abolition of perquisites and a new minimum pay of 70.5¢ an hour.

The year 1946 marked a measure of success in the Filipinos' long struggle against conditions of plantation life, and all plantation workers finally united into "one big union." An assessment of the early period makes it clear, however, that at no time, especially during the strikes, did the majority of Filipinos favor active militant organization in the face of threats and intimidation by the HSPA and the government. Support for the unions was neither widespread nor sustained, and most workers seemed to try to make do with a precarious and difficult situation. Hilario C. Moncado and his Filipino Federation of America also must have had some effect on the thinking of Filipinos about labor organization and striking, although it is not clear how many beyond his followers he was able to influence. Moncado became antiunion as labor agitation and emigration during the Depression threatened a serious loss of labor supply to the sugar industry. He warned Filipinos against returning to their homeland, saying that nothing awaited them there, and his followers were used as scabs in the 1937 strike (Thompson 1941:31-32).[9]

Yet it is also quite clear that the vast majority of plantation workers did suffer and therefore stood behind the demands of the unions for a better life and wage. The eagerness with which all joined the ILWU and were involved in the 1946 strike, once legal barriers and threats against strikers were removed, goes far to substantiate this assessment.

Relations with Other Workers

Before the successful establishment of the "one big union" that united all workers regardless of race, Hawaii's labor history was crosscut by the detrimental effects of capital's divide-and-rule tactics, which kept workers separated along racial and ethnic lines. As discussed above, these tactics were implemented on the plantations by the policies of job discrimination, differential pay scales, and residential segregation. When this was combined with the inherent difficulties of communicating across cultural and linguistic barriers, it comes as no surprise that almost half a century of work and struggle was needed to unite all workers. The most conspicious way in which management used these carefully cultivated differences was consistently to employ workers of other ethnic groups as strikebreakers.

In 1909 the HSPA refused to negotiate with the Japanese or to consider their demands. Hawaiians and Portuguese were recruited as strike-breakers in Honolulu and paid almost double what the workers were demanding (Lind 1938:234; *Honolulu Record* 1953:4). In 1916, a strike by the International Longshoremen's Association, a small local of mostly Hawaiians, Filipinos, and some Japanese, was broken by the use of Japanese strikebreakers (Fuchs 1961:243). Although the 1920 strike was the first major interracial plantation struggle, the planters focused on anti-Japanese propaganda to divide them from the Filipinos, depicted as "ignorant cat's paws of the Japanese" (Reinecke n.d.:97). In this strike, as well, the HSPA hired 2,200 strikebreakers of other nationalities at $3.00 a day when the strikers had been earning 77¢ (Reinecke n.d.:107). The big strikes of 1924 and 1937 followed the same pattern.

Despite the shared class position and the common suffering from racism experienced by plantation workers of all ethnic groups, plantation management successfully used such divisive tactics until 1946. The racial lines that divided workers from one another also spilled over into their personal relations. There appears to have been little friendship or intimacy across ethnic lines between the Filipinos and their Japanese coworkers, for example. Although living in separate racial camps for the most part, there was some contact between the two groups in the fields, in the schools, and in the stores. Some Filipinos married Hawaiians, Portuguese/Spanish, and Puerto Rican women between 1912 and 1931, but few married those of East Asian ancestry (Adams, 1937:179, table xxxii; Lind 1967:109-110). Stereotypes of the "bayaos" and "poke-knives" as flashy and hot-tempered (e.g., Cariaga 1936:34; Eubank 1943:96; Mitamura 1940:151) coexisted with the general planters' provincial stereotype of the Ilocanos as "hardworking and thrifty" (cf. *Star Bulletin*: 3 April 1924).

Some Japanese independent growers also appear to have preferred Filipinos over their own countrymen as cheap labor in their fields. A pineapple grower stated:

> For two years I have been hiring Filipinos. The reason being that there is no need of providing them with decent living houses. They built usually a small shack and they live in it. We don't have to give them very good food because they are used to living on cheap food. The best of all I can tell them when to look for another job. It is not hard to tell them this: "Hey, you bayao, no hanahana. You go alright. Bye and bye when me got hanahana, I call you." (Since I have no work for you now, it is better for you to go and look for another job. When I have work to

do, I shall go and ask you to come). I do not have to pay them while they are not working. However, I cannot do this to a Japanese man. He would not stand for it in the first place. (Masuoka 1931:158).

Impediments to Class Differentiation Within the Filipino Community

It may not be an incorrect assessment to say that Filipinos in Hawaii were more differentiated along lines of provincial origins (Tagalogs, Visayans, and Ilocanos) than they were along lines of class. This factor did not go unnoticed by the planters. They stepped up Ilocano labor migration in 1920, for example, for use on plantations where Visayans (i.e., Cebuanos) had been striking.

By 1930, 90 percent of all employed Filipinos were still unskilled workers, and four-fifths of these remained on the plantations (Fuchs 1961:146; Lind 1967:77). The number of Filipino-owned businesses remained miniscule, and most were precarious small-scale enterprises. In Honolulu during 1931, there were four Filipino printing shops, two groceries, and three barber shops; and in 1934, the "biggest event in the history of Philippine business in Hawaii" occurred, when the Insular Life Assurance Company of Manila established a branch there (*Wagay-way* 1941, I:7). A 1939 roster of Filipino businesses lists thirty-nine, three of which had gone out of business since compilation of the list. Tailor and barber establishments were the most numerous (Interchurch Federation of Honolulu 1936:7). Cariaga noted the consistent failure of Filipino-owned businesses, which apparently could not be supported by their own community (1936:74). The Depression put Filipinos in dire straits and must have hit these small shops hard. Another considerable factor hampering the rise of a business class (even petit bourgeois) was the fact that Filipinos were sending most of their savings back home to support families and investments there. Capital accumulation in Hawaii progressed slowly among this immigrant group. By 1928 they owned just .03 percent of the total amount of gross assessed real and personal property (Moe 1929:46).

Widespread illiteracy was certainly another hurdle to class differentiation, as was the bar on noncitizens from becoming professionals. There were no Filipino physicians, surgeons, or dentists in 1930; there were two lawyers and three teachers. Professionals accounted for .6 percent of the total Filipino population in 1940 and had increased only imperceptibly by 1950 and 1960 (1.2 and 1.8 percent respectively; Lind 1967:80, see tables 10, 11, 12, 19). Filipinos were least employed in managerial or clerical work and have consistently had the lowest income level of all ethnic groups in Hawaii. While, for example, 21.1 percent of all Japanese male workers earned $2,000 to $2,999 in 1949, 40.2 percent of all Filipinos earned this little. Similarly, 21.1 percent of all Japanese workers were in the $3,000 to $3,999 category, whereas only 7.6 percent of all Filipinos were (Lind 1967:82, 100).

At the same time, there does appear to have been some nascent differentiation of class interests among Filipinos, which found expression in their more than twenty-eight journals and papers published in Hawaii between 1914 and 1946. The pages of these magazines are filled with ads reflecting the petit bourgeois nature of the business community among Filipinos. *Wagayway (Philippines Commonwealth Outlook), The Filipino Outlook,* and *Philippine Press of Hilo,* for example, solidly supported the planters against the interests of the workers. Not only do they contain articles such as "Oh, for the Life of a Plantation Laborer" (*Philippines Commonwealth Outlook* 1947, I: March 3), but their editorial policy gave the following injunctions: give gratitude to plantation managers for their generous perquisites; remain docile and loyal to the plantations and do not leave them in search of better positions or federal jobs in Honolulu; resist engaging in labor strikes or altercations; understand the system of plantation passes; and praise the sugar bonus system and the outlawing of cockfights.[10]

Filipino journals aside, the slower mobility rate of this ethnic group is reflected in the fact that twenty-five years after most had arrived, more than half were still classified as laborers. In 1960 the proportion of Filipino men so designated remained nearly three times greater than that for all other males in Hawaii. This should not be taken as a reflection of the ability or ambition of Filipino immigrants, but rather as an indication of the handicaps the latest arrivals encountered. Perhaps no handicap was greater for Filipinos than the fact that they alone, among all workers in Hawaii, were colonial subjects of the United States. This had a profound effect on their status and class formation.

RACE AND CLASS: COLONIAL OPPRESSION AND CLASS FORMATION

The discussion of the plantation microcosm and the living and working conditions it imposed upon Filipino workers must be seen within the wider context of colonial oppression and the specific pattern of discrimination against Filipinos. The impact of U.S. oppression served to further the control that plantation managers were able to exert over Filipino workers. This was a direct result of their being a noncitizen labor force and, as colonial subjects, having no protection at all from their home country. Lack of redress for their grievances, in turn, affected the nature of their class formation and their involvement in militant labor struggles.

Filipinos in Hawaii were put in direct contact with the colonial overlords, most often represented by plantation managers. The planters' control over workers in this situation was not mitigated by the moral and personalistic tie evident in local political activity in the homeland. Instead, the Filipinos had to struggle against political apathy and neglect and a system that had established a sad record of successive failures and consistent betrayals at the hands of governmental investigators and commissioners. Whereas other nationalities had representatives of their governments to whom they could theoretically go in cases of ill-treatment (although their rights were not always protected), the Filipinos did not even have a consul or an ambassador in Washington. The Philippine resident commissioner there was too overburdened to look after the needs of so many of his countrymen scattered over such a large area. Especially in Hawaii, Filipinos remained "forgotten men" (Manzon 1938: 17; see also *Wagayway* 1941, 1:August, p. 2; 1946, VI: April, p. 2).

Labor Investigations in Hawaii

Between the arrival of the first HSPA-sponsored laborers in 1906 and the last, coming in 1946, some nine labor investigations were conducted, one resident commissioner was appointed, and numerous other officials representing the Philippine government visited the territory. None of this resulted in any concrete measures to alleviate the problems and conditions of the laborers, and it is doubtful whether the colonial officials who sent them seriously had this in mind. The first investigator, Joaquin Balmori (a delegate from Pangasinan and chairman of the Commission of Labor and Immigration), was asked by Governor Pinkham to conduct an inquiry into charges made against the HSPA by a former employee. Clearly, the motive for the inquiry was not out of any concern for the Filipinos. Balmori spent thirty-nine days visiting twenty-eight sugar plantations. He concluded that work and living conditions were adequate and that the laborers were satisfied (Balmori 1912; Gov. Files: Pinkham, U.S. Depts., Int. Dept., Oct-Dec. 1915; Pinkham to Lane, 21 Nov. 1915). Seven years later, in 1919, Prudencio A. Remigio came and reported that conditions were lamentable. Nothing was done about this (report Del Comisionado). The next official investigator came to the islands twice for lengthy periods of time and also concurred with Remigio's view. Francisco Varona visited almost all the plantations during 1920. He found that "on the whole the laborers were dissatisfied and discontented and that an unwholesome attitude between managers and laborers was apparent on most of the plantations," which was mainly a racial problem (cited in Dorita 1954:55).[11] No attention was paid to this finding either. He succeeded, however, in effecting the "Honolulu Agreement," which was a new contract offered to those who were previously not eligible for free passage home. Varona was sent to the territory again in 1935 by Quezon and gained a one-year extension of the agreement. After an abortive attempt to bring about unity among Filipino labor leaders, Varona called for a Filipino Labor Conference in mid-1938. Its major achievement was drawing up a set of resolutions recognizing H. C. Moncado, a militant anti-unionist, as a representative of Filipino labor (Dorita 1954:103-104).

Demands for a resident labor commissioner increased in the early 1920s, concern over which led the Filipino labor leader, Pablo Manlapit, to hold meetings at Aala Park in Honolulu. Resolutions were adopted regarding representation in the territory. When news of the growing labor unrest reached Governor-General Wood in the Philippines, he dispatched Cayetano Ligot in 1923 to report on conditions and to remain on in Hawaii as resident labor commissioner. Most of Ligot's report was concerned with his own expenses and a request to increase his $250 a month salary (while he discouraged workers from fighting to get more than $20). He blamed the workers for their own troubles; they were either "bad eggs" or were fooled by parasitic so-called leaders. He also denigrated the activities of labor leaders, especially Manlapit, documenting the growing antagonism between the two men. Ligot undertook another investigation in the company of Hermenegildo Cruz, the director of the Bureau of Labor in Manila. Cruz's minimal estimate of the cost of living ($15 a month for a single man, $9 for his wife, and $2.25 for each child) clearly revealed that many plantation workers with families were below the minimum subsistence line. He also admitted that Ligot did not inspect plantations often enough nor deal adequately with the complaints of the workers (Cruz 1926:8, 16, 19). Cruz's report further acknowledged that not all workers were satisfied, though he still maintained that "a spirit of mutual harmony and tolerance generally existed" (Cruz 1926:16; Quezon Papers: Ligot to Cruz, 22 May 1923; see also Duckworth-Ford 1926). Many of those who repatriated in 1932 and 1933 complained bitterly that both Cruz and Ligot were HSPA "stooges."[12] Cruz was even threatened with a suit for giving the HSPA a monopoly to recruit workers from the Philippines (Dorita 1954:97).

Charges against Ligot intensified, especially after his role in the 1924 strike, as did his quarrel with Manlapit. A petition was sent by Jose Bulatao, secretary of the Filipino Economic Movement on Kauai, asking for the abolition of the resident labor commissioner's office as it was of "no practical value or usefulness to Filipino laborers" (Quezon Papers, Bulatao to Quezon, 1 Oct. 1931). Consequently, Ligot was recalled in 1933, his office abolished, and Jose Figueras sent to investigate the accusations and report on labor conditions. His arrival and activities were praised by all. Although Figueras commended the planters and advised against striking, he actually did undertake to settle issues and complaints fairly. However, when he accused Ligot's newspaper—*Ti Salaw*—of being subsidized by the HSPA, collected testimony against Cruz, and prepared a list of some twenty specific demands for better treatment of laborers, the HSPA (through Governor Judd) asked for his removal. Figueras was recalled in 1934 (*Filipino Outlook* 1934, I, 4; *Philippine Press*, 1934, I; Quezon Papers, Filipino Labor Union to Quezon, 20 Dec. 1933; Dorita 1954:97, 98; Fuchs 1961: 236; *Wagayway* 1946, VI: April, p. 2).

Letters and petitions requesting representation in Hawaii were sent to the Philippine government following the departure of Figueras. Francisco Varona and Hilario Moncado, president of the Filipino Federation of America, were recommended for the post of commissioner. These requests went unheeded. Perhaps the worst affront to the rights of Filipinos came in 1939 when Don Joaquin M. Elizalde, the resident commissioner in Washington, passed through Honolulu on his way to the Philippines. He is reported to have "traveled incognito" and "deliberately insulted the Filipinos. . . . Upon his return, there were organized groups to meet him and banners denouncing him and condemning him" (Quezon Papers: C. R. Gorospe to Vice-President Osmeña, 19 Dec. 1939). When Dr. Carmilo Osias came with his wife to make still another investigation, he traveled widely and gave many speeches promising that something would be done within six months. By 1946, still nothing had been done. *Wagayway* commented in an editorial, "An elastic six months, eh?" (1946, VI:April, p. 2).

There was little workers could do at the time to cope effectively with this situation, rooted as it was in their status as colonial subjects. They were colonials of the United States without a spokesman for their interests either in the Philippines or in Washington. They could not effectively participate in the political activity of their homeland; nor was political participation open to them in Hawaii, as they were not citizens. All their attempts to limit the further importation of their countrymen—

who were used against them both as strikebreakers and as a surplus labor force causing depressed wages and unemployment—were futile (Dorita 1967:22 ff.; Quezon Papers: Cariaga to Quezon, 12 April 1934; Manlapit to Quezon, 4 May 1934; Benitez to Kahuku Quezon Club, 8 June 1949).

Colonial Status of Filipino Workers

Workers' demands for protection were stymied further by the fact that the Filipinos were in the anomalous position of being considered U.S. nationals until 1934—neither aliens nor citizens. Only those few who had served in the navy were eligible for citizenship through naturalization. In the territorial election of 1934, there were 102 registered Filipino voters, 88 of whom voted. Some were native-born citizens, but most were naturalized (Cariaga 1936:179). Filipinos could contribute to the public economy but could not take part in public decision making because, as one scholar of Filipino immigration remarked, citizenship was "denied Orientals" and political power remained "in the hands of the Caucasian and Hawaiian minority." Lasker further noted that a large group of temporary laborers without rights was an "ideal" arrangement, as it "avoids those large, social, economic, and political complications resulting from a large increase in permanent population" (1931:289).

With the passage of the Philippines Independence Act of 1934, the status of all Filipinos was changed from national to alien. Immigration was limited to fifty persons a year to the continental United States, with a special clause for Hawaii. U.S. citizens and corporations in the Philippines, however, were declared to have the same rights as citizens of that country. The American corporations were given tax exemptions and tariff reductions.

The denial of citizenship became particularly incongruous during the war years and shortly thereafter. First, plantation laborers were frozen into their jobs by a "gentleman's agreement" between the military, contractors, and plantation officials. The plantations kept their labor in the face of more attractive federal jobs, while they loaned labor, when necessary, to fulfill defense work. The workers, however, soon learned that this "loan" was made at their expense and much to the profit of the planters. The latter received almost double what they paid their workers from the government (Clark 1947:156-158). Had the plantation workers been citizens, they would have been free to assume much higher paying positions.

Second, the war also demanded declarations and specific examples of patriotism by alien ethnic groups in Hawaii. Filipinos were solidly pro-American, and their publications are replete with exhortations to demonstrate loyalty to Uncle Sam. They invested heavily in war bonds and made other contributions. Back home, thousands of their brothers were dying by the sides of their colonial overlords to save those islands for America so that they could be returned once again to its people. Filipinos felt strongly about a situation where "Philipinos are good enough to die under the American flag on Bataan and Corregidor and good enough to pay taxes in Hawaii—but not good enough to vote, hold public office, practice law or medicine" (*Wagayway*, 1945, V:November, p. 4, and 1943 issues).[13]

Perhaps the earliest public agitation for naturalization came from an editorial appearing in *Wagayway* in March of 1943 that pleaded for the option of citizenship for those who desired it (III:5). The following month, Ricardo Labez of the *Hilo Tribune* staff, and the first Filipino secretary of the Hilo Lions, engineered a meeting of a group of Honolulu's civic leaders which led to the organization of the Filipino Equal Rights Committee. They drafted a resolution to the U.S. Congress requesting naturalization; in 1946, such a measure was passed. It was more than a decade after the war was ended, however, that Filipinos began to have any representation at all in Hawaii's electoral politics.

CONCLUSION

The migration of Filipino laborers to Hawaii that began in 1906 transformed barrio-based peasants into an agri-industrial proletariat living and working on numerous sugar plantations through World War II. Most of the 125,000 or more immigrants were single, illiterate men from the Ilocos region. In their home country, economic and political relationships were expressed through a moral and personalistic patron-client tie. Ideally, the bond was mutual and reciprocal; social life placed great emphasis on family, kin, and community as well as on mutual aid characterized by reciprocity. By contrast, the need for cheap labor to work in Hawaii's sugar fields set the general characteristics of the Filipino population there, while the racist attitudes of the dominant haole elite and the policies of the planters who brought them to the islands provided the working environment. Labor contracts signed in the homeland specified rates, perquisites, and length of service, while the plantation regime exercised control over and demanded conformity from the laborers in a regimented and impersonal system. Filipinos had no rights within this system, as they were colonial subjects without the benefits of representation either in the Philippines or in Hawaii. Finally, the planters had created an artificial environment in which the highly unequal sex ratio worked against the reconstruction of much that was meaningful in the face-to-face interaction of the barrio.

An increasingly circumscribed economic situation in Hawaii held decreasing opportunities for movement off the plantation, as is reflected in the slow rates of both Filipino urban migration and occupational differentiation. Their position as an agri-industrial proletariat was thus reinforced, and the vast majority of Filipinos remained as unskilled workers dependent upon the plantations throughout the period. Workers' struggles and participation in strikes quickened the process of class formation. Labor agitation, organization, and three main strikes represent the response to stringent and controlled economic conditions. A persevering leadership also arose from among the Filipinos which, while not always consistent or farsighted in its policies, took up a struggle against tremendously weighted odds.

Filipino class formation was also fostered by the slow rate of internal differentiation. Only a small nucleus of a business and semiprofessional class had developed that wished to establish a successful community life in Hawaii. There was no capital accumulation to speak of, as all Filipino savings were remitted back home. During this period of their stay in Hawaii, Filipinos remained immigrants who, for the most part, saw themselves as temporary sojourners. Even many of those with Hawaiian-born children still thought of returning to their homeland. Yet by 1940, only about half who had come, had left the territory. Of these, two-thirds went back to the Philippines and the remainder moved on to California. The goal of those who stayed in Hawaii seemed to have been the same as when they first came—to make enough money to return home. Those who could not do this kept up a constant flow of remittances to the Philippines.

Filipinos' status as colonial subjects provided an added critical dimension to their persistently low level of internal differentiation. The workers' unsolved problems and unheeded requests to government officials represented the status quo supported by the convergence of interests between the U.S. rulers in the Philippines and the planters in Hawaii. Lack of satisfaction from these quarters forced the workers to fall back increasingly on their own resources and to participate in (or support) the struggle to organize labor on their own and to engage in militant strikes.

Scattered as they were over large distances in relatively isolated areas, and characterized by a mobile population, the Filipinos did not develop any strong cohesive community-wide organizations. For the most part, their associations were parochial, temporary, and localized and unable to act either within the community as a whole or effectively with the outside. Nonetheless, the bonds of ethnic unity and class solidarity were forged among the Filipinos in Hawaii between 1906 and 1946, owing in part to the planters' concern with preventing interracial solidarity and their associated policies of divide and rule, racial segregation, and other discriminatory practices.

NOTES

1. Much of the research for this article was accomplished under a National Endowment for the Humanities fellowship. It also draws heavily on parts of an earlier publication (Sharma 1980).

2. During the early experimental period of Visayan immigration, wives were briefly required to accompany their husbands.

3. Life histories I have collected contain similar statements. The rigorous schedule presented by Cariaga (1936:53) would seem to contradict his later statement (p. 53) that laborers were only eight or nine hours in the fields and came home with "enthusiasm for games and athletics."

4. The Philippine peso was tied to the U.S. dollar at the rate of 2:1 until independence in 1946.

5. Lind notes also that, even by 1957, more than one-half of the total Filipino population of Hawaii was still housed within a radius of less than one-half mile from that intersection.

6. While the generic model of Eric Wolf (1966) and Scott (1972) perhaps most accurately reflects conditions in Central Luzon, it has relevance for the Ilocos and other regions. Lewis (1971:49, 123) points out that the traditional relationship between the landlord and tenant continued in the Ilocos area, which was not noticeably affected by the increasing commercialization of agriculture that characterized Central Luzon by the 1930s. Lasker noted, as early as 1931, that the *obrero* system of daily wage contract labor had eliminated this relationship on the big haciendas in the Philippines (1931:242).

7. Lind points out that the earlier intimacy that existed between managers and laborers on Hawaiian plantations had disappeared by the first decade of this century. Lines of economic and social stratification

were more rigidly drawn with the formation of corporate agriculture, dispersed ownership through stockholders, and the increasing use of managers to concentrate on making a profit (1938:237 ff.).

8. Felipe states that this claim of a 15 percent increase was discounted "according to an explanatory note on the agreement issued by the NLRB representative, Arnold L. Willis, on 27 November, 1940" (1970:17).

9. I have no accurate figures on the number who followed Moncado, but at its height the Federation could not have had more than several thousand members in Hawaii.

10. Filipino publications often seem to have walked a tightrope between not disturbing the status quo of plantation life or invoking the displeasure of the planters, and attempting to wrest certain benefits for their community from the government in the Philippines.

11. It is not exactly clear what is meant when she states in a later work that "there was little, if any, racial antagonism in Hawaii against the Filipino" (Dorita 1967:22).

12. Dr. Macaraig, of the University of the Philippines, also told the secretary of the HSPA (J. K. Butler) that Ligot neglected the workers and would not attend their meetings. From what Ligot told Butler, it seems that Macaraig also intimated that Mr. Cruz "was purchased and bribed" by the HSPA and that this was the case with other Philippine investigators (Quezon Papers: Butler to Babbitt, 10 Aug. 1926).

13. Even the going-home benefit societies came under pressure during the war years. Prominent officials of Hawaii lauded the demise of the Inanama Mutual Society in 1942, stating, "We want to do away with racial organizations at this time" (*Wagayway 1942*, II: December, p. 3).

References

Adams, Romanzo
    1937   Interracial Marriage in Hawaii. New York: Macmillan.
Alcantara, Rueben R.
    1973   "The Filipino community in Waialua." Ph.D. dissertation, University of Hawaii.
Alexander, Arthur C.
    1937   Koloa Plantation, 1835-1935: A History of the Oldest Hawaiian Sugar Plantation. Honolulu: Star-Bulletin Press.
Aller, Curtis C., Jr.
    1957   Labor Relations in the Hawaii Sugar Industry. University of California, Berkeley: Institute of Industrial Relations.
Balmori, Joaquin
    1912   Report on the investigation made by the Hon. Joaquin Balmori, Delegate from Pangasinan, about conditions under which the Filipino laborers are working on sugar plantations in the Territory of Hawaii. Manila. On file at the University of Hawaii, Hawaii and Pacific Collection.
Bottomley, A. W. T.
    1924   Statement concerning the sugar industry in Hawaii. Honolulu. On file at the University of Hawaii, Hawaii and Pacific Collection.
Bouslog, Harriet
    1948   Memorandum on the history of labor and the law in the Territory of Hawaii, in the United States District Court for the District of Hawaii, Civil no. 828 and no. 836. Mimeo.
Cariaga, Roman R.
    1935   Filipinos in Honolulu. Social Science 10:38-46.
    1936   "The Filipinos in Hawaii: A survey of their economic and social conditions." Master's thesis, University of Hawaii.
Clark, Thomas Blake
    1947   Hawaii, the 49th State. Garden City: Doubleday.
Cruz, Hermenegildo
    1926   Report of the Director of Labor to his Excellency the Governor General of the Philippine Islands. Manila. On file at the University of Hawaii, Hawaii and Pacific Collection.
Dorita, Sister Mary
    1954   "Filipino immigration to Hawaii." University of Hawaii, Master's thesis.
    1967   "The Hawaiian Sugar Planters' Association and Filipino Exclusion." Pp. 11-29 in Josefa M. Saniel, ed., The Filipino Exclusion Movement, 1927-1935. Quezon City.
Duckworth-Ford, R. A.
    1926   Report on Hawaiian sugar plantations and Filipino labor. Manila.
Eubank, Lauriel E.
    1943   "The effects of the first six months of World War II on the activities of Koreans and Filipinos Toward the Japanese in Hawaii." Master's thesis. University of Hawaii.

Felipe, Virgilio A.
    1970   The Vibora Luviminda and the 1937 Puunene Plantation Strike. University of
           Hawaii, History 424. Honolulu.
Filipino Outlook. Honolulu.
Fuchs, Lawrence H.
    1961   Hawaii Pono: A Social History. New York: Harcourt, Brace, & World.
Gorospe, Otilio R.
    1933   "Making Filipino history in Hawaii." Mid-Pacific Magazine 45 (March): 241-255.
Griffiths, Stephen
    1978   "Emigrants and entrepreneurs: Social and economic strategies in a Philippine
           peasant community." Ph.D. dissertation. University of Hawaii.
Governors' Files
           Hawaii State Archives, Honolulu.
Hawaiian Sugar Planters Association
    1949   Sugar in Hawaii. Honolulu.
Honolulu Record
Honolulu Star
Interchurch Federation of Honolulu
    1936   Filipino Life in Hawaii. Honolulu.
Johannessen, Edward
    1956   The Hawaiian Labor Movement—A Brief History. Boston: Bruce Humphries.
Kent, Noel
    forth- Islands Under the Influence. New York: Monthly Review Press.
    coming
Kim, Bernice B. H.
    1937   "The Koreans in Hawaii." Master's thesis. University of Hawaii.
Krauss, Bob, and William P. Alexander
    1965   Grove Farm Plantation. Palo Alto: Pacific Books Publishers.
Lasker, Bruno
    1931   Filipino Immigration to the Continental United States and to Hawaii. Chicago:
           Institute of Pacific Relations, University of Chicago Press.
Lewis, Henry T.
    1971   Ilocano Rice Farmers, A Comparative Study of Two Philippine Barrios. Hono-
           lulu: University of Hawaii Press.
Liebes, R. A.
    1938   "Labor organization in Hawaii." Master's thesis. University of Hawaii.
Lind, Andrew W.
    1935   "Voting in Hawaii." Social Process in Hawaii 1:2-5.
    1938   An Island Community. Chicago: University of Chicago Press.
    1967   Hawaii's People. 3rd edition. Honolulu: University of Hawaii Press.
Lord, Virginia, and Alice W. Lee
    1937   "Taxi Dance Hall in Honolulu." Social Process in Hawaii 3:46-49.
Luis, Anastacio, and Herman Sensano
    1937   "Some aspects of the Filipino family." Social Process in Hawaii 3:64-69.
Manlapit, Pablo
    1959   "Pablo Manlapit." Handwritten copy for Roderick Minford, student. Honolulu.
           On file at the University of Hawaii, Hawaii and Pacific Collection.
Manzon, Maximo
    1938   The Strange Case of the Filipinos in the United States. New York: American
           Committee for Protection of Foreign-Born.

Masuoka, Jitsuichi
    1931 "Race attitudes of the Japanese people in Hawaii: A study in social distance."
          Master's thesis, University of Hawaii.
Mitamura, Machiyo
    1940 Life on a Hawaiian Plantation: An Interview. Pp. 144-151, in B. L. Hormann,
          ed., Community Forces in Hawaii, Honolulu: University of Hawaii Press.
Menor, Benjamin
    1949 "Filipino plantation adjustments." Social Process in Hawaii 13:48-51.
Moe, Kilmer O.
    1929 "The outlook for Filipinos in Hawaii." Honolulu Mercury, October 5:38-52.
Norbeck, Edward
    1959 Pineapple Town, Hawaii. Berkeley and Los Angeles: University of California
          Press.
Quezon, Manuel L.
    1914- Papers on Filipinos in Hawaii. University of Hawaii, Honolulu. Photocopy.
    1943
Philippine News Tribune
Philippine Press of Hilo
Philippines Commonwealth Outlook
Polk-Husted Directory
    1913- Honolulu: Polk-Husted Directory & Co.
    1920
Probasco, H. A.
    1965- "Japanese and Filipino Labor Unions and the 1920 Strike in Hawaii." Paper for
    1966 History 665, University of Hawaii.
Reinecke, John E.
    1966 Labor Disturbances in Hawaii, 1890-1925. Honolulu: n.p. On file at the Univer-
          sity of Hawaii, Hawaii and Pacific Collection.
    n.d. The Sugar Strike of 1920: Catalyst. Honolulu: n.p. On file at the University of
          Hawaii, Hawaii and Pacific Collection.
Remigio, Prudencio
    1919 Report Del Comisionado Filipino en Hawaii a Su Excelencia, El Gobernado
          General, Respecto de las condiciones de los obreros en el Territorio. In Quezon
          Papers.
Robinson, Clarence C.
    1935 "Occupational succession on the plantation." Social Process in Hawaii 1:21-25.
Scott, James C.
    1972 "The erosion of patron-client bonds and social change in rural Southeast
          Asia." Journal of Asian Studies 32:5-38.
Sharma, Miriam
    1980 "Pinoy in paradise: environment and adaptation of Filipinos in Hawaii, 1906-
          1946." Amerasia VII (2):91-117.
Smith, Jared G.
    1924 Plantation Sketches. Honolulu: The Advertiser Press.
Thompson, David
    1941 "The Filipino Federation of America, Incorporated: A study in the natural his-
          tory of a social institution." Social Process in Hawaii 7:24-35.
United States Bureau of Labor Statistics
    1903, 1906, 1916, Report of the Commissioner of Labor Statistics on Labor Conditions
          in Hawaii. Washington, D.C.: Government Printing Office.

United States, Bureau of the Census:
    1910, 1920, 1930. 1940, Washington, D.C.: Government Printing Office.
United States Congress, House, Committee on Immigration and Naturalization.
    1921   Labor Problems in Hawaii. Washington, D.C.: Government Printing Office.
Wagayway (formerly Philippines Commonwealth Outlook)
Wakukawa, Ernest K.
    1938   A History of the Japanese People in Hawaii. Honolulu: The Toyo Shoin.
Wentworth, Edna Louise
    1941   Filipino Plantation Workers. New York: Institute of Pacific Relations.
Wolf, Eric
    1966   Peasants. Englewood Cliffs, N.J.: Prentice-Hall.
Yamamura, Douglas
    1935   "Attitudes of Hotel Workers." Pp. 20-24 in B. L. Hormann, ed., Community
        Forces in Hawaii, Honolulu: University of Hawaii Press.

Index

Designer: UC Press Staff
Compositor: Etc. Graphics, Inc.
Printer: Braun-Brumfield, Inc.
Binder: Braun-Brumfield, Inc.
Text: 10/12 Andover Medium
Display: Andover